EXAMPLES&EXPLANATIONS

Property

Property

Fourth Edition

Barlow Burke

John S. Myers & Alvina Reckman Myers Scholar
and Professor of Law
American University
Washington College of Law

Joseph Snoe

Professor of Law
Samford University
Cumberland School of Law

Wolters Kluwer
Law & Business

To contact Customer Service, e-mail customer.service@wolterskluwer.com, call 1-800-234-1660, fax 1-800-901-9075, or mail correspondence to:

Wolters Kluwer Law & Business
Attn: Order Department
PO Box 990
Frederick, MD 21705

Printed in the United States of America.

1 2 3 4 5 6 7 8 9 0

ISBN 978-1-4548-0229-7

Library of Congress Cataloging-in-Publication Data

Burke, D. Barlow, 1941-
  Property : examples & explanations / Barlow Burke, John S. Myers & Alvina Reckman Myers Scholar and Professor of Law, American University Washington College of Law, Joseph Snoe, Professor of Law, Samford University Cumberland School of Law. — Fourth edition.
    pages cm
  Includes index.
  ISBN 978-1-4548-0229-7
  1. Property — United States — Cases. 2. Property — United States — Problems, exercises, etc. 3. Casebooks I. Snoe, Joseph A. II. Title.

  KF560.B87 2011
  346.7304 — dc23

2011050004

About Wolters Kluwer Law & Business

Wolters Kluwer Law & Business is a leading global provider of intelligent information and digital solutions for legal and business professionals in key specialty areas, and respected educational resources for professors and law students. Wolters Kluwer Law & Business connects legal and business professionals as well as those in the education market with timely, specialized authoritative content and information-enabled solutions to support success through productivity, accuracy, and mobility.

Serving customers worldwide, Wolters Kluwer Law & Business products include those under the Aspen Publishers, CCH, Kluwer Law International, Loislaw, Best Case, ftwilliam.com, and MediRegs family of products.

CCH products have been a trusted resource since 1913, and are highly regarded resources for legal, securities, antitrust and trade regulation, government contracting, banking, pension, payroll, employment and labor, and healthcare reimbursement and compliance professionals.

Aspen Publishers products provide essential information to attorneys, business professionals, and law students. Written by preeminent authorities, the product line offers analytical and practical information in a range of specialty practice areas from securities law and intellectual property to mergers and acquisitions and pension/benefits. Aspen's trusted legal education resources provide professors and students with high-quality, up-to-date, and effective resources for successful instruction and study in all areas of the law.

Kluwer Law International products provide the global business community with reliable international legal information in English. Legal practitioners, corporate counsel, and business executives around the world rely on Kluwer Law journals, looseleafs, books, and electronic products for comprehensive information in many areas of international legal practice.

Loislaw is a comprehensive online legal research product providing legal content to law firm practitioners of various specializations. Loislaw provides attorneys with the ability to quickly and efficiently find the necessary legal information they need, when and where they need it, by facilitating access to primary law as well as state-specific law, records, forms, and treatises.

Best Case Solutions is the leading bankruptcy software product to the bankruptcy industry. It provides software and workflow tools to flawlessly streamline petition preparation and the electronic filing process, while timely incorporating ever-changing court requirements.

ftwilliam.com offers employee benefits professionals the highest-quality plan documents (retirement, welfare, and non-qualified) and government forms (5500/PBGC, 1099, and IRS) software at highly competitive prices.

MediRegs products provide integrated health care compliance content and software solutions for professionals in healthcare, higher education, and life sciences, including professionals in accounting, law, and consulting.

Wolters Kluwer Law & Business, a division of Wolters Kluwer, is headquartered in New York. Wolters Kluwer is a market-leading global information services company focused on professionals.

Summary of Contents

PART I. POSSESSION, PERSONAL PROPERTY, AND ADVERSE POSSESSION

PART II. COMMON LAW ESTATES AND INTERESTS IN REAL PROPERTY

PART III. THE LAW OF LANDLORD AND TENANT

PART IV. TRANSFERS OF LAND

PART V. PRIVATE LAND USE CONTROLS

PART VI. PUBLIC LAND USE CONTROLS

Contents

Contents

Contents

PART II. COMMON LAW ESTATES AND INTERESTS IN REAL PROPERTY

Chapter 9   Common Law Estates and Present Interests   105

Contents

PART III. THE LAW OF LANDLORD AND TENANT

Contents

PART IV. TRANSFERS OF LAND

Contents

PART V. PRIVATE LAND USE CONTROLS

PART VI. PUBLIC LAND USE CONTROLS

Chapter 31   Constitutional and Statutory Constraints on Zoning   557

Chapter 32   Variances, Special Exceptions, and Zoning Amendments   571

Chapter 33   Zoning Extended and Challenged   589

Contents

Preface

Property, the study of the rights and duties among persons with respect to objects, land, and other assets, is perhaps the least intuitive of all the required courses taught during the first year of law school. The course blends a mixture of abstract relationships and concrete rules, at once a remnant of laws introduced in bygone centuries and a dynamic reflection of changes occurring today.

Property: Examples & Explanations discusses the fundamental definitions, rules, and concepts covered in Property courses. Most of this book's readers will be first-year students either preparing for class, supplementing class discussion, or studying for examinations. We aim to make the book useful at each of these stages of your semester. It will help bring the course materials into focus and provide the many perspectives to help you "think like a lawyer."

Each chapter contains an introductory overview that supplements (but does not supplant) your daily class assignments and aids in your review for examinations. Each overview provides a clear and accessible exposition of the fundamentals of the law of property, with the object of helping someone focusing on the subject for the first time.

Each chapter also includes a series of Examples that test your understanding of the material and your ability to apply the law to specific problems. We recommend that you think about, analyze, and write answers to as many Examples as you can. Writing out your responses is good practice for writing final examinations. It also forces you to analyze the facts and the law, evaluating possible solutions and ramifications of each choice you make. Alternatively, you might discuss each Example with a study partner or study group, gaining insight from the discussion.

Following the Examples in each chapter are Explanations that give our solutions. The Explanations discuss majority and minority rules and offer insights not readily grasped in class discussions or in the introductory overviews of the chapters themselves. Some Explanations will help you identify your weak areas; others will reinforce your conclusions and analysis. We have strived to make each Explanation a stepping stone on the path to success in your Property course.

There are no exhaustive citations of authority in this book. What citations are used in the text or in our Explanations we consider helpful either to orient the student reader to casebook materials or to indicate basic writings and leading cases in the field.

We enjoy our magnificent subject and want students to grasp its fundamental rules and concepts, all the while enjoying their experience.

B.B.
J.S.

December 2011

Acknowledgments

Barlow Burke acknowledges the helpful and patient research of five research assistants, Les Anderson, Athena Cheng, Stephanie Quaranta, Rachel Rueben, and Meryl Eschen Mills, while they were law students. He also acknowledges with appreciation the financial support, over several summers, of the Washington College of Law, American University. Joseph Snoe appreciates Judy McAlister, Tracy Luke, Grace Simms and Jeff Whitcomb for their help with the manuscript. He also thanks the Cumberland School of Law, Samford University, for its financial support.

We are both grateful for the guidance of the several anonymous reviewers of this manuscript provided by Wolters Kluwer, the many comments of students and professors on the first three editions, and for the editorial work of Carol McGeehan, Jessica Barmack, Eric Holt, John Lyman, Vincent Nordhaus, Sarah Zobel, and Margaret Rehberger at Wolters Kluwer — all gave their professional best. Aside from the above, we acknowledge our limitations, inevitable and otherwise, in attempting to pull so diverse a subject within the covers of one book, and look forward to the diverse suggestions of readers for the improvement of this fourth edition.

B.B.
J.S.

Property

PART I

Possession, Personal Property, and Adverse Possession

CHAPTER 1

The Law of Property

INTRODUCTION

Some courses on property law begin with the analysis of cases — sometimes they concern the acquisition of personal property, sometimes wild animals; and sometimes they introduce the subject with a U.S. Supreme Court case concerning the Fifth Amendment's takings clause or with a case about Native American claims to property that puts our American system into perspective. Historical and philosophical readings about property law's development might also be used to gain perspective.

Different perspectives on the institution or the idea of property have been around for a long time. These perspectives have long been controversial. Plato and Aristotle disagreed as to property's role in society. Since that time, property has been viewed variously as the product of one's labor (John Locke), as an extension of one's will (Georg W. F. Hegel), as the product of a person's settled expectations (Jeremy Bentham), and as the foundation of capitalism and class conflict (Karl Marx).

In the first year of law school, property is studied along with the two other wide-ranging areas of private and commercial law, the law of torts, and the law of contracts. The three subjects are studied in separate classes, but even though the signs on the classroom doors are different, this curricular separation should not lead you to the conclusion that the three subjects are entirely distinct. They are not. They are constantly intersecting. Property and torts, for example, have in common an historic origin in the cause of action for trespass, and often a substantive statement of a rule of property law begins or ends with the phrase "absent an agreement to the contrary" — meaning that persons involved are free to make a contract providing what the rule does not. In particular, the law of landlord and tenant (pertaining to leases) is a recently developed combination of contract and property law. Property, contract, and tort doctrines constantly arise and intersect in any law practice.

The subject matter of a course on property typically covers several topics. There may be a roadmap to your course in contracts, but with property there is no *one* roadmap; instead, there are at least six roadmaps. Thus, to the beginning student, the course's subject matter may seem huge. Personal property, common law estates and concurrent interests, landlord and tenant, real estate transactions, easements and covenants, and public land use regulation are the topics most frequently mapped in the first-year course on property.

Although some of these subjects will be unfamiliar if you are reading this during your first semester or quarter of law study, you will quickly realize that each has its origins in a different historical era of our legal system's development. The economic and social context in which the rules of each arose shaped it in different ways: Each developed in spurts and at different times. For example, common law estates developed rapidly in the late Middle Ages, while the law of landlord and tenant developed most quickly over the past several decades. Our legal system's rules for real estate transactions developed in response first to the system of estates, then to the development of the executory contract in the eighteenth century, and finally to American modifications in the English system designed to suit our own needs. The law of easements and covenants developed rapidly in the nineteenth century in response to the industrialization and urbanization then taking place. Our system of land use regulation developed gradually over the last century, but did so more rapidly during some decades — the 1920s, the 1950s, and the 1970s — than during others.

Add to this variety of origins the many intersections of property law with that of torts and contracts, and the teaching and study of property law becomes a challenge of a different dimension than is encountered in the latter subjects. As the topics change, beginning students need to treat each change as if it were the start of a new course, steeping themselves in both the context and the body of rules and doctrines governing each new topic.

Putting the various contexts you study into perspective should help you realize that the study of property is often the study of **tenures** — using an old-fashioned word for the study of the many ways in which property may be possessed or held — rather than the study of property itself. Thus the study of property is of the various interests that define the rights of its holder and of the documents conveying various interests in property and defining how it may be used, kept, or sold. It is also the study of deeds, leases, and the various other documents that purport to create or transfer it or an interest in it.

Property is not a thing wanted for itself, and property law is not about one person's relationship to a thing. Instead, it is about relationships between and among persons with regard to a thing. Property permits one person to exclude another from using a thing; to use it personally to gain rents, profits, or income from it; to sell it; or to give it by will to one relative and not another. All this is possible only when one's relationship to property is clear insofar as others are bound to respect it.

Property law is a series of rules defining a person's relationship to a thing that others must respect. That person is called an owner. The primary right of an owner is the right to exclude others from using or profiting from a thing. If the thing is movable, the thing becomes **personal property**. Land and the improvements on it become **real property**. The study of property generally includes both personal and real property, with a touch of intellectual property.

Defining property as a three-way relationship (owner to thing, others to thing, and owner to others) requires that the legal rules pertaining to it have widespread support. Support in this sense is the result of an appeal to the terms of a legal rule, its underlying policies and historical precedent, the judicial procedures in which the rule was formed, and the philosophy of law or jurisprudence underlying all of these.

Property law is the creation of society, useful to make society function, and not a product of natural law, although most would also say that property supports and enhances a person's identity and that a person's acquisitiveness is as close to a natural instinct as one can come.

COMMON LAW CASES

Property law is largely **state law**. Each of our states, territories, and the District of Columbia, with the exception of Louisiana, adopted for its legal system the common law of England in all of the jurisdictional, decisional, and analytical senses in which that phrase is used. So property law is typically state law, as opposed to federal law. As in the law of torts or contracts, courts often speak of the New York, the Pennsylvania, or the California rule. Such references make the point that, technically, it is too facile to speak of a law of property — instead, each state in our country has its own law. Even when a federal court decides a case involving property, it uses the law of the state whose law applies and, in the absence of a federal constitutional or statutory issue, must follow state court precedent.

A party who felt the trial court erred as to matter of law or finding of fact can appeal to an appeals or appellate court to review the challenged matter.

Most cases reproduced in casebooks are appellate cases. Usually seven to nine judges sit together on a state's intermediate or highest appellate court, the latter typically called the state's supreme court or court of appeals.

An appellate opinion has four parts. First, there is a statement of the facts of the case. These are facts found as such by the jury or, in a nonjury matter, by the judge sitting as a fact-finder in the trial court, and accepted as such by the appellate court. In an appeal from the trial court's decision, the facts are not retried, unless they are so unreasonable that the record of the case in the trial court does not provide any basis for them. So facts recited in an appellate opinion typically accept the factual determinations of the trial court.

Second, there is a statement of the legal issues involved in the case, followed, third, by a statement of the rule(s) resolving the issues and applying the rules to the facts. This third portion may be brief, but sometimes is lengthy. There the judge articulates a rationale for the rule — perhaps a public policy underlying it and an explanation as to why it is fair to apply it to the case at hand; how it promotes ethical behavior in attorneys, litigants, or the public at large; or how it might be efficiently administered or used in the future. Articulating a rationale usually involves the application (or not) of cases with precedential value for the court. The judge may explain what facts are particularly important to the decision or what is not being decided (see below, dicta). In the fourth part of the opinion, the judge gives the holding and the decision in the case.

The cases in casebooks are selected for their facts and details, their analysis, their influence, or their widespread acceptance. They may have more than one opinion — they may produce a (1) majority opinion, in which most of the judges on the court agree on the statement of the law, the analysis, and the result — the judgment or other remedy given in the case; (2) a dissenting opinion, with which some but not most of the judges agree; or (3) a concurring opinion, in which some judges agree with the majority's result, but not with some other aspect of their opinion. If there is more than one, the comparisons and contrasts between them may produce interesting statements as to the law, analysis, or remedies involved.

The cases studied may not represent the law of the state in which you eventually will practice law. The **precedential rules** of authority — looking first to a judge's own state or jurisdiction, then for similar cases in other jurisdictions, then to secondary (or non-case) authorities such as law reviews and legal treatises — produce a tendency to make the law of many jurisdictions into one uniform body of law, and many opinions into works of considerable scholarship.

Amid the secondary authorities, some of the more formal organized methods of legal expression, backed by large sectors of the legal profession, also re-enforce this tendency to uniformity. First, there are the American Law Institute's **Restatements of the Law**. Its first Restatement of the Law,

Property, was published in 1944. Restatements of the Law (Second), Property, have been published more recently: for Landlord and Tenant in 1977, for Security (Mortgages) in 1996, and for Servitudes (Easements and Covenants) in 1998. Other property subjects are in draft. Restatements are secondary authorities publishing their drafters' versions of the rules of law taken from decided cases, although not always the rule settled by a majority of cases deciding a particular issue. Sometimes drafters prefer what they see as a trend in the decided cases and extract their rule from the cases they see as representing that trend, rather than a rule representing the law established in a majority of states. Sometimes there is no majority; sometimes the law is unsettled or open. Whatever approach the Restatement takes, its decision is influential and its text will disclose the reasons and the authorities behind its choice.

Second, the Commissioners on **Uniform State Laws** have published Model Laws for adoption by American jurisdictions. The Uniform Commercial Code that you study in contracts class is the most successful of these laws. The Uniform Landlord Tenant Act, the Uniform Land Transactions Act, and the Uniform Probate Code are examples that have been influential, if not widely or completely adopted, in the law of property. Such laws may codify, modify, or repeal common law rules and, like the Restatements, may be cited by judges deciding common law cases as embodying a legal rule.

Third, there are **treatises** with discussions of the law attempting to make sense of disparate decisions and statutes. The *American Law of Property* (1952) is a collection of essays by (mostly) law professors specializing in the law of property. *Thompson on Real Property* (1994) is a more recent collection of such essays. Roger Cunningham, William Stoebuck, and Dale Whitman, *The Law of Property* (2d ed. 1993), is an excellent one-volume treatise. More specialized treatises, such as Raymond Brown, *Personal Property* (3d ed. 1975); Jon Bruce & James Ely, *Easements and Licenses in Land* (rev. ed. 1995); and Daniel Mandelker, *Land Use Law* (5th ed. 2003), perform the same function within narrower limits. Although there are many excellent treatments on common law estates and interests in the previously mentioned works, John Makdisi & Daniel Bogart, *Estates in Land and Future Interests* (5th ed. 2007), is an excellent workbook on a subject some students find challenging.

CASE ANALYSIS

Much law is gleaned from the analysis of cases. Case analysis is an essential skill for attorneys. If the case is concerned with the substantive law of property, the case is probably one involving a common law rule — i.e., a rule formulated by judges for cases that they heard and decided. Case law or **common law** rules are established by court decisions, as opposed to those made by legislatures enacting a statute. A judge deciding a case tries to resolve the issues in the case by following or drawing from prior decisions by judges in his or her jurisdiction. This doctrine of precedent is unique to the common law as opposed to civil law or code systems of law used in other countries.

The **doctrine of precedent** (or stare decisis) is fundamental to case analysis. It rests on the idea that people in similar situations should receive similar treatment at the hands of a court. Similar cases should be decided in a similar way so that people are treated as equally and fairly as possible, and so that people not in court who find themselves in a situation similar to one that a court has decided may predict what the law will be if and when they go to court. A judicial decision, published or reported in an opinion, not only binds the parties to the litigation that produced it, but also has predictive value for others.

An opinion has predictive value only when another court is bound to follow it. At the state level, this means that the opinion of a state Supreme Court binds all courts lower in the judicial hierarchy of the state, thus binding any intermediate appellate court and all trial courts. A trial court decision, at the other end of that hierarchy, is not binding outside the county or municipality in which the court sits, although it may be **persuasive authority**.

The root idea is that of providing equality for persons in similar situations. Deciding who is in a similar situation — not an identical situation (that almost never happens) — involves analysis of a reported case. Appellate or reported cases may be distinguished — i.e., read narrowly to avoid their applications — or applied — i.e., read for similarities.

Distinguishing case precedent is often necessary because courts have no control over who brings a case to court. In formulating and enacting a regulation or a statute, a legislature or an administrative agency might consider all the possible or predictable situations to which its work product might apply and draft a regulation or statute encompassing them; a court has no such opportunity. If a judge in an opinion writes more generally about the law than the facts of the case require, that part of the opinion will be considered *obiter dictum* — Latin for a statement "made in passing" — or **dicta**. Dicta may be included to explain a decision, or to limit its applicability to the facts found at trial — particularly when the facts were contested at trial. While not binding as legal precedent, dicta may be a persuasive authority even so.

Lots of cases, with lots of rules, may eventually form a body of law encompassing most aspects of a subject (some attorneys refer to rules synthesized from many cases as legal **doctrine** — but such terms of art have various and variable meanings). From many cases, a synthesis of the law may emerge. Producing this synthesis is a form of inductive reasoning — deriving a general rule from the individual cases. The generalization takes place using the materials the judge finds at hand — case(s), statute(s), and secondary authorities. If necessary (nothing else being available), even one case might be generalized for use in an opinion in another case.

Application of a case to another situation is a process of making analogies between the case and the situation at hand. It is often arranged in an opinion as a syllogism, a form of deductive reasoning, as in the following:

(1) Possession of land is necessary to bring an action of trespass.
(2) Alex has possession of land.
(3) Alex may bring an action of trespass.

Here the first proposition (1) is a major or general premise or rule, (2) is a minor or factual premise, and (3) is a conclusion, permitting a general rule to be applied to a particular situation.

The reasoning found in judicial opinions is either deductive or inductive — not unlike the forms of reasoning in other modes of expression. Analysis of any one opinion involves separating it into its parts and extracting its reasoning, but this task is complicated by the use of citation to cases and other authorities as it proceeds, by the judge's doing two or more things at once, and by the opinion's haphazard or blurry organization, as in the following opinion written for illustrative purposes by one of the authors. (The facts in this opinion have been taken from the opening chapter of James Fenimore Cooper's novel *The Pioneers*, published in 1826.)

Alex Hunter, Plaintiff v. **Mo Montour**, Defendant

in the Supreme Court of the State of Grace

LEARNED, J., delivered the opinion of the Court.

The plaintiff, Alex Hunter, was deer hunting in unposted woods in the unincorporated portions of Green County. After spying a large buck, Hunter's son, accompanying him, accidentally tripped and discharged his rifle, grazing the buck's flank and startling it. Hunter aimed at the startled animal, fired and hit it, not where Hunter aimed, but as the buck started and jumped, putting a bullet in its lungs. As a result of being thus fatally hit, the deer ran onto the land of Owen Owner, who held it and reached for a hunting knife. Just as Owen was about to plunge the knife into the buck, it leaped up a final time and was just about to run into the roadway abutting Owen's land when the passing defendant, Mo Montour, seeing the commotion of all this pursuit, brought his automobile to a halt and sprang from it. The defendant Montour then fired a pistol into the buck's head and seized it, carrying it off from the side of the road.

1. The Law of Property

The plaintiff Hunter brought a complaint sounding in trespass[1] against the defendant Montour in order to recover the buck or its value. The defendant Montour moved to dismiss the case, but this motion was denied and it was tried before Judge George Judd, sitting in the Circuit Court of Green County. The Circuit Court jury rendered a verdict for the plaintiff and Judge Judd gave judgment accordingly. The defendant appealed to this court. We now reverse.

Trespass is an action brought for the taking of personal property. It involves carrying off the goods of another. Its first element is a showing that the "goods" in question are in the plaintiff's possession. Spying the buck by the plaintiff's son, for example, did not amount to possession because the son's spying the animal shows neither an intent to possess it nor an act of possession. Both are essential to sustain the plaintiff's complaint. That the buck was unintentionally and slightly wounded adds nothing to the plaintiff's case. However, the plaintiff's fatally wounding it is a different matter. If accomplished intentionally, it shows that the plaintiff did intend to kill the buck and, if pursuit ensues, the pursuit itself might be the functional equivalent of taking actual possession of the buck. Here, however, the wound was accidental, and so the ensuing pursuit proved nothing.

Owner by seizing the buck all but possessed it; but even here, when the animal is still capable of bolting as a wild animal might be expected to do, it is just as likely to regain its natural liberty as lose it. The defendant, seemingly on Owner's behalf, raises another claim: that Owner in any event has a better right to the buck than does the plaintiff. This other claim is to the animal, as one on Owner's land: A landowner has a right to start wild animals naturally on their land, *ratione soli*.[2] However, here the animal was not naturally on Owner's land, having been pursued there by the plaintiff Hunter. Moreover, if the buck bolted onto the land of a neighbor, instead of going onto the roadway, Owner's right to it would likely end when Owner began his trespass onto the neighboring land — although this result would be stronger if the neighbor's land was posted, warning off hunters and trespassers. So Owner's claim to the animal by the landowner's right fails. In any event, this is not an argument open to the defendant to make. Owner is no part of this litigation and his rights may be asserted

---

1. The phrase "sounding in trespass" may itself seem strange. It is lawyer talk, and means that the theory on which Hunter brought his lawsuit was trespass. Every course in law school is full of such talk, and getting comfortable with it will permit you to do what lawyers do with much of their time — talk about law.

2. A Latin phrase meaning "on account or with reference to the soil." That is, the ownership of the soil is the basis for the right to start hunting there, just as a landowner owns a bee hive on his or her land. The law is full of such strange words and phrases, so keep your law dictionary handy: lawyers, judges, and professors will freely use terms that you as a lawyer will be embarrassed not to know.

in a future case. The defendant must win this one on his own merits, not on the weakness of the plaintiff's.

Under the law of this state, it is an open and unsettled question as to whether the defendant interfered with the plaintiff's or Owner's hunt. This court need not resolve this issue, however, as the defendant, firing a fatal wound showing his intent to take the buck, was also the first to actually seize the animal. He there has its possession to a degree that trumps the plaintiff's, and so the plaintiff's right to bring an action of trespass.

The plaintiff's complaint is dismissed. Judgment reversed.

LIVINGOOD, J., dissenting. I respectfully dissent. If the plaintiff's pursuit was an active one and the defendant had notice of it, I see no reason in law or policy why the defendant should be privileged to interfere with the plaintiff's hunt. The plaintiff's activity is a lawful one, the land through which it was pursued was unposted, and the plaintiff was in full view of the defendant when seizing the buck. The defendant's interference is to me an event highly likely to result in a breach of the peace, even if it occurred by the side of a public road and did not disturb the rights of an abutting owner.

It might be said that the rule of actual possession laid down by the majority will give the law a crispness and ease of administration that is highly desirable where the public must know the rules of the hunt, but to my mind, the certainty of the law is in no way diminished if a pursuit in plain view of the defendant of a fatally wounded animal is found the equivalent of actual possession. The aim is the capture of the buck, and the animal must first be pursued in order to be captured; otherwise, hunters will go at it with ever more powerful rifles and guns, endangering us all. Finding a constructive possession in pursuit such as this will surely result in the capture of the buck, without the defendant firing an additional shot. That the additional shot prevented the buck from running onto a public roadway points out that, at the kill, the plaintiff had just as much right to be there as did the defendant.

Finally, if this suit fails as a proposition pled under the law of possession and property, I foresee it refiled as a tort suit in which the quantum of possession required may well be less and in which the plaintiff might well succeed. This being so, it seems to me that the law of property should conform itself to the expectations of the jury below.

I would affirm their verdict and the ensuing judgment of Judge Judd.

Examples

1. Is the *Hunter* opinion binding on the courts of another state deciding a case with similar facts? Would it matter whether the other court was a trial or an appellate court?

11

2. After Hunter v. Montour is decided, Owen Owner sues Mo Montour for the buck that the result in the *Hunter* opinion permitted him to keep. May Owen do so?

3. Suppose that Owner's land abutted not a road, but Larry Lander's land, and the buck escaped Owner and ran onto Larry's land. Would the *Hunter* opinion prevent Owner from pursuing the buck there?

Explanations

1. The *Hunter* opinion is not binding on the courts of any other jurisdiction. It does not matter whether the other court is a trial court or an appellate court. The *Hunter* opinion is binding as legal precedent on all state courts in the State of Grace. The opinion is useful in other states, however, as persuasive authority. A judge in another state may read the opinion for its logic and reasoning, and may decide to agree with the *Hunter* opinion and adopt its reasoning as the judge's own.

2. Yes. Owen Owner's rights, including the right to sue, are unaffected by a lawsuit to which he was not made a party. If the court never gained jurisdiction over Owner, its judgment does not bind him. As the facts are stated in the opinion, for example, it is unclear whether Owen's lands were posted, and so it is also unclear whether Mo and Alex were trespassers at the time of the hunt and the kill. Whether Mo was a trespasser would affect his rights to the buck. Moreover, the effect of any trespass, if found, would make the case sufficiently different from the precedent established in the *Hunter* opinion, so even if found to be binding on the court in which Owner sues, it need not control the outcome of Owner's suit.

3. Once Owen Owner joins the hunt, as the opinion suggested in dicta, his trespass on the land of another might well prevent him from obtaining legal possession of the buck. The discussion in *Hunter* as to Owner is dicta, and while persuasive authority to courts in the state of Grace, it is still merely persuasive and not binding authority. Moreover, the *Hunter* dicta may not apply to Owner's situation perfectly. For example, Owen might be asserting not only his right to hunt, but also his right to take game from his own lands and, by extension of that right, to take game found on his land that, when pursued there, went elsewhere. If Larry's land were posted, that might prevent Mo and Alex from starting their hunt there, but might not prevent Owen from continuing an ongoing hunt there, pursuing an already wounded animal. So Owen Owner's position is distinguishable from Alex and Mo's: Owner is participating in a hunt that started rightfully, while Alex and Mo's hunt was tainted, with regard to Owner's rights, from the moment they entered the boundaries of

Owner's land. Property rights are relative to the rights of other people, particular people finding themselves in a context laden with facts. However, if Larry Lander's land was posted — i.e., had signs saying "No trespassing or hunting: Keep out" — the posting would affect Owner's rights.

CHAPTER 2

Personal Property and First Possession

INTRODUCTION AND DEFINITIONS

Property falls into two broad categories: real property and personal property. (Intellectual property has some aspects of both.) **Real property, real estate,** or **realty** refers to land and the improvements attached to the land. Buildings, fences, and dams, for example, are included with land as real property. **Personal property** or **personalty** is all property other than real property. Automobiles, books, tables, clothes, computers, and corporate stock are examples of personal property.

A **fixture** is personal property that has been permanently attached to real property, but that could be removed. A dishwasher installed into a kitchen cabinet is a fixture, for example. Fixtures' hybrid nature subjects them to rules applicable to personal property and sometimes to rules applicable to real property.

Property may change character. For example, trees and crops in the field are real property. When cut or harvested, the cut trees become personal property. Cut trees turned into lumber are personal property but once incorporated into a building, become real property.

Personal property may be tangible personal property or intangible personal property. **Tangible personal property** includes property of a physical nature. You can see it and touch it. Examples include automobiles, books, clothing, lumber, jewelry, paintings, furniture, and coins. **Intangible personal property** includes assets that cannot be touched or seen but that have value nonetheless. Examples include stock in corporations, bonds, patents, copyrights, notes or accounts receivable, goodwill, and contract rights. Intangible personal property often is represented by a writing (tangible property) but the asset itself (e.g., a patent, corporate stock, or a note receivable) is an intangible asset. Recently recognized intangible assets are the rights of publicity and privacy that prohibit others from using a person's name, face, or other attribute of that person for commercial purposes without permission.

POSSESSION, RELATIVITY OF TITLE, AND FIRST-IN-TIME

As discussed in Chapter 1, the word "property" has multiple connotations. It may be the thing itself; or it may define relationships and priorities, rights, and obligations among persons with respect to a thing. The study of the relationships among persons with respect to personal property is helpful in understanding three basic concepts: possession, relativity of title, and first-in-time.

Possession is the controlling or holding of personal property, with or without a claim of ownership. It has two elements: (1) an intent to possess on the part of the possessor, and (2) his or her actual controlling or holding the property. As to the second element, control is the key. Both the intent and the control elements must be present to acquire the rights of a possessor. A court will manipulate the two elements of possession according to the needs of the case. Possession need not be actual possession. More on this topic will follow.

Possession is basic to our law of personal property. Because proving ownership is so difficult and burdensome, we rely on possession as a surrogate for ownership and title. A possessor is said to have superior rights to personal property against all except those having higher rights or title, and a possessor can recover possession of an item of personal property, or recover damages for its injury or destruction. You probably own a wristwatch: How would you prove it if you were asked to do so?

Relativity of title is the idea that a person can have a relatively better title or right to possession than another, while simultaneously having a right inferior to yet another person. This doctrine is necessary because, in a common-law system, few acquire a perfect title. That would require that the person acquiring title litigate its relative strength against all other persons who have, or might conceivably have, any right or interest. Thus, an attorney speaks of a relatively better right to possession, or of a superior title or right.

One way to prioritize several individuals' rights is by a rule of **first-in-time, first-in-right**, establishing a priority of rights based on the time of acquiring the right in question. Under such a rule, all other things being equal, the chronologically first possessor has the better title.

All things are not always equal, however. Sometimes subsequent possessors prevail over prior possessors: A good faith purchaser or an adverse possessor can acquire title superior to those who came into possession before they did, for example. In contrast, persons taking their interests from a thief acquire no title to the thing: Title from a thief is a void title.

ACTUAL POSSESSION AND THE FOX CASE

Wild animal cases serve as the prototypes for problems in other areas of property law. Hunters of wild game provide a seemingly endless number of situations in which one or the other elements of possession is present — or missing. Whether a hunter has taken possession of an animal is the issue here.

The leading wild animal case in American law is Pierson v. Post, 3 Cai. Rptr. 175 (N.Y. Sup. Ct. 1805). Post was hunting on a beach. While he was in pursuit of a fox, Pierson intervened, shot the fox being chased by Post, and carried the animal off.

Post sued Pierson, and won in the lower or trial court. Pierson appealed. Post lost on appeal because he did not physically seize the fox before defendant Pierson shot and carried it off. Since Post never actually controlled the fox, the appellate court ruled Post never took legal possession. Control, the second element of possession (called **occupancy** in parts of this opinion), was not present.[1] Without it, the plaintiff does not have a sufficient interest in the thing sued for to warrant the court's hearing his complaint.

Pierson involved a rule of possession formulated so that the first hunter to capture a fox wins. This is a rule of first-in-time, first-in-right. It is into this rule of priority in time, reworded for the situation of two or more claimants for the same thing, that the concept of possession fits — as in, first-to-possess, first-in-right.

The hunter's race for the fox is without a fixed starting line — that is, without a starting line that all the hunters share. So we have Post, huffing and puffing over a distance longer than Pierson's, but Pierson wins. Put this way, the outcome hardly seems fair. Post expends considerably more effort and labor, and still he loses! Why? One answer is that there are no rules about the permissible gear that a hunter can use — more precisely, no restrictions on gear. One hunter can carry a high-powered rifle, another a pistol. Why is this? One answer might be that the courts think it is a bad idea for the law to have such restrictions; they might be taken for an attempt to make one set of laws for the hunter rich enough to afford the rifle, and another for the hunter using the cheaper pistol. Another answer might be that the cheaper pistol can be more skillfully and accurately used than the more expensive rifle — and the outcome of the hunt may change accordingly.

---

1. The two elements of possession are (1) the intent to possess and (2) actual control of or holding the property, discussed above.

Yet another answer might be one of necessity — if the law is to devise a rule for a race without a common starting line, then the end of the race is all that matters because it is all the court has to work with. Add to that the majority opinion's own justifications — wanting a rule that keeps the peace, damps down litigation, and is clear and easy to administer — and you have the justifications for the majority's decision.

Another version of the holding found in Pierson v. Post is in the opinion's discussion of several writers of legal treatises; that is, close pursuit after a **mortal wounding** gives a hunter a right to possession of the fox that is superior to another hunter's intervention. In the hypothetical opinion Hunter v. Montour in Chapter 1, Alex Hunter had the same argument in his favor, and it was no more successful for him than it was for Post. A "mortal wound" is one that, (1) on an objective basis, is likely to prove fatal to the animal — it will, given time, "deprive the fox of his natural liberty" — and (2) shows subjectively a "manifest intention" to seize the animal — that the pursuer intended to follow the hunt with a kill and is not just out for the enjoyment of the chase. Again, as with mere pursuit, intention alone will not do — or else Owen Owner would have won the hypothetical lawsuit whose opinion you read earlier. Instead, the intention must be manifest, or clearly shown by the wound. With this discussion of wounding, the court shows the two elements of possession coming together. In a sense, a mortal wounding is constructive possession of the animal.

The Pierson v. Post holding accepts as public policy that killing foxes is a socially useful enterprise. The dissenting judge in *Pierson* elaborates on this idea by saying that killing foxes saves chickens or, more precisely, protects the activities of chicken farmers. As you study cases in Property and other courses, look for public policy reasons why a court adopts a given rule of law.

The underlying ideas of both the majority and the dissenting opinions are not far apart, except that dissent would define possession in order to protect Post's pursuit of the fox. For both the majority and the dissent, the underlying rationale for the case drives the definition of "possession." Both the majority's rule of capture and the dissent's rule of pursuit are means to the same end — as are the ideas of "possession" and its kin, "constructive possession."

Constructive Possession

Constructive possession denotes possession that has the same effect in law as actual possession, although it is not actual possession in fact.[2] The term

---

2. The word "constructive" means "established by construing the facts of a case so that the facts give rise to an inference of [whatever — here, possession]." Attorneys also speak of constructive bailments, constructive conversion, constructive delivery, constructive fraud, and constructive notice; and that is just a limited sample of constructive legal concepts. You will encounter the same word in other areas of law as well.

"constructive" identifies a legal fiction mandating a legal conclusion or fact. A court treats a "constructive" matter as being the same as the actual matter. Thus, for example, a person in constructive possession of an item may not be in actual possession but will be deemed legally as being in actual possession. As a good example, the dissent in *Pierson* argued that Post's pursuit put him in constructive possession of the fox, in that it gave him a right to possession that was not yet actual possession. Attorneys also speak of constructive bailments, constructive conversion, constructive delivery, constructive fraud, and constructive notice; and that is just a limited sample of constructive legal concepts. You will encounter the same word in other areas of law as well.

In the context of natural resources law, constructive possession has also proven useful: The owners of land with oil, gas, or other minerals lying beneath its surface might not be in actual possession of those minerals, but they are often said to be in constructive possession of them. Hence, the legal maxim is that whoever owns the surface also owns to the depths of the earth.

The *Pierson* opinion says that prior cases involving hunters were decided under some type of regulation or statute, or involved litigation between hunters and the owners of private land on which the hunter captured the wild animal and in which the landowner usually prevailed. These factors are all potentially limiting facts in this case.

An English version of *Pierson* is the case of Young v. Hichens, 115 Eng. Rep. 228 (Queen's Bench, 1844). The plaintiff, from his boat, had enclosed a very large quantity of mackerel worth £2000 sterling in his net 140 fathoms long, drawn in a semicircle completely around the fish, with the exception of a space five to seven fathoms wide. Before the plaintiff could completely encircle the fish using a second net, the defendant's boat rowed through the gap, enclosed the fish, and captured them.

The court gave judgment for the defendant, except that the defendant had to pay a nominal amount for damage to the plaintiff's net: The court held that the plaintiff had not yet taken actual possession; neither did the plaintiff have constructive possession, because "all but reducing to possession" is not the same as possession. Were it otherwise, the plaintiff would be able to allege that he had a property interest sufficient to protect the fish in an action of conversion or trespass.

CUSTOM

Pierson may also have been decided in a way that most hunters in the locale might have found offensive. Judge Livingston suggests in his dissent that Post's hotfooted pursuit may have given him possession of the fox according to the custom of local hunters. Used in this way, custom is another basis for determining possession, custom being a use or practice long adopted by acquiescence, having the force of law. The majority of the court chose to ignore this basis. For example, the custom might be that the first hunter to put a bullet into an animal has the right to pursue it and reduce it to possession. Or, the custom might be that the hunter eventually taking possession of an animal must split the animal with the first shooter, so that the possessor and the shooter share the spoils. However, whatever the form of the custom, unless the first wound produced is a mortal wounding, it will typically not be seen by other hunters, who (assuming they recognize the custom) then will not know whether to observe it.

Customs are market- or locale-specific. For example, among hunters pursuing wild animals with a bow and arrow, the custom like the ones described may be somewhat more workable — an animal with an arrow sticking out of its body may be assumed to be an animal that is being pursued. In addition, in the whaling industry the use of harpoons makes the custom still easier to observe.

The judge in the case of *Ghen v. Rich*, discussing a segment of the nineteenth-century whaling industry, suggested that the custom of any group or industry should be recognized only under certain circumstances, to wit:

- when its application is limited to the industry and limited to those working in it,
- when the custom is recognized by the whole industry (or fishery in *Ghen*),
- when the custom "requires in the first taker the only act of appropriation that is possible" (e.g., the whale in *Ghen*, once harpooned and dead, quickly sinks to the ocean floor),
- when the custom is necessary to the survival of the industry, and
- when the custom "works well in practice."

Although custom dictated the result in *Ghen*, not many customs are likely to survive all these tests. In this sense, when setting out so many tests, the *Ghen* opinion really represents a triumph of the common law over custom in our legal system. Why is the court so suspicious of custom? A first answer might be that the custom of the industry will be formulated for the benefit of the industry, not for society as a whole. Second, although of benefit to an industry, a custom might be dangerous to those employed in it and the courts should consider that as well. Third, the custom can be wasteful of the resource. In *Ghen*, by custom the "owner" of a dead whale was the person who killed it by harpoon. Whales when killed by harpoon sank and resurfaced days later. Many of the dead whales washed ashore. A person finding the whale would notify the owner. The owner would retrieve the whale blubber and pay the finder a fee (or salvage) for his efforts. Not all dead whales were recovered, however: Some of the whales in the Cape Cod finback fishery "floated out to sea" and were "never recovered." Finally, a custom can lead to overinvestment in technology — the bomb-lance here. A bigger bomb-lance, with a rope attached to a bigger boat, could have meant immediate capture of the whale, but at what cost? The rule of capture taken from Pierson v. Post might lead to both waste and overinvestment.

In *Ghen*, the custom along Cape Cod's whaling areas required specially made equipment. Whaling ships elsewhere, using a harpoon with a rope attached to strike the whale, required a different custom. Herman Melville's novel *Moby-Dick*, chapter 89, describes various rules in the industry. Those other customs, untested in court, were not given the force of law; no custom should be imposed on wider regions or for a longer time than its use coincides with the law's needs.

THE DOCTRINE OF CUSTOM GIVING THE PUBLIC ACCESS TO BEACHES AND OTHER LANDS

Custom has not just been used in cases involving the creation of property by capture; it has also been used to create a common law right of access to certain types of real property. When, for example, a beach has been considered accessible to persons in a locale, their access may be said to arise by custom. A custom giving rise to access must be long-continued, uninterrupted, and reasonably asserted as a right. It is an inheritance from English common law, used to permit a local population to cut peat from a certain bog, use a certain spring for drinking water, or harvest timber for firewood in a certain forest, although the customary right to take away a substance will be more limited than the landowner's right to do so. Limitations for domestic or personal uses were often customary, and assertions of the custom in excess of that were regarded as unreasonable.

Blackstone said that the access must be so long continued "that the mind of man runs not to the contrary." In the United States, the custom must typically have been exercised from the beginning of the state's existence within the Union and uninterrupted thereafter. That's a long time! This is known as the doctrine's antiquity requirement. See State ex rel. Haman v. Fox, 594 P.2d 1093 (Idaho 1979) (finding 60 years insufficient). The people in theory possessed the land before the state did. The state was created subject to the preexisting custom, and so the persons benefiting from the custom had a right prior to any power of the state. As the examples from England have indicated, the custom must also be certain and reasonable as to place, subject matter, and persons benefiting from it.

NATURAL RESOURCES AND OTHER CONCERNS

First possession and rules of capture have been applied in at least two other contexts — in the law of natural resources and in water law. As to natural resources, a surface owner also owns the minerals underneath, such as coal or gold. Two minerals — oil and gas — are found in "pools" and flow through the ground to points of low pressure, much as water does. The first driller to tap and produce oil or natural gas from a pool underlying the lands of several owners has acquired possession of the resource brought to the surface, even though it may drain the pool under neighboring lands. Whereas lateral drilling is a trespass, drilling straight down from one's surface is legal, no matter that it is conducted close to a surface boundary line. Because this first-in-time rule resulted in inefficient overproduction of oil and gas, today state statutes and regulations allocate common pools of an oil or gas resource.

WATER LAW

The second use of a rule of first-in-time first-in-right in the context of natural resources concerns water. Water rights can be divided into rights to surface water (lakes, rivers, and streams) and those to underground or groundwater.

(a) Surface Water Courses

First-in-time applies to the acquisition of **surface water in a water course** — in a stream, creek, or river with a steady or seasonal flow — but the application of the rule differs in different parts of the country. Roughly divided, the water-rich eastern states are known as **riparian states.** Each person with land abutting a water course may take water from it for any **reasonable use.** In times of scarcity, a riparian landowner cannot use the water to benefit his non-riparian lands. Many riparian states go further and limit the use of the water to benefit the land parcel abutting the surface water. (Nonriparian lands are those that do not abut the water source.) Likewise, some riparian states limit the use of water to the surrounding watershed, so that the riparian user returns the water to the water course from whence it came.

Because water is scarcer in western states, water is allocated based on **prior appropriation.** While initially developed by custom and common law, prior appropriation allocations are controlled by state statute today. Under a prior appropriation system, the first person to make beneficial use of water gains a vested right to continue that use. The only way to prove a first-in-time allocation is to file an administrative action with the state water agency or engineer. The first person to file has the first priority; the second person to file has the second priority, and so on. A water right allocated in this manner entitles its holder to divert a set amount of water (often measured in "acre feet"), at a certain location, in a certain ditch, and for a defined use. In many ways, once allocated, water is treated like personal property: the right to use the water can be transferred, the water can be moved out of the watershed, and the water is treated separately from the land on which it is used. In a drought, persons with lower priorities may be prohibited from using any water until those whose claims have higher priority have satisfied their needs.

(b) Groundwater

Groundwater is underground or subsurface water. Groundwater (subsurface water) can be classified into two categories. Groundwater that flows in a channel is called an underground stream. The rules on use of water from underground streams follow the same rules applied to surface water.

The second type of groundwater is water not in a channel. These are known as **percolating waters.** As with oil and natural gas, the owner of the property at one time had an absolute right to withdraw percolating water and use it as he willed, either on the land or elsewhere. The absolute rule has often been supplanted by a **reasonable use doctrine**, also known as the American rule. Under the reasonable use doctrine, the water must be used solely on the overlying land if use elsewhere would cause hardship to other landowners with access to the common underground pool of water.

Some states follow a rule that dispenses with first-in-time and allocates the water based on land acreage owned, not a per-owner equality. This is known as the **correlative rights doctrine.**

The Restatement Second of Property §858 combines these approaches and allows a person to withdraw and use percolating groundwater unless the withdrawal unreasonably harms neighboring lands by lowering the water table or decreasing the water pressure; exceeds the landowner's reasonable share of the water; or reduces the level of surface lakes, harming users of the lakes.

As water becomes a scarce resource, state and local laws will become more technical and sophisticated. Even riparian states increasingly regulate its use.

ACTIONABLE INTERFERENCE

Keeble v. Hickeringill, 103 Eng. Rep. 1127, 11 Mod. 74 (Queen's Bench 1707), involved a decoy pond for ducks. Plaintiff Keeble brought an action against the defendant for discharging guns with the object of frightening the ducks away from the plaintiff's pond. The jury found for the plaintiff and awarded him £20 sterling. On appeal, defendant argued that there was no cause of action to redress the actions of which the plaintiff complained since the plaintiff did not own the ducks. Rejecting this argument, the appellate court held that the plaintiff had a cause of action. The court stated that "the true reason [for this holding] is that this action is not brought to recover damage for loss of the fowl, but for the disturbance" of the plaintiff's taking possession of them.

The opinion of Judge Holt in 103 Eng. Rep. makes three points. First, the plaintiff is a tradesman, using the decoy pond in a lawful manner for his business; second, the defendant, even as a competitor of the plaintiff, was acting illegally; and third, the general welfare is best served by promoting the social goal of providing ducks for English dinner tables. The first two points are related and do not depend necessarily on who owns land or who owns the ducks. The issue for lawyers reading the case is whether the earlier ones are preconditions (e.g., having a trade to protect, or being a competing tradesman) for a plaintiff's bringing and winning this action. If so, they discuss factors limiting the pool of future plaintiffs in these actions. If, however, the third point is the dispositive one, then it makes no difference whether the plaintiff is a tradesman. Whether the three points are equally crucial to the holding, or whether the last point is "where the judge is going" and so controls all others, depends on whether you take a formalistic or a functional approach to the law of this case. An attorney must learn to treat the case both ways, both as a way of defining possession and as a method of achieving some greater social good.

Compare *Keeble* with Pierson v. Post. Post's hunt in Pierson v. Post was ostensibly for sport, while the plaintiff in *Keeble* had improved the pond for his particular purposes and was hunting ducks there as his trade or business. The court recognizes that certain types of activity in competition with another business are acceptable while others are not, even though the end result of each may be to cause one competitor to be no longer able to conduct his business profitably (or at all). The stark example given by the court is that one person may (and is even encouraged to) set up a new school to compete with an established school, even if the new school recruits faculty and students such that the old school must close. In contrast, the court deems it impermissible (in fact, do not ever advise anyone to do this) to "lie in the way with his guns, and fright the boys from going to school, [so that] their parents would not let them go thither."

In contrast to Post, who was hunting on "wild lands," Keeble was in possession of Minott's Meadow, where his pond was. Thus, Keeble was in possession ratione soli — a term meaning that the owner of land has sufficient possession of the wild animals on the land to start a hunt for them, as well as the right to pursue them while on that land. Possession ratione soli is a specific instance of constructive possession — again, not actual possession, but a type of possession treated as if it were actual possession, in other words, a legal fiction. This is the rationale for the case as reported in 11 Mod. 74, a case report available and cited by the majority in *Pierson*, and on the basis of which the majority distinguished the *Keeble* case.

Judge Holt in *Keeble* concluded that "decoy ponds and decoy ducks have been used . . . whereby the markets of the nation may be furnished." Whether the case involves ducks or venison, the opinions in both *Keeble* and *Pierson* define "possession" in such a way as to get animals to market. To do that, constructive possession suffices for the plaintiff in *Keeble*, while actual possession is required in *Pierson*.

MISAPPROPRIATION

Taking possession of an already existing object of personalty is not the only way to acquire the thing as property. A person might invent or create a thing, and be entitled to obtain a patent or copyright under federal law, or a right to sue to prevent its misappropriation generally. See International News Service v. Associated Press, 248 U.S. 215 (1918) (holding that as between two competing news services, the systematic misappropriation of "hot news" stories by one competitor (the INS) was sufficient to justify an injunction against the INS until the commercial value of the stories dissipated). The **doctrine of misappropriation** has been used and discussed in many judicial opinions. See National Basketball Ass'n, Inc. v. Motorola, Inc., 105 F.3d 841 (2d Cir. 1997) (discussing and confirming the doctrine for a "sports score" reporting service). So when a plaintiff has by substantial investment created an intangible thing of value not protected by patent, copyright, or other intellectual property law, and the defendant appropriates the intangible at little cost so that the plaintiff is injured and plaintiff's continued use of the intangible is jeopardized, an action for misappropriation will lie. Some courts are hostile to the doctrine because copying many things results in useful competition and lower prices, and often respects the limits of existing patent and copyright statutes. See Cheney Brothers v. Doris Silk Co., 35 F.2d 279 (2d Cir. 1929) (refusing to use misappropriation doctrine against dress-design copiers).

Examples

Post-*Pierson* Problems

1. Assume the facts of Pierson v. Post: Post chasing the fox with hounds leading the way.
    (a) Suppose further that the record at the trial in Pierson v. Post proved that Post's hunt was interrupted by nightfall, and he camped and slept while his dogs continued to pursue the fox overnight. Post

resumed the hunt in the morning, and thereafter the facts of *Pierson* are the same as reported in the opinion. Pierson happened by as Post closed in on the fox, and Pierson killed the fox before Post did. Would this proof change the outcome of the case?

(b) Suppose that the record at the trial in Pierson v. Post proved that Pierson saw Post running after the fox, and just as Post closed in on the animal, Pierson muttered, "That no-good Post can't have that fox," and that, just after saying that, Pierson shot the fox and carried it off right under Post's nose. Would this proof change the outcome of the case?

(c) Suppose Pierson captured and caged the fox. A week later the fox escaped the cage. The next day Post killed the fox. Pierson sues for damages. What result?

(d) Suppose Pierson captured and caged the fox. Under cover of darkness, Post then entered Pierson's land and took the fox from the cage. Pierson discovered what happened and sued Post to recover the fox. What result?

(e) What types of pursuit — short of actually resulting in possession — do you think might give rise to a judicial finding of possession?

Custom-Made Law

2. (a) Ghen is a whaler pursuing a finback whale off Cape Cod. He shoots a bomb-lance and hits the whale, which instantly dies of the wound. The whale (as whales do when dying) sinks and two days later is discovered on a beach by Ellis, who sells it to Rich. Who owns the whale? See Ghen v. Rich, 8 F. 159 (D. Mass. 1881).

(b) Why wouldn't the *Ghen* court decide its case just on the basis of the law as stated in *Pierson*? (And why wasn't *Pierson* decided according to the custom of hunters, as Judge Livingston suggested in his dissent in Pierson v. Post?)

(c) The *Ghen* opinion states: "Neither the respondent (Rich) nor Ellis knew the whale had been killed by [Ghen], but they knew or might have known, if they had wished, that it had been shot and killed with a bomb-lance, by some person engaged in this species of business." What do you think might have been the effect of this trial court finding in *Ghen* on a case like *Pierson*?

Ownership of Fish in a Creek

3. A manufacturing company discharges chemicals from its plant into a nearby creek, causing a fish kill. The state attorney general's office sues the company for the value of the fish, alleging a property interest in the fish. In this suit, what result and why?

Oil Depletion

4. Who has possession of the empty underground space left after mining or after the extraction of oil or gas from a cavity in the earth? If oil or gas was injected into the cavity, would the surface owner have a trespass action against the injecting party?

Running Interference

5. Today, almost all states have enacted hunter harassment statutes, making it at least a misdemeanor to interfere intentionally with lawful hunting, and including in the definition of "interference" actions that are intended to affect the natural behavior of a hunted wild animal. What is the likely effect of such a statute on the outcome in *Pierson*?

Explanations

Post–*Pierson* Problems

1. (a) No. The only difference is the interruption in Post's hunt — and, if anything, that interruption seems to give the result in favor of Pierson more, rather than less, support. Post would likely argue that his dogs carried on the hunt for him, so the hunt never really was interrupted, and that the dogs put Post in constructive pursuit all the while. But pursuit is not possession.

   (b) It might. With this additional proof, Pierson's intent is not to seize the fox, but to deprive Post of it. A court that considers the subjective intent or an objective manifestation of spite or maliciousness might rule in Post's favor, or more specifically might rule against Pierson because of Pierson's bad conduct. Alternatively, a court may conclude Pierson does not have the requisite intent to possess that the law requires for legal possession — i.e., two requirements are necessary for possession: intent to possess and control. Control by itself is not enough. Other courts may not look to Pierson's motives but may conclude his action of picking up the fox exhibited the requisite intent to possess and control.

   (c) Post owes no damages. An escaped wild animal is deemed to have returned to nature and once more belongs to no one. There are exceptions. If the animal is not native to the area such that a reasonable person would gather that the animal belonged to someone, the original owner remains the owner. A person seeing a kangaroo hopping though the streets of San Francisco, for example, should expect that the kangaroo belongs to someone. Second, under the doctrine of *animus revertendi*, a person does not lose his interest in an animal that has the habit of returning to its owner's property.

This usually applies to domesticated animals, and is easy to apply to cats, dogs, horses, and cattle. The doctrine is less predictable for traditionally wild animals such as deer and raccoons.

(d) Easy question. Post must return the fox. Pierson's property interest in the fox remains in full force as long as the fox is caged. Post's unlocking the cage is a wrongful interference with Pierson's rightful possession. It might even be larceny — the carrying away of chattel in the possession of another. Post's trespass onto Pierson's land, moreover, factors against Post. The law frowns on trespassers, with the result that trespassers usually lose out to landowners.

(e) It might be a pursuit (1) halted by an interference that gives rise to tort liability; or (2) halted by a person like Pierson, but whose actions also violate the hunting regulations of the state; or (3) halted by a person who commits a crime or violates some other public policy by interfering. That is, the interference by an outside party might be of such a nature as to render his activity illegal, tainting his acts from the start and so focusing the court's attention on the actions of the inter-meddler, rather than the rights of the plaintiff claiming possession.

In addition, as indicated in dicta in Pierson v. Post, use of traps or nets or wounding such that escape is highly improbable might constitute constructive possession, which results in possession being in the owner of the traps or nets, or whoever did the wounding.

Custom-Made Law

2. (a) Ghen inflicted a mortal wound and so arguably had constructive possession of the whale at that point, even though he did not have actual possession of the whale. See Ghen v. Rich, 8 F. 159 (D. Mass. 1881) (reaching this result on another ground). The trial judge in *Ghen* reported: "The usage on Cape Cod, for many years, has been that the person who kills a whale in the manner and under the circumstances described, owns it. . . ." The custom of the industry as quoted is the ground on which *Ghen* was decided.

(b) The court could have followed Pierson v. Post, but the holding would have upset an entire industry that had operated successfully under the custom of awarding the whale to the person whose iron holds the whale, with a finder receiving a salvage (a reward). The judge limited the custom-as-law holding to cases where the custom had been recognized and acquiesced in for many years, and that undoing the custom may destroy the industry. It also helped that the finder received a salvage for finding the whale and notifying the whaler. Why wasn't Pierson v. Post decided by custom? The dissent in *Pierson* wanted to do just that. One argument may be that the custom should be limited to issues unique to an industry, and Pierson and Post were not professional fox hunters. It may be that this custom was not essential to the survival of fox-hunting businesses, even if there was one at the time, or that fox hunting was not critical to the economy of the region. It may be that no one presented evidence as to what the custom was adopted in the area. It may be that, as the majority stressed, the first-to-kill (or take actual possession) criterion is easier to apply in practice. The custom of hunters, moreover, may not be in the best interests of the wider society — farmers, families, and so on.

(c) The judges in *Pierson*, relying on *Ghen*, might have said that while in pursuit Post was in constructive possession of the fox for purposes of protecting his right to hunt that fox. If so, the court would have ruled in favor of Post this time. More likely, the majority in *Pierson* would have distinguished *Ghen* on the grounds that in *Ghen* the plaintiff killed the whale. Mere pursuit of a whale conferred no benefit. *Pierson's* majority opinion, in (nonbinding) dicta, said that intercepting an animal (fox or whale) so as to deprive it of its natural liberty and make its escape impossible may be considered possession. Using this logic, harpooning and killing a whale is much like "intercepting" it, but not sighting and chasing it.

Ownership of Fish in a Creek

3. A state government may have sufficient "possession" of wild animals to regulate the hunting of them. Geer v. Conn., 161 U.S. 519 (1896). Yet this possession is for regulatory rather than hunting purposes, and so may be insufficient to justify the state's bringing an action based on ownership of the fish. *See* Commonwealth v. Agway, Inc., 232 A.2d 69 (Pa. Super. Ct. 1967). The state might be authorized by statute to do so, and this case shows the need for statutes governing water pollution and protection of wild animals, fish, and fowl.

Oil Depletion

4. The surface owner regains "possession" of the mined-out space after the minerals have been extracted. It may be a trespass, therefore, when already captured oil or gas is pumped back into the cavity for storage. Another thought, following the rule of wild animals, is that the oil has returned to its natural state (given its "natural liberty" again, if you will), and thus is owned by the first landowner to pump it back out. In that case, the injecting party does not have sufficient possession of it to commit a trespass with it — or, put another way, the surface owner could claim ownership by drilling for the oil himself. Compare Hammonds v. Central Kentucky Natural Gas Co., 75 S.W.2d 204, 206 (Ky. 1934) (holding that the injecting party does not have possession

after the injection), with Texas American Energy Corp. v. Citizens Fidelity Bk. & Tr. Co., 736 S.W.2d 25 (Ky. 1987) (overruling *Hammonds*). *Hammonds* is not the law in the major oil-producing states.

Running Interference

5. Two outcomes seem reasonable here. First, the purpose behind these statutes may be to resolve disputes between hunters and nonhunters (environmentalists and animal rights advocates), so that disputes between two hunters, such as is presented in Pierson v. Post, would be unaffected and the outcome the same as under the common law. Second, and more broadly, Post would win if the effect of such a statute was to extend the unlawful interference policy in *Keeble* to the facts of *Pierson*. Pierson's actions may reasonably be argued to have influenced the behavior of the hunted animal, and so the statutory definition of interference is met and the statute applies. The policy behind these harassment statutes further argues that the "interference" cause of action recognized in *Keeble* should be extended to the facts of *Pierson* and that the factual distinctions between the two cases — i.e., between sportsmen and commercial hunters — should be ignored today. Viewed in the light of the policy and provisions of these statutes, the plaintiffs in both cases should be seen as having a "possession" sufficient to bring their actions.

Law of Finders
and Prior Possessors

As noted in the first two chapters, possession is important in determining relative rights to things. Although familiar sayings such as "possession is nine-tenths of the law" and "finders keepers, losers weepers" are inaccurate as statements of the law, they do echo the law's recognition that a person in possession of a thing has greater rights to that thing than do most other persons.

The study of finders of personal property (property other than real property) serves many purposes. For one, the concept is easy: Someone lost something; someone else found it; now who owns it? More importantly, some rules have evolved when the original or true owner cannot be found, and the finder and the owner of the place of the find (the *locus in quo*) may each claim possession.

The study of finders law gives you the opportunity to apply the rules and rethink the law. How should a court resolve issues pertaining to finders? Should it try to fit the facts into a box of the existing rules to determine who has the superior right to the thing? Or should the court determine who prevails based on instrumental goals — i.e., considerations other than black-letter rules? Or should the court simply say, "Finders win"? The common law holds that a finder of lost property has greater rights to the found property than the entire world except the true owner. The rule is often stated, "The title of the finder is good as against the whole world but the true owner." See Raymond A. Brown, *The Law of Personal Property* 25 (3d ed. 1975). If the true owner is located, the true owner can recover the lost property. The goal of the common law here is to facilitate the return of lost property to its true owner. Many times, however, the issue is who gets the property if the true owner never surfaces.

3. Law of Finders and Prior Possessors

A finder of lost property is a person who (1) takes control of the lost property and (2) has the intent to maintain possession of the property. To illustrate, three children, Andy, Brad, and Charlie, are playing. Andy finds a bag weighty enough to be tossed. Andy tosses the bag to Brad. As Brad catches the bag, the bag breaks open and money spills on the ground. Charlie snatches up the money. To which child would you give the money, assuming the true owner cannot be located?

One answer, of course, is to say the boys are acting in unison and thus should split the money equally. Another is to say Andy took control of the bag with the intent to possess it, and thus he should get the money since the money was in the bag. A third option gives the money to Charlie since it was Charlie who took control over the money with the intent to possess it. Brad, it seems, never had the requisite control or intent to possess. The issue may turn on whether you feel Andy ever had actual control or, more likely, any intent to possess the bag or the money. See Keron v. Cashman, 33 A.1055 (N.J. 1896).

Let's explore the practical application of the general rule that a finder of lost property has greater rights to the property than the entire world except the true or rightful owner. First, the easy case: TO (true owner) loses her watch; F1 finds the watch. F1 lays the watch on a table surrounded by a group of people. While F1 is standing there, F2 picks up the watch. F1 demands F2 return the watch. F2 refuses. Which of the two has the right to leave with the watch? Answer: F1. F1 has greater rights to the watch than the entire world except the rightful owner. F2's only argument is that F1 is not the true owner, but that argument does F2 no good. F1 as finder has greater rights to the watch than does F2 and all other persons except the true owner.

The result is a good one as a practical matter since it would be very difficult for a person to prove he or she owns that which he or she possesses. For example, you probably do not carry "proof" that you own your case-book, your laptop, or your backpack.

Now a more difficult scenario: TO loses her watch; F1 finds the watch. A week later F1 loses the watch in the park. Four days later F2 walks into a room, with F1 present, and announces that she found a watch in the park. F1 asks if the watch has certain characteristics. The watch does. F1 claims the watch. F2 does not want to give the watch to F1. Question: Who should get the watch? F1 or F2?

The answer is that F1 has greater rights to the watch than the whole world except the rightful owner, and thus F1 gets the watch. F1 and F2 are both finders. The common law rule as stated does not anticipate our scenario. The rule must be modified to say a finder of lost property has greater rights to the found property than the whole world except the rightful owner, a prior or rightful possessor, or a person holding through the rightful owner or rightful possessor. F2 has greater rights than everyone except TO and F1. Once F1 appears, however, F1 gets the watch. This is another application of the first possession rule.

CONVERSION, REPLEVIN, AND TROVER

Generally, a finder will return found property to the rightful owner if the rightful owner appears. But what happens if the finder, a borrower, or another person to whom the property has been entrusted refuses to return the property, has sold or given it to another person, or has modified the property such that it may not be acceptable to the true owner? When a person wrongfully exerts control over property inconsistent with the true owner's rights to the property, that person has engaged in an act of conversion.

Conversion is a common law tort of using another's property inconsistent with the rights of the true owner or rightful possessor. The true owner or rightful possessor can recover the property. The action or remedy to recover the asset itself (plus money damages for injury to the asset) is called **replevin**. Alternatively, the rightful owner or rightful possessor can seek monetary damages for the asset. The action for monetary compensation for conversion of personal property is called **trover**. In effect, trover is a forced sale. A person who is compensated pursuant to a trover action loses his rights to have the asset returned. The decision whether to seek trover (compensation) or replevin (the return of the property) lies with the true owner or rightful possessor, not with the present possessor. Actions for conversion, replevin, and trover most often are brought by true owners, but as the following case indicates, may be brought by finders and other prior possessors.

ARMORY v. DELAMIRIE

Most casebooks introduce finders through the brief opinion in the case of Armory v. Delamirie, 1 Str. 505, 7 Term R. 396 (King's Bench, 1722). There a chimney sweep found a piece of jewelry and delivered it to a goldsmith's shop for an appraisal. The goldsmith's apprentice removed the stone and then refused to return it to the sweep. The jewelry's appraisal without the stone was for three half-pence. The goldsmith offered the sweep that sum of money for the jewelry, but the sweep refused to accept and brought an action in trover — for the value of the jewelry — against the goldsmith.

The *Armory* court held that "the finder of a jewel, though he does not by such finding acquire an absolute property or ownership, yet he has such a property as will enable him to keep it against all but the rightful owner, and consequently may maintain trover." 7 Term R. at 398. In this holding, the term "prior possessor" might be substituted for the word "finder" — and the rightful or true owner then stands for any person whose possession is prior to that of the litigating parties.

The sweep wins this case because he is the prior possessor of the jewel. He could have stolen it from the house whose chimney he last cleaned and, still, as against the goldsmith, he would be the prior possessor, even though the rule of law is that "a thief's title is void" against the true owner's. Anderson v. Gouldberg, 53 N.W. 636 (Minn. 1892) (a replevin action for stolen logs); and see Gissel v. State, 727 P.2d 1153, 1156 (Idaho 1986) (stating, "[m]ere possession alone is sufficient to sustain a trespasser's cause of action for conversion against all but the true owner," over a strong dissent that a thief should receive no reward for her crime). In the litigation here, the goldsmith is the greater wrongdoer, even assuming that the sweep was a thief.

EXTENSIONS OF THE *ARMORY* RULE — AND A RIGHT OF SUBROGATION

Suppose that the jewel's true owner found out about the facts and outcome in *Armory* and brought a lawsuit against the goldsmith. What might be the theory of such a suit? It might be brought for conversion. Why? Because the goldsmith treated the jewel as his own when refusing to return it, as he was bound to do. And because the goldsmith does not have the jewel itself anymore, the suit will have to be brought for trover (money) rather than replevin (return of the jewel). The complaint says, in essence, "You converted it, you bought it." In this suit, the court applying the rule in *Armory* will give judgment for the owner. By paying the judgment, the losing party — here, the goldsmith — acquires the rights in the jewel upon which the owner based his suit — i.e., the right to sue for the conversion of the jewel perpetrated by the goldsmith.

This goldsmith's acquisition of the true owner's rights is an example of the doctrine of **subrogation**. The owner had a right to sue, sued, and by winning transferred her rights to the defendant goldsmith. Subrogation is a succession to another's right or claim. It puts another in the place of a person originally holding the claim. By paying the true owner for the jewel, the goldsmith acquired the true owner's rights.

Suppose further that the smith uses the right acquired by subrogation to sue the chimney sweep. In this second suit, the smith is here attempting to put the parties back *status quo ante*.[1] Because (1) the smith now holds some of the rights of the owner, and (2) that owner is the holder of a right to the jewel prior in time to the sweep, the judgment should be given to the smith. Up to now, the smith has run the risk that the sweep will take the money from the

---

1. This Latin phrase means "the state of affairs at a previous time" and Latinists might say that it should read *status in quo ante*.

Armory suit and move beyond the jurisdiction of the court. It is better for the smith to bear that risk than it is for the owner to do so, but now things can be put right by returning the money to the smith. The law should do so.

LOST PROPERTY, MISLAID PROPERTY, ABANDONED PROPERTY, AND TREASURE TROVE

The law of finders discussed to this point has a semblance of rationality. Unfortunately, judges over the centuries have complicated the analysis so that someone other than the finder may get the found property. Often the courts look at various factors to determine who keeps found property.

The most typical disputes occur between the finder of the property and the owner of the land or building where the property was found. Courts have categorized ways the true owner was separated from his property. Without overruling *Armory*, over time judges began to characterize found property as lost property, mislaid property, abandoned property, or treasure trove.

Lost property is property the true owner unintentionally and unknowingly dropped or lost. Property concluded to be lost property belongs to the finder (unless and until the true owner is located). To be contrasted with lost property, **mislaid property** is property the true owner intentionally placed in a given location and then left, or intentionally left intending to return for it later. Mislaid property belongs to the owner of the *locus in quo* (the premises owner or lessee) (unless and until the true owner is located). The idea is that the possessor of the real estate on which the property is found is in a better position to give the found property back to the true owner if the true owner comes back looking for it. Judges created this second category — mislaid property — to justify giving the found property to the possessor of the *locus in quo* in an attempt to preserve the true owner's rights.

To illustrate, a finder finds a watch with a broken watchband in a shop. If the true owner's watchband broke and the watch fell to the ground, the watch is lost property; and the finder keeps the watch. On the other hand, if the true owner put the watch on a table after discovering the watchband was broken and left without picking up the watch, the property is characterized as mislaid property and the owner of the shop keeps the watch.

The difficulty with this approach is that the only person who truly knows whether the object was lost or mislaid is the true owner, who never appears. If the true owner appears and claims the watch, the ownership issue as between the finder and the shopowner is moot.

The judicial inquiry becomes only slightly more complex when two more categories are introduced. **Abandoned property** is property the true owner intentionally and voluntarily relinquished, with the intent no longer to own the object, and without transferring his rights to another person. Like

35

possession, abandonment has two elements: an act of abandonment, and the intent to abandon. Intent is not presumed: Itmust be proved. The mere passage of time gives rise to no presumption of abandonment. Abandoned property belongs to the finder.

The finder also keeps **treasure trove**, which is gold, silver, and, in some jurisdictions, currency, intentionally concealed or placed underground, with indications it has been so long concealed that the true owner has long since died. Treasure trove carries a sense of antiquity. In England, treasure trove belongs to the crown; in the United States, treasure trove goes to the finder.

OTHER CONSIDERATIONS

Some courts find other factors to be important. These remaining factors carve out exceptions to the general rule that the finder keeps found property. The exceptions favor employers and owners of the locus in quo. For example, courts disfavor trespassers. Therefore, a trespasser who finds lost property, abandoned property, or treasure trove will lose out to the landowner (unless the trespass is "trivial").

Similarly, a finder who is on premises for a limited purpose must relinquish any found property to the landowner. In an abstract way, the finder does not have permission to find things, and so is acting outside the scope of his authorized entry.

Many cases have held that employees are acting for the benefit of their employers and therefore must give all found items to their employers (mislaid objects still go to the owner of the locus in quo). Other courts require the employee to turn over the object to the employer only when the employee found the object in a place not open to the public. Hotel staff, for example, often are required to give objects found in guest rooms to the hotel; many courts would rule in favor of the hotel employee if the employee found the object in a public area such as a lobby, however.

Notwithstanding the lost/mislaid dichotomy discussed earlier, many judges will award even lost property (as well as mislaid property) to the owner of the premises if the object was found in a private place, such as a private office, rather than in a public part of the premises.

Items found in a residence belong to the owner or renter of the residence, assuming the owner or renter lives there. In Hannah v. Peel, 1 K.B. 509 (1945), the finder prevailed even though the item was found in a residence because (a) the owner had never used the house as his residence and (b) the current tenant, the British Royal Artillery, did not use the house as a residence either.

Another analytical distinction that results in a landowner rather than a finder getting possession of found property centers on whether the found object was embedded in the soil or was on the surface of the property. Objects embedded in the soil belong to the property owner and not to the finder, even if the object is foreign to the native soil. See, e.g., Goddard v. Winchell, 52 N.W. 1124 (Iowa 1892) (aerolite/meteorite), and Allred v. Biegel, 219 S.W.2d 665 (Mo. App. 1949) (ancient Indian canoe). Objects found on the *surface* might stay with the finder subject to all the earlier rules that award found property to the owners of the premises or others (mislaid property, private place, residence, limited purpose access, employee). While a few states even award treasure trove embedded in the soil to the landowner, many courts modify the embedded/surface dichotomy to award treasure trove to the finder unless the finder is a trespasser.

INSTRUMENTAL VIEW

As a policy matter, should labels of lost, mislaid, abandoned, or treasure trove; or the happenstance of where the property was found; or who found it dictate who should get ownership rights of found property? Many commentators think not, and favor an instrumental view that asks what conduct or goals should be encouraged. All, for example, agree that any rule should facilitate the return of the property to the rightful owner. You can argue that giving the finder the property encourages disclosure; otherwise, the finder may not disclose to anyone that he found the property. The same instrumental goal of returning the found object to its rightful owner also justifies giving the found object to the owner of the premises. The true owner is more likely to return to the premises where the object was lost than he is to happen upon the finder of the object. The premises owner, moreover, must store and care for the found object in case the true owner returns to claim it. As an exercise in evaluating laws, list the reasons why the finder should keep the found object and the reasons why the premises owner should get it. Once you have your lists, draft what you think would be the best statute on this subject.

LEGISLATION

About 20 states have statutes addressing this issue. Many are patterned on statutes regarding estrays.[2] Some simply modify common law or provide that finders keep the property if the true owner cannot be found. Others require a finder to report the find to the local police department. The police

---

2. A legal term for strayed, domesticated farm animals.

will take custody of the found object. After a period of time, if the true owner does not claim the property, the finder may claim not just possession but title to the property as his own. Some statutes provide that the true owner either pays a reward based on the value of the property to the finder, or else reimburses the finder for the costs and expenses of keeping the property.

Examples

I Know the Owner

1. Would the result in Armory v. Delamirie be the same if the true owner were known? Assume the same facts as *Armory* except that the chimney sweep found the jewel outside the Pickering home. The chimney sweep sues the goldsmith as before. As a defense, the goldsmith proves the jewel belongs Mrs. Pickering rather than to the sweep. What result?

The Oil Painting Caper

2. Owen purchased an expensive painting to hang in his home. Owen thereafter gave the painting to Seth, his son, with a letter saying, "If and when you don't have a place to hang it, I want it back." Owen kept the bill of sale for the painting. Seth moved to a studio apartment with no place to hang the painting. Seth consigned it to an art dealer for sale. Ted stole the painting from the dealer. Ted sold the painting to Ben. The police recovered the painting from Ben. Who should the police give the painting to? Clue: Who has the right to present possession of the painting?

Cash Preserves

3. In YEAR 1 Charles buried $25,000 in coins and paper money in tin cans and glass jars in his backyard. It was commonly known that Charles did not trust banks and hid money on his property. Charles died in YEAR 12. All his property passed to his son Ozzie. Ozzie sold the land to David in YEAR 20. Later David hired Ellison to tear down and replace a garage. In removing the garage Ellison found the tin cans and glass jars containing the $25,000.
   (a) Ozzie, David, and Ellison all claim the $25,000. Who prevails?
   (b) Was the money lost, mislaid, abandoned, or treasure trove?
   (c) Assume Ozzie cannot be found. Who gets the cash: David or Ellison?

Finders Keepers

4. Omar collects stamps. A decade or so ago he purchased a set of stamps for $150,000. Last year Omar donated a dresser to charity. Pete bought the dresser for $30. Pete found the stamps in the dresser and advertised them for sale in a nationally circulated stamp catalog. Omar saw the ad and

demanded the stamps be returned to him. Pete refused. Omar sued. Pete defended by arguing, "Finders keepers, losers weepers."

(a) Is Omar's action one for replevin or one for trover?

(b) As a judge, how would you rule on Pete's "finders keepers, losers weepers" argument?

Plane Old Money

5. Central Bank repossessed an airplane when the owner defaulted on a loan. Four months later Central Bank took the plane to Lindner Aviation for its annual inspection. Lindner Aviation conducted its business in a hanger leased from the City Airport. Benjamin, an employee of Lindner Aviation, inspected the plane. As part of the inspection Benjamin removed panels from the wings. Although these panels are supposed to be removed annually at the inspection, a few screws were rusted into place. Benjamin used a drill to remove the rusted screws and panels. Inside the left wing, Benjamin discovered two packets of $20 bills with mint dates of forty years ago. The bills totaled $80,000.

(a) As between Benjamin and Lindner Aviation, who gets the $80,000?

(b) As between the prevailing party in (a) and City Airport, who gets the money?

(c) As between the prevailing party in (b) and Central Bank, who gets the money?

(d) As between the prevailing party in (c) and the previous owner of the airplane (who defaulted on the loan to Central Bank), who gets the money?

The Horsey Set-To

6. Opal owned a racehorse. Abel acquired the title certificate to the horse from the jockey club. Abel, noticing Opal's name on the title certificate to the jockey club had been forged, transferred the title certificate to the racehorse to Ben in full payment of a debt Abel owed Ben. Ben, thinking the title certificate was legal, sold the horse and endorsed the title certificate to Cory, another trainer. Under Cory's training, the horse won several races. Opal, watching one of these races, recognized the horse as her horse. What advice would you give Opal?

Explanations

I Know the Owner

1. The case of Jeffries v. The Great Western R.R. Co., 119 Eng. Rep. 680 (Queen's Bench 1856), was a trover action for the value of "trucks" or railroad cars. It held that the outcome would be the same as in *Armory*. The rationale of *Jeffries* was that a defendant in a prior possession case should win (if at all) on the strength of his own claim to the chattel, not

because someone else not before the court has a better claim than the plaintiff

The Oil Painting Caper

2. The police should give the painting to Owen, as Owen has the present right to possession. Seth, his son, was given the painting subject to a condition that he return it upon the happening of a certain event. That event occurred. Seth's consignment to the dealer attempted to give the dealer a power (to sell) that Seth did not have. Ted, the thief, has void title — i.e., no title, and cannot transfer good title. Ben consequently acquired no rights from Ted. (The result may have been different if the dealer sold the painting in the ordinary course of his business. The power of someone legally entrusted with property to transfer legal title to an innocent purchaser is developed in Chapter 5, "Good Faith or Bona Fide Purchasers.")

Cash Preserves

3. (a) Ozzie gets the money. He inherited all of George's property, including the money and the land. He is the rightful owner of the money and prevails over David, the current landowner, and Ellison, the finder.

David's main argument is that by selling him the land, Ozzie included everything buried on the property. The money and land, however, are separate assets. The sale of one is not the sale of the other. See Ritz v. Selma United Methodist Church, 467 N.W.2d 266, 269 (Iowa 1991). David loses. Any right Ellison might have is subject to the rights of Ozzie, the rightful owner.

(b) The money was not lost. The money could be mislaid. The fact that the money is in cans and jars is some indication Charles intentionally placed the money in the ground. The value of the money and the manner of its burial indicates it was not abandoned. It might be treasure trove, but it lacks that essential feel of antiquity characteristic of treasure trove. The characterization that fits best is that the money was mislaid — intentionally placed in the ground and the whereabouts forgotten, or at least not told to Ozzie.

(c) This Example is based loosely on Corliss v. Wenner, 34 P.3d 1100 (Idaho App. 2001). Ellison must argue that the money was lost, abandoned, or treasure trove since David as owner of the premises wins if the money was mislaid. As discussed in (b), the money was mislaid. Mislaid property goes to the owner of the land. Hence David, the landowner, gets the cash.

David, moreover, could persuade a court that Ellison was on David's land for a limited purpose that did not include finding and claiming the money. Anything Ellison found in or on David's land belongs to David.

Finally, David could argue the money was embedded in the soil and not on the surface. Embedded objects belong to the owner of the soil rather than to the finder. David gets the money if Ozzie is not located.

Finders Keepers

4. (a) Omar brought an action for replevin to obtain possession of personal property wrongfully detained by another.
   (b) Under the holding of Armory v. Delamirie, Pete had greater ownership rights against the whole world except the true owner. Once Omar proves he is the true owner, he wins and Pete loses. The sale or contribution of the dresser to the charity was not a gift of the stamps inside. Finders keepers, losers weepers is not the law. See Gantor v. Kapiloff, 516 A.2d 611, 613-614 (Md. App. 1986).

Plane Old Money

5. (a) The Example is based on Benjamin v. Lindner Aviation, Inc., 534 N.W.2d 400 (Iowa 1995). Using the labels and categories, Benjamin is the finder, but as he is also an employee in a place solely because of his employment, a court likely would award the money to his employer, Lindner Aviation. From an instrumental view, if a court finds that the true owner may return, it may award the money to Lindner Aviation as being the easiest for the true owner to locate.

   On the other hand, giving the money to Benjamin rewards honesty and encourages people to publicize their findings. Despite the instrumental view, most courts would characterize the find as one by an employee and award the money to Lindner Aviation.
   (b) As between Lindner Aviation and City Airport, Lindner Aviation prevails. Although City Airport owned the land and hanger, Lindner Aviation had legal possession. While courts often speak in terms of the owner of the locus in quo, the legal possessor — the tenant in this case — keeps the money.
   (c) As between Lindner Aviation and Central Bank, the issue is whether the packets of money were "lost" or "mislaid." The packets do not have the taint of antiquity to be treasure trove. While debatable, it does not seem the money is abandoned. The very circumstance of its being $20 bills placed in packets that ended up inside the wing of an airplane suggests that someone intentionally placed the money there. Therefore, the money was mislaid and not lost. Mislaid property belongs to the owner of the place where the money was found.

The money was found in an airplane owned by the Central Bank, even though the plane was in a hanger under Lindner Aviation's control. Central Bank wins.

(d) As between Central Bank and the owner of the plane before Central Bank foreclosed, Central Bank as current owner of the plane prevails. The only chance the previous owner has is to show he was the true owner of the money. Merely owning the plane at one time avails him nothing unless there is evidence he owned the money before it was placed in the wing.

The Horsey Set-To

6. Opal may elect to sue any one of the successive convertors of her property — Abel, Ben, or Cory — in trover for money damages, probably making this election depending on the value of the horse at the time of each conversion. While Opal may obtain a judgment against each separately, only one of these judgments may be satisfied. Otherwise Opal would wind up overcompensated. So once one of them is satisfied, she cannot sue the others on the theory of the forced sale: Opal will then have exchanged the title to the horse for whatever one of the possible defendants pays. See Baram v. Farugia, 606 F.2d 42 (3d Cir. 1979). Presumably a winning horse is worth more, so the suit should be against Cory.

Assume Opal sues Cory in trover and obtains a judgment against him, but Cory is judgment proof and offers to give the title certificate back to Opal. May Opal refuse the certificate and sue Abel? Yes. Opal is not required to accept the horse back. If Opal elects not to take the horse back, the theory of her case against Abel will be based on a bailment — the bailee might redeliver the horse, but when he cannot, he is strictly liable for his failure or refusal. (Bailments are the subject of the next chapter.) What is the measure of damages for this failure to redeliver the horse? Does it include lost profits, or is it limited to the value of the horse when the bailee converted Opal's right to it? Some cases say the former, but the latter is the traditional measure of damages.

Bailments

At this point, we turn from a discussion of acquiring ownership to transferring ownership or the right to possession. Bailment, gift, and sale are the three methods of transferring possession and ownership of personal property. This chapter considers bailments. Gifts and sales are introduced in the next two chapters.

DEFINITIONS

A **bailment** is the transfer and delivery by an owner or prior possessor (the **bailor**) of possession of personal property to another (the **bailee**):

(1) whose purpose in holding possession is often for safekeeping, repair, transportation, or for some other purpose more limited than dealing with the object or chattel as would its owner, and

(2) where the return of the object or chattel in the same, or substantially the same, undamaged condition is contemplated.

This transfer of possession of property for a limited purpose, once accomplished, requires the transferee or bailee to redeliver the property to the transferor or bailor. A failure to redeliver renders the bailee strictly liable.

Bailments affect everyday life. When a person rents a car or parks it in a commercial parking lot, a bailment arises. When you leave your clothes at the cleaner's or a package at UPS, a bailment is created. Even borrowing a book from a friend gives rise to a bailment.

Bailments are common in commercial transactions. For banks, pawn-brokers, common carriers, warehouses, and hotels, bailments are at the heart of their businesses. Some commercial bailments, as with warehouses, are treated in detail in the Uniform Commercial Code, Article 7. Thus bailments represent a pervasive form of transfer transaction, arising frequently and in many commercial and noncommercial contexts.

A bailment is the result of a contract or agreement, express or implied, or the conduct of the parties — or some combination of agreement and conduct. Some jurisdictions require an express agreement to create a bailment, but also may imply agreements and bailments from conduct. Identifying a bailment requires that you look not only at the parties' agreement, but also at their conduct — if only as evidence of their implementation of an implied agreement. More generally, a bailment may be regarded as the implementation of a contract, as a transfer of property, or as some sui generis hybrid of both contract and property law.

Bailments typically also are limited to tangible personal property, but this term includes pieces of paper representing rights in other things. It is now well settled that securities, bonds, and negotiable instruments may be held in a bailment as well. Whether intellectual property may be held in a bailment is a controversial subject.

A bailment requires a delivery of possession: without delivery there is no bailment. No particular ceremony is necessary. Delivery may be actual, constructive, or symbolic. With an **actual delivery** of an object, the bailor physically hands the property over to the bailee. A **constructive delivery** occurs when one gives the keys to a safe deposit box or to a heavy or bulky object, such as a bureau or chest of drawers, to the transferee; this transfers control of the object without actually delivering it, and is the gist of a constructive delivery. A **symbolic delivery** occurs when the bailor gives the bailee a thing symbolizing the object of the bailment. While this may be something associated with the object, a symbolic delivery usually means transfer by use of a written instrument.

In addition to delivery, a bailment requires the bailee's **acceptance** of the delivered property. Like the delivery element, acceptance might not be actual. Constructive acceptance is found when a person comes into possession of an object by mistake or takes possession of it when it is left or lost by its owner.

Without a consensual delivery and acceptance, some courts refer generally to the possibility of a constructive bailment without identifying the missing element. A **constructive bailment** arises when possession of personal property is acquired and retained under circumstances in which the recipient should keep it safely and return it to its owner. See Shamrock Hilton Hotel v. Caranas, 488 S.W.2d 151 (Tex. App. Ct. 1972) (involving a purse left in a hotel dining room and found by a hotel employee). In *Caranas*, there was no intentional delivery of the purse, but the court found that a constructive bailment arose because the hotel patron would expect that, if found, the misplaced purse would be retained and kept safe for her eventual return. Thus, where there is evidence that the bailee received and accepted the object, but not that the bailor intended to deliver it, a constructive bailment arises for purposes of allocating the loss or damage to the object upon its misdelivery or damage.

OVERVIEW OF NEGLIGENCE AND STRICT LIABILITY

Some of the following material discusses when a bailee is strictly liable and when it is liable only for negligence. **Strict liability** means an actor is liable for damages notwithstanding any actions he took or failed to take. **Negligence**, on the other hand, demands the actor be at fault. Negligence depends on state law creating (1) a duty or standard of care, and (2) the defendant's action or inaction breaching that duty and so falling short of the applicable standard of care. If the actor's conduct falls below the applicable standard of care, the actor is negligent.

For the defendant to be liable for his negligence, however, the negligence must be the cause of a plaintiff's injuries. Thus injury or damage is the third element of a negligence action. In addition, the defendant's negligence must be the proximate or legal cause of the plaintiff's injury. The proximate or legal cause considerations are matters of law, including whether the legal system believes a defendant should be liable in circumstances of the case. Finally, the plaintiff must suffer actual damages. An actor's "standard of care" varies based on the circumstances and is often a determination by a jury or trier of fact as to how a "reasonable person" should act under the circumstances. As this discussion indicates, it is easier for a plaintiff to win a strict liability case than it is to win a negligence case.

SPECIALIZED BAILMENT ISSUES

(a) Pledges

Some bailments have more specialized uses. A **pledge** is a bailment to secure a debt or obligation of the bailor. It is a bailment for security. The transfer of possession need not be made to the pledgee (the creditor or obligee). Instead, it can be to a third party.

(b) Park-and-Lock Cases

One tricky area of bailments is distinguishing a bailment from a lease or license. Identifying a transaction as a bailment — instead of a lease, say — is an important step for the alleged bailor because of the duty placed on the bailee to redeliver the chattel. A failure to redeliver raises a presumption that the bailee negligently handled the chattel in her care.

Take, for example, a parking lot that requires that you pull a ticket to lift a gate at entry, choose the space in which to park, and lock your car so that it cannot be moved by the management. If parking the car in the lot constitutes a bailment, the parking lot operator becomes a bailee, and with it comes the responsibility to care for the car. If the lot operator merely gives the car owner a license to use space to park his car, no bailment results and the car remains under the owner's control. If the space is leased for a definite period of time, the car remains under the control of the car owner, and no bailment exists.

Such a park-and-lock arrangement would have at one time created no bailment. Control over the car, coupled perhaps with an exculpatory clause on the ticket, negated the delivery requirement for a bailment. A license to use the parking space was instead created, or if you paid a fee at entry, perhaps a lease was found. Today a park-and-lock arrangement in some jurisdictions creates a bailment. See Allen v. Hyatt Regency–Nashville Hotel, 668 S.W.2d 286 (Tenn. 1984) (holding that a bailment was created when a car owner parked and locked his car in an indoor multistory garage operated in conjunction with a hotel).[1]

Peeling away the facts in *Allen* shows the difficulties with these cases. What if the lot were outdoors (in a setting in which the operator has less control over the parking spaces)? What if it were not associated with a hotel? The owner of an open park-and-lock lot, in which each space has a separate meter, is an unlikely bailee. See Rhodes v. Pioneer Parking Lot, Inc., 501 S.W.2d 569 (Tenn. 1973). A license or a lease is a more likely characterization of the arrangement in such a parking lot.

The New Jersey Supreme Court has ruled that the traditional elements of a bailment are inadequate for the enclosed park-and-lock lot cases and has found that a parking lot owner has a duty of reasonable care under all the circumstances of a case and that when the parked car is damaged upon its owner's return, there is a presumption of negligence by the owner of an enclosed lot because (1) the owner is in the best position to absorb and spread the risk of damage; (2) the car owner's expectation is that he will reclaim the car in the condition he left it; and (3) were it otherwise, the

---

1. Absent a statute, an innkeeper was strictly liable at common law for his guests' personal safety and property.

owner's proof of negligence while he was away "imposes a difficult, if not insurmountable, burden" on him. See McGlynn v. Parking Authority of City of Newark, 432 A.2d 99 (N.J. 1981).

Even when a bailment is recognized in a transaction, identifying the subject of the bailment may provide further problems. In a jurisdiction in which park-and-lock parking creates a bailment, the bailee will be liable for any vandalism that damages the exterior of the parked car, but might still argue that no bailment was created as to valuables found in — and stolen from — its glove compartment. The ground for this argument is that valuables might be expected to be found in, say, a safe deposit box in a bank, but not in the glove compartment of a car. There are exceptions, however. The operator of a parking garage in a well-known tourist location, such as the French Quarter of New Orleans, however, may be held to know that tourists carry valuables in the trunks of their cars.

(c) Safe Deposit Boxes

The same preliminary issues occur when a person rents a safe deposit box at a bank: Is the renting of the box a bailment, license, or lease? Despite the use of the word "rent" in transaction, courts usually find a bailment has occurred. The box remains under the bank's control.

MISDELIVERY OF BAILED PROPERTY

(a) Strict Liability and Negligence

The relationship between bailor and bailee gives rise to a standard of care and liability for the misdelivery or misredelivery of the object. Causes of action involving bailments are styled in their complaints in either contract or tort. For misdelivery of the bailed object, the bailee is strictly liable in tort absent a special agreement or a statute. A bailee is liable even if the bailee is not at fault for the misdelivery. An important example of a statute absolving a bailee from strict liability for misdelivery is found in the Uniform Commercial Code sections applicable to warehouse operators. UCC §7-404 (imposing no duty if reasonable commercial standards are used by the warehouseman). Otherwise, the bailee is strictly liable for a misdelivery of the chattel. In some states, a rule of strict liability has been replaced by a presumption of negligence — i.e., by a rule that says that unless the bailee can account for the loss of the bailed item in some nonnegligent way, a presumption arises that its loss was the result of the bailee's negligence.

(b) Burden of Proof

The burden of proof in a negligence case of misdelivery is on the bailee—who is generally the defendant in such cases—to show that he did not act in a negligent manner. This asks the bailee to prove a negative—that he was not negligent—and this is a very difficult task.

This burden of proof is assigned to the bailee for five reasons. First, the bailee knows the history of the bailment best. Second, the bailee has the right to sue thieves and converters of the chattel. Third, the bailee is in the best position to take steps to secure or recover the chattel. Fourth, the bailee can spread the risk of damage or misdelivery in its charges to customers. Fifth, and finally, the assignment serves to prevent the bailee from engaging in fraudulent misdeliveries or other acts. Many of these justifications also support holding the bailee strictly liable for damaged or misdelivered goods. To some extent, then, the assignment of this burden to the bailee serves as a stand-in or surrogate for strict liability.

Even if the bailee took reasonable care, a failure to take steps to secure the recovery of the chattel would render the bailee liable, unless the steps would have been futile.

A bailee who deviates from the terms of the bailment must show that the deviation made no difference to the loss or damage. Examples arise when the bailee takes a different route than instructed, or when the bailee entrusts the goods to a third party without authority, or where the chattel is stored elsewhere than as authorized. The deviating bailee in effect becomes the insurer of the goods and strict liability follows, unless the bailee can show that the deviation was harmless.

(c) What Must Be Redelivered

Generally it is obvious that property must be returned to the bailor. The issue in some cases, however, is what must be delivered back to the bailor. Consider the following four examples: First, a deposit of money in a bank. Here the same bills are not expected back, so no bailment arises; rather, a debtor-creditor relationship arises between the bank and its depositor.

Second, consider the deposit of grain into a silo or a grain elevator for its operator to hold for delivery to a railroad. Here the depositor expects that a similar quality of grain will be given over or back, but not the exact grains deposited. If the silo operator goes bankrupt, will the depositor have a lien on the silo's contents in order to recover the value of the grain? Does the lien suffice as a remedy for the depositor? The purpose of the bailment sometimes determines its presence or absence.

Third, a herd of cattle is put in the care of a farmer. Only if all the animals perished in the hands of the transferee would a court find this to be a bailment. The herd can be expected to suffer attrition if it is mostly bulls, but not so if it is mostly cows. Some courts might hold that the herd as a whole is the subject of a bailment, but that there is no bailment of the individual animals in it.

Fourth, consider seed delivered to a farmer by a merchant. There is no bailment when the merchant expects a mature crop in return. If bailor and bailee expect a change in the basic nature of the chattel, there is no bailment. But what if a transferee delivers grapes and expects to get wine back, delivers apples and expects cider, or delivers leather and expects shoes? That the bailed property is due back in some altered state is no reason not to find a bailment, unless there is some type of "net yield" clause in the agreement, in which case the bailee might keep the excess over the agreed-upon yield and the transaction might be seen as a partial sale of the property.

WHEN BAILED PROPERTY IS LOST OR DAMAGED

The bailee is liable not only for misdeliveries, but also if the bailed goods are lost or damaged. Strict liability does not apply in lost or damaged property cases. The bailee is liable only in negligence.

The **standard of care** traditionally required of the bailee varies with the degree of reward or benefit the bailee receives. A three-pronged rule is used, as follows:

(1) When the benefit of the bailment to the bailee is slight, the care required of the bailee is slight; the bailee is liable only for **gross negligence**. This is typically a **gratuitous bailment** such as a person taking care of an object for a friend or neighbor, or one created by a mistake. Ordinarily, a finder is such a bailee.

(2) If the bailment benefits both bailor and bailee mutually and is equally beneficial to both, the standard of care imposed on the bailee rises and the bailee is liable for negligence and has a duty of reasonable care under the circumstances. Leaving an item in a packet with the desk clerk of a hotel was found in one case to be a bailment benefiting both the bailor (the guest) and the bailee (the hotel). Peet v. Roth Hotel Co., 253 N.W. 546 (Minn. 1934); Shamrock Hilton Hotel v. Caranas, 488 S.W.2d 151 (Tex. App. Ct. 1972) (involving a purse left in a hotel dining room and found by a busboy). In Caranas, for example, leaving the purse unattended on the floor might not create a bailment, but the subsequent assumption of its possession by an employee does—and its subsequent disappearance from the hostess's desk will make the hotel liable for a misdelivery.

(3) Finally, if the bailment benefits the bailee, as with a borrowed object, the bailee's standard of care rises again and the merest neglect or any damage renders the bailee liable. This higher standard of care also applies to certain commercial bailees such as transport companies and repair shops.

This three-pronged standard has been challenged as too mechanical or too focused on a bailee's rewards instead of on the parties' conduct. Consequently, some courts have abandoned this three-pronged standard of care either expressly or with opinions that tend to combine or blur the several standards. These courts adopt, expressly or in fact, a rule of reasonable care under the circumstances (including as a circumstance the degree of benefit received by the bailee), making a bailee's liability dependent on the exercise of such reasonable care. This reasonable-care rule juxtaposes the risk and the bailee's conduct; the relationship between the risk and the conduct determines how much care is reasonable under the circumstances.

Examples

Honor Among Thieves

1. Armas steals a valuable wristwatch from its true owner and then takes it to Burrell's shop for repairs. Clayton sees the watch on Burrell's shop counter and takes it. Can Burrell replevy the watch from Clayton?

Parking Lot Tribulation

2. During the early evening hours, Darrell parks his car in an attended parking lot. He gives the keys to the attendant, who asks him how long it will be before Darrell returns. Darrell says that he will return at midnight, two hours after the lot closes. The attendant moves the car into a space visible from the booth and Darrell pays the parking fee for the hours up to closing. The attendant says that at closing he will put the keys to Darrell's car under the floor mat. Darrell nods to the effect that he has heard the attendant, but when he returns at midnight, his car has vanished. Darrell sues the parking lot owner for conversion of the vehicle. In this suit, what result and why?

High-Priced Free Parking

3. Florence went shopping. On the way, she stopped at a drive-through sandwich shop. After paying for her food, Florence put her wallet on the passenger seat. Florence parked her car at Barney's Clothes, Inc., which maintains a free parking lot for its customers. An attendant tends the lot. At the request of the parking lot attendant, Florence left her keys with

him. When Florence left her car to go shopping, she inadvertently left the wallet on the car seat.

When trying to pay for a new outfit, Florence missed her wallet and immediately returned to her car. Neither she, the attendant, nor the police could find Florence's wallet. The wallet contained $350. Florence sues Barney's Clothes for the value of the wallet but mainly for the $350. Who prevails?

Borne Away Bearer Bonds

4. A messenger employed by Stock & Co., a corporate securities brokerage firm, is instructed to deliver some bearer or demand bonds of Harmony Company to Bond Brothers, Inc., another securities firm. The messenger is given the bearer bonds of Harman, Inc., instead of those for Harmony Company. He carries the Harman bonds to Bond Brothers. He enters the Bond Brothers' office, approaches the receiving teller's window, rings the bell, deposits the bonds in a secure box to the side of the window, turns away, and returns to Stock & Co. An employee of Bond Brothers quickly notices the mistake, calls "Stock" through the window, and is approached by a man who says, "Yes, stock." The employee hands the Harman bonds to the man, who takes them and vanishes. Has a bailment for the bonds been created at Bond Brothers' office?

Organ Solo

5. The biotechnology industry is in part founded on the use of other people's body parts. Is a bailment created when a diseased organ is removed surgically from a patient by a doctor and later used in research that produces valuable medicine?

Are My Pictures Back?

6. Is a photography laboratory that accepts undeveloped film for processing into prints or slides a bailee of the film? Is this a bailment where the same thing, or a different chattel, is expected back? If there is a bailment, is the lab liable for the value of the film or the value of the prints? Can the fine print on the box of film or the receipt for the film exculpate or limit the liability of the lab?

Two Bailors

7. Orlando asked Aron to take some jewelry to Ben to be cleaned. Aron delivered Orlando's jewelry to Ben as directed. On the promised date Orlando called for the jewelry and demanded possession. Must Ben deliver them to Orlando?

Explanations

Honor Among Thieves

1. Yes. The issue is whether the bailee (Burrell) of a thief (Armas) acquires the right to sue third-party wrongdoers (Clayton) in replevin. The orderly conduct of bailments requires that although the thief has no possessory right to transfer, a second thief or other person without right should not be able to set up a weakness in bailor's (Armas') ownership as a defense.

Parking Lot Tribulation

2. The transfer of the keys, as well as the moving of the car by the attendant to a space selected by the attendant, suggests that there is a bailment. Assuming the attendant was acting within the scope of his employment, the crucial question is whether there was a constructive redelivery of the car. Because the action of the attendant made possible the theft, the rule of strict liability or the presumption of negligence should apply. See System Auto Parks & Garages v. Am. Economy Ins. Co., 411 N.E.2d 163 (Ind. App. Ct. 1980).

High-Priced Free Parking

3. This Example derives from Swarth v. Barney's Clothes, Inc., 242 N.Y.S.2d 922 (1963). Barney's Clothes wins. Barney's was bailee of the automobile under the facts, but it does not necessarily follow that Barney's was bailee of the wallet. The elements of the bailment are actual physical control with intent to possess — i.e., delivery and acceptance. Assuming the wallet was "delivered," there was no acceptance or intent to possess. A wallet is not usually possessed by the operator of the parking lot, and the attendant had no notice of the wallet. No bailment of the wallet; thus no liability under the bailment rules.

Borne Away Bearer Bonds

4. These are the facts of Cowen v. Pressprich 192 N.Y.S. 242 (N.Y. Sup. Ct. App. Term), rev., 194 N.Y.S. 926 (1922). The intermediate appeals court first held that a bailment was created. It was at first an involuntary or gratuitous one, to which only the slightest duty attached. When the Bond Brothers employee picked up the Harman bonds, however, it became a voluntary one, and a duty of reasonable care attached. Not having seen the messenger from Stock & Co., the Bond Brothers employee should have required identification, sent the bonds back using its own employees, or called Stock & Co. to check the identity of the messenger. Instead, the court said, when Bond Brothers undertook to redeliver the bonds, it took

the risk of misdelivery upon itself, and so should pay damages for its conversion of the bonds. The intermediate appeals court opinion in *Cowen* was issued over a strong dissent.

On further appeal, the state's highest appellate court adopted the lower court dissenter's analysis based on the fact that Bond Brothers took possession by mistake, and promptly noticed and honestly tried to remedy the mistake, without any intent to interfere with the plaintiff's ownership of the bonds and by an action consistent with the plaintiff's ownership. The highest appellate court concluded that Bond Brothers never accepted delivery and hence did not take on the responsibilities of a bailee. Because no bailment was created in Bond Brothers, Bond Brothers was not strictly liable for misdelivery of the Harmon bonds.

Organ Solo

5. Several issues arise. Many are discussed in Moore v. Board of Regents of the University of California, 793 P.2d 479 (Cal. 1990) (finding a breach of fiduciary duty and no patient consent, but not conversion). The first is whether a human organ can be the object of a bailment by the donor. Many courts and statutes frown on treating the human body as an object to be bought and sold in commerce. Many states refuse to recognize the organ as personal property; hence the bailment rules would not apply.

If the bailment rules do apply, the issue turns on whether the patient intended to give the organ to the surgeon for any purpose or for a limited purpose of destroying it according to law, whether the patient abandoned or released all interest in the organ, or whether the patient retained a property interest in the organ. Since there is no evidence that the patient intended to deliver the organ to the surgeon for research purposes, if the state permits a bailment in this situation, a finding of bailment — or at least constructive bailment — and conversion seems appropriate.

Are My Pictures Back?

6. The laboratory is a bailee. The photos to be returned can be traced to the original film, which distinguishes this case from one of fungible goods. The lab is liable for the price of the film. This may be a case where the lab can limit its liability. Some courts may not allow a bailee to limit its liability for its own negligence, however. This Explanation also assumes the laboratory has no reason to know of any "special circumstances" about this film's importance. See Carr v. Hoosier Photo Labs, 441 N.E.2d 450 (Ind. 1982) (holding, first, that it was a bailment to return the film, though in a new form; second, that the photographer accepted the terms of the exculpatory provision on both the box of film and the receipt for the film given by the lab; and third, that the provision was neither unconscionable nor void). *Carr* involved an experienced amateur

photographer, also an attorney with a business law practice, who took a European trip and brought back 18 rolls of exposed film for processing to a major film manufacturer's lab. Four of the rolls were lost and never accounted for. The photographer won a $13.60 judgment for the value of the film, but lost a lower court's award of $1000 for the value of his prints to him.

Two Bailors

7. Yes, Ben must deliver the jewelry to Orlando when Orlando provides proof of ownership. Older cases might add that Orlando should obtain a court order mandating that Ben deliver the jewelry to him. See Hentz v. The Idaho, 93 U.S. 575 (1876). In either event, delivery of the jewelry to the true or rightful owner should justify their later non-delivery to the bailor. Acceptance of the bailment should not estop the bailee from inquiring into the rights of the bailor. Acceptance raises only a rebuttable presumption of the bailor's right. An otherwise silent bailment agreement implicitly provides that the bailee will restore or redeliver the goods, deliver them at the direction of the bailee, or else account for their delivery. The bailee accounts for the goods when he delivers them to one whose rights are superior to the bailor's. A rule of judicial economy justifies this result.

Good-Faith or Bona Fide Purchasers

Chapter 4, on bailments, explained that the bailee (possessor of the property belonging to another) is obligated to redeliver the property to the bailor or to the rightful or true owner. This chapter deals with the rights of the true owner against a third party if the bailee wrongfully sells the object to the third party. It also addresses the rights of the true owner against good-faith third-party purchasers who purchased from thieves or other persons with voidable title. From the good-faith purchaser's perspective, the issue is the risk she takes that she must return a purchased item to the true owner.

A **good-faith** or **bona fide purchaser** (BFP) of personal or real property is a person who buys honestly and without notice of any conflicting claim on the property bought, whether or not the purchaser is negligent. A BFP must act in good faith and without notice that the wrongdoer did not have good title. In addition, the BFP must pay valuable consideration. If she signed a note or IOU or has not made payment, she has not yet suffered a loss. Hence she needs no protection. She has no obligation to pay. A donee — a recipient of a gift or a person who inherits from the wrongdoer — is not a purchaser and is not protected under this rule. The price paid by the BFP must provide adequate consideration, not necessarily fair market value, as long as the price is not so inadequate as to warrant a conclusion the purchase was not bona fide.

Example: Bert buys a television set from Andy, intentionally giving Andy a bad check. Bert later sells the television to Peter. Peter might not inquire about the identity of the prior owner or he may inquire and be told that Bert has forgotten who that was. Even though Peter does not insist on finding out who the former owner is, he still qualifies as a BFP, even though, had he insisted, he would have learned of Bert's fraud. Bert can give a better right to the television than he had.

This situation illustrates one of the two exceptions to the maxim that no one acquires greater rights in an object than one's vendor has to transfer. The first exception is for **good-faith purchasers** and the second is for **entrustments**. Both apply only in some limited, but important, situations. They are important because, as in the example in the previous paragraph, when and if one of the two exceptions applies, a person can transfer more rights to property than he has.

VOID TITLE, VOIDABLE TITLE, AND BONA FIDE PURCHASERS

At early common law, the law favored owners over all persons. A person could transfer only the rights he enjoyed; he could not transfer more rights than he had. Under this approach, a good-faith purchaser who bought an item from someone who did not have good title to it would return the item to the rightful owner without compensation. If the seller could not be found, the bona fide purchaser would be out his money too.

The rule that a person cannot transfer better title than he has is still the rule in cases where the transferor has a void title. **Void title** means no title. A bailee, for example, has no title, and generally cannot transfer good title (but see *entrustment, infra*). A thief has no title. A person buying stolen goods can be forced to relinquish the goods to the rightful owner.

When commercial markets developed, good-faith purchasers needed protection. It would stymie market trade if every seller had to document all owners in his chain of title for every item sold. Thus exceptions developed to the concept that a person without good title could not transfer good title. The first exception to the general rule occurs when the true owner is tricked by fraud or misrepresentation into voluntarily parting with title. The wrongdoer can transfer good title to a good-faith purchaser. The above Bert and Peter example is one such case. In another, the fraud or misrepresentation might happen because the dishonest purchaser misrepresented his identity. For example, the wrongdoer may negotiate a purchase by convincing the true owner he is wealthy when he is not, or he may trick the true owner into signing a document that transfers title, the true owner thinking the document is another instrument.

The courts label the title in these cases **voidable title**. The title is voidable in that the true owner can rescind the transaction and get the property back. Voidable title in the wrongdoer is good until the true owner rescinds, at which time the wrongdoer's title becomes void. If, however, the wrongdoer sells the object to a bona fide purchaser (BFP) — a person who pays fair value without notice the wrongdoer does not have good title — the BFP receives good title and will prevail even against the original owner. Thus, while the true owner can void the title of the wrongdoer, the true owner cannot void the title of the BFP.

The reason the wrongdoer can transfer good title has nothing to do with the wrongdoer. The courts, faced with two innocent parties having to suffer a loss, lay the loss at the feet of the true owner since she was the one who helped create the situation by transferring title to the wrongdoer. Of the two innocent parties, the innocent person who most easily could have prevented the problem or misunderstanding must suffer the loss. The true owner still has recourse against the wrongdoer, if she can find him.

As a reminder, the BFP prevails only if the true owner transfers title to the wrongdoer. A thief cannot transfer good title, even to a good-faith purchaser.

THE UCC AND BONA FIDE PURCHASERS

The following section of the Uniform Commercial Code (UCC), adopted in some form in all states but Louisiana, has been very influential in the law concerning bona fide purchasers.

> **UCC §2-403 (1962).** (1) purchaser of goods acquires all title which his transferor had or had power to transfer except that a purchaser of a limited interest acquires rights only to the extent of the interest purchased. A person with voidable title has power to transfer a good title to a good faith purchaser for value. When goods have been delivered under a transaction of purchase the purchaser has such power even though (a) the transferor was deceived as to the identity of the purchaser, or (b) the delivery was in exchange for a check which is later dishonored, or (c) it was agreed that the transaction was to be a "cash sale," or (d) the delivery was procured through fraud punishable as larcenous under the criminal law.

The first sentence in subsection (1) states that no vendor can transfer a better title than he or she has. It also restates, by implication, the void title rule, to the effect that a vendor with a void title cannot transfer any title at all. Subsection (1)'s second sentence expressly restates the voidable title rule, and so gives the true owner the power to revoke a transfer of goods in the hands of the transferee, while also giving that transferee the power to render it absolute by himself transferring it to a BFP. A voidable title is defective, but not wholly so. Instead, it is a title subject to a right of rescission in the transferor or the true owner of the object.

The UCC's bona fide purchaser is a person who acquires title (1) in a transaction in which a fair market value of the object is the consideration, (2) with an honest belief that he was acquiring title to the object, and (3) under circumstances that would not lead him to think otherwise. These requirements are not unusual; they merely restate the law as it existed prior to, and the law made as a result of, the UCC. The first requirement means again that a donee would not qualify as a BFP; some new and separate consideration must be given by the purchaser. The second requirement means that the transaction must be complete before the purchaser has knowledge — actual or implied — of the true owner's claim. The third requirement has been expanded under the UCC to require a purchaser to investigate the title offered with due diligence. See, e.g., Porter v. Wertz, 416 N.Y.S.2d 254 (N.Y. App. Div. 1979), affirmed, 421 N.E.2d 500 (N.Y. 1981) (involving the sale of a painting, and requiring that the gallery purchasing it investigate the title of its transferor, but without providing guidelines for that investigation). Such due diligence is important when the personalty is expensive — as with works of art or racehorses.

The UCC states that a person is not prevented from becoming a bona fide purchaser "even though . . . the transferor was deceived as to the identity of the purchaser. . . ." UCC §2-403(1)(a). What is deceptive is seen from the transferor's point of view. However, the intent of the UCC might be said to protect bona fide purchasers from both elegant and crude deceptions. The drafters' comment on this section says generally that it is specifically aimed at protecting the bona fide purchaser in situations "troublesome under prior law" (without ever saying what the trouble was). UCC §2-403, Comment 1 (1962).

If the UCC does abolish the distinctions of prior law, the con artists and rogues of the world might then extract a voidable title from owners — not to protect themselves, but to protect those of their transferees who pay value and can show bona fide ownership. Thus, whether the con artist uses face-to-face impersonation, the mail, the fax machine, or other means of deception should not matter. However, under this provision of the UCC, a theft accomplished by fraud and not by misrepresentation still leaves the thief with a void title.

ENTRUSTMENT

The second exception to the maxim that no one acquires greater rights in an object than one's vendor has to transfer occurs when a true owner "entrusts" her property to a merchant who deals in the type of goods entrusted. Under common law, a bailee did not have title and could not transfer good title to a good-faith purchaser. Recognizing that commerce would operate best if purchasers were assured they could keep objects they bought from merchants, first courts and then the UCC stepped forward to protect people who purchased from "merchants." UCC §2-403 provides:

> (2) Any entrusting of possession of goods to a merchant who deals in goods of that kind gives him power to transfer all rights of the entruster to a buyer in ordinary course of business.
>
> (3) "Entrusting" includes any delivery and any acquiescence in retention of possession regardless of any condition expressed between the parties to the delivery or acquiescence and regardless of whether the procurement of the entrusting or the possessor's disposition of the goods have been such as to be larcenous under the criminal law.

In this statutory exception to the void title rule, when a chattel's owner delivers the property to a bailee who is a merchant, and the bailee wrongfully sells the property to a person who buys it "in the ordinary course" of the bailee's business, the owner is estopped to deny the title of the purchaser. See Zendman v. Harry Winston, Inc., 111 N.E.2d 871 (N.Y. 1953). This exception is intended to keep trade and commerce with merchants humming by safeguarding purchasers' rights to what they think they have bought.

The definition of "entrustment" expressly states that the merchant can transfer good title to a purchaser in the ordinary course of business, regardless of any agreement between the entrusting person and the "entrustee." A former owner or possessor may not raise or assert objections to the subsequent extraordinary transfer, based on what the person dealing with an entrustee could not know. To illustrate, a person takes a diamond necklace to a jeweler solely to have the necklace appraised. The jeweler sells the necklace to a customer who happened to see it in the shop. UCC §2-403 protects the purchaser who bought from a merchant in the ordinary course of the merchant's business. The necklace's original owner's only remedy is against the merchant for damages.

A "buyer in the ordinary course of business" is "a person who in good faith and without knowledge that the sale to him is in violation of the ownership rights or security interest of a third party in the goods buys in ordinary course from a person in the business of selling goods of that kind." See UCC §2-201(9) (1962). Excluded from this definition is a pawnbroker, who is governed usually by special state statutes and regulations.

Examples

Broaching the Brooch

1. Joan, the owner of a valuable brooch, transfers it to TCo, a trust company, to hold in trust for Bess. A trust involves TCo's retention of the legal title, while Bess as the so-called beneficiary of the trust has the right to use it (the so-called equitable interest). Before giving it to Bess,

59

however, TCo mistakenly sells the brooch to Pete, a bona fide purchaser. Does Pete get to keep the brooch?

A Man of Wealth and Fame

2. Odetta meets Ricardo. Odetta is induced by Ricardo's false representation that he is JR (a man of wealth and good reputation), so that Odetta parts with possession of a jewel. Ricardo sells the jewel to BFP, a bona fide purchaser. In a suit between Odetta and BFP, what result and why?

The Trusting Entruster

3. (a) Oprah purchases an expensive painting to hang in her home. Oprah thereafter delivers the painting to Dan, an art dealer and conservator, for cleaning. A week later, Bridget sees the painting hanging in Dan's gallery and showroom and purchases it from Dan for a fair price and without any actual knowledge that Dan does not own it. Who now owns the painting?

   (b) Same facts, except that Bridget sees the painting in Dan's conservator shop, rather than in Dan's gallery. Bridget purchases as before. Who owns the painting?

   (c) Same facts as in (a), except that Bridget is another art dealer and owner of an art gallery. Should another merchant have the benefit of the UCC's entrustment provision, or is it just a "consumer statute"?

Stolen Goods

4. (a) Olive removes her brooch during dinner at a restaurant. When Olive is distracted, Rolfe picks up the brooch and walks away with it. Rolfe sells the brooch to Benny, a good-faith purchaser. In Olive v. Benny, who prevails?

   (b) Same facts as in (a), except Rolfe sells the brooch to Benny, a good-faith purchaser who sees the brooch in Rolfe's jewelry store. Who prevails between Olive and Benny?

Explanations

Broaching the Brooch

1. Yes. Joan intended to split the title into a legal and an equitable component, so the title in TCo's hands was voidable (one that Joan could rescind to prevent TCo from misusing it), so, if as stated, Pete was in fact a bona fide purchaser, Pete's ownership now trumps Joan's. Bess still has a remedy: she has the right to sue TCo for a breach of TCo's fiduciary duty as a trustee, measuring damages by the lost value of the brooch, but no right to replevin the brooch from Pete.

A Man of Wealth and Fame

2. Odetta intended to deal with Ricardo and, because Ricardo posed as JR, Odetta transferred the jewel to him. Odetta assumed the risk that Ricardo was not JR when she could have checked the facts and the representation made, but did not do so. If she had checked and discovered that Ricardo was not JR, then she would have had a right to rescind. Ricardo had a voidable ownership or a title that ripened into absolute title once in the hands of a BFP. Moreover, as between Odetta and BFP, Odetta had the ability to prevent the problem, and did not do so. On the equities of the situation, judgment for BFP. See Phelps v. McQuade, 115 N.E. 441 (N.Y. 1917). Although mistaken as to the identity of the purchaser, the owner's primary intent was to sell the chattel to the person he met face to face.

The Trusting Entruster

3. (a) Bridget owns the painting because she has dealt with a merchant to whom the painting has been "entrusted" — i.e., transferred to a "merchant who deals in art work." Although the painting was given to Dan for a limited purpose (this transfer creates a bailment), its hanging in the gallery of an art dealer gives Bridget the undisputed impression that Dan deals, in the ordinary course of his business, in works of art of a similar type. So under UCC §2-403(2), Dan has authority to transfer absolute ownership of the painting to Bridget.

   (b) Oprah does. With the change in the location of the painting, the doctrine of entrustment is not available to Bridget. Bridget's seeing the painting in the shop would not give her the impression that Dan has the authority to sell it. Bridget might then be tempted to fall back on the argument that Dan has a voidable title, not a void one, and then on proof that she is a bona fide purchaser. Although Bridget gives every indication of being a bona fide purchaser, the transfer by Dan defrauds Oprah and gives Bridget only a void title, one that can never ripen into absolute ownership for Bridget.

   (c) A good question. There is authority that because the Code is not clear on this, the provision's protection should also extend to other merchants. Mattek v. Malofsky, 165 N.W.2d 406 (Wis. 1969) (so long as the merchant has observed reasonable commercial standards of care in the acquisition).

Stolen Goods

4. (a) Olive wins. Rolfe had no title. His title is void and he cannot transfer good title to Benny.

   (b) Olive still wins. Rolfe had void title, not voidable title. Rolfe stole the brooch. Olive did not entrust it to him, so Benny cannot rely on UCC §2-403.

Gifts

CHAPTER

6

Gifts play an important role in life and law. We saw in Chapter 5 that a donee — the recipient of a gift — is not a bona fide or good-faith purchaser because she is not a "purchaser." Similarly, as you will study later in your course, real estate recording acts do not protect donees the way they protect good-faith purchasers and creditors. However, many uses of common law estates and interests, discussed later in this book, begin with a gift or a bequest.

A **gift** is a noncontractual, gratuitous transfer of property. It is made without legal consideration. If there is consideration, the law of gifts does not apply. A transfer for consideration is a sale, and the law of contracts applies.

There are two types of gifts: first, a gift between living persons is called an **inter vivos gift**; second, a gift made on account of a donor's impending death is called a **gift causa mortis**. A transfer of property by will after a person's death is called a **devise** or **bequest** and not a gift.

INTER VIVOS GIFTS

An **inter vivos gift** is a gift between living persons. Three elements are necessary for an effective gift:

1. Donative Intent: The donor's intent to transfer ownership of the object to the donee.

63

2. Delivery of the object to the donee.
3. Donee's acceptance of the object.

Thus, the donor's **donative intent**, plus physical **delivery** and **acceptance** are the three elements required for a valid gift.

(a) Donative Intent

For a gift to be effective the donor must **intend** to make the gift. Mere delivery is not a gift. The delivery, after all, may have been part of a loan, or a bailment. Courts are suspicious of the claim that a gift was made, and will scrutinize the facts of a transfer to ensure that the donor had the requisite intent. Indeed, the donor's intent controls the gift, and an otherwise silent deed of gift is construed in the donor's favor — unlike a bill of sale, whose terms are construed in favor of the transferee or buyer.

The donee bears the burden of proof to show that the donor had the donative intent. The evidentiary standard for a showing of donative intent — i.e., clear and convincing evidence — is high. Often, vague terms evidence a transfer of an object, as when someone says, "Take charge of this." It will be up to the alleged donee to show that a gift was intended. Thus the law's suspicion about gifts is soundly grounded in a skeptic's view that a person would not freely give away property.

Having the intent to make an oral gift and delivery of that gift usually occur simultaneously, but not always. If someone lends a book to a friend, but later discovers that he has two copies of it and says that the friend can keep the loaned copy, the donative intent exists. Proving that an oral gift of the book was intended can be very difficult, however, since its delivery and the intent to deliver it occurred at different times. Certainly the lender's statement that the friend can keep the book is evidence of a donative intent; while evidence after the time of delivery is admissible, it is not as convincing as evidence of intent at the time of delivery. On the other hand, a donor's saying, "I'll give you the book next week," is evidence of intent and the delivery and acceptance that next week by the donee will complete the gift transaction. In a third transaction, when the donor says, "I'll give the book to you, friend, if I find out that I have a second copy of it," there is no gift until there has been a delivery. A gift cannot be subject to a condition precedent (an act or event that must occur or not occur before the gift will be made or become effective).

Note that if the donor makes a gift of a book because he thought he had two copies of it and discovers after delivering the book that he did *not* have two copies of it, he cannot demand the book back. The gift was complete — and irrevocable — when the gift was accepted by the donee. Even if the donor says that having a spare copy is a condition of the gift, that condition will not survive the donee's acceptance. An oral condition on a gift is invalid on the acceptance or completion of the gift. The difficulties of proof, and the temptation the donor might feel to make up conditions after the fact, are simply too great. The law's treatment of gifts is, after all, rooted in its distaste for perjury.

(b) Delivery

Delivery is a necessary element of a gift. Usually, delivery entails the actual physical delivery of the object. An agreement that a donor will transfer, and another receive, an object is insufficient for a delivery. A mere promise to make a gift, moreover, is unenforceable by the donee because the consideration necessary for a binding contract is missing: the donor can decide not to make the gift (revoke the promise) any time before delivery. Once the gift is completed, however, ownership shifts and the lack of consideration is no longer a concern.

When physical delivery is impossible (the chattel is large or heavy) or impractical (it is in the hands of a third party, or in a bailee's possession), physical delivery is not required and courts have shown a willingness to recognize other types of delivery. In such circumstances, the delivery element may be satisfied by a symbolic delivery. A **symbolic delivery** occurs when the thing delivered stands in the place of the property. Symbolic delivery occurs, for example, when a picture of a large chest of drawers is delivered to the donee; that would be a symbolic delivery of the chest. Another example involves the delivery of one item (a necklace for example), along with a written inventory of similar items: The one in such a situation stands for the many. A symbolic delivery in these situations may be either representational (the chest of drawers situation) or representative (the necklace example). Generally, a sale deed or deed of gift stands for the thing itself; likewise, a corporate share certificate stands for the interest in the entity.

A delivery may also be **constructive**. The property itself is not transferred, but something giving access to and control over it is. Examples involve giving the keys to an automobile or the keys to a safe deposit box to the donee. Here a constructive delivery gives the donee access, or the means of exercising possession and control, over the chattel. Other examples of this type of delivery occur when the donee is already in possession, or has possession in some other capacity, as a bailee or employee. Actual delivery would be a fruitless action, one that most persons would not think worth taking.

Still another example of constructive delivery involves hidden property, the donor giving instructions to the donee as to how to go about finding it: Upon its recovery by the donee, the property has been constructively delivered. Intent and delivery are separate elements. Clear evidence of the donor's intention is needed to complete the gift. Although physical delivery is evidence of the intent to make the gift, delivery is only one bit of evidence and not a conclusive substitute for evidence of intent: It is too easy to obtain the keys to a chest, or a car, and claim it was the subject of a gift. This is particularly true when the donor is in ill health, is dying, or is otherwise unable to put his or her hands on the property at the moment. Constructive delivery only emphasizes that the rationale for the concept of delivery is to have the donor relinquish possession and control over the chattel.

(c) Acceptance

For a completed gift, the recipient must accept the gift. Although a donee may refuse or reject a gift, acceptance is generally presumed from the benefit received by the donee; thus, acceptance has not been the subject of much reported litigation. Without evidence to show rejection, there is no rejection. The presumption of acceptance is a rebuttable one. No one is required to accept whatever "gift" someone else thinks would be to his or her benefit. Property may not be forced on the unwilling.

Why might a person not accept a gift? There may be tax or continuing upkeep or other obligations that flowed from the gift, or the donee may wish for the gift to go to the alternate donee. Or something like this: In 1877, Ed Singleton was hanged in Beeville, Texas, for murder. Singleton directed that his body be skinned and the hide given to the attorney who prosecuted him. Some prosecutors may accept gifts (or bequests) like this; others may not.

GIFTS CAUSA MORTIS

A **gift causa mortis** is made when the donor has an apprehension or expectation of his or her own impending death and delivers the chattel with the intention that possession over the subject of the gift takes effect immediately, but ownership becomes absolute only upon the donor's death. Jewelry is often the subject of gifts causa mortis.

There is a presumption that a gift made while death is impending is a gift causa mortis, rather than a gift inter vivos. This presumption is rebuttable by proof of the donor's intention to part unconditionally with the property given.

The expectation of death required is subjective; an objective or reasonable expectation is not required. Whether or not the expectation of death is present is a question of fact. The illness, disease, or peril prompting the expectation must be objectively present, however. A threatened assassination, minor surgery, and a perilous journey or an enterprise undertaken voluntarily have all traditionally been found insufficient.

The donor must have a present intention to deliver absolute ownership of the property in the future, at death; an attempt by the donor to reserve control over the property until death invalidates this type of gift.

The title of the donee causa mortis is not absolute until the donor is dead. Death must result from the same illness, disease, or peril producing the donor's initial expectation, not some other illness or event, although it is not necessary that the sole cause of the donor's death be the same as that causing the donor's expectation of death.

Gifts causa mortis are revocable. In some jurisdictions, revocation is automatic if and when the donor recovers from the illness, accident, or other event that made death seem likely. Recovery is seen as a determinable event.[1] In some jurisdictions, however, a gift causa mortis is revoked only if the donor affirmatively revokes the gift after recovery. An automatically revoked gift causa mortis belongs to the donor as though no gift causa mortis had ever been made. The gift is not thereafter revived by a relapse or another, equally grave, illness. To illustrate, if just before heart surgery Mother gives her wedding ring to her youngest daughter at her bedside, and Mother survives surgery, Mother gets her wedding ring back. If Mother a month later dies from a heart attack or any other reason, Mother's wedding ring passes according to her will or the canons of descent, and her youngest daughter has no superior claim to the ring because Mother at one time made the ring the subject of a gift causa mortis.

A person cannot make a gift causa mortis to escape the claims of creditors. Gifts causa mortis are subject to the claims of creditors when other assets of the donor are insufficient to repay the debts. Whether such gifts are subject to marital rights is generally a matter for state probate codes and statutes — and generalizations about this subject are hazardous. Real estate may not be the subject of a gift causa mortis.

The gift causa mortis is the functional equivalent of a devise (a transfer of property by will). Every state has enacted elaborate requirements in a Statute of Wills that must be fulfilled to give effect to a will or testamentary transfer. The gift causa mortis is thus an extraordinary power and, being in derogation of the jurisdiction's Statute of Wills, is not favored. A high standard of proof — that of clear and convincing evidence — is generally required to uphold such gifts. Courts are also likely to strictly construe statutes and cases upholding such gifts. As with inter vivos gifts, the judicial rationale for strictly construing the elements of this type of gift has to do

---

1. A determinable event (or condition subsequent) automatically terminates the donee's ownership and returns title to the donor without any action on the donor's part.

with the evidentiary problems associated with them. In the instance of gifts causa mortis, however, the evidentiary problems are acute because the donor is dead.

Examples

Dresser Delivery

1. Is the giving of the keys to a dresser a symbolic or a constructive delivery?

Revocation and Donative Intent

2. Owen executed an otherwise valid deed of gift. The deed contained a power to revoke. Does the power to revoke indicate a lack of donative intent sufficient to invalidate the gift?

Christmas Carol

3. (a) In September, Lee handed Peter a signed paper promising that Lee will give Peter 10,000 shares of Profit Corporation as a Christmas present. Lee died in November, devising all his "stock and bonds" to Carol. Carol and Peter both claim the Profit Corporation stock. Who gets the stock?

   (b) In September Lee transfered 10,000 shares of Profit Corporation stock to Peter, with the qualification that Lee (the grantor) will receive all dividends paid by Profit Corporation on the stock on or before Christmas. Lee died in November, devising all his "stock and bonds" to Carol. Carol and Peter both claim the Profit Corporation stock. Who gets the stock?

He Loves Me, He Loves Me Not

4. Larry Love proposed marriage to Hilary Hart, buying and placing on Hilary's finger an engagement ring. Six months later Hilary broke off the engagement when she learned of Larry's infidelity. Larry Love brought a replevin action for the return of the engagement ring. What result?

The Uncashed Check

5. Odysseus writes, signs and delivers a check to Don, drawn on Odysseus' checking account as gift, but dies before Don cashes it. Does Don have a right to cash the check?

Suicide and the Gift Causa Mortis

6. Ollie, contemplating suicide because of recent business and personal problems, executed a deed of gift of the contents of her safe deposit

box to Del. Is suicide a life-threatening illness justifying a gift causa mortis?

War

7. Fred is a member of the armed forces and is about to go to war. Is he contemplating death in the way required to make a gift causa mortis?

Explanations

Dresser Delivery

1. Giving the keys may be a symbolic delivery of the piece of furniture, but could be a constructive delivery of the contents of the dresser, found in the drawers. These two concepts are easily confused, but both are useful means for courts to uphold a gift when there is sufficient evidence of donative intent but no actual delivery.

Revocation and Donative Intent

2. No. If the deed adequately indicates a present donative intent — i.e., an intent at the time Owen delivered the deed to make a gift — the gift is good. The donee owns the property. Owen made the gift with a qualification, and retains the right to demand that the property be returned to him. The gift was complete and belongs to the donee until and unless Owen affirmatively revokes.

   Some courts refuse to enforce revocation clauses as a matter of public policy. See dicta in Gruen v. Gruen, 496 N.E.2d 869 (N.Y. 1986) ("Once the gift is made it is irrevocable . . . and the donor is not an owner.") As you will learn, revocable trusts are common. A revocable trust arises when a grantor transfers property to a person (the trustee) to hold for the benefit of a third party (the beneficiary). The grantor can retain the right to revoke the trust and get the property back. If the revocable trust is permissible, the revocable gift should be permissible. The only reason to differentiate between the two is that revocation rights in a trust usually are in writing, whereas many gifts are oral.

Christmas Carol

3. (a) Carol wins. Lee's promise is unenforceable because Peter gave no consideration. When Lee died, he was the legal owner and the stock passed according to his will.

   (b) Peter keeps the stock. The gift in September was a present gift, with a present intent to make a gift, delivery, and acceptance. Lee's retaining the income for four months does not make the gift incomplete.

He Loves Me, He Loves Me Not

4. Larry Love gets the engagement ring. Although a few courts disagree, most courts hold an engagement ring is given in contemplation of marriage and therefore is a conditional gift: The marriage is an act or event that must occur before the gift is completed (a condition precedent). This Example is based on Carroll v. Curry, 912 N.E.2d 272 (Ill. App. 2009). See also 38 Am. Jur.2d Gifts §70 (2010).

The Uncashed Check

5. No. The donor could have stopped payment on the check any time before it was cashed, and the donor's death revoked the authority of the bank to cash it, so the gift was incomplete because of the donor's retention of a power to revoke the gift. The donor could have cashed a check and given the donee the money. The check is not a deed of gift, and the power to cash it is not the same as a gift. See Woo v. Smart, 442 S.E.2d 690 (Va. 1994) (holding that the delivery of a check is an incomplete assignment of the funds on account).

Suicide and the Gift Causa Mortis

6. A person contemplating suicide has traditionally not been regarded as being in imminent peril of death sufficient to justify an exception to the Statute of Wills, so older authorities would answer this query in the negative. Suicide is traditionally an insane act. A few more recent cases reason that mental illness is just as pressing a backdrop for a gift causa mortis as physical illness. They hold that the contemplation of suicide should be treated as one in contemplation of death. Scherer v. Hyland, 380 A.2d 696 (N.J. 1977). The analogy between a person facing major surgery (being allowed to make a gift causa mortis) and a suicide makes it difficult to deny a person contemplating suicide donative power. The recent view is that some mental illnesses (e.g., depression) are accompanied by an irresistible urge to commit suicide, putting a person in contemplation of death. More generally, it might be said that if a jurisdiction recognizes (as most do) that a person contemplating suicide may have testamentary capacity, his will becoming valid on that account, it should also be possible for a person contemplating suicide to make a gift causa mortis.

War

7. A person about to go to war is not facing an imminent peril giving rise to an expectation of death. There are, however, English cases to the contrary.

CHAPTER 7

Fixtures

Most property may be characterized as real property (land and permanent improvements) or personal property (all other property) (tangible personal property in some historical contexts is called chattel). Real property includes land as well as buildings and other immovable, permanent improvements attached to the land. Personal property includes a broader range of property, from tangible items such as furniture, cars, books, and machinery, for example, to intangible items such as stock and bonds. The distinction between real property and personal property informs many areas of the law. This chapter explores a hybrid asset: the fixture.

A **fixture** is a form of chattel or personal property that, while retaining a separate identity, is so connected to the real property that the law considers it a part of the realty. A furnace, for example, is commonly thought of as a fixture in a house. Other common fixtures in a house would be a dishwasher, light fixtures, bathtubs, and toilets. A fixture thus stands on the definitional border between personal property and real property.

A fixture has three elements, all of which are essential. First, the personal property must be annexed to the realty. **Annexation** means attachment to the realty. It may be either actual or constructive. In older cases, this is the most important of all three elements.

Second, it must be adapted or applied to a particular use or purpose beyond itself and made a part of some larger component of or function on the realty. Parts of a heating or cooling system are examples. This second, *adaptation* factor has sometimes been absorbed into the first, by a doctrine of constructive annexation. Under this doctrine, although not physically annexed, the item at issue is taken to be essential to the functioning of the property. In some jurisdictions, this second aspect of the elements of a fixture has tended to drop away.

Third, there must be an **intention to annex** it to the realty. Whose intention controls is the question here. In many American decisions, intention is the most important — perhaps the most confused — element of the three-prong test for a fixture. The most cited American case on the subject, Teaff v. Hewitt, 1 Ohio St. 511 (1853), uses the intent of the annexor, actual or inferred from a combination of several factors: the nature of the property annexed, the relation and situation of the annexor, the method of annexation, and the purpose or use of the personal property. The element of intention does not refer to the annexor's subjective mental state; instead, it is the objective intention of a reasonable person acting within the facts and circumstances of the transaction(s) in dispute.

The law of fixtures is context-specific. A theater seat is a fixture, whereas a living room chair is not. A pipe organ is a fixture in a church, but not in a house unless its removal would cause substantial destruction. A woodstove may not be a fixture in an urban residence (where other means of heating are available), but might be in a cabin in the north woods. An air conditioner may well be a fixture in Tucson, but not in Seattle.

What difference does it make that personal property is called a fixture? The consequences can be seen in two situations, the first involving vendors and purchasers of the underlying real property. Absent an agreement to the contrary, a fixture is automatically transferred to the next grantee of the realty. This transfer occurs, then, when the contract of sale and the deed to the real property are silent on the matter. It is said to happen "by operation of law." The best advice for the parties to such a transfer is to agree what will and will not pass with the title to the realty. Otherwise, what a vendor (seller) of property might consider personal property may, upon transfer to a purchaser, become a fixture. If an item is expressly bargained over, and the vendor is given an express right to remove it in a contract of sale, the vendor has a license to enter the property and do so within a reasonable time. In the vendor/purchaser context, that reasonable time is likely to be until the day the vendor delivers the deed to the property to the purchaser. After that time, the vendor is deemed to have waived his right of removal.

A second situation occurs when the real property is used as security or collateral for repayment of a loan (in a word, "mortgaged"). If the debtor does not pay back the loan, the mortgaged real property may be sold and the sales proceeds used to pay back the loan. The issue arising in this context is whether a particular piece of equipment or attached personal property is part of the collateral securing the loan and can be sold to satisfy the debt. The answer depends on whether the law regards the disputed property as a fixture. Here, again, the issue is context-specific: Personal property alleged to be a fixture, but not necessary to lend its value to the property in order to repay the debt, will likely not be found a fixture. On the other hand, the property necessary to provide security or to attract purchasers to a forced sale of the property will likely be regarded as a fixture.

Examples

Range Removal

1. Vendors executed a contract of sale to sell their house, but had another house on the real property they sold. The second house was rented to a tenant. The contract reserved the right to remove a gas range from the vendor's house. Can the vendors remove an identical stove from the rental house?

Farm Fixture

2. The Farmers and Mechanics Bank holds a mortgage on Fred's farm in a semi-arid region of the country. The farm's fields are watered by a standard irrigation system that has three components: first, lightweight and portable gated pipes of various lengths and diameters, with gates or windows on one side that can be opened or closed and thus regulate the flow of water onto a field; second, riser pipes permanently connecting the gated pipes to underground water pipes buried under the fields; and third, the underground water pipes attached to the water supply. Fred defaults on the repayment of the mortgage loan, and the bank forecloses. At the sale of the farm, will the gated pipes, riser pipes, and underground water pipes be included in the real property and sold as fixtures?

Explanations

Range Removal

1. No. The rental house was presumably sold as a unit, not in discrete parts. What seems important to the purchasers about the rental house is that it is an economic unit for collecting rent money. What is a fixture in one setting (e.g., the main house) may not be so in another (e.g., the rental unit). Here the reservation of the right to remove the stove in the main house is presumed to be exclusive unless the vendors reserve further items in the contract. In this instance, they did not do so.

Farm Fixture

4. The gated pipes are not fixtures. They are portable, are used in the various lengths and diameters needed for irrigation, and can be easily removed without damage to the underground and riser pipes. It is also possible that the risers could be attached to sprinklers, hoses, and other devices, and so the fields could be irrigated in other ways and without the use of

the gated pipes. With all these features, these pipes are not fixtures. See Wyoming State Farm Loan Bd. v. Farm Credit Sys. Capital Corp., 759 P.2d 1230 (Wyo. 1988).

In contrast, the underground water pipes are part of the realty, or at least fixtures, and will remain with the farm. The riser pipes are a closer issue. Since they are permanently attached to the underground water pipes, however, they likely will be found to be fixtures passing with the farm.

CHAPTER 8

Adverse Possession

The preceding chapters dealt mainly with personal property. This chapter introduces adverse possession, a legal process to gain (or lose) title to either real or personal property.

INTRODUCTION

A landowner can have a person wrongfully on his land, such as a trespasser, removed from the property. The legal action to remove a trespasser is called **ejectment**. On the other hand, a person who is not the legal owner of property, and who in fact may have entered as a trespasser, who uses the property for enough years becomes the owner of the property and defeats all rights of the true or rightful owner, even if the latter had legal or record title, under a process known as **adverse possession**.

Every state has enacted an adverse possession statute. Each state's statute sets out the number of years the adverse possessor must use the property before its true owner will be prohibited from ejecting the adverse possessor. After that period of time, a trespasser becomes the owner and his subsequent purchasers, heirs, and descendants succeed to his rights. The former legal or record owner has no further rights to the property and cannot claim damages for his or her loss.

If the true owner of property fails to sue a trespasser within the period of time allotted for bringing an action in ejectment, the trespasser thereafter acquires its title. The adverse possessor obtains an original title to property. His title, in other words, is not derived from its former owner's.

The number of years an adverse possessor must use the property, also known as the **statute of limitations period**, the limitations period, or the statutory period, varies widely among the several states, and may vary within a state depending on whether the adverse possessor has a faulty deed (known as **color of title**) or bought the property at a tax sale. In Iowa, for example, the statutory period is 40 years without color of title, but only 10 years with color of title. Texas has shorter statute of limitations periods: 10 years without color of title and 3 years under color of title. California and Idaho have 5-year statutes of limitations for use both with color of title and without color of title. Most states fall between these extremes, requiring between 7 and 30 years for the statute to run.

Although all authorities, courts, and legislatures embrace the idea of adverse possession, they do not agree on why we allow adverse possession and on the underlying rationale for adverse possession.

There are several traditional rationales. First, adverse possession *punishes* true owners who sit on their rights for too long. "You snooze, you lose." True owners are encouraged to monitor their property. This rationale deals with the abandoning owner; it was most useful in the nineteenth century, when pioneers traveled from region to region, never intending to return to their origins and abandoning land in the process. Our society is more comfortable if someone uses and lays claim to property. Rights must be asserted, or lost.

Second, adverse possession laws *reward* the person who uses, works on, or improves property for a long time, becoming in the process known in the community as its owner. In this vein, some state statutes require the adverse possessor to improve, cultivate, or enclose the claimed property for the statutory period.

Beyond these punishment or reward rationales, a third rationale views the elements of adverse possession as *evidentiary* tools. Evidence decays as time passes, and stale claims to property should be barred. Another evidentiary function is to confirm lost grants or otherwise correct conveyancing mistakes and oversights. Landowners, moreover, are not required by law to record deeds and other documents affecting real property. Thus long and visible possession and use becomes a substitute for documentary proof of a lost or misplaced deed. And some deeds are invalid for technical reasons. The person signing a deed may not have authority to do so; its drafter may have described the property incorrectly; or the possessor may have received the property as an oral or parol gift, ineffective because real property transfers must be in writing under the Statute of Frauds. With the passage of time, adverse possession laws eliminate these problems.

Fourth, adverse possession laws serve a *structural* purpose, facilitating the efficient transfer of property. Land, in particular, does not wear out. A purchaser or other possessor of property should be free from potential ownership claims originating decades earlier when the putative legal owner has not indicated she even knows or cares that she owns the property. Courts in many contexts begin with a premise that no person should be forced to "buy a lawsuit." Adverse possession serves to quiet titles, reinforce the reliability of land records, and allow transferability of land at lower cost than would otherwise be possible. To some commentators, the integrity and reliability of the deed records alone justifies denying relief to long unenforced claims.

Finally, adverse possession preserves the *status quo*. As O.W. Holmes wrote, "Man, like a tree in the cleft of a rock, gradually shapes his roots to his surroundings, and when the roots have grown to a certain size, can't be displaced without cutting at his life." When ejecting the adverse possessor would result in more of a loss than the true owner would gain, there is no longer any point in denying the adverse possessor title.

Adverse possession cases concerning land fall into two broad categories. In one, the adverse possessor claims a parcel of land completely unrelated to any other land the adverse possessor owns or claims. The second category concerns boundary disputes, where neighboring landowners dispute who has the right to a strip of land used by one party but included within the legal description of another. Despite the potentially different concerns applicable in each of these two categories, courts resort to the same statutory and common law principles in resolving both categories of cases, but may interpret the elements of adverse possession differently.

ELEMENTS OF ADVERSE POSSESSION

While state adverse possession statutes differ, a typical case may arise when the legal or record owner brings an action in ejectment to oust the defendant, whom the legal or record owner claims is a trespasser. The defendant counters, claiming to own the property by adverse possession. Alternatively, a person may bring a declaratory judgment action asking the court to rule that the person owns the property by adverse possession. In either scenario, the person claiming ownership by adverse possession bears the burden of proof to prove every element of adverse possession.

In evaluating an adverse possession claim, a court considers the elements contained in its state's adverse possession statute and, invariably, several judicially developed elements to determine whether the adverse possessor "adversely possesses" the property. Thus, to assert a successful adverse possession claim, an adverse possessor must show that the adverse possession met each of the following common law elements:

1. Actual
2. Open and notorious

3. Exclusive
4. Hostile or adverse
5. Continuous

In addition, some courts add other elements, by common law or by statute, including the following:

6. Claim of title or claim of right
7. Good faith or bad faith
8. Improvement, cultivation, or enclosure
9. Payment of property taxes

While some courts list claim of right or claim of title as separate elements and require either good faith or, conversely, bad faith as a separate element, commentators seem to agree these are subsets of the hostility element (hostile or adverse).

An adverse possessor must satisfy each required element to prevail. Courts apply a checklist approach. Failure to satisfy even one element defeats the action. In analyzing a case for the following elements, note that the same acts may satisfy several elements. As a general guideline, an adverse possessor who acts with respect to the property as would an owner of similar property in the community for the period of limitations usually satisfies each element.

(a) Actual Possession

An adverse possessor must be in **actual possession** of the property. Actual possession serves several purposes. It gives notice to the true owner and others who come to the property that the adverse possessor is using the property. It also indicates that the adverse possessor may be claiming the property and has ousted all other persons. Finally, the date the adverse possessor entered onto the property triggers the true owner's cause of action in ejectment or trespass, and the adverse possession statute of limitations period starts running.

What constitutes actual possession is a function of the type of property involved, where the property is located, and what uses of the property would be expected in the community. A person is not required to live on the property, though in most cases the adverse possessor does live on or adjacent to the claimed property. In one early leading case, the adverse possessor lived across the street from the lot he claimed, stepping onto it as needed to sell the right to dig sand and gravel to some, refusing it to others. These actions were confirmed by several witnesses at trial. His adverse possession claim was successful. See Ewing v. Burnet, 36 U.S. 41

(1837). Building a house, farming, fencing, even cutting timber or hunting and fishing in the right situations, may constitute actual possession. While paying taxes helps establish actual possession, unless the state law requires payment of taxes as an essential element, an adverse possessor is not required to pay taxes and, in fact, may claim adverse possession even though the legal owner pays the taxes. Selling the land, mortgaging it, or renting it to others could constitute actual possession.

Generally, an adverse possessor gains ownership of only so much of a tract of property as the adverse possessor actually occupies. The adverse possessor bears the burden of proving the boundaries to the land used adversely. The true owner continues to own any unoccupied land. Proving adverse possession can be extremely vexatious if the adverse possessor gradually expands the land being possessed. The statute of limitations period runs only from the time the particular part of the land being claimed is actually used, not from when any part of the parcel is being used

Example 1: Teresa, a trespasser, occupied and used a 20-foot strip beginning in Year 1. She started using 10 more feet in Year 5, and another 30 feet in year 10. Teresa brought a declaratory judgment action in Year 11 that she owned the 60 foot wide parcel of land by adverse possession. The state's adverse possession statute provided for a 7-year statute of limitations period. Assuming she can prove the other elements, she may claim only the 10-foot strip she entered in Year 1. If she cannot identify the boundaries of this strip, a court may rule she cannot prove actual possession of any of the land for the requisite period.

A major exception to this rule occurs when the adverse possessor claims the land under **color of title**. A person enters under color of title when he claims ownership pursuant to a written document, usually a deed, purporting to transfer the property to him, but the document is defective in some manner. Thus a faulty deed, or a deed from someone not owning the property, or owning a part or fractional share of the property, or a sheriff's tax sale deed that is defective because some part of the sale was improperly conducted does not convey legal title to the purchaser, but does clothe the purchaser with color of title.

Having color of title benefits the adverse possessor in two ways. First, as noted earlier, many state statutes reduce significantly the statute of limitations period for persons taking possession of property with color of title. In North Carolina, for example, the 20-year period is reduced to 7 years if an adverse possessor has color of title. Second, the adverse possessor with color of title who successfully proves an adverse possession claim based on actual possession of a part of the tract described in the document constituting color of title is deemed to be in **constructive possession** of the whole tract.

Example 2: Wally owned Blackacre, a 500-acre parcel of heavily wooded land in Arkansas. Wally sold and deeded Blackacre to Edwin, who lived in St. Louis. Five years later, Wally died. Wally's daughter, Serena, believing she inherited Blackacre, sold and deeded Blackacre to Judy. The deed to Judy did not convey good title to Judy since Serena did not own Blackacre. The faulty deed to Judy, however, was color of title. Judy cleared 5 of the 500 acres and used the 5 acres as her residence. Judy lived there for the statutory period. Because Judy has color of title, she has adversely possessed the entire 500 acres described in her deed, not just the 5 acres she actually possessed.

An exception to the constructive ownership by color of title rule is that the true owner's actual possession of a part of the described land negates the constructive possession, and thus the adverse possession is limited to the land actually possessed. As explained by the U.S. Supreme Court in *Deputron v. Young*, 134 U.S. 241, 255 (1890) (applying Nebraska law), "Where the rightful owner is in the actual occupancy of a part of his tract, he is in the constructive and legal possession and seisin of the whole, unless he is disseised by actual occupation and dispossession; and where the possession is mixed, the legal seisin is according to the legal title, so that in the case at bar there could be no constructive possession on the part of the defendant or his grantors, even if that might exist if he had had actual possession of a part, and no one had been in possession of the remainder."

Example 3: Assume the facts in Example 2 above except that shortly after buying Blackacre Edwin moved to Arkansas, cleared five acres of Blackacre, and lived there. Edwin remained unaware that Judy was residing on another five acres of Blackacre. After the limitations period has passed, Judy may claim only the five acres actually possessed.

Constructive possession benefits the adverse possessor in a variety of transfer situations. An adverse possessor occupying one lot has constructive possession of several lots conveyed separately if all lots are enclosed as a unit. Likewise, constructive possession reaches several lots conveyed in one document even if the lots are separately described in the deed. If the deed describes multiple lots — some occupied, others not — constructive possession even extends to lots that do not adjoin the occupied land.

(b) Open and Notorious Possession

Open and notorious possession means the adverse possessor's use of the property is so visible and apparent it that gives notice to the true owner if he checked his land that someone may be asserting an adverse claim to the land. The adverse possessor's use must be of such character under the circumstances as would indicate to a reasonably attentive owner that someone else might be claiming the property. Buildings, fences, crops, or animals might constitute an open and notorious presence. Fences or crops — enclosure or cultivation — are sometimes statutory requirements as well. If the true owner has actual knowledge of the adverse possessor's claim, however, the open and notorious element is met even though no one else has reason to know of the adverse claim.

Normally, the adverse possessor is not required to give actual notice to the true owner that the adverse possessor is on the land or that he is claiming the land as his own. As a major exception, the adverse possessor must give actual notice when the adverse possessor is claiming adversely against a co-owner. A co-owner is someone who owns land concurrently with the adverse possessor, as when two or three people buy the property together as a unit, or where they inherit from parents. For more on cotenants and concurrent ownership see Chapter 13.

(c) Exclusive Possession

Exclusive possession means that the adverse possessor holds the land to the exclusion of the true owner. Possession cannot be exclusive, moreover, if two or more adverse possessors use the property adverse to each other's ownership. If, however, one adverse possessor has a superior legal right — by holding under color of title or having entered the property first, for example — the adverse possessor with the superior right may oust the other adverse possessor and continue possession, the statutory period running from the time the first adverse possessor initially occupied the property. Generally, the first adverse possessor may eject or oust subsequent adverse possessors even though the first adverse possessor has not occupied the property for the statutory period. Some states, to the contrary, hold that exclusive possession means exactly what it implies — that only one person can claim adverse possession.

Exclusive possession does not mean only one person can ever gain title by adverse possession. Most states permit persons acting in concert to adversely possess property. They become co-owners or co-tenants.

(d) Hostile or Adverse Possession

There are three theories as to what constitutes hostile or adverse possession.

(1) The Majority or Objective View

Hostile or **adverse possession** in most states means simply that the adverse possessor uses the occupied property without the true owner's permission, and inconsistent with the true owner's legal rights. A person entering property with the true owner's permission cannot claim adverse possession. A tenant leasing the property for more than the statutory period, for example, cannot claim ownership, since her possession was never hostile. The fact that the true owner gave permission to an adverse possessor already on the premises might not destroy the hostility element, however, if the possessor intends to remain on the property with or without the true owner's permission.

If a person enters onto the property with permission, or his occupation is consistent with the true owner's title, the possessor's continued stay could become hostile, but the hostility claim must be unequivocal. In most cases a tenant or co-owner must give actual notice to the true owner or engage in some act that clearly brings home the fact that the possessor is claiming full ownership as against the landlord or co-owner. Arguably, a tenant refusing to vacate property after a lease ends and denying any continuing obligation to pay rent may exhibit the hostility element. In some states, however, the tenant must vacate the property and then re-enter to begin the running of the statute of limitations.

(2) The Minority, Bad Faith, or Intentional Trespass View

Courts and commentators favoring the objective view discussed previously agree that a possessor using land on his neighbor's property under the mistaken belief as to the exact location of the boundary line can adversely possess the land as long as he claims the strip used as his own. Some courts, however, deem important the adverse possessor's subjective intent, and look to the possessor's state of mind. The issue, particularly acute in boundary disputes, is whether the possessor's subjective intent is relevant.

A small minority of jurisdictions hold that mistaken possession does not constitute hostility. These courts find no hostility if the adverse possessor intended to claim only the property described in his deed, and was on neighboring land under the mistaken belief that the land was described in his deed. The subtle difference between the possessor's intending to claim the property whether or not described in the possessor's deed and not intending to claim unless the disputed strip was contained in the possessor's deed, to be determined after the statutory period has run, tempts the possessor, who may never have thought about it, to lie. Because of the tendency to tempt otherwise honest people to lie, and because a rule that disfavors mistaken possession rewards bad-faith adverse possessor and penalizes good-faith possessors, most but not all courts conclude that the possessor's intent is irrelevant.

(3) Good Faith View

A few cases courts go the other direction and require the adverse possessor in a boundary dispute to be on his neighbor's land in good faith, actually believing it to be included in his deed description. Only if the adverse possessor is on the neighboring land mistakenly thinking the neighboring land is included in his deed will the adverse possessor be able to satisfy the hostile and adverse possession element. As with the bad-faith discussion above, however, most courts hold the possessor's good faith irrelevant.

(e) Continuous Possession

To satisfy the statute of limitations for adverse possession, a claimant must be in **continuous possession** for the entire limitations period. Continuous does not mean uninterrupted. It does not mean the person must be on the property 24 hours a day, or even every day. It simply means the possessor must use the property as would a true owner under the circumstances. Intermittent use usually does not constitute continuous possession, but seasonal use may be continuous, as in the use of a hunting cabin during hunting seasons, or the cutting of timber when appropriate. In one interesting case, a court held that two prison sentences of four and nine months each did not interrupt the possessor's continuity of possession. See Helton v. Cook, 219 S.E. 2d 505 (N.C. App. 1975).

The continuity element focuses on the adverse possessor's time on the property, rather than on how long the true owner has been dispossessed. If an adverse possessor abandons the property, and a second adverse possessor independently enters into possession, the statute of limitations starts anew. If an adverse possessor leaves the property with the intent to return and returns to find a new adverse possessor on the property, the returning possessor can eject the second adverse possessor and continue the running of the statute.

PRIVITY AND TACKING

The adverse possessor gains a limited interest in the property even though he has occupied the property for less than the time necessary to gain title and is subject to ejectment by the true owner. An adverse possessor may eject other trespassers and adverse possessors even before the statute of limitations runs, as long as the adverse possessor entered the property first.

The adverse possessor, moreover, may sell or give his interest to another person. The purchaser or donee succeeds to the adverse possessor's attributes, including the time the first possessor occupied the property. This adding of time the first adverse possessor used the property to the time the second possessor used the property is called **tacking**. The relationship necessary to allow tacking is called privity. **Privity** occurs by contract of sale, gift, will, or other inheritance (intestate succession).

DISABILITIES AND TOLLING THE RUNNING OF THE STATUTE OF LIMITATIONS

Many states provide that the statute of limitations for an adverse possession claim will not run against a true owner who is under a legal **disability** when the adverse possession commences. States consider various conditions or situations to be disabilities. Infants (minors) and the mentally ill generally are deemed disabled. Other common groups include persons in prisons and those in military service.

If a true owner of property is under a disability, the statute of limitations will not run against him or her until the disability is removed. Meanwhile the statute is said to be **tolled**. To illustrate, if a statute provides for a ten-year statute of limitations, the state law deems a minor to be under a disability until the minor reaches age 21, and the true owner is 15 years old when the adverse possession begins, the statute of limitations is tolled and does not begin to run until the true owner turns 21. In this example, therefore, the statute is tolled for six years and the true owner has until he or she turns 31 to bring an ejectment action against the adverse possessor. Some statutes reduce the limitations period following a period of disability (but the person under a disability has at least the standard limitations period to bring suit).

Some guiding principles seem common to most states. First, the disability must exist on the date of the adverse possessor's entry onto the land. A disability that arises after the adverse possession begins will not toll the running of the statute. To illustrate, if an adverse possession begins in year one, and in year two the true owner is sentenced to 20 years in the state penitentiary, the statute is not tolled. If the true owner had been sentenced in year one and the possession began in year two, however, the statute would be tolled until the true owner was released from prison.

Second, there is no tacking of disabilities, although when the true owner is under more than one disability, the one of most benefit to him may be elected. If a true owner under a disability when the adverse possession begins falls under a second disability during the time of the adverse possession, the statute is tolled only during the continuance of the first disability. For example, if the true owner is 15 when the possession begins, and is sentenced to prison for ten years when he is 19, the statute is tolled until he reaches majority (say, age 21), and will run against him after that date even though he still is in prison.

Third, a person taking from or through the true owner under a disability generally can take advantage of the tolling statute to the same extent as the person with the disability, except that the disability is deemed to end on the day of the sale or gift. The logic behind this rule is as follows: Without the rule, if the statute ran against the new owner from the first day the adverse possessor entered onto the property, the person under a disability might not ever be able to sell the property because the property might immediately vest in the adverse possessor. Or, from the new owner's perspective, he could lose all rights in the property before having an opportunity to discover and eject an adverse possessor.

TEMPORAL AND PHYSICAL SEVERANCE AND ADVERSE POSSESSION

Adverse possession laws protect persons who have a "future interest" in property. Land ownership can be divided temporally — i.e., by time. In a simple scenario, O, the true owner, may transfer property to A to use during A's life, and give to B the right to possess the property after A dies. A is said to be the life tenant in this example. B is called the remainderman. The general rule is that the statute does not begin to run against a person having a future interest until the future interest becomes possessory. In the life tenant–remainderman scenario, the remainderman has no right to possess or use the property until A dies. If an adverse possessor enters the property *after* the ownership has been divided in time between the life tenant and the remainderman, he can divest only the life tenant and the statute does not begin to run against the remainderman until A, the life tenant, dies, and B, the remainderman, gains the right to possession. If the adverse possessor enters the property *before* O, the original owner, makes the transfer to A and B, however, the statute runs against both the life tenant and the remainderman.

Likewise, land ownership can be divided vertically — into air rights, surface rights, and subsurface (typically mineral) rights. If minerals have been sold separately from the right to use the surface, and thereafter an adverse possessor enters the property, he can divest only the holder of the surface rights — unless he opens a mine, at which point he starts to run the statutory period against the person holding the mineral rights. If the adverse possessor enters the property before the surface and the mineral rights are severed, however, the statute runs against both the surface and the mineral owner.

In one famous case, Marengo Cave Co. v. Ross, 10 N.E.2d 917 (Ind. 1937), the discoverer of a spectacular cave, owning the land where the cave's mouth was located, mistakenly believed that the whole cave was located under his land. It wasn't, and the owner of the land whose surface lay adjacent and partly above the cave sued the discoverer's successors in title, but only after the cave's users had, over a period of 50 years, improved its accessibility and made extensive efforts to turn it into a profitable tourist destination. Ross, the adjacent owner, sued Marengo, the current operator of the enterprise, to quiet title to that portion of the cave under Ross's land. A court-ordered survey disclosed that the cave was indeed under Ross's land. The court held that Marengo's possession "tacked" onto that of prior operators of the cave. It also held that the use was actual, hostile, and continuous, but not exclusive and open and notorious, even though Ross had occasionally toured the cave, buying a ticket to do so.

As to the open and notorious element, you might argue that the development of the cave enterprise, exploiting the cave as its true owner would, is sufficient. On the other hand, the underground nature of the cave might not give Ross notice that his property was being used. Ross could not locate the cave without entering it, which he could not do without a court order. Just as when a miner exceeds the extent of his mineral rights when extending a mine under land he does not own, there is something secret and fraudulent about the trespass. Either argument is reasonable, but the *Marengo Cave* court concluded the possession of the cave was not open and notorious.

PERSONAL PROPERTY AND ADVERSE POSSESSION

Personal property can be acquired by adverse possession, but the mobility of personal property creates tricky issues. In early cases, domesticated animals could be acquired by adverse possession, but if the animals were taken out of their original locale to places where their true owners were very unlikely to find them, or if personal property such as paintings were fraudulently concealed, the statute of limitations was tolled.

Additionally, as to some of adverse possession's elements — actual possession, exclusivity, hostility, and continuity — the law worked reasonably well. But other elements such as open and notorious possession presented problems. A person can wear his or her wristwatch, but who will notice? Or an adverse possessor may keep the property in his home away from public view. Under such circumstances, is it sensible to let the limitations period run out in the usual fashion?

These questions are the more pressing because the statutes of limitations for personalty — for actions of trover, conversion and replevin (see Chapter 3) — are shorter (typically between four and eight years) than similar ones for realty. These questions have been a source of debate, and two rules have developed to answer them. The first, traditional rule is that the statute of limitations for actions for personalty does not start to run until the action "accrues" — that is a lawyer's way of saying that the last element of the cause of action is in place. So, for example, when a work of art disappears and then reappears on the wall of a purchaser, the cause of action to recover it does not accrue until its true owner discovers its whereabouts and makes a demand for its return. This gives the purchaser an opportunity to return it, but upon refusing to do so, the true owner's action is complete — the demand and refusal being the last element in it. This "demand and refusal" rule means that the statute runs only from the date of the refusal and that the statute was tolled beforehand. See Solomon R. Guggenhein Fdn. v. Lubell, 569 N.E. 426 (N.Y. 1991).

The second rule is the rule of due diligence. Here, after the personal property disappears, the true owner may toll the statute for the period of time that he or she searches diligently for it, but if the search is discontinued, the statute runs. The true owner bears the burden of proof on the issue of diligence. Meanwhile, the cause of action does not accrue until the true owner discovers, or by the exercise of reasonable diligence should discover, the facts which will permit the action to accrue. See O'Keeffe v. Snyder, 416 A.2d 862 (N.J. 1980). Discovery of the facts is here the key; no demand is necessary.

Both the "demand and refusal" and the "due diligence" rule have advantages and disadvantages. They both, rather than modifying the elements of adverse possession, focus on when the statute of limitations starts and stops. Consider, for example, a cause of action in replevin: its elements are (1) the loss of personal property, (2) the plaintiff's right to it up to the time of the action, and (3) a demand for and a refusal to return it. The due diligence rule's focus is on the second element; the demand and refusal's rule is (obviously) on the third element, and differs in the extent to which the court is willing to prefer the rights of the true owner over its present possessor. The demand and refusal rule is easier to apply and consistent with the traditional preference of the common law for a true owner's rights. The due diligence rule is more flexible, considers the disadvantage at which possessors find themselves showing adverse possession, and allows the true owner to show how much she valued the chattel. Yet both rules attempt to inhibit the fencing or thievery of personal property (if in different ways), and both are fact-based enough to take account of the many ways in which the true owner might be "diligent" in searching for lost chattel.

Examples

Hunting Lodge

1. Arthur obtained a defective tax deed to a section of land on which he constructed a hunting cabin. When the cabin was destroyed by fire several years later, Arthur rebuilt it on a cement foundation, cleared the acreage around the cabin, planted grass, and posted a sign along a

nearby road indicating an access road to the cabin. Arthur occupied the cabin during hunting seasons and occasional other weekends over the course of the limitations period, but never resided there or attempted to keep others off the land around the cabin. He never otherwise improved the land or posted it against other hunters, but he did pay the taxes, and sold the scrub timber on the land for pulpwood. Has Arthur acquired adverse possession?

Timing Is Everything

2. In a state with a 20-year statute of limitations, Alie entered and began adversely possessing Blackacre. Nineteen years later, trespasser Tom destroyed Blackacre's crops. May the record owner of Blackacre (the true owner, or TO) sue Tom for damages to Blackacre on the day after the statutory period ends in favor of Alie?

Interim Transfer

3. Ten years ago Adam entered and began adversely possessing TO's White-acre, located in a state with a 20-year statute of limitations for adverse possession. This year, Adam deeds Whiteacre to Xeno, a bona fide purchaser. What estate does Xeno obtain?

It's Yours? Really?

4. A quarter century ago Angie entered and immediately began adversely possessing TO's Brownacre. TO now arrives and tells Angie it is TO's land. A surprised Angie says she is sorry; she thought it was her land and didn't know it belonged to TO. In a state with a 20-year statute of limitations, does Angie own Brownacre?

With Your Kind Permission

5. TO told Andy, "Stay as long as you need a place." Andy did and, after the statutory period passed, sued TO in order to establish adverse possession. Will Andy's claim succeed?

One Farm, Two Deeds

6. Amy gave Brad a deed to Amy's farm. Amy then gave Charlie a similar deed to the same farm (except, of course, for the name of the grantee — here, Charlie). Brad started to cut timber on the farm. Charlie moved into the farmhouse and farmed the fields. Both Brad and Charlie continued in this manner for the limitations period. Charlie then sued Amy and Brad for adverse possession of the land described in the deed from Amy. What result and why?

Dispossessing Future Estate Holders

7. (a) AP entered Blackacre adversely. TO held a life estate in Blackacre, remainder to Bobbie and her heirs. The prescriptive period in the jurisdiction is ten years. Eleven years later, TO died and Bobbie brought suit to oust AP. In this suit, what result and why?

   (b) AP entered Blackacre adversely. TO, the true owner of Blackacre, then died and left a will devising a life estate in Blackacre to Angelina, remainder to Bobbie and her heirs. The statue of limitations period in the jurisdiction is ten years. Eleven years later, Angelina died and Bobbie brought suit to oust AP. In this suit, what result and why?

Calculating Time in Possession

8. Owen owned Blackacre. In a state with a 20-year statute of limitations Ayn began adversely possessing Blackacre. After satisfying all the elements for adverse possession for 10 years, she left Blackacre (and the state). Hearing Ayn has moved, Bessie moved onto Blackacre adversely and stayed for the next 15 years. Then Owen sued Bessie in ejectment, claiming he owned Blackacre and Bessie was a trespasser. What result and why?

This Land Is My Land

9. Assume a 20-year statute of limitations in the following Examples:

   (a) In Year 1, Odie, the true owner, is ousted (forceful or wrongful exclusion) from Blackacre's possession by Arthur, who in Year 5 is ousted by Betty, who in Year 15 is ousted by Cory, who in Year 20 is ousted by Dan. Who has title to Blackacre in Year 31?

   (b) If, in Year 22, Cory had sued Dan in ejectment to regain possession, what result?

   (c) What result if Dan had sued Cory for damages in polluting the soil on Blackacre's wheat fields?

   (d) Ossie owned Blackacre. Addy entered upon Blackacre in Year 1. Addy stayed in possession until year 25. In that year, Ossie sold to Ben and Ben then sued Addy in ejectment. In this suit, what result and why?

   (e) Same facts as in (d) except Ossie sold to Ben in Year 15, and Ben sued Addy in Year 15. What result?

   (f) Same facts as in (e) except Ben waited until Year 25 to bring his ejectment action. What result?

Disabled Advice

10. O was insane when ousted by A in Year 1. A was in adverse possession from Year 1 to Year 15 when O, in a lucid moment, conveyed the property to his insane son S. Assuming a 20-year statute of limitations, what would you advise O to do?

Bad Fences Make Bad Neighbors

11. A fence was mistakenly constructed between Arden's and Ben's lots 20 feet into Ben's property, and for ten years Arden used the extra 20 feet as his own. Ben then constructed an improvement on his land on his side of the fence and, during the construction, tore down the fence to get construction equipment onto the land and around his new improvements. After the construction, the fence was rebuilt, but in a different place, eight feet from the boundary indicated in the record title. Another ten years passed, with Arden and Ben fully using the land on their respective sides of the new fence. In a state with a 20-year limitations period, Arden sued Ben for adverse possession of the 20 feet now in dispute. What result?

Intent on Ownership

12. Twenty-one years ago, the true owner, Owen, left Blackacre. Annie told two persons that she was the new owner, and was in adverse possession thereafter for 20 years. Annie's witnesses are dead and, upon Owen's return, Owen sues Annie for ejectment. Annie's defense is her adverse possession. Assuming a 20-year statute of limitations, what result and why?

Step Neighbors

13. This case is based on Mannillo v. Gorski, 255 A.2d 258 (N.J. 1969). The New Jersey adverse possession provision at the time of the dispute stated: "Every person having any right or title of entry into real estate shall make such entry within 20 years next after the accrual of such right or title of entry, or be barred therefrom thereafter." In the summer of 1946 Gorski made certain additions and changes to her house. Among the improvements were a concrete stoop with steps on the west side of the house for use in connection with a side door, and a concrete walk from the steps to the end of the house. The concrete walk was the same width as the steps. The steps and concrete walk encroached 15 inches upon her neighbors' (the Mannillos') land. The Mannillos brought an action in 1968 for an injunction to stop the continuing trespass. Gorski countered for a declaratory action that she owned the 15-inch strip by adverse possession. Gorski did not know that the steps and walk encroached on the Mannillos' property until shortly before trial.

    (a) Does the New Jersey adverse possession statute provide that an adverse possessor, such as Gorski, prevails by using the property for 20 years; or does it provide that the record or true owners, such as the Mannillos, lose all rights to eject anyone who has been in possession for 20 years?

(b) Was Gorski's possession actual?

(c) Was Gorski's possession open and notorious?

(d) Was Gorski's possession hostile and adverse? Could the fact that Gorski did not know the steps encroached on the Mannillos' property affect your answer?

(e) Was Gorski's possession exclusive?

(f) Was Gorski's possession continuous for 20 years?

(g) If the Mannillos prevail, should the court force them to sell the disputed land to Gorski? If Gorski prevails, should the court order her to pay the Mannillos for the disputed land?

(h) The platform, steps, and walk were in place and visible when the Mannillos bought their property. A survey at the time should have discovered the encroachment. Should either of these facts affect your analysis of this dispute?

Tack and Toll Time

14. A state has a ten-year statute of limitations period for adverse possession claims. The state also authorizes an extension of the statute of limitations period if the true owner is under a disability. It allows possessors in privity to tack holding periods for purposes of the adverse possession statute. The state's disability provision reads as follows:

Tolling for Disabilities:

(1) If a person entitled to bring an action is, at the time the cause of action accrues, either under the age of 20 years; or insane; or imprisoned on a criminal charge, the action may be commenced within 2 years after the disability ceases, except that where the disability is due to insanity or imprisonment, the limitations period prescribed in this chapter may not be extended for more than 5 years.

(2) Subsection (1) does not shorten a limitations period otherwise prescribed.

(3) A disability does not exist, for the purposes of this section, unless it existed when the cause of action accrues.

(4) When two or more disabilities coexist at the time the cause of action accrues, the two-year period specified in subsection (1) does not begin until they all are removed.

Assume for the following Examples that the adverse possessor has met the actual, open and notorious, hostile and adverse, exclusive, and continuous elements of adverse possession.

(a) Bryan, born December 1, 2000, inherited property on July 1, 2006, when he was five years old. Poe entered upon the property on January 1, 2011, claiming it as her own. When does Poe gain title by adverse possession?

(b) Same as (a) except Bryan was convicted of robbery and sentenced to prison on July 1, 2019, when he was 18. He served four years, and was released on July 1, 2023. When does Poe gain title by adverse possession?

(c) Same as (a) except on January 1, 2016, when Bryan was 15, Bryan (by his trustee) sold the property to Michelle, who turned 18 on January 1, 2016. When does Poe gain title by adverse possession?

(d) Same as (c) except Bryan sold the property to Michelle on July 1, 2021. When does Poe gain title by adverse possession?

(e) Lance was 18 when he inherited property on January 1, 2010, while serving in the armed forces. Addie entered on the property on July 1, 2010, claiming it as her own. On January 1, 2011, Lance died in an automobile accident, leaving the property to his one-year-old son, Kevin (born July 1, 2009). When does Addie gain title by adverse possession?

(f) Same as (e) except Addie sold the property to Ed Verse on January 1, 2004, giving him a deed for the property. When does Ed Verse gain title by adverse possession?

(g) Same as (f) except the state statute reduces the limitations period to five years if the adverse possessor has color of title. When does Ed Verse gain title by adverse possession?

Explanations

Hunting Lodge

1. Yes. Arthur used the property as would a true owner. A true owner using the property as a hunting lodge would not clear the land or necessarily fence in the land. The posting of the directions to the cabin, the road to the cabin, and the cabin itself are open enough possession to give notice to the true owner. Holding pursuant to the tax deed satisfies the adverse and hostile element. Even though Arthur does not reside on the land, his use as would a true owner of a hunting cabin, especially as reinforced by the presence of the road and the cabin itself, is enough to satisfy the continuing possession element. Arthur had exclusive possession. The faulty tax deed is a color of title, so any problems Arthur may have in establishing exactly how much of the property he used at all — much less continuously for the limitations period — are overcome since Arthur is deemed to be in constructive possession of all the land described in the tax deed. Some states require payment of property taxes to claim by adverse possession; most states do not. Either way, Arthur is okay because he paid them. See Monroe v. Rawlings, 49 N.W.2d 55 (Mich. 1951).

Timing Is Everything

2. The record owner may sue in some states. Once the title to Blackacre is transferred to Alie, TO no longer has any right to sue Alie in ejectment to recover possession and title. However, that does not necessarily mean that rights against trespassers such as Tom that arise before the limitations period runs end as well. See 10 *Thompson on Real Property*, §87.03, at p. 86 (David Thomas, ed., 1994) (indicating that in some states the owner's suit will lie). On the other hand, in other states the title acquired by adverse possession relates back to the date of the adverse possessor's entry and, when this rule is given its broadest effect, the TO might now be held to have no right to sue Tom.

Interim Transfer

3. Xeno acquires all of the right, title, and estate that Adam had. Thus, Xeno can tack her own possessory right onto Adam's ten years of adverse possession, so that Xeno can acquire title by adverse possession in ten more years in a state with a twenty-year statute of limitations.

It's Yours? Really?

4. Yes. The post-limitations period admission is irrelevant to the passage of title to Angie by adverse possession. The statute is a statute of repose. Once perfected, title by adverse possession is as good as any title, and nothing said by the claimant will divest it. Adverse possession creates a new title, not just a defense to the former owner's title. Land transfers are subject to the Statute of Frauds, which requires a writing to transfer title. For Angie to return Brownacre to TO, she must execute a deed. An oral statement is inadequate to transfer title. While Angie's possession was not consciously hostile to TO, she was on the property other than with TO's permission, and that is all the hostility most states require.

With Your Kind Permission

5. No. TO's permission immunizes his holdings from Andy's claim. Andy's possession must be hostile and adverse to TO's ownership. TO can stop Andy's claim dead by showing that Andy had permission to take possession (as a tenant with a lease has permission to do so).

One Farm, Two Deeds

6. Judgment for Charlie as to the farmland. Charlie has color of title and constructive possession of the land described in the deed as to Amy. Constructive possession, however, must give way to Brad's actual possession of the forest: Both Brad and Charlie have constructive adverse

possession of the whole farm—fields and forests—against Amy. Against each other, however, the doctrine of color of title does not resolve the dispute. The second deed to Charlie does not annul the first; indeed, the usual rule is "first in time, first in right," so that Brad's deed would control, except for lands in Charlie's actual adverse possession. Thus, Charlie gets the farmland; Brad gets the timberland and any land not used by either. Land in constructive adverse possession must, in other words, bear some reasonable relationship to land actually possessed. See 3 Am. L. Prop. §15.11, at 820 (James Casner, ed., 1952).

Dispossessing Future Estate Holders

7. (a) Judgment for Bobbie. You will study future interests later in the course. Return to this Example after studying future interests. TO holds a life estate, which means he owns Blackacre as long as he lives. Once he dies, Blackacre automatically passes to Bobbie. The adverse possessor used the property for the full limitations period, but only against TO, the holder of the life estate, not against Bobbie. AP owns Blackacre as long as TO lives. Once Bobbie's remainder vests in possession at TO's death, however, AP must run the statute against Bobbie all over again. Even if the adverse possessor fully and efficiently used the land during the life tenant's tenure for the full limitations period, title is not transferred to the adverse user in this instance. No amount of honest labor will be rewarded by transferring Bobbie's title to AP, because Bobbie is not the sleeping owner the law means to penalize. Both theories of adverse possession cannot be satisfied in this instance.

(b) This time, judgment for AP. The adverse possession began at a time when TO held Blackacre in fee simple absolute (TO owned it potentially forever), so the statute continued to run against all persons, including Bobbie, who had interests in Blackacre originating in TO's ownership. When TO died and left Blackacre partly to Angelina (life estate) and to Bobbie (remainder after Angelina's death), each took subject to AP's rights already established in the property. AP successfully acquired the fee simple absolute that TO held at the time of AP's entry.

Calculating Time in Possession

8. Judgment for Owen. Bessie is not in privity with Ayn and therefore cannot tack Ayn's time to Bessie's possession period. The statute of limitations for Bessie began running when she entered onto Blackacre in late 1990. Owen, although a true owner sleeping on his rights for more than the statutory period, still prevails over the adverse user, who has not

herself been in possession and satisfied the elements of adverse possession for the statutory period. This result shows that the "sleeping owner" statute of limitations rationale is not as important as the reward theory in these circumstances.

This Land Is My Land

9. (a) Odie still owns Blackacre because no one adverse possessor has run the statute for the required 20 years. Dan held it the longest, 11 years, but still fell short of the required 20 years. For the successive disseisers, one must be in possession for the statutory period to oust the true owner thereafter. None of the disseisers can tack preceding possessors' time on the land since they were not in privity. If Betty had sold or willed her rights to Cory, and Cory had deeded or willed his rights to Dan, Dan could tack both Betty's and Cory's times of possession and prevail, but that's not what happened.

   (b) Judgment for Cory. The prior possessor has a right to possession superior to the right of a later adverse possessor, even if the latter is satisfying all the elements required for adverse possession up to the time of the suit. Adverse possession is a method of transferring title after the statute has run, not an exception to the doctrine of relativity of title. The prior adverse user has a right superior to any successors, assuming she can prove that she did not abandon the property. Cory can eject Dan, but does not have the title yet. Does Cory get credit for Dan's possession? This is an open question.

   (c) Judgment for Dan. Dan has a separate interest in the wheat crop, assuming that he planted it and intends to harvest it, no matter that Cory has a right of prior possession. Protecting the crop presents an issue separate from the prior right to possession of the soil. Here Dan seeks not possession, but damages.

   (d) Judgment for Addy, who has acquired (assuming that proper proof is presented in this suit) Ossie's title by adverse possession, so that, in Year 25, Ossie had no rights to transfer to Ben. Ben cannot acquire more than his vendor had to give and so acquires nothing. Ben is not without a remedy, as he likely has a suit against Ossie for failing to convey good title.

   (e) Ben prevails. He acquired all of Ossie's rights as legal owner. The statute of limitations has not run on Addy's adverse possession, so Ben can eject her.

   (f) Addy wins. Ben waited too long to sue. He has 20 years to bring suit. The statute of limitations is measured by the time the adverse possessor is in possession, not by the time a record title owner has title.

Disabled Advice

10. Absent some special statutory provision on this problem that adjusts the time a person can bring suit once a disability is removed, your advice to O should be to sue A in his son's name before Year 35, when the limitations period will run in A's favor in a majority of states. The statute of limitations is tolled while O is insane since insanity is a disability. We do not tack disabilities, however. Only the disabilities in effect at the time the adverse possessor entered the land toll the statute. Though O's son S was insane when taking his interest, the statute of limitations begins running in A's favor as soon as the title is transferred to S: S's disability does not stop or toll the statute's running.

Bad Fences Make Bad Neighbors

11. Ben's construction interrupted the prescriptive period. Judgment for Ben. See Mendonca v. Cities Service Oil Co., 237 N.E.2d 16 (Mass. 1968). For certain the limitations period was disrupted as to eight feet. An argument could be made that Arden used twelve feet continuously for the entire 20-year period. A better argument can be made, however, that if Arden was truly claiming adversely he would have challenged Ben's taking down the fence and using the eight feet. Having failed to assert his rights in a situation where the true owner would have challenged Ben's actions, Arden lost his adverse claim to the entire 20 feet and started the limitations period anew as to the remaining twelve feet after the fence was back up. The degree of the intrusion matters. Ben reclaimed 40% the challenged land unopposed, not just a relatively small fraction of it (a few inches for example).

Intent on Ownership

12. Judgment for Annie in states adopting the objective view of hostility and for Owen in states requiring subjective good faith on the adverse possessor's part. Actually, this problem is really an argument for the majority rule. Annie's possession (if she can prove it), regardless of what she told people about it, should control. Adverse possession cases often turn as much on matters of proof as on questions of law. Annie, for example, may not be able to prove when she took possession, or that she took hostilely, because her main witnesses are not able to testify. In practice, adverse possessors entitled to have a title decreed theirs should actively pursue a judgment saying so. At a minimum, witnesses' affidavits at the beginning and at the end of the limitations period and a record of the possession over the required length of time should be made and kept.

Step Neighbors

13. (a) The New Jersey adverse possession statute provides that the record or true owners, such as the Mannillos, lose all rights to eject anyone who has been in possession for 20 years. The statute says anyone having a right to enter can bring suit, in this case for ejectment. The person with the right to enter is the legal owner, in our case the Mannillos. According to the statute the true owner can bring the action as soon as the action accrues, which is as soon as the Gorskis' stoop, steps, and walk encroach onto the Mannillos' land. The statute says if the person with the right to bring the action fails to bring the action within 20 years after the cause of action accrues, the true owner is barred from ever bringing the suit. Since the legal owner cannot bring a suit to oust or eject the trespasser after the statute of limitations has run, the trespasser in effect and legally has the right to the property.

    (b) Gorski's possession was actual. She claims only the land where her stoop, steps, and walk sit.

    (c) A critical issue in the opinion in Mannillo was whether Gorski's possession was open and notorious. Although the stoop, steps, and walk were visible (and in all likelihood walked on by Mannillo at times), the New Jersey Supreme Court concluded the encroachment onto the Mannillo property was not open and notorious. Beginning with an assertion that the foundation of adverse possession is the failure of the true owner to commence an action for the recovery of the land involved, the court concluded the possessor's use must be of such character

    > as to put an ordinarily prudent person on notice that the land is in actual possession of another. . . . Generally, where possession of the land is clear and unequivocal and to such an extent as to be immediately visible, the owner may be presumed to have knowledge of the adverse occupancy. . . . However, when the encroachment of an adjoining owner is of a small area and the fact of an intrusion is not clearly and self-evidently apparent to the naked eye but requires an on-site survey for certain disclosure as in urban sections where the division line is only infrequently delineated by any monuments, natural or artificial, such a presumption is fallacious and unjustified. . . . Accordingly, we hereby hold that no presumption of knowledge arises from a minor encroachment along a common boundary. In such a case, only where the true owner has actual knowledge thereof may it be said that the possession is open and notorious.

    > While the New Jersey court's approach is sensible in urban settings, it causes enough practical problems that most other states have not expressly adopted the "minor encroachment" rule. One

troubling issue that arises, for example, is what constitutes a minor encroachment and what a major encroachment. In a later case, a New Jersey trial court and the supreme court disagreed over whether a strip of land one foot wide and 152 feet long was a minor or a major encroachment ("minor encroachment," ruled the supreme court). The rule also makes more difficult determining whether long-used property may be claimed by adverse possession when prior owners' knowledge is unknown. Another issue, as discussed in Explanation (h), below, is whether a survey taken when Mannillo purchased the property should have given Mannillo actual, inquiry, or constructive notice. Because Gorski's possession was not open and notorious under the New Jersey approach, Gorski's adverse possession claim fails no matter how she fares under the other elements.

(d) A major issue in *Mannillo* was whether an entry and continuance under the mistaken belief that the possessor has legal title to the land in dispute exhibits the requisite hostile and adverse possession to sustain an adverse possession claim. Until this case, New Jersey held adverse possession could not be bottomed on mistake. In *Mannillo*, New Jersey held that the adverse possessor's intent is irrelevant.

New Jersey's former rule, called the "Maine Doctrine," required as an essential element of adverse possession that the adverse possessor intend to claim the property whether or not his deed describes the land, and whether or not it is eventually determined he had no right to enter upon the property. "If, on the other hand, a party through ignorance, inadvertence, or mistake occupies up to a given fence beyond his actual boundary, because he believes it to be the true line, but has no intention to claim title to that extent if it should be ascertained that the fence was on his neighbor's land, an indispensable element of adverse possession is wanting. In such a case the intent to claim title exists only upon the condition that the fence is on the true line. The intention is not absolute, but provisional, and the possession is not adverse." 255 A.2d at 261. Thus the Maine Doctrine favors a person with hostile ambitions and disfavors an honest but mistaken person. A minority of states adhere to the Maine Doctrine. If New Jersey had not disclaimed the Maine Doctrine in *Mannillo*, Gorski would not have satisfied the hostile and adverse element, and thus could not avail herself of the adverse possession statute.

In *Mannillo*, however, New Jersey aligned itself with the vast majority of states and commentators that adhere to the Connecticut Doctrine that the possessor's mental state is immaterial. Besides treating intentional wrongdoers better than honest possessors, the Maine Doctrine encourages dishonesty at trial. A person who knows she might prevail if she testifies that she intended to claim the disputed property but definitely loses if she says she used the property by mistake will be tempted to testify that she intended to claim the property as her own even though it was not described in her deed. We disfavor laws that encourage dishonesty and lying. The Connecticut Doctrine, on the other hand, posits an objective rule that the very nature of the entry and possession of the property is an assertion of an adverse and hostile possession when that possession is without the consent of the true owner. Adopting the more objective Connecticut Doctrine, the New Jersey Supreme Court concluded that Gorski satisfied the hostile and adverse element. In the end, it was a short-lived victory, since the court held that Gorski's possession was not open and notorious. See Explanation (c), supra.

(e) Gorski's possession was exclusive. Even though guests and invitees used the stoop, steps, and walk (including, presumably, the Mannillos when they visited Gorski), Gorski was the only one to claim possession. You might have noticed that although Gorski used a small portion of the Mannillos' lot, the Mannillos resided on the biggest portion of the lot, used the lot daily, and used it more intensely than Gorski. Only by treating the one lot as two pieces of property can Gorski be deemed to be in exclusive possession. Courts in fact do treat a portion of the property as separate property for determining exclusivity.

(f) Gorski's possession was continuous for more than 20 years. The stoop, steps, and walk were in place from 1946 until 1968, which exceeds 20 years. It is the possessor's use and possession of the land that must exist during the limitations period. It also does not matter that the Mannillos had owned their house for only 15 years (since 1953). The time the possession was adverse to the Mannillos' predecessor in interest (their seller) is deemed to run against the Mannillos.

(g) The general rule is that the successful adverse possessor does not have to compensate the former owner and that the true owners are not required to sell to trespassers. Some commentators have criticized the all-or-nothing approach, arguing that adverse possessors — especially in boundary disputes — should have a right to purchase the land, but not to take the land without payment. Some states, through betterment statutes, force the true owner in some cases to elect to pay for improvements made in good faith by an innocent improver or to sell the property to the innocent improver. It seems unfair to require Mannillo to compensate Gorski since Mannillo cannot benefit in the slightest from the stoop, steps, and walk. The New Jersey court held that since its holding could result in undue hardship in boundary disputes, "if the innocent trespasser of a small portion of land adjoining a boundary line cannot without great expense remove or eliminate the encroachment, or such removal or elimination is impractical or could be accomplished only with great hardship, the true owner may be forced to convey the land so occupied upon payment of the fair value thereof without regard to whether the true owner had notice of the encroachment at its inception" where "no serious damage would be done to the remaining land as, for instance, by rendering the balance of the parcel unusable or no longer capable of being built upon by reason of zoning or other restrictions." 255 A.2d at 264.

(h) Although it may be tempting to consider the pre-existing condition because the Mannillos got what they expected when they bought the home and the surprise discovery is more of a psychological windfall than a loss of expectations, adverse possession and trespass laws do not take into account the fact that the encroachment existed at the time the true owner bought the property. Nonetheless, under New Jersey's minor encroachment rule, a survey may have given the Mannillos actual notice of the encumbrance, thus making Gorski's possession open and notorious. Even if the survey did not give the Mannillos actual notice because, hypothetically, they did not look at the survey and no one told them of the problem, a court might conclude a reasonable person should have known what the survey shows and treat the Mannillos as having **constructive notice** or that they should have asked about the survey results (known as **inquiry notice**). Unfortunately for Gorski, treating the survey as giving the Mannillos notice of any type would not have helped her since the Mannillos purchased (and thus would have received notice) in 1953. The case was filed in 1968, so only 14 or 15 years had elapsed, preventing Gorski's adverse possession from meeting the 20-year requirement.

Tack and Toll Time

14. (a) Poe would gain title by adverse possession on December 1, 2022. Under the statute, the earliest Poe could gain title by adverse possession would be January 1, 2021. Bryan, a minor or infant under the statute until he turns 20, cannot be dispossessed until two years after his disability ceases. Bryan turns 20 on December 1, 2020. Two years later is December 1, 2022. Poe gains title on the later of

the normal adverse possession period or the special disability period, in this case on December 1, 2022.

(b) Poe would gain title by adverse possession on December 1, 2022, the same time she would have possessed had Bryan not gone to prison. Provision (3) of the state statute, as do all or virtually all state statutes, provides that a disability does not exist for purposes of adverse possession unless it existed when the cause of action accrued. Bryan's only disability when the action accrued — when Poe entered onto the land — was his age. Bryan's going to prison does not toll the running of the limitations period.

(c) Poe gains title by adverse possession on January 1, 2021. Under the statute the earliest Poe could gain title would be January 1, 2021. The statute provides that a person is entitled to an additional two years after the disability ends to bring an action. The "action" that may be brought is an ejectment action against Poe, the trespasser (adverse possessor). The "person entitled to bring an action" includes Bryan and any person taking through Bryan, including his estate should he die, his successors, devisees, or heirs, including in our Example the purchaser, Michelle. Bryan's disability ceased on January 1, 2016, the date he sold to Michelle. Two years later is January 1, 2018, which is earlier than if Bryan had no disability. The statute sensibly provides that the two-year extension rule cannot shorten a limitations period otherwise prescribed. The prescribed period ends on January 1, 2021. Poe gains title then. The limitations period does not begin anew when ownership changes hands. Michelle has only five years to bring an action to eject Poe, not twenty years.

(d) If Bryan sold to Michelle on July 1, 2021, Poe gains title on December 1, 2022. Again, the earliest Poe could claim title by adverse possession is January 1, 2021. Since Bryan's disability ended on December 1, 2020, he and any person claiming through him, including Michelle, have until November 30, 2022, to bring an action to eject Poe. Michelle bought after January 1, 2021, but bought while Bryan (and, through Bryan, Michelle) had almost a year and a half to bring an action. Michelle must bring an action before December 1, 2021. The statute continues to run against Michelle, however. The limitations period does not begin anew when Michelle purchases the land from Bryan.

(e) Addie gains title by adverse possession on July 1, 2020, the earliest day possible under the statute. Lance had one disability when he acquired the land: being under age 20. Note that the statute does not include being in the military as a qualifying disability. Lance died in 2011. His disability ended on that date. The two-year extension would not benefit Lance or Kevin. The main issue is whether Kevin can toll the statute because he was a minor or an infant both when Lance acquired the land and when Lance devised the land to him. Unfortunately for Kevin, he was not a "person entitled to bring an action at the time the action accrued." Kevin could not bring suit, and in fact had no right to the land at all, until the land passed to him under Lance's will. Despite his age, therefore, Kevin may lose all rights to eject Addie on July 1, 2020, when Kevin just turns 11. Let's hope Kevin's parent, legal guardian, or trustee looks out for his interest!

(f) Ed Verse gains title by adverse possession on July 1, 2020. Ed Verse is able to "tack" the time Addie was on the land. Addie sold the land to Ed Verse, and thus was in "privity" with Ed Verse, so he succeeds to her attributes, including time she adversely possessed the property.

(g) Ed Verse would gain title by adverse possession on July 1, 2020. This is tricky. Under the analysis in Explanation (f), above, the latest Ed Verse would gain ownership would be July 1, 2020. The shorter limitations period for holding under color of title should benefit rather than hurt Ed Verse. Under the color of title provision, Ed Verse, acquiring the property on January 1, 2014, normally would gain title by adverse possession on January 1, 2019. If Ed Verse could tack Addie's time, he would have acquired title on July 1, 2015. Ed Verse cannot tack Addie's time, however, since either the statute would provide the five-year period begins when the adverse possessor receives color of title, or a court would require the adverse possessor to satisfy the complete five years under color of title. Otherwise, an adverse possessor not under color of title could deed her property to a person qualifying for the shorter limitations period before the true owner filed suit (and maybe arrange for that person to deed the land back to her). Because Ed Verse entered under the color of title statute rather than the general adverse possession statute, he entered for purposes of the color of title statute when Kevin was the owner and when Kevin was a minor or infant. So Kevin would be able to toll the statute until he reaches 20, plus two years, or until July 1, 2031. Since Ed Verse prevails sooner under the ten-year general limitations period — whether or not he has color of title — by tacking Addie's time and avoiding a tolling of the running of the limitations period due to Kevin's disability, Ed Verse would rely on the general limitations period and gain title by adverse possession on July 1, 2020.

Common Law
Estates and Interests
in Real Property

Common Law Estates and Present Interests

Real property ownership can be divided several ways. O, owning 100 acres of real property, might transfer 50 acres to A and the other 50 acres to B. Alternatively, O might sell the surface rights to A and the mineral rights to B. If he wanted, O could transfer the management rights to A (a trustee of a trust, for example) and the income and profits interest to B (the beneficiary of the trust). The next few chapters develop a fourth method of dividing up ownership: over time. O, for example, might transfer acreage to A for a period of time (say, 10 years) and then give it to B for the rest of the time, or might give it to A "for life" (this is known as a life estate, meaning it lasts as long as A lives, and no longer) and then give it to B for the rest of the time, meaning that B will wind up, after A dies, owning the property in perpetuity. In other words, property can be divided physically, but may also be divided along a timeline.

The study of who owns what interests in property over time is known as the study of estates and of present and future interests. Studying estates and present and future interests requires more than reading for and attending class. You should work problems outside of class. In addition to the Examples in this book, you can find more practice problems in John Makdisi and Daniel Bogart, *Estates in Land and Future Interests* (5th ed. 2007), and Linda H. Edwards, *Estates in Land and Future Interests: A Step-By-Step Guide* (2d ed. 2005).

SOME HISTORY

We start with a very brief history of the origin of estates and future interests. In 1066, at the battle of Hastings, a Norman archer shot the Anglo-Saxon king, Harold, in the eye socket, killing him and leading to the conquest of England by William I, the Conqueror. After the battle, William parceled out the countryside to his knights; what he gave them was a use right, or **tenure** — the right to hold.

William initially parceled out lands for limited periods of time, usually for the life of a particular knight, the estate which today we call a "life estate." William, as king, prized personal loyalty above all, and rewarded it with land. But that loyalty had to be tested and affirmed anew with each generation, and so the land reverted to the king at death. The knights, once in possession of their holdings, quickly became interested in their families and children holding the land after their deaths. Over time, the knights and other landed persons were allowed to pass property along to male heirs.

The landed persons, however, became increasingly interested in two additional rights: the right to transfer or dispose of their property by will after death (**testamentary power**, or **devisability**) and the right to dispose of their land during their lifetimes (a **power to alienate**, or **alienability**). The right to alienate land was recognized by the Statute *Quia Emptores* (Latin for "concerning purchasers") in 1290.[1] The Statute of Wills in 1540 authorized all Englishmen to transfer or devise property by will at their death.

As society evolved, the meaning of the granting language evolved. Initially, for example, a grant "to *A*" meant *A* owned a life estate — i.e., owned the property for his life — and the property at his death reverted to the grantor (often the king). Later a grant to "*A* and his heirs" meant *A* owned the property for his life and at his death the property passed to his heirs — usually his eldest son. After 1290, a grant to "*A* and his heirs" meant *A* owned the property outright, and his heirs owned nothing unless and until the parent died still owning the property. After 1540, a person owning land could devise the property to anyone by will. Heirs had only an expectancy but no absolute right to succession. Finally, the presumption that a grant "to A" conveyed a life estate was reversed so that today a grant "to A" is presumed to convey a fee simple absolute unless language in the conveyance limits the grant.

The landowners were also interested in transferring land not only to one person, but to a line of successors who could hold tenure, accounting for spouses, children, and grandchildren. From that desire evolved the system of estates in land. It was and is still possible today to create interests in property that are split along a timeline running successively from the present into the future. Such a split in ownership is the major feature of our common law

---

1. Throughout this book, you'll notice common law forms of action and procedures based initially on late-thirteenth-century statutes. Many are the result of the work of Edward I, known as a law reformer in his day and to this day. These are not statutes in the modern sense — they are the product of "the King sitting in Parliament" with his nobles, and so are more like executive orders issued with the consent of the nobles.

interests and estates, created first for England's nobility but available to all of us today.

Split ownership — fragmented over time — enabled a transferor or testator to control the ownership of property after the transfer or, in the case of a will, after the testator's death (a **testator** is a person dying and leaving a will, a/k/a a **decedent**; and whatever property is transferred by will is often referred to as a **decedent's estate**, administered by an **executor**). Most rules for transfers and wills discussed in this chapter were either formulated for testators interested in such control or by their children, heirs, and transferees resisting that control. The history of common law estates may be seen as a series of intergenerational conflicts, as well as a series of devices designed to achieve that age-old aim of the propertied classes, tax avoidance.

ESTATES AND INTERESTS

The study of estates and interests is, for the beginner, one of concepts and vocabulary. We'll begin by defining and distinguishing "estates" and "interests." A person may have an ownership interest in property. That interest may refer to an estate (ownership along a time continuum). Elsewhere in the course you will encounter other interests a person may have in land, such as easements, restrictive covenants, equitable servitudes, liens, mortgages, and leases. A later chapter, for example, explores concurrent interests — when more than one person shares the same possessory rights to specific property.

Estates categorize ownership over a timeline. Estates are divided into present possessory interests (commonly called present interests) and future possessory interests (commonly called future interests). A person owns a present interest in property if he or she can take possession and use the property currently — in the present time. In contrast, a person who owns a future interest must wait until some future time to take possession of the property. Although the owner of a future interest in property, being without the right to immediate possession, in effect gets no present enjoyment or economic benefit (other than appreciation in value) from owning the land, the person owning the future interest is an owner of the property nonetheless.

Estates also refer to when and how ownership ends. Some estates last forever or into infinity, some for a person's life, some until something happens. Thus, in classifying estates and interests, it is said that "Owen has a present interest (or future interest, as the case may be), held in an estate known as a. . . ." You will spend the best part of the next several chapters learning to fill in that last blank. This task will require constant study — cramming the subject won't suffice.

ESTATES: FUNDAMENTAL FRAGMENTS OF TIME

Fragmentation of ownership interests over time is the basic concept underlying present and future interests. Judges in early England wanted to visualize ownership of property for all time. Moreover, land was considered to last forever. An oft-used diagram shows a dot representing today and a line extending to infinity to identify all estates in property from today to infinity:

A **fee simple absolute** is what we think of as complete ownership, lasting until the end of time. Its owner can enjoy the property, transfer it away by sale or gift during his life, or devise it (by will) at his death. If he dies without a will and still owning the property, the property passes to his descendants, usually family members, designated in a state statute known generally as the Canons of Descent or the Intestacy Statute. The above diagram illustrates the fee simple absolute.

The diagram indicates that beginning at the present, the dot, on the facts known today, all persons who can use or possess the property from now to infinity must get their rights from or through the fee simple absolute owner. Obviously the owner cannot personally use the property until infinity. Human mortality precludes that. The owner, however, controls who gets the property from now until infinity. The owner during his life or at his death will pass the right to control use and possession to others.

A common transfer is from the property owner (O) to A for life, remainder to B. This grant would be diagrammed:

A has a present interest, held in a life estate. A can use the property during his lifetime (or transfer the rights to others to use the property during A's lifetime).

B has a future interest, a (vested) remainder, held in a fee simple absolute. B must wait until A's life ends before B can possess and use the property. B has the right to possess the property or designate who will control the use of the property until infinity after A's death.

If O had granted A a life estate and not stipulated what happens after A dies, the law stipulates the property will revert back to O (or O's later designee) at A's death. The timeline would look like this:

A has a present interest, held in a life estate.

O has a future interest, a reversion, held in a fee simple absolute. That is, once A dies, the property reverts to O, and O again has a fee simple absolute, and once more is free to possess the property or designate who will.

There are four core estates, categorized based on the potential longevity or duration of the possessory interests.

Estate	Duration
Fee Simple	Forever (Infinity)
Fee Tail (fee simple conditional)	Until original grantee's lineage dies out
Life Estate, or Term for Life	For the life of the grantee
Term of Years	Fixed period measured in years, months, or days

The first three estates for historical reasons are known as **freehold estates**. As you can see, this category of estates, or types of tenure, has nothing to do with how they begin; the key is that they have different ways of ending. Possession of a freehold estate is denoted by a special word: **seisin**—pronounced "seez-in." So lawyers say, "land must always be seised of some person" or "O has seisin."

The fourth estate listed here, the term of years, along with the periodic tenancy, the tenancy at will, and their documentary cousin, the leasehold, are all known as **nonfreehold estates.** Historically and today, a nonfreehold estate is a less complete form of ownership than a freehold estate. An apartment rental, for example, is a nonfreehold estate.

A person may hold each of the estates as present interest or as a future interest. Hence a person may own a present interest in a life estate, or a future interest in a life estate. The same is true for the other estates.

Example: Olivia deeded Blackacre to Adam for his life, then to Barbara for her life, then to Carla and her heirs. Adam owns a *present interest* in Blackacre, held in a life estate. Barbara owns a *future interest* in Blackacre, held in a life estate. She must wait for Adam to die before she takes possession. Carla owns a future interest, a vested remainder held in fee simple absolute.

THE IMPORTANCE OF TERMS — AND SOME MORE TERMS

Much of the study of estates is the study of nomenclature, or labels. Therefore it is important to master precise labels. There are different categories of fees simple, for example: fee simple absolute, fee simple determinable, fee simple subject to a condition subsequent, and fee simple subject to an executory limitation. Master the differences between them and use precise labels in referring to them. Do not label a reversion a reversionary interest, for example, because you will only confuse yourself and other people. Some aspects of each estate require careful scrutiny as you study each estate.

First, master the wording used to create each estate. There may be seemingly subtle differences in wording to distinguish different estates. There is a big difference, for example, between a grant to "Jill and her heirs" (fee simple absolute) and one to "Jill and the heirs of her body" (fee tail or fee simple conditional).

Next, know the characteristics of each estate. One on which you need to concentrate refers to its **termination** — how or when the estate's duration ends. A fee simple absolute may not end; it potentially lasts into infinity. A life estate, on the other hand, lasts only for the life of some person and ends on that person's death. An estate can end either naturally or by a condition subsequent. A **condition subsequent** is the occurrence or non-occurrence of an event that can cut short an estate. An estate may end naturally, for example, on the death of a person or at the end of a given time period, say ten years. An estate may be terminated by a condition subsequent, for example, if the grant conditions the continued ownership on the property not being used for some purpose, or the grant conditions the continued ownership on the property being used for some purpose and the property ceases to be used for that purpose. A grant to "Local School Board, but if the land ceases to be used for school purposes, then to the Lion's Club" creates a fee simple in Local School Board that might last forever, but School Board's fee simple estate could be terminated unnaturally if the condition subsequent (land ceases to be used for school purposes) happens.

Finally, know whether and in what ways the estate or interest holder can transfer the interest. Property is **devisable** if the owner can transfer ownership by a will — a testamentary transfer. Property is **descendible** or **inheritable** if the property can pass by the state's intestacy statute to heirs if the owner dies without a will. Property is **alienable**, **assignable**, or **transferable** if the owner can sell or give it away during his lifetime — an *inter vivos* transfer. Most estates and interests are devisable, inheritable, and alienable to some extent today, but there are exceptions.

(a) Fee Simple Absolute

A *fee simple absolute* is an estate with an infinite or perpetual duration. A person owning a fee simple interest theoretically can possess the property forever. There is no inherent end to the ownership. The owner may sell or give the property away, devise it by will, or die without a will and have the property go by operation of law under the canons of descent to his heirs. Hence a fee simple absolute is alienable (transferable or assignable), devisable, and descendible (inheritable). Most land sales are for a fee simple absolute.

The language traditionally used to create a fee simple absolute is "**to A and his heirs.**" Today the phrase "**to A**" also transfers a fee simple absolute, as do phrases such has "**to A, his heirs and assigns.**"

Diagramming the grant:

to *A*	and his heirs
Words of Purchase	**Words of Limitation**

The critical language to determine who owns the estate are the **words of purchase**. Property transferred "to *A*" belongs to *A*. They denote who takes the estate. Property transferred "to *A* and his heirs" still belongs solely to *A*. The remaining language, "and his heirs," are **words of limitation**. They tell experienced lawyers what was granted, that the grantor intended the estate to be one greater than a life estate, and that the estate lasts in perpetuity — i.e., that the grantor transferred a fee simple absolute. Despite the language of the grant, *A*'s heirs get absolutely nothing from this transfer. Only *A* gets the property.

(b) Life Estate

(1) Attributes of a Life Estate

The life estate — as the name implies — means the owner owns the property for life. The life estate is the oldest type of freehold estate. The life tenant (the holder of a life estate) has seisin. As long as the life estate lasts, its holder may use the property, collecting all the rents and profits generated from it. The life estate's duration is measured by the life tenant's life. The life estate is neither devisable nor descendible (by the life tenant) because the life estate ends on the death of the life tenant. The life estate, however, is alienable *inter vivos* (transferable during the life tenant's life) by the life tenant for a term lasting so long as the original life tenant lives. The third party's right to continue using the property ends with the original life tenant's life.

Because the life estate was the dominant estate for more than 100 years, courts for centuries interpreted transfers "to *A*" as life estates. That is, when in doubt whether the grantor meant to transfer a life estate or a fee simple absolute, English courts 900 years ago would find the grant "to *A*" to be a life estate. The reverse is true today. Either by statute or judicial decision, a person transferring property today is deemed to transfer his or her entire interest in the property unless the words of grant or other evidence indicate that the grantor intended to transfer a lesser interest. Today a grant from O to A would transfer a fee simple absolute to A.

There are no mandatory words required to create a life estate. "To A for life" may be the most common, but "to A for her natural life," "to A during her lifetime," "to A for the term of her life," and "to A as long as he lives" all create a life estate. The language to create a life estate may be diagrammed:

The words "To A" are **words of purchase** indicating who gets the property. The words "for life" are **words of limitation** indicating the grantee A's ownership of the property ends on her death.

Example 1: Owen transfers Blackacre "to A for life." A has a present interest, held in a life estate. When A dies her interest in Blackacre ends. She cannot devise it to anyone, nor will Blackacre pass by inheritance to her heirs.

Because a life estate has limited duration, some other person also must own an interest in the property. If the grant to the life tenant does not stipulate who takes the property upon the life tenant's death, the original grantor (or his estate if he is deceased) takes possession. When a grantor is to receive possession back when the life estate ends, the grantor's future interest is labeled a **reversion**.

Example 2: Owen transfers Blackacre "to A for life." A has a present interest in a life estate. Owen owns a future interest, a **reversion**. A owns the present possessory interest. Owen cannot use Blackacre while A is alive, but Owen (or someone taking through Owen) will take possession of Blackacre in the future when A dies.

A transferor or grantor may provide that some third party will take the property after the life estate ends. The future interest following a life estate owned by a third party (not the grantor) is called a **remainder**. A remainder is a future interest in a third party that "remains" after the interests and estates prior to it end *naturally*. In practice, the remainder follows the life estate, fee tail, and the term of years. Remainders may be vested remainders, contingent remainders, vested remainders subject to divestment, or vested remainders subject to open. The distinction between the various remainders, and between a remainder and a reversion can lead to have critically different consequences. For now, master the difference between a remainder and a reversion.

Example 3: Owen transfers Blackacre "to A for life, then to B and her heirs." As in Example 2, A owns a present interest in a life estate. A future interest follows A's life estate. The future interest, being in a person other than the grantor, is called a *remainder*. In a few pages we learn B's remainder is a vested remainder in fee simple absolute. B's heirs own nothing under the grant.

While a life estate is frequently measured by the life tenant's life, it can be measured by the grantor's life or by the life of a third party. Thus, O's conveyance "to A for O's life" gives A possessory rights until O dies. The words of purchase "to A" give the property to A. The words of limitation "for O's life" limit the duration of A's ownership to O's life. The "O to A for O's life" conveyance might be a means to confer benefits on A when O wants the property to go to someone else after O dies.

When a person's interest in a life estate is measured by the life of a third person, say X, the life estate is called a **life estate pur autre vie** X — that is, a life estate measured by the life of X. A person owning a life estate pur autre vie may transfer or assign the life estate to another party during his life; and because the life estate continues as long as the other person lives, the life estate pur autre vie may is devisable (by will) and descendible (inheritable) (if no will). The life estate pur autre vie ends on the death of the person who is the measuring life.

Example 4: Owen in Year 1 transferred Whiteacre "to A for life." In Year 5 A transferred her interest in Whiteacre to B. B died in Year 10 while A was still alive. B by will devised all his real property to C. Question: Who owns what interests in Whiteacre? In year 1, A owned a present interest, held in a life estate. Owen owned the reversion, a future interest, to become possessory when A died. In Year 5, B acquired a life estate pur autre vie A. Owen maintained his reversion. When B died, he devised the life estate pur autre vie to C. C can use Whiteacre until A dies. Owen retained his reversion. If A died in Year 20, C's life estate pur autre vie A ends and Owen owns Whiteacre in fee simple absolute.

Example 5: Same facts as in Example 4 except A died in Year 8 while B is still alive. Since B owned a life estate pur autre vie A, B's interest in Whiteacre ended on A's death. Owen's future interest, his reversion, becomes a present possessory interest, a fee simple absolute.

(2) Marketability Problems

In practice, legal life estates are difficult to market. Lenders may be reluctant to take property held as a life estate for security for a loan for fear the life tenant may die before the loan is repaid. Purchasers who wish to improve the property likely will not purchase a life estate and invest millions of dollars in constructing improvements since they would lose the improvements and land as soon as the life tenant dies. There are other problems with life estates, so much so that England no longer recognizes the *legal* life estate (the *equitable* life estate — one held in trust — is recognized). The legal life estate continues to be recognized in the United States, although most life estates are equitable life estates held in trusts.

A transferor may choose the legal life estate to impose obligations on the life tenant, to avoid the fees and costs involved in administering a trust for property, or to preserve the property in its present use. There may be reasons driven by the federal and state estate tax codes as well since by definition the legal life estate expires on the life tenant's death, and will not go into the life tenant's decedent's taxable estate. Income taxes might figure in the transferor's calculations too: The transferor can carve out a future interest for a charity and obtain a charitable deduction for the value of that interest, with the transferor or his family enjoying the property in the mean time in a life estate.

(3) Conflicts Between the Life Tenant and the Remainderman

Besides the lender and sales problems discussed above, legal life estates create problems between the holder of the legal life estate and the person who owns the property once the life estate ends (the original grantor who has a *reversion*, or a third party who has a *remainder*). Often a life tenant will want to use the property in a manner contrary to what the future interest holder would. Some rules have evolved to resolve these conflicts.

First, logically enough, the holder of the life estate can exclude others from the property, including any holder of a future interest (either a reversion or a remainder). Thus, the life tenant can treat the future interest holder as trespasser should the future interest holder attempt to use the property or remove anything from it.

Second, the life tenant keeps all the income, rents, and profits from the use of the land during the life estate. The life tenant who farms the land, for example, may keep the crops or the proceeds from the sale. Likewise, a life tenant who rents the property to another keeps the rent and is not obligated to share the net rents with the future interest holders.[2] Special rules under

---

2. The renter or lessee loses rights to continued possession of the leased premises on the death of the life tenant unless he has or makes an agreement with the future interest holder.

the rubrics of "waste" and "open mines doctrine" balance the rights of the life tenant to extract minerals and change the use of the land with the life tenant's obligation to preserve the property in its current condition for the future interest holder. Those rules are developed more fully later in this chapter.

Third, a life tenant has duties and obligations. The life tenant must keep the premises in ordinary repair, must pay taxes, must pay the interest on any mortgage for all the property, and in some jurisdictions must pay insurance premiums. A life tenant is not entitled to contribution or reimbursement from the future interest holder for these expenses. The repairs required to be made are ordinary repairs only. The life tenant, on the other hand, is not obligated to improve the property; to repair extraordinary damages caused by storms, earthquakes, fires, etc. (but it may be his duty to repair damages from ordinary wear and tear). Likewise, a tenant who constructs improvements on the land cannot seek partial payment from future interest holders. We take this up in detail later in this chapter in the discussion of the cause of action for "waste."

Sometimes the life tenant acquires land subject to a mortgage and or notes secured by the property. The life tenant is responsible for the interest payments. Some states say he is not liable for the principal of any loan secured by the property; others say the life tenant is liable for the principal included in any installment payment due during the life estate.

Although some states require the life tenant to insure buildings on the land, most do not. In these states, a life tenant who insures the building anyway cannot seek reimbursement from the future interest holder. Some states hold a life tenant may keep any insurance proceeds received on any claim made against the policy, while other states hold the life tenant and the remaindermen must split any insurance proceeds according to the relative values of each person's interest (which can be calculated using actuarial tables).

Further, a life tenant has a duty to pay real property taxes. This duty includes an obligation to buy the property at a tax sale. This makes sense: if the life tenant has the duty to pay taxes, then he has the duty to remedy the situation when the taxes fall into default and the local government seeks to sell the property to satisfy that default. Moreover, if the government makes a special assessment against the property for permanent improvements, such as streets, sidewalks, sewers, and so on, most states hold the life tenant and the remainderman liable for each person's proportionate share (based on relative values of each person's interest).

(4) Life Estate or Fee Simple

Some drafters of wills (testator) and deeds (grantor), often nonlawyers, do not use "to A and his heirs" or "to A for life" to identify what estate the recipient is to take; or a testator or grantor might include a purpose or an unclear explanation of his intent. A classic example occurs when a testator favors one or more parties by guaranteeing the party the right to continue living on the property. Usually the favored party is someone who shared a home with the decedent for many years. The grant or will may be worded, "I want my home to go to A to live in." The issue in these cases is whether the transferor or grantor intended to give the transferee a fee simple absolute, a life estate, or some nonfreehold estate.

A judge trying this issue will first read the plain language of the document, attempting to ascertain the grantor's or testator's intent. If that does not resolve the issue, the judge will resort to rules of construction. **Rules of construction** are not laws, but are accepted suppositions that can be rebutted by evidence. One rule of construction is that a testator (deceased person with a will) intended to give away all his property through his will. An interpretation that disposes of all the testator's property in the will rather than resorting to the state's intestacy statute is favored. A corollary of the first rule is that a partial intestacy (i.e., a will that does not dispose of all the testator's property) is disfavored. Another rule of construction is that a grantor or testator conveys her full interest in the property unless the intent to pass a lesser estate is clearly expressed or necessarily implied by the terms of the deed or will.

(c) Fee Tail and Fee Simple Conditional

Desiring to maintain large estates as a unit for generations so as to preserve a family's wealth and social standing, a grantor might have created a fee simple conditional or fee tail. The **fee simple conditional** and **fee tail** in effect were a series of life estates. A enjoyed a life estate; on A's death the property automatically passed to A's eldest son for his life; on his death the property passed to that son's eldest; and so on until the family line ended (died **"without issue"** is the traditional phrase for this event), at which point the property reverted back to the grantor (or more likely to one of the grantor's heirs). The ending of the grantee's bloodline is called **failure of issue**. The fee tail thus thinks in dynastic, not individual, terms.

The fee tail and fee simple conditional are related estates — in fact, one replaced the other and both are created by the same language: **"to A and the heirs of his body."** In the transfer "to A and the heirs of his body," the words "to A" are **words of purchase**, and the phrase "and the heirs of his body" are **words of limitation** — sometimes called in this instance **"words of procreation."** Each generation of A's heirs has a life estate.[3]

---

3. At common law, a fee tail could be a **"fee tail special"** — e.g., "to A and the heirs of her body by her husband Ben" — or **"fee tail male"** or **"fee tail female"** — e.g., "to A and the male (or female) heirs of his body."

At one time, "heir" meant a male heir, the system of inheritance then in use being **primogeniture**, or inheritance limited to the eldest son. Before the birth of a son, the holder of the fee simple conditional had a fee simple conditioned on the birth of an heir. If its holder died without an heir, the property reverted back to the grantor. By the Statute *De Donis Conditionalibus* (1285), the fee simple conditional was changed into a fee tail, and thereafter, when O conveyed "to A and the heirs of his body," a fee tail, inheritable to the last member of the grantee's family line, was established. And a younger son inherited and became the heir if his elder brother died before inheriting. South Carolina is the only jurisdiction recognizing the fee simple conditional today. Today heirs are determined by state intestacy statutes and do not favor males or first-borns.

Can you think of a family still using a line of succession dictated by primogeniture? If you are thinking of the English royal family, the House of Windsor, you have probably the most famous example of the use of the fee tail in the world. Daughters don't inherit the English throne unless there is no son — which is how the current Queen Elizabeth II came to sit (seisin again) on her throne.

Fee tails, like life estates, are not devisable or generally inheritable because the property passes from one generation to the next under the terms of the fee tail grant. The fee tail, when used in conjunction with a principle of primogeniture, served to preserve the largest English estates intact rather than to split them up among the children of the nobility. It was also early used to return land transferred to a child to the family's estate should the line of that child die out. This second use of the estate was particularly useful in transfers of land to a second or third son, who normally would not inherit the family's main estate under the system of primogeniture. (During the time the estate was first created, mortality rates due to war, disease, and the limited ability of farmers to produce enough food were such that it took on average a minimum of four children in a family to ensure the continuation of a family dynasty.)

Today all but four states have abolished the fee tail by statute, many doing so in the early nineteenth century. States still recognizing the estate are three New England states (Maine, Massachusetts, and Rhode Island) and Delaware. In these four states, the holder of the fee tail can break the entail or **disentail** the property simply by conveying his interest in fee simple absolute to a third party, who takes it in fee simple absolute. Often the beneficiaries of disentailing are creditors of the estate holder, and often the third party is the entailed owner's attorney, who serves as straw man, or someone bound to convey it right back in fee simple absolute. In all other states, the fee tail is abolished by statute.[4]

---

4. Often these statutes simply said something like "the estate in fee tail is abolished." Thus, to know whether the statute applies, one must know the words necessary to create the estate in the first place.

The statutes abolishing the fee tail interpret the traditional fee tail grant as creating one of several estates: Most states give the first grantee a fee simple absolute; other states give the first taker a life estate after which the heirs of his body take a fee simple absolute. Only about seven states use the second configuration. A few states preserve the fee tail for one generation.

Fee tails, even where authorized, are seldom used. More than that, the use of the fee tail was unusual even at common law, because grantors and testators did not want to chance a failure of issue after their children and grandchildren died. Better to have used the conveyance "to *A* and his heirs" or some variation or to split the fee into more acceptable present and future interests.

(d) Term of Years

The term of years, a nonfreehold estate, resembles a leasehold and is treated under that topic. See Part Three, "The Law of Landlord and Tenant." In general, a term of years lasts for some fixed period. The fixed period may be for centuries, decades, years, months, or days. Because the term of years ends naturally and is not divested (unless some condition is attached in the grant), the future interest following a term of years is a reversion if the grantor owns the property again after the term of years ends or a remainder if a third party takes possession. A term of years is alienable, inheritable, and devisable.

WASTE

(a) Voluntary, Permissive, and Ameliorating Waste

A life tenant is obligated to deliver the property in essentially the same condition or use as when the life tenant took possession. Waste occurs when the possessory life tenant permanently impairs the property's condition or value to the future interest holder's detriment. In general, it involves the abuse, alteration, or destruction of realty by a person not a trespasser and not holding a fee simple.[5] A future interest holder may bring an action for waste for substantial injury to these future interests caused by

---

5. Waste is used to regulate two other relationships in the law of real property — the landlord-tenant and the mortgagor-mortgagee relationship.

the life tenant The future interest holder may collect damages and an injunction to prevent waste.

A grant or transfer can be made "to A for life, without impeachment for waste." Under this grant, the holder of the life estate is immune from suit by the future interest holder.

Waste falls into several categories. **Affirmative** or **voluntary waste** occurs when the life tenant actively changes the property's use or condition, usually in a way that substantially decreases the property's value. A court will enjoin affirmative waste. A second category of waste, **permissive waste**, is akin to nonfeasance — the life tenant fails to prevent some harm to the property. For example, one court found that not making normal repairs to a water pump that resulted in dead lawn, shrubs, and trees was permissive waste. See Kimbrough v. Reed, 130 Idaho 512, 943 P.2d 1232 (1997). The life tenant was required to pay damages to the remainderman. The law of permissive waste evolved to become the duties discussed earlier: to make ordinary repairs, to pay interest on debt, to pay taxes and assessments, and in some jurisdictions to pay insurance premiums.

A variation of affirmative waste is **meliorating** or **ameliorating waste**, or waste that benefits the remainderman's interest. In England, the law of waste was strict: A life tenant could not stop growing crops and begin grazing cattle, for example, even if it made the property more productive or valuable. Even changing crops may have been waste. Courts in the United States have allowed reasonable changes in use and condition. For example, in Melms v. Pabst Brewing Company, 79 N.W. 738 (Wis. 1899), a life tenant owned a stately mansion in the midst of a brewery complex. Over time other commercial activities encroached on the mansion to the point at which it was no longer suitable for use as a residence, and not efficiently convertible to commercial purposes. The court held under the circumstances that demolishing the mansion and replacing it with a commercial building would not be waste. In effect, meliorating waste is non-compensable waste. In evaluating whether it will be permitted, courts look at the life tenant's expected remaining life, the need for change, and the good faith of the life tenant and future interest holder in proposing or opposing the change.

(b) Open Mines Doctrine

The open mines doctrine sets out rules applicable to natural resources, particularly minerals. Under the **open mines doctrine**, a life tenant may mine and remove minerals (and keep the profits) if the grantor had opened the mines or began the mining and removal before he granted the life estate. The presumption is the grantor intended the life tenant to continue using the property as the grantor had been using it. That same presumption swayed courts to conclude, unless the future interest holder consented, that the life tenant could not begin or conduct mining operations if no mining took place before the life estate began. While England applied the same rule to timber cutting, American courts in some cases allow timber cutting using the ameliorative waste analysis.

(c) Economic Waste

A variation on waste is economic waste. **Economic waste** occurs when the income from property is insufficient to pay the expenses the life tenant has a duty to pay: ordinary maintenance, real estate taxes, interest on mortgages, and in some jurisdictions, insurance. Economic waste does not mean the property is not being used for its highest and best use, only that it does not pay for its own upkeep. The life tenant — and in some cases the remainderman — can bring an action to sell the property if economic waste occurs.

In an illustrative case, Baker v. Weedon, 262 So. 2d 641 (Miss. 1972), the life tenant, Anna Weedon, experienced personal economic distress and wished to sell land (her life estate interest and the remaindermen's interest) and put the money in a trust so she could use the income from the trust to pay for her personal living expenses. The court held that economic waste does not mean the life tenant personally would be better off financially, or that a court can act when a life tenant needs to sell (not just her interest but the remaindermen's as well) for economic reasons. Only if the income from the property is insufficient to "pay taxes and maintain the property" could a court order a sale. The property in that case generated just enough money each year to pay the taxes and maintenance. Hence the court found no economic waste.[6]

DEFEASIBLE FEE SIMPLE ESTATES

The three freehold estates developed to this point — fee simple absolute, life estate, and fee tail (and the fee simple conditional) — are subject to several variations, particularly of the fee simple absolute, that may end prematurely because of a condition subsequent. A **condition subsequent** is an event whose occurrence or nonoccurrence will terminate the estate. Once the condition

---

6. Ultimately, the remaindermen in the case had a change of heart, agreed to sell all but five acres of the 150-acre farm, set up a trust, and allow Anna Weedon to take the income from the trust.

subsequent occurs, the estate holder's interest ends and the property either reverts to the original grantor or passes to a third party.

Example: Armas transferred Blackacre "to Britney and her heirs, but if Britney sells alcohol on Blackacre, then to Carrie." Armas has transferred a fee simple to Britney but it is not a fee simple absolute since Britney may lose all her interest in Blackacre if she sells alcohol on Blackacre.

The example illustrates the concept of a defeasible estate. A life estate may also be defeasible, but most defeasible estates are defeasible fee simples. Three distinct defeasible fees have evolved, each with its own label and characteristics. Britney's estate in the above example is called a fee simple subject to an executory limitation. If the property were to return to Armas, the grantor, Britney's interest would be called a fee simple subject to a condition subsequent. The grant could have been worded differently to create the third defeasible fee simple, the fee simple determinable. It is important to learn the words to create each defeasible fee simple and the attributes of each estate.

(a) Fee Simple Determinable

A **fee simple determinable** is an estate that would be a fee simple absolute but for a provision in the transfer document that states that the estate shall *automatically* end on the happening of an event or nonevent. An example is "to A and her heirs so long as the property is used for church purposes," or "to A and his heirs unless liquor is sold on the property." Although it is sometimes said that no words of art are necessary to create such estates and that the transferor's intent controls, the words typically employed to create a fee simple determinable are "so long as," "during," "while," "unless," and "until." All these words, with the phrases that follow, are words of limitation, indicating a fee simple determinable.

The significant difference between a fee simple absolute and a fee simple determinable is that while both potentially have an infinite or perpetual duration, the fee simple determinable might terminate automatically if the condition subsequent occurs. Historically a grantor could not provide that the property would pass to a third party if the condition subsequent eventuated and the fee simple determinable ended. The only option was to have the property return to the original grantor (or his heirs if the original grantor was dead). The chance that the property might return to the grantor if the condition subsequent happened is called the **possibility of reverter.** In sum, absent words to the contrary, a fee simple determinable is a present possessory estate followed by a possibility of reverter in the grantor. Sometimes the possibility of reverter is expressed in the deed or will creating the fee simple determinable; if not expressed it will be implied as part of the nature of a fee simple determinable.

The timeline for a fee simple determinable would look like this:

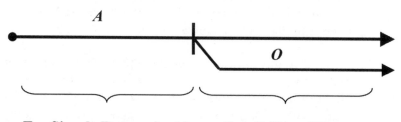

Fee Simple Determinable   **Possibility of Reverter**

Example: Armas deeded Blackacre to Britney "so long as Britney does not sell alcohol on Blackacre." Britney owns a fee simple determinable estate in Blackacre that could last forever. However, if Britney sells alcohol on Blackacre, the property automatically returns to the grantor, Armas, who owns a possibility of reverter.

(b) Fee Simple Subject to a Condition Subsequent

Closely related to the fee simple determinable is the **fee simple subject to a condition subsequent**. Like the holder of a fee simple determinable, the holder of a fee simple subject to a condition subsequent may hold the property forever, but could lose it entirely if the condition subsequent occurs. The difference between a fee simple determinable and a fee simple subject to a condition subsequent is that the fee simple determinable ends automatically upon the happening of the condition subsequent, whereas the grantor of a fee simple subject to a condition subsequent must assert his right of entry (also called "right of reentry" or "power of termination"). Until the grantor exercises his right or entry, the holder of the fee simple subject to a condition subsequent continues to own the property. As is the case with the fee simple determinable, the only person who can retake the property on the event of the condition subsequent is the grantor or his heirs.

The fee simple subject to a condition subsequent usually can be identified by some of the following language in the granting instrument: "provided that," "but if," "on the condition that," or "provided, however." Compare these phrases with the one used to create a fee simple determinable.

The timeline for a fee simple subject to a condition subsequent would look like this:

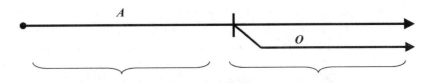

Fee Simple Subject to a Condition Subsequent   Right of Entry (in the Grantor)

Example: Armas transferred Blackacre "to Britney; provided, however, if Britney sells alcohol on Blackacre, then Armas may re-enter and retake the land." Britney owns a fee simple subject to a condition subsequent in Blackacre. Her interest may last forever. If she sells alcohol on Blackacre, however, Armas can elect to take back the property. Armas owns a right of entry (right of reentry; power of termination).

There are some different legal consequences between a fee simple determinable and a fee simple subject to a condition subsequent. First, when the conditioning event occurs under a fee simple determinable, the owner of the fee simple determinable loses all interest in the property immediately and the title automatically reverts to the holder of the possibility of reverter. Once title reverts, it is too late for a waiver. A new deed is required to undo the effect of the broken condition. On the other hand, the holder of a fee simple subject to a condition subsequent owns the land until the holder of the right of reentry elects to retake the property. The holder of a right of entry does not automatically gain possession upon a broken condition. The holder may waive any breach of the covenant. Until the owner of the right of entry retakes the property, the owner of the fee simple subject to a condition subsequent continues owning the land.

Second, unless modified by statute (which many states have done), the running of the statute of limitations for adverse possession starts at different times. The adverse possession statute starts running against the holder of a possibility of reverter (as to a fee simple determinable) on the day the condition subsequent happens. In contrast, since the owner of a fee simple subject to a condition subsequent continues owning the property even if the designated event occurs, the adverse possession limitations period does not begin to run until the holder of the right of entry exercises that right. A few states by judicial decision or by statute equate the two estates for adverse possession purposes and begin the running of the statute of limitations as soon as the condition occurs.

Third, while most states have adopted a uniform rule on the power of the holder of the possibility of reverter and right of entry to transfer or devise the future interest — either both are assignable or neither is — in a few states the possibility of reverter is transferable, while the right of reentry is not.

Commentators have long urged that the two estates be consolidated by statute since the remaining differences are too small to warrant continuing both. These critics contend that despite the fact that the fee simple determinable has an automatic termination feature and the fee simple subject to a condition subsequent does not, a reentry is never automatic. To them the view that O turns up and A gives up possession is simply unrealistic. Further, as a matter of policy, any exercise of O's rights ought to be judicially supervised in any event, no matter what words the grantor uses. Many states have merged the two.

Some state legislatures have responded to the problems that possibilities of reverter and rights of reentry create for conveyancing attorneys by enacting statutes that limit their duration to a period of 20 or 30 years. These interests must be asserted within the statutory time period or else be forever barred. A few courts have done the same thing without waiting for their legislatures by limiting the life of a possibility of reverter or right of reentry to a reasonable length of time. See, e.g., Mildram v. Town of Wells, 611 A.2d 84 (Me. 1992) (holding that not asserting a right of reentry for 82 years vested the holder of the present interest with a fee simple absolute). Other courts have found, based on the language used by the drafter, that the future interest was personal to the grantor or transferor and not intended to be alienable, devisable, or descendible for the benefit of his or her heirs.

(c) Distinguishing a Fee Simple Determinable from a Fee Simple Subject to a Condition Subsequent from a Covenant

At times it may be critical to determine whether a given grant is a fee simple determinable or a fee simple subject to a condition subsequent. If properly drafted, the determination is easy. A grant using the words "as long as," "so long as," "during," "while," "unless," or "until" creates a fee simple determinable. A grant using the words "provided that," "provided, however," "but if," or "on condition that" creates a fee simple subject to a condition subsequent. Problems arise when the grant uses words from both categories or the grant is otherwise ambiguous.

A judge will try to ascertain the grantor's intent as expressed in the document as a whole. Because courts disfavor forfeitures, when in doubt, as a matter of construction, a judge will construe a grant as a fee simple subject to a condition subsequent rather than as a fee simple determinable because the fee simple subject to a condition subsequent allows the possessor to continue ownership until the holder of the right of entry (power of termination) acts to retake the property.

In some cases a court may interpret the qualification to the title as not being a divesting condition at all, but instead a covenant. A **covenant** is a promise to do or not do some act. A grantor may seek injunctive relief or damages for a breach of a covenant, but the owner of the fee simple will not forfeit ownership. In some cases a court may even interpret limiting language as **precatory language** instead of as a condition or a covenant. Precatory language expresses a desire, suggestion, hope, or expectation, but does not rise to the level of a covenant or condition.

(d) Fee Simple Subject to an Executory Limitation

One shared characteristic of the fee simple determinable and the fee simple subject to a condition subsequent is that only the original grantor or his heirs can hold the future interest (the possibility of reverter or the right of reentry). For more than 200 years in England, a grant could not divest a defeasible fee in favor of a third party. The grantor had to retain a future interest for himself. Finally, by the Statute of Uses enacted in 1536, grantors could pass future interests following a defeasible fee simple to a third party. After more than 200 years of judges and lawyers repeating the mantra "only the grantor can have a future interest following a defeasible fee," the English legal community settled on a new label for the expanded rights.

The same granting language that would create either a fee simple determinable or a fee simple subject to a condition subsequent creates a **fee simple subject to an executory limitation** (also known as a fee simple on executory limitation) if the future interest goes to a third party. Only one label for the possessory interest was coined, not two. The new label given to the future interest to a third party following a fee simple subject to an executory limitation is the **executory interest**.

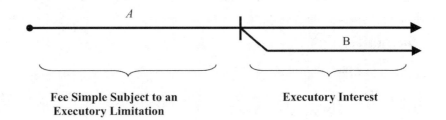

Fee Simple Subject to an
Executory Limitation

Executory Interest

Example: Armas transferred Blackacre "to Britney as long as Britney does not sell alcohol on Blackacre, then to Carl and his heirs." Britney's estate is a fee simple subject to an executory limitation. Carl's future interest is an executory interest (technically a *shifting* executory interest, as will be discussed in Chapter 10).

CLASSIFYING ESTATES IN FEE SIMPLE — A FLOWCHART

If an estate is alienable, devisable, and descendible, then ask yourself the following questions, in the order presented in the following flowchart:

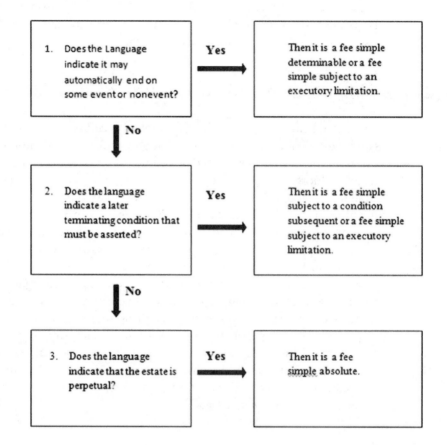

Examples

A Present and a Future Estate

1. (a) O, having full ownership, conveys Blackacre "to A for ten years." What is A's estate?
   (b) What is O's interest?
   (c) What estate will A and O have in ten years?

Words of Purchase and Limitation

2. In the following conveyances, does A hold an estate in fee simple absolute?
   (a) O conveys "to A."

(b) O conveys "to A and his heirs."

(c) O conveys "to A and his heirs, but if A dies, to B and his heirs."

No Issue

3. O conveys "to A and his bodily heirs, but if A dies without issue, to B and his heirs." A has a daughter, C, who predeceases A. This may occur, for example, if a farmer, Orville, dies, leaving his farm to his eldest son, "Arnold, and his bodily heirs, but if Arnold dies without issue, to Bart and his heirs." What estates are created?

An Estate for Joint Lives

4. O conveys "to A and B for the lives of A and B." When does the estate end?

Insurance Proceeds

5. O conveys Blackacre "to Larry for life, remainder to Freda and her heirs." Larry the life tenant insures Blackacre against fire for $100,000. Improvements on Blackacre are worth $75,000. They burn to the ground. Larry claims the proceeds of the policy. Freda appears and claims the bulk of the proceeds. Can she do so successfully?

She Meant Well

6. O writes, "I give my house and lot to you for your residence. Don't sell it. Let your sister have the rest of my property." What estate is transferred?

A Slew of Estates

7. What estates are created in the following transfers?
   (a) O conveys "to A and his heirs so long as the property is used as a residence."
   (b) O conveys "to A and her heirs, on the express condition that Blackacre be used only for residential purposes, but if it ceases to be used for such purposes, then O and her heirs shall have the right to reenter."
   (c) O conveys "to A, provided that the estate granted shall cease and determine if liquor is sold, used, or stored on the premises."
   (d) O conveys "to A and his heirs, it being my wish and purpose in making this conveyance that the property be used for residential purposes."
   (e) O conveys "to A and his heirs, provided further that O and A agree and promise that the property shall only be used for residential purposes."
   (f) O conveys Blackacre "to A so long as he wishes to live on the property."
   (g) O conveys Blackacre "to A, provided that he lives on the property, but if he does not live there, then to O."

(h) O conveys "to A for life, then if B graduates from law school, to B and her heirs so long as the land is used for a law office." What interests do the parties have before B graduates from law school?

(i) What interest do the parties have when B graduates from law school?

(j) O conveys "to A so long as the property is used as a residence solely, provided, however, that if it is not so used, the estate shall cease and revert to B and his heirs, who have the right to repossess the property." What estate does A have?

Explanations

A Present and a Future Estate

1. (a) A has a term of years or a leasehold, a nonfreehold estate. It is a present possessory estate.

   (b) Just after the conveyance, O has a reversion in fee simple absolute. It is a future interest (currently nonpossessory). See infra Chapter 10.

   (c) After a term of years ends, A no longer has any interest in Blackacre. O will possess, among estates, the grandest of them all — a fee simple absolute, which is what we think of when we say that a person has "ownership" of real property.

Words of Purchase and Limitation

2. (a) Yes. Today A holds an estate in fee simple absolute. The words of purchase are "to A" and the words of limitations are supplied by the canon of construction that a fee simple absolute is preferred, unless the language of the deed or will indicates the grantor or testator meant to transfer a lesser estate.

   (b) Yes. Although other words might be used, "to A and his heirs" are the recommended words to create a fee simple absolute.

   (c) No. A's estate is something less. The words of purchase are the same, but the words of limitation are "and his heirs, but if A dies to B and his heirs," and indicate that the grantor intends that descendibility and devisability not be part of A's estate; thus no fee simple absolute was intended. Since A must die, A's death is considered the natural termination of his interest and not a condition subsequent. A holds a life estate. See Mark Reutlinger, *Wills, Trusts, and Estates: Essential Terms and Concepts* 92 (1993).

No Issue

3. "A and his bodily heirs" is interpreted to mean the same as "A and the heirs of his body." Hence A has a fee tail (or fee simple conditional), where it is recognized.

Since *A* has a child, *C*, who predeceased him, it matters how the jurisdiction handles the failure of issue. If the state is one of the few that retains the fee tail, the land would belong to *A* as long as he lived, then to *A*'s eldest child as long as he lived, then to his eldest child as long as he lived, until *A*'s bloodline ended, at which point the land would go to *B* (or his heirs). In the Example, *A*'s line died with him and his daughter, *C*; so on *A*'s death *B* would get a fee simple absolute estate in the farm.

States that have abolished the fee simple conditional and the fee tail have interpreted language that historically created one of the two estates in two different ways. The majority of states treat the "and the heirs of his body" and "and his bodily heirs" language as words of limitation indicating a fee simple absolute — i.e., just like "and his heirs." In those states, *A* received a fee simple absolute, and *B* got nothing.

In other states *A* has a life estate and if he dies with children living at his death (or grandchildren if no surviving child) the child (or grandchild) takes the land in fee simple absolute. If *A* dies without issue, the property passes to *B* in fee simple absolute.

Which interpretation applies makes a big difference in the Example since *A* died without a surviving child (*C* predeceased *A*). In the first instance *A* owns the farm in fee simple absolute and can devise it in his will or it passes to his heirs (siblings, cousins, etc.). In the second instance, *A*'s interest in the farm ends on *A*'s death and *B* owns the farm in fee simple absolute.

An Estate for Joint Lives

4. The estate ends either (1) when the first of *A* and *B* dies, or (2) when the last of the two dies. The intent of the transferor or grantor, *O*, controls the choice. That choice involves either construing the greatest estate granted by the transferor or freeing the title of this life estate at the earliest possible time and vesting the transferor's reversion. Thus, policies of either presuming the words of conveyance against the grantor or freeing up the alienability of the title conflict here. The transferor's intent should control. If there were added to this conveyance a "remainder to the survivor of them in fee simple absolute," the length of the life estate would be clear. (This remainder would, as we will see, be a contingent remainder, lacking as it does ascertainability of the identity of the survivor until the death of either *A* or *B*.) See 1 *American Law of Property* §2.15, at 128 (James Casner, ed., 1952).

Insurance Proceeds

5. Some courts hold that a life tenant has no duty to insure the property. If Larry has no duty under a state's law to insure the improvements, then the proceeds should be wholly his, and some courts have so held. There

may be insurance law questions as to what Larry can insure, but Freda as the holder of the remainder has no standing to raise those questions. (The moral here is for the present and future interest holders to get together and purchase insurance, making sure that everyone's interest is adequately covered — or for the person creating the tenancy to impose the duty to insure on the tenant.) See 1 *American Law of Property* §2.23, at 159 (James Casner, ed., 1952).

She Meant Well

6. Several aspects of this language are relevant. The "for your residence" language may indicate a life estate; dead people don't need a house. Similarly, the "don't sell it" language perhaps negates the alienability aspect of a fee simple absolute. On the other hand, perhaps the drafter intended merely to reenforce and define the purpose of the writing — to provide a residence for the transferee — i.e., precatory language. The restraints on use and alienability on the holder of the estate may be consistent with either a fee simple absolute or a life estate. If the court finds it to be a fee simple, the court will independently review the "don't sell it" language to decide whether the restraint is an unreasonable restraint on the alienability of land. Still, perhaps the "rest of my property" language indicates a future interest to follow a life tenancy in the house and lot. If this is a lay drafter, however, one cannot put too much store in such a person's knowledge of future interests. Also relevant to a determination of the issue of how to define the estate are the other provisions of the transfer. Is the sister otherwise well provided for by the "rest of my property" language? As things stand, the jurisdiction's statutes preferring the larger estate, such as a fee simple, most likely will control. See White v. Brown, 559 S.W.2d 938 (Tenn. 1977), discussed and distinguished in Williams v. Estate of Williams, 865 S.W.2d 3 (Tenn. 1993).

A Slew of Estates

7. (a) A has a present interest in fee simple determinable, followed by O's future interest, a possibility of reverter, held in fee simple absolute. See Thomas Bergin & Paul Haskell, *Preface to Estates in Land* 48 (2d ed. 1984).

   (b) *A* has a present interest in fee simple subject to a condition subsequent. O's future interest is a right of reentry or a power of termination. If, after the terminating event is described, the last clause were to read instead "B and his heirs shall have the right to reenter," *A* would hold a fee simple subject to an executory limitation, and B would hold an executory interest in fee simple absolute.

(c) This is a conveyance with words indicating a fee simple determinable (the "cease and determine" phrase, indicating an automatic shift of the fee simple back to grantor O) and with words indicating a fee simple subject to a condition subsequent (the "provided that" language). In this ambiguous grant, the modern canon of construction disfavoring forfeiture and preferring finding the larger estate in the grantee leads to this conveyance being a present interest in A, held in fee simple subject to a condition subsequent, O's retaining a right of reentry at the moment of the conveyance.

(d) A has a fee simple absolute. The additional language is precatory language, indicating O's desire, but is neither a condition nor a covenant, and therefore is unenforceable.

(e) A has a fee simple absolute. The language neither makes the interest into a fee simple determinable nor subjects it to a condition subsequent. Rather, the promise is a covenant to use the property as a residence; when he does not, the breach of this promise subjects A to contract remedies (e.g., damages or an injunction). The difference between a condition and a covenant is that breach of a condition results in a forfeiture of the property while the owner retains ownership when a covenant is breached, but may be subject to monetary damages or, more likely, an injunction.

(f) This conveyance creates either a determinable life estate or a fee simple determinable in A. A court will try to ascertain the grantor's intent based on the surrounding facts and circumstances. Today a court would tend to find that O transferred the fee simple determinable, the larger estate, to A, the grantee. If the grant is a fee simple determinable, O retains a possibility of reverter. If, on the other hand, the grant is a determinable life estate, O has a reversion, getting Blackacre back when A ceases living on Blackacre and no later than A's death. If A's interest is a fee simple determinable and A continued to live on the property up to his death, A has satisfied the condition and, as a result, at the moment of death he holds the property in fee simple absolute. Some good it will do him! This result will, however, benefit his heirs or assigns.

(g) A has a fee simple subject to a condition subsequent. The terms "provided" and "but if" are words denoting a fee simple subject to a condition subsequent. A does not own a fee simple subject to an executory limitation since Blackacre returns to O and does not vest in a third party. The drafting, however, is extremely sloppy: Instead of "then to O," better to have said that "O has the power to terminate A's interest and the right to reenter the property." This makes plain that the termination is not automatic and that O must do something, through either self-help or at law, to reenter. See 1 *American Law of Property* §4.6, at 417 (James Casner, ed., 1952).

(h) *A* has a life estate, B has remainder (a contingent remainder since B must satisfy a contingency — graduating from law school — to take after *A* dies). Because it is possible *A* may die before B graduates, O the grantor retains a reversion. O also has a possibility of reverter, but as a matter of tradition, lawyers only mention the first interest O holds, the reversion.

(i) B's remainder interest is no longer contingent. It is a vested remainder in fee simple determinable. Contingent and vested remainders are developed more fully in the next chapter. Since B's remainder is vested, O's reversion has ended, but O's future interest, the possibility of reverter, remains. Thus, B has a vested remainder in fee simple determinable, and O has a possibility of reverter. See 1 *American Law of Property* §4.12, at 427 (James Casner, ed., 1952).

(j) *A* has a fee simple subject to an executory limitation. The language is ambiguous, indicating either a fee or a life estate. The preference for the larger estate permits this language to be construed as a fee simple subject to an executory limitation. B has an executory interest (in the next chapter we learn that B has a *shifting* executory interest).

Future Interests

INTRODUCTION

The previous chapter introduced present interests and estates, and, to a lesser extent, future interests. An estate held in fee simple absolute, for example, is perpetual ownership or ownership until the end of time. A fee simple absolute can be diagrammed on a timeline as follows:

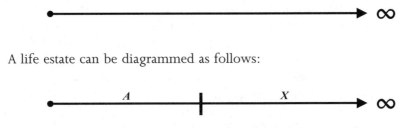

A life estate can be diagrammed as follows:

where *A* has a life estate. X has either a remainder in fee simple absolute or a reversion, depending on who X is.

Perhaps the most important feature of these two diagrams is the ∞ symbol at the end of each timeline. From the earliest years of English and American common law, judges and lawyers classified interests and estates by visualizing who controlled ownership of land from the moment of the effectiveness of a deed, will, or other instrument until infinity. If a person owned a life estate, the legal mind wanted to know who (or whose heirs or assigns) took possession once the life estate ended.

Example: Orville transferred Blackacre to *A* for life. *A* has a life estate or, more fully described, *A* has a present interest held in a life estate. Because he transferred less than his full interest in Blackacre and will take back possession of Blackacre once Andrew dies, Orville has a future interest, a reversion. A reversion is a future interest since the holder does not have a present possessory right to the land. Orville has a present property right, but the possession is deferred until a later time. Nothing else being said, Orville holds that reversion in fee simple absolute.

DISTINGUISHING PRESENT INTERESTS AND FUTURE INTERESTS

A person's interest in property has two analytical components. First, the interest is either a present interest or a future interest. Second, the interest is held in some type of estate. For shorthand purposes, lawyers normally think and classify future interests into those held by the transferor or grantor, and those held by a third party, meaning someone other than the transferor or grantor. A reversion is an example of a future interest held by a grantor, and a remainder is an example of the equivalent future interest held by a third party.

Example: Orville transferred Blackacre to *A* for life, then to B for life, then to C. *A* owns a present interest held in a life estate. It is a present possessory interest, meaning *A* can use Blackacre and exclude all others, including Orville, B, and C from Blackacre. B has a future interest, a vested remainder held in a life estate (more about vested remainders later). The term "vested remainder" indicates a future interest, a particular future interest with its own legal attributes. C too has a future interest, a vested remainder held in fee simple absolute.

B and C currently own property interests in Blackacre, but cannot use the property and are not entitled to possession until a later date, so they merely have *future possessory* interests. Once *A* dies, B's interest becomes *a present possessory interest* — she will have a "present interest held in a life estate." Until both *A* and B die, C's interest remains a vested remainder in fee simple absolute. Once *A* and B die, C's interest becomes possessory as a fee simple absolute.

FUTURE INTERESTS RETAINED BY THE GRANTOR OR TRANSFEROR

The future interest (currently owned interest that becomes possessory at a future date) retained by the transferor (or his heirs or assigns) are three:

1. Reversion
2. Possibility of reverter
3. Right of entry (a/k/a "right of re-entry" and "power of termination")

These three interests were introduced in the previous chapter.

The **reversion** is retained by the transferor or grantor when he transfers an interest less than the one he owns to another. It follows a life estate, fee tail, or term of years (i.e., estates that end naturally).

The reversion differs from the possibility of reverter and the right of entry in that the reversion does not depend on the occurrence (or nonoccurrence) of a condition precedent. Stated otherwise, the grantor's reversion follows the natural termination of the preceding estate. Hence a grantor's future interest is a reversion when it follows a life estate (which ends naturally when the life tenant dies), a fee tail (which ends naturally when the grantee's family bloodline ends); and the term of years (which ends naturally at the designated time).

Example 1: Orville transferred Blackacre to *A* for life. *A* has a present possessory interest in life estate in Blackacre. Orville has a reversion. Orville gets possession of Blackacre when *A* dies, and *A*'s life estate ends naturally.

If the grantor or transferor can retake transferred property, usually a fee simple but it may be a lesser estate, only if the occurrence or nonoccurrence of some condition terminates the estate prematurely, the grantor's future interest will be a possibility of reverter or a right of entry depending on whether the grantor's interest vests automatically or whether the grantor must take some action to retake possession. The **possibility of reverter** is a future interest held by a transferor or grantor who transfers a fee simple determinable. The **right of entry** is the grantor's future interest that follows the fee simple subject to a condition subsequent.

The possibility of reverter and the right of entry demand a condition precedent — i.e., some event or condition — before the grantor's interest becomes possessory. The grantor's condition precedent will be the same event as the divesting event or condition subsequent divesting the present interest. Hence, the condition subsequent that divests a fee simple determinable or fee simple subject to a condition subsequent is also the condition that vests possession or the right to retake the property in the grantor.

Example 2: Owen transferred Blackacre "to Local School District, but if classroom teaching ceases on Blackacre, Owen may reenter and retake Blackacre." Local School District enjoys a present interest as a fee simple subject to a condition subsequent. Owen's future interest is a right of entry. Owen's future interest is not a reversion because the School Board's interest could continue to infinity. Owen's future interest will become possessory only if the condition that classroom teaching on Blackacre ceases is satisfied. If classroom teaching on Blackacre ceases, Owen can regain possession of Blackacre by reentering and demanding possession.

Example 3: Owen granted Blackacre "to Local School Board as long as classroom teaching is conducted on Blackacre." Local School District owns a present interest in a fee simple determinable. Owen's future interest is a possibility of reverter, not a reversion. Deciding whether to call the future interest in the grantor of a fee simple determinable a reversion or a possibility of reverter vexed early theorists. On the one hand, a fee simple determinable ends naturally once the condition occurs, in this case the ceasing of classroom teaching on Blackacre; hence reversion sounds plausible. On the other hand, a fee simple of any type by its nature lasts until infinity unless cut short; hence it could not be followed by a reversion. Ultimately, a consensus developed that a reversion cannot follow a fee simple determinable; hence the possibility of reverter characterization prevailed.

Once classified, a future interest in the grantor thereafter retains the same name though owners change: If the transferor dies or assigns his future interest to a third party, the name of the future interest remains the same. Thus, if O transfers his reversion in Blackacre to a third party A, A's interest retains the label 'reversion.'

Most present interests and future interests are assignable (transferable), devisable, and inheritable. Reversions, for example, are assignable, devisable, and inheritable. A grantor or other holder of a reversion can gift it or sell it while alive, devise it by will, or let it pass by inheritance. The transferability of possibilities of reverter or rights of entry are more muddled. Both are inheritable. In most states currently, both are assignable inter vivos, and devisable by will. A few jurisdictions, however, limit their transferability. A small number of states do not allow the grantor to assign inter vivos the right of entry. States that do not allow a grantor to assign a right of entry split on whether the possibility of reverter can be assigned.

All but four states allow decedents to devise rights of entry and possibilities of reverter.[1]

FUTURE INTERESTS IN THIRD-PARTY TRANSFEREES

Future interests in transferees can be divided into three fundamental types:

1. Vested remainders
2. Contingent remainders
3. Executory interests

Each of these types can be further sub-divided into more precise sub-categories.

(a) Remainders

The future interest called a reversion if retained by a grantor is called a remainder if granted to a third party in the same document creating a life estate, fee tail, or term of years. A **remainder** is a future interest in a third party that "remains" after the interests and estates prior to it end naturally. The remainder must be created in the same instrument of transfer — either a will, deed, or other document — as one or more prior possessory interests, and it must be possible to become possessory immediately following the natural termination of the prior estate. The remainder cannot divest or cut short the prior estate, or follow an interest that has been cut short by a condition subsequent. The remainder most commonly follows a life estate, but may follow a term of years or a fee tail.

Example 1: Ollie transferred Blackare to A for life, then to B and her heirs. A owns a present interest, held in a life estate. B owns a future interest. Because B's future interest was created in the same document as A's life estate, and becomes possessory immediately upon the end of A's life estate, B's future interest is a remainder. B's remainder will be held as a fee simple absolute.

Example 2: Ollie transferred Blackacre to A for life. A owns a present interest, held in a life estate. Ollie owns a future interest, a reversion. Five years later Ollie transferred all her interest in Blackacre to B. What is B's

---

1. The four states are Illinois, Nebraska, North Dakota, and South Dakota.

interest? It is a future interest, a reversion, because that was what Ollie had originally, and the reversion once classified in Ollie's hands, remains a reversion in any subsequent transfer. A remainder must be created in the same transfer document as the life estate, and here it was not.

To be a remainder, the future interest in the third party must become possessory immediately on the natural termination of the prior estate. To repeat, a future interest that does not become possessory immediately on the natural termination of the prior estate cannot be a remainder. As we will see, it may be an executory interest, but it cannot be a remainder.

Example 3:   Oscar transferred Whiteacre to *A* for life, then to B for life, then to C on the first day of the month after B dies. A owns a present interest, held in a life estate. B owns a future interest, a remainder to be held in a life estate since B's interest was created in the same document as *A*'s life estate and becomes possessory immediately upon the natural end of *A*'s life estate. C was granted a future interest, but it cannot be a remainder since it does not become possessory immediately upon the natural termination of B's life estate. There is a gap between B's death and C's interest beginning. (Hint: C's interest is an executory interest). Oscar retains a reversion to take effect upon B's death since someone must have legal possession at all times.

Declaring that a person has a remainder merely says he owns a future interest, an interest that may become possessory sometime in the future. The term "remainder" in and of itself does not say what estate that future interest is held in: The remainder may be in a life estate, a fee simple absolute, a term of years, a fee tail, a fee simple subject to condition subsequent, a fee simple determinable, or a fee simple subject to an executory limitation.

Example 4:   Orville transferred Blackacre to *A* for life, then to B and her heirs. *A* has a present possessory interest held in a life estate. B has a remainder. B takes possession of Blackacre immediately following the natural termination of A's life estate, which occurs at *A*'s death. B's interest in Blackacre at the time of the grant is a remainder, held in fee simple absolute. Once *A* dies, B's interest becomes a present interest, held in fee simple absolute. That is, future interests can become present ones, but once classified, an estate of whatever type stays the same.

Remainders play a critical function in the transfer of property to individuals, particularly in the creation of trusts, and in estate planning (wills). Much of the rest of this chapter develops various aspects of remainders. First, however, the next section explains the most recently created future interest in third party transferees: the executory interest.

(b) Executory Interests

In early England, judges required someone to be in legal possession of land at all times: that meant no gaps between a present possessory interest and a future possessory interest. The only future legal interest recognized in a third party was the remainder, which must have become possessory immediately on the natural termination of the prior estate. If a gap appeared, the attempted future interest was void. Thus, in a grant such as O to A for life then to B one year after A's death, B's interest would have been invalid in England 900 years ago (at a time when the foundation principles of English and American property law were being established, which is why it matters).

Similarly, only legal future interests in the grantor could follow a divested fee simple: those being the possibility of reverter and the right of entry. Any attempt to create legal rights equivalent to a possibility of reverter or right of entry in a third party in the conveyancing instrument was rejected and the attempted interest in the third party was held void and unenforceable. Lawyers wishing to accomplish the same result created the *use*, which was similar to the modern day trust, in which legal title was conveyed to a person or institution to hold for the use of the true beneficiaries. While the beneficiaries' equitable interests could not be enforced in courts of law, they could be enforced in courts of equity. In 1536 the English Parliament at King Henry VIII's exhortation enacted the Statute of Uses that "executed" the uses, which meant the beneficiaries' equitable interests became legal interests. Suddenly, grants to third parties that either followed a gap in time or that divested a fee simple were recognized and enforceable at law. Only, instead of being called remainders, possibilities of reverter, and rights of entry, these future interests in third parties were called executory interests. Likewise, the interest that was called a fee simple determinable or a fee simple subject to a condition subsequent earned a new name once the third party's right to the executory interest was recoginzed: the fee simple subject to an executory limitation.

Today an **executory interest** is a future interest in a third party (again, someone not the transferor) that takes effect only when the preceding interest is divested or cut short by a condition subsequent. The executory interest typically follows an interest held in some type of defeasible fee simple. Although similar to a possibility of reverter and a right of entry (which are interests in the grantor that follow, respectively, an estate held in a fee simple determinable and a fee simple subject to a condition subsequent), an executory interest is an interest following a defeasible fee if the property passes to a third party instead of to the grantor. The fee simple divested in favor of the third party is called a **fee simple subject to an executory limitation**.

Example 1: Orville transferred Blackacre "to A and his heirs, but if A does not graduate from law school by age 30, then to B." A's estate is a present interest, held in a fee simple subject to an executory limitation in favor of B, and B has a future interest, an executory interest held in fee simple absolute. B's interest does not wait patiently for the natural termination of A's interest — so B's interest cannot be a remainder. B's future interest is an executory interest.

The present possessory interest being divested may be that of a third party transferee or of the original grantor. If a third party transferee's interest is divested, as in the above example, the future interest is a *shifting executory interest*. If the grantor's interest is divested, the future interest is a *springing executory interest*. Remainders and executory interests are mutually exclusive types of future interests.

The **springing executory interest's** most common uses are transfers following a gap in time. Thus a conveyance from O "to A one year after O's death" is enforceable as a springing executory interest. It is not a remainder because A does not take possession immediately after the natural termination of a prior estate. For the same reason, A has a springing executory interest when O conveys "to A and his heirs twenty years after the date of this deed.

Example 2: O transferred Blackacre "to A for life, then one year after A's death to B and her heirs." A owns a present interest, held in a life estate, followed by a future interest, a reversion, in O, held in fee simple subject to an executory limitation in favor of B. B's future interest is a springing executory interest held in fee simple absolute. B's interest is not a remainder since it does not follow the natural termination of A's life estate, and it divests O's fee simple to become possessory.

Example 3: Grandpa deeded Blackacre "to Junior if and when he graduates from law school." Junior's interest is not a remainder since it does not follow the natural termination of a prior estate: Grandpa's interest is divested when Junior graduates from law school. Junior owns an interest in Blackacre, a future possessory interest labeled a springing executory interest, springing from the grantor, Grandpa. Until Junior graduates, Grandpa continues to hold his estate, a fee simple subject to an executory limitation in favor of Junior. If Junior does not graduate from law school during his lifetime, his interest never becomes possessory and, in effect, disappears.

The **shifting executory interest** is the more frequently encountered executory interest. The shifting executory interest follows an interest held by a third party that may be divested by a condition subsequent stipulated in the conveyancing document.

Example 4: O conveyed Blackare to "*A* and his heirs, but if *A* uses Blackacre for commercial purposes, then Blackacre is to go immediately to B and her heirs." *A* owns a present interest, held in a fee simple since *A*'s ownership of Blackacre may last until infinity; but it is not a fee simple absolute since *A*'s interest can be divested if *A* uses Blackacre for commercial purposes. Since Blackacre would go to B (someone other than the grantor, O), *A*'s interest is a fee simple subject to an executory limitation. B, who takes if *A* uses Blackacre for commercial purposes, owns a shifting executory interest. B's interest is not a remainder since B's future interest does not follow the natural termination of *A*'s interest: for B to take possession of Blackacre, *A*'s fee simple must be divested by the occurrence of a condition subsequent (*A*'s using Blackacre for commercial purposes).

Example 5: O by will devised Whiteacre "to *A* for life, then to B and her heirs, but if Whiteacre ceases to be used for farming within ten years of *A*'s death, to C and his heirs." *A* owns a present interest, held in a life estate. B owns a future interest, a (vested) remainder in a fee simple subject to an executory limitation in favor of C. C owns a future interest, a shifting executory interest.

B's interest is a remainder because it follows the natural termination of *A*'s life estate. B's estate is a fee simple because it may last until infinity, but it is not a fee simple absolute since B's fee simple can be divested if Whiteacre ceases to be used for farming within ten years of *A*'s death. B's interest is a fee simple subject to an executory limitation in favor of C. C's interest is not a remainder since B's fee simple must be cut short before C can take possession.

The good news for law students is that the legal consequences are the same for shifting executory interests and for springing executory interests. The only difference is that the *springing* executory interest divests the transferor, whereas the *shifting* executory interest divests a transferee (grantee). Here's a nice review of the possibility of reverter (held by a grantor), and shifting and springing executory interests (held by grantees).

Example 6: O transferred Blackacre "to *A* as long as Blackacre is used for farming, then it reverts to O." *A* owns a present interest, held in a fee simple determinable. O has a future interest, a possibility of reverter.

Example 7: O transferred Blackacre to "*A* as long as Blackacre is used for farming, then to B and his heirs." *A* owns a present interest, held in a fee simple subject to an executory limitation in favor of B. B has a shifting executory interest.

Example 8: O transferred Blackacre "to B to take effect if and when B agrees to farm Blackacre." O has a present interest, held in a fee simple subject to an executory limitation in favor of B. B has a springing executory interest.

The following chart summarizes present estates, words normally used in creating the estate, and names of the future interests held either by the grantor or by third persons:

Estates in Real Property, with Future Interests

Freehold Estates		Future Interest	
(Typical wording in italics in second column, followed by future interests in the two right-hand columns)		Grantor	Third Person
Fee Simple			
Absolute	*"to A"* *"to A and her heirs"*	None	None
Determinable/Subject to an Executory Limitation	*"to A so long as . . . "* *"while . . . "* *"during . . . "* *"unless . . . "* *"until . . . "*	Possibility of Reverter	Executory Interest
Subject to a Condition	*"to A provided that . . . "*	Right of Entry	Executory Interest
Subsequent/Executory Limitation	*"on condition . . . "* *"but if . . . "*		
Fee Tail	*"to A and the heirs of his body"*	Reversion	Remainder
Life Estate	*"to A for life"*	Reversion	Remainder Executory Interest

Non-Freehold Estate		Future Interest	
Term of years	*"to A for _____ years"*	Reversion	Remainder

VESTED AND CONTINGENT REMAINDERS

Most of the rest of this chapter develops remainders in depth. A critical distinction must be made between vested remainders and contingent remainders. Hence we start there.

Remainders in land can be either vested or contingent. These two sub-categories of remainders are mutually exclusive. A **vested remainder** is one that (a) is owned by an ascertained person or persons (persons who can be named) **and** (b) is not subject to a condition precedent. A **contingent remainder** is one where either the owner is unascertained **or** the right to the current or future possession of the property is subject to a condition precedent (a contingency).

Because they already are possessory, all present interests, whether a life estate, fee simple absolute, fee simple determinable, fee simple subject to a condition subsequent, or a fee simple subject to an executory limitation, are vested. In addition, all future interests in *the grantor* (or his later assigns or heirs) are deemed vested even if the interests become vested only upon the happening of a contingency. Distinguishing between vested and contingent interests, therefore, becomes critical only with regard to remainders and executory interests — i.e., future interests in third parties.

To review, a **vested remainder** is given to an ascertained person and is not subject to a condition precedent. The vested remainder becomes possessory upon the natural termination of the immediately preceding estate. It follows any life estate, fee tail, or term of years that ends naturally. A **contingent remainder** is a remainder that either is given to an unascertained person or is subject to a condition precedent. Executory interests, because they cut short a prior estate and thus do not follow a natural termination of the prior estate, are always contingent interests (but not contingent remainders).

(a) Ascertained Persons

Assuming no condition precedent, a remainder is vested if it is given to an ascertained person and contingent if it is given to an unascertained person. A person is ascertained if he or she can be specifically determined at the time a transfer or devise is effective.[2] One foolproof way to have an ascertained person is to name the person. Thus a remainder to "Paul Property" or to "my son, Paul Property" would be to an ascertained person. In discussing interests and estates, lawyers reduce a transfer to its essentials: an ascertained person is by convention designated by a letter. Thus a gift to "*A*" is a gift to an ascertained person.

There is some difficulty, though not much, when a transferee is identified by a label or description. If the description can apply to only one person or individually identifiable person, that person is ascertained.

_____

2. A deed or deed of gift is effective at the time of its execution and delivery. A will or devise is effective at the time of the death of the decedent.

If further developments are necessary before a specific individual can be pinpointed, the recipient is an unascertained person. The most common unascertained persons are unborn persons. For example, if Orville dies, his will devising Blackacre to his daughter, Andrea, for life and then to Andrea's first-born child, but she has no child: the remainder to Andrea's first-born child is to an unascertained person and thus is a contingent remainder.

Example 1:   O conveyed Blackacre "to A for life, then to B and his heirs." Both A and B are ascertained persons.

Example 2:   O conveyed Blackacre "to A for life, then to B's children." B is childless. The remainder to B's children is to a group of unascertained persons. Therefore, B's children have a contingent remainder.

Example 3:   O conveyed Whiteacre "to A for life, remainder to B's heirs." B is married to C and has one son, D. Even though B has a wife (or husband) and a son, the grant to "B's heirs" is a gift to unascertained persons because no living person can have heirs. B's heirs can be definitely identified only when B dies. The remainder, therefore, is a contingent remainder. Once B dies, however, B's heirs can be identified; they will then be ascertained persons. Since there is no further condition precedent, B's heirs once ascertained at B's death will have a vested remainder in fee simple to take possession on A's death.

Example 4:   O conveyed Whiteacre "to his son, A, for life, and then to A's children (O's grandchildren)." A is alive. A has three children (B, C, and D). B, C, and D are ascertained persons. The gift to "A's children" is a class gift. When one person in the class is identified, the class is vested. Nonetheless, as will be developed more fully later, for a very important purpose — applying the Rule Against Perpetuities — a gift to a class that is vested but subject to more people being added to the class will be treated as a contingent remainder until the class "closes" (i.e., all persons who might take are ascertained).

Example 5:   O conveyed Greenacre "to A for life, then to A's widow." A is married to B. A's widow is an unascertained person. B and A's widow may be different people. B may expect to be A's widow, but she may predecease A, or she may divorce A. A's widow has a contingent remainder. B has an **expectation** only, which is not a recognizable property interest.

(b) No Condition Precedent

A vested remainder has no condition precedent. A remainder with a condition precedent is a contingent remainder. A **condition precedent** is an event (condition) that must occur (or fail to occur, depending on how it is worded) *before* an interest becomes vested (for a remainder) or possessory (for an executory interest). To illustrate, if O conveys Blackacre to A for life, and then to B if B becomes a lawyer before A dies, the requirement that B become a lawyer before A dies is the condition precedent. It must occur before B's contingent remainder becomes a vested remainder.

A condition precedent must be contrasted with a condition subsequent that terminates a possessory or vested interest. The fee simple determinable, fee simple subject to a condition subsequent, and fee simple subject to an executory limitation all incorporate a condition subsequent. The holder can be divested if the condition subsequent occurs. A condition divesting a fee simple on executory limitation and giving possession to an executory interest is both a condition subsequent and a condition precedent. Since a remainder by definition follows the natural termination of a life estate or other freehold, a remainder cannot follow an estate terminated by a condition subsequent.

Example 1:   O conveyed Blackacre "to A for life, then to B and her heirs if B marries during A's lifetime." A owns a life estate. Since A's life estate ends naturally at his death and B's interest can become possessory immediately upon A's death, B owns a remainder. Is B's remainder a vested or a contingent remainder? B's remainder is a contingent remainder because a requirement that B marry while A is alive is a condition precedent to B's remainder becoming vested. A's interest will end naturally no matter if B marries or not; but B will not take possession unless she satisfies the condition precedent. As soon as B marries, assuming B marries while A is alive, B's remainder becomes vested. B or her designee will take possession of Blackacre after A's death.

Example 2:   O conveyed Whiteacre "to A and his heirs, but if B marries before A dies, to B and her heirs." B does not own a remainder. She can take possession only if A's fee simple estate is divested by B's marrying during A's lifetime. B owns a shifting executory interest. A owns a fee simple subject to an executory limitation in favor of B.

WHY WE DISTINGUISH VESTED AND CONTINGENT REMAINDERS

We distinguish vested remainders from contingent remainders for several reasons, many only of historical importance in most jurisdictions. For example, at one time a person could assign and devise vested remainders but not contingent remainders. Today both vested and contingent remainders are assignable and devisable. In addition, persons holding vested remainders had rights to prevent waste by the present possessor. Finally, some special rules destroyed contingent remainders or rendered them void. The Rule of Destructibility of Contingent Remainders (mentioned in footnotes in this chapter), the Rule in Shelley's Case, the Doctrine of Worthier Title, and the Rule Against Perpetuities are the common judicially created rules developed to terminate contingent remainders. These rules, to the extent they remain in force, do not apply to vested remainders. We delve into these rules more in Chapter 11 and discuss the Rule Against Perpetuities in Chapter 12.

INTERPRETING TRANSFERS WITH CONDITIONS PRECEDENT AND CONDITIONS SUBSEQUENT

IMPORTANT: *When interpreting grants, read them in the order written, usually interpreting each part up to a comma or semicolon.* The order in which a grant is written can change the type of interest created and whether any remainder created is vested or contingent. Consider the following examples.

Example 1: O conveyed Blackacre "to A for life, then if B survives A, to B and her heirs." B's interest is a remainder since it follows the natural termination of A's life estate. For B to take possession, however, B must outlive A. The survivorship requirement[3] is a condition precedent. B has a contingent remainder. In the actual conveyance the drafter should provide who takes if the condition precedent is not satisfied. Since no provision was made, O (or O's heirs) as the holder of the reversion takes Blackacre on A's death if A survives B.

Example 2: O conveyed Blackacre "to A for life, and when A dies, to B and her heirs." A has a present interest, held in a life estate. B's interest is a remainder since it follows the natural termination of A's life estate. B has a vested remainder, held in a fee simple absolute. The words "and when A dies" do not constitute a condition precedent—they merely state the fact that B takes following the natural termination of A's life estate. A life estate naturally terminates on the death of the life tenant. The natural termination of a life estate is neither a condition precedent nor a condition subsequent.

---

3. In contrast, in a conveyance "to A for life, then to B and her heirs" there is no survivorship requirement—that is, B need not survive A to take the remainder. If B does not survive A, B's assigns, heirs, or devisees take on A's death. Unless explicit, there is no survivorship requirement for a future interest.

Example 3: O conveyed Blackacre "to *A* for life, then to B and his heirs, but if B does not survive *A*, then to C and his heirs." *A* has a present interest, held in a life estate. B's interest, by reading just between the commas, is a vested remainder since the interest follows the natural termination of the preceding life estate and there is no condition precedent. After the second comma comes a condition subsequent, however, that can divest B's interest. B's interest, therefore, is a vested remainder, subject to divestment, held in fee simple absolute. Compare Example 1 above, where essentially the same grant was labeled a contingent remainder. The difference in the two is the order in which the grant was written. In Example 1 the condition came first and was a condition precedent; here it came after the interest was vested and is a condition subsequent. C does not have a remainder because a condition must divest or cut short B's vested remainder before C can possess Blackacre. C, therefore, has a shifting executory interest in Blackacre.

Example 4: O conveyed Blackacre "to *A* for life, remainder to B's children." B is alive and has two children, C and D. *A* has a life estate. Stop at the comma. After the comma, B's two children, C and D, have vested remainders subject to open (more on subject to open later). B's children's interest follows the natural termination of the preceding life estate and there is no condition precedent (B's children do not have to survive *A*). Hence the children's interest is vested. Their interests are subject to partial divestment (subject to open), however, if B has another child, who when born would share in the grant.

Example 5: O conveyed Blackacre "to *A* for life, remainder to B's children who attain age 18." B is alive and has one child, C, who is ten years old. B's children, including C and any later-born children, have a remainder since their interest in Blackacre could take possession following the natural termination of *A*'s life estate. Reading after the comma and to the period, the children's remainder is a contingent remainder because to take Blackacre the child or children must reach age 18. Reaching age 18 is the condition precedent. Until C or some other child of B reaches age 18, the interest remains a contingent remainder in fee simple absolute. Since O did not make a provision as to what happens to Blackacre if none of B's children attains age 18, O retains a reversion.

ALTERNATIVE CONTINGENT REMAINDERS

Whenever a grantor fragments ownership rights into present and future interests, parties must be able to identify an owner for all periods of time and all events and contingencies. Of special importance, a grant of a contingent remainder should include a determination of who takes if the condition precedent fails to develop. There are two main options. First, explicitly or by default if the grantor makes no provision, the grantor retains a reversion. Second, the grantor may provide that another person take if the contingency fails, creating an alternative contingent remainder. An **alternative contingent remainder** results where one of two named persons (neither of whom is the grantor) takes to the exclusion of the other based on whether or not a condition precedent occurs. If the condition or event happens, one party will own the property; if the condition or event does not happen, the other party will own the property.

While they serve similar purposes and intents, alternative contingent remainders must be distinguished from a vested remainder in one person and a shifting executory interest in another. Generally speaking, if the remainder in the first person is a contingent remainder, the interest in the second person will also be a contingent remainder; hence they have alternative contingent remainders. If, on the other hand, the first person's interest is a vested remainder that may be divested and another person (other than the grantor) takes if the condition or event occurs, the first person owns a vested remainder, held (usually) in a fee simple subject to an executory limitation, and the second person owns a shifting executory interest.

Example 1: O conveyed Blackacre "to A for life and then to B if B reaches 21, but if B does not attain age 21, then to C." A has a life estate. B and C have alternative contingent remainders. O has a reversion. B owns a contingent remainder since her interest can become possessory immediately after A's life estate ends but only if B reaches age 21. Alternatively, C owns a contingent remainder since his interest can also become possessory immediately after A's life estate ends, but only if B dies before she reaches age 21. B or C will own Blackacre after A's death, but only one of them will. Since which of A or B will own Blackacre after A dies depends on whether B reaches age 21, B and C own alternative contingent remainders. If B attains age 21, B gets Blackacre on A's death and C gets nothing. If B dies before turning 21, C gets Blackacre on A's death, and B (and her heirs or devisees) gets nothing. In a third scenario, if A, the life tenant, dies before B turns 21 while B is still alive, O gets back Blackacre until either B celebrates her twenty-first birthday, in which case B gets Blackacre, or B dies before reaching 21, in which case C gets Blackacre.[4]

Example 2: O conveyed Blackacre "to A for life, then to B if B attains the age of 21; but if B does not attain age 21, to O." Reading the grant in the

---

4. If the Rule of the Destructibility of Contingent Remainders applied, and A died before B reached age 21, both B's and C's alternative contingent remainders would be destroyed.

order written, *A*'s interest is a life estate. B, an ascertained person, has a contingent remainder because she must live to age 21. If B does not attain age 21, O at *A*'s death once more owns the property. O therefore has a reversion (and not a contingent remainder, nor a contingent reversion (no such thing as a contingent reversion)).

Example 3: O conveyed Blackacre "to *A* for life, then to B if B attains age 21." B is 15. The result here is the same as in Example 2. *A*'s interest is a life estate, B has a contingent remainder, O has a reversion. O has a reversion since he transferred less than his full interest. The grantor retains a reversion when he transfers a life estate followed by a contingent remainder. If B turns 21 during *A*'s life, B's contingent remainder becomes a vested remainder and O's reversion disappears. If *A* dies before B attains age 21, O once more owns Blackacre, subject to a springing executory interest in B if and when B attains age 21.[5]

Example 4: O conveyed Blackacre "to *A* for life, then to B and her heirs, but if B does not use Blackacre for a residence, to C and his heirs." *A*'s interest once again is a present interest, held in a life estate. Reading between the commas, B owns a vested reminder in a fee simple, but immediately after the comma creating the vested remainder is a condition subsequent, B's not using Blackacre as a residence, that that might divest B's fee simple. Since C takes if B ceases to use Blackacre as residence, B owns a vested remainder in a fee simple subject to an executory limitation in favor of C; and C owns a shifting executory interest. Neither B nor C owns a contingent remainder.

VARIATIONS ON VESTED REMAINDERS

Vested remainders are remainders in which the holders are ascertained persons and no condition precedent exists. There are some analytical variations of vested remainders. The sheer variety indicates courts have a preference for construing a remainder as vested rather than contingent.

---

5. In four jurisdictions (Indiana, Kansas, New Hampshire, and Oklahoma), a contingent remainderman must satisfy the contingency before the prior estate ends; otherwise, the contingent remainder is destroyed. This Rule of the Destructibility of Contingent Remainders is developed more fully in Chapter 11. If B's contingent remainder is destroyed, O gets Blackacre back as a fee simple absolute (which is also why there must a reversion after alternative contingent remainders).

(a) Indefeasibly Vested Remainder

The **indefeasibly vested remainder** is a remainder with no condition subsequent and is not a class gift subject to open. A gift "to A for life, remainder to B and her heirs" illustrates the indefeasibly vested remainder. B has a future interest, a vested remainder held in fee simple absolute. B's vested remainder is certain to become possessory. Her interest cannot be divested; she need not worry about any class gift complications (class gifts are addressed below in "Vested Remainder Subject to Open").

(b) Vested Remainder Subject to Divestment

Because of the canon of construction favoring vested remainders over contingent remainders, courts favor vesting remainders as soon as possible. Such a construction leads to a vested remainder that may be subject to divestment. These remainders are **vested remainders subject to divestment**. The vested remainder subject to divestment must be distinguished from two other interests: the contingent remainder, and the fee simple subject to an executory limitation. In addition, some authorities categorize various types of vested remainders subject to divestment based on whether the divestment occurs before or after the future interest can become possessory.

The key to distinguishing a vested remainder subject to divestment from a contingent remainder is whether the determinative condition is a condition precedent (so the remainder is a contingent remainder) or a condition subsequent (so the remainder is a vested remainder subject to divestment). The following examples illustrate the distinction:

Example 1: O conveyed Blackacre "to A for life, then to B and her heirs." B has an indefeasibly vested remainder held in fee simple absolute.

Example 2: O conveyed Blackacre "to A for life, then to B and her heirs if B attains age 21, but if B does not attain age 21, to C and his heirs." B has a contingent remainder held in fee simple absolute, the condition precedent being B's attaining age 21. C has an alternative contingent remainder, the condition precedent being B's not attaining age 21. O has a reversion.

Example 3: O conveyed Blackacre "to A for life, then to B and her heirs; but if B does not attain age 21, to C and his heirs." B's remainder is vested because the divesting condition occurs after the clause granting B her interest; the divesting condition is a condition subsequent. B has a vested remainder subject to divestment held in fee simple absolute because B's interest may be divested before B takes possession. Contrast this with Example 2, where the condition is part of the grant itself, and is a condition precedent. Because B's interest is a vested remainder that may be divested or cut short, C's interest cannot be a contingent remainder. C's interest ripens into possession only if B's interest is divested. Hence C has a shifting executory interest in fee simple absolute.

Vested remainders subject to divestment may be segregated further into those vested remainders subject to divestment that must be divested, if at all, before the future interest holder takes possession, and those they may divest a future estate after it becomes possessory. The distinction results in the divestment language being associated with either the vested remainder or with the estate, whichever is applicable. If the divesting event or condition must occur before the holder of the vested remainder takes possession, the divestment language is attached to the vested remainder label before the resulting estate is mentioned, as in a "vested remainder subject to divestment in a fee simple absolute." In contrast, if the divesting event or condition may occur after the holder of the future interest takes possession, the divestment language follows the name of the resulting estate, as in a "vested remainder in a fee simple subject to divestment" or "vested remainder in a fee simple defeasible."

Example 4:   Same facts as in Example 3: O conveyed Blackacre "to *A* for life, then to B and her heirs; but if B does not attain age 21, to C and his heirs." B's remainder is vested because the divesting condition occurs after the clause granting B her interest; the divesting condition is a condition subsequent. B has a vested remainder subject to divestment held in fee simple absolute because B's interest may be divested before B takes possession. The divestment language, "subject to divestment" modifies "vested remainder." C owns a shifting executory interest.

Example 5:   O conveyed Blackacre "to *A* for life, then to B and her heirs; but if B stops farming Blackacre, to C and his heirs." B has a vested remainder. B's remainder is not subject to a condition precedent and so is not a contingent remainder. Further, B's vested remainder is not subject to divestment before B takes possession (i.e., while it is still a vested remainder); therefore, it is incorrect to label it a vested remainder subject to divestment in fee simple. Her interest is a future interest, a vested remainder in a fee simple subject to an executory limitation (or a vested remainder in a fee simple defeasible or a vested remainder in a fee simple subject to divestment). C has a shifting executory interest. Contrast this Example with Example 3 and Example 4.

(c) Vested Remainder Subject to Open

A common estate-planning device is for a testator (a decedent) to leave property to a child for life, then to the testator's grandchildren (the life tenant's children), even if none then are born. For example, Owen may devise Blackacre to "my son, Albert, for life, then to Albert's children." The remainder to Albert's children is a **class gift** since it is to a group of persons identified by description rather than by names. Albert may or may not have any children. Assuming Albert has two children when Owen died, the two children have a vested remainder since their interest follows the natural termination of their father's life estate and there is no condition precedent; but it is not an indefeasibly vested remainder. Albert may have more children who, when born, will share in the grant to "Albert's children." Albert's living children's remainder in Blackacre is vested — they will have a shared right to possession of Blackacre on Albert's death — but that vested remainder is subject to partial divestment in favor of later-born siblings. Hence we label the children's interest a **vested remainder subject to open**, indicating others can enter the described class; or, synonymously, a **vested remainder subject to partial divestment**, indicating the vested members of the class may lose some interest in the property.

(1) Class Closing Physiologically or Naturally

For practical reasons, at some point the class of persons who will share in a class gift must *close* (no more persons can enter the class even if later born). Two rules have evolved. First, a class closes **physiologically** or **naturally** whenever biologically no one else can be born into the class.

Example: O died, devising Blackacre "to my wife, Edna, for life, then to my son Franklin's children." Franklin has one child, Greta. Greta has a vested remainder subject to open. If Franklin has a second child, Harold, Harold shares equally with Greta in the vested remainder subject to open. If Franklin has a third and a fourth child they, too, would share in the vested remainder subject to open. Once Franklin dies, however, or more precisely nine months after Franklin dies, Franklin can have no more children. The class is complete with however many children are then born. Assuming Franklin dies with two children, Greta and Harold, in the class, the two children will be co-owners of Blackacre, with no chance Franklin will have another child.[6]

---

6. For purpose of class closing — and also for the Rule Against Perpetuities — acceptable procreation techniques are limited to those used two centuries ago. Frozen embryos and cloning are not possibilities in class closing and Rule Against Perpetuities applications.

(2) Class Closing by the Rule of Convenience

A class also may close by the rule of convenience. The **rule of convenience** states that a class closes whenever any member of the class can demand possession or distribution. The class does not necessarily close when a person is identified and satisfies any condition precedent, but only when some member of the class can demand possession. A vested member can demand possession usually no sooner than the natural termination of the preceding life estate or term for years, or until the divesting condition occurs in a fee simple subject to an executory limitation. Living persons — including those born within nine months — who are identifiable members of a class when the class closes by convenience, but who have not satisfied any condition precedent, may still share in the property if they later satisfy the condition precedent. In other words, the class closing rules merely circumscribe the persons who might take; it does not limit the number of persons who are in the class to those already vested. Consider the following successive events in the lives of *A*'s children:

Example 1: O's will devised Blackacre "to *W* for life, then to *A*'s children who attain age 21." *A* has two children: K (age 8) and L (age 5). K and L have contingent remainders, contingent on attaining age 21. The class of *A*'s children remains open to any after-born children of *A*.

Example 2: When K is age 15 and L is 12, *A* has another child, M. The three children (K, L, and M) have contingent remainders. The class is still open for *A*'s children who may be born later.

Example 3: K reaches age 21, and now has a vested remainder subject to open. The class does not close physiologically since *A* is still alive and can have more children. Likewise, the class is not closed by the rule of convenience since K, although vested, cannot demand possession of Blackacre until *W*'s life estate ends.

Example 4: *A* has a fourth child, N. N has a contingent remainder and shares ownership of Blackacre as long as N attains age 21.

Example 5: K dies at age 23. K is still vested. The condition precedent is attaining age 21. There is no condition precedent requiring any of *A*'s children to survive the life tenant, *W*. *K*'s devisee or heir will take *K*'s share of Blackacre on *W*'s death.

Example 6: *W* dies when L is 21, M is 9, and N is 2. *A* is still alive. The class of "*A*'s children" closes pursuant to the *rule of convenience* since K and L have satisfied the condition precedent — attaining age 21 — and *K*'s devisees or heirs and L can demand possession of Blackacre as soon as W's life estate ends, which it did when she died. While the class closes, the class is "A's children," not "A's children who have attained age 21." Thus M and N are still members of the class and will be vested if and when they attain age 21.

Example 7: Two years after the events in Example 6, A has a fifth child, X. X is A's child, and just as cute as were K, L, M, and N. However, X was born after the class of A's children closed and so will not share in Blackacre. The rule of convenience sometimes is unfair, but nonetheless makes land more alienable and marketable. Without it, A's children could not sell Blackacre until A died since A may have another child at any time.

Example 8: Continuing the example, N died in car wreck at age 18. N will not attain age 21, and thus neither N's devisees nor heirs will own any share of Blackacre. Blackacre will be co-owned in equal shares by K's devisee, L, and M (age 27 at N's death).

RESTATEMENT (THIRD) OF PROPERTY (TENTATIVE DRAFT)

The American Law Institute (ALI) is a private association of judges, lawyers, and professors organized to promote the clarification and simplification of the law. The ALI is best known for the publication of its "Restatement" of various areas of the law. The ALI's pronouncements are not law, but often are given serious consideration by judges and state legislators. The ALI as of this writing is drafting the estates and future interest component of the Restatement (Third) of Property. This hint of what the ALI might propose comes from Tentative Draft No. 6 (March 28, 2010).

The Restatement (Third) would combine and reduce the number of estates held as present interests to four: Fee simple absolute, fee simple defeasible, life estate, and term of years. The fee tail would not be recognized. Language traditionally creating the fee tail would create a fee simple absolute (or a life estate followed by a remainder depending on the wording of the grant). The fee simple defeasible would encompass the fee simple determinable, the fee simple subject to a condition subsequent, and the fee simple subject to an executory limitation.

The Restatement (Third) would propose more dramatic changes to future interests, limiting future interests to reversions (that may be vested or contingent), remainders (that may be vested or contingent), or postponed class gifts (that may be subject to open). Disappearing would be the possibility of reverter, the right of entry, the executory interest, and the vested remainder subject to divestment. The Restatement (Third) would eliminate the Rule of Destructibility of Contingent Remainders in the few states that currently retain it.[7]

Examples

Reversion Review

1. Consider which of the following conveyances creates a reversion:
   (a) O (the holder of a fee simple absolute) conveys Blackacre "to A for life."
   (b) O conveys Blackacre "to A for life, but if B marries C, then to C and his heirs so long as B and C use the property as a residence."
   (c) O conveys Blackacre "to A for life" and A transfers "to C for C's life."

A Has a Life Estate

2. Identify the interests created by the following transfers: O conveys Blackacre "to A for life . . .
   (a) "then to B and his heirs."
   (b) "then to B's children." B is childless at the time of the conveyance.
   (c) "remainder to B's heirs." B is alive.
   (d) "but when A dies, to B and his heirs."
   (e) "then if B survives A, to B and his heirs."
   (f) "then to B if B survives A, but if B does not survive A, to C and his heirs."
   (g) "then to B for life, then to C and his heirs."
   (h) "then to B and his heirs, but if B does not survive A, then to C and his heirs."
   (i) "then to A's surviving spouse and her heirs."
   (j) "then to B; but if B does not murder C and burn his house down, to C and his heirs."

B Has a Vested Remainder

3. Identify the interests created by each of the following transfers in which O transfers Whiteacre . . .
   (a) "to A for life, then to B for life, then to C and her heirs."
   (b) "to A for life, then to B for life, then if C survives A and B, to C and her heirs."
   (c) "to A for life, then to B for life, then when A and B die, to C and her heirs."

---

7. The Rule of Destructibility of Contingent Remainders is discussed more fully in the next chapter.

More Future Interests

4. Identify who has what interest in what estate in the following transfers of Brownacre from O . . .
   (a) "to A for life, remainder to B's children." B is alive and has two children, C and D.
   (b) "to A for life, remainder to B's children who attain age 18." B is alive and has one 10-year-old child.
   (c) "to A for life, remainder to B's heirs." B is divorced and has one child, C (age 10).
   (d) "to A for life, remainder to B if she graduates from law school; if not, to C."

Minor Gift

   (a) O conveys Blackacre "to my son A for life, then to his children who reach 21." A has two children, B (age 8) and C (age 13). What interests and estates do B and C have?
   (b) If C were to die after reaching 21 while A is alive, who owns what then?
   (c) Assuming the facts in (a), A dies, leaving B (then age 10) and C (age 15). What interests and estates are created at A's death?
   (d) What happens six years later, when B is 16 and C is 21 years old?

A Class Gift

6. Edna owned a 100-acre farm at her death. Her will provided that the farm passed to her sister, Faye, for life; at Faye's death, the farm passed to Faye's son, George, for life; it then went to George's children who survive George. George has one child, Trudy.
   (a) What interests do the respective parties have at Edna's death?
   (b) George has a second child, Sam. Does Sam have an interest in the farm?
   (c) Faye dies. A year later George has a third child, Robert. A month after Robert is born, Trudy dies, her only heir being her father, George. Who owns what interests in the farm?
   (d) George dies, survived by Sam and Robert. Who has what interests in the farm?

Implementing Your Client's Wishes

7. O has two children, a son A and a daughter B. O's son A is married without children. O is not fond of A's wife. O wants to transfer a farm to A. O wants

the farm to go to A's children or grandchildren if any after A dies, but not to A's wife.

(a) Which of the following conveyances would you recommend? ("Issue" are lineal descendants such as children, grandchildren, etc.)

   (1) O conveys the farm "to A and his heirs, but if A dies without issue, to B and her heirs."

   (2) O conveys the farm "to A for life, remainder to A's issue, but if A dies without issue, to B and her heirs."

   (3) O conveys the farm to A for life, remainder to A's children then living, but if A dies without children, to B and her heirs.

   (4) O conveys the farm "to A for life, remainder to A's children then living, and if any child not surviving A is survived by any child or children, said child or children shall share in the parent's share; but if A dies without any issue, then to B and her heirs."

   (5) O conveys the farm "to A for life, remainder to A's children then living if they reach age 21, and if any child not surviving A is survived by any child or children, said child or children shall share in the parent's share; but if A dies without any issue, then to B and her heirs."

   (6) O conveys the farm "to A for life, then to B and her heirs, but if A has any issue surviving him, to A's issue."

(b) Draft a conveyance transferring the farm to A if O thinks A's wife is wonderful.

Vest and Divest

8. Identify the interests and estates created in the following conveyances:

   (a) O conveys Blackacre "to my daughter A for life, then to my grandchild B and his heirs, but if any issue of my grandchild B survive A, then to those surviving issue."

   (b) Same facts as in (a). B dies, survived by his wife, C, and his child, D. B's will devises his interest to his wife, C.

   (c) Same facts as in (a) and (b). A dies.

   (d) O conveys Whiteacre "to A for life, remainder to B and her heirs, but if B marries C, then to C and his heirs."

   (e) O conveys Whiteacre "to A for life, then to B and his heirs, but if B sells alcohol on Whiteacre, then to C and her heirs."

   (f) O conveys "to A for 99 years if he lives so long, then to B and his heirs."

   (g) O conveys "to A for life, then one day after A is buried, to Bentham and his heirs."

   (h) O conveys "to A for life, then if B survives A, to B and his heirs, but if B does not survive A, to C and his heirs."

Explanations

Reversion Review

1. (a) O has a reversion, even though it is not stated in the grant itself. O transferred less than his full interest in Blackacre. What O retains is a reversion to take possession as soon as A's life estate ends.

   (b) O has a reversion until B marries C. If A dies before B marries C, O retakes possession of Blackacre. Once B marries C, O's reversion ends. O still has an interest, but it is not a reversion. O's interest is a future interest, a possibility of reverter, that follows C's fee simple determinable.

   (c) Both O and A have reversions. O has a reversion upon the end of A's life estate. A has a reversion upon the end of C's life estate if A outlives C.

A Has a Life Estate

2. A has present interest held in a life estate, and then . . .

   (a) B has a vested remainder in fee simple absolute. There is no implied condition that B survive A. If B dies before A, upon A's death B's heirs or devisees take both possession and the remainder.

   (b) B's children have a contingent remainder because they are not yet born. They are unascertained persons until born. O has a reversion in case B has no children. When a child of B is born, then that child will be said to have a vested remainder subject to partial divestment or "subject to open" (upon the birth of that child's siblings, when that second child, and each subsequent sibling, will partially divest his or her older siblings, gradually and pro rata reducing their share of the property). This is an example of the law's preference to classify remainders as vested.

   (c) B's heirs have a contingent remainder. No one is an heir of a living person — one may only be an heir apparent — a putative heir maybe, a hopeful heir certainly, but not legally an heir until the death of B, at which time the remainder becomes vested. If this conveyance were contained in B's will, the remainder would be vested because B's heirs are known at her death. A will is effective or "speaks" for this purpose at death, no matter how long before the fact it was executed.

   (d) B has a vested remainder in fee simple absolute. The words "but when A dies" do no more than indicate when A's present interest will naturally terminate. The words are not a condition precedent to the remainder.

   (e) While A is alive, B's estate is a contingent remainder. The condition of survivorship is express and is a condition precedent. Unless clearly expressed as a condition precedent, surviving the life tenant is not a condition to taking a remainder. In this case, however, O expressly conditioned the vesting of the remainder on B's surviving the life tenant, A. O keeps a reversion in case B does not survive A.

(f) When the words "but if B does not survive A, to C and his heirs" are added to this conveyance shown in (e) above, B's and C's remainders are both contingent; they are alternative contingent remainders, meaning that the condition precedent attached to one interest is the opposite of the condition attached to the other. At the time of the termination of the life estate, one of the two conditions will be satisfied and so one of the two remainders will become vested. While the remainders are both contingent, O would retain a reversion in fee simple absolute. Alternative contingent remainders were much used in England during the age of Queen Elizabeth I to ensure that when two sons were alive at the conveyance, if the elder son and heir were to die before his parents, the family property would devolve on the younger.

(g) B has a vested remainder in life estate. It is vested even though B may die before A's life estate ends. The reason B might never actually possess Blackacre is that her estate ends on her death, which may occur prematurely; surviving A is not a condition precedent to the grant but an end to her estate. C has vested remainder in fee simple absolute. C takes possession of Blackacre after both A and B die.

(h) B has a vested remainder subject to divestment in fee simple absolute. The survivorship condition is a condition subsequent, not a condition precedent. Since C can take only if B's vested remainder is cut short or divested, C cannot have a contingent remainder. C has a shifting executory interest in fee. If B dies before A, then B's interest is extinguished and C takes on A's death.

(i) A's surviving spouse owns a contingent remainder, contingent for two reasons. First, A's surviving spouse is an unascertained person: while A's current spouse very likely may be A's spouse at A's death, it may be someone else. Second, A's spouse must meet the condition precedent of surviving A.

(j) Trick question. A transfer — or a devise for that matter — intended to induce an illegal act — here murder and arson — is unenforceable and the inducing language is stricken. The grant will be rewritten to read, "then to B." B's interest is a vested remainder, held in fee simple absolute. C has no interest. Crime does not pay (or shouldn't).

B Has a Vested Remainder

3. A has a present interest held in a life estate, and then . . .
   (a) B has a vested remainder in life estate (or for life). Remainders designate the interest is a future interest. What estate is held is a different query. Here B's future interest is a life estate or an estate held for life. C has a vested remainder as well, his being a vested remainder in fee simple absolute.

(b) B has a vested remainder held in a life estate. C's remainder is subject to a condition precedent — C's surviving both A and B. Thus C has a contingent reminder in fee simple absolute. O has reversion in case C fails to survive A and B.

(c) B has a vested remainder in life estate (or for life). C has a vested remainder in fee simple absolute. The clause "then when A and B die" states the law as to when a remainder takes possession: Life estates end at the death of the life tenant and remainders take immediately thereafter. It is superfluous language. It is not a condition to C's taking. C (or her heirs or devisees) will possess Whiteacre after A and B die.

More Future Interests

4. A has a present interest held in a life estate, and then . . .

(a) The two children, C and D, have a vested remainder subject to open in fee simple absolute (or, alternatively labeled, a vested remainder subject to partial divestment). If B has more children, the after-born or adopted children will share in the remainder with C and D. The children's age are irrelevant to this classification.

(b) B's 10-year-old child has a contingent remainder in fee simple absolute, contingent on attaining age 18. O has a reversion in fee simple absolute to take effect on A's death if either B's child dies before he reaches 18 (and B has no more children who have attained age 18 by A's death), or B's child is still a minor. Once B's child turns 18 he will have a vested remainder subject to open in fee simple absolute.

(c) Assuming B is alive, B's heirs have a contingent remainder: Only decedents have heirs, so B's heirs are unascertained. C may have an expectation, but no interest yet; C may be an heir apparent but is not an heir until B dies (and C survives B). O has a reversion in fee simple absolute. If, on the other hand, B is dead, B's heirs (may be only C on the facts) are ascertained and have a vested remainder in fee simple absolute.

(d) B has a contingent remainder, contingent on B's graduating from law school. C also has a contingent remainder, contingent on B's not graduating from law school. B's and C's remainders here are alternative contingent remainders, one taking if there is a graduation, the other if there is none. If both remainders are contingent, the logic of the common law dictates that O has a reversion in case the life tenant, A, should die before B dies or graduates from law school.

Minor Gift

5. (a) B and C, then ages 8 and 13, respectively, have a contingent remainder, being subject to a condition precedent (their reaching the age of 21). O has a reversion.

(b) When C reaches 21, the remainder vests as to C, so C has a vested remainder subject to open (subject to partial divestment) upon B's reaching 21. C's heirs or devisees would take his interest in this vested remainder subject to open. B is included in the class of A's children but still holds a contingent remainder since B at age 16 has not reached 21 yet.

(c) Assuming the Rule of Destructibility of Contingent Remainders is not the law in this jurisdiction (the Rule is discussed in the next chapter), O's reversion becomes the present interest at the time of A's death, held in fee simple subject to an executory limitation. A's children, B and C, hold a springing executory interest. Either B or C reaching age 21 is the divesting event.

(d) Six years later, once C turns 21, C's springing executory interest divests O's reversion. C or C's heirs hold in fee simple subject to partial divestment by B when B reaches 21.

A Class Gift

6. (a) Faye has a life estate. George has a vested remainder in a life estate. Trudy has a contingent remainder, the condition precedent being her surviving her father, George. Edna (or Edna's estate) has a reversion in case George dies with no child surviving him. This question was intentionally written with names instead of letters so you can practice word problems, but if it is easier for you to visualize, rewrite the problem using letters: E conveys to F for life, then to G for life, then to G's children who survive him.

(b) Yes. Sam is "George's child" so Sam has a contingent remainder, the same as Trudy.

(c) George has a present interest held in a life estate, it becoming a present possessory estate when Faye's life estate ended. Sam and Robert still have contingent remainders, contingent on surviving their father. Neither Trudy's heirs nor her devisees have any interest since Trudy did not satisfy the condition precedent of surviving her father. Edna's heirs or devisees (we need more facts to know for sure which) have a reversion in case none of George's children survives him.

(d) Robert and Sam own the farm in fee simple absolute. They will own the farm in equal proportions as tenants in common (tenants in common are covered later).

7. Implementing Your Client's Wishes

(a) (1) Option 1 does not carry out O's intent. A owns a fee simple subject to an executory limitation in favor of B if A does not have any children. A is free to devise the property to his wife as long as they have a child. The grant does not guarantee *A*'s children will receive any interest in the farm after *A*'s death.

(2) Option 2 may work although there is a possibility *A*'s children may die young and the property pass by intestacy to *A*'s wife. There's also a construction problem. Since "issue" includes grandchildren, who would take what percentage interest if, for example, *A* has two children, one child childless and one child with three children? Or who would take what shares in what interests if *A* died with one surviving child who was childless, and a second child who predeceased *A*, but left three children? A lawyer's job is to prevent future litigation if possible.

(3) Option 3 carries out *O*'s interest to prevent *A*'s wife from owning any interest in the farm. It does not address the situation where one of *A*'s children predeceases *A*, but is himself or herself survived by a child (*A*'s grandchild).

(4) Option 4 seems to carry out *O*'s intent. *A* owns a life estate and the farm passes to *A*'s children or grandchildren. The grant as a practical matter makes it very difficult for *A* to sell the farm during his lifetime. Before formalizing this grant, the attorney should clarify that is *O*'s intent. If not, either a further revision needs to be made or perhaps a transfer to a trust giving the trustee (who might be *A*) power to sell might be a better option, with trust document including the Option 4 grant as the trust terms.

(5) Option 5 adds a condition precedent that *A*'s children must reach age 21 as well as survive *A* to gain a possessory interest. On one hand, this option eliminates the possibility that a minor child could die after being vested with *A*'s wife inheriting that child's share. On the other hand, it hampers the sale of the farm until *A*'s youngest child reaches age 21.

(6) Option 6 seems to be a variation on Option 2, but reverses the order of who takes the vested interest and who gets the executory interest. B owns a vested remainder subject to divestment in fee simple absolute because B's interest will be divested, if at all, before it becomes possessory. *A*'s issue surviving *A* own a shifting executory interest.

(b) "*O* hereby transfers the farm to *A* and his heirs." *A* owns a fee simple absolute interest in the farm and may sell, devise, or have it pass by inheritance.

Vest and Divest

8. (a) *A* has a present interest held in a life estate; B has a vested remainder subject to divestment in fee simple absolute. B's children who survive *A* have a shifting executory interest. There is no condition precedent

to B's remainder so it is a vested remainder, but B may be divested of his interest if a child of his survives A (whether or not they survive B); so B has a vested remainder subject to divestment in fee simple absolute. B's issue who survive A have a shifting executory interest.

(b) A has a present interest held in a life estate. C has inherited B's vested remainder subject to divestment in fee simple. B's surviving issue, D, has a shifting executory interest in fee simple absolute. Final disposition awaits A's death.

(c) After A's death, C's vested remainder is divested. When child D survives A, D's shifting executory interest shifts the fee simple held by B's devisee, C, to D. D owns Blackacre in fee simple absolute. Modern canons make the words "and his heirs" unnecessary.

(d) A has present interest held in a life estate. B has a vested remainder subject to divestment in fee simple absolute. C would have a shifting executory interest in fee simple absolute if C married B.

(e) A has present interest held in a life estate. B has a vested remainder in fee simple subject to an executory limitation. It is not a vested remainder subject to divestment since B must sell alcohol on Whiteacre to be divested, and this cannot occur until after B takes possession. Hence B's interest cannot be divested while it is still a vested remainder. C has a shifting executory interest.

(f) A owns a determinable term of years. B has a shifting executory interest in fee simple absolute. A's interest has a definite maximum term, but can be cut short by his death before the end of the term. It is not a life estate even though in all likelihood A will die before the 99 years have passed.

(g) A has present interest held in a life estate. O has a reversion. Bentham has a springing executory interest (springing from O, not A). At common law, Bentham's estate was void because there was a gap in seisin. No one could be buried before his or her death, unless he or she was buried alive — a possibility the law did not admit. Today the gap in seisin, as well as the shift in seisin, is permitted and Bentham's estate is a springing executory interest in fee simple absolute.

(h) A's life estate is followed by two alternative contingent remainders in fee simple absolute in B and C, respectively, and followed further by a reversion in O. The condition determining who will take the property is whether B survives A. If B survives A, B gets a fee simple absolute interest in the property. If B does not survive A, the property goes to C in fee simple absolute. O has a reversion even though one of the remainders, B or C, has to take. This is because at common law a life estate terminated by forfeiture before the death of A if the life tenant was found to be a traitor or disloyal to the king.

Special Rules of Construction

Several rules of law or construction developed in England long ago to decrease the control that grantors, testators, and other transferors have over real property, and later on, to increase the alienability of property. Most states no longer follow many of them, but some do and in some instances, understanding them is necessary to see the extent to which they are and are not followed. This chapter covers these rules, except for the Rule Against Perpetuities, which is discussed in Chapter 12.

THE RULE OF DESTRUCTIBILITY OF CONTINGENT REMAINDERS

In England during the fourteenth and fifteenth centuries, seisin had to be continuous. It could not ever be in abeyance, for if it was to be, the lord of the manor could not know who was responsible for the land within his domain. Lawyers and judges consequently were troubled when a life tenant died and the holders of a remainder were not yet ascertained, or when a named contingent remainder holder had not satisfied the condition precedent. Early examples generally involved the naming of heirs.

Example 1: Owen conveyed Blackacre "to *A* for life, remainder to B's heirs." B is alive. *A* living person's heirs are unascertained (common law lawyers said that "no living person has heirs"), so the remainder in B's heirs is contingent. If A died before B, then, the remainder had not vested, being that seisin had not rested on anyone — a nightmare in the feudal system since no one was responsible for paying taxes and providing soldiers for the King.

In addition, because the common method of transfer was by enfeoffment with livery of seisin, judges came to require that all transfers had to take place at once. A vested remainder relaxed this requirement, and the judges regarded the remainder as being capable of taking possession when and if the prior freehold estate ended — at which time seisin passed instantly to the remainderman. A contingent remainder required a further relaxation of the rule that seisin had to be continuous. The judges balked — and wouldn't do it. Given the choice between having the property revert back to the grantor until the remainderman satisfied the condition precedent or voiding the contingent remainder, the judges chose to void the contingent remainders that were still contingent when the preceding life estate ended. A remainder, they said, had to vest at or before it came into possession. From thence developed the rule of destructibility of contingent remainders.

The **rule of destructibility of contingent remainders** states that a contingent remainder is destroyed if it has not vested at or before the termination of all preceding life estates.

Example 2: O conveyed Blackacre "to A for life, then to A's children who attain age 21." A died when A's only child, C, was age 15. Since C's remainder was not vested (i.e., it is still contingent on C turning 21) upon or before the end of A's life estate, according to the rule of destructibility of contingent remainders, C's contingent remainder was destroyed. It is void. O (or O's heir or devisee) takes Blackacre by way of a reversion. Put differently, in this case, the rule prefers the reversion over waiting for the remainder to free itself of uncertainty.

Example 3: O conveyed Blackacre "to A for life, then to B for life, then to A's children who attain age 21." B died when A's only child, C, was 15. C's contingent remainder was not destroyed since C's remainder does not need to be vested until A's life estate ends.

Example 4: Same facts as in Example 3 except A rather than B died when C was 15. C's contingent remainder still was not destroyed since B had possession after A dies. Only if both A's and B's life estates ended before C turned 21 would C's contingent remainder be destroyed.

The rule of destructibility of contingent remainders has its limits. First, the rule applies only to contingent remainders in real property. It does not apply to remainder interests in personal property. Thus, the rule does not apply to transfers of artwork, stocks, bonds, furniture, and other personal property. Second, it does not apply to equitable interests — i.e., interests held in trust. Thus a transfer of real property to a trustee in trust to benefit A for life, then to B if B attains age 21, will continue to be valid even if A dies before B turns 21. Third, it applies only to contingent remainders. It does not destroy executory interests. In fact, a major impetus for the development of executory interests as legally cognizable ownership vehicles was to circumvent the rule of destructibility of contingent remainders. Fourth, the rule does not apply to vested remainders subject to divestment since the remainder is vested (even though it may never become possessory). This is one reason it is important to distinguish contingent remainders from vested remainders subject to divestment. See chapter 10. Finally, the rule is simply not a factor in the vast majority of states. Only a few states retain it.[1]

American judges worked hard to contain the rule, since it often thwarted a transferor's intent.

Example 5: Ted devised Blackacre "to Alex for life, then to Ben's children" at a time when Ben was already dead. Alex died the next day. Although Ben was dead, Ben's wife was pregnant with Ben's later-born child Charlie. Charlie was allowed to take the remainder. A person ascertained within the period of gestation preserved the remainder that would otherwise be destroyed by the rule of destructibility of contingent remainders.

Example 6: O transferred Blackacre to "A for A's life or five years, whichever is greater, then to B if B attains age 21" at a time when B is 16. B's contingent remainder will not be destroyed since A or his heir or devisee will own the land for at least five years, long enough for B to turn 21. That is, the rule of destructibility of contingent remainders can be avoided by structuring the transfer of property as a grant of a term of years rather than as a life estate, long enough to guarantee an age condition is met.

Example 7: O conveyed Blackacre "to A for life, remainder to T (a trustee) in trust for the life of B, remainder to B's children who survive B and their heirs." T's interest is a remainder to preserve contingent remainders in the surviving children. This devise was the creation of a great seventeenth century English conveyancer by the name of Orlando Bridgeman (who also argued the case creating the Rule against Perpetuities, discussed in Chapter 12). T's remainder was a vested one that would last until the second

---

1. Four states to our knowledge retain the rule: Indiana, Kansas, New Hampshire, and Oklahoma.

remainder (the contingent remainder in "B's children who survive B" in this Example) vested.

THE MERGER RULE

Other rules work to destroy or void contingent remainders. The merger rule is one such rule. The basic idea of the **merger rule** is simple: If a person holding a vested life estate acquires the next vested estate in the same property, the two vested estates merge into one. For example, if a person holding a vested life estate acquires a vested remainder in the same property, instead of the person owning a life estate and the vested remainder in the same property, the two estates "merge" into one larger estate, the fee simple absolute. Similarly, if a person owns a vested remainder and later acquires the immediately preceding vested life estate, the two estates merge into one.

Example 1: Owen conveyed Blackacre "to A for life, remainder to B." If A acquired B's vested remainder, A then owned both the present interest held in a life estate and a vested remainder held in fee simple absolute. Historically, recognizing that in substance B owned the rights to Blackacre from now to infinity, a court would combine ("merge") the two legal estates into one. In this Example, the resulting estate is a fee simple absolute.

The common law went further, however, and gave such a high priority to vested estates that any contingent remainder separating the two vested estates was destroyed, as in the following example.

Example 2: Owen conveyed Blackacre "to A for life, remainder to B for life if he attains the age of 21, remainder to C and his heirs." At this point, A owned a present interest held in a life estate; B owned a contingent remainder to be held in a life estate, contingent on reaching age 21; and C owned a vested remainder to be held as a fee simple absolute. Assume A acquired C's vested remainder when B was 16. The Merger Doctrine held the two vested estates merged, and the merger of two successive vested interests destroyed B's intervening contingent remainder. B's contingent remainder was destroyed because he could not take the seisin at the time he needed to — the date of A's acquisition of C's interest. B's interest could not be vested at the termination, through merger, of the prior estate because B was only 16 and he needed to attain age 21 for his remainder to vest.

There is nothing inerrant about the result in this example. It's just the law, and one reason that some commentators regard the merger rule as a component of the rule of destructibility of contingent remainders.

As the example pointed out, if a person owning a life estate acquires a vested remainder that follows a contingent remainder held by some other person, the life estate and the vested remainder merge, destroying the contingent remainder. The rule works the other way too. So if a person holding a vested remainder that immediately follows another person's contingent remainder in the same property acquires the possessory life estate that immediately precedes the contingent remainder, the life estate and vested remainder merge, destroying the contingent remainder. That simplifies the title, but at the expense of the holder of the contingent remainder.

The merger rule has its limitations. For the two vested interests to merge to destroy an intervening contingent remainder, for example, the two vested estates must be acquired at different times. Two vested interests acquired in the same document do not destroy intervening contingent remainders.

Example 3: O conveyed Blackacre "to A for life, then to B for life if B attains age 21, then to C." B is age 15. A has a present interest held in a life estate, B has a contingent remainder held in a life estate, and C has a vested remainder held in fee simple absolute. No merger occurs because *A* and *C* are different people. B's contingent remainder is good.

Example 4: Same facts as in Example 3, except two years later A buys C's vested remainder. A now owns a (vested) life estate and a vested remainder in the same property, the two vested interests having been acquired at separate times. The two vested interests merge into a fee simple absolute, destroying B's contingent remainder in life estate. A then owns Blackacre in fee simple absolute. The same result follows if C had acquired A's life estate — that is, the life estate is absorbed into the fee simple absolute.

Example 5: O conveyed Greenacre "to A for life, then to B for life if B attains age 21, then to A." A has a present interest held in a life estate and a vested remainder in fee simple absolute. In between A's two vested estates is B's contingent remainder in a life estate. A's two vested estates do not merge to destroy B's contingent remainder since the three estates were created in the same document.

As another limitation, the merger rule merges only vested estates, not contingent remainders.

Example 6: O conveyed Whiteacre "to A for life, then to B for life if she attains age 21 (B is 14), then to C if C attains age 21 (C is 5)." Three years later A acquired C's interest. After the acquisition, A had a (vested) present interest held in a life estate and a contingent remainder held in fee simple (contingent on C's attaining age 21). B's intervening interest is a contingent remainder held in a life estate. A's two estates do not merge since A has one vested estate and one contingent estate. A person must own two *vested* estates for the two to merge. B's contingent remainder remains valid.

The merger rule simply merges vested estates. In the process the merger rule may destroy a contingent remainder but that is not its primary function. Thus a contingent remainder that does not intervene the two vested estates remains valid.

Example 7: O conveys Brownacre "to A for life, then to B for life, then to C if C attains age 21" (C is 14). A has a (vested) present interest held in a life estate, B has a vested remainder in life estate, C has a contingent remainder in fee simple absolute, and O has a reversion (in case C does not reach 21). Two years later B acquires A's life estate. Since B now owns two vested interests, the two interests merge into one possessory life estate for the longer of A's or B's life. The merger does not destroy C's contingent remainder, however, since C's interest follows the two vested estates and is not an intervening estate.

Example 8: O conveys Redacre "to A for life, then to B for life, then to C." A has a present interest held in a life estate, B has a vested remainder in a life estate, C has a vested remainder in fee simple absolute. Two years later A acquires C's vested remainder. A has a vested life estate and a vested remainder in fee simple absolute, but the two estates do not merge to destroy B's intervening interest since B's remainder in life estate is vested and not contingent.

FORFEITURE

A contingent remainder might have been destroyed centuries ago in England by its being subject to **forfeiture**. If O conveyed Blackacre to A for life, remainder to B if B attained age 21, and when B was 16, A's life estate was forfeited for treason or some other crime, or A committed waste on Blackacre and the remedy was forfeiture (as often it was in the early cases), the contingent remainder was destroyed. Today A might forfeit his property used in a drug transaction, and the same rules would apply: the contingent remainder would be destroyed.

THE RULE IN SHELLEY'S CASE

The **Rule in Shelley's Case** is simply stated: When a devise or conveyance transfers a freehold estate to a person and in the same instrument also transfers a remainder to that same person's heirs or the heirs of his body, and either both estates are legal or both are equitable, both are considered to be held by the first-named freeholder, either for life, in fee simple absolute, or in fee tail; and the person's heirs get nothing under the grant. In its most common application, a remainder in favor of a life tenant's heirs is deemed held by the life tenant. Stated this way, the rule can be seen to depend on the merger rule and a preference for vested remainders. See Wolf v. Shelley, 1 Co. Rep. 93b (1581) (Lord Edward Coke reporting the case). This rule is usually broken down into three requirements: (1) a freehold estate (usually a life estate) given to a first transferee, (2) a remainder limited to the heirs of the first transferee in the same instrument, and (3) a freehold and a remainder of the same quality — i.e., either both being legal or both being equitable in nature.

Thus if O conveys "to A for life, remainder to A's heirs," by operation of law, A comes into ownership of both the life estate (under the terms of the conveyance) and the remainder in his heirs. Early cases using the rule interpreted this remainder as meaning ". . . then to A and his heirs." The words creating the remainder ("remainder to A's heirs") are all construed in this case as words of limitation, thus construing these words toward the fee simple absolute. Thus, too, by operation of law, the courts changed the contingent remainder into a vested remainder — and the full conveyance into "to A for life, remainder to A and his heirs." Pursuant to the merger rule previously discussed, A's two estates merged. A then held his merged interests in fee simple absolute.

The Rule in Shelley's case is a rule of law, not a canon of construction for ascertaining the transferor's intent. See Perrin v. Blake, 96 Eng. Rep. 392 (K.B. 1769) (Lord Mansfield, J., holding the rule a canon of construction), reversed, 98 Eng. Rep. 355 (Ex. Chamber, 1770) (Blackstone, J., holding the rule one of law — a holding that he later embedded in his famous treatise, much read by early American lawyers). The grantor's intent makes no difference to the question of whether the rule in Shelley's case applies. Today many call the rule an anachronism, but many defend it still as a means of rendering land alienable sooner.

The remainder to A's heirs need not follow the first freehold estate directly; there may be an intervening estate, as when O conveys "to A for life, remainder to B for life, remainder to A's heirs and their heirs." Under the rule, A holds both the present interest in the life estate and a future interest, the vested remainder held in fee simple absolute. The same result would occur if a condition precedent were added to the remainder to A's heirs, as where the words "if the land is still used as a farm" were added to the conveyance. That the remainder is not vested makes no difference. The rule applies to both vested and contingent remainders.

In some cases the Rule in Shelley's Case gives A two interests in property, but not the complete ownership of the property in fee simple absolute.

This is so because the Merger Rule will not operate if there is an intervening estate created by the same document or if the remainder is a contingent remainder. Only when there is no impediment to merger will *A* wind up with a fee simple absolute. In other words, all the Rule in Shelley's Case does is transform a grant to "*A*'s heirs" to a grant "to *A*" if *A* also receives a freehold estate (usually a life estate) in the same document. Once that transformation is done, whether the Merger Rule applies depends on the Merger Rule guidelines.

The Rule in Shelley's Case has been abolished by statute in well over 40 states. Where wholly abolished, a conveyance to *A* for life, then to *A*'s heirs, creates the following interests: a life estate in *A*, a contingent remainder in *A*'s heirs, and a reversion in *O*. Some states have partially abolished the Rule: for example, Indiana abolished it for trusts, but not for wills, and Oregon and New Hampshire abolished it for wills, but not for non-testamentary trusts. The Rule is still the law in two or three states. The state statutes require a close reading.

Moreover, many statutes abolishing the rule provide simply that "The Rule in Shelley's Case is hereby abolished." Reading such a statute, you are no better off if you do not know what the rule is in the first place — hence your need to know it. In some states the rule has been abolished only prospectively, meaning that it still controls conveyances made before the effective date of the abolition statute.

The Rule applies to transfers of real property but not usually to personalty. If *O* deeds his farm equipment "to *A* for life, remainder to *A*'s heirs," the rule does not apply in nearly all states. Where it does not apply, the interests created take as written. What if *O* deeds Blackacre and its farm equipment to *A* for life, remainder to *A*'s heirs? Maybe the Rule should apply to personalty in cases like this — or the deed should be interpreted so that the equipment are trade fixtures (fixtures not otherwise fixtures but necessary to the operation of Blackacre) to stay with Blackacre.

Example 1: *O* conveyed Blackacre "to *A* for life and then to *A*'s heirs." *O* intended for *A* to have a life estate followed by a contingent remainder in fee simple in *A*'s heirs (contingent on *A*'s heirs being identified at *A*'s death). Notwithstanding *O*'s intent, the Rule in Shelley's Case converted the contingent remainder in *A*'s heirs to a vested remainder in *A*. Since *A* owned a life estate and the immediately following vested interest, pursuant to the merger rule, *A*'s two interests merged into a fee simple absolute.

Example 2: *O* conveyed Whiteacre "to *A* for life, then to B for life, then to *A*'s heirs." The Rule in Shelley's case converted the contingent remainder in *A*'s heirs to a vested remainder in *A*. *A*'s heirs have no interest. Even though *A* owned a (vested) life estate and a vested remainder, the two estates did not merge because there was an intervening vested remainder in life estate in B. Merger would not apply even if B's interest were a contingent remainder since the interests were all created in the same document. The intervening estate delayed full application of the Rule. A can convey a fee simple subject to B's life estate. B can have a cause of action in waste if needed against A as a life tenant.

Example 3: O conveyed Greenacre "to A for life, then to B's heirs." The Rule in Shelley's Case does not apply since B received no other interest in the grant. Therefore, B's heirs have a contingent remainder in fee simple absolute, contingent on being identified at B's death.

Example 4: O conveyed Brownacre "to A for life, then to A's heirs if the land is used for a farm at A's death, and, if not, to B and her heirs." The Rule in Shelley's Case transformed the contingent remainder in A's heirs to a contingent remainder in A, contingent on Brownacre being farmed at A's death. No merger resulted because A must own two vested estates for merger, and here he owned one vested estate (the life estate) and one contingent estate (the contingent remainder). Contrast this result with that in Example 16, where the contingent remainder was transformed into a vested remainder. The reason for the different result is that the Rule in Shelley's Case merely converts a grant "to A's heirs" to one "to A." Rewritten, the grant in Example 1 is to "A for life, remainder to A" — the contingency of being an heir disappears automatically. In this Example, on the other hand, if rewritten after application of the Rule in Shelley's Case, the grant is "to A for life, then to A if the land is used as a farm at A's death" — the contingency remains.

Example 5: O conveyed Blackacre "to A for life, then to A's children, but if A has no children, to A's heirs." The Rule in Shelley's Case does not apply here because the remainders are alternate contingent remainders — courts tend to require the precise formula of a life estate in A and a remainder in A's heirs in order to apply the Rule — and the application of the Rule is delayed again by the intervening estate.

Example 6: O conveyed Redacre "to Amy for life, then to Amy's heirs, excluding her sisters Bea and Carlotta." The Rule does not apply because any limitation on the class of heirs renders it inapplicable. Likewise, a conveyance "to Abby for life, then to Abby's heirs and Beatrice," would render the Rule inapplicable.

Example 7: O conveyed Whiteacre "to A for life, remainder to A's heirs and their heirs." The Rule applied because to hold otherwise would turn a rule of law into a canon of construction.

THE DOCTRINE OF WORTHIER TITLE

The Doctrine of Worthier Title works similarly to the Rule in Shelley's Case, except the Doctrine of Worthier Title applies to conveyances to the grantor's heirs. The Doctrine of Worthier Title changes ownership from "O's heirs" to "O" in grants such as O "to A for life, then to O's heirs" or "to A for life, then to my heirs." As with the Rule in Shelley's Case, the transferor in olden England was either attempting to avoid taxes due to the King on the descent of property or was looking to narrow the rights of creditors to A's life estate. The courts responded in a similar fashion. They voided O's heirs' remainder and held that instead O had a reversion. The Doctrine of Worthier Title started as a rule of law, but survives today (where it has not been abolished altogether) as a rule of construction to ascertain the grantor's intent.

The **Doctrine of Worthier Title** states that when there is a conveyance or devise to a person, with a remainder or executory interest to the grantor's heirs or next of kin (but not to the heirs of the grantor's body), no future interest is created in the grantor's heirs; rather, the grantor retains a reversion. Once deemed to hold the reversion, O can transfer it again and, being a vested interest, it can be subjected to levy and sale by O's creditors. The Doctrine applies to real, personal, legal, and equitable property. The Doctrine is in effect a prohibition against remainders in a transferor's heirs.

Why is the reversion "worthier" than a remainder? First, a reversion is always vested—and thus the Doctrine is an example of a preference for vested interests. Second, it promotes the alienability of property. And third, descent at common law was worthier than a devise. That third rationale seems strange today. At common law it made sense because descent (inheritance) was a taxable event; landowners tried to use the remainder to O's heirs device as a tax dodge since the property passed by an earlier grant not by descent. The Doctrine of Worthier Title quashed that ploy.

Today the Doctrine of Worthier title is widely applied only to inter vivos transactions—to deeds and similar instruments of transfer. The Doctrine's so-called wills branch (applying it to devises) is not much used, being abolished by statute or judicial decision in about 30 states. Where abolished, a devise from O "to A for life, then to O's heirs" will be enforced as written.

The Doctrine of Worthier Title continues to apply to deeds in many states. It survives only as a rule of construction, to which the grantor's intent is relevant, and not as a rule of law. As a rule of construction, a gift over to O's heirs creates a rebuttable presumption that O did not in fact intend the gift over to take and intended instead that the grantor retain the reversion. The grantor's heirs have no interest, only the hope or expectation that they will inherit if the grantor does not sell or devise it to others.

The presumption can be rebutted. The use of a word other than one commonly meaning "heirs" in the limitation is one way to rebut the presumption. O's conveying "to A for life, remainder to those persons who would be my heirs at A's death" does the trick, changing the common meaning of the word just enough. So does "to A for life, remainder to my heirs, the latter persons to take as purchasers," as does "to my children" or "to my issue."

The doctrine has been abolished in about 30 states (including California, Illinois, and New York). Even where abolished by statute, the statute's express language may not provide for its retroactive effect (affecting documents drafted before abolishment). When the state statute is silent on the issue of retroactivity, a court may refuse to abolish the doctrine retroactively. In order to avoid running afoul of the Doctrine of Worthier Title, a drafter should specifically name the person to whom the transferor intends property to go.

"O's heirs" must refer to all of "O's heirs" and not some subset of heirs before the Doctrine is invoked. Thus the Doctrine of Worthier Title would not affect a conveyance "to A for life, then to O's lineal heirs," or "to A for life, then to O's heirs living at A's death." Similarly, the Doctrine would not apply to a conveyance "to A for life, then to O's heirs in equal shares." because heirs generally take, under the canons of descent, in representational shares (per stirpes), not per capita (per individual equally): that is, when one of Grandma's children is deceased, that child's children takes the share of the deceased parent and does not take in her own right. Likewise, when O conveys "to A for life, then to B and her heirs" when B is in fact the sole heir of O, the Doctrine would not apply: B takes the remainder by way of words of purchase, not descent or limitation, so the Doctrine is inapplicable.

Examples

The Rule of Destructibility of Contingent Remainders

1. Unless stated otherwise, assume that the state recognizes the Rule of Destructibility of Contingent Remainders.
   (a) O conveyed Blackacre to "my son A for life, then to his children who reach 21." A has two children, B (age 8) and C (age 13). What interests and estates do B and C have?
   (b) Same facts as in (a). A died when B was 10 and C was 15. Who owns what interests in Blackacre?
   (c) Same facts as in (a). A died when B was 19 and C was 23. Who owns what interests in Blackacre?
   (d) Same facts as in (b), except the state does not recognize the Rule of Destructibility of Contingent Remainders. Who owns what interests in Blackacre?

The Rule in Shelley's Case

2. (a) O conveyed Whiteacre "to *A* for ten years, then to *A*'s heirs." Does the Rule in Shelley's Case apply?
   (b) O conveyed Whiteacare "to *A* for life, and then two days after *A*'s death, to *A*'s heirs." Does the Rule in Shelley's Case apply?
   (c) O conveyed Whiteacre "to *A* for life, and on *A*'s death, to *A*'s children." Does the Rule in Shelley's Case apply?
   (d) O conveyed Whiteacre "to *A* for life, then to B for ten years, then to *A*'s heirs." Does the Rule in Shelley's Case apply?

The Doctrine of Worthier Title

3. (a) O conveyed Blackacre "to *A* for life, then to O's next of kin." Does the Doctrine of Worthier Title apply?
   (b) O conveyed Blackacre "to *A* for life, then to B and her heirs," where B is an heir of O. Does the doctrine apply?
   (c) O conveyed Blackacre "to *A* for life, but if *A* does not live on Blackacre, to the heirs of O." Does the doctrine apply?

Explanations

The Rule of Destructibility of Contingent Remainders

1. (a) *A's* interest is a present interest, held in a life estate. *A*'s children, alive and after-born, have a contingent remainder, contingent on their attaining age 21. O has a reversion. The Rule of Destructibility is not implicated while *A* is alive.
   (b) Pursuant to the Rule of Destructibility of Contingent Remainders, the contingent remainders to B and C are destroyed. O owns Blackacre in fee simple absolute.
   (c) C owns Blackacre subject to partial divestment if B reaches 21. Once C turned 21, *A*'s children's interest became a vested remainder subject to open. The Rule of Destructibility of Contingent Remainders does not destroy any type of vested remainder.
   (d) Because of the reversion, O owns Blackacre. O's present interest is held in a fee simple subject to an executory limitation. B and C own springing executory interests.

The Rule in Shelley's Case

(a) No. *A* does not hold a *freehold* estate, as the rule requires. Instead *A* holds a nonfreehold estate, a term of years. Thus a variance in wording produces a different legal result, so be alert — for example, O transferring "to *A* for 99 years should *A* live so long, remainder to *A*'s heirs" is a way to avoid the Rule in Shelley's Case: This is a term of years, rather than a life estate, followed by a remainder in *A*'s heirs.

(b) No. The heirs' interest here is a springing executory interest, not a remainder. The rule applies to remainders, not to executory interests. *A* has a life estate; *O* has reversion in fee simple subject to an executory limitation, *O*'s reversion to become possessory when *A*'s life estate ends. *A*'s heirs have a springing executory interest. *A*'s heirs' interest is not a remainder since it does not immediately follow the prior life estate; it follows *O*'s fee simple and it must cut short the fee simple to become possessory. Historically, the fact that the Rule in Shelley's case does not destroy executory interests was the impetus for creating executory interests in the first place.

(c) Still no. The remainder in "*A*'s children" is not the same as "*A*'s heirs" even though children constitute a major category of "heirs." The Rule in Shelley's Case applies only to "heirs," not to "children" or "issue" or even to "persons who would be my heirs." From these three Examples you see how attorneys avoid the impact of the rule. There are other ways to avoid the Rule in Shelley's Case. For example, the use of two instruments — one to the life tenant, another to the heirs of the tenant — will avoid the rule since the Rule in Shelley's Case requires the interest to be created in the same document. Another stratagem would be to put either the life tenant's or the heirs' interest in a trust, making it an equitable interest, so that the requirement that either both interests be legal or both be equitable is not satisfied and so (again) the rule does not apply. The Rule in Shelley's Case may be avoided by leaving the remainder to the life tenant's widow or widower, for example, or to named heirs. This would conform to the typical estate plan of many people and still avoid the rule with a slight change in the wording of the transfer. When the rule is so easily avoided, it becomes a trap for the unwary. For some, this argues also for the Rule's abolition.

(d) Yes. The document purported to create a life estate in *A* and a remainder in *A*'s heirs. Thus the remainder becomes a vested remainder in *A*. *A* then owns both a life estate and a vested remainder in fee simple absolute. The two interests do not merge to form a fee simple absolute, however. The merger rule demands the two vested interests be acquired at different times. In addition, merger will be allowed to destroy an intervening interest only when the intervening interest is contingent. Here *A* received both interests in the same document, and B's term of years is vested. So there was no merger in this case.

The Doctrine of Worthier Title

(a) Yes. The words "next of kin" are sufficiently close to "heirs" to render the doctrine applicable since the Doctrine today is a canon of construction, not a rule of law.

(b) No. The limitation must use just the term "heirs" or its equivalent.

(c) Yes. An older, shortened statement of the Doctrine is that a "limitation over to an heir is void." Why? Because an heir cannot be a purchaser, meaning that the word heirs cannot be words of purchase under the Doctrine. An executory interest is arguably just as much "a limitation over" as a remainder, so the Doctrine of Worthier Title transforms the executory interests in O's heirs to a right of reentry in O. But James Casner, an eminent authority on future interests, has disagreed. See James Casner & Barton Leach, *Property* 343 (2d ed. 1969). Professor Casner, like many traditionalists, strictly construed the Doctrine. It was fully formed by the time executory interests became established, so a strict construction of the Doctrine required that executory interests be excluded from its reach.

CHAPTER 12

The Rule Against Perpetuities

INTRODUCTION

The Rule Against Perpetuities (RAP) is a judicially created rule to encourage the alienability (transferability) of property. The Rule Against Perpetuities balances a tension between landowners who want to maintain land in the family unit for many generations and judges, merchants, and members of future generations who want land to be freely alienable. After centuries of legal invention and counteractions, the courts in a series of cases between 1682 and 1833 settled on a Rule Against Perpetuities that allows a landowner during his lifetime (or at his death through a will) to control ownership into some future generations, but only for a limited time. The Rule requires "vesting" within a certain time. The Rule will void or invalidate future interests that "vest too remotely."

The classic statement of the Rule Against Perpetuities, formulated by Professor John Chipman Gray,[1] *The Rule Against Perpetuities* §201 (4th ed. 1942) in its totality reads:

> No interest is good unless it must vest, if at all, not later than twenty-one years after some life in being at the creation of the interest.

---

1. John Chipman Gray (1839-1915) graduated from law school in 1861, served in the Civil War, and then entered practice in Boston. He began teaching law in 1869, was an early advocate of the case method, and was the author of the first property casebook.

The Rule of Perpetuities, while easy to state, can be challenging to apply. The Rule is best mastered by working practice problems. This chapter gives many examples to use as practice and reinforcement. Try to understand the analytical reasoning of each sentence in each illustrative example. You can find more practice problems in John Makdisi and Daniel Bogart, *Estates in Land and Future Interests: Problems and Answers*, 5th ed. (Aspen 2007).

Part of the difficulty in applying the Rule Against Perpetuities is that you first must master the present and future interest and estate rules discussed in the previous chapters before applying the Rule Against Perpetuities (RAP). In addition, applying the Rule may turn on events not immediately apparent, and may involve your imagining untimely births and deaths of many.

PART I
THE RULE AGAINST PERPETUITIES EXPLAINED

In general, the Rule Against Perpetuities encourages the early vesting of interests by voiding contingent interests that vest too remotely. Interests that vest within the relevant period ("not later than twenty-one years after some life in being at the creation of the interest"), on the other hand, are valid or "good." A **vested interest** is one where the takers are ascertainable persons (they can be named) *and* there is no condition precedent to the interest becoming vested.

Future interests to unascertained persons *or* that are subject to a condition precedent are **contingent interests**. The Rule Against Perpetuities voids or invalidates *contingent future interests that vest too remotely*. Those contingent future interests that conform to the Rule are "good" under the Rule and, as long as the interests do not violate some other rule, will be enforceable. Those contingent future interests that do not vest within the time specified by the Rule, however, are "not good" and will be stricken from the grant so that the grant must be read as though the invalidated future interest was not included.

The courts in developing the Rule Against Perpetuities exempted from the Rule's reach all interests *vested* at the creation of the interest (vested remainders subject to open being the exception — see below). Three categories of interests are always "good" under the Rule Against Perpetuities because they are deemed vested at the creation of the interest:

1. All *future interests* in the *grantor*: The Rule Against Perpetuities will not void reversions, possibilities of reverter, and rights of entry, which are interests held by the grantor and deemed vested.
2. Any *present possessory interests* in third parties: The Rule will not void any immediately present possessory interest such as a life estate, fee tail,

term of years, fee simple absolute, fee simple subject to a condition subsequent, fee simple determinable, or fee simple subject to an executory limitation to a third party.

3. Any <u>future</u> <u>interests</u> held by third persons if the interests are *vested* immediately upon creation. Hence the Rule will not void vested remainders (except for some vested remainders subject to open as explained below).

To emphasize, the Rule Against Perpetuities' potential to invalidate an interest is limited to future interests (a) in third parties (not the grantor), where (b) the third party is unascertained (cannot be named) or there is a condition precedent to the interest becoming vested.

The following three kinds of future interests,[2] then, are the ones subject to the Rule Against Perpetuities:

1. Contingent remainders (including alternative contingent remainders)
2. Executory interests (springing and shifting executory interests)
3. Vested remainders subject to open (class gifts)

The following chart is useful in identifying those interests that are and are not subject to the Rule:

Subject to RAP	Not Subject to RAP
Contingent remainder	Vested remainder[3]
Vested remainder subject to open	Vested remainder subject to divestment
Executory interest	Reversion Possibility of reverter Right of entry

---

2. A fourth classification subject to the Rule is the option to purchase. Options to purchase are commercial rights to purchase property in the future. Some courts subject options to purchase to the Rule Against Perpetuities scrutiny. Because options differ from traditional estates in land, discussion of them is postponed until later in the chapter.

3. It is sometimes said that the Rule does not apply to indefeasibly vested remainders. This statement is more like a legal conclusion that there is a person alive at the time of the effective date of the instrument, who is able to provide a measuring life and by whom one is able to prove that the remainder will vest, or not, within the period permitted by the Rule. The person vesting the interest provides, in other words, the validating life required under the Rule.

A judge applying the Rule Against Perpetuities may seem to have two personalities. At first, the judge will interpret the deed or will to establish who owns what interests and estates according to the instrument. At this stage the judge attempts to carry out the grantor's intent, resorting to the canons of construction as necessary, and to apply the other rules of law studied in the prior three chapters to determine who has vested interests and who has contingent interests.

Once the judge determines what interests and estates are created under the conveyance, the judge shifts from trying to carry out the grantor's intent to ruthlessly seeking *any* possibility that a contingent future interest violates the Rule. In this stage, the judge need find only one possible scenario, no matter how remote the possibility, in which a contingent future interest violates the Rule to void the contingent interest.

PRELIMINARY OBSERVATIONS

(a) Creation of the Interest

The last words of Professor Gray's formulation are "at the creation of the interest." When is an interest created? In an inter vivos transfer (during the grantor's lifetime) the interest is "created" when the deed creating the interest is first delivered to some third party having an interest, or to a trustee of an irrevocable trust for the benefit of a third party.[4]

Example I: O delivered a deed to A transferring Blackacre "to A for life, then to B if B survives A, otherwise to C." A's, B's, and C's interests are created when O delivers the deed to A. As a review, A has a present interest held in life estate. A's interest is vested at the creation of the interest and thus is "good" under the Rule Against Perpetuities. B and C own alternative contingent remainders, which are subject to closer scrutiny under the Rule. As you will see, the interests in this Example are "good" under the Rule Against Perpetuities since A is a life in being at the creation of the interest and it will be known no later than immediately upon A's death whether B survived A.

A grantor may create the contingent future interest in a will. Interests created in a will are "created" for purposes of the Rule Against Perpetuities at the time the testator (grantor) dies, not on the day the will is executed (signed).

---

4. Irrevocable means the grantor cannot end the trust or otherwise get the property back at her election. A revocable gift is not yet the creation of the interest since the grantor can revoke the gift or change beneficiaries at will.

Example 2: O signed her will in Year 1. Her will granted Whiteacre "to A for life, then to B and her heirs if B survives A, otherwise to C." O died in Year 12. The interests to A, B, and C were created in Year 12 for purposes of applying the Rule Against Perpetuities.

(b) Vesting Versus Possession

The next preliminary point distinguishes "vesting" and "possession." The Rule Against Perpetuities stresses vesting, not possession. Thus a vested interest that may not become possessory for a century or more is still good.

Example 1: O's will transferred Blackacre "to his wife, W, for her life, then to his son B in fee simple absolute." W has a present interest held in life estate. Present possessory interests are vested under the Rule Against Perpetuities. W's interest is "good." B's interest is a vested remainder in fee simple absolute, vested because B is ascertained and there is no condition precedent to B's vesting. Even though B's interest is vested, B's right to possess Blackacre is postponed until W's life estate ends.

Example 2: O's will transferred Blackacre "to his wife, W, for her life, then to his son B (age 10) if B lives to age 21." W has a present interest held in life estate. Present possessory interests are vested under the Rule Against Perpetuities. W's interest is "good." B's interest is a contingent remainder in fee simple absolute, contingent because B must turn 21 for his interest to vest. If and when B celebrates his 21st birthday in eleven years, his remainder in Blackacre becomes vested. Even though B's interest will be vested, B's right to possess Blackacre is postponed until W's life estate ends.

Remainders when they vest are said to be "vested in interest." In Example 1 and in Example 2 when B turned 21, for instance, B's remainder is said to be "vested in interest." Executory interests, on the other hand, "vest in possession." Since the holder of an executory interest by the nature of the interest takes when the prior interest is divested or cut short, the executory interest vests and becomes possessory simultaneously.

Example 3: O transferred Whiteacre "to A and his heirs as long as Whiteacre is used for residential purposes, then to B and her heirs." A owns a present interest held in fee simple subject to an executory limitation in favor of B. Under O's grant, B owns a shifting executory interest. The divesting event is Whiteacre's no longer being used for residential purposes. If that occurs, A's fee simple interest fails, and B's interest begins. B immediately is vested and acquires a possessory right simultaneously. (As a preview, B's executory interest is subject to the Rule Against Perpetuities and, as we will see, the Rule would void B's executory interest since White-acre may be used for residential purposes for centuries — i.e., much longer than 21 years after O, A, and B are dead — before being used for nonresidential purposes.)

The difference between *vested in interest* (remainders) and *vested in possession* (executory interests) will not change the Rule Against Perpetuities analysis. It is very important, however, to remember that a remainder can vest without becoming currently possessory.

(c) Rule Applies to Legal and Equitable Estates

The next preliminary point is that the Rule Against Perpetuities applies to all contingent future interests, both legal interests and equitable interests. The Rule, therefore, applies whether legal interests are granted directly to persons, or whether equitable interests are created by transfers to trustees to hold in trust for third-party beneficiaries.

(d) Certain Contingent Remainders to Charitable Organizations

The final preliminary point is that a gift of a present interest in one charity followed by a contingent remainder or executory interest in a second charity escapes the Rule Against Perpetuities scrutiny. This exception encourages charitable giving. The scope of the exception varies from state to state. Like contingent interests held by charitable organizations, contingent interests held by the State and its subdivisions are not subject to the Rule.

Example: O deeded Blackacre "to Local School Board, but if the land is not used for school purposes, then Blackacre shall pass to the Red Cross." The Red Cross interest is a shifting executory interest that would be invalidated by the Rule if to a noncharitable organization or individual. Because both Local School Board and Red Cross are charitable organizations, however, the Rule Against Perpetuities will not void the Red Cross' interest.

AN ANALYTICAL APPROACH

Several approaches have been advanced to apply the Rule Against Perpetuities to future contingent interests. If your professor has a favorite approach, learn it.

As a reminder, all it takes for the Rule of Perpetuities to void an interest is just one possible series of events in which the contingent interest will not vest "within 21 years of a life in being at the creation of the interest." One approach, therefore, is to imagine one scenario where the contingent interest will neither vest nor be certain to fail to vest within the relevant time period. This approach entails imagining people die at the most inopportune time, people are born who in all likelihood will never be born, or an event occurs decades after all logic dictates the event will happen in the normal course of human affairs.

Another approach is to find a person alive at the creation of the interest who either must control the reason the vesting event occurs or fails to occur, or at whose death (or within 21 years after his death) the contingent interest must vest. Such a person is called the "validating life." The validating life may be, and often is, someone named in the grant, but may be someone not named in the grant. Often overlooked by students is that the validating life may be the person owning the contingent interest itself.

Example 1:   O transferred Blackacre to A for life, then to B if and when B attains age 50. B is 12 years old. O, A, and B are lives in being. The interest to B is good since B is a life in being and we will know at or by his death whether B attained age 50. The 21 year period won't factor in the analysis.

Usually relevant persons not named in the grant control vesting by being necessary for the birth of someone described, but not named, in the grant.

Example 2:   O transferred Whiteacre "to A for life, then to B's grandchildren." Even though they are not mentioned in the grant, B's children (B's grandchildren's parents) might be the validating lives (sometimes called measuring lives) — and will be the validating lives if B is dead at the creation of the interest; more on this later.

Unless your professor directs you otherwise, follow these steps:

Step One: Determine the intended interests and estates in the original grant as written.

Example: O deeded Blackacre "to A for life, then to B if she survives A, otherwise to C." A owns a present interest in a life estate. B owns a contingent remainder in a fee simple, contingent on surviving A. C has an alternative contingent remainder, contingent on B not surviving A.

Step Two: Identify which if any of the interests are contingent remainders, executory interests, vested remainders subject to open, or options to purchase. If none, all interests are vested and therefore good under the Rule Against Perpetuities.

In the example in Step One, *A*'s life estate is vested and thus not subject to the Rule. *B*'s contingent remainder and *C*'s alternative contingent remainder are subject to the Rule Against Perpetuities scrutiny, however.

Step Three: Determine the vesting event, which is the event or events that must occur before the contingent future interest vests.

In the example in Step One, the critical event is *A*'s death and whether B survived *A*.

Step Four: Determine if the grant sets an outside number of years no greater than 21 years from the creation of the interest. (The example in Step One did not set an outside number of years). If so, the interest is good. If not, either the event clearly may occur long after all current lives in being have died and hence the contingent interest is void or, just as likely, you may need to proceed to the next step.

Example 1: O granted Blackacre "to *A* and his heirs if the bridge over Raging River is opened in the next ten years." Under the terms of the grant, O owns a fee simple subject to an executory limitation in favor of *A*. *A* owns a springing executory interest. *A*'s executory interest must be analyzed under the Rule Against Perpetuities since it is a contingent future interest. *A*'s interest is good under the Rule since the vesting event must occur within ten years of the creation of the interest, or *A*'s interest will never vest. *A*'s executory interest is valid. If the bridge opens within the ten year period, *A* takes possession and ownership of Blackacre. If the bridge is not opened at the end of ten years, *A* will never possess Blackacre under this conveyance (due to the terms of the grant, not because of the Rule Against Perpetuities).

Example 2: O granted Blackcare "to *A* and his heirs when the bridge over Raging River is opened." Under the grant, O owns a fee simple subject to an executory limitation in favor of *A*. *A* owns a springing executor interest. *A*'s executory interest must be analyzed under the Rule Against Perpetuities since it is a contingent future interest. In contrast to Example 1, *A*'s executory interest here violates the Rule Against Perpetuities because the grant does not stipulate an outside limitation on the number of years either directly or indirectly on when *A*'s interest may vest (and Steps Five and Six below don't apply). The bridge may not be opened for 100 years after O and *A* died.

Step Five: Determine if a named person is essential to the happening or nonhappening of the vesting event. If so, determine if the event must occur (or be certain to fail to occur) during that person's life (or within 21 years of her death if 21 years or less is stipulated in the original grant). If, for example, the vesting event depends on Eileen's getting married, surviving someone, reaching a certain age, opening a business, or whatever, the contingent interest will be certain to vest or fail to vest by the time Eileen dies; and hence will be "good" under the Rule.

Example 1: O granted Whiteacre "to A and her heirs if A is elected governor." O currently owns Whiteacre as a fee simple subject to an executory limitation in favor of A. A owns a springing executory interest. A's shifting executory interest must undergo scrutiny under the Rule Against Perpetuities. If A becomes governor, A divests O and becomes the new owner. We will know one way or the other during A's lifetime whether A becomes governor and her executory interest in Whiteacre vests. If A dies without becoming governor, the interest is certain to fail to vest as soon as A died. Hence, A's future executor interest is valid under the grant. All she must do now is become governor to own Whiteacre.

Example 2: O granted Whiteacre "to A and her heirs if A or any of her children are elected governor." O's and A's interests in Whiteacre are the same as in Example 1 except the divesting event is either A or one of her children becoming governor. Since "A's children" is not limited to a named person or persons, we can imagine A giving birth to an after-born daughter who outlives her mother and siblings by more than 21 years without becoming governor. That exceeds the RAP's allowed time period. Hence the Rule of Perpetuities would void A's springing executory interest. O owns Whiteacre in fee simple absolute.

Step Six: Determine if an unnamed but described person or class of persons is essential to the happening or nonhappening of the vesting event (even if all they must do is die, have children, or survive someone). The described person or persons may be the ones receiving the contingent future interest but just as likely could be a group serving as parents of the recipient group. If the critical person is described but not specifically named, there is a good chance some person not alive at the creation of the interest will fit the description, and thus the vesting event may not occur until after the perpetuities period expires.

Described but unnamed persons or classes of persons cannot be validating lives unless no one not yet born can fit into the description (i.e., the class is closed). Be careful not to rush your analysis on this one: To illustrate, A's children may be a closed group, hence validating lives, if A is already dead but not be a closed group and hence not validating lives if A is alive since A may have another child after the interest is created (more on class closings later).

Example 1: O granted Brownacre "to A for 90 years, then to whomever is the principal of Central High School at that time." A (and his heirs or assigns) own a present interest as a term of years. The principal of Central High School 90 years from now owns a contingent remainder, contingent because the principal is unascertained until *A*'s term of years ends. The contingent remainder must be analyzed under the Rule Against Perpetuities.

The present interest owners consist not only of *A* but of his heirs or assigns, at least one of whom may not be a life in being at the creation of the interest, and the person who will be principal of Central High School very likely will be someone who is not born yet. Therefore, since the term of years is for 90 years, thus it could easily exceed 21 years more than the last to die of all relevant lives in being, the attempted grant to the principal is void. Striking the invalid contingent interest from the original grant, *A* still owns a present interest, a term of years for 90 years; and O owns a reversion.

Example 2: O granted Blackacre "to *A* for 90 years, then to B's grandchildren who are alive at B's death." *A* (and his heirs or assigns) own a present interest as a term of years. B's grandchildren who are alive at B's death own a contingent remainder since they will not be ascertained until B dies. Since B's grandchildren are not named, they cannot be validating lives themselves. Even those alive at the creation of the interest may die before B and hence not become vested.

B's children, even though not named in the grant, potentially could be validating lives even though they are not named. Since B is alive, however, B's children cannot be validating lives since B can have more children after the grant (no matter how old B is at the time); therefore B's children in this example cannot be validating lives.

Luckily for B's grandchildren, B is alive and named; and B's death is the vesting event, or more specifically being B's grandchild and alive at B's death. Since B's surviving grandchildren will be ascertained and the condition precedent of surviving B met on B's death such that B's grandchildren who survive him will have vested remainders on that date, the contingent remainder to B's grandchildren is valid.

Note that B's grandchildren may all be dead before the 90 year term of years ends and hence personally may never use and enjoy Blackacre. Their interest is good under the Rule Against Perpetuities, however, because all that is required is that their interest vests. Immediate possession is not required.

Step Seven: If the contingent future interest does not vest or be certain to fail to vest immediately upon the death of a named person or of an identifiable person or class of persons essential to the vesting who are alive at the creation of the interest, use your imagination to create scenario where the contingent future interest does not vest or is sure to fail to vest within the perpetuities period. One of the more popular examples follows.

Example: O in his will devised Blackacre "to *A* and her heirs after [O] receives a Christian burial." *A*'s interest is a springing executory interest. It does not vest until O receives a Christian burial. Nothing in the devise stipulates an outside number of years, nor does it stipulate in whose lifetime the Christian burial must occur. With a little thought you imagine a series of events by which O does not receive a Christian burial within 21 years of some life in being at the creation of the interest. Here's one such scenario: O is dead already. A is alive but she might die before O receives a Christian burial because, for example, O's body might be lost in an airplane crash in the middle of the Amazon jungle. Somebody might find O's body 100 years after A's death (and the death of everyone else alive at the creation of the interest), and give him a Christian burial. Since we have imagined one possibility of A's executory interest not vesting or being certain not to vest within 21 years of a life in being, the Rule Against Perpetuities voids A's springing executory interest. A gets nothing by this devise. Blackacre instead goes to whomever gets Blackacre under O's will if the specific devise to A was never included. Sound weird? Welcome to the Rule Against Perpetuities.

Step Eight: If the Rule Against Perpetuities voids a contingent future interest, the invalidated interest is stricken from the grant. Rewrite the grant with the invalidated interest stricken and determine what interests and estates remain after the invalidated interest is omitted from the grant.

Example: O granted Blackacre "to Local School Board as long as Blackare is used for school purposes, then to B and her heirs." Under the grant, Local School Board owns a fee simple subject to an executory limitation in favor of B, the divesting event being Blackacre not being used for school purposes. B owns a shifting executory interest to become vested and possessory when Blackacre is not used for school purposes. Local School Board's interest is vested and not subject to the Rule Against Perpetuities. B's shifting executory interest, however, is subject to the Rule. Since the vesting event is not limited in time by the grant and is not tied to a life in being, we can imagine Blackacre being used for school purposes well beyond 21 years after all lives in being have died, for example 200 years, before the land is no longer used for school purposes. Consequently, the Rule Against Perpetuities voids B's executory interest. After striking B's interest, the grant reads "to Local School Board as long as Blackacre is used for school purposes." Under the grant as rewritten, Local School Board owns a fee simple determinable and O, the original grantor, owns a possibility of reverter, neither interest subject to the Rule Against Perpetuities.

UPDATED VERSIONS OF THE RULE

Based on the foregoing discussion, it is possible to restate the Rule in plainer, modern English. Here are three updated versions:

A.

Any interest, other than one in the testator, grantor, or transferor, is invalid when it might (1) vest or fail to vest as a remainder, or (2) become possessory, or not, as an executory interest, at a time more distant than 21 years after a life in being at the effective date of the transferor's instrument.

B.

No contingent remainder, executory interest, or vested remainder subject to open is valid at its creation unless it must (1) become vested in possession, become vested in interest, or become a vested remainder in a class no longer subject to open, or (2) fail by its own terms, not later than 21 years after a life in being at the time of its creation. For purposes of this Rule, the time of creation shall be the date of (1) the delivery of an inter vivos deed or (2) the death of the testator for an interest created by will, or (3) a trust's becoming irrevocable.

C.

For a contingent future interest in a transferee to be valid and enforceable, we must be able to determine on the day the interest is created that the date we'll know for certain whether the contingent future interest will vest or fail to vest is no later than twenty-one years after the death of all relevant lives in being at the creation of the interest. If a possibility exists the interest still will be contingent after that time, the interest is unenforceable and must be stricken from the grant.

PART II
APPLICATION OF THE RULE AGAINST PERPETUITIES TO SPECIFIC SITUATIONS

Following the preceding steps will resolve most Rule of Perpetuities problems. This part of the Chapter discusses the Rule in its more common applications: First off are contingent future interests dependent on the occurrence or nonoccurrence of an event.

INTERESTS DEPENDENT ON AN EVENT

The Rule Against Perpetuities is likely to invalidate a contingent interest (contingent remainder, executory interest, or vested remainder subject to open) that depends on the occurrence or nonoccurrence of an event to vest unless the event must be accomplished by a life in being, during (or within 21 years after) a life in being's life, or within a definite period of time less than 21 years. In all likelihood, all other interests dependent on the occurrence or nonoccurrence of an event will violate the rule, no matter how improbable the chances, we will not know one way or the other within the perpetuities period. When a condition is an event or act, look for a life in being — known as the validating life — who must accomplish the act, or in whose life (or no longer than 21 years after that person's life ends) the event will occur or forever be unable to occur. If there is a validating life, the contingent remainder or executory interest will be good. If there is no validating life, the future interest most likely will be invalid.

Example 1: Owen devised Blackacre "to my grandchildren alive twenty-one years after my death." This interest is valid under the Rule. The twenty-one-year period does not, for purposes of the Rule, have to be preceded by a measuring life. The interest is vested or not within the twenty-one-year component of the perpetuities period.

Example 2: Ollie devised Blackacre "to *A* for life, remainder to such of *A*'s children who attain the age of 21." *A* survived *O*. "Children" under the Rule is construed to mean "children whenever born." Hence the grant to *A*'s children in most cases is either a contingent remainder or a vested remainder subject to open. Since *A* is alive, *A* may have more children including children born more than 21 years after Ollie's death. *A*'s children's contingent remainder is valid under the Rule, however, because it will "vest" within 21 years of *A*'s death. *A* is a validating life. *A* is alive and *A*'s children must be conceived or born (allowing for post-death gestation) within *A*'s lifetime.[5] Since they must turn 21 years old within 21 years of *A*'s death, the children's future interest is good. If the grant had said "age of 22," the children's interest would be invalid. Do you see why?

Example 3: Example 3 revisits the Christian Burial example introduced earlier: *O* conveys Blackacre "to *A* for life, then to *B* and his heirs if *A* is given a Christian burial." Step one determines each person's interest as intended by the grantor. *A* has a present possessory interest held in a life estate. *O* has a reversion. Neither is subject to the Rule. *B*, however, has a springing executory interest. (*B* does not have a contingent remainder since it does not follow immediately after *A*'s life estate ends; there is a break between the time *A* dies and the time *A* is buried — or so we hope. Blackacre returns to *O* in that interim period.) Only *B*'s springing executory interest is subject to the Rule.

The Rule of Perpetuities applies to *B*'s springing executory interest. The odds against *A*'s either receiving or not receiving a Christian burial within 21 years of his death (and *O*'s and *B*'s deaths since they are lives

---

5. Fortunately, the Rule Against Perpetuities does not mandate application of science developed after 1900. So do not consider frozen embryos, cloning, time travel, or the like, as much fun as it would be to do so.

in being also) are infinitesimal. Unfortunately, the Rule is a rule of logical proof (not a rule of common sense). A judge can imagine a scenario in which *A* dies and his body is not discovered until 21 years after all lives in being have died, or in which the undertaker failed to act in the requisite time; and *A* is given a Christian burial more than 21 years after all lives in being have died. Nothing in the original grant requires *A*'s Christian burial occur within 21 years of any life in being or within 21 years of *A*'s death. In this case B's springing executory interest violates the Rule and is invalid.

Once an interest is invalid under the Rule, a judge literally will draw a line through the invalid part of the conveyance. A line would be drawn through "then to B and his heirs if *A* is given a Christian burial." What remains is "to *A* for life," with an unstated but implied reversion in 0.

Example 4: 0 conveyed Whiteacre "to Local School District so long as Whiteacre is used for a school, then to *A* and her heirs." Local School District owns a fee simple subject to an executory limitation. *A* has a shifting executory interest. Local School District's fee simple subject to an executory limitation is a present possessory interest and is not subject to the Rule. *A*'s shifting executory interest is subject to the Rule, however. Nothing in the grant requires the divesting event to occur within 21 years of a life in being. There is no validating life. Since Local School District may use Whiteacre for a school for a time lasting at least 21 years after all lives in being have died, the Rule voids *A*'s executory interest. Drawing a line through "then to *A* and her heirs" leaves a grant "to Local School District so long as Whiteacre is used for a school." After applying the Rule, Local School District has a fee simple determinable. 0 has a possibility of reverter (which is again not subject to the Rule).

Example 5: 0 conveyed Brownacre "to Local School District; but if Local School District ceases to use Brownacre for a school, to *A* and his heirs." The analysis parallels that of Example 4, but with a twist. Before applying the Rule, Local School District owns a fee simple subject to an executory limitation. *A* has a shifting executory interest. Since Local School District may use Brownacre well beyond the perpetuities period, *A*'s executory interest violates the Rule and thus is void. Drawing a line through "but if Local School District ceases to use Brownacre for a school, to *A* and his heirs" leaves a grant "to Local School District." Local School District has a fee simple absolute. Neither *A* nor 0 has any interest in Brownacre. Contrast this with the result in Example 4.

Red flag conditions and events that run afoul of the Rule are events such as "when a decedent's estate is settled," "when all the gravel is taken from the land," "when my estate is settled," "when a bridge [or building or road] is completed," "as long as used for school purposes" (or church purposes, or park purposes, or lodge purposes), and "after the next Democrat (or Republican) is elected President." Consider the next three examples:

Example 6:   O transferred Blackacre into a trust, directing his trustee to "work the gravel pit until it is exhausted, and then to sell Blackacre and distribute the proceeds to my issue then living." Because the pit possibly might be worked well beyond the perpetuities period, the grant to O's issue living at the exhaustion of and sale of Blackacre is invalid. This is sometimes called the "Magic Gravel Pit" example.

Example 7:   O devises Whiteacre "to my relatives who survive the war." The possibility exists that the war might last longer than the perpetuities period, so the entire interest of the relatives is invalid under the Rule. This is the "Interminable War" example.

Example 8:   O devised Brownacre "to my issue living at the distribution of my estate." While in all likelihood O's estate will proceed through probate and be distributed in a reasonable period of time, the grant does not stipulate an outside time limit for the distribution; and so the possibility that the administration and distribution of O's estate might not occur until well after 21 years after all lives in being have died means the devise to O's issue living at the distribution of O's estate is invalid under the Rule. Brownacre will pass to whoever receives the residuary of O's estate or, if no residuary clause, to O's heirs. This is the so-called administrative contingency or the "slothful executor" example.

Not all events can occur past the perpetuities period. If a life in being must be the one to satisfy the condition, the condition or event must happen no later than that person's death.

Example 9:   O conveyed Greenacre "to A and his heirs, but if A sells alcohol on Greenacre, to B and her heirs." A has a fee simple subject to an executory limitation, an interest not subject to the Rule. B has a shifting executory interest that is subject to the Rule. Applying the Rule, B's shifting executory interest is good since either A will sell alcohol on Greenacre during his life (in which case B gets Greenacre) or A will not sell alcohol on Greenacre during his life (in which case A can devise Greenacre or his heirs get it, and B gets nothing). A is the validating life because the condition must occur, "if at all" (the phrase used in Gray's formulation of the Rule), during A's lifetime. If the grant were changed to read "to A and his heirs, but if alcohol is ever served on Greenacre, to B and her heirs," the Rule would void B's interests since alcohol might not be sold on Greenacre until at least 21 years after all lives in being have died.

Example 10:   A Property professor funds a trust with $10,000, to be paid to the first person in her current Property class who becomes a U.S. senator. The trustees have legal title and each person in the class — used in two senses here since the gift is a "class gift" — has an opportunity to claim the $10,000 by becoming a U.S. senator. Every student in the current class is a validating life. Since we will know at least by the death of the last student in the class whether any one became a U.S. senator, the gift is valid under the Rule. The probability that any student in the class will become a senator is irrelevant; only the certainty that we can tell one way or the other during the lives in being matters.

Example 11:   Contrast Example 10 with these facts: A Property professor funds a trust with $10,000 to be paid "to the first student who ever was or ever will be enrolled in my Property class who becomes a U.S. Senator." In this case none of the students qualifies as a validating life since the students who can be named may all die and someday a person not yet born on the day of the grant will become a student and live well past 21 years after all lives in being have died. It is possible, for example, that a person, X, may be born a year after the trust is established, thus not a life in being, and enroll in the professor's Property class 25 years later. Then at least 21 years after the last of the professor and all her Property students who were lives in being at the creation of the trust died, student X, who was not a life in being, may be elected U.S. senator, or may live another 50 years without holding any office. Since we might not know at the end of the perpetuities period whether anyone was vested, the interest is invalid. The Property professor gets her money back.

This example helps transition to the next common application: A grantee described but not named in the grant.

GRANTEES IDENTIFIED BY DESCRIPTION RATHER THAN NAMED

A second scenario that raises Rule Against Perpetuities concerns occurs when a measuring life or a recipient of a contingent remainder or executory interest is described by a label rather than a name. The rub comes because a person who was not a life in being at the creation of the interest can fit the description. The most troublesome situation arises when some person already seems to fit the description, and likely will be the person to fit the description, but a remote chance exists that some other person ultimately might be the one described. A famous example in this category is the unborn widow — or, as some today might call it, the Anna Nicole Smith example.[6]

Example 1: **The Unborn Widow:** O conveys Blackacre "to *A* for life, then to *A*'s widow, if any, for life, then to *A*'s issue then living." This is an understandable grant, especially if *A* is married at the time of the grant. Unfortunately, *A*'s current spouse may not be *A*'s widow, and the person who will be *A*'s widow may not even be a life in being at the creation of the interest. *A*, for example, may divorce or become widowed himself, and many years later may marry someone who had not been born at the time of the original grant. *A* has a present interest held in a life estate not subject to the Rule. *A*'s widow has a contingent remainder in a life estate, contingent on being identified: we must wait until *A*'s death to identify *A*'s widow. "*A*'s issue then living" also own a contingent remainder, contingent on being ascertained and alive when *A*'s widow dies.

A's widow's contingent remainder is valid under the Rule. *A*'s widow (if he has one) will be identified immediately upon *A*'s death, and once identified her interest is vested. *A* is the validating life for his widow's interest. *A* was a life in being at the creation of the interest so *A*'s widow's interest will be vested well within the perpetuities period. If *A* dies without a widow, that fact is known at *A*'s death also.

The contingent remainder in *A*'s issue then living at *A*'s widow's death, on the other hand, fails to satisfy the Rule. *A*'s issue then living must satisfy two contingencies. First, *A*'s children must be identified, which they will be by *A*'s death (or nine months thereafter), so that causes no RAP problem. Second, the children must survive *A*'s widow. *A*'s widow is not a validating life since she might not have been a life in being at the creation of the interest. It is possible to imagine that *A* will divorce his current spouse, then 30 years later marry a woman who was not born when the interest was created. All of *A*'s children from his first wife may die. *A* and his new spouse may have children, also not lives in being at the creation of the children's contingent remainder. Then *A* dies (finally), leaving a widow and children, none of whom were lives in being at the creation of the children's contingent remainder. *A*'s widow easily might live another 21-plus years, so it is possible we will not know within the perpetuities

6. When Anna Nicole Smith married Howard Marshall in 1994, she was 63 years younger than he was on the date of his marriage. Such marriages do not happen very often — but their frequency is irrelevant to the Rule. Such a marriage could happen and when they do, the Rule assumes that the Howard Marshalls of this world are fertile — an assumption known often as the "fertile octogenarian" rule — and might conceive a child on the wedding night and die the next day. See Marshall v. Marshall, 126 Sup. Ct. 1735 (2006).

period which of *A*'s children survive *A*'s widow. *A*'s children's contingent interest, therefore, is invalid under the Rule.

Drawing a line through "then to *A*'s children then living," the remaining grant as rewritten reads, "to *A* for life, then to *A*'s widow, if any, for life." *A* has a present interest held in a life estate, *A*'s widow has a contingent remainder held in a life estate, and *O* has a reversion (not subject to the Rule).

The unborn widow example is but one of several types of daydreams that can void an interest under the Rule. It relies on the assumption that any living person, no matter how old, could marry at any age and then could have a child.

Example 2: *O* conveys Whiteacre "to *A* for life, then to *A*'s children for life, and at the death of all of *A*'s children, to the principal of City High School." *A* owns a life estate, which is a present possessory interest not subject to the Rule. *A*'s children have either a contingent remainder (if none alive) or a vested remainder subject to open (if at least one is alive). Because all of *A*'s children become vested no later than *A*'s death (or nine months after *A*'s death), *A*'s children's remainder is valid. The grant to the City High School principal is invalid, however. The contingent remainder to the principal of City High School depends on someone holding that position at the last to die of *A*'s children. Since the principal and the last to die of *A*'s children may not be lives in being at the creation of the interest, and both may outlive all lives in being by at least 21 years, the Rule of Perpetuities invalidates the remainder to the principal. Drawing a line through "and at the death of all of *A*'s children, to the principal of City High School," the remaining grant as rewritten gives *A* a life estate, and *A*'s children a contingent remainder in life estates. Since someone must take after the two life estates, *O* owns a reversion.

Labels such as husband, wife, widow, mayor, minister, president, and so on, present similar difficulties under the Rule. When testing interests held by a person identified by or following an interest held by a person identified by a descriptive label, separate the possible ultimate recipient from the identifiable person currently wearing the label.

VESTED REMAINDERS SUBJECT TO OPEN (CLASS GIFTS)

Vested remainders subject to open are grants to more than one person (a class gift), where the recipients are identified by description rather than named, and/or at times must satisfy a condition precedent. As soon as one person in the class is identified and satisfies any condition precedent, that person's interest becomes vested. The interests of the remaining people in the class may still be contingent, however. Vested remainders subject to open are considered to be contingent interests for purposes of the Rule Against Perpetuities.

The Rule against Perpetuities is harsh on class gifts: All persons receiving a class gift must pass muster under the Rule or no member's interest can be good. Professor Dukeminier called this special rule "the all-or-nothing rule." Instead of holding the class is vested if any one of the class members becomes vested, or holding that the interest of any member in the class whose interest is sure to vest (or sure to fail to vest) within the perpetuities period is valid even if other members' or prospective members' interests are not, the Rule demands each and every person in the class be certain to vest (or certain to fail to vest) within the perpetuities period or everyone in the class loses. If even one *potential* member of the class can be identified or envisioned who will not vest (or fail to vest) within the required period, the grant to the entire class fails and is void.

Example 1: O conveyed Blackacre "to A for life, then to B's children who attain age 35." B is alive and has one child, C, age 6. A has a present interest held in a life estate — not subject to the Rule. B's children (C and any child born to B in the future) have a contingent remainder, contingent on being identified and on attaining age 35 — so subject to the Rule. O has a reversion — not subject to the Rule. Thus the contingent remainder to B's children is subject to the Rule's analysis.

The contingent remainder to B's children is a class gift. All of B's children (living and potential children) are members of the class; each child to take must reach age 35. C is alive (and hence a life in being) and we will know whether C reaches age 35 on or before his death, but the test is not whether one member will vest or fail to vest within the time period, or whether one member of the class is a "life in being," or whether we can envision one scenario where all members vest or fail to vest in time. The test is, can we imagine or dream up one scenario, however improbable, in which we will not know within 21 years of all lives in being whether all potential members of the class will vest or fail to vest? Yes, we can envision a chain of events where we will not know within 21 years of a life in being whether all of B's children either will or will not reach age 35. B could have another child, X, not a life in being at the creation of the contingent remainder. O, A, B, and C (all the relevant lives in being) could die soon after X is born. Since X is not even one year old when all relevant lives in being die, we will not know in 21 years whether X reaches age 35. The contingent remainder "to B's children who attain age 35," therefore, violates the Rule and is void. B's children's interest is struck from the grant. After B's children's contingent remainder is stricken from the grant, A has a life estate, and O has a reversion.

Example 2: O conveyed Whiteacre "to *A* for life, then to B's children in fee simple, provided if any of B's children fail to attain 35 that child's interest passes to B's surviving children." B is alive and has one child, C, age 6. As in Example 1, *A* has a present interest held in a life estate not subject to the Rule. C has a vested remainder subject to open (partial divestment) if *A* has more children, and subject to complete divestment if C does not reach age 35. Vested remainders subject to open must undergo the Rule Against Perpetuities analysis. Attaining age 35 in this example is a *condition subsequent* potentially divesting a child's interest; it is not a *condition precedent* to taking an interest. Since we will know at B's death who B's children are (B cannot have a child after his death),[7] B's children's interest will vest no later than B's death. At that point, B's children will have a vested remainder subject to an executory limitation. Thus the remainder to B's children is valid under the Rule. While the conveyances in Examples 1 and 2 may be alternative wordings to achieve the transferor's intent, the conveyance in Example 2 succeeds while the one in Example 1 fails to accomplish the transferor's goals.

Here is more to go, however. The original transfer in Example 2, before applying the Rule, divests the vested interest of any child who does not attain age 35. Any divested interest passes to B's surviving children, if any, who therefore have a shifting executory interest in any divested interest. The shifting executory interest is subject to the Rule. It fails to satisfy the Rule in this example. The reasoning: B may have another child and after every life in being (O, *A*, B, and C) dies, we still might not know if that child's interest will pass to the heirs of B's children who did reach age 35. The executory interests are void and must be deleted from the grant. After deleting the offending language, the conveyance reads, "to *A* for life, then to B's children in fee simple." *A* has a life estate; B's children have a vested remainder in fee simple absolute. The divesting condition disappears.

INTERGENERATIONAL FAMILY TRANSFERS

A special situation involving class gifts concerns the intergenerational family transfer. Overly simplified, the Rule Against Perpetuities allows a grantor to control ownership of property "from the grave" for persons he knew plus one generation, while not allowing control beyond that generation. Thus the Rule prevents a person from devising property to his children for life, to his grandchildren for life, to his grandchildren's children for life, and so on for centuries.

---

7. Recall that a child in gestation is considered born for purposes of the Rule.

Class gifts are evaluated on an all-or-nothing rule. If any one of the potential persons of the class possibly will not vest (or fail to vest) within the perpetuities period, the grant to every member of the class fails. Generally, the contingent interest granted to the first class (if it is the first generation) of persons will not violate the Rule (unless there is another condition precedent other than then being ascertained or born), but any contingent interest to a class in the next generation or any subsequent generation likely will violate the Rule. Stated another way, if the parents (the first generation) of a designated class of beneficiaries (the second generation) are themselves a class that someday may include a person who was not a life in being at the creation of the contingent interest, the contingent interest to the designated class of beneficiaries (the second generation) very likely violates the Rule Against Perpetuities.

Example 1: O devised Blackacre "to his son A for life, then to A's children for life, then to A's grandchildren in fee simple." A has no children. A in this devise owns a present interest held in a life estate that is not subject to the Rule. A's children have a contingent remainder held in a life estate, contingent on being born; and A's grandchildren have a contingent remainder held in fee simple absolute, again contingent on being born. The last two interests are contingent remainders subject to the Rule Against Perpetuities. The first, the grant to A's children is valid since we will know at A's death whether A had any children and who they are. A is the validating life for A's children's interest. The class of A's children closes biologically immediately on A's death.[8]

The interest in A's grandchildren, on the other hand, violates the Rule. The members of the class can be increased by A's children having children. "A's children" (or any of them) cannot be validating lives since an after-born child can become a member of the class of "A's children." In one scenario, for example, A could have a child, X, who was not a life in being at the creation of the interest. A could die suddenly. X may not have a child until more than 21 years after A dies. Since under this scenario we will not know whether the interest to A's grandchildren will vest until after the perpetuities period ends, the entire contingent remainder to A's grandchildren fails (under the all-or-nothing rule). The transfer to A's grandchildren fails because the class of persons who can give birth to new members of the class itself can grow to include persons who were not lives in being at the creation of the interest.

Finally, after striking out the grandchildren's interest, the devise is rewritten as O devises Blackacre "to his son A for life, then to A's children for life." A has a present interest held in a life estate, A's children have a

---

8. For more on class closings biologically and by the rule of convenience, see supra, Chapter 10.

contingent remainder held in a life estate (contingent on being born), and O's heirs or devisees have a reversion.

Example 2:   O conveyed Whiteacre "to *A* for life, then to *A*'s children for life, then to B's grandchildren." *A* and B are both alive and childless. O intended to give *A* a present interest held in a life estate, *A*'s children a contingent remainder held in a life estate, contingent on *A*'s having children, and a contingent remainder held in fee simple absolute to B's grandchildren, contingent on B's grandchildren being born (no survivorship requirement). Under the Rule, the interests given to *A* and to *A*'s children are valid: as to *A* because he is already vested, and as to *A*'s children because we will know at *A*'s death whether *A* had any children (and who they are). B's grandchildren's contingent remainder, contingent on B's grandchildren being born, violates the Rule, however. The group that can increase the members of the class of B's grandchildren are B's children. Since B is alive she may have one or more children, none of whom would be lives in being at the creation of the interest. Neither B nor B's children are validating lives. B's after-born children could live at least 21 years after the last to die of *A*, B, and O, before procreating any of B's grandchildren. The contingent remainder to B's grandchildren, therefore, is invalid under the Rule since it is possible a grandchild may be born after the perpetuities period has run. By drawing a line through "then to B's grandchildren," the grant is "to *A* for life, then to *A*'s children for life." *A* has life estate, *A*'s children have a vested remainder held in a life estate, and O has a reversion. B's grandchildren have no interest in Whiteacre.

Not all grants to grandchildren are invalid, however. Sometimes a descriptive class can be the validating lives if no after-born person can enter the class. Compare the above Example with the following:

Example 3:   O conveyed Greenacre "to *A* for life, then to *A*'s children for life, then to B's grandchildren." *A* is alive; B is dead, survived by two children, C and D. As in the prior example, *A*'s life estate and *A*'s children's contingent remainder are valid under the Rule. Before applying the Rule, B's grandchildren have a contingent remainder in fee simple absolute, contingent on being born. The class of individuals that can procreate and so add more people to the class of B's grandchildren are B's children. In contrast to the prior example, when B herself could have more children, here B, being dead, cannot have any more children. Thus the class of B's children is fixed at two children, C and D, both of whom are lives in being at the creation of the interest. C and D are validating lives. Since we will know whether B had any grandchildren, and who they are, no later than the death of the last to die of C and D, B's grandchildren's contingent remainder will vest at that time if B has any grandchildren, or never vest if B has no grandchildren by that time. The contingent remainder in B's grandchildren is valid.

EFFECT OF CLASS CLOSING RULES ON INTERGENERATIONAL TRANSFERS

As explained in Chapter 10, classes can close physiologically (naturally or biologically) or by the Rule of Convenience. A class closes *physiologically* whenever no one else can enter the class; usually this means, be born into the class. The preceding three examples illustrate a class closing physiologically. No new child could enter a class after the potential parents and grandparents died. A class closes pursuant to the **Rule of Convenience** when any member of the class can demand possession of the property. See supra, Chapter 10, for a fuller explanation.

Closing a class does not end the inquiry. Even though a class closes, either physiologically or by the Rule of Convenience, the contingent interests of all persons who comprise the class must be certain to vest (or fail to vest) within the perpetuities period. If the contingent interest of just one member of the class is not certain to satisfy the Rule Against Perpetuities, the grant to everyone in the class fails. That bears reiterating: All it takes is one member or hypothetical member of a class to fail to satisfy the Rule Against Perpetuities for the grant to the class to fail, even to those members already vested. This can happen by the class remaining open past the perpetuities period. In addition, it can happen even if the class is closed, if the members cannot satisfy a condition precedent within the perpetuities period.

Example 1: Owen conveyed Blackacre "to Abby for life, then to such of Abby's children then living." Abby's children own a contingent remainder, contingent on being alive at Abby's death. The contingent remainder is subject to the Rule Against Perpetuites. Abby is a life in being — i.e., alive at the effective date of the conveyance, so there is no need for the 21-year period of the Rule (Abby being the validating life) since the remainder will vest or fail at the end of Abby's life.

Example 2: O devised Blackacre "to A for life, then to B's children who attain age 20." B has no children. O intended A to have a life estate and B's children to have a contingent remainder, contingent on attaining age 20. Applying the Rule Against Perpetuities, A's life estate is valid since it is a present interest. Likewise, the contingent remainder to B's children who attain age 20 is good. B is the validating life. The class of B's children — the class is B's children, not B's children who attain age 20 — closes *physiologically* when B dies, and will all reach or fail to attain age 20 within 21 years of B's death. Hence, B's children's contingent remainder is valid.

The class may close before B's death. If B is still alive, the class of B's children can close by the Rule of Convenience at the later of A's death or after A's death when at least one of B's children has turned 20. That is because the class closes when one member of the class can demand distribution; in this case when a child turns 20. Only B's children alive when the class closes can receive anything from the grant (the children are not required to have to met the condition precedent; only to be alive, to be a member of the class); B's after-born children if any get nothing. Any member of the class who satisfies the condition precedent of attaining age 20 will share in the ownership of Blackacre.

Example 3: O devised Whiteacre "to A for life, then to B's children who attain age 30." B has no children. The only difference between this and the prior example is that in this example B's children must attain age 30. Because of this difference, however, the contingent remainder to B's children fails. B is not a validating life. The class may close when B dies but the contingency of attaining age 30 presents an insurmountable obstacle. B may die the day her youngest child is born, and A may also die that day. In 21 years B's youngest child may be 21, but it will still be uncertain whether the child will attain age 30. RAP does not tolerate uncertainty. B's children's interest fails. Drawing a line through the interest to B's children, A has a life estate, and O's heirs or devisees have a vested remainder in fee simple absolute.

Example 4: Same facts as in Example 3, except B has two children, K, age 33, and L, age 28, when the devise is effective at O's death. Before applying the RAP, K has a vested remainder subject to open and L has a shifting executory interest becoming possessory if L turns 30. Applying the Rule, the interest to B's children is invalid. The reason is the class of B's children does not close until either A or B dies. Once the class closes, the last person — living or hypothetical — to enter the class must satisfy the condition precedent within the perpetuities period. An invalidating scenario envisions B having another child, X, who was not a life in being at the creation of the interest, while A, B, K, and L die soon after X is born. In that case we won't know for certain within 21 years whether one-year-old X will reach age 30. Hence the gift to the entire class of B's children fails, even though one member already satisfies the condition precedent, and one will or will not do so within a couple of years. Drawing a line through the interest given to B's children, A has a life estate, and O's heirs or devisees have a vested remainder in fee simple absolute.

Example 5: O devised Brownacre to A for life, then to B's children who attain age 30. B is dead, survived by K, age 33, L, age 28, and M, age 15. The class is closed physiologically since B, the parent, is dead. Since we will know within 21 years of lives in being (K, L, and M are all lives in being so we will know during their lives in being) which of B's children attain age 30, the vested remainder subject to open is valid.

Example 6: Same facts as in Example 5, except M is age 3. The vested remainder subject to open is still valid. The class is closed physiologically because B is dead, and all three children (K, L, and M) were lives in being at the creation of the interest. So we will know at or before the last of B's children to die whether they attain age 30. B's children themselves are the validating lives. No more children can enter the class. Recall that the perpetuity period is 21 years after all lives in being have died, which includes three-year-old M.

Example 7: Same facts as Example 5, except B is alive and *A* is dead when O's devise becomes effective. The grant to B's children is valid. Since K is age 33 and thus meets the condition precedent, K has a vested interest. A second consequence of K's being vested is that at the end of *A*'s life estate (which never began here since *A* predeceased O), K can demand distribution of her share of Brownacre to own in fee simple subject to partial divestment if her siblings attain age 30. Under the Rule of Convenience, since K can demand distribution, the class of B's children closes. If B has another child, that after-born child cannot share in Brownacre. Once the class closes, the question becomes whether we are certain to know within 21 years of a life in being if all the members of the class will reach age 30. Since all the members in the class of B's children in this Example are lives in being — and are validating lives since the class is closed — we will know within seconds of the last to die of K, L, or M which of B's children reached age 30. The grant to B's children is valid.

COMMERCIAL OPTIONS

Early Rule Against Perpetuities issues centered on intergenerational transfers. Interests frequently challenged under the Rule today are options and rights of first refusal. A person may sell land, for example, and stipulate that if the purchaser ever finds a buyer for the property, the original seller has the right to repurchase the land for the price offered by the third party. The seller here has a right of first refusal. It is possible no buyer will be found until after all lives in being have been dead for at least 21 years. Alternatively, a person may acquire an option to purchase land without an outside time limit on the right to exercise the option.

Some commentators dislike extending the Rule to options, favoring instead a more direct inquiry into whether the option is an unreasonable restraint on alienation. Such a restraint is concerned with the duration of an interest. RAP, on the other hand, is concerned not with an interest's duration, but whether or not it vests beyond the perpetuity period. RAP is not a Rule that voids interests that last too long, but instead voids interests that vest too remotely. Nonetheless, many courts have concluded that an option to purchase is a property interest akin to a springing or shifting executory interest; therefore, they invalidate options to purchase that have no expiration date. Most courts relying on the Rule will not imply a reasonable time period in the agreement, using instead the 21-year period allowed by the Rule. Other courts have refused to extend RAP to options and rights to repurchase.

Example 1: In a state that subjects options to the Rule Against Perpetuities, O gives A the option to purchase Blackacre for $100,000, the option to be good for six months after the State Highway Department completes the Lane Road Bridge over Green River. Since the state may not complete the bridge over Green River within 21 years of any lives in being, the option violates the Rule.

Example 2: Ozzie granted "to Acme Corporation an option to purchase Blackacre when its appraised value is greater than $1,000,000 an acre." Is the option to purchase held by a "life in being"? No. Although Acme Corporation is a legal entity with many useful purposes in our legal system, it is not a "life in being." Such a life must be that of a natural person. So the perpetuities period as to the option, is 21 years, measured in gross, and because the possibility exists that the appraised value won't rise this much over the perpetuities period, the interest is invalid. Ozzie could also become the validating life, but he might die the day after the conveyance, leaving the option to be exercised 22 years later, so with him, the interest is also invalid.

Good drafting can save an option or right of first refusal from a RAP challenge. First, a drafter can establish a time period of less than 21 years in which the holder of the interest can exercise the option or right. Second, the optionee can be given the sole right to exercise the option or right, specifying that it is not exercisable by the optionee's heirs, assigns, or successors. Third, the option or right can be exercisable only by named persons, such as the president of the optionee corporation or other legal entity. Fourth, the option or right can be subject to termination at regular intervals, each of which is within the gross period of the Rule (called the savings clause).

STATUTORY REFORMS OF THE RULE

The Rule Against Perpetuities in its pure form remains the law in a handful of jurisdictions. Some six states have abolished it. Most of these substituted a statutory provision prohibiting unreasonable restraints on alienation instead. In addition, some states have modified the Rule substantially.

(a) The Wait-and-See Doctrine

Wait-and-see means what it says. It changes the inquiry from what may happen to what did happen. First, an interest is found — or not found — to violate the Rule Against Perpetuities in its common law form. Second, if a violation is found, then the courts await the end of the perpetuities period set up in the instrument — deed, will, or trust — to see what actually are the facts at the end of the period. Courts thus use actual facts, not possible ones, permitting consideration of facts arising after the creation of the challenged interest. With an "actual fact" test to apply, if the contingent interest vests by the end of the traditional Rule Against Perpetuities period, the interest is good and enforceable — if not, it is invalid and a declaration of invalidity is available. The wait-and-see doctrine was introduced into the law both by statute and judicial decision and has, since the 1960s, reduced the number of reported RAP cases dramatically. About a dozen states today have adopted some form of this doctrine.

> **Example:** O devised Blackacre "to A for life, remainder to A's children reaching age 25." A is alive. A's children X and Y are ages 10 and 2 respectively. Under the traditional Rule, the contingent remainder to A's children X and Y would be void since we can envision A giving birth to another child, Z, and A, X and Y dying one day after Z is born. Since we won't know within 21 years whether Z reaches age 25, the contingent remainder to A's children would be void. In contrast, under the Wait-and-See doctrine, the parties wait to see if X or Y (or any other child of A) reaches age 25 within 21 years after the last to die of A, X, or Y. In most cases A's children would be in their 40s, 50s, or 60s by the time their parent A died and so that their interests had vested years earlier. Only if A died with a child (or children) under the age of 4 (and no other living children) would the contingent remainder not be able to vest within 21 years (it could of course fail to vest if the child died before reaching age 25). If A died with at least one child who was alive at the creation of the interest, however, even a child under the age of 4 may reach age 25 during a life in being since the sibling was a life in being.

(b) The Uniform Statutory Rule Against Perpetuities

A second wave of RAP reform followed the introduction of the Wait-and-See doctrine. Twenty-two states have adopted a statutory approach set out in the Uniform Statutory Rule Against Perpetuities (USRAP), promulgated in 1986 by the Commissioners on Uniform State Laws, and made part of the Uniform Probate Code. Under USRAP, a court will wait and see what happens instead of imagining one scenario under which the Rule would be violated. If the interest vests (or it becomes certain the interest will never

205

vest) within the waiting period, the interest is valid; otherwise, it is not. Unlike the Wait-and-See doctrine, however, the waiting period under USRAP is a definite period of time — usually a period of 90 years — at the end of which the "actual fact" test is applied. In contrast to the Wait-and-See example above, *A*'s only child under the age of 4 could be able to satisfy the Rule Against Perpetuities under USRAP if she reaches age 25.

Thus the Wait-and-See doctrine and USRAP both use a cumulative approach to reform: the interest that is challenged and found void under the common law RAP is given a second chance and evaluated under the Wait-and-See doctrine in either its basic or USRAP form. Kentucky, Mississippi, New Hampshire, Ohio, Pennsylvania, Rhode Island, and Vermont still use the Wait-and-See doctrine in its original form. Many other states that had adopted that form have since switched to the 90 year, USRAP version, finding it easier to apply.

(c) The Cy Pres Doctrine

In a few states, a court will also reform an instrument to validate contingent interests, attempting to carry out the transferor's intent in a way that does not violate the Rule Against Perpetuities. Cy Pres mean "as near as possible" in Latin and so provides a judicially applied rule of construction, not a rule of law. As such, this equitable doctrine is used to construe the transferor's intent so as to save, rather than to destroy, the challenged interest.

(d) The Rule and Trust Law

Creating a trust separates the legal from the equitable title to property. The trust agreement conveys the legal title of designated real or personal property to a trustee (either a natural person or the trust department of a bank), and the equitable title to a person or persons who benefit from the trust, known as its beneficiaries. A trustee is a fiduciary. Property held in trust is known as trust property, or the *corpus* or *res* of the trust. Property in trust may be added to over time by the person creating the trust — known as the settlor. A trust may be created inter vivos or by will at death. Some of the strongest advocates for reforming the common law Rule Against Perpetuities have been the trusts and estates departments of banks and the law firms that counsel them. The express trust is useful to convert wealth and to transfer it from generation to generation. Typically, the res of a trust is stocks, bonds, or other financial instruments. Here the Rule gets in the way.

One method of reform is to abolish the Rule as it applies to trusts. Another is to establish a perpetuities period for trusts that is a fixed number of years — sometimes so long that the trusts permitted as a result are known as "**dynasty trusts**."[9] About one-fourth of the states have modified the Rule to exempt dynasty trusts from the Rule if the power to alienate the trust property is not suspended beyond the new perpetuities period. Some states permit trusts to last a long time (1000 years in Colorado and Utah; 360 years in Florida and Nevada; 150 years in Virginia, Ohio, and a few other states). The Rule in these states still applies to legal estates, but not to equitable interests held in a trust.

Estate tax problems aside, there are several reasons for wealthy persons to use trusts. First, trustees are usually sophisticated investors of a trust's assets, swelling their value over the long term. Second, few restraints on the alienation of trust assets by a trustee exist. Third, assets held together grow over time at a rate often exceeding assets without such continuity. Finally, a beneficiary's ability to withdraw some trust assets annually further makes an equitable interest in a trust more like ownership.

(e) Generation-Based Perpetuity Period

The American Law Institute (ALI) in its Restatement (Third) of Property proposal concluded the "mechanism embodied in the common-law Rule was ill-chosen." The ALI also condemned the trend toward lengthening the statutory perpetuities period to hundreds of years as "ill-advised." The ALI emphasized a "rule that curbs excessive dead-hand control is deeply rooted in this nation's history and tradition, and for good reason." The ALI prefers a new Rule Against Perpetuities, one that does not rely on "lives in being," favoring instead a "generation-based perpetuity period." The ALI's proposed Rule "limits dead-hand control to granting benefits through but not beyond two generations younger than the transferor." The proposed Rule also switches the Rule's focus from the time of vesting to when a trust or other donative disposition terminates by requiring the trust or other donative disposition to terminate on or before the end of the perpetuity period. The perpetuity period ends on the death of the last measuring life. The measuring lives are the transferor and beneficiaries of the transferor who are no more than the equivalent of two generations younger than the transferor. A trust or other donative disposition that runs afoul of the perpetuity period is not void but is subject to judicial modification in a manner that "most closely approximates the transferor's manifested plan of

---

9. While best explained in a study of estate and gift taxation, the reform of the Rule, the rise of these trusts, and amendments to the federal estate provisions of the Internal Revenue Code are intertwined in numerous ways. Attempts to tax so-called generation-skipping trusts have occurred alongside RAP reforms.

distribution and is within" the Rule's perpetuity period (i.e., similar to the Cy Pres doctrine discussed above).

Example: O devised property to trustee T in trust to pay income "to my son A for life, then to A's children for their respective lives, and on the death of A's last surviving child to distribute the principal of the trust to A's then-living descendants." At O's death, A had two children B-1 and B-2, and no other descendants. A's third child, B-3, was born after O's death. A, A's spouse, B-1, and B-2 died soon after B-3 was born.

Under the traditional Rule Against Perpetuities analysis, the contingent remainder in "A's then-living descendants" would be void since we could imagine, as actually occurred in this Example that A has another child (B-3), who could outlive all the lives in being at the creation of the interest by more than 21 years so that it would still be unknown at the end of the perpetuities period which, if any, of A's descendants would survive A's child, B-3. Likewise it is very likely the interest to A's descendants then surviving would also fail under the Wait-and-See approach since B-3 most likely would live past the end of the 21-year perpetuities period. While the USRAP's 90-year period may save the day, it is possible B-3 would live another 90 years.

The ALI Restatement's proposed Rule changes the focus from "lives in being" to "measuring lives" — i.e., beneficiaries who are no more than two generations younger than the transferor. A's child B-3, even though she was not a life in being, qualifies as a measuring life under the generation-based perpetuity period approach. Since A's descendants who survive B-3 will be known at B-3's death, the contingent remainder to A's then-living descendants is valid.

Examples

Unless otherwise stated, assume the common law Rule of Perpetuities applies to the following Examples.

Grandpa's Class Gift

1. O executed a will six years ago, devising Blackacre to A for life, then to A's children for their lives, then to A's grandchildren. At the time, O, A, and A's two children (L and M) are alive.

   O died this year. A died two years before O's death, survived by L, M, and A's newborn daughter, P, and one grandchild, R.
   (a) Who are the lives in being at the creation of the interest?
   (b) Are the devised interests valid under the Rule Against Perpetuities?
   (c) What result if A were alive at O's death?

Another Grandpa Story

2. O devised Greenacre "to A for life, then to A's children for their lives, then to A's grandchildren living at the death of A's last surviving child." At O's death, A and his two children, X and Y, are living. Is the Rule Against Perpetuities violated by this devise?

The Big Event

3. (a) O conveyed Whiteacre "to A and his heirs so long as a commercial use is not made of the property, and, if it is used for a commercial purpose, then to B and her heirs." How does this grant fare under a Rule Against Perpetuities analysis?

   (b) What result if O's grant was "to A and his heirs; but if used for commercial purposes, to B and her heirs"?

   (c) What result if O's grant is to "to A and his heirs so long as A does not use Whiteacre for commercial purposes, and if A uses Whiteacre for a commercial purpose, then to B and her heirs"?

RAP Session

4. (a) O conveyed Blackacre "to A for life so long as A uses Blackacre as a residence, then to B and her heirs, but if liquor is sold there, to C and her heirs." Do B's and C's interests violate the Rule Against Perpetuities?

   (b) O conveyed Brownacre "to A for life, then 30 years after A dies, to B and his heirs." B dies, leaving C as his heir. Does B's interest violate the Rule Against Perpetuities?

   (c) O conveyed Whiteacre "to A for life, then to A's children for their lives, then to B." Is B's future interest valid under the Rule Against Perpetuities?

   (d) O, in his will, devised Redacre "to my grandchildren who attain age 21." O is survived by his son, A, but no grandchildren. Is the grant to O's grandchildren valid?

   (e) O while alive conveyed Greenacre "to such of my grandchildren who attain 21." O has one child, A, and one grandchild, GC. Is this interest valid under the Rule Against Perpetuities?

Wait and See

5. Assume the following occur in a wait-and-see jurisdiction:

   (a) O devises Blackacre to "to A for life, remainder to A's child first reaching the age of 25." A has no children either at O's death or at A's death. The remainder to A's child would be void under the common law Rule Against Perpetuities. How does it fare in a jurisdiction with a wait-and-see statute?

(b) What if, in the devise in (a), *A*'s only child is born after the interest is created, and is three years old at *A*'s death? Is the remainder valid in a wait-and-see jurisdiction?

(c) What if *A* died and is survived by his two children born after O died, two-year-old B and four-year-old C? C soon thereafter dies. Is the gift valid in a wait-and-see jurisdiction?

(d) What if, in (c), it was C rather than B who died just after *A*'s death?

(e) On January 1, Year 1, O conveys Whiteacre "to *A* and his heirs so long as a commercial use is not made of the property, and if it is used for a commercial purpose, then to B and her heirs." What result in a wait-and-see jurisdiction?

Explanations

Grandpa's Class Gift

1. (a) A will becomes operational upon the testator's death. Until that time the will can be revoked or amended, and the owner can sell, assign, or gift any property mentioned in the will. The interests, therefore, were created at the time of O's death, rather than when O executed his will six years previously. The lives in being at the time of the death were L, M, P, and R. O and *A* were both dead and thus not lives in being at the creation of the interests.

(b) Step one is to determine what interests O intended his will to create. Since *A* is dead, under the will, *A*'s children, L, M, and P, have vested possessory life estates and *A*'s grandchild, R, has vested remainder subject to open in fee simple absolute. The possessory life estates are vested and thus not subject to the Rule Against Perpetuities. The vested remainder subject to open must be tested by the Rule Against Perpetuities since it is a class gift and every member of the class must satisfy the Rule for the class gift to be good: a class gift passes or fails as a unit.

As tested, the class gift to *A*'s grandchildren is good. The validating lives are *A*'s children since we must know at their deaths who their children are. *A*'s children were lives in being at the creation of the interest (i.e., at O's death) and no more children can be born to *A* and added to the class of *A*'s children. The class of *A*'s grandchildren closes physiologically when the last of *A*'s children dies. Since the class of *A*'s grandchildren closes at the last to die of *A*'s children, the gift to *A*'s grandchildren is good.

(c) R's vested remainder subject to open and any executory interest in future-born *A*'s grandchildren violate the Rule Against Perpetuities if *A* is alive at O's death. O intended a life estate in *A*, a vested remainder subject to open in life estate in *A*'s children, and a vested remainder subject to open in fee simple to R and A's other grandchildren when born. The gift to A is valid since A owns a possessory life estate. The vested remainder subject to open in A's children is valid since the class of A's children closes physiologically and by the Rule of Convenience when A dies, and it becomes both possessory and vested immediately upon A's death. A is the validating life.

The vested remainder subject to open in A's grandchildren, including R, is invalid, however. An interest is invalid if there is any chance we could not be certain that every possible holder would either be vested or be certain to fail to vest within 21 years of a life in being. In this case, R, L, M, and P could all die suddenly. A could have another child, X. A could die shortly after X is born, and X could live well past 21 years before having any children, or could live a hundred years without having any children. Either way, the class gift to A's children would not be closed until the perpetuity period lapsed.

The interest to R (and A's grandchildren) being invalid, the devise is to A for life, to A's children for life, then to O's heirs or devisees.

Another Grandpa Story

2. The answer is yes, in part. A's present interest in a life estate is vested, so the Rule is inapplicable to it. The remainder to A's children is a vested remainder subject to open in life estate. A is a validating life — meaning A is alive, no persons who were not lives in being can enter the same class as A (or fit his description), and a class of "A's children" must of logical certainty close at or before A's. Hence the class of A's children will close and be vested immediately at A's death. A's children's vested remainder subject to open in a life estate is valid under the Rule.

The remainder to A's grandchildren is invalid, however. The interest is a contingent remainder. The two conditions precedent are the grandchildren being ascertained (which can be done by being born) and surviving until the death of the survivor of A's children. So the Rule applies. Envisioning the worst of all scenarios, A could have another child, Z, born after O's death. A, X, and Y could then die. After the 21-year perpetuities period passed, Z could have a child, GC (a grandchild of A). GC possibly being born 22 years after all lives in being have died already is an event indicating we will not know within 21 years of a life in being at the creation of the interest which, if any, of A's grandchildren will survive the last to die of A's children. In addition, Z is not dead yet, and easily could live another 50 years, making it at least 70 years since the last life in being died before we will know if GC survived Z. The Rule does not permit 70 years of uncertainty in this situation.

Striking the invalidated grant to A's grandchildren's, A owns a life estate, A's children own a vested remainder subject to open in a life estate, and O's heirs or devisees own the reversion.

The Big Event

3. (a) As written, A has a fee simple subject to an executory limitation and B has a shifting executory interest. A's fee simple subject to an executory interest is a vested possessory interest and not subject to the Rule. The shifting executory interest in B is subject to the Rule, however, and is invalid under the Rule. The condition subsequent to A's interest, and thus the condition precedent to B's executory interest, is an event, use of the property for commercial purposes. Since Whiteacre may be used for noncommercial purposes for centuries after all relevant lives in being have died, B's shifting executory interest therefore is invalid. Just because the grant mentions two lives in being (A and B) does not mean the condition must occur during their lives. Drawing a line through B's shifting executory interest, the grant reads, "To A and his heirs so long as a commercial use is not made of the property." As rewritten, A has a fee simple determinable. O (or his heirs or devisees) has a possibility of reverter.

   (b) A's interest is a fee simple subject to an executory limitation, and B has a shifting executory interest. A's interest is a present possessory vested interest and thus not subject to the Rule. B's shifting executory interest is invalid under the Rule since the event, using Whiteacre for commercial purposes, may not occur until A and B, the relevant lives in being, have been dead for decades. Drawing a line through B's invalid executory interest, the grant reads, "to A and his heirs." A owns Whiteacre in fee simple absolute. O and B have no interest in Whiteacre. Compare the result in (a).

   (c) O intended A to own a fee simple subject to an executory limitation, and B to own a shifting executory interest. A's present possessory interest is vested and not subject to the Rule. B's shifting executory interest dependent on a condition precedent, A's using the land for commercial purposes, is subject to the Rule. In contrast to B's interest in (a) and (b), this time B's interest is good. A is the validating life here. The divesting event by its terms must occur during A's lifetime and A was a life in being at the creation of the interest.

   LESSON: When drafting transfers dependent on an event to shift an interest, write the condition so that it can occur only during a life in being at the time the interest is effective — i.e., write it as follows: "to A and her heirs so long as A resides there, then to B and her heirs." This ties the interest to A and limits its force to the length of A's life. It is impossible then for this executory interest to vest only after the lives in being plus 21 years. Stated another way, unless a divesting event must occur during a life in being, the executory interest following a fee simple subject to an executory limitation violates the Rule.

RAP Session

4. (a) B has a vested remainder subject to an executory limitation (alternatively, give yourself bonus points if you said B received a vested remainder subject to divestment in fee simple absolute since B may lose her interest if *A* sells liquor on Blackacre). As a vested interest, it is not subject to the Rule Against Perpetuities. B's interest is valid.

   C has a shifting executory interest. It is invalid under the Rule. The divesting event, liquor being sold on Blackacre, may occur during *A*'s life estate determinable, during *A*'s life, or decades after all lives in being have died. This is another "events" type RAP question. Rewriting the grant after striking out C's executory interest, *A* has a life estate determinable and B has a vested remainder in fee simple absolute. O and C have nothing.

   (b) Yes, B's interest violates the Rule. The original grant gave *A* a life estate, O a reversion in fee simple subject to an executory limitation, and B a springing executory interest. *A*'s life estate and O's reversion are not subject to the Rule. There is no survivorship requirement for B to take, only the passage of time. An executory interest must vest in possession (rather than just vest in interest) to be valid, however. Unfortunately, the 30 years that must pass after *A*'s life estate ends before the springing executory interest becomes possessory is way too long. O and B could die about the same time *A* does. If so, 21 years later still no one would be entitled to possession of the executory interest. As rewritten after striking B's springing executory interest, *A* has a life estate, and O has a reversion.

   (c) *A* has a life estate; *A*'s children have a contingent remainder in life estate, contingent on being ascertained; and B has a vested remainder. *A*'s life estate is not subject to the Rule. *A*'s children's contingent remainder is subject to the Rule. *A* is the validating life for a grant to *A*'s children. We will know at *A*'s death who *A*'s children are. Therefore, the contingent remainder in life estate in *A*'s children is good. B's interest is a vested remainder. Unlike executory interests, vested remainders need only be vested in interest not vested in possession. B's vested remainder is good.

   (d) Yes, O's grandchildren's interest is valid. The example does not say who owns Redacre until O's grandchildren turn 21, but at any rate O intended the grandchildren to have an executory interest. An executory interest must vest in possession within 21 years (or, more precisely, 21 years plus 9 months' gestation period) after all lives in being at the creation of the interest have died. *A* is a validating life since O's grandchildren are the same as *A*'s children, *A* is a life in being, and no other person can enter the class of O's children. Once *A* dies, the class of O's grandchildren closes physiologically. Each member of the class will have either attained age 21 or died before reaching age 21 in the 21 years after *A* dies. The interest to O's grandchildren, therefore, is good.

Note, however, that if O's grandchildren must attain age 22, the gift would be invalid since *A* might die days after his youngest child is born, and 21 years later we still won't know if that child will reach age 22. The Rule would void the interest of that child and every child in the class of O's grandchildren, even those who have already reached age 22.

(e) O's grandchildren would receive a springing executory interest. It is not a vested remainder subject to open since the interest does not follow the natural termination of a life estate or estate for years. It cuts short O's fee simple. What might happen? *A* and GC might die soon after the interest is created. O might have another child, B. O then could die, survived by B, who was not a life in being. In 21 years we might not know if B has any children (if O will have any grandchildren, and how many), much less whether all of O's grandchildren will attain age 21. The gift to O's grandchildren is void. O still owns a fee simple absolute. Compare (d).

Wait and See

5. (a) In a "wait-and-see" jurisdiction, we may not know if the contingent remainder in "*A*'s child first reaching the age of 25" is met within the 21-year perpetuities period until 21 years after *A* dies. No decision can be made either way on O's death. We must wait to see if *A* has any children during his life. If *A* dies childless, as in this Example, no one will satisfy the condition precedent. So at this point, whether *A*'s first child is a valid gift or not becomes an irrelevant issue since no one can take. O's reversion becomes a fee simple absolute at *A*'s death. If, instead of using the 21-year perpetuities period, the state adopted a 90-year wait-and-see period, as long as *A* has a child survive him, no matter the child's age, we wait to see if that child attains age 25.

   (b) In a jurisdiction adopting the common law perpetuities period, the remainder is not valid, because *A*'s life is now the only measuring life. B was not a life in being. Since it is clear a three-year-old cannot attain age 25 in the 21-year perpetuity period, the interest is invalid. If, on the other hand, the jurisdiction has adopted a fixed 90-year perpetuities period, we must wait and see if B turns 25 in the 90 years after the interest is created. Assuming B was born within 65 years of O's death, the Rule poses no barrier to B's taking; the condition precedent that he must attain age 25 might, but the Rule does not.

(c) We must wait and see. The determination of validity cannot be made at O's death or at A's death. The decision is deferred in a "wait-and-see" jurisdiction. B's death means in the wait-and-see jurisdiction that B will be certain not to vest within the 21-year period (or thereafter). C, at four, is the eldest child and thus may attain age 25. The Rule is not a barrier to C's taking. If C turns 25, he gets the property.

(d) B at age two cannot turn 25 in 21 years. In states using the common law perpetuities period or the wait-and-see 21-year period, B's interest is invalid. O has a reversion. In states using the 90-year perpetuities period, as long as B was born within 65 years of O's death, which is almost certain, the Rule will not keep B from taking. B's interest is also good under the ALI's proposed generation-based perpetuity period since B would be a measuring life.

(e) In a wait-and-see jurisdiction using the common law perpetuities period, the parties must wait until 21 years after the last of the relevant lives in being. Here, O, A, and B's being mentioned in the grant would serve as measuring lives. If Whiteacre is used for commercial purposes during the perpetuities period, A is divested and B takes pursuant to the shifting executory interest. If no commercial use is made of the property during that period, B's interest disappears. The condition subsequent to A's interest remains. A continues with a fee simple determinable and O (or his heirs or devisees) has a possibility of reverter. Compare Example 3(a), above.

In a jurisdiction adopting the 90-year rule, the parties must wait 90 years after the interest was created (i.e., from January 1, Year 1, until January 1, Year 91, to see if the property is used for commercial purposes. If so, B gets Whiteacre. If Whiteacre is used for commercial purposes after January 1, Year 91, it reverts back to O and his heirs.

CHAPTER 13

Concurrent Ownership

As we have seen, property ownership can be divided up in several ways. A landowner of 100 acres, for example, may give 50 acres to one person and 50 acres to another; the landowner may give one person the whole 100 acres as a life estate and another the remainder; the landowner may sever the surface from the subsurface by granting away the mineral rights; or the landowner may transfer legal title to a trustee with rights to manage and sell the property for the economic benefit of beneficiaries who have the right to income and value appreciation.

Finally, two or more persons may concurrently own the same interest in the same land. There are three major concurrent interests developed in England and recognized in the United States: tenancy in common, joint tenancy with right of survivorship, and tenancy by the entirety. Each may be found in any present or future interest, and may be held in any estate—for life, in fee simple determinable or subject to a condition subsequent, in fee simple absolute, etc.

TENANCY IN COMMON

The most common form of concurrent ownership is the tenancy in common. Each tenant in common owns a share of the same piece of property. The default rule is that each co-tenant has an equal right to possess the whole property and to share equally in rents and appreciation in value. Thus, it is said that their interests are "undivided"—that is, each has *seisin* and the right to possess the whole. In practice, they frequently own varying proportional interests in the land. Tenants in common (or co-tenants) are presumed to own a property in proportion to the amount each contributed to purchase the property, but this presumption is rebuttable and subject to an agreement to the contrary.

Tenants in common normally share in rents and sales proceeds according to their respective interests. Even if co-tenants own varying interests in property, each co-tenant enjoys the right to possess the entire property. Thus if A owns a 50% interest and B and C each own a 25% interest in Blackacre, as tenants in common, A would receive 50% of any net rents from the property, but all three would have equal rights of possession.

Concurrent ownership sometimes breeds conflict and disagreement. Common law default rules have evolved to resolve possession, use, profit-sharing, and expense-sharing issues that may arise when concurrent owners cannot agree.

A tenancy-in-common interest is assignable (transferable), devisable, and inheritable. Transferees become tenants in common with the remaining tenants in common. A co-tenant can mortgage his interest to secure a loan or can sell his interest, but cannot sell his co-tenants' interests in the property.

Example 1:   O transfers Blackacre, a 100-acre farm, to A and B as tenants in common. No more being said in the deed of transfer, A and B each own a 50% undivided interest in the entire 100 acres. Three years later A dies, devising his interest in Blackacre to M. M now owns a 50% interest in Blackacre. B and M own the 100-acre farm as tenants in common.

Example 2:   O transfers Whiteacre to A and B as tenants in common. A then dies without a will, survived by two children, C and D. Without a will, C and D take A's interest under the canons of descent or intestacy, again in equal proportions, so that B owns a 50% interest and C and D each owns a 25% interest in Whiteacre.

Example 3:   O transfers Greenacre, along with its farm equipment, to A and B as tenants in common. In a majority of states, it is possible to have a tenancy in common in personalty as well as real property.

JOINT TENANCY WITH RIGHT OF SURVIVORSHIP

The joint tenancy with right of survivorship is a form of concurrent ownership with a survivorship element. When a joint tenant dies, her interest ends. The last surviving joint tenant owns the property outright, and may sell or devise the property. The joint tenancy with right of survivorship is often used as a will substitute: It avoids the cost and time of probate administration since a decedent's interest in the property ends on her death and the other joint tenant takes the title. Often the property involved is the family residence.

> **Example:** Ann and Brady are joint tenants with right of survivorship in Whiteacre. Ann dies, her will devising all her real property to Donna. Donna gets no interest in Whiteacre. Brady is the sole owner. A year later Brady dies, his will devising all his real property to Emmylou. Emmylou owns Whiteacre.

The preferred language to create a joint tenancy with right of survivorship is "to *A* and *B* as joint tenants with right of survivorship and not as tenants in common." The most significant difference between a joint tenancy with right of survivorship and a tenancy-in-common is the right of survivorship.

At one time — and still today in many states — a joint tenancy could be created and maintained only if all the tenants shared the four unities:

(1) Unity of Time — The joint tenants' interests must vest at the same time.
(2) Unity of Title — The joint tenants must acquire title in the same deed or will.
(3) Unity of Interest — Each joint tenant must own equal shares of the same estate.
(4) Unity of Possession — Each joint tenant has a right to possession of the whole property.

Historically, a joint tenant could change his interest from a joint tenancy with right of survivorship to a tenancy-in-commom by destroying any one of the four unities. That absolute rule is no longer the law either for creating or destroying joint tenancies in many states. An agreement between joint tenants that one tenant have sole possession, for example, does not destroy the unity of possession. Likewise, a court in equity may look to the respective contributions each joint tenant made to acquire the property and divide any sales proceeds in proportion to each joint tenant's respective contribution.

Unity of title is still required in some states, but it has been abolished by statute or judicial opinion in most states, after decades of being circumvented by use of a straw man or straw. A **straw man** is a person who briefly takes legal title for the sole purpose of re-conveying the property back to his grantor. Usually the straw is someone in the lawyer's office, a secretary or a paralegal — someone who can be trusted to re-convey the property.

The process worked this way: A person holding land solely in his own name wanted to own the property as a joint tenant with right of survivorship. He may have wanted to pass the property to his spouse or child outside of probate.

Let's assume the landowner wanted to transfer the family residence to himself and his wife as joint tenants with right of survivorship. At early common law, a joint tenancy with right of survivorship did not result when a person made a direct transfer to his spouse or a transfer to himself and his spouse since the deed attempted to create an interest in the spouse at a different time and under a different title (deed). The landowner could not deed an interest in the property to his spouse as a joint tenant or to himself and his spouse as joint tenants with right of survivorship. A tenancy in common and not a joint tenancy with right of survivorship resulted. The solution to this dilemma was for the landowner to transfer the property to a straw man, who immediately deeded the land to the original landowner and his wife as joint tenants with right of survivorship.

Many states have recently concluded that there is no reason to require a straw. These states allow a direct transfer from one person to himself and another as joint tenants with rights of survivorship, particularly when the other is the spouse. Be cautious here, as many states still require resort to a straw man for one spouse to transfer property to himself and spouse as joint tenants with right of survivorship.

A joint tenancy is created by a deed or a will. A joint tenancy cannot arise by intestate succession: Two or more persons inheriting the same property become tenants in common. On the other hand, it is possible under proper facts — usually taking the land under a faulty deed naming the co-tenants as joint tenants with right of survivorship — that joint adverse possession could yield a joint tenancy held by two or more adverse possessors.

When two joint tenants die simultaneously, most courts treat half the property as if one tenant survived and the other half as if the other tenant survived — effectively treating the property as a tenancy in common, giving the heirs of each tenant an equal share.

Sometimes, rarely we hope, one joint tenant murders the other joint tenant. When one of two co-tenants murders the other one, the murderer forfeits the right of survivorship, but not his interest. In effect, murder turns the joint tenancy into a tenancy in common.

Since her interest in the joint tenancy ends on her death, a joint tenant cannot devise her interest in a joint tenancy with right of survivorship; nor is her interest inheritable. A joint tenant may transfer or assign her interest during her life, however. The assignment ends the joint tenancy at least as to the transferee, who thereafter holds his interest as a tenant in common with the other tenants, who continue to hold their fractional share in a joint tenancy with right of survivorship. Ending a joint tenancy with right of survivorship interest in property and transforming it into a tenancy in common interest is called a "severance."

SEVERANCE

In some states, when one or more of the four unities of a joint tenancy with right of survivorship no longer exists, the joint tenancy interest is said to be **severed** from the joint tenancy relationship and becomes a tenancy in common ownership interest. A severance, in short, turns a joint tenancy into a tenancy in common between the severed interest and the remaining joint tenants. The remaining joint tenants continue holding their interests in the property as a joint tenancy with right of survivorship. Thus, when the joint tenancy is created in three or more persons, a unilateral act of one of them leaves the joint tenancy intact as between the remaining tenants, who together then would hold a tenancy in common with the severing tenant. Courts in these states look for some action or relationship that destroys one of the four unities to find a severance.

Courts in other states do not focus on the four unities, but look instead for an act or instrument that indicates an intent by one of the joint tenants to terminate the survivorship element.

Joint tenancy interests can be severed voluntarily or involuntarily The most common voluntary severance occurs when one joint tenant unilaterally transfers her interest to another person, as when A, a joint tenant, deeds her interest to a third party. The most common involuntary severance is a foreclosure sale or a sale in bankruptcy proceedings.

Example 1: O, the holder of a fee simple absolute in Blackacre, conveys "to A, B, and C, as joint tenants with right of survivorship." Five years later C conveys her interst to D. The deed to D is a severance of D's interest in the joint tenancy. A and B continue in joint tenancy with each other, but are in a tenancy in common with D, each of the three having a one-third interest in Blackacre. If A dies, leaving a will devising her interest in Blackacre to M, M gets nothing. A's interest ends on her death and B owns a two-thirds interest in Blackacre as a tenant in common with D, who owns a one-third interest.

Example 2: Same facts as in Example 1, except A and B survive while D dies, leaving a will devising his interest to N. D held an interest as a tenant in common at his death. A tenancy in common is devisable, so N owns a one-third interest in Blackacre. A and B continue to own the remaining two-thirds interest in Blackacre as joint tenants with right of survivorship as between themselves, but as tenants in common with N.

Example 3: Same facts as in Example 1, except A, B, and D all survive. A sells her interest to L. This severs A's interest from the joint tenancy. Since joint tenancy requires more than one person (and B cannot be in a joint tenancy by herself), the joint tenancy is now a tenancy in common, with B, D, and L as tenants in common.

(a) Leases

Generally, a short-term lease by one joint tenant does not sever a joint tenancy. The lease ends on the death of the leasing joint tenant. The lessee's possessory rights derive from the lessor joint tenant; when the lessor joint tenant no longer has an interest due to his or her death, the lessee also loses his right of possession. The lease terminates with the death of the leasing co-tenant even though the lease term has not run its course and the lessee has no notice in the lease or elsewhere of the extent of the lessor's rights: the surviving, non-leasing joint tenants do not take subject to the lease.

Some older cases held that a lease with a long term might work a severance, at least for the term of the lease. More recent cases have concluded that even a long-term lease by one joint tenant will not sever the joint tenancy.

The modern trend rests on a couple of rationales. One is that the lease is not a freehold estate and hence there is no severance of title and the tenant enjoys the rights of possession through the leasing co-tenant, not in his own right. The second is that in a state no longer holding the four unities as essential to the joint tenancy, under a principle of "equal dignity," the parties who intended to hold as joint tenancy with right of survivorship should manifest their intent to terminate the survivorship element more definitely. Likewise, an option to purchase the leasing joint tenant's interest, when contained in the lease, does not sever the joint tenancy, either.

Lesson to the wise: Because a lessee's right to continue occupying the premises through the term of the lease might end on the death of his lessor, a wise lessee should require all joint tenants execute the lease.

(b) Mortgages

The issue in many cases is whether one joint tenant unilaterally granting a mortgage to secure a debt severs a joint tenancy with right of survivorship. As background, a mortgage is a document by which the owner of real property pledges the property to secure the payment of a debt (a promissory note) owed by the owner of the property or by someone else. If the debtor fails to pay the debt, the creditor may "foreclose" on the mortgaged property, selling it to raise money to pay off the debt.

The vast majority of states are **lien theory states**, meaning a mortgage provides security for a loan. Title remains with the debtor. Since legal title remains with the debtor joint tenant, the giving of a mortgage by one joint tenant to secure his personal debt does not sever the joint tenancy. Only when the interest is sold following foreclosure proceedings does a severance occur.[1]

States differ on what happens to the mortgage if the debtor joint tenant dies while the mortgage is outstanding. Conceptually, the mortgage should be worthless since the deceased debtor no longer owns an interest in the property, and the creditor's rights depend on the debtor's interest. The deceased joint tenant's interest, moreover, does not pass to the other joint tenants; rather, the interest just ends, similar to a life estate. Some states, by statute or judicial opinion, however, conclude that the property continues to be subject to the mortgage. Lesson to be learned: Lenders should have all joint tenants sign the mortgage, even if they are not personally liable for the debt.

About a dozen states are known as **title theory states**, where a mortgage conveys legal title to the creditor. The creditor owns the debtor's interest in fee simple determinable, to revert to the debtor when the debt is retired. Some courts, especially a few decades back, viewed the transfer of legal title as destroying at least one of the four unities, and thus severed the debtor's interest from the joint tenancy. While that is still the law in some title theory states, most recognize that the mortgage is a security device, and the debtor remains the true owner. In these title theory states the mortgage, as in the lien theory states, does not sever the joint tenancy.

(c) Judgment Liens

Just as a completed foreclosure of a mortgage will sever a joint tenancy, so also will a levy and sale of a joint tenant's interest sever it. The docketing of the lien, however, does not sever it because the service of a sheriff's writ of execution does not disturb the possessory rights of the joint tenants, so it works no severance.

---

1. In many states, even the foreclosure sale does not sever the joint tenancy until the time to exercise a statutory right of redemption passes. Under the right of redemption, the owner of the foreclosed property can "redeem" or buy the property from the purchaser at the foreclosure sale by paying the purchaser his purchase price (plus costs and interest) within a statutory period of time after the foreclosure sale (the period ranging from three months to two years).

(d) Unilateral and Secret Severances

As noted earlier, a joint tenant unilaterally can sever a joint tenancy by transferring her interest to a third party. Sometimes a joint tenant wants to sever her interest from the joint tenancy but continue to maintain her interest in the property as a tenant in common rather than as a joint tenant. In some states the joint tenant must resort to the use of a straw man to sever her interest. A few states from among those that allow the direct creation of a joint tenancy with right of survivorship without the use of a straw man see no reason to prevent the direct severance without using a straw.

The possibility exists, however, that the severance is done secretly and does not come to light until one or the other joint tenant dies. The secret severance opens up the possibility of fraud: A joint tenant may execute a severance deed to himself or to another as a tenant in common without telling anyone else or even recording the deed in the public deed records. If he dies first, a severance will be found to have occurred, with the joint tenant's assignee, devisee, or heir taking the joint tenant's interest as a tenant in common. If he is the survivor, he might destroy the severance document and take the whole of the property. The law does not countenance this ruse. Thus, where courts approve direct severances that do away with the use of straw men, they more closely scrutinize the completely secret severance. To prevent this fraud on the other joint tenants, some states require either public recording or notification to the other joint tenants. See, e.g., Cal. Civ. Code §638.2 (1986) (statute likely enacted to counter the holding in Riddle v. Harmon, 162 Cal. Rptr. 530 (1980)).

DISTINGUISHING JOINT TENANCIES FROM TENANCIES IN COMMON

Centuries ago in England, the joint tenancy was the default concurrent interest. A transfer from O "to A and B" created a joint tenancy with right of survivorship. English courts were anxious to avoid splitting ownership. Creating a joint tenancy with right of survivorship was presumed to be the parties' intent when there was any ambiguity as to whether a document created a tenancy in common or a joint tenancy. The purpose of the presumption was to maintain family estates intact.

Today, however, this presumption is reversed. The tenancy in common is preferred. Statutes in many states provide that a grant to concurrent owners is presumed to be a tenancy in common unless the deed clearly establishes that the grantor intended to create a joint tenancy with right of survivorship. From our earliest times, state legislatures were anxious to encourage widespread ownership of land.

A major caveat with regard to married couples is in order here. In many states that recognize the tenancy by the entirety (an estate exclusively reserved for married couples — to be developed in the next section), a grant to a husband and wife is presumed to create a tenancy by the entirety unless the deed expresses a clear intent to create another interest. In some states that do not recognize the tenancy by the entirety, a grant to a husband and wife is presumed to create a joint tenancy with right of survivorship unless the deed or will clearly manifests intent to create a tenancy in common. In some states that do not recognize the tenancy by the entirety, only married couples can hold property as joint tenants with right of survivorship, but the presumption is that the grant creates a tenancy in common unless the grant evidences a clear intent to create a joint tenancy with a right of survivorship. In the remaining states, a grant to a husband and wife is treated like any other grant to multiple persons, and is presumed to be a tenancy in common unless a clear intent to create another concurrent interest is expressed.

The most popular words to create a joint tenancy with right of survivorship are "to A and B as joint tenants with a right of survivorship and not as tenants in common." Some courts will find the requisite intent to create a joint tenancy with right of survivorship in a grant "to A and B as joint tenants," but many courts refuse to find a joint tenancy with right of survivorship unless the deed or will contains words of survivorship. "To A and B jointly" creates a tenancy in common for example, not a joint tenancy with right of survivorship. A specific indication of an intention to establish the right of survivorship, along with a negation of a tenancy in common, is the best course for the conveyancer.

A grant to "A and B as joint tenants, remainder to the survivor of them" creates joint life estates, with a contingent remainder in the survivor. It is not the same as a joint tenancy with right of survivorship, however, and dramatically different legal consequences may follow. As discussed in the next section, any joint tenant can unilaterally "sever" her interest from the joint tenancy and become a tenant in common with the other co-tenants. Severance destroys the survivorship character as to her interest. When she dies, her heir or devisee takes her interest. In contrast, persons holding joint life estates with a contingent remainder cannot unilaterally terminate the survivorship requirement.

TENANCY BY THE ENTIRETY

A third form of concurrent ownership is the tenancy by the entirety. The tenancy by the entirety is limited to husbands and wives, who own the property as a unit, not by equal shares. The same four unities necessary to form a joint tenancy with right of survivorship are essential to form a tenancy by the entirety, and in addition, the couple must be married at the time they acquire the property. Thus marriage is the fifth unity required for this type of tenancy. Engaged to be married is insufficient. Hence, a couple buying a home to live in after their marriage will not hold the home in a tenancy by the entirety. Divorce terminates the tenancy by the entirety and a tenancy in common results in most states (a joint tenancy with right of survivorship results in a minority of states).

Like the joint tenancy with right of survivorship, the tenancy by the entirety is characterized by a right of survivorship in the surviving spouse. Unlike in the joint tenancy, one spouse cannot unilaterally sever the tenancy by the entirety. Moreover, neither spouse can seek judicial partition.[2]

About half the states recognize the tenancy by the entirety. In the majority of those, a grant to a husband and wife is presumed to create a tenancy by the entirety unless a different form is indicated in the deed. In other states, a grant to a husband and wife creates a presumption that a tenancy in common is created unless the deed indicates a tenancy by the entirety or joint tenancy with right of survivorship is intended. To avoid confusion, parties intending to create a tenancy by the entirety should convey to "H and W, husband and wife, as tenants by the entirety."

At one time, a husband and wife owning property as tenancy by the entirety were deemed one — and that one was the husband. He had management rights, rights to the income, and the power to sell. The wife had survivorship rights — even if the husband sold the property, the wife's survivorship rights continued in force. A wife relinquished her survivorship rights if she signed the deed. As a practical matter, therefore, husbands and wives both signed deeds conveying the property to third parties

Since the husband could sell the property, he also could pledge it as security. His creditors, secured and unsecured, could foreclose on the property. A purchaser at foreclosure was entitled to possession of the property, and to all rents and income from the property. If the husband outlived the wife, the purchaser kept the property in fee simple absolute. If the wife survived her husband, she got the property back.

Well over a century ago, states began enacting Married Women's Property Acts (MWPA) giving married women rights to control property. Courts and legislatures applied MWPA to fashion three theories of a modern tenancy by the entirety in all states recognizing this tenancy. Today, in the majority of tenancy-by-the-entirety states, a creditor can foreclose on the tenancy by the entirety property only if both spouses are liable for the

---

2. Judicial partition is explained later in this chapter.

underlying debt or both have executed a mortgage. The husband and wife, moreover, both must execute the deed on the sale of the property. In a second group of states, a creditor of one spouse's separate debts may foreclose on the debtor spouse's half interest (the half interest being a fiction, since the couple holds the property as whole) subject to the other spouse's survivorship rights. Thus the creditor can get rents from the property if any are collected, but will lose all rights in the property if the nondebtor spouse outlives the debtor spouse.

Finally, in two states — Kentucky and Tennessee — creditors can reach a spouse's survivorship interest, but not the right to current possession and rents. Hence creditors have no interest while both spouses are alive, and will have an interest only if the debtor spouse survives the nondebtor spouse.

RIGHTS AND OBLIGATIONS BETWEEN CO-TENANTS

(a) Possession, Ouster, and Payment of Rent

Each co-tenant (tenant in common, joint tenant, or tenant by the entirety) has the right to possess the entire property. As such, the majority rule is that a co-tenant using the whole property, absent ouster, does not owe rent to the other co-tenants. In a small minority of states, a co-tenant using the property owes a fair rental to the remaining co-tenants.

In the majority of states where a co-tenant owes no rent to his co-tenants for using the property, the rule changes if the occupying tenant ousts the other co-tenants. **Ouster** occurs when the occupying tenant acts to prevent the other co-tenants from using the property. Ouster may occur if the occupying tenant changes the locks or if the occupying tenant makes use of the property in a way that no other use can be made of any part of the property and refuses to make room for another's use. Generally, before the ousted co-tenant can bring an action for ouster, the co-tenant must make a demand for access to the property and be denied access.

Example: H and W, husband and wife, own Blackacre as tenants in common. H abandons W and Blackacre. C, a judgment creditor of H, levies on Blackacre to satisfy the judgment, and purchases H's interest in Blackacre at the judgment sale and then demands half of the fair rental value of Blackacre from W, who is using Blackacre. W refuses. C is not automatically entitled to rent from W. C must first demand possession and be refused it by W (the common term for this is "ouster"). Only then is C entitled to half Blackacre's rental value.

(b) Contribution

A co-tenant who expends money for some matter related to the commonly owned property sometimes may seek reimbursement from his co-tenants for his expenditures. There are three distinct judicial causes of action with which a co-tenant may seek reimbursement from his co-tenants: contribution, an accounting, and a final settlement on sale or partition. A co-tenant seeks **contribution** when he demands his co-tenants pay for their pro rata share of expenses. If a co-tenant refuses to contribute voluntarily, the paying co-tenant may bring a judicial action for contribution.

(1) Taxes, Interest, and Insurance

Assuming no one is using the property, a co-tenant who pays the annual property taxes, government assessments, or interest on mortgages may seek contribution from the other co-tenants.[3] Taxes and interest are usually known as **carrying charges.** All co-tenants have a duty to contribute their share of taxes and interest on mortgages. In a minority of states, property insurance is a carrying charge. Where insurance is a carrying charge, a co-tenant paying insurance premiums can seek contribution. Otherwise, no contribution is allowed for insurance premiums.

Co-tenants must contribute to pay carrying charges since, in the case of property taxes and mortgage interest, nonpayment may result in the property being foreclosed on and sold. In addition, the amount owed and the obligation to pay are established by outside parties and not by an individual co-tenant.

If the paying co-tenant is the only co-tenant using the property, no contribution is permitted for carrying charges up to the fair rental value of the property. Because the occupying co-tenant is not obligated to pay rent to her co-tenants, she is responsible for the taxes and interest on the mortgage since she is the principal beneficiary of the payment (plus, it serves as a substitute for the payment of rent). If the occupying co-tenant does pay rent to her co-tenants, she may offset the others' share of the carrying charges against the rent due.

Unless the other co-tenants agree, a co-tenant has no right to compensation for services performed by the co-tenant.

---

3. Co-tenants are responsible only for interest on mortgages existing when the concurrent ownership began, or the mortgage secures a debt for which all co-tenants are personally liable. If one co-tenant mortgages the property or her interest in the property, she is solely liable for the interest payment and cannot get contribution.

(2) Mortgage Principal

A co-tenant who makes a mortgage principal payment when due or past due may seek contribution from his co-tenants. A co-tenant who prepays the principal of a mortgage, on the other hand, cannot seek contribution, but must wait until the principal payment comes due and payable under the original mortgage before seeking contribution.

(3) Repairs and Maintenance

A co-tenant cannot get contribution for repairs, even necessary repairs. While on first blush it would seem best if the paying co-tenant received contribution for necessary repair and maintenance — say, to fix a broken window, replace a roof, or mow the lawn — courts have been reluctant to decide on a case-by-case basis which repairs were necessary, what type of repair (quality and extent) was needed, and how much should have been spent for the repair. Hence courts have concluded that no co-tenant has a duty to make repairs.

> ***Example:*** A co-tenant in possession pays to repair property and clean up its yard after city officials order him to do so pursuant to a city ordinance. Here contribution would be appropriate if a failure to obey would result in enforcement of the ordinance by seizing the property. The repair costs in this example are government assessments and hence are carrying charges.

(4) Improvements

A co-tenant who improves property cannot compel contribution from his co-tenants. The rationale is that no one has a duty to improve property, and no one who chooses to improve the land should force his co-tenants to contribute. Were it otherwise, rich co-tenants might "improve" poorer co-tenants out of their interest.

(c) An Accounting

Even though a co-tenant cannot seek contribution for repairs and improvements, he may get some reimbursement indirectly in an accounting. An accounting occurs when a co-tenant maintains records (and furnishes a copy to her co-tenants) as to income and expenses from renting the property to a third party. Even though a co-tenant can solely possess co-owned property and keep any profits generated from that sole possession, once he leases or rents the property to others he must account for any profits and share the net proceeds with his co-tenants. See Statute of Anne, ch. 16, §27 (1705) (adopted by all American states either as part of the common law or by statute).

In an accounting the co-tenant collecting rent payments may offset the costs associated with generating and collecting the rent. The co-tenant may offset rent revenues by the amount he expended on taxes, interest, mortgage principal, and insurance. In addition, he can offset other expenses, such as advertising, management fees, *actual* amounts spent on repairs or maintenance, and utilities. The co-tenant can offset his monetary outlays only to the extent of any rental income received. The accounting in effect reduces how much of the rental proceeds the co-tenant must distribute to his co-tenants. Absent an agreement to the contrary, an accounting does not allow him to demand contribution from his co-tenants if expenditures exceed revenues. Notwithstanding this limitation on the accounting, the paying co-tenant can still demand contribution if rent revenues are insufficient to pay the property taxes, government assessments, interest, and currently payable principal payment on a mortgage. Unless the tenants agree, a co-tenant receives no compensation for time spent managing the property.

Example: *A, B,* and *C* own raw land as tenants in common. *A* pays the annual taxes of $3000 and the interest of $5000 on the outstanding mortgage. *A* rents the land to a local farmer who will cut the grass on the land to use as hay to feed his livestock. The farmer pays *A* $2000 rental. *A* can demand *B* and *C* each contribute $2000 ($8000 total carrying costs less $2000 rents equals $6000, divided by 3 equals $2000 per co-tenant).

The co-tenant cannot offset the total cost of improvements in an accounting. He can offset only so much of the cost of the improvements as is traceable to an increase in rents received because of the improvements, but no more.

(d) Final Settlement on Sale

If the co-tenants sell the property, either voluntarily or by a judicially ordered partition sale (discussed below), a final settlement takes place. A co-tenant who expended money and has not been reimbursed for taxes, interest, mortgage principal, repairs, maintenance, insurance, and other common expenses associated with owning the property will be reimbursed out of sales proceeds.

Improvements are a special case. A co-tenant who paid for improvements will receive the sales proceeds attributable to the value added by the improvements. The amount paid for the improvement is irrelevant.

As was the case under contribution and an accounting, a co-tenant who spends time managing and selling the property is not entitled to any compensation for her labors unless the other co-tenants specifically agree.

Example 1: Adam, who owns a one-third interest in Blackacre as a tenant in common, builds a house on Blackacre for $100,000. Five years later the three co-tenants sell Blackacre for $250,000. The land is worth $75,000; the building is worth $175,000. Adam receives the $175,000 attributable to the building and one-third of $75,000 ($25,000) as his share of the sales proceeds.

Example 2: Maurice, who owns a one-third interest in Whiteacre as a tenant in common, spends $20,000 to install a swimming pool. Two years later the co-tenants sell Whiteacre for $215,000. The land and building are valued at $210,000. The swimming pool added $5000 to the property's value. Maurice receives $5000 for the swimming pool and one-third of the $210,000 ($70,000) for the land and building as his share of the sales proceeds.

(e) Tax Sales and Foreclosure Sales

If the co-tenants fail to pay taxes or mortgage payments, the state or the mortgagee (the creditor) may seek a judicial sale of the property to pay either the taxes or the mortgage. The co-tenants share excess proceeds from these sales as explained above.

Co-tenants may have a statutory right to redeem the property from the purchaser at the foreclosure sale for a short time after the foreclosure sale (usually from three months to two years). The rights of redemption are alienable and persons to whom co-tenants assign these rights take their assignments as tenants in common.

If a co-tenant purchases the property at the tax sale or foreclosure sale (or after the foreclosure sale by exercising the statutory right of redemption), the majority rule is that the purchasing co-tenant is deemed to be acting in her fiduciary capacity as a co-tenant. The remaining co-tenants have the option of remaining co-tenants by contributing their share of the taxes or mortgage. If the other co-tenants choose not to contribute, after a reasonable time the purchasing co-tenant will own the property outright.

In a minority of states, if the other co-tenants have an opportunity to bid at the tax sale or foreclosure sale, the purchasing tenant represents himself and not the co-tenancy. There are exceptions — if the other co-tenants are not adults, if the purchasing co-tenant deceived the other co-tenants into believing he was representing the co-tenancy, or if the purchasing co-tenant intentionally did not pay the taxes or the mortgage because he was in a superior financial position to successfully purchase the property at the forced sale.

(f) Adverse Possession

Since each co-tenant has the right to possess the co-owned property, it is difficult for a co-tenant to adversely possess the property. It can be done, however. To begin running the statute of limitations the co-tenant claiming by adverse possession must give clear notice to the other co-tenants that she is claiming adversely. Notice in writing certainly gives the requisite notice, but it is not the sole method to give notice. Ouster alone may not suffice, but ouster combined with acts so inconsistent with a concurrent ownership that co-tenants must be deemed to be on notice of the adverse possession might suffice.

PARTITION

Tenants in common or joint tenants with right of survivorship are not obligated to continue a concurrent ownership and they are not required to sell just their interests to separate themselves from the co-tenancy. Instead, the tenant in common or the joint tenant has an absolute right to petition a court to partition the property. (Neither spouse can seek partition of property held in a tenancy by the entirety.) A partition action is today statutory in nature, although it began as a common law cause of action. There are two distinct categories of partition: partition in kind and partition by sale.

(a) Partition in Kind

Courts favor **partition in kind**, or physical partition. A partition in kind offers the least upset to the original co-tenancy, and it does not force a person to sell who does not wish to do so. In some states, the presumption favoring a partition in kind is statutory. In a partition in kind, the court divides the property into parcels of equal value; each co-tenant receives a separate parcel. When fewer than all co-tenants seek partition, they receive separate parcels and the others own the rest of the property as co-owners. If a court cannot partition the property into parcels of equal value, the court may order a money payment from one party to another to equalize the division. This payment is known as **owelty.** Because a partition is seldom likely to involve equally valuable parcels distributed to each tenant, owelty is a common feature in a partition in kind.

Example: Anne and Bruce own Blackacre as tenants in common. Blackacre is a forty-acre farm with a farmhouse. Anne seeks a partition in kind. A court awards Anne five acres and the farmhouse with a total value of $200,000; and awards the remaining 35 acres valued at $210,000 to Bruce. Bruce must pay an owelty of $5000 to Anne to even out the value each party receives.

(b) Partition by Sale

Partition in kind is not always practicable or advisable. In these cases, a court may order a **partition by sale** wherein the property is sold and the proceeds split among the concurrent owners. A single-family residence, for example, is not suited to partition in kind. Other factors, including a large number of co-tenants, the terrain, and the size of the tract, may convince a judge that a partition in kind is inadvisable. Similarly, when the appraisals necessary to justify a partition in kind are costly, or the appraisals are unreliable, a court may order a **partition by sale.** Judicial discretion in administering the partition by sale is generally recognized as a matter of equity, subject to the rules governing accounting and contribution (discussed earlier in this chapter).

A judicially ordered partition by sale may be appropriate even if all competent parties agree to a sale because a minor or unascertained (unborn) person owns an interest. The court approves the sale if it is in the best interest of the minor or unborn persons.

Some states permit a co-tenant to purchase at the sale — others do not. Where permitted, a purchasing co-tenant must pay a fair value and that amount is subject to judicial scrutiny. The proceeds of the sale are distributed as in a final accounting and settlement discussed above. Any co-tenant who has not accounted for any rents must do so. Sales proceeds from improvements will be allocated to the improver equal to the *value* of the improvements added to the overall value of the property, and not the *cost* of the improvements.

An agreement between the co-tenants prohibiting judicial partition normally is invalid as a restraint on alienation, but such restrictions will be sustained when limited to a reasonable time. For example, limitations on sale of a residence embodied in a divorce settlement and prohibiting a co-tenant's filing a partition action have been found reasonable.

Whether a restriction is reasonable may depend on whether the co-tenant wanting partition acquired his or her interest with knowledge of the restriction, the expertise of the co-tenant in possession, or the terms of an agreement on the subject between the parties. Nonetheless, an agreement to limit access to the judicial process is not to be inferred lightly. Partition is favored by the law and agreements to limit the remedy will be strictly construed.

Examples

Drafting Exercise

1. Now that you know the basic characteristics of all three of the major concurrent interests, please draft the granting clauses in a deed to create a tenancy in common, a joint tenancy with right of survivorship, and a tenancy by the entirety.

Dying to Know What Happened

2. (a) O, the holder of a fee simple absolute in Blackacre, conveyed Blackacre "to A, B, and C as joint tenants with right of survivorship." A year later C conveyed all his interest in Blackacre to D. Who has what interest in Blackacre?

   (b) A died five years later, devising his interest in Blackacre to E. Who owns what interest in Blackacre?

   (c) Three years later B died, devising his interest in Blackacre to F. Who owns what interest in Blackacre?

Surviving Joint Tenancies

3. O conveys Blackacre "to A and B and the survivor of them." What interest or estate is created for A and B?

Creating a Tenancy by the Entirety

4. Toby purchased his home when he was single. Now he is married to Veronica and wants to own the home as a tenant by the entirety with Veronica. How would you advise Toby to create the tenancy by the entirety?

On Second Thought

5. Kent and Richard own their law office building as joint tenants with right of survivorship. Kent was recently diagnosed with cancer. He wants to sever the joint tenancy and drafts a deed conveying his interest in the office building to himself as a tenant in common. What is the result of such a conveyance?

Mortgage Business

6. In a jurisdiction that does not clearly adhere to either a lien or a title theory, how would you recommend that a mortgage lender proceed in a loan for the purchase price of a residence whose title is to be held in the name of a husband and wife as joint tenants?

Our Land, His Debt

7. H and *W*, husband and wife, held title to Blackacre as joint tenants with right of survivorship. They separated. Later that year H borrowed $100,000 and executed a mortgage on Blackacre to secure payment of the debt. H died the next year. The state condemned Blackacre to build a new sports arena. The state agreed to pay $500,000 for Blackacre. The debt secured by the mortgage ($100,000) was unpaid, but was not the subject of a foreclosure action. H's executor claimed a portion of the condemnation award for H's estate. Is this claim valid?

He Did *What?*

8. (a) Anthony and Barlow held title to Blackacre as joint tenants with right of survivorship. Barlow executed a mortgage in a lien theory state. Barlow defaulted on the mortgage loan and the creditor brought a foreclosure action. The court hearing the foreclosure ordered that Blackacre be sold through a judicial sale, conducted at an auction. Barlow showed up at the sale, was the highest bidder for the property, and obtained a deed confirming the title to the property to him in fee simple absolute. Anthony came forward to claim his interest in Blackacre. Barlow sued Anthony to quiet title in fee. What result?

   (b) Same facts as in the previous problem, but a third party, not Barlow, obtained title through the foreclosure sale. Would this affect the result?

   (c) What result in (a) if Anthony and Barlow had both signed the mortgage, and Barlow was the highest bidder at the foreclosure auction?

Future Interests Intrude

9. (a) O conveyed Whiteacre "to *A* for life, remainder to B and her heirs." *A* and B cannot agree on the management of Whiteacre and *A* sues B for partition. What result?

   (b) O conveyed Blackacre "to *A* and B as tenants in common for life, remainder to C and her heirs." *A* and B disagree about the management of Blackacre and *A* sues B for its partition. May *A* bring this action?

Contribution and Accounting

10. (a) Shane, a widower, died intestate, survived by his three children: Homer, who lives one mile from Shane's residence; Louise, in Louisiana; and Ken, in Kentucky. Shane's residence passed to his three children under the state's intestacy statute. In what concurrent interest do the three children own the home?

(b) The house sat vacant for four months after Shane's death. Homer looked after the house but did not reside in it. He paid the monthly water and electricity bills totaling $120 for four months, paid a junior high school student $240 over four months to mow the lawn, and paid $90 for the annual termite inspection. Homer sent a $1000 check monthly to Mortgage Company ($4000 total in four months). Of the $4000, $1200 was interest, $1800 went against principal of the note, $600 went to property taxes, and $400 went to insurance on the house. Homer asked Louise and Ken to reimburse him. Assuming Ken and Louise do not want to pay anything, but will pay the minimum the law requires, how much will Homer collect from Ken and Louise?

(c) After four months of the house sitting empty, Homer hired a painter to paint both the exterior and the interior of the house for $4500. He could have a hired a painter for $3600, but felt more comfortable with the one he hired. After the house was painted, Homer paid $90 to advertise the house for rent.

　　Homer leased the home for $1500 a month. Homes in the neighborhood similar to the house rented for $1800, but Homer was happy to get $1500. Homer continued paying the $1000 each month to Mortgage Company. The tenant paid for the utilities and lawn maintenance.

　　What are the financial ramifications to Homer, Louise, and Ken after the first month's rental?

(d) After two years, Homer collected enough rental revenues to reimburse himself for expenditures out of his personal funds. In the first month after that he collects $1500 rent and pays Mortgage Company $1000, $120 for the annual termite inspection, and $80 to repair a clogged toilet. What are the financial consequences to the cotenants?

(e) A year later the tenant moved out. In the first month there was no rent income from the house, but Homer paid the $1000 due that month to the Mortgage Company ($900 carrying charges and $100 insurance premium). Instead of sending Louise and Ken the $100 a month they had come to expect, Homer sends a letter demanding each contribute $300. Louise does not want to pay and demands to know why she did not receive her $100. Homer, frustrated, filed a suit seeking judicial partition. Should the judge order a partition in kind or a partition by sale?

(f) Homer engaged a real estate broker, who located a buyer to purchase the house for $180,000. The broker's commission was $10,800. Other expenses of sale were $4200. To retire the note and mortgage, $15,000 of the sales proceeds were paid directly to Mortgage Company. Homer tells the closing agent that he spent 45 hours on the sale of the house and dedicated 450 hours to managing the property for the benefit of the three co-tenants since their father's death. He figures conservatively his time was worth $20 an hour, for which he has never been compensated, and for which he wanted to be compensated out of the sales proceeds ($900 for time on the sale of the house; $9000 for his labors all those years). How much does each co-tenant get from the sale of the house?

Alimony and Child Support

11. The tenancy by the entirety was established in an era without widespread divorce, when a person was expected to marry for life. Would it be wise to remove the immunity from levy and sale enjoyed by entireties property when a former spouse seeks to collect support payments — including child support — due from an ex-spouse now remarried and presently holding property in a tenancy with a subsequent spouse? What are the legislative alternatives?

Explanations

Drafting Exercise

1. To create a tenancy in common, you might say that O conveys to "A and B, in equal shares, as tenants in common." For a joint tenancy, say O conveys to "A and B as joint tenants with right of survivorship and not as tenants in common." For a tenancy by the entirety O conveys to "A and B, husband and wife, and to the survivor of them as tenants by the entirety, and not as tenants in common or joint tenants." Some of these suggestions are the product of caution or some make use of a default rule, but the intent in each case is made clear.

Dying to Know What Happened

2. (a) C's deed to D severed the joint tenancy. A and B continue in joint tenancy with each other, but together reform as a tenancy in common with D, each of the three having a one-third interest in Blackacre.
   (b) A's interest in Blackacre ended on his death. He had nothing to devise to E. B, as a joint tenant, gets A's interest. D is a tenant in common and will not increase her ownership. A now owns a two-thirds interest and D owns a one-third interest in Blackacre as tenants in common.
   (c) B died owning her interest as a tenant in common. A tenant in common can devise her interest. Therefore, F owns a two-thirds interest and D owns a one-third interest in Blackacre as tenants in common.

Surviving Joint Tenancies

3. Because a survivorship right is indicated (though not as clearly as it might be), many state courts say that this conveyance creates a joint tenancy with a right of survivorship in *A* and *B*. However, some state courts — a minority — hold that *A* and *B* have a concurrently held life estate, lasting as long as they both live, followed by a contingent remainder held by the survivor in fee simple absolute. States using the minority rule sometimes do so in order to prevent a partition action that would otherwise defeat the survivorship right. See William Stoebuck & Dale Whitman, *The Law of Property* §5.2, at 181 n.39 (3d ed. 2000).

Creating a Tenancy by the Entirety

4. When one party to a proposed joint tenancy already owns the property to be held in the tenancy, the parties should proceed in a two-step transaction. First, Toby should transfer the title to the property to a straw (a/k/a straw man) (an intermediary to temporarily hold legal title). Second, the straw should retransfer the title to Toby and Veronica as husband and wife in a tenancy by the entirety. They then would receive the title with the four unities present at the moment of the tenancy's creation. A straw is used when a jurisdiction does not clearly permit the unilateral creation of a joint tenancy by one of the tenants. The straw serves some function. The formalities of the process bring home to the sole owner the legal significance of what he or she is doing. They also prevent a layperson from accidentally creating a tenancy by the entirety when a tenancy in common was intended.

On Second Thought

5. It depends on the jurisdiction. If the jurisdiction allows a joint tenant unilaterally to sever a joint tenancy, Kent's deed severs the tenancy. This assumes Kent abides by any other requirement the state may impose, such as recording in the public deed records or notifying Richard.

    If, on the other hand, a jurisdiction requires a straw for a sole owner to create a joint tenancy in himself and another, then it is also likely to require the use of a straw to end the joint tenancy (unless a joint tenant transfers his interest to a third party). Some jurisdictions allowing a person to create a joint tenancy directly without the use of a straw may require a straw for a joint tenancy to sever his interest. In either of these jurisdictions, Kent's deed to himself is ineffective to sever the joint tenancy; and the joint tenancy continues.

Mortgage Business

6. The simplest and safest method is for both husband and wife to sign both the note and the mortgage.

Our Land, His Debt

7. The executor's claim is not valid. The mortgage, even given without *W*'s consent, does not sever the joint tenancy in lien theory states and in many title theory states so long as H has the financial ability to repay the loan and eliminate the mortgage. In most states the mortgage is extinguished with H's death (H's estate still is liable on the loan, however; only Blackacre does not serve as security for nonpayment). The survivorship right is still effective on H's death and on H's death *W* owns Blackacre. As owner of Blackacre she is entitled to the entire condemnation award. The separation does not affect how the title is held. See People v. Nogarr, 330 P.2d 858, 861 (Cal. Dist. Ct. App. 1958). In some title theory states, however, H's mortgage severs the joint tenancy with right of survivorship. In these states H's estate owns a one-half interest in Blackacre as tenant in common and will receive half the condemnation proceeds. The executor can use $100,000 to retire the outstanding note. *W* keeps her half of the condemnation proceeds.

He Did *What?*

8. (a) Anthony prevails. Barlow will neither win nor quiet the title. The mortgage did not work a severance of the joint tenancy when executed, but when the property was put into foreclosure and beyond Barlow's power to recall, a severance occurred. Thus, when the court ordered that the results of the sale were binding on Barlow, a severance of the joint tenancy had destroyed the survivorship right and Anthony and Barlow became tenants in common. Only Barlow's interest in Blackacre was auctioned. The title obtained in foreclosure was subject to Anthony's rights and, by decree, the court in Barlow's suit will find that Anthony and Barlow hold Blackacre as tenants in common. A deed claiming to give Barlow sole ownership in fee simple absolute may have been color of title for an adverse possession action, but Anthony acted well within any limitations period.

   (b) Only Barlow's interest could be sold at auction. The sale severed the joint tenancy with right of survivorship. Anthony and Barlow would still be tenants in common at the point when the court ordered the sale. After the sale, the third party becomes a tenant in common with Anthony.

(c) First, since both parties executed the mortgage, a third party purchasing at a foreclosure sale would own the whole property, not just a one-half interest. The issue is whether Barlow will receive the same favorable treatment allowed a third-party purchaser. In a majority of states Barlow would be deemed to purchase the property on behalf of the joint tenancy. If he had the money to buy at the foreclosure sale he had the money to make the mortgage payments and so he had a duty to make the mortgage payments. Anthony would be allowed to continue as a joint tenant with right of survivorship. In most states Anthony would be required to contribute funds for his share of the purchase price.

If, however, Anthony and Barlow lived in a state where a joint tenant is treated the same as a third party as long as the other joint tenants have an equal opportunity to bid and there was no indication Barlow engaged in fraudulent conduct or was in a fiduciary relationship with Anthony, Barlow would own Blackacre outright. Any excess sales proceeds over the amount of the mortgage would be divided between the two in a final settlement.

Future Interests Intrude

9. (a) Judgment for B: no partition. A has a present interest held in a life estate; B has a vested remainder held in fee simple absolute. A and B do not have concurrent possessory rights and so neither has a right to bring a partition action against the other.
   (b) Yes. A and B have a concurrent right to possess the life tenancy, so each has a right to bring partition against the other, but only as to the life estate they both hold, and not as to C's remainder. C does not have any concurrent rights to possession with them. Concurrent life tenants may bring partition inter se. An analogous result: If T1 and T2 both hold a joint leasehold, they have a right to partition the lease inter se, but have no such right against their landlord.

Contribution and Accounting

10. (a) A tenancy in common is presumed unless the deed or will stipulates another form. Here there was no deed or will, only a statute. Homer, Louise, and Ken own the residence as tenants in common.
    (b) Ken and Louise are obligated to pay carrying charges, which are the interest of $1200, the property taxes of $600, and the mortgage principal reduction payments of $1800. In some states the $400 for insurance is also a carrying charge; in others it is not. The law of the state where the property is located controls the definition of a carrying charge, not the state where the various co-tenants live.

Assuming insurance is not a carrying charge, the total of the carrying charges is $3600. The three siblings own equal shares and are equally liable for the carrying charges. Thus Ken and Louise should both contribute $1200 to Homer.

While it seems in fairness the co-tenants should all contribute to pay the reasonable costs of societally acceptable (and even mandated) expenses, a court will not force Louise and Ken to contribute for the yard maintenance, the utilities, the termite inspection, and, in most states, the insurance premiums. An annual termite inspection in some states is mandated by statute, so this may not be an elective expense everywhere. A good argument could be that this should be a carrying charge when it is state mandated and outside the control of any co-tenant. On the other hand, a co-tenant must select the inspector and that may result in a range of costs within the discretion of one co-tenant.

(c) Homer keeps the entire first month's rental of $1500. Under the Statute of Anne, Homer must share net rental proceeds with his co-tenants, Louise and Ken. In an accounting, Homer can reduce the amount to be split with Louise and Ken by the interest ($300), the mortgage principal reduction ($450), and the taxes ($150) (total of $900). In addition, he can offset the other $4690 of expenses related to the rental — insurance ($100), advertising ($90), and painting (repairs and maintenance are not an improvement) ($4500).

In the accounting the revenues are the actual amount collected, not what *could* have been collected, so rent revenues are $1500, not $1800. Likewise, deductions are actual amounts paid, not what *could* have been negotiated, so the painting expense is the full $4500. Homer cannot be reimbursed in the current month by more than the rent collected. Thus Homer can receive only the $1500 this month. Homer could have demanded contribution if the rent revenues did not cover the carrying charges, but here they did. Nothing prohibits Homer from requesting Ken and Louise pay their share if Louise and Ken are willing to pay, but he cannot force them to contribute. Expenditures not offsetting revenues are carried forward to offset any excess revenues in the next month, months, or years.

(d) Homer can offset the carrying charges, the insurance premium, and the termite inspection costs (total of $1200). Homer keeps the $1200. He then splits the remaining $300 equally among himself, Louise, and Ken; or $100 to each.

(e) Partition by sale. It's hard to imagine any of the three co-tenants even arguing for a partition in kind. Assuming one does, the judge begins with the presumption that a partition in kind is preferred.

But here, where the property is a single-family rental house, the impracticalities of a partition in kind are so great that a partition by sale is an easy decision.

(f) First, no co-tenant is entitled to compensation for representing the co-tenancy unless the co-tenants agree. Therefore, Homer gets no money for his efforts in the sale or for the many years he managed the property. After that, the math is simple. Sales proceeds of $180,000 less the commissions ($10,800), the other fees ($4200), and the mortgage payment ($15,000) leaves $150,000 to be divided among the three co-tenants, or $50,000 each.

Alimony and Child Support

11. There are at least two alternatives. First, legislation might authorize a court to issue a lis pendens (a recorded document in the deed records giving notice of a potential claim against the property) for a tenancy-by-entirety property, so that when the present spouses seek to sell or transfer it, the proceeds of that sale or transfer will be available to support the spouse of the former marriage to the extent of the ex-spouse's interest. This recognizes the continuing usefulness of the tenancy for the subsequent marriage, but only so long as the property itself is needed to support that marriage. This approach might, however, encourage evasion — as when the property is leased under a long-term arrangement, rather than sold outright — and so might be difficult to enforce. Another drawback is the spouse seeking alimony or child support may need the money currently, not at some distant future date.

Second, the docketing of a judgment or order for support of the former marriage might convert the tenancy in the subsequent marriage into a tenancy in common for purposes of the lien attachment/execution with regard to the support order. Here, the legislature recognizes the primacy of the first marriage over the second. This alternative is best suited to situations in which an ex-spouse has failed to meet support obligations for children of a former marriage. When the second spouse of the nonsupporting ex-spouse relies on the tenancy, this approach might work a hardship, and might deny the partners of the second marriage a future domicile of equal quality. The choice among alternatives is perhaps best left to a legislature.

Marital Property

At common law, a spouse was not an heir of her husband or his wife. By virtue of the marriage, however, each spouse held a life estate in some types of property of the other. These life estates were implied by law, not created by a deed or in a will.

COMMON LAW DOWER

At common law, a wife had a claim in the form of a life estate to a one-third share of all of the real property of which the husband was solely and beneficially seised in fee simple at any time during his marriage. This estate is called **dower.**

Dower is available from the moment of marriage. In early England dower designation of the dower house and lands was a part of the marriage ceremony: This designated property was called "named dower." Originally, the bride's family met with the groom and determined the lands to serve as his bride's house and lands, should she outlive him — hence the term "dowager," meaning a resident of a dower house. Often a large estate had a permanent dower house on its grounds. Kensington Palace in London, for example, is the dower house of the House of Windsor. Dower expanded from that beginning to include a fraction of all the husband's lands — a/k/a "unnamed dower."

Dower is intended to provide economic and social security for a widow, assuring her that she will live as she had become accustomed during her marriage. Originally it permitted her to live in the same locale as during the marriage. Today it permits her to maintain the same social position. In an age of primogeniture, it also provided in some measure for younger sons and daughters, who could continue living with their mother.

Before a husband's death, the wife's dower interests were called **inchoate dower** — not yet a legal estate in the husband's real property, but giving her a basis for suit in case the husband attempted to defeat a later dower claim by a fraudulent conveyance during the marriage.

After the husband's death, dower was termed **choate or consummate dower.** On the basis of it, when the husband in his will provided for the wife less than dower would, the wife had the right to have the court probating the will survey the husband's property and set aside one-third of each parcel of his land — the dower lands — for her life. Dower is thus a life estate that arises by operation of law.

DOWER REFORM

States are abolishing dower. Where it continues, it is a claim to a one-third or one-half life estate in all of the spouse's real property. Although in most states retaining dower, the wife (and in some states the surviving spouse — dower being extended to husbands as well as wives) has a dower in all lands, unless barred or released, of which the deceased spouse was ever seised during marriage; a few states limit dower to lands held by the decedent spouse at death. In Kentucky a wife has a dower of one-third of the lands the decedent did not own at death and of half the lands held at the husband's death. Moreover, contrary to the trend of most states to abolish dower, Kentucky extended dower to personal property. See Ky. Rev. Stat. Ann. §392.020 (Michie 1999).

A spouse cannot defeat his spouse's dower by selling or mortgaging the property. Purchasers and lenders thus are best advised to get the dower-owning spouse's signature releasing her dower in the property.

THE ELEMENTS OF DOWER

Today, the first element of a dower claim is a **valid marriage** when the property is owned. A marriage that is annulled or otherwise void ab initio is insufficient. A final decree in divorce may extinguish the dower claim by agreement. If no agreement is reached at divorce or in some other postnuptial agreement, the dower continues, but will not attach to property acquired after the divorce.

The second element is **sole and beneficial seisin** in the deceased spouse of the property at any time during the marriage. Property transferred before the marriage or acquired after the marriage ends cannot be subjected to a dower claim.

Seisin is always in a person holding a present possessory freehold estate. If the deceased spouse was a co-tenant, no dower lies because he or she was not solely seised. If the deceased spouse was a trustee for another, there is no dower in the property held in trust because there was no beneficial seisin. Similar results obtain when the spouse held as a straw man or otherwise held bare legal title. If the spouse, for example, executed a binding contract of sale to sell the property before the marriage, there is no dower in it. That title was held for the purchaser pending the closing and transfer of title.

Example 1:   A husband acquired land in fee simple absolute, subject to an option to buy it held by a third party. The wife's common law dower is also subject to the option since the estate is derivative and cannot outlast its source. A similar result would obtain if the husband took title to land subject to a mortgage during the marriage.

The estate of which the deceased spouse is seised cannot be one that ends at the deceased spouse's death. Dower does not apply to remainders and executory interests since the husband never had seisin in the property. A right of entry, exercised or exercisable by the time of death, is subject to dower. As to whether a possibility of reverter must be exercised, there is a split in the cases: Some courts do not require exercise because the right of possession given in the possibility of reverter is automatic.

In summary, dower does not apply to a deceased spouse's . . .

1. term for years. It is a nonfreehold estate and has no seisin. It does not matter that the term is 99 or 999 years.
2. life estate. It has seisin, but not inheritability. The purpose of dower is to give the surviving spouse a share of what the deceased's spouse's heirs take, for her security and for the security of younger children of the marriage. The life estate ends at the death of the deceased spouse and the heirs have no further interest in the property to which it applied.
3. joint tenancy. Where the deceased spouse is not the surviving tenant, the latter's right of survivorship prevails over a dower claim.
4. partnership interest in real property. A partnership interest is not subject to common law dower because the interest is regarded as personalty rather than real property. Any restrictions on transfer should be limited to those in the partnership agreement. (Similarly, if the deceased spouse owned shares in a corporation or other legal

entity whose sole assets were real property, there would still be no dower, and for the same reason — the shares are personalty.)

Dower does apply to a . . .

1. fee simple determinable. Dower attaches, but is subject to the occurrence of the stated condition. Dower rises no higher than the estate to which it attaches (which, as a general rule, also explains why it does not attach to a life estate).
2. fee simple subject to a condition subsequent, or to an executory limitation. Same answer as in the prior paragraph: Dower attaches, but subject to the condition.

Dower applies to legal, rather than equitable, estates. There is no equitable action to protect a dower claim.

Dower applies, moreover, whether the spouse held property in fee simple absolute or fee tail. Only in the instance of a fee tail special — i.e., a fee tail limited to the issue of a prior spouse — did dower not apply.

Example 2:   A conveyed Blackacre to B in fee simple absolute. B then conveyed to C, who conveyed to D. A died, leaving W1 his widow. B then died, leaving widow W2. C soon died, leaving widow W3. Finally, D died, leaving widow W4. All four widows survived and claimed dower. If each widow has a common law dower right, then W1 has 1/3 life interest, W2 has 1/3 of the remaining 2/3 — or 2/9 of Blackacre. Now 1/3 + 2/9 = 5/9 of Blackacre, are already in widows W1 and W2's hands, so W3 has 4/27 and W4 8/81.

DOWER AND ADVERSE POSSESSION

Property acquired by adverse possession is subject to dower. If the deceased was in the process of adversely possessing property and so was still subject to disseisin or ouster by its true owner, so is the spouse claiming dower: He or she cannot acquire more rights than the deceased spouse had acquired by the time of death.

DOWER AND WASTE

In this country, widows were early permitted by statute to protect their inchoate dower rights with a cause of action in waste, and were protected from suits in waste when clearing uncultivated lands held through dower.

RELEASE OF DOWER

A wife can release dower by signing away her rights. Release of dower claims is necessary, or at least customary where dower has not been repealed, upon the transfer of the property. Buyers and lenders insist wives join in executing deeds with their husbands even if the husband is the sole legal owner of the property. Dower also can be released by a prenuptial or postnuptial agreement. Since dower survives divorce unless the wife (or husband) agrees to release her (or his) rights, a final divorce decree (as opposed to a pending action for one) may and should make express provision to release a spouse's estate from a dower claim by the ex-spouse.

BARRING DOWER

Dower claims can sometimes be barred in two ways. The first way is by putting property into a trust prior to marriage because, historically, dower applied only to legal estates, not to equitable interests like trusts. Thus real estate held in a trust was considered personal property and not real property subject to dower. This is not a foolproof method of barring dower today because dower may apply to personal as well as real property — and trust proceeds are regarded as personalty.

Second, dower is barred by giving the deceased spouse a life estate in property, with a power of appointment created prior to the marriage. This may be a surer method of barring dower, but it is more inflexible than a trust.

FORCING AN ELECTION

Some states retaining dower stipulate that the surviving spouse must choose between taking her dower or taking under the husband's will (or by inheritance if there is no will). In states that allow a wife to take dower in addition to taking under the deceased husband's will, a husband can force a surviving spouse to elect between her dower rights and her rights under his will.

CURTESY

Dower was a wife's life estate in one-third of her husband's real property at common law. Her interest could last for her life long after her husband's death. The husband at common law had a right to his wife's property too. The extent and longevity of his rights can be broken into three steps. First, upon marriage, at common law a husband received a life estate in all — not just a third — of his wife's real property of which she was seised. This estate arose at the time of the marriage. It lasted until either the husband or the wife died. It was called the **estate by the marital right**, or the estate (in Latin) **jure uxoris** — all this while the wife was entitled only to the equivalent of walking-around money. The husband's estate by marital right was a right of use and occupation — a right to possess the eligible property and use its rents and profits. This right continued for the life of his wife.

A husband received a second, more beneficial right in his wife's property at the birth of issue born alive to the husband and wife during their marriage. At the birth of the first child, the husband acquired a life estate measured by his life — called tenancy for life by the **curtesy initiate** (intended to support children and maintain their father in the same economic condition as existed throughout the marriage). So long as the issues of the marriage were born alive, whether or not they survived, the estate *jure uxoris* merged into a larger estate — the husband acquired a life estate in the wife's freehold estates inheritable by the children. This estate lasted so long as the marriage did, and was followed by a reversion in the wife, should she outlive her husband.

Finally, the husband at common law, upon the death of a wife by whom there was a child born, owned a tenancy for life by the **curtesy consummate** (or curtesy). Thus the curtesy initiate became a curtesy consummate, and it continued to the end of the husband's life. Unlike dower, both claims to curtesy by the husband required the birth of issue born to the couple during their marriage; no such requirement attached to a dower claim. So curtesy was, like dower, a life tenancy, except that it applied to both legal and equitable estates of the wife in any lands she held during the marriage. Like dower, it is a derivative estate, but for the husband to claim curtesy, the wife need not have had seisin in the lands claimed; some cases said that "seisin in fact" (bare possession) would suffice.

One of the principal legislative results of the first women's movement, begun at the Seneca Falls Convention in 1848, was the enactment by state legislatures of the Married Women's Property Acts. Courts interpreted the Married Women's Property Acts to have abolished the estate *jure uxoris* (husband's estate by the marital right). Curtesy soon was abolished. States retaining dower extended dower to husbands so that husbands and wives were treated the same.

Comparing Dower with Curtesy	
Dower	Curtesy
attaches to a fraction	attaches to all
requires seisin in law	requires (actual) seisin in fact
attaches to legal estates	attaches to legal and equitable estates
does not require issue	requires birth of issue

THE MODERN ELECTIVE SHARE

States abandoning dower and curtesy give a surviving spouse an *elective share,* also known as a *statutory share* or *forced share.* At common law, a spouse was not an heir of her husband or his wife. The elective share is a right of the surviving spouse to elect between (a) taking her husband's property as though she were an heir under the state's intestacy statute or under a provision in the elective share statute, or (b) taking under the deceased spouse's will.

The elective share is usually one-third or one-half of the deceased spouse's estate. It is generally one-third of the estate when there are lineal descendants of the decedent, and one-half when there is none. It applies to both real and personal property and to both legal and equitable interests in property, so long as the property is owned by the deceased at death.

The elective share is not self-executing. It provides nothing until the surviving spouse — during probate of the estate or as part of an intestate distribution — files an election to take it after the decedent's death. Typically, the election must be made within nine months of the spouse's death, or within six months after the will is probated, whichever occurs later. The survivor taking the elective share must forego all devises under a decedent's will.

CALCULATING THE AMOUNT OF THE ELECTIVE SHARE

Calculating the amounts of an elective share is complicated. As background, not all of a decedent's property passes by will or by intestate succession (through probate). Much passes outside probate. We have studied tenancy by the entirety and joint tenancy with right of survivorship. Other nonprobate assets include trusts (i.e., one spouse transfers valuable assets to a trustee making himself, his spouse, or a child the beneficiary), life insurance policies, retirement plans, and inter vivos gifts.

An issue is to what extent nonprobate assets should be considered in calculating the elective share. Some states do not consider nonprobate assets; others include only some. The Uniform Probate Code lumps most nonprobate assets into an **augmented estate**, which is the total of the probate estate and a reclaimable estate.

The **reclaimable estate** is comprised of the following:

1. Assets owned by the electing spouse received from the deceased. This prevents the electing spouse from getting a larger share than is due by getting inter vivos gifts, for example, and then electing an intestacy share of what remains in the decedent's estate.
2. Assets held in trust for the spouse that originated with the decedent.
3. Insurance and pension plans of the decedent naming the spouse as beneficiary.
4. Assets held by others, often in a trust, if the decedent had a power of appointment (a right to designate who would receive the income or principal of the trust on a yearly basis or at his death), or had a right to revoke the trust.
5. Assets transferred by the decedent to another where the decedent retained a life estate, possession, or income, or with a right of survivorship. This keeps the decedent spouse from depleting the surviving spouse's share.
6. Any assets gratuitously transferred to anyone within two years of the decedent's death (i.e., gifts). There is a $3000 per donee exception.
7. A 1990 revision to the Uniform Probate Code would bring into the reclaimable estate all the assets held by the surviving spouse, not just those received from the decedent.

The reclaimable estate is added to the probate estate to get the augmented estate. The applicable fraction (normally one-third or one-half) is multiplied against the augmented estate to determine the surviving spouse's elective share. The spouse's elective share is reduced by the assets already in his or her possession, and by the assets passing to the electing spouse outside of probate. That leaves the net elective share, which comes from the decedent's estate.

HOMESTEADS

Some state statutes and state constitutions protect a family's residence or "homestead" against creditors' claims. The **homestead exemption** protects eligible property from the claims of unsecured creditors and many secured creditors of either spouse. The homestead property cannot be foreclosed on by secured creditors unless the mortgage or lien being foreclosed was given for delineated purposes — a mortgage to purchase or improve the homestead property; a lien for past-due property taxes; a federal tax lien; or as a lien from a property settlement in a divorce, for example.

The main homestead property is the principal residence. The residence is defined as a dwelling and the land on which it is located, the acreage sometimes being limited to a certain area or acreage, or value, or both. Some states protect other assets, such as a car or motorcycle, farm animals, or tools of a trade, but it is the family residence and sometimes one business location that constitutes the major protected asset. Not only is the residence protected against creditors, but purchasers cannot defeat a spouse's homestead rights unless the spouse signs the deed. Hence both spouses are required to sign the deed to a residence even if the house is in the name of only one spouse. In some states a homestead right is not self-executing; there must be a recorded declaration of homestead defining its extent.

The homestead is of limited effectiveness as a shield against the claims of creditors in most states. The homestead exemption is typically limited to a stated value and often that value, adequate when enacted into law, is outmoded and too low. If a residence is worth more than the homestead value, the house gets sold and the creditors can claim the excess value. In other states, however — Texas being the prime example — the homestead exemption can safeguard some valuable assets with no limitation on value (200 acres plus improvements for land outside a city; up to 10 acres of land with improvements including the residence and maybe a business in a city).

SEPARATE, MARITAL, AND COMMUNITY PROPERTY

Eight states — Louisiana, Texas, New Mexico, Arizona, California, Nevada, Washington, and Idaho — were founded as community property states, derived from the civil laws of Spain and France, which were brought by early settlers from those countries to these states. Two other states — Wisconsin and Alaska — have chosen to become community property states in recent years. The remaining, common law states, derive their concepts of property ownership from English common law.

In **common law states,** also known as **separate property states,** property is owned by the spouse who paid for or inherited it. A person's property is separate from his or her spouse's property. In practice, for most of our history, that meant the husband owned most of the marital assets since he earned income, while the wife cared for the house and children. On divorce the husband got the assets. Common law states developed alimony and support laws to prevent divorced women from becoming destitute. On the death of the husband, he controlled who got his assets, unless dower or the elective share rules protected the widow. Many common law states have passed legislation that mimics those of community property states in cases of divorce. These statutes differ primarily in the extent to which they require a judge to accept either the legal rules classifying or the spouses' designation of property as separate or marital property. To varying degrees, these statutes assume that judges have equitable discretion to divide spousal property upon divorce, no matter which spouse holds title, marriage being in some sense a partnership.

Community property states view the marital unit as one — a partnership — in which the husband and wife work as a unit for their mutual benefit. Hence, whatever one earns is deemed owned by both. Property bought with the husband's wages, for example, is deemed owned half by the husband and half by the wife. All property acquired during the marriage is presumed to be community property.

That community property presumption can be rebutted, however. Property acquired before the marriage is **separate property** and belongs to the spouse who owned the property before the marriage. Property acquired during marriage as a gift, an inheritance, or a devise is the separate property of the recipient spouse. In most community property states, a couple can enter into a prenuptial agreement, providing assets purchased with income earned by one party shall remain that person's separate property. This may occur, for example, on second or third marriages, where both spouses have independent sources of income and also likely children by prior marriages.

The biggest divergence among the community property states centers on income earned from separate property. In three community property states (Texas, Louisiana, and Idaho) income from separate property is community property. In the five other states, income from separate property is separate property. Gains from the sale of separate property are separate property and considered a return of the principal asset.

If separate property is commingled with community property (usually this concerns money in bank accounts), the rebuttable presumption is the separate money was spent first and for living expenses rather than for assets. In other words, commingled funds most likely will be found to be community property. To illustrate, if W owns corporate stock as a separate asset and receives dividends from the corporation, in the majority of community property states the money received as dividends remains her separate property (in the minority of community property states the income is community property). If, however, W deposits that money into a joint banking account or any account with both separate funds and community funds in it, unless W kept meticulous records classifying the separate funds and the community funds, the funds will be presumed to be community funds.

The spouses can **transmute** separate property into community property (or vice versa) by agreement — required to be written in most of the eight states, oral in some. Both spouses must agree. One spouse cannot act unilaterally.

Recognizing that some married couples move from common law states to community property states, some community property states say property continues to hold its character as separate or community property, as it had when acquired. Others say all separate property acquired during a marriage is considered to be quasi-community property once the couple moves to a community property state.

Each state has its own rules as to who can manage which assets and which assets creditors can reach. A typical statute may require creditors of only one spouse to exhaust that spouse's separate assets before resorting to the community property. A creditor of one spouse cannot reach the other spouse's separate property. A creditor of both spouses can reach community property, as well as the separate assets of both spouses.

In marriages of any length in community states, most assets will be community property. Upon divorce each spouse is entitled to half the community property. If one spouse has a business, generally that spouse gets the business's assets, and other assets of equal value will be awarded to the other spouse. On death, the deceased spouse may devise his or her half of the community property.

Until 1948, there was a decided federal income tax advantage given to married couples in community property states, but the Internal Revenue Code that year was amended to permit married persons in all states to split their income with their spouse for purposes of income tax liability, hence the category of "married, filing jointly" on IRS Form 1040.

Much of the community property system is embodied in the Uniform Marital Property Act, enacted in Wisconsin in a modified form. Its aim is to bridge the gap between common law and community property jurisdictions by providing for shared management of property during the marriage, no matter who holds title to it, and to protect the non-owning spouse if the owner dies first or upon dissolution of the marriage.

ANTE-NUPTIAL AGREEMENTS

Ante-nuptial or prenuptial agreements are agreements between persons contemplating marriage concerning management and ownership of property acquired and held during and after marriage. So long as the agreement is not solely for the purpose of sexual relations, the scope of such agreements under the Uniform Ante-Nuptial Agreement Act (adopted by about 20 states) may include a definition of rights of each spouse in the property of the other, including the disposition of property on death, the elimination or modification of spousal support rights on divorce, inheritance rights, and alienation rights during marriage. Some courts are wary about ante-nuptial agreements and may annul an ante-nuptial agreement because one party did not have legal counsel, or time to consider the agreement's consequences, or for some other procedural deficiency. Full disclosure and time to consider are preconditions to a valid agreement.

PUTATIVE SPOUSES

Persons who think that they are validly married when they are not are known as *putative spouses.* In most states, marriages must be validly performed by someone with authority to do so, witnessed, etc. State statutory requirements pertain. Only a very few states recognize so-called common law marriages — typically based on lore like "live together for seven years and you are married." In some states putative spouses have been protected by theories of estoppel, implied contract, or unjust enrichment. Where such theories have been successful, they have protected one person in a long-term relationship that ended with the other party to it retaining an unreasonable amount of the property accumulated during the relationship and acquired through the efforts of both parties. Lesson to be learned: Don't count on it! The law everywhere has proceeded on a case-by-case basis, making no progress except by litigation. It might be safer to say that two persons, with support or other rights originating in divorce decrees from prior marriages, don't lose those rights just because they have entered into new co-habitation relationships.

Examples

Dower Power

1. Harry and Wanda married. Harry in his own name acquired Blackacre in fee simple absolute. They divorced. Years later, Harry died. Does Wanda have a common law dower claim on Blackacre (in states that recognize dower)?

Elective Share

2. Darrell held title to Blackacre in fee simple absolute. Darrell transferred that title to his son Steven for "one dollar ($1.00), love, and affection." Shortly after the transfer, Darrell died. Is the value of Blackacre subject to the elective share otherwise available to Darrell's spouse, Wynona?

Will Substitutes

3. Does the elective share apply to will substitutes — e.g., gifts causa mortis, gifts to another's bank account, and joint bank accounts?

The Tax Man Cometh

4. H and W, husband and wife, own their residence, Blackacre, as tenants in common. H and W file separate federal income tax returns, as they have done for years. H becomes delinquent in the payment of his taxes. The Internal Revenue Service is authorized by Int. Rev. Code §§6321 and 7403 to seize and sell any property in which the delinquent taxpayer has any right, interest, or title. Thus, the IRS seeks to satisfy H's delinquency by asserting its statutory lien on and selling Blackacre. H and W seek to block the sale, saying that under state law the homestead is exempt from such a sale. Are they correct?

A Community Effort in Common

5. Larry and Melinda have been married for six years. Larry received a $100,000 year-end bonus at work. He bought $100,000 of Capitol Co. stock. Melinda's grandfather died soon thereafter, leaving Melinda $100,000 in Capitol Co. stock. A year later Capitol Co. sent Larry a dividend check in the amount of $5000. Capitol Co. also sent a $5000 dividend check to Melinda. Larry and Melinda deposited their dividend checks in separate bank accounts (Larry into his account and Melinda into hers). Six months later they divorced.
   (a) Assuming Larry and Melinda live in a common law state, who gets the Capitol Co. stock, and who gets the $10,000 from dividends?
   (b) Assuming Larry and Melinda live in a community property state, who gets the Capitol Co. stock, and who gets the $10,000 from dividends?

Explanations

Dower Power

1. Yes, Wanda has a dower claim in states that recognize common law dower. Absent a contrary provision in the divorce decree, dower is not terminated by divorce, and so Wanda's dower claim is not barred even though it is asserted years after the end of the marriage. This is a rule that was formulated long ago, well before the divorce rate rose so steeply. It indicates the strong attachment of the common law to dower claims.

Elective Share

2. Under the Uniform Probate Code, the value of Blackacre is subject to the elective share otherwise available to Darrell's spouse, Wynona, since it was a gratuitous transfer within two years of Darrell's death. If Darrell's intent in effectuating the transfer is to give Steven what he would otherwise inherit under Darrell's will, but takes Blackacre out of his estate, the courts in some states would include the payment in the reclaimable estate. If, on the other hand, Steven had paid full consideration for the asset, then the money Steven paid would be included in Darrell's estate and subject to Wynona's elective share, but the property Steven bought would be excluded.

Will Substitutes

3. Does the elective share apply to will substitutes — e.g., gifts causa mortis, Totten trust bank accounts, and joint bank accounts? Yes, unless the state statute modifies the result as to a particular asset class. This is a variation of the issue in the previous problem. The answer, then, is essentially the same, but with regard to any particular will substitute, the answer will often be a matter of statute and part of the state's probate code. So check the applicable code. When the code is silent, it makes sense to include within the elective share any assets and funds governed by any functional equivalent of a valid will. The intent of the transferor is the same as that of a decedent, and the decedent's estate would be depleted if the use of the substitute robs the estate of its value. The value of the elective share is lost if the value of the substitute is not included in the share's calculation.

The Tax Man Cometh

4. No. A homestead provides an exemption from many debts, but not from tax liens. The IRS may levy on the whole title to property held in co-tenancy by a delinquent taxpayer with a nondelinquent one, so long as the nondelinquent co-tenants receive just compensation for their interest as a result of the IRS sale. See United States v. Rogers, 461 U.S. 677, 698 (1983).

A Community Effort in Common

5. (a) In a common law state, each marital partner owns separate property. Larry's bonus is his, and his purchase of the stock with his money means he owns the $100,000 worth of stock. The dividends earned from his property are his money. Likewise Melinda's inheritance is hers, and the dividends she receives from her stock are her money. Larry and Melinda each get $100,000 in stock and $5000 in cash.

(b) In a community property state, all income earned by either spouse is community property and belongs equally to both spouses. Larry's bonus, therefore, is community property. The dividends on community property are community property. Gifts and inheritances received by a spouse during a marriage are the separate property of the recipient spouse. Thus the $100,000 in stock Melinda inherited is Melinda's separate property. The community property states differ on the character of the dividends on separate property. Some say income earned on separate property is community income; others say income earned on separate property is separate property.

Larry gets $50,000 of Capitol Co. stock and $2500 in cash for his half of the community property. Just as certainly, Melinda gets $150,000 worth of Capitol Co. stock (her $100,000 separate property and her $50,000 share of community property) and $2500 in cash from the community property dividends. In some community property states, Larry and Melinda split the $5000 dividends Melinda received on her separate stock; in other states Melinda gets the entire $5000.

The Law of
Landlord and
Tenant

PART III

15

The Landlord and Tenant Relationship

In a **lease** the owner of property (the landlord or lessor) contracts to grant a tenant or lessee exclusive possession of specific real or personal property. It typically is — but need not be — for a definite term and it also is typically given in exchange for rent. (Rent is not necessary for a lease's validity, just as a deed for the conveyance of any interest or estate need not be based on consideration to be valid.) Thus, a lease is either a grant or a contract transferring the right to exclusive possession for an agreed, if indefinite, period of time. The lessor retains a reversion. Leased real property, after being described in detail, is usually known as "the premises."

No particular words of art are necessary to create a lease. Under the provision for real property interests in the Statute of Frauds, states require that a lease with a term longer than one, two, or three years — depending on the jurisdiction — must be in writing. If a lease is for a term exactly one, two, or three years, then it too should be in writing because most states' Statute of Frauds will require some writing for a lease to be enforceable. A few states require all leases to be in writing. If the Statute of Frauds requires that a lease be in writing, so must any agreement modifying or terminating it. The real property recording acts of many states require a lease with a term of more than one, two, or three years (depending on the state) to be recorded to be protected against bona fide purchasers.[1]

Leases originally were considered conveyances of nonfreehold estates in land. Consequently many rules applicable to the conveyance of land still apply to leases. The law of contracts strongly, even predominantly,

---

1. A chapter on recording acts can be found later in this book.

influences landlord-tenant law today. In some regards, tort law intrudes, and in the past 60 years or so governments have expanded regulation of the landlord-tenant relationship.

Whether a lease is a conveyance under property law or a contract can affect the outcome of an issue. For example, if a lease is not considered a conveyance of an interest or estate in real property, a landlord could, any day of the week, walk onto the premises, jerk his thumb at the door, and say "Get out. I'll pay your damages." Which law applies may be a function of the type of issue at hand; or a court may label the lease a property conveyance or a contract to justify its substantive law or the remedy.

Because different approaches and rules apply, sometimes an issue in a case is whether the parties created a lease or some other interest: a life estate, an estate for years; a license; or employee lodging. Evaluate the underlying relationship and not just the name given to the document.

To illustrate, if a person buys a ticket to a sporting or entertainment event, or to ride an airplane, and the event or airline personnel demands the ticket holder leave the premises, the ticketholder's (and premises owner's) rights vary if the arrangement is a lease and not a license. Likewise whether the ticket authorizing a person to park her car in a parking lot is a license or lease affects whether the premises owner is liable if the car is stolen.

TYPES OF LEASE

Leases fall into four distinct categories. Three are voluntary: the term of years, the periodic tenancy, and the tenancy at will. The fourth, the tenancy at sufferance, arises when a lessee rightfully in possession pursuant to a lease stays on the property after the lease ends. The law applicable to each type has some unique characteristics.

(a) Term of Years

A **term of years** or **tenancy for years** is a lease for a fixed period of time. A term of years arises from any lease or rental agreement that expires at the end of a defined period, whether for a day, a week, a month, a year, several years, or 999 years. The emphasis is on the word "term," not "years." An example of a short term of years may be the rental of a hall for a dance or wedding reception, or a beach house for a week. A longer term of years may be a 99-year lease on land on which the lessee intends to construct a building. The common law put no limit on the length of a term of years.

A landlord who grants, demises, and lets "to Tenant for five years" creates a term of years. ("Demise" and "let" are the traditional verbs used to transfer this interest, and "grant" is a verb indicating that a document is used to accomplish the transfer.) A transfer "to Tenant for 100 years if Tenant so long lives" is a term of years, or more precisely a determinable term of years. A fixed maximum term is clearly stated, although this term could end before a century has passed. The fact that it might end earlier is irrelevant for classifying the grant as a term of years: When a conveyance is for a fixed term, the interest is a lease not a life estate or some other freehold estate.

A term of years need not commence when the lease is executed or delivered, but may commence at a time in the future. The reversion retained by the landlord is a future interest, arising after the term ends. When the term ends, the reversion's holder takes back possession.

The term of years must recite the length of the term. A term of years requires that calendar dates be identified for the first and last days of the lease. The dates can be specified as a date — "November 30, 2020," for example — or based on a familiar day — "until Labor Day 2020," for example — or based on a fixed term — "for six months beginning January 1, 2014," for example. If no date of commencement is given for the term, it may be inferred to begin on the date that the lease is executed by the parties to it, or on the date of its delivery by the landlord to the tenant. To illustrate, "to Tenant starting six months from the date of this lease, and thereafter for five years" is sufficient when the lease is dated. Likewise, a reference to another document or event can provide the requisite defined period. For example, "to Tenant so long as he rents the property adjoining Blackacre" is sufficient when the lease to the adjoining property stipulates a term of years. In this sense, the law refers to the term as a determinate period.

A term of year is also alienable, devisable and inheritable unless a covenant or provision in the lease restricts the right to transfer. Only when the provisions of the term of years require that the tenant perform personal services will the lease not be inheritable. (Even an explicit restriction on the tenant's use of the premises will not deny a lease's inheritability.) Likewise, if the landlord dies during the term, the executor or administrator of his or her decedent's estate has a duty to recognize the lease's term and provisions.[2]

An important feature of the term of years is that the tenant need not provide the landlord with notice that she will vacate the premises at the end of the term. Likewise, absent a statute on the subject, neither must the landlord give the tenant a notice to vacate at the end of the term. In both instances, the lease itself provides that notice. The expiration of the term is self-executing and automatic.

A lease failing as a term of years becomes either a periodic tenancy, a tenancy at will, or a license, depending on the particulars of the lease and the case. A **license** is an authorization from an owner to enter premises without

---

2. But *see* joint tenancy with right of survivorship *supra* Chapter 13, "Concurrent Ownership."

liability for trespass; it is revocable at will by the licensor (and presumably by the licensee, too, on a principle of mutuality).

(b) Periodic Tenancy

The **periodic tenancy** has no defined ending date. The tenant possesses the leased premises for an indefinite term, paying scheduled periodic rent to the landlord. Thus, a periodic tenancy is one that continues or runs from day to day, week to week, month to month, or year to year. A month-to-month apartment lease, for example, is a periodic tenancy.

If the lease does not state the length of the lease term, the initial term's length will conform to the frequency of the rent payments. Thus, if rent is payable monthly, the parties will be found to have a month-to-month periodic tenancy, and if a lease has a starting date, but no termination date, stated in it, it is a periodic tenancy because by default it is governed by the rental period.

The periodic tenancy endures until one of the parties gives the notice to end it. An express notice is required to terminate the periodic tenancy. Generally, unless the lease stipulates a different notice period, either party can terminate a periodic tenancy by giving notice at least equal to the length of the tenancy. To be effective, the notice must state the termination date. A tenant in a periodic tenancy for six months must give six months' notice; one in a month-to-month tenancy must give a month's notice, and so on. Since giving notice to terminate a long-term lease term in advance is impractical and not necessary to protect the parties, periodic tenancies of one year or more can be terminated on six months' notice.

Many states statutorily have relaxed the time requirements when a notice must be given, some to as short a time as seven days for a tenant to terminate a residential lease, or three months to terminate a year-to-year lease. Some states retain the month's notice required for a month-to-month tenancy, but allow the lease to end a month after the notice is given, even if that date is not the end of the month or the lease period. In these cases, the last month's rent is prorated.

Like the term of years, a periodic tenancy may be created by express agreement. It may also be created by implication, however, as when a term for years with an annual term expires, and the tenant continues to pay rent as it comes due and the landlord continues to accept or collect the rent and does not attempt to reenter the premises. The terms and conditions of the lease for the original term are carried over into the new one.

(c) Tenancy at Will

A **tenancy at will** is a landlord-tenant relationship that endures only as long as the parties agree it shall. It continues only by mutual agreement and ends when one of the parties wants to end it. The tenancy at will is encountered mostly where the relation of landlord and tenant is an informal one, as where one friend permits another to stay in his or her house. A tenancy at will rarely is used intentionally in commercial transactions — business people need more certainty than the tenancy at will provides.

The tenant at will enjoys rights as a tenant. The tenant, for example, can sue to evict trespassers.

A tenancy at will may be either express or implied. It has been implied, for example, when a purchaser occupies property pending conveyance of title. In states where all leases must be in writing to satisfy the Statute of Frauds, not just leases of a duration greater than one, two, or three years, an oral lease by law is a tenancy at will. In several states, all oral leases are presumed to be tenancies at will.

A conveyance to Tenant "so long as he wishes," or "as long as he pays rent and resides on the premises" might be examples of a tenancy at will, but might also be determinable life estates and, construing toward the higher estate, perhaps the latter is the better view. Where it is clear on the face of the agreement that both parties intend to establish a tenancy at will, the lease will be a tenancy at will, and lease provisions such as for required notice to terminate and for the payment of rent at intervals do not create a periodic tenancy. On the other hand, even a very broad forfeiture clause in favor of a landlord in a commercial lease will not turn a lease otherwise qualifying as a term for years or periodic tenancy into a tenancy at will.

At common law a tenancy at will was terminable at either party's fancy with no notice period required. Many states by statute require the landlord to give 30 days' notice, and some allow only the tenant to terminate the lease at will.

A tenancy at will is not inheritable or devisable. It ends at the death of either party. Likewise, the tenancy at will is not transferable or assignable. A transfer of the landlord's title, or an assignment of the tenant's rights, ends the lease.

(d) Tenancy at Sufferance

A **tenancy at sufferance** is not a true estate — it is a type of wrongful occupancy. It occurs when a tenant enters into a valid lease of any of the three types mentioned previously and then holds over past the end of the lease term. The tenant's entry onto the premises was rightful, but continuing there is not.

The general rule is that the landlord has a choice of remedies when a tenant wrongfully holds over: The landlord may elect to evict or eject the tenant as a trespasser and recover damages or, alternatively, to extend the lease for a new term.

The landlord's election depends on the tenant's holdover being wrongful and nontrivial. The tenant's holding over must be voluntary, for example, and not for reasons out of his control. Similarly, a tenant may leave personal property on the premises after the term so long as what is left does not interfere with the landlord's or new tenant's possession. Further, a delay in vacating caused by the landlord's failure to provide services excuses the holdover. These limits are imposed on the holdover doctrine because of its harsh effects on, and the resulting judicial sympathy for, the tenant.

(1) Holdover as Trespasser

If the landlord elects to treat the tenant at sufferance (or holdover tenant) as a trespasser, she need not give a notice to quit and may eject the tenant at any time. Even though the tenancy by sufferance has no definite term and may be terminated at the will of either party, by statute in some jurisdictions a landlord may eject a holdover only through use of the judicial process, rather than through self-help. Once the landlord elects to treat the tenant as a trespasser, the landlord cannot change her mind and try to extend the lease.

In addition to ejecting the holdover tenant, a landlord will seek an amount equal to the fair rental value of the premises for the time the tenant at sufferance was on the premises past the termination of the lease. Many state legislatures impose a liability for double rent on tenants for each day of a holdover period. Some of these statutes require that the landlord make a demand for double rent before the liability arises, but this matter is not always addressed.

(2) Holdover as Renewing Lease

If the landlord elects to treat the tenant as having renewed the lease on the same or similar conditions and covenants, then the issue turns to the length of the new term. Some courts say the renewed lease will be the same duration as the original lease; others say the lease will last the period covered by one rent payment as a periodic tenant. For example, if a tenant holds over following a one-year lease, with rent payable monthly, in some states the new lease period would be one year, and in other states it would be one month. Because of the harsh effects of this election on the tenant, no court is likely to hold the tenant to a term longer than one year.

Some states by legislation have abrogated the landlord's option of extending the lease for an additional term without the tenant's consent and have limited the landlord's remedy to double rent for each day of the holdover period. Some but not all states require the landlord make a demand for double rent before the double rent accrues.

(3) Holdover in Other Situations

A tenancy at sufferance may also be found when a mortgagor holds over after a foreclosure decree is final, a vendor of property stays in possession after conveying title to a purchaser, or a purchaser or grantee keeps possession after defaulting on a contract to purchase or in disregard of a rightful assertion of a possibility of reverter or right of reentry. This type of tenancy is, after all, more a wrongful occupation than an estate in land.

THE LANDLORD'S DUTY TO DELIVER POSSESSION

Related to the holdover issue is the touchy subject of what to do when a new tenant arrives ready to move in but the previous tenant has not vacated. Courts early on established the landlord has the duty to convey to the tenant the legal right to take possession of the premises for the term. But legal right to possession is not the same as delivery of actual possession free of holdover tenants and trespassers.

To put the issue in concrete form, assume an incoming law student signed an apartment lease in May, to take effect in August in time for the beginning of classes. The appointed day to move in arrived, and the student found the previous tenant still living in the apartment. The prospective law student mentions this disconcerting fact to the landlord, who expresses his awareness and dismay. The issue now is whose responsibility is it to eject the holdover tenant.

The majority rule — the so-called English Rule — places the duty on the lessor (landlord) to oust the holdover tenant and any trespassers on the property at the beginning of the lease. A minority of states adopted the so-called American Rule that requires the landlord only deliver legal possession, not actual possession. Under the American Rule, the tenant must evict the holdover tenant and any trespassers. The two rules are default rules only; the parties to the lease can (and should) contract for or modify either rule.

The English and the American rule each has some rational arguments in its favor. The English Rule requires that the landlord deliver to the tenant not only the right to possession, but actual possession as well. First, this is what most tenants expect; they want to lease property, and do not expect to buy a lawsuit. Second, the landlord will likely know why possession cannot be delivered — why a previous tenant holds over, and if there is any interest paramount to the tenant's. The landlord is likely to be acquainted with the facts necessary to litigate such issues. If the tenant had the burden of litigation, he would find himself relying on the landlord for crucial testimony anyway. Third, the landlord, often in the business of leasing business or residential property, is the one with the experience and expertise in such matters. Fourth and finally, the landlord is often the one best able to bear the risk of holdovers.

A tenant under the English Rule has the option of voiding the lease and getting damages caused by the failure of the landlord to deliver actual possession on time or, alternatively, to accept possession, abate rent for the time the tenant is denied possession, and collect any damages resulting from her dispossession.

The American Rule holds that the landlord need only deliver the right to possession, not actual possession, to the tenant at the beginning of the lease. First, granting the right to possession is all the landlord promises to do when the lease is regarded as a conveyance of a term. If the landlord wants to extend a warranty or additional rights to the tenant, the parties should bargain over such matters. Every conveyance or contract can bring on a lawsuit; why should the possibility here be so troubling? Second, the tenant has the burden of litigation all during the term to eject trespassers — why should the rule be different on the first day of the lease? Conversely, the landlord is not responsible if the trespasser damages the premises after the first day of the lease — again, why should the law be different on the first day? The tenant can procure insurance to protect himself against trespassers. Third, the landlord may have expertise dealing with leased premises, but he has no special expertise in predicting which tenants will hold over and in effect become tortfeasors; he should not be responsible for the torts of a holdover tenant unless he contracts for this liability. Finally, the tenant has rights against the trespasser or holdover in trespass. If the landlord is crucial to the litigation, then under modern pleading rules he can be impleaded in the tenant's action.

On balance, which of these rules is better? See Hannan v. Dusch, 153 S.E. 824 (Va. 1930) (adopting the American rule, but including a full discussion of both rules). The English Rule is arguably the better one, particularly for residential leases. It conforms to most tenants' expectations and landlords may otherwise take advantage of a tenant's ignorance of the law. It requires that the landlord bargain for any variation in the rule, rather than the tenant. It requires the landlord to use his legal expertise to evict the holdover. It construes the lease against the landlord — its grantor, probably its drafter, and certainly its beneficiary.

Why, then, did the court in *Hannan* adopt the American rule? The lease involved there was a commercial, long-term lease. It was to last for 15 years. The opinion ignored both the implications of this 15-year term and the commercial use for the premises. Indeed, it makes nothing of either, wanting perhaps a uniform rule for both residential and commercial tenancies. The court noted that the tenant had a summary possession remedy under state law, but valued it so little that he did not assert it.

Some authorities have argued that which rule should apply depends on the situation. The English rule seems preferable for apartment rentals, for example. If the lease were for farm land, however, the American Rule may make more sense because it takes time to grow crops, and harvest time may occur after the end of the lease. In this situation, placing the burden on the lessee to resolve the controversy between the lessee and former tenant may be the better option. See Matthew J. Heiser, *What's Good for the Goose Isn't Always Good for the Gander: The Inefficiencies of a Single Default Rule for Delivery of Possession of Leasehold Premises*, 38 Col. J. of Law and Soc. Probs. 171 (2004) (from which this example was drawn).

Examples

Get a Lease

1. (a) Larry "leased" Blackacre "to Tom, to continue so long as rental payments are made." Is this lease a valid term of years?
   (b) Larry leased Blackacre "to Tom for five years, unless Tom graduates from law school within that time." Is this a valid term of years?
   (c) Larry leased Blackacre "to Tom so long as Tom remains a law student." Is this lease a valid term of years?
   (d) Larry leased a house to Tom, Tom's possession to begin on July 1, for a rent of $500 per month. No term was specified. What type of tenancy was created?
   (e) Same facts and question as in (d), except that the rent was "at an annual rental of $6000, payable at the rate of $500 per month and due on the first day of each month."

Look at the Time

2. (a) Larry leased Blackacre "to Tom, starting on July 1, Year One, and ending at midnight on June 30, Year Two, and continuing thereafter, year to year." On January 15, Year Three, Tom notified Larry that he would terminate the tenancy and vacate the premises on May 31, Year Three. Is this notice effective?
   (b) If Tom does no more, is the notice effective at the end of the next annual period?
   (c) If Lanny leased Blackacre to Tina, month to month, starting on July 1, is a notice of termination mailed 15 days before the end of the month effective to end the tenancy at the end of that month?
   (d) Would the notice in (c) be effective 45 days later, at the end of the next month, when the initial notice contained the following statement: "Whatever tenancy I hold as of the date of your receipt of this letter, I elect to terminate my tenancy at the end of the next period commencing after the date on which you receive this letter." Is this a clear enough statement of termination?
   (e) Is there an effective notification for a termination in 45 days if Tina hands Lanny the keys to the property, and Tina's notice contains the statement in (d) and, in addition, contains a statement that the landlord "can take possession immediately"?

Get a Lease — Part Two

3. (a) While Larry and Tom were negotiating for a lease, Larry permitted Tom to take possession and accepted a weekly rent payment from Tom. What type of tenancy was established?

(b) Larry leased a store to Tom "with rent payable on demand and computed" according to a fixed ratio of dollars to the volume of goods sold in the store. What type of tenancy was created?

(c) If a tenancy at will is created when both landlord and tenant have the right to terminate the estate, what is created when only one party has this right?

Holdover Hangover

4. (a) Larry leased a home to Tom for a term of years. At the end of the term, Tom planned to vacate the premises but could not find an alternative lease because of a shortage in the local housing market; so Tom remained in the house while he looked for a place to move. Is Tom's holding over a voluntary action?

(b) What if Tom holds over, but Larry does nothing for two months after the term? What is the legal effect of Larry's silence?

American Rules Decision

5. In a state adopting the American Rule, if the landlord and the tenant cannot agree on what cause of action to bring against the holdover — summary possession, trespass, or interference with a contract — who decides?

Co-Holders Over

6. Len was a co-tenant in a term of years lease. Len vacated the premises at the end of the term, but Lannie, his co-tenant, did not vacate. Is Len responsible in damages for Lannie's holding over?

Curtailed Negotiations

7. (a) Taft had a year to run on his remaining term of years on premises leased from Lonnie. Taft received an offer from Timmy to take over Taft's premises. Taft asked Lonnie whether Taft's lease would be renewed at its expiration in a year and enclosed a letter with the offer from Timmy. Lonnie orally represented that Taft's lease would be renewed; and Lonnie wrote a letter to Taft indicating that Lonnie "was glad that Taft would remain on the premises for many years to come." Taft discontinued talks with Timmy about taking over Taft's premises. Later Lonnie informed Taft that Lonnie would not renew the lease, but offered Taft other premises at double the rent. Would you advise Taft to sue Lonnie to enforce Lonnie's offer of a renewed term?

(b) Ted leased Redbrick from Larry for a term of five years, and after the fourth anniversary of the lease negotiated for a renewal of the lease.

Larry by letter confirmed that progress had been made for the new lease, but indicated in the letter that "we've got a way to go yet before a complete agreement is reached." Larry attached a form lease, unsigned but approved by Larry's agent. Negotiations continued past the expiration of the term, when Larry broke them off unexpectedly and declared Ted to be holding over, threatening suit to evict him or hold him to a new term. May Ted vacate Redbrick without further liability?

Taking His Home to Work

8. (a) Eddy was the caretaker of a swank residential club (C). Eddy's sole compensation was the right of occupancy of an apartment there. Eddy's "employment agreement" contained the occupancy right, but also gave C the right to terminate Eddy's employment without cause and at any time. C terminated Eddy's employment, padlocked Eddy's apartment, and removed Eddy's personal property from the apartment. In the applicable jurisdiction, padlocking has been found to violate the state's prohibition against a landlord's using self-help, and by statute, moving costs and triple damages are available against the landlord using self-help. What is Eddy's best argument for being treated as a tenant, with regard to self-help as well as, say, C's notice obligations and remedies?

   (b) Owen agreed to occupy Lawrence's land in exchange for driving off trespassers. Owen entered the land, improved it, and grew crops there. Is Owen a tenant?

Explanations

Get a Lease

1. (a) No. A term of years requires a definite termination date or the ability to ascertain an ending calendar date at the beginning of the lease. Even the occasion of Tom's death does not satisfy that requirement since his death is not determinable. Tom's interest is more akin to a determinable life estate, to end if Tom stops making payments; or to a month-to-month periodic tenancy, with options to renew.

   (b) It is a valid term of years. A maximum term of five years is stated, and anyone inspecting the lease can readily determine when it will be safe to let the same premises from Larry.

   (c) No (traditional rule). There is no stated term, and no commencement or termination date, and no way of knowing how long Tom will remain a law student, so no way of determining the term. Thus under the traditional rule the lease is a tenancy at will or periodic tenancy. Some courts, however, will enforce such a lease as a tenancy of years (or just enforce the lease on its own terms without classifying it). These courts realize the parties intended an event, not a date, as determining the termination date, such as a lease until another building is ready for occupation. This construction adds some uncertainty to the automatic termination inherent in a tenancy of years but believes the parties sensibly accepted that uncertainty at the beginning of the lease.

(d) A periodic tenancy from month to month, until terminated by proper notice.

(e) A periodic tenancy from year to year is established. The annual reservation of the rent establishes the longer of the two periods implied in the lease. The longer reservation of the rent shows that the parties contemplate the year-to-year term. This is the typical result. The reservation of rent clause overrides the rent payment clause.

Look at the Time

2. (a) No, for two reasons. First, this is a periodic tenancy. It cannot be terminated at any time other than the end of the period named in the agreement. Second, the notice provided is not long enough. To end a year-to-year periodic tenancy, a six-month notice is required. The notice given here is 15 days short of that and so is ineffective. This notice should be received by Larry by January 1, Year Three.

(b) In most states, the answer is no. An ineffective notice is forever ineffective. After all, the tenant providing the ineffective notice might change his mind about vacating. However, a minority of states answer in the affirmative: The ineffective notice is revived for use in the next period, when it might be effective. The rationale for the majority rule is that a periodic tenant has a duty to provide the landlord with a clear notice of termination, naming the date on which he or she will vacate the premises.

Tom would be well advised to give a second notice during Year Three, setting out clearly an intent to vacate on June 30, Year Four. The tenant must give clear notice of the intent to terminate. The rule (that an ineffective notice is forever ineffective, and not revived for use in the next period when it might be effective) forces the tenant to give a second notice, one that clears up any misunderstanding that the landlord might have. It is designed to force the tenant to be clear.

(c) No. Thirty days' notice is required, but the authorities are not uniform. Some states by statute authorize a shorter notice period. In many states the notice would be valid to end the tenancy on July 31. In other states authorizing the shorter notice period, however, the notice is not valid for termination to occur for July 31 either, since the notice does not mention July 31.

(d) When the lease is regarded as a contract, Tina has indicated a clear intention to vacate, so the answer is probably in the affirmative. The issue turns on whether reasonable persons would agree on the termination date. This one seems to pass the test. But it would have been far more sensible to state the termination date.

(e) The court in Worthington v. Moreland Motor Truck Company, 250 P. 30 (Wash. 1926), held this language would be sufficient to provide the landlord with notice ending the lease in 45 days, but indicating that if a date and time of termination were not fixed, the notice might be insufficient. Tina's actual possession ended on the day she turned the keys over; her legal possession continues until the termination date.

Get a Lease — Part Two

3. (a) A tenancy at will. It is not a week-to-week periodic tenancy, because the ongoing negotiations indicate that no secure term has yet been fixed: When the negotiations end, the lease for whatever term will commence, and the flexibility required in the negotiations should not be diminished by implying a term for the interim, unless the doctrine of estoppel applies. See Carteri v. Roberts, 73 P. 818 (Cal. 1903) (holding that a month-to-month periodic tenancy is created when a defendant, after notice to the plaintiff, begins to plow the plaintiff's agricultural land while farm lease negotiations between them are pending).

(b) A tenancy at will. Larry supplied the premises and Tom the sales effort that produced the rent; either can terminate what each brings to this arrangement at will. Since Tom is supplying business and sales skills, it is particularly important that he have the right to terminate — otherwise he would find himself indentured to Larry.

(c) This problem is often treated by avoidance; that is, many courts hold that when one party has the power to terminate, the other implicitly has such a right as well. Thus, by operation of law, a tenancy at will arises. A principle of mutuality of right (and remedy) supports this result, but in some instances, the intent of the parties is clearly expressed in the agreement to the contrary. What then? One response is to construe the interest as a determinable term of years, the lease fictitiously labeled a "perpetual lease." The presumption is that the landlord will terminate the lease when the tenant fails to pay the rent.

Holdover Hangover

4. (a) Yes. Although the hardship on Tom is great, this probably is not a holding over that would tempt the courts to excuse the tenant. Tom should have anticipated this problem. The harsh effects of the holdover doctrine encourage tenants either to settle with landlords on a

new lease or to vacate. The doctrine thus benefits all incoming tenants, who are, after all, just as affected by a housing shortage as Tom. A different answer may result if Tom could not move for one day because the former tenant in his new place had not vacated, and Tom's remaining on the premises did not inconvenience the landlord or any new tenant waiting for Tom to move. Likewise, not vacating because the tenant suffered a serious illness was involuntary and excused on that account.

(b) The obvious consequence is that the landlord, after a reasonable lapse of time, might be deemed to have consented to a periodic tenancy in most states. There is a time at which the landlord's silence will be deemed consent, but the lapse of two months or so is unlikely to bring about this result. A court's finding an implied election is unlikely, unless the silence lasts an unreasonably long time. See Beach Realty Co. v. City of Wildwood, 144 A. 720 (N.J. 1929) (tenant holding over two months and two days, without any communication from the landlord, is still a tenant at sufferance). This, however, is no reason to advise a landlord in such a way as to encourage her silence in a matter in which the doctrine seeks to encourage communication and clarity: If the landlord passes up opportunities to communicate, that fact might encourage a court to imply an election.

American Rules Decision

5. The tenant under the American Rule gets to decide who brings the action for possession, no matter what it is called — summary possession or trespass.

Co-Holders Over

6. No. The landlord's election is to treat the holdover as an intentional trespasser, and a vacating co-tenant like Len is not that. In addition, the holdover's extended lease is treated as a new lease and not a continuation of the old one — so Len is not a party to the extended lease. Further, the relationship of co-tenancy exists only so long as the parties hold a concurrent estate in the premises — and after Len vacates, they do not have any concurrent estate. In the same vein, if the lease had an option to renew, could one co-tenant's exercise bind the others? Again, no. The co-tenants would have to exercise it together. See *Bockelman v. Marynick*, 788 S.W.2d 569 (Tex. 1990) (so holding when Len and Lannie were husband and wife).

Curtailed Negotiations

7. (a) No. Although the reliance of the tenant on the landlord's letter is clear, it is not enough to enforce under an estoppel argument. Estoppel

requires (1) a promise, upon which there is a (2) reasonable reliance, causing (3) subsequent injury or damage to the relying person. The letter indicated Lonnie was glad Taft would remain on the premises. It never mentioned a lease renewal. The landlord's wish for a continuing relationship with the tenant does not amount to a promise that most courts enforce by estoppel. Since lease renewals must be in writing to satisfy the statute of frauds, Taft's reliance on an oral communication was not reasonable. See Peter E. Blum & Co. v. First Bank Bldg. Corp., 275 S.E.2d 751, 753 (Ga. App. Ct. 1980).

(b) Yes. The unsigned form gives the court something on which to base Larry's promise, which Ted relied on by holding over. Rendering Ted liable as a holdover would represent subsequent injury or damage that Ted can avoid by vacating the premises. Ted thus has an estoppel defense to any suit of Larry's, either to hold Ted over for a further term or to hold Ted liable as a trespasser. See Daehler v. Oggoian, 390 N.E.2d 417 (Ill. App. Ct. 1979).

Taking His Home to Work

8. (a) Eddy's best argument is that the title of the "employment agreement" does not control its substance, and that this agreement establishes both an employer-employee and a landlord-tenant relationship; that the latter is not an incident of the former, but independent of it; that the landlord-employer's dual status does not excuse noncompliance with both landlord-tenant and employment law; and that the performance of the employment contract is consideration for the lease. Rent may be paid in services as well as money, and a contractually enforceable lease results no matter how the rent is paid. See Grant v. Detroit Assn. of Women's Clubs, 505 N.W.2d 254 (Mich. 1993).

The argument to the contrary is that the overriding intent of the parties in the agreement is to create an occupancy right linked and incidental to an employment relationship. Occupying the apartment enables Eddy to perform the caretaker function of the job better; the agreement taken as a whole reserves no rent; and but for the employment Eddy would not be occupying the apartment in any event. This creates at least a presumption that the employment relationship is the principal one between the parties, and that Eddy's interest in the apartment is no more than a license. Thus labor and employment law should provide the controlling set of legal rules.

(b) Probably. This is, if anything, an easier case than the Eddy and C one above. Driving off trespassers provides continuing consideration for Owen's right of occupancy, so that Owen is Lawrence's tenant at will. Owen's driving off trespassers is the service, payment that allows Owen to use the land for purposes benefiting himself — i.e., his farming.

Transfers of the Lease

PRIVITY OF CONTRACT AND PRIVITY OF ESTATE

A landlord and tenant relationship, from the outset, involves both privity of contract and privity of estate. **Privity of contract** is a relationship existing between both parties to a contract. The lease is a contract. Thus the landlord and the tenant are in privity of contract with respect to the leased premises.

At one time only persons in privity of contract could enforce or be held liable for a contract. This caused problems when a tenant transferred her leasehold to a third party (assignee) and the landlord wanted to collect rent from the assignee who was not a party to the original lease, and hence was not in privity of contract with the landlord. The courts resolved this sticky problem by crafting another type of privity—privity of estate.

Landlord and tenant are also in the relationship known as **privity of estate** because both the landlord and the tenant have a mutual, immediate, and simultaneous interest in the leased premises—the tenant having the right to possession for a term, and the landlord having the reversion after the term. See *Restatement, Second, Property*, §16.1 (1977). Privity of estate permits a landlord to collect rent from the tenant's assignee, even though there is no direct contract between them.

ASSIGNMENTS AND SUBLEASES

There are two distinct categories of tenant transfers: assignments and subleases. An **assignment** is a transfer of the whole of the unexpired term of the lease. It need not be a transfer of all of the premises. An assignment of a portion of the premises for the unexpired remainder of the term is called an *assignment pro tanto*.

A *sublease* is a transfer of less than the full remaining term of the lease or, more precisely, when the subletting tenant (by becoming a sublessor) retains some interest in the lease. A sublease is an independent transaction creating a wholly new and distinct landlord-tenant relationship between the sublessor and the sublessee. It has no effect on the original lease — for a court to hold otherwise would be to sanction a unilateral change in an ongoing contract. The sublessee is not bound by the covenant to pay rent in the original lease — the original or head tenant remains bound by it — or by any other covenant in the original lease, also known as the primary or "head" lease. The sublessee, of course, is bound by the rent obligations and other provisions of the sublease.

No particular words of art are required to assign or sublet, but the Statute of Frauds may apply to either category of transfer. A sublease is treated just as a lease would be, and an assignment is subject to the Statute of Frauds depending on the length of the unexpired term. Good practice requires that assignments and subleases be in writing.

THE TRADITIONAL RULE

The majority and the traditional test for distinguishing between an assignment and a sublease is this: If the original tenant retains an interest in the premises, the transfer from the tenant to the third party is a sublease, but if the original tenant transfers the property for the entire remaining period of the lease, the transfer is an assignment. Transferring the lease for even one day less than the remaining time of the lease results in a sublease rather than an assignment. The traditional rule operates regardless of the actual intent of the parties.

If a tenant with one year remaining on a two-year lease transfers the remaining year of the term to a third party, the tenant has assigned the lease and the third party is the *assignee*. If the tenant transferred the leased premises to a third party only for the summer months while the tenant was on vacation elsewhere, that is a sublease and the third party is a *sublessee*. Similarly, if a tenant leases an apartment and then takes in another person to reside in the second bedroom, that is a sublease of a portion of the premises. Query: Is that the correct classification? Why isn't this considered a fractional assignment of the estate? Some older opinions call it an assignment; more recent ones a sublease.

Under the traditional rule, the retention of a right of reentry or a possibility of reverter by the original tenant creates a sublease, not an assignment. Likewise, a tenant's right to enter the premises for a breach of particular covenants in the original lease, in order to preserve that lease, likely would be held to be the right of a sublessor under the traditional rule.

RULE OF INTENT

A minority of jurisdictions have adopted a rule giving effect to the parties' intentions whether they created a sublease or an assignment. See, e.g., Jaber v. Miller, 239 S.W.2d 760 (Ark. 1951), followed in Ernst v. Conditt, 390 S.W.2d 703 (Tenn. App. Ct. 1964). What the parties call what they did — as transferring either a "sublease" or an "assignment" — does not control. Instead, the intent of the parties is ascertained from an interpretation of the document as a whole, just as it would be with any other written agreement or contract. This rule gives the parties the right, not to customize their transfer, but to choose whether to use an assignment or a sublease for it. When there is no evidence of the parties' intent in the matter, the traditional rule, once applied regardless of the parties' intent, will likely still be applied as the parties' presumed intent. While the rule of intent brings the law of leases into harmony with the general rules of contract law and interpretation, it provides less certainty in many situations, and perhaps for this reason it has been adopted in only a minority of jurisdictions.

THE EFFECT OF TENANT TRANSFERS ON PRIVITY

Privity of contract exists between a landlord and a tenant, but not between a landlord and a tenant's assignee or a tenant's sublessee. Privity of contract exists between landlord and tenant even after the tenant transfers (either by assignment or subletting) the lease and moves, unless the landlord expressly agrees to substitute the transferee for the tenant, looking only to the transferee for the rent payments and to satisfy all obligations under the lease (known as a **novation**). The landlord's consent to the transfer does not implicitly terminate the privity of contract between the original parties to the lease.

Privity of estate exists between a landlord and a tenant and a landlord and a tenant's assignee, but not between a landlord and a tenant's sublessee. Under privity of estate, the landlord can sue his tenant or an assignee (but not a sublessee) for back rent.

Example 1: Larry Landlord leased a building to Terry Tenant. The signed lease between them resulted in a privity of contract. There also existed a privity of estate between them because they each owned an interest in the leased building.

Example 2: Terry Tenant assigned her entire interest in the leased building to Abby Assignee. Larry landlord is not in privity of contract with Abby Assignee since they have not contracted with each other. Because they are not in privity of contract, at one time Larry landlord could not bring suit to collect rent from Abby Assignee. Courts circumvented this legal hurdle by concluding Larry Landlord and Abby Assignee were in privity of estate since they each have ownership rights in the leased premises. With privity of estate in place, Assignee became obligated to pay rent directly to Landlord.

Example 3: Instead of assigning the lease, Terry Tenant sublet the building to Sara Sublett. Larry Landlord is not in privity of contract with Sara Sublett. Moreover, he is not in privity of estate with Sara Sublett, either. Landlord's action for rent or for other breach of the lease terms runs against Terry Tenant, the original tenant with whom he is in privity of contract. Terry Tenant is in privity of contract with Larry Landlord; and is also in privity of contract and privity of estate with Sara Sublett, and can enforce the terms of her lease with Sara Sublett.

The landlord can have only one recovery, judgment, and satisfaction for the rent. In a sublet, the landlord's recourse is against the original tenant. In the assignment context, the landlord's primary action is against the assignee. The original tenant, however, remains secondarily liable on an assignment. The tenant, upon assignment, becomes liable for rent as a surety — someone against whom recovery may be had if the assignee does not pay. A *surety* is a person bound to perform an obligation when another (here, the assignee), who is primarily liable to do so, does not. For example, if the tenant is forced to pay the rent due from an assignee, the tenant may sue the assignee to recover what was paid. This suit is based on a principle of **subrogation** — i.e., the tenant steps into the shoes of the landlord for purposes of this suit.

If and when a tenant's assignee himself assigns the lease to another person, the original assignee thereafter has neither privity of estate nor privity of contract with the landlord. Because the assignee herself assigning her interest is not in privity of contract privity of estate with the original landlord, the assignee is not liable for future rent to the original landlord. He remains liable, however, on any past due rents related to his time in possession. Now the second assignee has privity of estate with the landlord, and is liable for rent on that basis.

If, on the other hand, the first assignee sublets, the landlord and the new sublessee are not in privity of estate. The assignee's sublessee is liable to the assignee for rent, but not to the landlord; the assignee and the landlord are still in privity of estate, however, and the assignee still owes rent to the landlord.

Example 4: Following Example 2 above, Abby Assignee assigned her lease to Lee Stranger. Lee Stranger failed to pay three months' rent. Larry Landlord may sue Lee Stranger for the rent since there is privity of estate between them. (but not privity of contract). Landlord cannot collect from Abby Assignee, however, since they no longer are in privity of estate.

REAL COVENANTS

Amid such chains of lease assignments, some particularly important covenants in the primary lease are said to be **real covenants** that "run with the land." Real covenants are those promises, obligations or burdens that may be enforced against persons who take the promisor's estate or interest in the leased premises. A promisor is the person agreeing to be bound by a covenant, and may be either a landlord or a tenant. Thus a real covenant will bind any successor of the promisor for the period of time he or she holds the estate of the promisor. Likewise, the promisee's successors also have the right to enforce the benefit of the covenant. The covenant for quiet enjoyment and the covenant to pay rent are important examples of real covenants. Real covenants provide another basis (in addition to privity of estate and privity of contract) for holding an assignee in possession liable for the obligations in the primary lease.

Lease covenants that do not meet the requirements of a real covenant are **personal covenants** binding only the promisor and not any successor to the promisor's interest in the leased premises. The requirements for ascertaining whether a covenant is real or personal are very technical, as fully developed in Chapter 28, infra, but in general they involve (1) the **intention** of the original promisor and promisee (here the landlord and the tenant) that they bind successors to the interests of each, (2) **privity of estate** (always present with a chain of assignments between the original landlord and any later assignee in possession), and (3) the requirement that the subject of the covenant **touch and concern** the leasehold premises or land. A restriction on the use of the premises imposed in the lease generally touches and concerns the land, as do the covenant to pay rent, the covenant for quiet enjoyment, a covenant restricting assignments and subleases, a covenant to repair the premises, and a covenant to renew or extend the leasehold's term.

LANDLORD'S CONSENT TO A SUBLEASE OR ASSIGNMENT

In general, leaseholds are freely transferable. Absent a provision in the lease to the contrary, the tenant has the right to alienate his or her interest or estate. A lease silent on the matter of transfer is construed by the courts as permitting a transfer without the landlord's consent.

For several legitimate reasons a landlord may not want just anyone to be a tenant; or may want only the original tenant to occupy the premises. The tenant's right to sublet or assign may be restricted by an express provision in the lease. Restrictions on alienation by a tenant are justified as a reasonable protection of the landlord's interest and income from the premises. An express restriction on assignment or subletting is strictly construed against the landlord, however. Often it is said that the restriction on alienation is to be construed against its beneficiary, the landlord — who is typically the drafter of the restriction in any event. A lease, like any contract or agreement, will be construed against its drafter.

LANDLORD CONSENT PROVISIONS

Leases often incorporate a provision that the tenant may assign or sublet a lease only if the landlord consents. Historically, and in most jurisdictions today, the landlord could refuse to consent for any reason or for no reason. A growing number of jurisdictions, however, oblige the landlord to have a *commercially reasonable basis* for withholding consent to a sublease or assignment when the lease provides that the landlord must give (generally written) consent to any assignment or sublease. This is a so-called **silent consent provision**, the lease being silent on the standards the landlord is to use when considering a request to consent to a sublease or assignment.

In these jurisdictions, the landlord may not arbitrarily refuse to approve a proposed sublessee or assignee and must have a commercially reasonable basis for a refusal. A commercially reasonable basis is a business reason rather than a personal or discriminatory reason, and rather than an excuse to extort more rent. See Kendall v. Ernest Pestana, Inc., 709 P.2d 837 (Cal. 1985) (interpreting a lease provision stating that "there shall be no sublease or assignment without the landlord's consent," holding such consent shall not be unreasonably withheld; and reviewing the reasons for the traditional no-mitigation rule, but adopting the minority rule forbidding unreasonable withholding of consent both as a matter of public policy and as a matter of enforcing an implied covenant of good faith and fair dealing into the lease), noted in 14 Pepp. L. Rev. 81 (1986). The *Pestana* holding is that "where a commercial lease [contains an approval provision, the lessor's] consent may be withheld only where the lessor has a commercially reasonable objection to the assignee or the proposed use." See *Kendall*, 709 P.2d at 849.

The tenant seeking to assign or sublet the lease must provide sufficient information to the landlord that the tenant has procured a satisfactory assignee or sublessor. A landlord may refuse to consent when a tenant, even if he has found a perfectly acceptable assignee, refuses to let the landlord review that assignee's credentials.

The rule requiring the landlord to have a commercially reasonable basis for refusing to consent to the assignment or sublease is justified in several ways. First, it promotes the free transferability or alienation of leases, and furthers the policy of the law of disfavoring restraints on alienation. Second, it arises from an implied covenant of good faith and fair dealing that applies to leases as well as to most agreements or contracts. Third, it carries out the reasonable expectations of the parties. The downside to requiring a landlord to have a commercially reasonable basis for refusing to consent is that inevitable disagreements between the parties will lead to prolonged legal disputes.

Where the landlord must have a commercially reasonable basis to refuse to consent to an assignment or sublease, the tenant has several remedies when the landlord unreasonably refuses to consent. A suit for damages is the most recognized remedy, but that exposes the tenant to expensive and time-consuming litigation. Some courts (but not enough to establish a clear trend) have permitted a tenant to abandon the lease if the landlord arbitrarily refuses to consent to the assignment or sublease. The underlying issue is whether, in effect, the burden of finding a transferee falls on the landlord who unreasonably refuses to consent to an assignment or sublease, or whether the burden remains with the tenant.

A lessor (landlord) may seek a clause in the lease that gives the landlord the absolute right to refuse consent or even to prohibit an assignment or sublease altogether. Courts to date have enforced these provisions. Alternatively, a lease may provide the tenant can assign or sublet the lease with the landlord's consent, and that the landlord's consent shall not be unreasonably withheld, and may list the reasons a landlord can withhold consent.

Since many leases are pre-printed form contracts, another issue that arises is whether the landlord and the tenant freely and fairly bargained over the consent clause. Because many clauses in a long lease may not be bargained over, many courts will strike an anti-assignment covenant as an illegal adhesion contract.

Assignment and subleasing provisions in commercial leases are among the most fiercely negotiated clauses of a commercial lease. As an illustration, when a jurisdiction's law requires that landlords have a commercially reasonable basis for refusal to consent to a sublease, landlords often insist on the insertion of a "rent recapture" provision in a lease, giving the landlord the right to collect all or part of any appreciation in the rent charged a sublessee. Such provisions are generally found reasonable.

Most cases and statutes regarding the commercially reasonable basis for refusing to consent to an assignment or sublease focus on commercial leases. There is a trend to adopt the commercially reasonable standard for residential leases, too, as opposed to just commercial leases. Residential tenants are likely to be in greater need of protection than are commercial tenants. Even in jurisdictions that do not imply a commercially reasonable standard for withholding consent, there is a tendency to imply some standard for reasonable conduct in the residential lease: If the proposed assignee or sublessee is as acceptable as the original (or "head") tenant, then the landlord cannot reasonably withhold consent. A landlord acting unreasonably in this context subjects himself to an action for damages by the tenant refused the consent.

The lease assigned or sublet without the landlord's consent is not void; rather, it is voidable at the option of the landlord, who may either elect to accept the rent and waive the benefit of the covenant prohibiting transfer without his consent, or else evict the transferee. No automatic forfeiture of the lease is implied. A landlord's accepting rent from the assignee or sublessee will be deemed a waiver of a landlord's right to withhold consent. After accepting the rent, the landlord is presumed to know of the transfer and to have consented to it.

THE RULE OF DUMPOR'S CASE

With a no-assignment-without-consent provision in the lease, once the landlord consents to a first assignment, without reserving a right to consent to future assignments, he is deemed to have waived the right to consent further, and future assignments can be made without consent. This is the Rule of Dumpor's Case, 76 Eng. Rep. 1110 (K.B. 1578), intended to promote the free alienability of the lease. It also, however, typically flies in the face of the expressed intent of the original parties to the lease.

The rule is a trap for the unwary landlord, who may defeat it with a statement that she consents to this particular assignment, rather than to all future ones. The issue is one of forcing one party or the other to be clear about a litigation-breeding silence, and on that ground is consistent with the majority rule adopted by courts for "silent consent" covenants. Many courts, however, accept the rule silently. It might be regarded as an early application (black-lettered) of the doctrine of estoppel. See, e.g., Childs v. Warner Bros. Southern Theatres, Inc., 156 S.E. 923 (N.C. 1931) (collecting the cases). Dumpor's Case does not apply to covenants prohibiting or limiting the right of a tenant to sublease.

TRANSFERS OF THE LANDLORD'S INTEREST

The landlord can sell or assign the leased premises. Any transfer will be subject to any outstanding leases (but see Recording Acts, discussed infra Chapter 25). A transfer of the landlord's reversion is made subject to outstanding leases. This is an application of the rule that a grantor cannot convey more than he or she has. Thus, the transferee does not have an immediate right to possession of premises subject to a lease. After the transfer, the new owner of the property is in privity of estate with the tenant, and all the real covenants (those running with the land) benefit and burden the new owner from that time forward. Thus, the transferee may, and the former landlord or the transferor may not, sue for rent accruing after the transfer. The transferee also has the burden of real covenants and becomes the party primarily liable for them. After transferring the reversion, the landlord's privity of estate with the tenant ends, but his privity of contract does not; thus, absent a release of liability by the tenant, the former landlord remains liable on his personal covenants in the lease, and secondarily liable on its real covenants.

As with the rules governing a tenant's transfers, these rules show that at root the law is protecting the interests of the non-transferring party to the original lease. With assignments and subleases, it is the landlord who is protected; when the landlord transfers the reversion, it is the tenant who has his lease carved out of the reversion. Moreover, these rules about transfers are default rules, subject to agreement to the contrary by the parties.

Examples

Assignments and Subleases

1. (a) LL leases Blackacre to T. T transfers his interest "to T1 so long as T1 farms the property." Is T1 a sublessee or assignee?

   (b) LL leases Blackacre to T, who transfers his interest to T1 "but if T1 does not pay the rent to LL, T has the right to reenter. . . ." What type of transfer is this?

   (c) LL leases Blackacre to T, who "sublets" his entire interest to T1 and agrees (in a separate document) with LL to remain liable for the rent if T1 does not pay it. What type of transfer is this?

   (d) Same facts as in (c), but T1 learns that T is still liable to LL for T1's unpaid rent. LL then sues T1 directly for the rent. T1 defends, arguing that he has neither privity of estate nor privity of contract with LL and so is not liable for the rent to LL, and that T's liability for T1's unpaid rent implies a right of reentry, re-enforcing the idea that T1 has a sublease. Is T1's defense a good one?

(e) LL leases a house to T. T "subleases" to T1, using the word "sublease" several times in the course of the T-T1 agreement. The agreement provides that T1 is entitled to possession for T's entire unexpired term. T1 remits the rent payments to T, thinking that he will pass them along to LL, but T does not; instead, he absconds and, six months later, LL notifies T1 that he has not received the rent since T1 took possession. Will T1 have to pay the rent twice, a second time to LL?

Landlord's Consent

2. (a) A lease provision provides that the tenant's interest may be assigned or sublet with the landlord's consent, but if the landlord's consent is not obtained and the tenant transfers his interest, the tenant shall pay the landlord $5000. Is such a provision enforceable?
   (b) A lease contains a prohibition on assignments. Is subleasing prohibited too?

Refusing Consent

3. Assume the following Examples take place in a state that requires a landlord to have a commercially reasonable reason for refusing to consent to an assignment or sublease.
   (a) LL and T execute a commercial lease that prohibits its sublease or assignment. Is this lease provision valid?
   (b) LL reserves a right of first refusal to take back the leased premises if LL agrees to accept the same terms as T offered the proposed assignee or subtenant. Is such a right of first refusal enforceable?
   (c) LL and T execute a commercial lease that expressly provides that "LL may withhold consent to any sublease or assignment in its sole and absolute discretion." Is this lease provision valid?
   (d) LL and T agree that LL may withhold consent to any sublease or assignment by T, "but only with having a reasonable basis for doing so," and that LL's "decisions in such matters shall be final." T wants to assign its lease to T1, but LL refuses to consent because he does not feel good about T1. Can LL refuse consent?
   (e) LL and T execute a lease that provides that T cannot sublease or assign the lease without LL's prior written consent, such consent not to be unreasonably withheld; that T shall give LL notice of any potential sublessee or assignee; and that, "upon T's sublease or assignment of T's leasehold, LL may, at its option, either consent to the sublease or assignment or reenter and repossess the leased premises and terminate all of T's rights under this lease therein." Is this lease provision valid?

(f) LL and T execute a commercial lease that "T may assign the premises with LL's prior written consent." T wants to assign the lease to T1. Must LL have a commercially reasonable reason for refusing to consent to the assignment?

(g) Same facts as in (f). T wants to sublet the premises to T1. The leased premises are in a shopping mall. The landlord considers national chain stores essential to the success of the mall. T, a national chain, wants to sublet the premises to a local resident opening her own business. This would be her first shop. Must T get LL's consent to sublet to T1?

Explanations

Assignments and Subleases

1. (a) T's retention of a possibility of reverter suggests that this is a sublease. See Anderson v. Ries, 24 N.W.2d 717 (Minn. 1946) (holding a transfer to X so long as he is in the armed forces is a sublease). The language used in this transfer is that required for T's retaining a possibility of reverter, a common law estate regarded as a vested one and sufficient to hold that this transfer is a sublease.

(b) Recent cases using the traditional rule would find this a sublease as well. It's a close case for many courts, and there are older authorities to the contrary. Even courts using the traditional rule might hold that this is an assignment. The right to reenter is express, but unless the right is asserted, T1 has the same estate as does T. That's good enough for most courts. At the start of T1's interest, T is for all practical purposes out of the picture. In fact, the condition sounds like a security device to guarantee the tenant can get the property back if he is forced to pay rent to the landlord. A minority of jurisdictions label this a sublease, the condition subsequent persuading courts there that the estates are not the same

(c) An assignment. Although T and T1 seemingly intend to make T1 a subtenant, the majority of courts would hold that when the entire interest of a tenant is transferred, an assignment results, no matter what the parties called the transfer. Even courts in states that follow the rule of intent will follow the traditional rule where, as here, evidence of that intent is thin. (Indeed, the rule of intent has in the last half century gained few adherents.)

(d) No. It's still an assignment. Even though once T pays the rent he could sue T1 for possession and so assert the functional equivalent of a right of reentry, most courts would still follow the rule that a transfer of a tenant's entire interest is an assignment. Further, T's continuing liability is contractual; if a right of reentry is reserved, it should be reserved expressly because the law does not readily imply a new type of estate. Here, one would not be implied from T's payment of T1's rent, on the theory that T and T1 could easily have provided for a right of reentry and did not do so. T1's defense would fail.

(e) The T-T1 agreement is intended to be a sublease, and the rental payments paid to T are consistent with this intention. Most likely, however, the transfer of all of the unexpired term trumps the payment ritual. This argues that the "sublease" is really an assignment — and that is how most courts would classify it. The substance and actions of the parties trump their intent under the traditional rule. T1 may thus owe the rent twice, on a theory of privity of estate established between the landlord and an assignee. T1 has an action against T, if he can locate T — not always easy to do. This Example illustrates the importance of a subtenant or assignee to clarify with the original tenant and landlord who should receive the rent checks.

Landlord's Consent

2. (a) No. See Fish v. Robinson, 106 N.E. 1057 (Ohio 1913) (prohibiting the enforcement as a forfeiture or penalty and a violation of the policy proscribing unreasonable restraints on alienation).

(b) No. Although the cases on the subject are split, the lease should be construed against its beneficiary or drafter and no implication that a prohibition against the lesser act of subletting is included or implied from the express prohibition of the greater or more inclusive act of assigning the tenant's interest. This accords with the weight of authority. The tenant may thus sublease his or her interest.

Refusing Consent

3. (a) Yes. The commercially reasonable refusal standard is an implied covenant and can be overruled by an express provision in the lease. Nothing there holds that the landlord may not, at the start of the lease, bargain for and give the tenant notice (in the lease) of an absolute prohibition on assignments or subleases.

(b) Yes. See *Restatement, Second, of Property* §14.2, Comment i (1977). The landlord's willingness to pay the tenant the premium or excess rental the assignee or subtenant would pay eliminates one of the concerns underlying the commercially reasonable standard.

(c) The provision is valid. If an absolute prohibition is valid (see Explanation 3(a), supra), so should this somewhat lesser prohibition be.

The provision establishes a standard, the landlord's sole and absolute discretion. The commercial tenant is on notice.

(d) Probably not without a more concrete reason. The express lease provision overrides the implied commercially reasonable standard. The two provisions in the lease establishing the standard applicable to the landlord's discretion appear to be inconsistent. A court would try to reconcile the reasonable basis provision against the landlord's final decision provision. Since contracts have an implied covenant of good faith and fair dealing, a court could and should conclude that the landlord must act in good faith in refusing to consent to the assignment. Good faith here would approximate the commercially reasonable standard for refusing to consent.

(e) The provision is valid in most jurisdictions. The provision provides for forfeiture if the landlord decides it is in his best interest to force the forfeiture. The majority of courts imposing a commercially reasonable standard would interpret the contract as written. Courts in a minority of jurisdictions would hold the provision valid but scrutinize the specific scenario where the dispute arose. The judicial concern is that a forfeiture provision allows the landlord to reap the benefit of increased rentals otherwise accruing to the tenant. These courts consider the landlord's refusal to consent so the landlord can collect higher rents an abuse of the landlord's power. The context of the leasehold might matter here. A court might strike this provision from a clause in a long-term commercial lease but accept it in a bedroom apartment lease in a private home.

(f) Yes. The lease provides for the landlord's consent to an assignment but does not establish the standard to guide the decision maker. The default rule applies; that requires a commercially valid reason for refusing to consent.

(g) T does not have to get LL's consent. The lease provision required LL's consent for an assignment, not for a sublease. Courts disfavor restraints on alienation and will construe restraints on alienation narrowly. A provision requiring a tenant to get consent before assigning the lease will not be interpreted to require consent to a sublease, even when the lease is essential to the success of a larger enterprise. The lease required the landlord's consent only to an assignment, not to a sublease. LL's attorney should have required a consent for a sublease in the lease (as well as for the assignment).

17

Waste, Duty to Repair, Destruction of Leased Premises, and Security Deposits

---

WASTE

A tenant has a duty to his or her landlord not to commit waste. Waste is the unauthorized destruction, alteration, misuse, or neglect of the leased premises. Waste traditionally involves a change in the physical identity of the premises. There are two principal types of waste: It may be either (1) voluntary and intentional, or (2) permissive. **Voluntary or affirmative waste** is a direct, willful, or intentional injury to the premises. **Permissive waste** is the result of neglect or omission, such as allowing a structure on the premises to deteriorate or become exposed to injury by the weather.

Traditionally, a tenant's making material or substantial change in the premises was voluntary waste, regardless of the fact that it increased its fair market value. Such an approach has been modified in many jurisdictions to depend on the express or implied intention of the parties, with the result that a reasonable change in the premises — that is, one reasonably necessary to use the property as contemplated in the lease — is now permitted.

The tenant has the duty (implied in every lease) to redeliver the premises to the landlord in the same *condition* as it was received, wear and tear excepted. This implied covenant to redeliver is the minimum duty that the tenant owes the landlord due to the duty not to commit waste. A tenant's unauthorized changes to the premises' physical condition more likely will be found to constitute waste. This view may not apply, of course, to a long-term leasehold — i.e., to a lease whose term is long enough to amortize or depreciate the value of the tenant's changes, so long as the tenant restores the premises to its original condition.

More generally, the tenant has the duty not to injure the *value* of the landlord's reversion. This duty is subject to two exceptions. First, a tenant may make such changes as are reasonably necessary to use the premises in a way contemplated by the parties to the lease. Sometimes this is stated as a tenant's right to make temporary or minor changes in the premises during the course of the lease, subject to a duty to restore the premises as they were at its beginning. Second, as previously mentioned, a tenant is not liable for damage to the premises caused by wear and tear. However, a tenant is liable for damage resulting from his or her own negligence and, of course, for willful and intentional damage.

The parties are free to agree that the tenant may use the property "without impeachment for waste," thus waiving the tenant's liability for waste.

REMEDIES AND DAMAGES FOR WASTE

If the tenant fails to return the premises to its original leased state, a landlord can receive compensation equal to the loss of value due to the waste or the cost to return the premises to its prior condition. By statute, in some states the measure of damages for waste is double or triple the amount of the actual damages. See, e.g., 6 Edw. 1, ch. 5, §1 (1278) (the Statute of Gloucester, imposing triple damages), enacted as D.C. Code §45-1301 (1976). Injury to freehold estates (the jewels of the common law estate system) by nonfreeholders was the rationale for awards of multiples of the actual damages involved. Equitable relief available to a landlord includes an injunction to prevent future waste, or in some extreme cases judicially ordered termination of the lease. Parties to a lease can and usually do contract as to rights and remedies concerning waste and maintaining the condition of the premises.

FIXTURES

The law of fixtures is an offshoot of the law of waste. As discussed in Chapter 7, a **fixture** is personal property annexed and attached to the premises so as to become real property, not being removable without substantial damage to the premises. Fixtures need not be annexed to the premises, but when they are annexed, they cannot be removed by the tenant at the end of the term.

A fixture has three definitional elements: (1) annexation, either actual or constructive; (2) adaptation of the thing to the use or purpose of the premises to which it is annexed; and (3) an intent to make the thing a permanent feature of the property. An intent to make the thing a permanent feature of the leased premises is the critical element in the United States. If intent is found, a court likely will find constructive annexation, if not actual annexation. In practice, too, the adaptation element has tended to decrease in importance over the years.

The intention of the tenant to annex property to the premises is the traditional test used to determine whether the property is a fixture. See Teaff v. Hewitt, 1 Ohio St. 511 (1853). Intention will be inferred from the circumstances, not the tenant's subjective state of mind. In many cases, whether the fixture can be removed without damaging the premises becomes the crucial issue. Because the fixture was personalty and initially the tenant's, there is an inference in these cases that the tenant should be able to remove his property unless the landlord can show that doing so would cause substantial damage to the premises. Thus, the intention and damage elements in the definition of a fixture coexist today in an uneasy tension. If the property cannot be removed from the premises without damaging the leased premises, the property becomes a fixture and remains on the leased property even after the lease ends.

THE DUTY TO REPAIR

At common law the tenant took the leased premises with all its defects. The rule of caveat lessee — tenant beware — applied. The wise tenant inspected the premises for fitness and adequacy of purpose before executing the lease.

Once the tenant took possession, the tenant, not the landlord, had a duty to repair the leased premises. The tenant's duty to repair was sometimes implied from the duty not to commit waste. Generally the tenant had a duty to maintain the premises in its current state but not a duty to rebuild any buildings in case of a building's destruction (unless the tenant destroyed it), or to restore the premises from the effects of wear and tear. The tenant's duty ran from the time he took possession, not from the execution of the lease, and only as to the improvements then in existence. If the premises were to be improved after that time and before the lease move-in date, the tenant had a right to inspect them for fitness and adequacy for the leased purpose. The commercial tenant still has a duty to repair today. The landlord has no duty to repair the leased premises absent an express covenant in the lease.

The residential tenant is responsible for minor repairs. States by judicial opinion and statute, however, have modified the traditional duty to repair in the case of leased residential premises to impose a duty on the landlord to insure the premises meet basic health and safety standards. The landlord, moreover, must maintain the premises in a habitable condition — the so-called warranty of habitability, developed more fully in Chapter 19, infra. The standards for habitability are often measured by the housing and building codes of the jurisdiction; but, as we will see, some courts have required more of landlords, invoking a rule of reason.

Even under the common law rule imposing the duty to repair on the tenant, the landlord has some duties to repair. (1) The landlord is responsible for the public or common areas of an apartment building — which are, after all, not part of any tenant's leased premises. Halls, entryways, yards, stairs, elevators, common porches, and the roof are examples. (2) Some areas under the landlord's exclusive control are his or hers to repair as well — the furnace room, for example. (3) The landlord may be liable to repair latent defects of which he or she knew or should have known (and of which the tenant had no knowledge). When the landlord makes a repair, whether or not under a duty to do so, the repair must be performed without negligence.

Example: Tenant leased a single family house, described by its postal address in the lease. Tenant agreed "to keep the premises in good repair and condition and to return them in as good a condition as received." The landlord insisted that Tenant mow the lawn more frequently that Tenant does. Whether Tenant has to or not might turn on the definition of "premises" or "good condition" in the lease. If the house's floor plan were attached to the lease, Tenant probably need not mow more frequently.

THE DESTRUCTION OF THE PREMISES

(a) Termination of the Lease

At common law, absent a contrary lease agreement, a tenant could not terminate the lease or refuse to pay rent on the destruction of a building or of other improvement on the premises. The assumption was that the land was the basis for the lease. See Bunting v. Orendorf, 120 So. 182 (Miss. 1929). That the land was flooded and useless for farming for a season, or that a wildfire swept over it, made no difference. The assumption was fitting when leases were for agricultural purposes, and homes had few if any modern conveniences. When improvements are the most valuable component of leased premises, continuing the lease makes little sense when the improvements are destroyed by a storm, fire, or other unforeseen event.

Most states have changed the law to place the risk of sudden destruction of the premises on the landlord, except where the land itself is the subject of the lease or when the tenant caused the destruction. This is especially true for residential leases. In case of the improvement's substantial destruction, the tenant, but not the landlord, has the option to terminate the lease. Generally the damage to the essential structure must be great enough that the structure is uninhabitable. Parties to a lease often stipulate in the lease when a structure would be considered so damaged that the tenant may terminate the lease or if the lease shall continue or be abated while the landlord (or tenant) repair or rebuild.

(b) Duty to Rebuild

At common law, absent an agreement in the lease to the contrary, the landlord had no obligation to rebuild after a sudden destruction. The tenant could not terminate the lease, either. The tenant had a duty to maintain and repair the premises, but the common law had no clear rule assigning a duty on the tenant to rebuild destroyed structures. Typically, leased property was agricultural lands and the only improvements were barns and sheds. Even when the tenant was called on to rebuild such structures, the replacement cost, in relation to the value of the lease, fell within the "ordinary repairs" required of tenants.

Imposing a duty on the tenant to rebuild urban property where the land is substantially improved with a building or other structure, and the building's value is substantially more than the value of the underlying land, is inappropriate — as most, but not all, courts have recognized. Courts, moreover, have resisted attempts by landlords to combine a duty to repair and a duty to redeliver the premises at the end of the term in substantially its initial condition to impose a duty on tenants to rebuild destroyed structures.

In some leases, tenants covenant to keep and maintain the premises in the condition that they received them, or to repair the premises. Courts interpret this covenant to be the tenant's duty to make ordinary, incidental, nonstructural repairs, not substantial, major, or structural ones. This interpretation is often an example of courts construing the lease for the benefit of the tenant and against its likely drafter, the landlord.

In some leases, the landlord undertakes to "put" the premises in good condition, but not to "keep" it there. The former implies only a first-day duty, the latter a broader duty continuing throughout the term of the lease. For clarity, to prevent the duty to repair from spilling over into a duty to rebuild after a fire or similar occurrence, the lease should address what happens if the improvements are substantially destroyed in a provision separate from the one that sets out the duty to repair. The landlord, for example, might agree "to put, but not keep" the premises in repair during the term of the lease. The lease could provide the landlord rebuilds, the tenant rebuilds, or the tenant could terminate the lease if the improvements are destroyed.

SECURITY DEPOSITS

Landlords customarily require a cash payment as a **security deposit** to cover damages to the premises by the tenant beyond ordinary wear and tear. Thus, the security deposit secures the tenant's performance of the lease covenants, particularly the covenant not to commit waste. The security deposit payable at the execution of the lease is held by the landlord pending an inspection of the premises at the end of the term. The security deposit is not refundable until the tenant has complied with all covenants of the lease.

Because of the possibility of landlord abuse of this device, particularly wrongful retention at the end of the term, nearly every American jurisdiction limits by statute the landlord's rights in such deposits in various ways. Common statutory restrictions on the landlord's use of security deposits include (1) a maximum dollar amount to be assessed, set typically at not more than one or two months' rent; (2) a requirement that the deposits be held in an escrow account, and not commingled with the landlord's other funds, or held in trust, with a duty to pay interest on them; (3) a procedure for the landlord to account for expenditures (if any) and to return the deposit in whole or in part to the tenant; (4) safeguarding deposits from claims of the landlord's creditors; and (5) multiple damages (usually double or treble damages) and the landlord paying the tenant's attorney's fees when a landlord willfully retains a deposit without accounting for its use. Often these statutes apply only to residential tenancies. California, Colorado, New Jersey, and Texas have particularly detailed legislation in this area. Because of the legislative fear that landlords will simply pocket the security deposit and wait for the departing tenant to sue, courts generally require strict compliance with the procedures imposed on residential landlords by these statutes.

For commercial leases, substitutes for a security deposit are sometimes used — so substituting a letter of credit, a surety bond, or financial collateral of some type provides the landlord with equivalent protection against a tenant's trashing the premises.

Examples

The Injured Tenant

1. A landlord installed carpeting in Tony's apartment. Tony caught his foot in a hole in the carpet, fell, and threatened to sue the landlord for his injuries. Should you take the case?

Building Code Violations

2. A commercial tenant covenants to repair one wall of improved premises during the term of the lease, and does so, but repairs it in such a way that although it is structurally sound, it lacks fire-retardant qualities required by the local building code. Upon discovering this fact, must the tenant redo the repair to comply with the code?

A Burning Issue

3. Larry leased improved premises to Terry, who undertook in the lease "to restore the premises to the condition in which they were received by me." The premises were totally destroyed by a fire of unknown origin. Larry insisted that they be rebuilt as they were received. Must Terry do that?

Last Month's Rent

4. Ted, a tenant, executed a lease with Lisa, a landlord, and provided Lisa with one month's rent as a security deposit to assure the condition of the premises. Can Ted substitute the deposit for the last month's rent?

Explanations

The Injured Tenant

1. You should, but the landlord's duty to install the carpet does not automatically confer a duty to inspect it for defects. That is an issue of negligence, whether the landlord acted reasonably under the circumstances. The relative abilities of both the landlord and the tenant to inspect and the tenant's particular use of the premises will affect the outcome of the case. Premises liability is developed further in Chapter 20, infra.

Building Code Violations

2. Maybe. The duty to repair the wall assigned in the lease is not necessarily the same as the duty to comply with governmental codes. The two duties are related, but the duty to repair involves maintenance of the premises and is particularly related to the tenant's duty to redeliver them in as good a condition as they were at the start of the lease. Complying with the building code may upgrade the existing facilities. For example, the fire-retardant qualities demanded by the city may require that the tenant spend twice what it would have cost to fix the wall without the fire-retardant materials. Both types of covenants may be found in many leases and both must be consulted before assigning the duty to repair in compliance with codes. Perhaps the landlord is in the best position to be

familiar with such codes, due to a longstanding ownership of the premises, or his or her having seen the premises used in different ways, or using it for his or her own purposes. In ruling on the matter, a court likely would consider the length of time remaining on the lease, which party benefits the most from the compliance, and the intent of the parties as can be best ascertained from the lease.

A Burning Issue

3. Some courts would require Terry to rebuild; most would not. A tenant may agree to *restore* the premises at the end of the lease to its first-day condition. Some courts have used this duty to restore as imposing an obligation *to rebuild* the premises after its substantial destruction by a storm or by fire. However, agreeing to restore is different from agreeing to repair or rebuild. The distinction between "repair" and "restore" or between "restore" and "rebuild" is well established in the case law, but not appreciated by the public or many lawyers; the use of such verbal distinctions can ignore the lease's plain meaning, its other provisions, and the surrounding transaction.

   The better view is that an obligation to "restore" takes its meaning from the law of waste; that is, it implies a right of the tenant to make temporary or minor changes in the premises during the term of the lease. Such changes may be defined as those that are consistent with the tenant's use, do not affect the structural features of the premises (e.g., the walls, foundation, and so on), can be amortized during the term, and may be removed without material damage to the premises. Under this view, there is no obligation to rebuild after a fire. In any event, such temporary changes must be removed and the premises restored to their original condition at the lease's end. When a fire of unknown origin destroys the premises, the tenant is not at fault and so is not liable in waste — and on this account, will not be liable to "restore" the premises.

   If the lease imposed a duty on the tenant to insure the premises and then imposed a duty to apply the proceeds of the insurance claim to the damaged premises, a duty to restore or rebuild might reasonably be inferred to have been allocated to the tenant. The mere fact that the tenant had taken out a fire insurance policy does not affect the answer — presumably the landlord could have (and in the real world, would have) insured the premises as well. The law pertaining to insurance and the covenants in the lease are two different things.

Last Month's Rent

4. The answer is no. Unless the lease identifies the deposit as the last month's rent, the deposit safeguards the lessor by providing funds in

hand to pay for any damages to the leased premises. The tenant has a duty to make ordinary repairs and not to damage the property or commit waste. The security deposit serves as the source of the payments to repair when the tenant fails to fulfill his duty to repair or leave the premises in its original condition, normal wear and tear excepted.

CHAPTER 18

Termination and Abandonment of the Lease

Either the landlord or the tenant may wish to terminate the lease prematurely. The landlord may tire of the tenant's complaints, or the tenant's rent may be in arrears. The tenant may need or want to move elsewhere. We have already discussed one option open to the tenant — that is, to assign or sublet the premises to a third party. See Chapter 16, supra.

This chapter develops two situations. In the first the landlord wants to evict the tenant for some reason, often for nonpayment of rent, or the tenant has not vacated the premises after the lease ended. In the second the tenant wants to turn the leased premises back to the landlord before the lease ends.

LANDLORD'S EVICTION OF TENANT IN DEFAULT

A landlord may want to evict a tenant who defaults on a lease covenant, normally for nonpayment of rent, but maybe for violating some other lease term, such as being too rowdy, having unauthorized pets, or engaging in an illegal activity. Alternatively, the tenant may be a holdover tenant who remains on the premises after the lease ends. The landlord has various options for evicting a tenant in default. We begin with self-help.

SELF-HELP

Eviction by *self-help* takes place when the landlord evicts the defaulting tenant without resort to the judicial process. At one time in England, a landlord could use reasonable force to evict a tenant. No more. First, and most importantly, in no American jurisdiction is a landlord authorized to use excessive force to regain possession of leased premises, no matter what the landlord's rights are under the lease. A few states still allow reasonable force, but not many.

In a majority of states today, a landlord can still resort to self-help for retaking possession of the premises if (a) the landlord has a right to repossess the leased premises; and (b) the landlord's exercise of the remedy is peaceable. As liberating as self-help may sound to a landlord, do not become too enamored with it. While self-help is still the rule in a majority of American jurisdictions, the trend is to restrict it, and a growing number of jurisdictions prohibit self-help altogether.

Where self-help without excessive force is permitted, the landlord must have a right to repossess the premises. Otherwise, the tenant has the legal right to possession and any eviction, actual or constructive, is wrongful, subjecting the landlord to liability for trespass and interference with the tenant's quiet enjoyment of the premises. It may also subject the landlord to criminal prosecution for disturbing the peace, breaking and entering, and so forth. The landlord would have a right to possession if the tenant breaches any lease covenant and does not remedy the breach within a reasonable time after notice.

In addition to having a right to repossess, the landlord's self-help eviction must be "peaceable." At one time — and still today in a small number of states — the landlord was allowed to use "reasonable force" to regain possession. Most states that still permit self-help, however, demand that the retaking be peaceable.

States differ on the meaning of "peaceable." For some, no violence is permitted, and the landlord must leave if the tenant puts up any resistance. Some states permit force against objects but not against people. A landlord can force open doors and windows and move furniture and belongings when the tenant is not there, for example. Other states do not permit forcing doors and windows, but do allow the landlord to change the locks. Other jurisdictions say even changing locks is forcible and not peaceable (the theory here is that the lock-out is the equivalent of forcibly keeping the tenant out and is, in any event, often the distraint or unlawful detention of the tenant's personalty). Some say turning off water and utilities is not peaceable. Some say the even that threat of violence is the same thing as violence. In these states, self-help becomes almost illusory. The trend is for states to prohibit self-help in favor of using the judicial process.

Example: Landlord evicts Tenant by non-peaceful actions while Tenant is in default of a provision of the lease prohibiting rowdy behavior. Tenant sues Landlord to regain possession of the premises and prevails — otherwise the rule about peaceable actions would be nugatory.

Some states will enforce lease provisions giving the landlord the option of self-help. Other states refuse to enforce the self-help provisions, considering them to be against social policy.

EJECTMENT

A landlord can bring a suit in ejectment to oust a defaulting or holdover tenant. Ejectment is the traditional common law cause of action for the recovery of possession or real property and for damages due to the withholding of possession. One problem with the ejectment proceeding is that months or years may pass before a final judgment is reached. While the landlord at that time can seek damages and past due rent from the tenant, the tenant at the end of the process may turn out to be judgment proof. A second problem is that to cover losses suffered while the legal proceedings take place, landlords will want to raise the rents of other tenants but due to market constraints may not be able to do so.

SUMMARY POSSESSION STATUTES

Recognizing that the twin extremes of self-help and suits of ejectment were unsatisfactory solutions, all states have enacted summary eviction procedure statutes, variably called **summary proceedings, summary ejectment, forcible entry and detainer (a/k/a FED)**, or **summary possession**. The idea is to give the landlord a prompt hearing to evict defaulting tenants. The landlord gives notice to the tenant to remedy the default or to vacate. States prescribe the number of days the tenant has to cure any default, usually no more than ten. If the tenant does not cure the default or vacate, the landlord can pursue the summary possession procedure, which moves quickly through the judicial system. Summary possession suits move to the head of the judicial docket and are often heard in special landlord-tenant courts. Despite their popularity in landlord-tenant cases involving private residential housing cases, summary proceedings are not allowed to evict tenants in federally assisted public housing.

To insure speedy proceedings, some states limit the summary action to nonpayment of rent, with no defenses, offsets, or counterclaims available to the tenant (except a defense that the rent was paid). Landlord claims not allowed in summary possession proceedings must be brought in ejectment or other time-consuming civil cases. Other states expand the list of claims the landowner can bring, but this opens up the need for the tenant to rebut, and maybe for each side to conduct discovery. Expanding the options open to the landlord and the defenses available to the tenant prolongs the proceedings, which defeats the purpose of the summary possession actions.

Statutes and judicial opinions, moreover, authorize the tenant to withhold rent in certain circumstances, most notably in residential leases. For example, states have authorized residential tenants to withhold rent if the premises are not habitable. See Chapter 19, infra. Many states allow a tenant to defend against eviction by proving the landlord sought the eviction in retaliation for the tenant's exercising her legal rights. See Uniform Landlord and Tenant Act §5.101. Each additional defense or safeguard brings with it the potential for further delays in the proceedings.

A check-the-box complaint form, see below, permits the landlord to recover rent due — i.e., back rent, not rent for the time the landlord says that he or she is entitled to possession, not future rent, and not rent due to the anticipatory repudiation of the lease by the tenant. The traditional bargain that the landlord implicitly strikes by bringing a summary possession action is giving up rent or damages in exchange for a quick procedure to regain possession.

18. Termination and Abandonment of the Lease

D.C. Super. Ct., Landlord and Tenant Form 1, 558 A.2d @ LXXXIX-XCII (1989):

SUPERIOR COURT OF THE DISTRICT OF COLUMBIA
CIVIL DIVISION, LANDLORD & TENANT BRANCH

L&T. _____

_____   vs. _____
Plaintiff/Landlord   Defendant/Tenant

_____   _____
Address   Address

_____   Washington, D.C. _____
                 Zip Code   Zip Code

COMPLAINT FOR POSSESSION OF REAL ESTATE

DISTRICT OF COLUMBIA, ss:

☐ _____ being first duly sworn, states: ☐ he or she is the landlord and/or ☐ licensed real estate broker or ☐ the landlord's authorized agent of the house, apartment or office located at_____, Washington, D.C. The property is in the possession of the defendant, who holds it, without right,_____. The landlord seeks possession of the property because:

A. ☐ The tenant failed to pay: $_____, total rent due from _____ to _____ : $ _____ late fees; and/or $ _____, other fees (Specify) _____. The monthly rent is $ _____. The total amount due to the landlord is $ _____. Notice to quit has been: ☐ served as required by law ☐ waived in writing.

B. ☐ Tenant failed to vacate property after notice to quit expired. (copy attached).

C. ☐ For the following reason: (explain fully).

_____

_____

Notice to quit is: ☐ not required   ☐ waived in writing   ☐ either

_____

Therefore, the landlord seeks the Court for:
    ☐ judgment for possession of the property described.
    ☐ judgment for rent, late fees; other fees and costs in the amount of $_____.
    ☐ an order of the Court that all future rent be paid into the Registry of the Court until the case is decided.
Subscribed before me this _____ day of _____,
_____.

                                                          _____
                                                          Plaintiff/Landlord or Agent

(Notary Seal and Signature here.)

SUMMONS — TO APPEAR IN COURT. YOU ARE HEREBY SUMMONED AND REQUIRED TO APPEAR ON _____, 19 _____ AT 9:00 A.M. PROMPTLY, in Landlord and Tenant Court, Courtroom . . . to answer your landlord's complaint for possession of the premises listed in the above complaint. If you live on the premises and you are not named as a tenant you must come to court if you claim a right to possession of the premises.

IMPORTANT INFORMATION FOR TENANTS — ACT PROMPTLY. WHEN YOU MUST COME TO COURT, ALWAYS BRING THIS COMPLAINT WITH YOU. The form above is a complaint filed by your landlord asking the Court for the right to take back the property you occupy. On the front is the Court date. You must come to Court or you may be evicted. If the landlord seeks a money judgment against you for rent due, and a judgment is entered against you, your wages, bank account, or other property may be attached. When you come to Court, bring your lease, rent receipts, pictures and other papers that may help explain your side. Before you come to Court, you may get your own lawyers, or you can represent yourself. If you wish to have legal advice and you cannot afford a lawyer, contact the Legal Aid Society . . . for more information about where to obtain such help. If you need help to pay the rent, go to the Department of Human Services Center in your neighborhood or when you come to Court ask about Emergency Assistance. Although you are not required to do so, you may enter into an agreement with your landlord to pay the rent, to correct any other problem or to move. Be sure that all promises that either you or the landlord make are in writing before you sign the agreement.

TENANT'S ABANDONMENT AND SURRENDER

Sometimes a tenant wants to end the lease early. As one example, in one case a man signed a lease on an apartment in anticipation of his marriage. When the engagement and wedding were canceled, he wanted out of the lease because as a single student he could not afford the apartment. See Sommer v. Kridel, 74 N.J. 446 (1977). What should the tenant do? One option is to assign or sublet the lease. Alternatively, the tenant may surrender the premises back to the landlord or abandon the premises with or without communicating with the landlord.

SURRENDER

The tenant **surrenders** a lease by transferring the lease back to the landlord, with the landlord accepting the return. Many courts require the surrender to be in writing to satisfy the Statute of Frauds if the lease originally had to be written to satisfy the Statute. If the landlord accepts surrender, the tenant is relieved of responsibility for future rent payments. Where the facts indicate the landlord intended to treat the lease as surrendered, a court will find a **surrender by operation of law** even if there is no writing. If a landlord engages in activity so inconsistent with the tenant's continuing obligations under the lease, a court will find surrender by operation of law. A landlord should thus be counseled not to treat the premises as his own if he doesn't want to be found accepting a surrender.

ABANDONMENT

Most complications with mid-lease terminations occur when the tenant abandons the lease with or without notifying the landlord, or the landlord refuses to accept a surrender. Once a tenant abandons the lease, a landlord can elect one of three or four options.

(1) The landlord can treat the lease as continuing, do nothing, and sue the tenant on the covenant to pay rent as the rent falls due.
(2) The landlord can treat the lease as continuing and relet the premises for the tenant's account, reserving the right to sue the tenant for any unpaid balance of the rent.
(3) The landlord can accept the surrender of the lease, and relet on the landlord's own account.

(4) The landlord can treat the abandonment of the lease as an anticipatory repudiation, suing the tenant for either (a) damages — the difference between the reasonable rental value of the unexpired term and the present value of future rent — or (b) unpaid future rent — the difference between the contract rent and the amount received from a new tenant, both damages and future unpaid rent being recoverable in one judicial proceeding.

Options 1, 2, and 3 provide the most traditional and widely accepted statement of the landlord's options. Options 2 and 3 require careful action — and a paper trail documenting whether the landlord is acting for the tenant or on his own behalf. Option 4 is accepted in some jurisdictions.

(a) Lease Continues — Landlord Does Nothing

The landlord is given this election because the tenant cannot unilaterally terminate the lease. The landlord is within his contractual rights to treat the lease as continuing even if the landlord lets the unit sit empty. The rent is owing and the landlord can collect past due rent. This may entail several successive lawsuits since the landlord in most jurisdictions can seek only past due rent, not future rents receivable over the remaining term of the lease. As a practical matter, the landlord should not wait until the lease is over to collect, since the longer she waits to collect, the greater the chances the tenant has left the jurisdiction, died, or become insolvent.

A few states that by statute permit the landlord to do nothing require the landlord to give notice to the tenant that the landlord is letting the premises lie idle and will sue for the rent as it is due. In jurisdictions without such a statute, failing to provide this notice is seldom found to be an obstacle to collecting rent over the remaining term of the lease. The landlord thus may sit back and sue for the rent from the abandoning tenant, whether the tenant fails to take possession at the beginning of the term, or takes possession and then later abandons. Inevitably, however, the passive landlord runs the risk of the tenant's skipping the jurisdiction or becoming insolvent and judgment proof.

The option to do nothing in its purest form is dying out. Viewing the lease as a contract, courts increasingly impose a duty on the landlord to mitigate her damages, usually by finding a new tenant.

(b) Landlord Relets on Tenant's Behalf

The second option open to the landlord is to treat the lease as continuing and relet the premises on the abandoning tenant's behalf. The tenant remains liable for the difference between rents received and rents owed, and is entitled to any excess rents collected. This option won't be used when the landlord expects to relet for a higher rent as the landlord rationally will elect to treat the abandonment as a surrender.

In many states the landlord has a duty to mitigate damages when a tenant abandons. The landlord who fails in this duty to mitigate may recover only those future unpaid rents and other damages that she could not have avoided by reletting. Even in states where the landlord does not have a duty to mitigate, the landlord might still relet to get some money from the premises, to help out the tenant, or because the landlord wants the unit occupied.

The duty to mitigate serves several public policies. It is consistent with contract law for the wronged party to a contract to mitigate damages. Moreover, the duty to mitigate encourages landlords to keep leased premises in use and to return them to the rental market as quickly as possible. Finally, it decreases the likelihood of physical damage to the premises through vandalism and neglect.

The tenant often must give the landlord notice of the abandonment before the duty to mitigate is imposed. Until then, the landlord may continue to do nothing. The tenant's merely walking away from the premises could leave the landlord confused about what to do, in part because the landlord's election has its hazards. The tenant may later claim he did not abandon and the landlord trespassed on his property. Alternatively, the landlord's reletting may be found to be an acceptance of the tenant's surrender of the lease, with the consequence that the tenant is traditionally relieved of any obligation to pay any future rent.

Where imposed, a landlord's duty to mitigate is to make reasonable efforts to mitigate. What satisfies the duty to mitigate depends on the facts and circumstances of the situation. One court said the owner of multiple vacant units must treat the vacated premises as "one of his vacant stock." Summer v. Kridel, 378 A.2d 767 (1977). Merely listing the premises for rent is insufficient to satisfy the landlord's duty, but it is not clear that the landlord has to move the tenant's premises to the top of its list of vacant apartments and show it first to prospective tenants. The landlord need not attempt to relet using a lease with fewer or more lenient covenants than those imposed on the abandoning tenant or for a use substantially different from the abandoning tenant's use — nor need the landlord relet at a below-market rent.

Courts split on whether the landlord has the burden of proving she mitigated or the tenant has the duty to show the landlord failed to mitigate. Some courts justify putting the burden on the landlord because the proof will be within the landlord's control and this allocation of the burden makes sense on that ground. Putting the burden on the abandoning tenant, on the other hand, may expedite the finding of a new tenant because the abandoning tenant in monitoring the situation may present likely prospects to the landlord as evidence the landlord did not mitigate, and the landlord may accept the new tenant.

(c) Landlord Treats Abandonment as Surrender

A landlord may elect to treat an abandonment as a surrender because the premises can be leased for a higher rental, because the landlord sympathizes with the tenant, or because it is not worth the hassle to attempt to hold the tenant liable for the remaining term of the lease. Since some tenants may return and argue that the landlord should have relet on the tenant's behalf, and that the tenant is thus entitled to any excess rent collected over the amount the tenant owed on the lease, the landlord should give written notice to the tenant that she is retaking the property or should decisively relet to make clear the landlord is acting for herself and not on the tenant's behalf. Even after giving a notice, the landlord is well advised to relet for a term different than that remaining on the abandoning tenant's lease, changing the leasehold premises slightly, changing the fixtures, or renovating the premises to suit the new tenant. Such actions have been held to show that the landlord acted for herself.

On the other hand, if the landlord intentionally relets on the tenant's account, likely when there is a falling market for rentals, the landlord will not want any reletting activity to be taken as an acceptance of the surrender; instead, the landlord wants this activity to be consistent with standing on the lease's rights. So, to preserve the landlord's rights, the landlord should notify an abandoning tenant in writing that, whether or not the landlord has any duty to relet, she is doing so for the benefit of the tenant and intends to hold the tenant for the difference in rent collected and rent owed. The landlord should keep a separate ledger for the unit so as to prove costs and revenues when necessary.

Some landlords insert a so-called "survival clause" in their leases. Such clauses provide that the landlord may relet without terminating the abandoning tenant's lease. Even with such a clause, courts are likely to hold that the clause only creates a presumption that the landlord did not accept the surrender — and that the facts and circumstances of any reentry may still provide substantial evidence otherwise.

(d) Abandonment as Anticipatory Repudiation

Since the lease mixes contract and conveyancing principles, courts in some jurisdictions let the landlord accept the surrender of the tenant's lease and still sue for rent or damages. The abandonment is viewed as an anticipatory repudiation of the lease by the tenant, thus breaching the covenant to pay rent. If the landlord establishes the tenant abandoned the premises for the unexpired term, the landlord can collect an amount equal to the present value of rents due under the lease over either the fair rental value of the lease or the actual rentals of any subsequent lease. Such an election, critics say, gives the landlord an opportunity to increase his damages — not an efficient result. Samuel Williston attacked the doctrine's use on this basis in the landlord-tenant context, urging that the doctrine of independent covenants created no debt to be repudiated until the time for payment of the rent arrived. Proponents of using the doctrine (e.g., Professor Henry Ballentine) thought that Professor Williston did not distinguish between repudiating performance and repudiating the promise to perform — and that repudiating the promise justified use of the anticipatory repudiation doctrine here.

Examples

Peaceable Self-Help

1. (a) In a state in which a landlord's changing the locks has been held to be a forcible entry, is the landlord's entering with a pass key and removing the tenant's goods to a storage facility a forcible entry or a peaceable entry?

   (b) In a state in which locking out the defaulting tenant is not peaceable, may the landlord cut off the utilities?

The Duty to Mitigate

2. (a) In a state requiring the landlord to mitigate, can the landlord recover the costs of reletting: advertising the premises, the costs of an agent's time, the brokerage fee, if any, and so forth?

   (b) LL and T enter into a lease that contains both a covenant to pay rent and a provision that permits free assignability and subleasing. How does this provision affect the applicability of a mitigation rule to the lease?

   (c) Should the duty to mitigate be the rule of commercial leases as well as of residential leases?

   (d) Can the duty to mitigate be abrogated in a residential lease by agreement?

Malled

3. (a) Travel Agency had been a tenant of Mall Inc. for twelve years when it executed a new 3-year lease to run from January 1, Year One to December 31, Year Three. For several months before executing the new lease Travel Agency discussed with Mall Inc. its need for more space. Over the summer of Year One, Travel Agency located larger premises elsewhere, but did not tell Mall Inc. Mall Inc. learned that

Travel Agency was moving when the Mall manager arrived on September 14, Year One, to find the premises vacated and a sign on the window giving Travel Agency's new address. Mall Inc. on September 20 by letter notified Travel Agency it was in default under the lease and should act to cure the default by returning to the premises. Instead, Travel Agency delivered the keys to the leased premises to Mall Inc. on September 30, Year One. Mall Inc. accepted the keys. In Year Two Mall Inc. sued Travel Agency for back rent. Travel Agency claimed its obligation for rent ended on September 30, Year One, when Mall Inc accepted the keys. Mall Inc. disagreed. Who is correct?

(b) Two months before Travel Agency vacated the leased premises, Travel Agency talked with the owner of Collector's Gallery about taking over Travel Agency's premises. Travel Agency encouraged Collector's Gallery to talk with Mall Inc about leasing space, but cautioned Collector's Gallery not to mention Travel Agency might vacate since Travel Agency did not want anyone to know. Travel Agency's space was 900 square feet. Collector's Gallery told Mall Inc. it was looking for around 2000 square feet. Another Mall tenant, the Flower Pot, was looking to move from a kiosk to a store location about the size of Travel Agency's space. Mall Inc. negotiated with the Flower Pot about the vacated space but never mentioned the space to Collector's Gallery. Negotiations with the Flower Pot proved unsuccessful and ended December 15, Year One. Mall Inc. mentioned the vacated space to Collector's Gallery after December 15. Collector's Gallery executed a lease for the vacated space on January 15, Year Two. At trial Travel Agency argued Mall Inc. failed to properly mitigate damages when it did not lease the premises to Collector's Gallery, who was a willing and acceptable tenant, on October 1, Year One. Mall Inc. disagreed. Who is correct?

(c) Pursuant to Mall Inc.'s policy, under the lease agreement executed on January 15, Year Two, Collector's Gallery would not owe any rent until it opened for business (provided it opened within 120 days). This provision allowed the tenant to remodel the premises, bring in stock, and set up for business before rent accrued. Collector's Gallery opened for business on March 15, Year Two. Mall Inc. at trial argued Travel Agency owed it the rent for the time between January 15 and March 15. Travel Agency disagreed, saying (even if it owed rent past September 30 or October 1, Year One) it should not be held liable for further rent once Mall Inc. executed the new lease and Collector's Gallery took possession. Who is correct?

(d) Would the answer to (c) change if Travel Agency owed $3000 a month rental, and Collector's Gallery under the new lease owed $2500 a month rental?

(e) Would the answer to (c) change if the lease with Collector's Gallery was a five-year lease ending on December 31, Year Six, at a rental of $2500 a month?

Slow Down on Acceleration Clauses

4. In a jurisdiction requiring the landlord to mitigate the abandoning tenant's damages, a landlord inserts a covenant in the lease accelerating the rent for the unexpired term upon the tenant's abandoning the premises. When the tenant asks why this covenant is there, the landlord (or her counsel) replies that it is necessary because the courts have not held that the doctrine of anticipatory repudiation is available to landlords in the jurisdiction. Acceleration clauses of this type are common, the landlord reports, in mortgage loan documents. How do you evaluate such a response, and how do you reply to it?

Waiting for a Better Tenant

5. In a jurisdiction following the mitigation rule, a shopkeeper approached the landlord and asked if abandoned premises in a shopping center were available for rent. The landlord replied that they were not, and that they had already been relet. This was untrue, but the landlord was then awaiting an appointment with a prospective tenant willing to agree to a higher rent. Four months later, the landlord was successful in renting to a national chain store at a higher rent. Can the landlord charge the abandoning tenant for rent due under its old lease for the four months the store was vacant?

The Abandoning Assignee

6. If the landlord relets on an abandoning tenant's account and as her agent, and the transferee of the tenant's interest defaults and himself abandons, who is responsible for the unexpired term, and for pursuing the transferee?

Explanations

Peaceable Self-Help

1. (a) In the majority of states, any action inconsistent with a tenant's continued possession will be a nonpeaceable eviction and hence a forcible entry.

   (b) It depends on the state. Many states forbid as little as walking through an unlocked door and cutting off utilities without the tenant's consent. Most states, however, would hold this to be peaceable, especially if the utilities can be turned off without confronting the tenant or entering the premises. In fact, most states would allow changing locks; only the most restrictive states prohibit changing locks and turning off utilities.

The Duty to Mitigate

2. (a) Yes. Ordinarily tenants must bear the cost of any reasonable expenses incurred by the landlord in attempting to relet. The rationale for such a result is that if it is clear that the landlord, who, with reasonable diligence, relets at a rent lower than in the original lease, can still recover the difference money from the defaulting tenant, she should recover the attendant transaction costs as well.

(b) It theoretically could have an effect, but it doesn't. The argument that it should have an effect is that when a tenant has the contractual right to sublease or assign, the tenant should have the duty to use that right to find a new tenant when abandoning the lease. This argument is appealing because the tenant should attempt to minimize both her own damages and disruptions of rent flow to the landlord as much as the landlord should mitigate the tenant's damages. The tenant's having a right to sublet or assign the lease is a plausible reason not to impose a duty on the landlord at all. After all, the landlord has no continuous duty to seek new tenants and here such a duty does not appear to have been part of the parties' initial bargain.

The tenant's right to assign or sublet does not relieve the landlord of her independent duty to mitigate damages, however. The reasons given for imposing the duty to mitigate on the landlord — the landlord is in the business of leasing, even the wronged party should mitigate damages he can avoid (often labeled the doctrine of avoidable consequences), the landlord's best interest is to keep units occupied, productive, and not subject to waste — remain even if the tenant can sublet or assign the lease. A tenant has some incentive to find a new tenant. A tenant can start searching for a new tenant to take over the lease the day the tenant vacates, whereas the landlord often must wait until the tenant abandons before seeking a new tenant, so that the unit will be vacant at least a month in most cases if the landlord must find a new tenant.

(c) Yes. There is no policy reason why the holding should not be applicable to commercial leases. Some states require mitigation in commercial as well as residential leases. Some limit as a matter of policy the duty to residential leases. Others, as a matter of statutory construction, limit the duty to mitigate to residential leases if the state legislated the mitigation rule in a law similar to the Model Residential Landlord-Tenant Code or the Uniform Residential Landlord and Tenant Act, but has no similar legislation for commercial leases. About half the states do not require mitigation either for residential or commercial leases.

(d) Probably not. The duty to mitigate is based on public policy that recognizes the landlord's superior knowledge in the residential rental market and superior bargaining position because the landlord can hand the tenant a preprinted lease on a take-it-or-leave-it basis. In that instance the landlord's duty to mitigate should be non-waivable in a residential lease. A court's ruling may depend on whether the abrogation was a bargained-for provision, or whether it was a provision in an adhesion lease.

Malled

3. (a) The issue is whether Mall Inc.'s acceptance of the keys is an acceptance of Travel Agency's attempted surrender. This Example is loosely based on Grueninger Travel Service v. Lake County Trust Co., 413 N.E.2d 1034 (Ind. Ct. App. 1980). The actual court ruled in favor of Mall Inc. The court recognized acceptance of keys is evidence of acceptance of surrender of the lease; but acceptance of the keys here was consistent with continuing to hold Travel Agency liable under the lease as Mall Inc. sent the letter and accepting the keys was consistent with Mall Inc.'s obligation to mitigate damages by finding a new tenant.

(b) Mall Inc. acted properly. The issue is whether Mall Inc. acted responsibly to relet the vacated premises. Considering Mall Inc. was negotiating with the Flower Pot in good faith and Mall Inc. was under the impression Collector's Gallery was looking for more than twice the space the vacated premises offered, the court concluded Mall Inc. acted responsibly, or at least did not fail to try to mitigate. The court was also cognizant that Travel Agency contributed to the confusion by imploring Collector's Gallery not to mention it knew of Travel Agency's plans to vacate.

(c) Mall Inc. prevails again. The new lease does not replace or nullify the original lease. It is the vehicle to mitigate damages. The proper formula is to calculate the rent due from Travel Agency first; and reduce that amount by the amount collected under the new lease. That formula leaves Travel Agency liable for accrued rent up to March 15.

(d) The answer to (c) would not change. Mall Inc. is not required to lease the premises for the same amount as Travel Agency owes. As long as Mall Inc. acted in good faith, Travel Agency remains liable for the entire lease term less the amount Mall Inc. was able to mitigate. In this case Travel Agency remains liable for the full rent until March 15. After March 15, Travel Agency will be liable for $500 monthly as the difference between its $3000 a month liability and the $2500 Mall Inc. collects from Collector's Gallery.

(e) The issue here is whether leasing the premises for a period longer than the original lease amount to Mall Inc.'s acceptance of surrender. If so, Travel Agency is not liable for rents after the new lease was executed. The court in *Grueninger* indicated the longer term could be evidence of a surrender (but not in the actual case since the lease there authorized Mall Inc. to lease for a longer term). Under this holding the result is the same as in (d) above.

Slow Down on Acceleration Clauses

4. Rent acceleration clauses are common in older leases. Their use in loan documents is no reason to use them in leases, however. In states where the landlord is not required to mitigate, the rent acceleration clause allows current collection of the present value of future rents, which is beneficial to the landlord, who then is not required to bring periodic suits for past due rent. In jurisdictions requiring landlords to mitigate damages, however, acceleration of all future rents in addition to receiving any rents received from a new tenant during the lease's original period awards the landlord a double benefit: the actual value of the premises in the new rental, and a penalty against the initial tenant. Penalty provisions in contracts are unenforceable, and courts have so held in this context. A properly worded and implemented clause reducing the present value of the contracted future rents by the present value of the current rental value of the premises or the amount of actual rentals expected on a reletting of the premises may pass judicial review; as might a liquidated damages provision calling for two or three months' rent as approximating the lost revenue for the time it takes to find a new tenant.

Waiting for a Better Tenant

5. No. The duty to mitigate requires that the landlord not discourage offers to rent; while the landlord is free to make the decision to refuse to entertain a prospective offer to rent, the landlord cannot then charge the tenant with the risk and costs of that decision and recover rent for the extended waiting period it chose. See O'Brien v. Black, 648 A.2d 1374, 1378 (Vt. 1994) (holding just that).

The Abandoning Assignee

6. The easy answer is, not the landlord, who would have the same series of options as when the original abandonment occurred. See Novak v. Fontaine Furniture Co., 146 A. 525 (N.H. 1929). However, once a jurisdiction accepts a duty to mitigate in some form and it is imposed once, then in order to simplify matters and the law, the landlord should

have a duty to mitigate damages by making reasonable efforts to relet each time. The landlord has the prior experience in reletting, is in control of the premises, and is in a position to show it to prospective tenants. Certainly after the originally abandoning tenant is given notice of the default, the original liability of that tenant reemerges, and thereafter that tenant also has a strong incentive to make some efforts to find a new tenant, if only to check up on the landlord's renewed activity.

CHAPTER 19

Achieving Habitable Premises

EVICTIONS — ACTUAL AND OTHERWISE

When a landlord and a tenant enter into a lease, the landlord promises that neither she nor anyone else claiming through her will interfere with the tenant's lawful possession. This promise, implied in all leases, is called the *covenant of quiet enjoyment*. The promise arises either from the written words of the lease — demise, let, lease, used as verbs — or in oral leases, from the relationship of landlord and tenant. In a related doctrine, a landlord's actually or constructively evicting a tenant absolves the tenant of his obligations under the lease, including the duty to pay rent.

(a) Actual Eviction

The landlord's *total actual eviction* of the tenant from the leased premises occurs when the landlord excludes or locks the tenant out of the premises. A padlock on the door to an apartment is sufficient for this purpose. Wrongful actual eviction breaches the covenant of quiet enjoyment. The tenant's obligation to pay rent ends upon eviction and the tenant may sue for damages. An actual eviction may be a *partial actual eviction* as well, where the landlord renovates the property and makes some of the leased premises part of a common area of a multiunit property, such as a hallway or lobby. Even occupying a *de minimis* amount of the leased premises in this way may give rise to a partial actual eviction. In some jurisdictions, a tenant is completely relieved of rent liability for a partial actual eviction even if the tenant continues to use the rest of the premises. In other states, the remedy for a partial actual eviction is a partial abatement of the rent if the tenant continues using the premises.

(b) Constructive Eviction

Constructive eviction occurs when the landlord so substantially interferes with the tenant's use and enjoyment, or causes or allows inhospitable conditions to persist that the tenant is justified in vacating the premises, even though the landlord's actions or inactions fall short of being an actual eviction. When, because of a landlord's acts or failure to act when the landlord has a duty to act, the leased premises are rendered unfit for habitation, in whole or in substantial part, the tenant may elect to vacate after giving the landlord notice of the disturbance and a reasonable opportunity to cure.

The necessary elements of a constructive eviction are (1) intentional (actual or inferred) acts or failures to act by the landlord that breach a duty owed to the tenant and (2) that substantially interfere with the tenant's enjoyment of the premises, or render the premises unfit for the purpose for which it was leased; and (3) the tenant vacates the premises (4) within a reasonable time after the landlord's actions. Issues surround each necessary element. When these conditions for constructive eviction are satisfied, the tenant thereafter is relieved from the obligation to pay rent.

Constructive eviction is an affirmative defense, and a type of tenant self-help, best used when the tenant has somewhere else to go and rent. It is a clone of actual eviction, so that the tenant is required to vacate so that the constructive eviction looks as much like actual eviction as possible.

In the most obvious cases, a landlord acts with the intention of making the tenant's life so unpleasant the tenant voluntarily vacates. A landlord may turn off the water, heat, and electricity, for example. Generally, a tenant can show that the landlord acted with the intent to force the tenant to move. While obvious in concept, the landlord's intentionally trying to oust a tenant indirectly is rare compared to the situations where a landlord's failure to act (or acting with no intent to interfere with the tenant's use) constitutes a constructive eviction.

The failure-to-act form of constructive eviction occurs when a landlord has a duty to act or cure a problem and the landlord fails to act or cure the problem within a reasonable time after the tenant notifies the landlord of the condition. The landlord's duty can be a common law duty (usually related to common areas), a statutory duty, or a duty imposed under a lease provision.

In early cases, the landlord's action may have been a failure to control the common passageways of a building, with the result that bawdy or nuisance-like behavior of persons there affected the suitability of the tenant's premises. See Phyfe v. Dale, 130 N.Y.S. 231 (S. Ct., App. Term, N.Y. 1911) (noise and lewd conduct in halls). Or, it may be that the landlord's failure to control a noisy tenant disturbs other tenants in their premises. See Milheim v. Baxter, 103 P. 376 (Colo. 1909) (tenants on landlord's adjoining property).

A landlord's failing to maintain basic services to premises often forms the basis of a constructive eviction. Thus, a constructive eviction occurs when the landlord fails to supply heat, utilities, or water when needed if the landlord has agreed to supply heat, utilities, or water. The actions of the landlord have compelled the tenant to leave, just as when the landlord actually evicts the tenant.

Mere disagreement with the landlord, inconvenience or dissatisfaction will not amount to a constructive eviction. Likewise, a landlord's bringing an action for ejectment is not a constructive eviction unless the landlord is abusing the legal process in doing so.

Whether the landlord is under a duty to act when a third party, another tenant, or an off-premises condition creates the inhabitable condition arises in some cases. Conventionally, the landlord has no duty to control the actions of other people. Courts have refined the concept, however, and will find a duty if the landlord has the right and power to control the actions of the third party. For example, a landlord may be held to have constructively evicted a tenant when the landlord rents adjoining space to an aerobics studio or to a noisy bar. In several cases, tenants were picketed by protestors (fur selling, abortion clinics, etc.) and the police would not disperse the protestors unless the landlord signed a complaint. The landlord's failure to sign was enough of a breach of her duty to her tenant to serve as the basis for the tenant's successful constructive eviction claim.

(c) The Covenant of Quiet Enjoyment

The doctrine of constructive eviction is based on the landlord's breach of the covenant of quiet enjoyment. Pursuant to the *covenant of quiet enjoyment*, the landlord promises the tenant shall have quiet and peaceful possession of the premises for the term, as against the landlord, any person holding through the landlord, or any person with a title superior or paramount to the landlord. This covenant is implied in all leases — residential and commercial, written and oral. The parties can contract for quiet enjoyment and any express covenant of quiet enjoyment takes precedence over the implied covenant provided by operation of law.

Because of the common law doctrine of independent covenants, a landlord's breach of the covenant of quiet enjoyment traditionally gave rise only to a cause of action for damages, while the tenant remained liable for the rent. The covenant's breach as the basis for a constructive eviction, however, today lays the groundwork for the tenant's right to vacate the premises.

Absent a lease provision contrary, the covenant of quiet enjoyment is still an independent covenant — the tenant need not be in compliance with the leasehold covenants (including the covenant to pay rent) to enforce it. The tenant may vacate and then sue for damages. In this cause of action, the tenant's measure of damages under the covenant is for the difference between the rent reserved in the lease (often called "contract rent") and the fair rental value of the use that was in fact received, measured to include the unexpired period of the lease. This is a "difference money" measure of damages, using the values of what the tenant should receive and what the tenant in fact received.

Thus today a tenant has two options when the landlord breaches the covenant of quiet enjoyment. The tenant may stay in the leased unit and sue for damages or the tenant may vacate the premises and treat the breach as a constructive eviction. A constructive eviction requires the tenant to surrender the premises. There is dicta in some cases, particularly in New York, to the effect that upon a breach of the covenant the tenant must vacate; this is not generally so. The tenant must vacate to fulfill the last two elements of a constructive eviction, but not to sue for damages on the basis of the covenant itself.

(d) The Tenant's Dilemma

When asserting a constructive eviction due to a breach of the covenant of quiet enjoyment, the tenant runs the risk that after he or she moves out, a court will later find that no constructive eviction occurred. In such an instance, the tenant will owe the landlord rent. The tenant bears the risk of a wrong guess about the law. To avoid this predicament, in a few jurisdictions a tenant may seek a declaratory judgment that a constructive eviction has occurred before vacating. In at least one case, a court in a declaratory judgment action found a constructive eviction to have taken place before the commercial tenants vacated the premises. See Charles E. Burt, Inc. v. Seven Grand Corp., 163 N.E.2d 4 (Mass. 1959).

As stated previously, the tenant who remains in possession does not give up a suit for damages for breach of a covenant of quiet enjoyment, of fitness, or of use for a particular purpose. See Stewart v. Childs Co., 92 A. 392 (N.J. 1914) (holding that the covenant to pay rent and the covenant of fitness were independent covenants). The measure of damages is again difference money.

(e) Scope of the Covenant of Quiet Enjoyment

The covenant of quiet enjoyment requires that the landlord act in such a way as to interfere with the tenant's peaceful possession. Usually the covenant is breached when the landlord has a duty to do or not do something. Hence, the failure to supply hot water or heat when the landlord is contracted to provide hot water or heat can be a violation of the covenant of quiet enjoyment. The failure of the landlord to make major repairs; to provide essential services or habitable premises; to properly maintain the heating or air conditioning facilities; to obtain a needed governmental permit; to control vermin, insects, or rodents; or to police the activities in the hallways or in other apartments can be a breach of the covenant of quiet enjoyment.

(f) Partial Constructive Eviction

A landlord may be found to have constructively evicted a tenant from a portion of the premises. A partial constructive eviction must be clearly documented by the tenant who, after all, remains in possession of the rest of the premises. Because the tenant has not vacated, theories of partial constructive eviction are rarely used. The tenant's dispossession is less clear.

(g) Partial Actual Eviction

A *partial actual eviction* occurs when a landlord or her agent takes over part of the premises and denies the tenant use of a portion of the premises crucial to use of the whole. The underlying rationale for an actual partial eviction is that, absent some agreement to the contrary, the landlord conveyed the exclusive use of the demised premises to the tenant for the term and may not evict the tenant from any portion of the premises during the term.

Because the landlord is not permitted to apportion his wrong, courts have said that in this situation, there has been a total failure of consideration for the lease and, after providing the landlord with notice and a reasonable time to restore the premises to the tenant, the tenant is entitled to vacate the premises and is, in some jurisdictions, relieved entirely of the obligation to pay the rent. See Fifth Ave. Bldg. Corp. v. Kernochan, 117 N.E. 579 (N.Y. 1917) (Cardozo, J.) (denial of safekeeping area for jewelry store when safe was found to be under public sidewalk in the store's basement); Smith v. McEnany, 48 N.E. 781 (Mass. 1897) (Holmes, J.) (holding that an encroaching wall, making it impossible for dray wagons to deliver goods to retail premises, was such an eviction); Barash v. Pennsylvania Terminal Real Estate Group, 256 N.E.2d 707, 709 (N.Y. 1970) (attorney denied right to work weekends because landlord would not then heat or air condition a sealed office building. While useful to commercial tenants, partial actual eviction has not been of much help to residential tenants denied habitable premises.

THE IMPLIED WARRANTY OF HABITABILITY

The difficulty, from the tenant's perspective, with the remedy of constructive eviction is that the tenant must vacate to assert it. This is particularly difficult when the tenant is poor and has no place to go. Staying put but abating the rent is what many poor tenants want instead. Their desire coincides with a judicial recognition that the fastest method to get a landlord's attention fixed on the condition of the premises is to reduce the landlord's cash flow or rental income stream from the property.

In addition, most residential tenants (poor or not) are inexperienced at repairing their premises, but bargain for and expect the structures thereon to be suitable for habitation. Most treat their rented premises as a bundle of services and many low-income tenants have little choice of premises and little bargaining power, and so face standardized leases and sometimes even racial and ethnic discrimination. In short, many need the law's protection when leasing a residence.

Faced with such conditions, many courts have adopted an *implied warranty of habitability* requiring that rental premises be offered and maintained in a physical condition that provides safe, decent, and habitable housing for tenants. It is also consistent with the idea that landlords should comply with the standards found in building and housing codes enacted by many local governments around the country.

This implied warranty of habitability applies in most jurisdictions only to residential premises — and, on the facts of the cases that establish it, it is arguable that the warranty applies only to low-income housing, although there are no cases refusing to extend it to rental premises offered at high rents. It is both a warranty and a covenant. It is a warranty that residential premises are safe, clean, and fit for habitation at the time of the execution of the lease. It is also a covenant that the landlord will maintain and repair the premises so that they remain in that same condition throughout the term of the lease. It is both a representation of fact (a warranty) at the start of the lease, and a covenant (a contractual promise) of fitness during its term.

The warranty of habitability is implied and applies whether or not it is expressed in the lease. Any lease provision that purports to negate the warranty of habitability is void as a matter of public policy. The warranty of habitability applies to both written and oral leases. In most jurisdictions the tenant may not waive its benefits nor assume the risks inherent in uninhabitable premises, either in the lease or thereafter.

This warranty applies only to physical conditions that make the premises habitable. It requires that a landlord maintain the premises so that the basics of habitable living are afforded. Luxury items are not included. Heat, hot water, plumbing, safe kitchen appliances, and safe and sound structural conditions are warranted. The warranty is not breached, however, when the window blinds are broken, there are cracks in the plaster, or the premises need fresh paint. A landlord need not repaint the walls to satisfy the warranty, for example, but the warranty will require a landlord to remove any lead paint that constitutes a safety hazard to a tenant's child. Moreover, things like the presence of radon, a virus, or loud noise on an adjacent property may affect the health and happiness of the tenant but, unless the landlord is somehow responsible for their presence or they are the subject of a special purpose statute or ordinance, they do not affect the physical conditions on the premises and so do not breach this warranty.

The impact on this warranty on prior law is substantial, but precise. It partially abrogates the doctrine of independent covenants to the extent that it makes the tenant's covenant to pay rent and the landlord's duty to repair uninhabitable conditions into dependent covenants. It applies this duty to repair to both patent and latent conditions. And it greatly expands a tenant's remedies for such conditions.

(a) Basis for the Warranty of Habitability

The basis for the implied warranty of habitability is most often found in the housing code in the jurisdiction. Thus a substantial violation of the local housing code will breach the warranty. In some jurisdictions, the warranty of habitability derives from a common law concept of habitability. See Glasoe v. Trinkle, 479 N.E.2d 915 (Ill. 1985) (applying the warranty even where there was no housing code); Green v. Superior Court, 517 P.2d 1168 (Cal. 1974). Even when the housing code is not violated, the landlord may still be in breach of the warranty if the defect in the premises complained of makes the premises uninhabitable or unfit in the view of a reasonable person. Thus, an objectively reasonable standard of habitability is required by the warranty. No matter the source, the uninhabitable conditions complained of must be substantial to breach the warranty; de minimus defects will not do.

More than 40 states have adopted some form of the implied warranty of habitability, either by statute or judicial opinion. Some commentators argue that the imposition of this warranty is helpful to those tenants protected by it. Others respond that it just drives up rents to cover a landlord's legal liabilities for it. See Charles Meyers, *The Covenant of Habitability and the American Law Institute*, 27 Stan. L. Rev. 879 (1975) (arguing that it drives up rents); D. Kennedy, *The Effect of the Warranty of Habitability on Low Income Housing: "Milking" and Class Violence*, 15 Fla. St. U. L. Rev. 485 (1987) (arguing it is a benefit to tenants).

(b) A Breach of the Warranty

There are three elements to a successful warranty of habitability claim. First, the landlord must have notice of the defective condition. Second, the defect must be substantial, considering its violation of the applicable housing code, its effect on the tenant's health or safety, the length of time it has existed, and its seriousness. Third, the landlord must have been given a reasonable time to repair the defect and have not done so.

(c) Commercial Tenants and the Warranty of Suitability

In a few jurisdictions, the implied warranty of habitability has been extended, in a somewhat different form, to commercial leases. See Davidow v. Inwood North Professional Group, 747 S.W.2d 373 (Tex. 1988) (finding an *implied warranty of suitability* for intended use). Most courts that have considered this extension have not extended the warranty to commercial leases. See, e.g., Seoane v. Drug Emporium, Inc., 457 S.E.2d 93 (Va. 1995).

(d) Enforcement Remedies

If a landlord breaches the warranty of habitability, the tenant may (1) withhold rent until necessary repairs are made; (2) sue the landlord to collect damages, as will be discussed below; or (3) in some jurisdictions, repair the condition himself and deduct the reasonable cost of this repair from his next rent payment(s). A landlord cannot evict a tenant who pursues damages or withholds rent based on a breach of the warranty of habitability.

(e) Damages

A tenant may seek "difference money" contract damages: either (1) the difference between the fair rental value of the premises as warranted less the fair value in an unrepaired condition, or (2) the difference between the reserved or contract rent, as stipulated in the lease, less the fair value in an unrepaired condition. Difference money measures of damages have come in for a good deal of criticism. They often require litigation to establish and collect. This litigation is likely to require the use of expert appraisers to establish the fair rental value of the property with and without the conditions alleged to breach the warranty. This may be expensive and time-consuming, and in the end some courts have concluded that the result may not be worth the effort, being imprecise at best.

Some courts for practical reasons prefer a third measure of damages based on a percentage reduction formula (the percentage diminution measure of damages): Damages are equal to the contracted rent amount multiplied by a fraction equal to the percentage that the use and enjoyment of the premises was reduced by the presence of the uninhabitable conditions. In addition to damages, a tenant may seek to abate his rent or to withhold rent altogether. Under the percentage diminution measure of damages, a good deal of discretion is given the trial court, for the fact finder must figure out what, in percentage terms, a broken toilet or the lack of hot water is worth. In practice, this requires the buildup of case law and precedent on the subject, so that a judge can quickly determine that a broken toilet will permit the tenant to reduce the rent by (say) 20 percent, that the lack of hot water requires a 15 percent reduction, and so on. The advantage of this measure is a practical one: It simplifies fact finding and is cheap, expert-free, and sound in result, if not elegant in theory. See Wade v. Jobe, 818 P.2d 1006 (Utah 1991).

Emotional distress and punitive damages are possible as well, indicating that "slumlordism" has tort aspects, touching the personhood of the tenant. Punitive damages are likely when the landlord flouts tenant requests to repair up to code or puts exculpatory covenants into a lease, particularly after the jurisdiction has adopted the implied covenant of habitability.

(f) Withholding Rent

Perhaps the most important remedy given tenants using this warranty is rent withholding by the tenant. Often this remedy is authorized by state statute. When it is not, the tenant should deposit the rent into escrow or a special account. When rent withholding is authorized by statute, the statute should be followed to the letter. The rationale for regulating this withholding remedy is that because the purpose of the warranty is the improvement in quality of the housing supply, tenants should not be permitted to put their rents beyond the reach of the court or the landlord. Withholding the rent disciplines landlords, but at the same time they should not be denied the rent money once they do remedy the uninhabitable conditions, else they will have no cash flow with which to maintain the premises in the future.

When withholding rent the tenant should (1) give the landlord a notice of breach and an opportunity to repair, followed by (2) a reasonable time for the landlord to make the repair, followed in turn by (3) a notice of rent withholding, establishment of an escrow account, and later (4) deposit the withheld rent in an escrow account. This remedy amounts to tenant self-help and a substitute for a suit for damages: Thus, a tenant unilaterally withholds the rent and waits for the landlord to sue him for the amount withheld. It thus shifts the burden of bringing suit to the landlord.

RETALIATORY EVICTION AS A TENANT'S DEFENSE TO EVICTION

Because in many jurisdictions the implied warranty of habitability or the standards by which habitability is defined are based on a housing or building code, tenants should report code violations so they can be brought to the landlord's attention and repaired. A tenant who reports a code violation to government officials and is evicted as a consequence of exercising her right to obtain a governmental benefit (premises up to code standards) has successfully defended a summary eviction procedure action by pleading that the landlord sought the eviction action with a retaliatory motive. See Edwards v. Habib, 397 F.2d 687 (D.C. Cir. 1968), cert. denied, 393 U.S. 1016 (1969). In Edwards, the tenant, Mrs. Edwards, defended herself in a summary procedure action. The opinion held that summary procedure may not be used when the landlord acts with a retaliatory intent and that, until that intent is dissipated, there can be no eviction. In a later opinion, the same court held that when the eviction procedure is begun shortly after the tenant reported the violation, there is a presumption that the intent is retaliatory and the landlord has the burden of showing that it is not.

Edwards concerned a month-to-month periodic tenancy and so the effect of the holding was to say that the landlord could not refuse to renew the tenancy as long as he or she had a retaliatory intent. The court was clear that retaliatory intent provides the basis for an exception to the common law rule that the landlord "may evict for any legal reason or for no reason at all." The elements of a retaliatory eviction doctrine are (1) the enactment of an applicable housing code statute or ordinance, embodying the objective of insuring safe and decent housing conditions; (2) the landlord's business being leasing residential housing; (3) the tenant at the time of the reporting of the code violation not being otherwise in material default on the lease; (4) the landlord's primary (or substantial or partial) motive for eviction being the tenant's reporting the code violation; and (5) the tenant's report being made in good faith and with cause.

This doctrine works in tandem with the implied warranty of habitability, particularly in jurisdictions in which it, too, is housing code–based. As a practical matter, what violates the code will often also violate the implied warranty of habitability.

It is not necessary that the tenant give a notice of the code violation to the landlord in order to later invoke the retaliatory eviction defense. The defense's focus is on the report to public officials, rather than any preceding action by the tenant. The retaliatory eviction theory has also been the basis for a tenant recovering damages in a separate suit against the landlord, or as the result of a counterclaim when the landlord sues the tenant in an action other than summary possession. There is, however, a split in the cases on this issue.

The tenant must prove the elements of the retaliatory eviction, except when a statute provides to the contrary. Putting this burden on the landlord would be requiring proof of a negative. Putting it on the tenant seems to require what is seldom available — proof of the landlord's subjective state of mind. Thus, allocating this burden involves tough choices, and deciding whether it is satisfied often involves proof of objective actions that may indicate a subjective intent on the landlord's part to evict the tenant for reporting code violations to local authorities. Statutes are particularly helpful here in creating legal presumptions, usually rebuttable ones.

(a) Modifications to the Retaliatory Eviction Defense

Statutes have attempted to answer some of the questions raised by opinions such as *Edwards*. Some require that the retaliatory motive be dominant — not just one among many; others only require a substantial motive. See Minn. Stat. Ann. §566.03 (1971) (intent "in whole or part" may be deemed retaliatory), noted in 61 Minn. L. Rev. 523 (1977). Some courts have found a rent increase, or a decrease in services to a tenant, may be retaliatory as well. The presumption of a retaliatory motive may be dissipated after a certain time period — say, one year after the tenant reports the code violation. Without such a provision, the presumption might operate for a far longer period. See, e.g., Conn. Gen. Stat. Ann. §47a-20 (1986) (six-month period), interpreted in Murphy v. Baez, 515 A.2d 383 (Conn. Super. Ct. 1986).

The retaliatory eviction doctrine has great potential for tenants. Consider the possibilities: retaliatory rent increases, retaliatory use of self-help (when peaceful self-help is permitted a landlord), retaliatory repairs, even a retaliatory going out of business.

In addition, when the doctrine is used in tandem with the illegal lease doctrine, discussed in the next section, the tenant has a potent arsenal of rights to use against the landlord.

ILLEGAL AND FRUSTRATED LEASES

(a) The Illegal Lease

Some leases are illegal from the moment of their execution because they offend some strongly held public policy — e.g., a lease made for running a gambling establishment in a jurisdiction where gambling is illegal, a lease for running a house of prostitution, or a lease for an anticompetitive purpose violating the antitrust laws. Such leases are said to be void *ab initio*. Other leases may be made illegal during their term, as when a use stipulated as the only use that is to be made of the leasehold premises is prohibited by an amendment to the applicable zoning code.

In one case, a landlord sued a tenant in arrears on her rent in a summary eviction process. The tenant moved out, contending all the while that no rent was due because numerous and substantial housing code violations in existence at the start of the lease rendered the lease illegal when executed. The court agreed the lease was illegal because of the housing code violations. See Brown v. Southall Realty Co., 237 A.2d 834 (D.C. 1968).

When a lease is made for an illegal purpose or when it is illegal to lease the premises (say, for a use illegal under the zoning ordinance or building code applicable to the premises), the law "leaves the parties to it, as it finds them." There is a presumption that both parties to the lease knew the law and so violated it in executing the lease. It is the execution of the lease that is illegal — so when the housing code is used as a basis for illegality, the violations of the code must exist at the time of execution.

The same District of Columbia court in a later case refused to extend *Brown*'s illegality doctrine to violations not proven to exist at the lease's execution. The post-execution violation could not have been within the contemplation of the parties when the lease was made — so violating the housing code was not the purpose of the lease. A court may still find the lease to be illegal based on public policy. A court, more typically, will base the doctrine on the presumed knowledge of the parties and refuse to find an illegal lease for post-execution violations of the housing code. However, the supervening violations might render the lease impossible of performance, and this impossibility is another traditional ground for avoiding a lease. The illegal lease theory was more important before courts and legislatures recognized the warranty of habitability, which is the theory most residential tenants use.

The value of the illegal lease doctrine is that it works well in low-income housing contexts to remedy code or statutory violations in existence on the lease's first day; thereafter, the implied warranty of habitability extends a landlord's duty to keep the premises up to code. Rendering the lease illegal gives the tenant a ground for avoiding liability for future rent at the level reserved in the lease. Depending on local law, Brown and any applicable implied warranty cases and statutes would seem to provide the tenant with an election to use either the illegal lease or the implied warranty of habitability doctrine to seek a remedy for substandard housing.

(b) Frustration of Purpose

The doctrine of *commercial frustration* has been applied to commercial leases in many cases when the purpose for which the lease is made is nearly totally destroyed during its term. Thus, for example, a lease with a use restriction in its covenants is frustrated when that use is made illegal by a zoning change. Preexisting events do not give rise to frustration of purpose since, unless provided otherwise in the lease, tenants take the premises with all defects. Only supervening and unforeseen events can legally frustrate the purpose of the lease. Supervening events that make the business less profitable or even unprofitable or more burdensome to conduct, however, are insufficient to constitute a frustrated purpose.

Example: Tenant executes a five-year lease, intending to operate a bar. Six months after the execution of the lease, the county citizens vote to prohibit liquor sales in the county. Tenant can no longer sell alcohol. The change to Tenant's ability to sell alcohol does not qualify as a frustration of purpose since Tenant can still use the premises as a bar or restaurant that does not sell alcohol. The lease continues. If, on the other hand, the lease stipulated that the purpose was to sell alcoholic beverages, a court may find a frustration of purpose.

It is irrelevant that the lease has proven less profitable during its term than was anticipated at the start. The doctrine is not a means for investigating the level of profitability of leases and drawing lines between more and less profitable ones. Not surprisingly, then, its greatest use comes when the premises that were the initial subject of the lease are destroyed, or nearly so, such that the operation or use contemplated in the lease is no longer possible.

When (1) a frustrating event is not reasonably foreseeable, and (2) the value of the consideration or the counter-performance of the lease is totally or nearly totally destroyed by the frustrating event, a tenant's defense based on the doctrine of commercial frustration will be successful in a landlord's action for rent. The courts stress that these two elements constitute rigorous tests, that the doctrine is not to be applied liberally, or that the doctrine is applied only in cases of extreme hardship. Whether stated as a procedural canon or more substantively, these statements mean that courts, in cases of doubtful applicability for the doctrine, will not use it to rewrite the contractual aspects of the lease in dispute.

If an event is foreseeable, then the tenant is generally said to have assumed the risk that it will occur. Thus, when the tenant could have foreseen an event, the tenant must provide for it in the lease or otherwise (with, say, insurance) or else be deemed later to have assumed the risk.

Examples

Not So Easy Access

1. Branch Bank leased premises on the lowest floor of a three-story office building to Echo on a five-year lease. The lease provided that Echo could use a "common right of access" to enter and leave its offices. A year into the lease Branch Bank renovated the building. The renovation created noise, dirt, and an occasional disruption of electric service. The construction also made the rear parking lot inaccessible. During most of a 12-month period, many of Echo's employees used street-level parking in front of the building, and entered the building, through the main street-level door to the building, walking downstairs to Echo's offices. Late in the year Branch Bank changed the locks to the main street-level door for security reasons. After that, Echo's employees could not use the main entrance before or after regular business hours and were forced to use a rear door, which often was obstructed and difficult to use. Echo sued Branch Bank, claiming that Branch Bank's not letting Echo employees enter and exit through the main street-level door before and after regular business hours harmed Echo's business. What result under the following claims?
   (a) Total or partial actual eviction
   (b) Constructive eviction
   (c) Breach of quiet enjoyment
   (d) Breach of covenant of habitability

Wade in the Water

2. Lister and Wade entered into a five-year lease for commercial space in the basement of a building. A driveway abutting the building was improperly graded, so that after a rainfall water covered much of the basement's floor. Lister in writing promised to repair the driveway. Lister repaired the driveway, remedying the condition for a time, but not permanently. The water condition worsened until a rainstorm left five inches of water in the basement. Wade notified the landlord of the water, and vacated a short time thereafter. Lister sued for rent for the remainder of the term. In this suit, what result?

Worst House in Town

3. Lee showed Toni the worst residential premises in town and then leased it to Toni at $100 per month. Toni finds living there disgusting and wishes to sue Lee for damages. The jurisdiction recognizes a right to difference money damages, but not a percentage reduction formula. What would you advise?

Habitable Habitats

4. (a) Does the implied warranty of habitability apply to housing other than low-income residential units, particularly units in a multiunit apartment building?

   (b) Does the implied warranty of habitability apply to premises without air conditioning in the summer months in an area in which the temperature rises into the nineties?

   (c) Does the implied warranty of habitability apply to premises inhabited by the deadly Ebola virus, even though it does not affect the physical condition of the premises?

   (d) What if a strike of local government garbage collection employees means that rotting garbage piles up in the basement, creating a health problem and odors and attracting rats — does the implied warranty require the landlord to arrange for alternative pickup?

   (e) Does the landlord warrant that the premises are secure so that the tenant will be free of a criminal assault on the premises?

   (f) A shower pipe in an apartment covered by the implied warranty of habitability burst and water sprayed over the tub and bathroom floor. The tenant did nothing except promptly report the break to the building manager. Before the manager responded, water covered the bathroom floor and seeped into the ceiling of the apartment below. (The tenant's throwing a bathroom towel over the broken pipe would have kept the water in the tub.) The landlord quickly repaired the pipe and charged the tenant for the ceiling damage. The tenant refused to pay. The landlord sued for the payment. What result in this suit, and why?

   (g) Should the implied warranty of habitability apply to tenants in federally subsidized public housing?

   (h) Does the implied warranty of habitability apply when the owner of a condominium unit sues the property owners' association for a defective ceiling in a hallway leading to the unit?

Retaliatory Conduct

5. BulkCo rents space from the Metropolitan Port Authority (MPA) (a city-owned dock facility). In response to a newspaper article extolling the

benefits of the MPA's expanding its facilities for importing coal tar pitch, the BulkCo president wrote a letter published in the newspaper in which he claimed the MPA had made inadequate investments to ensure the environmentally safe discharge of coal tar. A month later the BulkCo president at a meeting with MPA officials expressed concern for the safety of his employees working close to the coal tar.

Three days later MPA sent BulkCo a letter terminating the lease effective one month later because continuing the lease would be "foolish" given BulkCo's president's comments. BulkCo did not vacate and at the trial BulkCo fought eviction by alleging retaliatory eviction for exercising its first amendment free speech rights. What result?

Explanations

Not So Easy Access

1. (a) No claim whatsoever for total actual eviction since Echo remained on the premises. The partial actual eviction claim is based on Echo's losing its rights to a "common right of access," particularly before and after regular business hours. As to partial actual eviction, the issue turns on whether Echo's employees should have a right to use the main access 24 hours a day or whether use of the rear door suffices (in which case no partial actual eviction). The court in Echo Investing Services, Inc. v. North Conway Bank, 669 A.2d 227 (N.H. 1995), concluded the lease provision giving Echo a "common right of access" required only that Echo's employees have access to the offices, not necessarily access through the main street-level door. No partial actual eviction.

    (b) The court in Echo also concluded no constructive eviction occurred. Branch Bank has a duty under the lease to provide access and not to interfere with Echo's quiet enjoyment of its premises. Here there was some interference with access and interference from dirt and noise. The issue turns on whether the noise and dust and use of the rear door after hours substantially interfered with Echo's use of the premises. That is a factual issue. The trial court in Echo had concluded Echo's use of its premises was not substantially affected and hence Echo was not constructively evicted — the premises were fit for Echo's business. The Echo court did not address but could have held that no constructive eviction occurred as a matter of law because Echo did not vacate the premises.

    (c) Most courts conclude the covenant of quiet enjoyment ensures the tenant maintains possession of the premises, and that its use is not substantially impaired by action or nonaction by the landlord. Unless the tenant is actually or constructively evicted, there is no breach of the covenant of quiet enjoyment. In these jurisdictions, Echo's loss on the constructive eviction claim disposes of this claim as well. The New Hampshire Supreme Court used the Echo case to expand the covenant of quiet enjoyment to include the denial of beneficial uses of the leased premises based on the tenant's reasonable expectations. Under this claim, the tenant need not vacate to prevail in its claim for damages. The practical difference in this covenant of quiet enjoyment and constructive eviction is that some landlord interferences with a tenant's quiet enjoyment justify a tenant's terminating the lease and collecting any damages that resulted from the landlord's action or nonaction. Other interferences do not justify the tenant's terminating the lease but do warrant damages for harm caused.

(d) The warranty of habitability applies to residential leases only, not to commercial leases. Echo has no warranty of habitability claim against Branch Bank. A few jurisdictions recognize a parallel warranty of suitability. Based on the trial court's finding the premises were fit for Echo's use, our guess is a court in New Hampshire would rule against Echo on a warranty of suitability claim.

Wade in the Water

2. Judgment for Wade the tenant. Rainfall covering the floors of the premises, particularly in a basement where, by force of gravity, it has nowhere to go, renders the premises unfit for use in heavy rains. The recurrences of the problem render it a substantial interference with the tenant's use of the premises: In this context, "substantial" need not mean continuing or permanent, it need only mean that the tenant cannot normally count on using the premises. All of the elements of a constructive eviction are present. The fact that commercial premises are involved is unimportant: The doctrine of constructive eviction applies to both residential and commercial leases. Its availability for commercial lessees remains an important feature of the doctrine in the many states adopting an implied warranty of habitability only for residential lessees. See Reste Realty Co. v. Cooper, 251 A.2d 268 (N.J. 1969).

Worst House in Town

3. Difference money damages can be either the difference between the fair rental value of the premises in a habitable condition and in its unrepaired condition, or the difference between the rent stipulated in the lease and the fair rental value in an unrepaired condition. If this is the worst housing, the two formulas are likely to produce the same result, and almost nothing by way of recovery. For instance, the contract rent has to be assumed to be higher than the fair rental value for the premises in its

unrepaired condition for there to be a difference greater than zero under the second measure of damages. Quite often, the efficient method of using both difference money formulas is to assume that the reserved or contract rent in the lease is the same as the fair rental value, and the amount recovered will then be the same as when the second measure is used. In effect, the landlord charged and the tenant is already paying the rental value of the premises in its uninhabitable condition. Thus, for slum housing, these measures of damages produce the least when they are needed the most. Moving out and then asserting the doctrine of constructive eviction may remain the best course of action for Toni (assuming she can afford to live somewhere else).

Toni might argue the lease was illegal and avoid rent altogether or withhold rent until Lee makes the premises habitable. A risk then is that Lee might board up the house or apartment and take it off the market, especially if the cost to repair exceeds any rental he might get from it.

Habitable Habitats

4. (a) Yes. In some jurisdictions, the earliest uses of the implied warranty of habitability were made by high-income tenants. Limiting some of the implied warranty cases to their facts, involving low-income and periodic tenancies, is unfair to other tenants. Creating one set of legal rules for low-income markets and another set for high-income markets requires less than crisp line drawing, and is unwise policy. There is no reason for public policy to deny a high-income tenant the benefits and the remedies of the warranty. See Timber Ridge Town House v. Dietz, 338 A.2d 21 (N.J. Super. Ct., L. Div., 1975) (permitting tenant a rent abatement for patio attached to an adjacent, expensive townhouse, but denying abatement for pool and playground).

   (b) Yes in Houston, Texas, but perhaps not in Vermont. The standards for habitability inevitably will vary by region and court. Another method of analysis would be to determine the source of the warranty, and then to answer yes in states that premise the warranty on the common law, but no in states that premise the warranty on the housing code. See Park Hill Terrace Associates v. Glennon, 369 A.2d 938 (N.J. Super. Ct., App. Div., 1977) (per curiam) (holding yes).

   (c) No, Ebola is a deadly virus, but not a breach of the implied warranty — which is not a cure for all of a tenant's health and safety concerns. The implied warranty concerns only the physical condition of basic services and features of the premises, and that is not the concern here. So the presumptive answer is no, unless the physical condition of the premises is implicated somehow: The landlord might be a jack-of-all-trades in repairing the premises, but he is no doctor.

(d) The garbage strike is an event beyond any one landlord's control, and this Example raises the issue of whether the landlord must be at fault in causing the condition for there to be a breach of the implied warranty. The warranty is implied from the relationship of a landlord to a tenant. The fault of one party seemingly has nothing to do with it, and the status of the landlord everything to do with it. See Park West Management Corp. v. Mitchell, 391 N.E.2d 1288, 1294 (N.Y. 1979) (finding warranty breached regardless of whether the landlord is at fault, but with statements to the effect that the landlord is not supposed to provide every amenity under the warranty).

Another issue is whether the garbage is like the virus issue — i.e., not based on a physical condition on the premises. When the strike has gone on long enough and the garbage is piled up, it might be argued forcefully that the area where it is usually contained awaiting pickup is not being maintained in a habitable manner, and so the warranty is breached. Likewise, extermination of pests such as rats is basic to a landlord's job of maintaining habitable premises, and the presence of the rats is good evidence of a breach.

(e) This Example presents a matter of considerable controversy. Unless the security system fails and the assault results because of the failure, the landlord does not warrant that the premises are free of crime. In this respect, a landlord is not the guarantor or insurer of a tenant's safety. Shifting the risk of crime to the landlord is different in kind from shifting the duty to repair uninhabitable conditions, and is an ineffective way to fight crime, whereas the implied warranty of habitability may well be an effective way to improve the quality of rental housing. At the same time, the presence of security devices like locks and alarms in high crime areas is a physical condition required to keep the premises free of breach. A good security system for such premises makes them habitable, and the system's failure renders them uninhabitable and may breach the warranty.

Courts in California, the District of Columbia, New Jersey, and New York think security from crime is covered by the warranty. See, e.g., Note, "Warranty of Security" in New York: A Landlord's Duty to Provide Security Precautions in Residential Buildings Under the Implied Warranty of Habitability, 26 Ford. Urb. L. J. 487, 488, n.11 (1988) (collecting the cases). If the courts are willing to have the landlord warrant against third-party acts such as garbage workers' strikes, a warranty against criminal actions caused by the premises' insecure nature isn't likely to be far behind.

(f) One of the authors thinks the landlord should prevail: Probably the landlord should obtain judgment if the implied warranty of

335

habitability were viewed as a contractual covenant. The landlord then has a plausible argument that the tenant should have contained the leak with the towel. If the implied warranty is enforced by contract remedies, then the tenant generally has a contractual duty to mitigate the damages that the uninhabitable conditions cause. So the issue is whether the tenant has a duty to mitigate damages caused by a breach of the implied warranty of habitability. Many of the cases adopting the warranty also discuss contract remedies for its breach; a duty to mitigate damages normally attaches to the remedy of damages for breach of contract. Moreover, in the context of vendors and purchasers of new housing, the implied warranty of habitability imposed on the developers of new housing incorporates a purchaser's duty to mitigate damages. See, e.g., Wawak v. Stewart, 449 S.W.2d 922 (Ark. 1970). Whether tenants have a similar — and similarly strong — interest in the property is a question not addressed by courts: The length of the lease as well as the need for quick action on the tenant's part will bear on the answer. There is no definite answer to this issue in the case law, but the probable answer is that the tenant, too, has a duty to mitigate damages.

The other author would not hold the tenant liable: First, the duty to mitigate acts to reduce damages, not to require the injured party (the tenant) to pay the person who is primarily responsible (the landlord). Second, the tenant is not demanding the landlord fix the ceiling — such a demand might be made by the tenant in the unit below — so the tenant is not mitigating her own damages. Third, any duty to mitigate here more closely resembles the duty element in a negligence action, which itself has two components. For the tenant to be deemed negligent, a reasonable person must know or should know that throwing a towel on the pipe would have kept the water in the tub, and would have recalled that when the crisis arose. In addition, to be liable in negligence, the tenant must owe a duty to the landlord to act. Placing that duty on the tenant here would require the tenant who saw a fire, for example, to have a duty to extinguish it or pay for the resulting damages. The general rule of tort is that no one must act absent a special relationship. Arguably, landlord-tenant relationship is not such a relationship. Finally, broken pipes and resulting repairs are normal operating expenses in a multiunit dwelling, and are more properly the obligation of the landlord, who can spread the expected costs to all tenants as part of the monthly rental.

Lesson to be learned: how a case is pled, and the theory of a case, matters. So take your choice. The authors of this book have different views of the answer. No matter which one of us is correct, the authors enjoyed arguing over this Example. Law is fun.

(g) The answer is a qualified yes; the warranty imposed on public housing authorities as landlords is usually somewhat narrower in scope than is the warranty imposed by state law. Because the rent roll is crucial not just to the apartment house but also to the program as a whole (and to payment of the government bonds guaranteed by the roll), the remedy of rent abatement is likely to be more closely supervised, and the opportunity for administrative action to remedy the defect given more time to work. See, e.g., Connille v. Secretary of Housing and Urban Development, 840 F.2d 105 (1st Cir. 1988) (imposing an implied warranty as a matter of federal common law). As a matter of policy, public housing tenants should have the same rights as tenants in private housing. Federal statutes generally require public landlords to extend roughly similar rights, but with different and more cumbersome enforcement mechanisms, as a condition of receiving federal grants and other assistance.

(h) In a condominium, each and every unit holder might generally think of the unit as his or her apartment, but in fact each holds a fee simple absolute to it, not a lease, so the conventional landlord-tenant relationship is absent. When the implied warranty of habitability is based on a state statute, its terms control the matter. Condominium regimes or developments are subject to detailed state statutes, and they are generally silent on this matter. See Agassiz W. Condominium Assn. v. Solum, 527 N.W.2d 244, 247 (N.D. 1995).

Where the warranty is based on the common law, however, the answer is less certain. Many condominium regimes were converted from rental apartments, and arguably landlords should not be able to escape the implied warranty just by converting. Moreover, insofar as common passageways and areas are concerned, the successor of the landlord is the unit owners' association, and applying the warranty to these areas is much less a reach than making an association liable for conditions within the units. The association, however, is a common agent of all the unit owners, so permitting the suit is like permitting owners to sue themselves. Nonetheless, the policy behind the implied warranty is to make "landlords" pay attention to the uninhabitable premises, and associations should be given the same incentives. See Pershad v. Parkchester S. Condominium, 662 N.Y.S.2d 993, 995 (N.Y. Civ. Ct. 1997) (taking jurisdiction over condo owner's complaint for defects on common areas). Like tenants, unit holders expect a package of services, may not have the necessary repair skills, and cannot repair common areas without association permission. Moreover, an association typically has remedies much like eviction when the unit owner does not pay assessments for maintaining the common areas, indicating that the association should be treated like a landlord as to those areas.

Imposing an implied warranty on an association may require that the remedies be limited. For example, assessment withholding probably is not a sound policy choice: If such withholding were permitted, all owners would be injured and the association would not be able to cover repair costs as expected. See Rivers Edge Condominium Assn. v. Rere, Inc., 568 A.2d 261, 263 (Pa. Super. Ct. 1990) (so holding). Thus, a unit owner might have a contract action against the association, but not be able to withhold assessments from it.

Retaliatory Conduct

5. The first and most critical issue is whether BulkCo can invoke the retaliatory eviction defense at all. Generally the retaliatory eviction defense is available only for residential leases, not commercial leases. But "generally" leaves open the possibility of an exception. Such was the holding of the court in Port of Longview v. International Raw Materials, Ltd., 979 P.2d 917 (Wash App. 1999), which under the facts of the Example held a commercial tenant could use the retaliatory eviction doctrine to defend against eviction for asserting its first amendment free speech rights against a *government* landlord as long as the speech addressed a matter of public concern and the speech was a substantial or motivating factor in the lease termination. That was the situation in the case and BulkCo prevailed. Several cases have indicated if the landlord was a private landlord, BulkCo would not have been able to use the retaliatory eviction defense.

Premises Liability of Landlords

PREMISES LIABILITY

Premises liability — the liability of landlords for injuries to tenants and nontenants — has undergone a major transition in the past century. Currently, the states' approaches to premises liability fall into three distinct camps.

(a) Landlord Liable for Injuries in Specific Situations

The majority of states fall into the first camp, which began with the old common law concept that the landlord's liability ended once the landlord delivered the premises to the tenant. It became the tenant's duty to keep the premises in repair. See Borders v. Rosenberry, 532 P.2d 1366 (Kan. 1975). The following exceptions to the general rule, however, have often become more important than the general rule.

(1) Latent Defects

The landlord must disclose latent defects where there is an unreasonable risk of physical harm present on the premises if the risk is known to the landlord but unknown to the tenant on the first day of the lease. (Some courts use the execution of the lease as the relevant date, and in most cases the different time frame is a matter of dicta.) Once the landlord discloses the defect to the tenant — either before, at, or after delivery to the tenant — the landlord's responsibility to the tenant and invitees ends.

(2) Prior Conditions Dangerous to Persons Off Premises

The second exception is for a landlord who transfers possession with the knowledge that there is a condition on the premises dangerous to persons off premises. This is a duty imposed on landlords on the first day of the lease. Typically, the landlord is liable for nuisances on the premises at the start of the lease. If the landlord was liable before the transfer, liability should remain and not be avoided just because of the transfer, even if the tenant is also aware of the dangerous condition.

(3) Leases for Public Use

Third, when the premises are transferred for a public use known to the landlord, the landlord has a duty to inspect and repair the premises in light of that contemplated use. A single-family residence would not be subject to this exception, but commercial premises, such as restaurants, theaters, and retail stores, typically are. If the landlord knows that the public will be admitted to the leased premises, the landlord is responsible for conditions that might foreseeably cause injury even if the tenant is aware of the condition and may be jointly liable.

(4) Negligence in Maintaining Common Areas

Fourth, the landlord remains responsible for negligence in maintaining common areas of multiunit premises and non-common areas if the areas are under the landlord's control. Hallway carpets that trip people, as well as lead paint used in hallways, are examples. The landlord is responsible for injuries caused by defects in a common area. This is a limited affirmative duty to inspect and repair.

(5) Landlord Contracts to Repair Leased Premises

Fifth, when the landlord contracts to repair, he assumes a duty to do so, no matter that the defect was in existence at the start of the lease or arose thereafter. Generally a landlord who contracts to repair but fails to do so is liable to persons injured because the landlord failed to act. The burden of proof is on the tenant to show the contract or agreement to repair.

(6) Negligent Repairs

Sixth, and finally, the landlord is liable for negligence in any repairs that he makes. This exception typically applies when the tenant neither knows nor should know of the negligence in performing the repair work. Thus, when the landlord makes the premises more dangerous with that work, or when the work has the deceptive appearance of being safe, the landlord is subject to liability for the physical harm caused thereby.

(b) Landlord Liable Under Negligence Standard

A few states have abandoned the classification scheme discussed above and will hold a landlord liable under the negligence standard based on how a reasonable landlord would prevent foreseeable harm. The landlord's duty under a negligence standard should extend to all persons likely to frequent the premises. The landlord's standard of care should be adapted to the right of access and the amount of control of the premises the landlord has. The negligence standard still leaves an injured tenant, as a plaintiff, the burden of litigation and proof as to the landlord's standard of care, its breach, actual and proximate cause, and duty; and subject to the defenses traditional in negligence cases such as assumption of the risk, contributory negligence, and comparative negligence.

(c) Landlord Strictly Liable

The California Supreme Court, for a few years, held a landlord strictly liable for all injuries to persons on leased residential premises, but has since reversed itself. Louisiana by statute holds landlords strictly liable for injuries to tenants resulting from the defective condition of the premises. As far as we know, no other state holds the landlord strictly liable for injuries resulting from defective conditions on the leased premises. See Raymaker v. Am. Family Mut. Ins. Co., 718 N.W.2d 154 (Wis. App. 2006) (rejecting strict liability).

LANDLORD LIABILITY FOR CRIMINAL ACTS

In most jurisdictions, absent some agreement to the contrary or the presence of a public or criminal nuisance on the premises, a landlord is not liable for the intentional criminal actions — murder, assaults, muggings, etc. — by third parties committed against tenants on the premises.

In other jurisdictions, however, a landlord has a duty to protect the common areas of a multiunit property against a known risk of foreseeable crimes, either under a general negligence standard or as an extension of the warranty of habitability. The same rationale used to impose premises liability for physical defects has been used to impose a duty on the landlord to protect tenants from criminals. See Kline v. 1500 Massachusetts Ave. Apartment Corp., 439 F.2d 477 (D.C. Cir. 1970). *Kline* arose in a large multiunit apartment house, and the court noted "the duty of protection is the landlord's because by his control of the areas of common use and common danger he is the only party who has the *power* to make the necessary repairs or to provide the necessary protection." Id. at 477. Once the landlord knows of the insufficiency of the existing protection devices (doors, locks, etc.), a duty to take the necessary precautions arises. The landlord must "take those steps which are within his power to minimize the predictable risk to his tenants." Id. at 481.

For the tenant, the duty in *Kline* translates into a burden of proving that (1) the landlord knew of the defect and had control over it, and (2) the defect foreseeably increased the risk of criminal acts. Plaintiffs have been most successful in meeting this burden when the defect relates to a criminal's means of gaining access to common areas. Broken locks, missing passkeys, and accessible outside fire escapes are more easily made the basis of a landlord's liability than, say, defective lighting or alarms. The landlord is not an insurer of the tenant's safety; she must only act reasonably. Moreover, the landlord's duty is measured—and limited—by the measure of protection afforded the tenant at the start of the lease, for it is that standard on which the tenant relies in executing the lease. The same security must be maintained by the landlord throughout the lease.

The foreseeability of the increased risk of crime is best shown by other crimes occurring on the premises when the criminal's access was by a similar means. Foreseeability is an important element because the duty being discussed is a duty to undertake to prevent crimes, not to control the conduct of criminals. It is a duty to reduce a criminal's capacity to commit crimes in the common areas of the property.

Thus, a defect, in the common areas, subject to the landlord's control, and subjecting the tenant to a foreseeably increased risk are the four elements of a landlord's liability in jurisdictions where it is imposed.

The cases involving criminal activity comprise both residential and commercial leases, and there is no reason why the same liability cannot be imposed in both settings. Shopping center landlords have been involved in litigation over crimes committed in parking areas around the center, for example.

Finally, there has been some legislative activity expanding the landlord's obligation to combat criminal activities. First, a landlord knowingly permitting his premises to be used for the conduct of a public nuisance is liable to have the premises closed down. Second, drug forfeiture statutes can result in the forfeiture of the landlord's interest in a property used routinely for drug trade. Finally, city ordinances have been upheld that require landlords in high crime areas to provide armed security guards in apartment houses with more than 100 rental units. See 515 Associates v. City of Newark, 623 A.2d 1366 (N.J. 1993) (upholding Newark, N.J., Ordinance §15:13-1 (1991)).

EXCULPATORY CLAUSES

A landlord may insert an **exculpatory clause** into a lease whereby the landlord is absolved from liability for injuries on the premises or is indemnified by the tenant if the landlord is found liable to any person. Exculpatory clauses are often enforceable in commercial leases, but the trend is for courts to declare them void as a matter of public policy in residential leases. Early exceptions to the exculpatory or indemnification clause included actively concealed hazards and unfit conditions, or when the landlord's active negligence led to the injury. Later courts struck the clause when bargaining power between the landlord and tenant was unequal. Statutes, such as the Model Residential Landlord-Tenant Act, prohibit or severely restrict the use of exculpatory clauses.

Examples

Premises for Liability

1. A statute provides that "the presence on premises, rented for human habitation, of a paint containing more than five-tenths of 1 percent of lead by weight shall be construed as rendering said premises unfit and uninhabitable." Does this statute make a landlord on whose property such paint is present strictly liable, liable for negligence per se, or liable generally in negligence for the harm to a tenant's child caused by exposure to this paint?

Liable for Premises

2. (a) A tenant was assaulted in his apartment after the person committing the assault gained access to the common area of the apartment house through a defective lock on an outer door. Does it matter that the criminal activity occurred in the apartment and not in the hallway?

   (b) Same facts, except that the criminal gained access to an outside fire escape, and thence up the fire escape to and through an unlocked window in the tenant's apartment. The landlord had provided the lock for the window, and it was in working order at the time of the assault. What result?

   (c) Same facts, except that the person committing the assault was another tenant. What result?

343

Take a Hike

3. Lawrence leased land to a church for the stated purpose of using the property as a summer camp. A 12-year-old camper slipped on a narrow pathway and was severely injured when he tumbled into a gulch by the pathway. Is Lawrence liable?

Shack Attack

4. Linda leased a farm to Fred. Linda showed Fred a storage shack and pointed out that the supporting posts for the shack had rotted. Six months later Edgar, a farm hand, climbed to the top of the shack. The shack collapsed, injuring Edgar. Is Linda liable?

Explanations

Premises for Liability

1. Absent a clear legislative history on this issue, the language of the statute controls. A child who might ingest the paint is certainly subject to the health hazard such paint presents. The statute expands the implied warranty of habitability to conditions created by lead-based paint. The landlord, therefore, has a duty to repaint premises affected by lead paint, but only after the landlord knows or has reason to know of its presence. Lack of notice of the condition, and denial of an opportunity to repaint, would be defenses to an action based on the statute. See Gore v. People's Savings Bank, 665 A.2d 1341 (Conn. 1995) (holding that the statute makes the landlord liable for negligence per se; that a jury need not decide the landlord acted (un)reasonably and (im)prudently—the statute establishes that the landlord acts imprudently when the lead paint is present—but that a landlord may defend that it had neither actual nor constructive knowledge of the paint on the premises).

Liable for Premises

2. (a) No, so long as the elements of liability are present. Aaron v. Havens, 758 S.W. 2d 446 (Mo. 1988). The landlord is not strictly liable and must know or should know of the defective lock before liability attaches.

   (b) There are two issues. First, is the window, set in an outside wall, part of a common area? The authorities are split on this matter. If the window is under the tenant's control, there is no liability on the landlord. Second, if it is a common area, is the landlord liable for its unlocked state? No court has held that the landlord must provide a locked fence around an apartment house, so a holding that it is a landlord's duty to insure that all windows remain locked is similarly unlikely. Finally, in states that hold that contributory negligence is a complete defense, the landlord may escape liability if a fact finder could find the tenant was contributorily negligent.

(c) A very few courts have imposed liability, and then only when the landlord knew or should have known of the other tenant's criminal history involving assaults. The issue therefore is the foreseeability of the assault, so that, even when the landlord knew of the other tenant's criminal history, foreseeability will be a fact question and difficult to show. An easier case might arise when the assault was committed by the landlord's employee.

Take a Hike

3. Lawrence very well could be liable. If the fact finder concludes the narrow pathway on the edge of a gulch was a defective condition, or if the fact finder concludes the summer camp was for public use, or in other jurisdictions if a fact finder concludes a reasonable person should have foreseen someone falling into the gully at that point, Lawrence may be found liable since the dangerous condition was there when Lawrence delivered possession to the church. Lawrence may defend successfully if the church had an opportunity to learn about the hazard — again, a factual determination will decide the outcome of this case.

Shack Attack

4. Linda is not liable. Linda would be liable for latent defects in the shack if the tenant had no knowledge of the effect. As soon as Linda informed Fred, her tenant, of the rotted posts, her liability ended. Linda was not obligated to notify Edgar of the dangerous condition. Notice to the tenant was enough.

PART IV

Transfers of Land

The Sales Contract

INTRODUCTION

This chapter concerns the purchase and sale of real property. An owner wishing to sell real property typically places it on the market by listing the property with a real estate broker. The broker is typically the potential seller's agent and the broker's employment agreement is known as a listing agreement. In practice, most sellers enter into these agreements without involving an attorney. Purchasers also often contact a broker to locate suitable property and they may also contract for the broker's services.

Once brought together, sellers and potential purchasers negotiate the terms of the sale, often through real estate brokers. The purchasers may conduct studies related to the suitability of the land for their needs. Assuming the parties agree on such matters as the sale price, the parties enter into a contract of purchase and sale, an earnest money contract, or other such name. Both seller and purchaser incur enforceable obligations when it is executed.

From the date the buyer and seller execute a sales contract to the date their transaction is completed (or "closed"), legal disputes may arise concerning the performance of the contract. Because between these two dates the contract is executory (meaning that it is in the process of being performed by the parties), the period of time between the two dates is known as the **executory period**.

Because of the importance of the contract, each party should be represented by an attorney before signing it. In most residential sales, however, the parties rely instead on a preprinted, standard form contract supplied by the seller's broker. The blanks on the form identify the parties, set the sale price or at least a method to determine the sale price, describe the property to be conveyed, include language that the seller will convey and the purchaser will acquire the property, set the closing date, delineate the manner of payment including cash and seller-financing, and acknowledge receipt of the deposit, down payment, or earnest money. Filling in these blanks is incidental to the broker's business, and so is not the unauthorized practice of law. Brokers often supply a form that contains a provision detailing the amount of the sales commission payable to the broker from the deposit. Additional preprinted terms in the typical form contract concern the remedies each party will have on the other's breach. The parties may insert other conditions, such as making the sale contingent on the purchaser's obtaining financing, having the land rezoned, or selling an existing residence.

CLOSING

After entering into the sales contract, the buyer may inspect the property, review title documents, survey the property, and secure loan commitments. The seller may need to correct any title imperfections or repair the property. Based on some findings or failures, one of the parties may decide not to complete or close the transaction.

At closing, then, the parties complete their transaction. The seller transfers the property to the purchaser by deed of some type. The seller might also assign all contracts, leases, and personal property on the premises to the buyer. The buyer will pay the seller cash or execute a note to the seller (or a combination of the two). The closing agent will prorate (allocate) the current year's taxes, insurance, and other items between the seller and the purchaser. If the purchaser borrows money to purchase the property, the buyer and the seller must execute documents to satisfy the lender's preclosing conditions, so that the title and the loan can be closed, in that order, on the same day.

REAL ESTATE BROKERS AND AGENTS

Sellers often engage real estate brokers or real estate agents or salespersons to market their property. Real estate agents may not sign a listing agreement, may not sue for a commission, and work under the supervision of a broker. An agent is thus, under the law of agency, a sub-agent of the broker. Both a broker and an agent owe fiduciary duties of loyalty, good faith, and fair dealing to the seller. Absent an express power of attorney, neither is empowered to negotiate or sign a contract or other documents on the seller's behalf—that is, the broker cannot obligate the seller to sell the property. A listing agreement is only an employment and personal services contract.

No broker unlicensed when executing a listing agreement may sue or collect a commission. No licensed broker may share a commission with an unlicensed one. Likewise, a listing agreement authorizes payment of a commission to the broker. It must be written. Either the jurisdiction's Statute of Frauds or a regulation of the state agency licensing brokers requires this. The listing agreement also sets out the terms of the listing. The commission must be stated in the listing. It is typically a percentage of the purchase price procured by the broker, split 50-50 between the listing broker and a cooperating selling broker, with a part of each commission split again with any salesperson who might be involved in the transaction or with the brokerage firm of each broker.

If the listing provides that the seller may still use another broker to sell the listed property, the agreement is an **open listing**. This is an offer to pay a commission without the owner's seeking a return promise: before a broker performs, it is a unilateral contract, an offer to sell to be accepted by a broker's performance and revocable beforehand.

Example: Broker B reading the morning newspaper sees the following ad: "City lights, vu, mint, 123 Wide Way, Nirvana, 3 br, 2 ba, hvac, $500,000, will co-op w/brokers, contact O." If B responds to this ad, will she have a valid listing? No, because there is no identification of a specific broker and no commencement or termination date for the listing; moreover, the owner has not signed it. If the broker responds to the ad, learns from O that the commission will be 5 percent of the purchase price obtained, and introduces O to P, who completes the sale, B will have an argument for a commission based on estoppel. Then the completed sale will have terms as definitive as a listing agreement stating the material terms for a broker's employment.

Exclusive listing agreements fall into two categories. In one, known as the **exclusive agency contract**, the seller is free to find her own purchaser; and if the seller finds a purchaser without the broker's assistance,and without any other broker's assistance, the seller owes no commission. In an exclusive agency, then, the seller promises in effect that "if I sell using another broker, I will pay you a commission anyway (even if I owe that other broker a commission too), but I reserve the right to sell the property myself." Under the second type, known as the **exclusive right to sell**, the broker receives a commission no matter who sells the property, whether it be the listing broker, another broker, or the listing owner.

Example: O lists Whiteacre with broker B. P drives by Whiteacre, sees B's for sale sign, and thereafter deals exclusively with O. Is B entitled to a commission? Yes if the listing agreement is an exclusive right to sell. This is the reason brokers overwhelmingly prefer this type of listing.

In most jurisdictions, unless the listing agreement provides otherwise, the seller's broker earns a commission when he procures a **ready, willing, and able** buyer, whether or not the seller actually enters into a sales contract with the buyer, and whether or not the sale closes. A sales contract may be the broker's best evidence that the buyer is ready, willing, and able to meet the terms of the listing, but it does not matter if the sales contract is executed or closed: A broker earns her commission just by introducing the seller to a prospective "ready, willing, and able" buyer. After all, the broker cannot negotiate the terms of the sale, so with the introduction, the broker's work is done. Even if the title proves unmarketable, the parties rescind the sales contract, improvements are destroyed in a fire, or a zoning change makes the buyer's proposed use illegal, the commission is still due. (Whether a broker would sue for it in all these situations is another matter, often involving a business decision.)

Example: Owen lists Blackacre with a broker in a state where the "procuring a ready, willing, and able buyer" rule determines when brokers are entitled to commissions. The broker locates a prospective buyer who signs a valid contract of sale with Owen. The contract provides that the broker's commission is "due at closing." The buyer breaches the contract and refuses to close. The broker is still entitled to a commission. There is a difference between being entitled to the commission and its being payable at closing. It might be convenient for Owen to pay the commission out of the sale proceeds, but the phrase "due at closing" does not make closing a condition precedent to the broker's receiving a commission, so the state's default rule controls.

In about a dozen states, the rule is that a broker's commission is not payable unless the sale is closed: No closing, no commission is their rule. This minority rule assumes that a prospective buyer cannot be shown to be "ready, willing, and able" until the closing. Only then, for example, has the buyer qualified for a mortgage loan and shown himself "able" to purchase. More generally, it does not allocate to the seller the risk that the buyer will turn out to be unready, unable, or unwilling to close. Thus the seller is not responsible for investigating the purchaser's personal and financial capacities before signing the sales contract. Further, the minority rule is consistent with the executory nature of most sales contracts.

Example: Owen lists Blackacre with a broker as in the previous Example, except that Blackacre is located in a "no closing, no commission" rule state and Owen breaches the contract and refuses to close. Does Owen owe the broker a commission? Yes, because Owen has breached the contract, caused the broker to lose a commission, and on that account, is liable to the broker for it. Owen's interference with the broker's entitlement gives the broker a cause of action in tort for interference with a contract or a prospective advantage. In contract, Owen has made an implied promise to close, breached that promise, and injured the broker. Both in tort and contract, Owen is liable.[1]

When a sales contract procured by a broker does not close because the buyer breaches, and the seller, as in the prior Example, does not owe the broker a commission, many courts force the breaching purchaser, who was not even a party to the listing agreement, to pay the commission to the broker as a third party beneficiary of the sales contract.

The majority and minority rules have a common element. Both rules require that the broker "procure the sale" of the listed property to a ready, willing, and able buyer. Under the majority rule, then, the broker must be the procuring cause of the sale, meaning typically a contract of sale, but "sale" is interpreted, in a minority rule state, to mean the closing. The requirement that the broker "procure" the buyer is the equivalent of what tort law recognizes as a rule of proximate cause. The broker can thus either set in motion a chain of events leading to the sale ("but for" the broker's action, no sale would take place) or the broker can oversee a chain of continuous events leading to a sale (an unbroken chain, in which the broker is responsible for every link — a "chain of events" test). Whatever the state's rule, the parties can specify in the sales contract precisely when the broker's fee is earned and what contingencies if any affect the broker's right to the commission.

Example: O lists Greenacre with broker B, who introduces P to O, but O and P do not execute a sales contract until the listing agreement has expired. Their contract's provisions are substantially different from those called for in the listing. Is B entitled to a commission? She is under a "but for" test for procuring cause, but not under a "chain of events" test.

Although brokers and agents are involved in the majority of home sales, a growing number of homeowners have begun using websites and yard signs to offer homes "for sale by owner." This option eliminates or reduces the broker's commissions, but places a marketing and appraisal burden on owners.

BROKER AS SELLER'S AGENT

The listing broker is the seller's agent and owes a duty of loyalty, good faith and fair dealing, and disclosure of material facts to the seller. The duty of loyalty includes a prohibition against self-dealing: The listing broker can

---

1. This tortious and implied contract suit works equally well in a majority rule jurisdiction.

buy property from his principal (the seller) but must disclose to the seller that the broker is buying the property and must disclose, if true, that the seller has set a below-market asking price. Similarly, a broker must promptly relay all offers to the seller and cannot intentionally delay efforts to sell the property until his principal lowers the listing price just so the broker, or a friend or relative, can buy the property at a lower price. Although not guaranteeing success, the broker must diligently seek a purchaser. The broker cannot perform any act showing disloyalty. In some states, this duty prohibits the broker from indicating to potential purchasers that the seller is desperate to sell or would accept a lower price.

In contrast, buyer's brokers often have more limited statutory duties replacing the common law's fiduciary duties — limited to a duty not to act negligently toward their employer.

Example: H and W, a young couple, have been driving around looking at homes with broker B. When getting out of B's car to inspect O's home, W says to H: "Let's offer $250,000, then we can go as high as $300,000." If B overhears this, must she report this to the listing owner? Yes, if B is the seller's broker, but no if B is a buyer's broker, even if as a buyer's broker B has an incentive to obtain a higher price (because the commission, shared with the seller's broker, is computed as a percentage of the purchase price).

Example: The facts are the same as in the prior Example, except that B is the seller's agent and responds to W, saying that "there is an outstanding offer of $275,000 for this home." Has B breached her duty of loyalty to O? Maybe not, because making the negotiations a realistic exchange is well within the broker's province. Saying that O would not accept less than $275,000 would be a breach. A broker is everywhere barred from disclosing a listing owner's lowest acceptable or "reservation" price: Most buyers will know that discovering that price is their role in a negotiation.

Example: Broker B offers to list O's Greenacre and makes notes about its defective condition during a walk-through with O. O lists Greenacre with another broker. B is employed as a buyer's broker by C. B shows Greenacre to C and tells C to have the property inspected. C contracts to buy Greenacre, closes the sale with O, and then learns of B's notes. C sues B, alleging that he would have paid less had he known of the defect. In C's suit, what result? Non-disclosure of the notes is constructive fraud on C (constructive fraud is one way of framing a breach of a fiduciary duty), unless the duty does not arise until the execution of the buyer-broker agreement. But a buyer hires a broker to gain knowledge of the real estate market: If the broker walked C through the property, noticed the defect for the first time, a duty to disclose it arises, and this situation is little different from the facts presented. The loss of the commission is the default rule for measuring damages for the breach of a fiduciary duty, but B may in some jurisdictions also be liable either for the decrease in fair market value due to the defect or the cost of repairing it.

Selling brokers, those brokers that show properties to prospective buyers, are typically sub-agents of the listing broker.[2] Their main contact, however, is with prospective buyers. In fact, they may show a single prospect many properties, all owned by different sellers, yet they are paid their commission pursuant to a sharing arrangement with the listing broker through a listing agreement with the seller. Selling brokers owe a duty to the seller despite having considerably greater contact with the buyer. Recognizing this reality, and in line with many buyers' expectations, a few jurisdictions hold the selling broker to be the buyer's agent. In any jurisdiction and with proper disclosures, a broker may become a dual agent, representing both the buyer and the seller, a situation rife with conflicts of interest. A small but growing number of prospective buyers employ the services of a buyer's agent, whose loyalty is to the prospective buyer.

Example: O, Brownacre's wealthy owner, lists it with B, who sells it to P through the effort of selling broker B1, who misrepresents its profit potential to P. P learns of the misrepresentation and sues O. In a jurisdiction using a chain of agents and sub-agents, this suit is not subject to dismissal. However, if B1 is P's agent, then the liability for the misrepresentation can go no farther than B1. O will have P's suit dismissed.

BROKER'S DUTY TO DISCLOSE LATENT DEFECTS TO PURCHASERS

A broker may have a duty to the buyer to disclose latent defects or, more specifically, she may have a duty to disclose facts materially affecting a residential property's value or desirability when the broker, using reasonable diligence and making a reasonable inspection, discovered or could have discovered them, even though the buyer did neither of those things. The broker usually has a duty independent of the seller's duty to make the same disclosures: The broker may be directly liable for her breach of the duty to disclose, and the seller may be liable both for his failure to disclose and for the broker's breach of her duty to disclose.

Traditionally, the broker and the selling owner had only a duty to refrain from **intentional misrepresentations**, from making any false statement about the

2. In major urban areas, both the listing and the selling broker are members of a multiple listing service (MLS) that shares listings among its members. Where available, MLSs are utilized for 80-90 percent of all residential listings.

listed property or from actively concealing defects or material facts about it. Mere non-disclosure was not actionable. They owed no further duty to disclose to buyers under a theory of **caveat emptor** ("let the buyer beware"). Caveat emptor is still the default rule in many jurisdictions. Most states also hold the broker liable for **negligent misrepresentations** — where a broker knows or should know of matters underlying a false statement. Negligent misrepresentation occurs when a broker gives erroneous information about a matter of general knowledge affecting the real estate market in the neighborhood. Eight states even hold the broker liable for **innocent misrepresentation**, in effect making the broker liable for good faith statements that turn out to be incorrect.

Example: Broker B tells client P that the house they are inspecting is "a three family house." Actually, the zoning ordinance locates it in a single family residential use district. Is B liable for a misrepresentation? Not in most jurisdictions because the ordinance is a public document available to P. B is not a zoning expert and has no duty to verify the zoning: P is best able to evaluate any prospective use of the house. While the broker might customarily check tax records to make sure the listing owner actually owns the house (this can often be done on the Internet), the zoning ordinance is not checked.

Example: Broker B obtains a listing for O's house. When submitting the listing to the MLS, a listing broker is typically obligated as an MLS member to state a house's square footage on the submission form and to indicate the source of the information — e.g., "as shown on tax records." B fails to show the source of the square footage. P obtains the listing sheet, buys the house, attracted to it by its potential for renovation, the cost of which P estimates by a dollar amount *per* square foot. P renovates, but the square footage is wrong and the renovation costs substantially higher than P estimated. Is B liable for the misrepresentation? Perhaps. If P's suit is for a negligent misrepresentation, then proof of reliance is necessary, but if intentional misrepresentation amounting to fraud is alleged, no reliance need be shown. (Or, put another way, reliance is shown by P's carrying out his renovation plans.) Knowing of the renovation plan, B might be expected to know that the square footage is material to P's purchase.

In states where caveat emptor is not the rule, a broker must avoid misrepresentations of material facts and must disclose latent and material defects that the broker either knew about or could have discovered upon reasonable inspection. **Latent defects** are those not discoverable by a buyer or his representative upon a reasonable inspection. In order to hold a broker liable, not only must the defect be latent, rather than open and discoverable on reasonable inspection, but the condition or defect must be a **material defect**, one significantly affecting the value or use of the property.

In most jurisdictions, listing owners are required by statute to fill out detailed, statutorily prescribed disclosure forms covering many of the major features of a listed property — for example, its roof, hvac systems, plumbing, and foundation. Their doing so entitles brokers to rely on these disclosures in representing a property to prospective buyers, thus making the owners ultimately liable for any misrepresentation.

Example: Broker B knows of a defect that should be disclosed in a disclosure form or by a professional inspection of listed property. The defect is undisclosed on the form. B advises P to obtain an inspection report. P does so, but the report does not disclose the defect. Is B liable for a silent misrepresentation? No, most courts dealing with the matter hold that the inspection report trumps B's duty to disclose. The proper remedy is against the inspector for negligent performance of the inspection. The net impact of the disclosure form and B's silence is blunted by the presence of the inspector.

THE STATUTE OF FRAUDS

Every American jurisdiction has enacted a Statute of Frauds. The Statute of Frauds requires that deeds and real estate contracts be in writing and signed by the person to be bound. The statute does not render non-complying contracts void, illegal, or unperformable; it renders them unenforceable in court.[3] The statute applies to transfers of any interest in real estate, including easements, real covenants, mineral rights, water rights, long-term leases, life estates, remainders, and liens. Some states also require that options to purchase be in writing. In most states, modifications of provisions included in a writing also must be in writing, and a slight majority of states allow a person entitled to rescind a contract to orally rescind it. In all states, a special statute or a regulation of a licensing agency requires listing agreements made by real estate brokers to be written.

Example: A sues B for specific performance of their sales contract for Brownacre. B successfully defends the suit on the ground that the contract does not satisfy the Statute of Frauds. The contract provides that in any litigation about it, the prevailing party may recover attorneys' fees. A responds that if the contract is unenforceable, so is the fee provision. Is A correct? No. The Statute does not affect the validity of this provision; it

---

3. Thus a court will not order specific performance of an oral contract even if all parties agree to it. An oral contract for real estate is said to be voidable. The parties may perform it and, if carried through to closing, the transaction will not be undone.

only provides a defense to the conveyance. Otherwise the contract is neither void, voidable, nor illegal.

Thus not all provisions of the real estate contract or deed must be in writing to satisfy the Statute of Frauds. Oral provisions will be enforced as long as a sufficient writing exists concerning the transaction. A memorandum of an oral contract satisfies the writing requirement. Although the Statute of Frauds does not itself set out minimum requirements of a "writing" (except the writing must be signed by the person to be bound), courts have established four essential requirements.

Although some courts demand more, the essential requirements of a writing that satisfies the Statute are that it must (1) identify the parties, (2) be signed by the party to be bound, (3) describe the property, and (4) state the price, or at least a method to determine it. These essentials do not have to be contained in the same document or even in formal documents. Courts have concluded that a series of letters can constitute a writing, for example, or that a check can be the writing or part of the series constituting the writing if it contains all the required information. Courts require at least one of the writings to reference the other writings before they consider the separate documents to be one writing.

Example: S, intending to sell Blackacre, places the word "assignee" in place of the name of a buyer. This is an insufficient designation of the parties to the contract and does not comply with the Statute of Frauds.

Example: S and A, the agent for B, execute a contract for the sale of Whiteacre by S. So long as the agent is identified, A's principal need not be. The principal might be a wealthy person afraid that if known to S, S will demand a purchase price above Whiteacre's market value.

Example: Assuming the same facts as in the previous Example, does A's signature on the contract, bind P? Yes, the signature requirement may be here a subscription or attestation of the contract at the direction of the "party to be bound" as long as A acted when signing within the scope of his agency. The party to be bound need not sign in her own hand.

Example: Assuming the facts in the two previous Examples, S discovers that A's agency is an oral agreement with the principal. Now the contract does not comply with the contract. If the contract must be written, so must the supporting documents or agreements underlying the essential requirements of the contract.

Example: V and P execute a brief contract of sale for Greenacre. The contract satisfies the Statute, except that P's "signature" is an electronic one contained in an e-mail. Most courts would hold that the "party to be bound" has "signed" the contract. Not every jurisdiction has a case holding this, but federal and state statutes have caught the law up with the advent of e-mails and the Internet.

Example: S and B execute a brief contract for the sale of Brownacre complying with the Statute in all respects except that the description of the property is a postal address as opposed to a legal description. Just as a document complying with the Statute need not be a formal one, so too the description need not be one required for a deed. So long as the property is described with a precision that permits later location, the description is sufficient. So if the postal address is "1234 Country Lane," the description may be sufficient; if it is "P.O Box 294," it isn't.

In addition to requiring essential terms, some jurisdictions require that to comply with the Statute, a contract contain its material terms. Material terms are subject to performance during the executory period. For example, a financing contingency may require that the buyer obtain third-party mortgage financing, and this contingency must be sufficiently definite so that the parties can tell when it is satisfied and when it is not. Similarly, a contract might call for rezoning the property or for the sale of the seller's present home before a closing can be held. If a term is non-material, then a court will supply it based on a rule of reason or custom and usage in the locale. For example, if a contract is without a date for closing, a court will say that the closing must take place within a reasonable time; if it does not say when possession of the property will change hands, a court will infer that it does so at the closing.

Example: Sam and Bea sign a sales contract for Blackacre. It contains all essential terms required by the Statute of Frauds and also provides: "Contract to follow." Is that phrase sufficient to prevent enforcement of the contract under the Statute? No, if the jurisdiction requires only essential terms, but perhaps in a jurisdiction requiring essential and material terms. When negotiations are ongoing when the contract is signed, there is as yet no enforceable contract: The negotiations have only taken some issues off the table. If negotiations are begun afterwards, terms added subsequently are entitled to a presumption that they are not material, but incidental to an already enforceable contract.[4]

In interpreting a contract with both oral and written provisions, courts do not allow testimony to contradict any written provision but will allow testimony to clarify it and to clarify or contradict oral provisions. Testimony

---

4. This Example tells you why traditionally most jurisdictions require that only essential terms be written. Were it otherwise, it is too easy for a party to fake the materiality of a term.

also will be allowed to contradict the terms of a memorandum of an oral contract.

PART PERFORMANCE AND OTHER EXCEPTIONS

Exceptions to the Statute of Frauds are based on equitable principles. They are granted when the facts and circumstances surrounding the otherwise unsatisfactory contract show that enforcing it will not work a fraud on the party seeking the protection of the Statute. In all cases, the moving party (1) must prove an oral contract exists, and (2) must persuade a court to excuse the party's failure to produce a writing containing the essential elements of the contract.

(a) Part Performance

A court will excuse a failure to procure a writing satisfying the Statute of Frauds when the buyer does some combination of the following in order to demonstrate part performance of a contract: (1) pays the purchase price, (2) takes possession of the property, and (3) improves it. Paying the purchase price alone is insufficient to warrant enforcement of the contract since the complaining party can be put back into the position he would have been in if there had been no contract simply by having the money returned to him (i.e., by restitution). Some courts accept partial payment, some require substantial payment, and some require full payment of the purchase price. Even with payment of the full purchase price, courts usually require at least one of the other two requirements before excusing noncompliance with the Statute. Taking possession entails more than delivery and acceptance of title: The buyer must physically move onto the property and perhaps even incur substantial moving expenses from another location. A party who substantially improves the property — i.e., the improvement must result in the property's value being increased more than the fair rental value accruing to the moving party during the time he possessed the property — may be excused from complying with the Statute. When the required elements of this exception are met, the acts constituting part performance serve as an alternative form of evidence of the contract.

(b) Equitable Estoppel

Under this exception, courts in a few states will excuse a contract's noncompliance with the Statute of Frauds if a party seeking performance, in justifiable reliance on an oral contract and the continuing assurances of the other party, so substantially changes his position that injustice would result unless the contract is enforced. The equitable estoppel or equitable fraud theory usually is invoked in cases involving persons, often family members, who move to the property to care for the property's owner, who also lives there, on the oral promise that the owner at her death will devise the property to the moving party. The consideration for the contract is the services performed. The following are the requirements for the equitable estoppel or equitable fraud theory:

A certain and definite oral contract;
Acts that refer to, result from, or are made in pursuance of the agreement; and
A refusal to fully execute the oral contract would operate as a fraud on, and place the moving party in, a situation not remediable by damages.

These courts recognize that substantial or full performance of the contract by one party is strong evidence of a contract. For these courts to accept performance in lieu of a written contract complying with the Statute, the acts constituting the performance must refer unequivocally to the otherwise unsatisfactory contract; that is, the acts must make sense only if they are in furtherance of it and the owner of the property has benefitted from it. Thus enforcing the contract in this situation avoids unjust enrichment. For example, if an elderly parent makes an oral promise to convey her home to a child who comes to live there and care for her until her death, performance of the agreement by the child may be shown by part performance.

Example: Stu and Beau agree to buy and sell a site for a gas station, but their agreement does not contain the essentials necessary to satisfy the Statute of Frauds. Meanwhile Beau engages an architect who draws up plans for the station, gets the necessary environmental approvals for the site, and makes arrangements to sell the fuel of the Hi-Price Oil Company. If Beau satisfies the requirements of the equitable estoppel exception, he can recover the cost of all of his off-site improvement plans, which he could not do under the part performance exception because it, among other things, requires a physical improvement on the site that is the subject of the agreement.

(c) Admission of a Contract in Court

A third exception used in a few states involves the judicial process: When a party to be bound is sued and properly defends on the ground that the Statute of Frauds is unsatisfied by the writing sued on, but admits in court that there was indeed a valid oral contract, courts divide on the issue of whether the defense will succeed. On the one hand, the contract is not in compliance with the Statute, but on the other hand, the party has brought the matter of the contract's enforceability before the court, where the safeguards against forcing fraudulent agreements on unwilling parties can be tested, using the rules of evidence, by direct and cross examination under oath. Thus to some the evidentiary purposes of the Statute seem capable of satisfaction in court by testing a party's admission. To other courts, testing that admission might encourage perjury, so confining the defense to the requirements of the Statute protects the judicial process.

Examples

Real Estate Brokerage

1. O experiences financial reverses, is unable to meet his mortgage payments on his home loan, and lists his home with broker B1 using an exclusive right to sell listing. B1 shows the home to clients of buyer's broker B2. B2 knows that these clients are in financial trouble. B2's clients execute a sales contract "subject to financing," but rescind the contract when financing proves unavailable to them. The home plummets in value. O then learns that the contract was never likely to close due to the buyers' inability to obtain financing. O sues B2, based on the lost opportunity to sell to someone else. Will O recover?

2. O owns Blackacre. The case law of the jurisdiction in which Blackacre is located and listed with broker B1, defines the duty of loyalty as a broker's "working solely in the interests of the broker's client." Buyer's broker B2 presents two offers from two clients. Is B2's duty of loyalty violated?

The Statute of Frauds

3. Mae owned an apartment complex at 6002 Broad Street worth $250,000. Due to her declining health, Mae felt she no longer could manage the units. Desiring to receive a steady stream of income for the rest of her life, she sold the apartment complex to Donnie, who lived in one of the apartments. He paid $25,000 cash and gave Mae a note for the remaining $225,000. The note provided for interest at the prevailing market rate and for monthly payments of interest only. The note's $225,000 principal was due in a lump sum in 15 years.

   As part of the sale, Mae agreed that if she received timely monthly payments, the unpaid balance of the note would be forgiven at her death. Mae declined to put this agreement in writing at closing, but acknowledged the agreement in the presence of others, and agreed to put it in a writing after closing. Three weeks after closing, Mae executed her will. Her will contained the following provision: "Any note still owing to me or my estate by Donnie should be given to Donnie. This gift is in accord with an agreement made when I sold my apartment units at 6002 Broad Street in Parkville to Donnie but never put in writing. I intend that this agreement be honored."

Eight years later Mae executed a new will revoking all previous wills. The new will made no reference to Donnie, the note, or the apartment complex. Donnie regularly paid monthly interest payments to Mae until he learned of her death, at which time he stopped making payments, relying on the understanding the remaining debt was canceled on Mae's death. Mae's heirs claim Donnie must pay the $225,000 note. Does the Statute of Frauds prevent Donnie from enforcing Mae's agreement to forgive the note at her death?

4. Sal and Sally, husband and wife, own a house as tenants in common. Ben and By, husband and wife, negotiate to purchase the house.
   a. Sal and Sally sign the sales contract and Ben signs on behalf of himself and By. Ben and By refuse to close. Does the Statute of Frauds prevent Sal and Sally from enforcing the sales contract?
   b. Sal signs the sales contract on behalf of himself and Sally, but Sally does not sign. Both Ben and By sign the sales contract. Sal and Sally refuse to close. Does the Statute of Frauds prevent Ben and By from enforcing the sales contract?
   c. If Sal signs but Sally does not sign the sales contract, as in (b), can Ben and By invoke the Statute of Frauds to rescind the sale if Sal and Sally seek specific performance?
   d. Sal signs; Sally does not sign; both Ben and By sign; and, in addition, the contract provides: "This sales contract to be effective upon the execution thereof by both sellers and both purchasers." Ben and By refuse to close. Can Sal and Sally enforce the contract?

5. Bess orally agreed to purchase 806 acres from Solomon for $1,000 per acre. Pursuant to the agreement, Bess gave Solomon a $10,000 check as a down payment and agreed to pay $400,000 at closing, and to pay the balance with interest later. Bess applied for and acquired a written loan commitment from Bank for the $400,000 to be paid at closing. Solomon refused to deed the property to Bess and conveyed the property to someone else instead. Bess brings suit seeking money damages. (a) Did the delivery of the check and securing the written loan commitment satisfy the Statute of Frauds? (b) If not, does the transaction fall within either the part performance or equitable estoppel exception to the Statute of Frauds?

6. Stan and Bob agree on terms that Stan will sell Whiteacre to Bob. They both go to the office of Ann, an attorney, and tell her that they want her to draft their sales contract. Ann listens to them discuss the terms of the sale, including an "all cash at closing" provision. Ann fills out a blank

deed, which Stan signs, giving it back to Ann for safekeeping. Stan and Bob then leave Ann's office and go together to a local bank to arrange financing for Bob for the cash he'd need to close. Later that day, Ann makes notes about Stan's and Bob's discussion of the sale terms. Is the Statute of Frauds satisfied in this situation?

7. Mr. Fox owned a farm when he died intestate. His heirs were his eight children. Wishing to unify ownership in himself, one of them, Sly Fox, made agreements with six of his siblings to purchase their undivided interests in the farm. One sister, Leona, did not want to sell. She desired a particular lot on the farm, a/k/a the knoll, on which she someday wanted to build a home. Sly and Leona orally agreed Leona would convey her undivided interest in the farm to Sly and in exchange Sly at some future time would convey the knoll to Leona. The seven siblings (including Leona) executed a deed transferring their interests in the farm to Sly. Sly paid six siblings (excluding Leona) $1,000 each for their respective interests in the farm. Leona was the only grantor who did not receive any money. Over the next ten years Leona often discussed "her lot" on the farm with Sly. Sly often complained about the costs and hassles of subdividing, but never disavowed the original oral agreement. Sly never developed the knoll, but he did sell some land from the farm. Following an argument between Sly and Leona, Leona by letter demanded Sly fulfill his agreement to transfer the knoll to Leona. Sly balked at transferring the land, offering instead to pay Leona the same $1,000 he had paid the others. Leona sues. Sly defends, citing the Statute of Frauds. Does the contract fall within the part performance or other exception to the Statute of Frauds?

Explanations

Real Estate Brokerage

1. O will recover. Because the prospects themselves had a duty to disclose their financial difficulties, B2 also had, as their agent, a duty to disclose. Moreover, B2 could have avoided this situation by suggesting that the buyers be pre-approved for financing, a short contingency period, or a financial statement from the buyers. Not to do so, and not to disclose the prospects' trouble, is unprofessional and a violation of the broker's fiduciary duty of loyalty and fair dealing. The suit will be more easily maintained in a jurisdiction where the selling agent is the sub-agent of the listing agent, but in other jurisdictions, the suit might be based in tort for interference with a prospective advantage.

2. Yes, B2's duty of loyalty is violated, particularly if B2 does not disclose the conflicting offers to the clients and even if the offers are received on

different days or if B2 gives one offer to another broker in his firm to present to O. If B2 discloses the fact of the competing offers (without revealing their terms) to each client, leaving it up to O to evaluate each, a court might hold that as long as the broker gives one of the offers to another of his firm's brokers to present, the fiduciary duty applies to the individual brokers involved, but not to their firm. Having a broker to advocate each offer then satisfies the rationale for a duty of loyalty.

The Statute of Frauds

3. No. (a) A writing satisfies the Statute of Frauds if it identifies the parties, sufficiently describes the property, states the purchase price, and states an intent that the property will be conveyed. If the seller finances the sale, the financing terms are material and the writing must document them, including the interest rate, if any. A provision that the balance (the principal) of a note is to be forgiven upon some condition other than full payment is an essential element related to the financing and must be included in a writing signed by the party to be bound. (b) Multiple and non-simultaneous documents may constitute the "writing" if a signed writing indicates they are related to the transaction. Prior to Mae's executing the first will, the agreement that the balance of the note was to be forgiven at Mae's death was merely an oral contract unenforceable under the Statute. Mae's first will referencing the sale of the apartments, including the note, and the contractual forgiveness of the note, memorializes the agreement and refers unequivocally to it. (c) Mae signed the will and thus she is bound. Donnie did not sign it, but since he is not being bound, he is not required to sign. Mae's revoking the first will is irrelevant since the debt forgiveness was a part of the original contract and was not a testamentary transfer: A will may serve as a writing for purposes of the Statute even if it is not valid as a will or is later revoked. Donnie must rely on the Statute to prevail. (d) The part performance exception is inapplicable because Donnie has not paid the purchase price. The equitable estoppel exception is also inapplicable: Donnie did nothing substantial beyond or in reliance on the agreement sufficient to excuse a failure to get a writing.

4. a. The contract is enforceable against Ben, but not By. A husband is not his wife's agent just because they are married. No husband-wife exception to the Statute of Frauds exists. By did not sign, so the Statute prevents enforcement of the contract against her. Ben did sign, and the contract can be enforced against him.

   b. Now the contract is enforceable against Sal, but not Sally, provided she shows that she never made Sal her agent. If Sal contracted to convey more than his half interest in the tenancy, he is liable in damages, but

Ben and By cannot be forced to accept the title (to Sal's half of the tenancy) in an action for specific performance.

c. No. Ben and By are still bound and Sal and Sally can seek specific performance of the contract after Sally either ratifies Sal's actions as her agent, signs the contract before Ben and By's offer is revoked, or sells her interest to Sal so he can seek specific performance.

d. None of the parties is bound. The contract is conditioned on all four parties' signing it. Even though the parties to be bound signed, it is not yet effective. Either side may rescind prior to all four parties' signing. Until then, the sale is contingent since the provision makes the sale an "all or nothing" proposition.

5. a. The $10,000 check may satisfy the Statute of Frauds if it contains enough information. While it may come close to satisfying the Statute, it probably will not contain all the essential information. The check might contain a notation describing the property on its memo line, name both parties (Solomon as payee and Bess' name printed on top of the check), and Solomon's endorsement on the back and Bess' signature on the front. But a check for the deposit lacks both a statement of the full purchase price and the terms of the financing. The loan commitment concerns the terms of the Bank loan, not the terms of Bess' purchase, so it adds no essential information. Together, the check and loan commitment do not satisfy the Statute. Bess has no action.

b. No. Oral contracts saved by part performance require more than the mere payment of earnest money. Even full payment of the contract price will not save the putative purchaser when she, like Bess, could be put back into her original position by the return of the deposit or the full price. Since Bess never took actual possession, much less made substantial improvements to the property, neither part performance nor equitable principles call for the transaction to be recognized. These facts do not excuse Bess' noncompliance with the Statute. Bess performed no acts other than payment of the earnest money referable to a contract and Solomon will not be unjustly enriched when retaining the property.

6. The first issue is whether the attorney's notes can be used to satisfy the Statute. Stan and Bob told Ann that the terms of the sale were already settled when they entered her office, making Ann the parties' disinterested agent. Thus the notes might well contain all the essential terms of the sale. (If Ann didn't ask about an essential term left out of the discussion, she might be acting unprofessionally.) Even if the notes were not made contemporaneously with the parties' discussion of those terms, they will suffice as long as they are made within a reasonably short time afterwards. (It's an attorney taking notes, after all!) If the notes do not suffice, then what about the deed left with Ann? If the deed with blanks is

completely filled in, it will contain all the essential terms (perhaps save one), but giving it to Ann for safekeeping is not to say that it has been delivered by Stan to Bob, and thus it is subject to modification before delivery and cannot satisfy the Statute. So it adds no essential information at this point. The one essential term that the deed might not contain is the purchase price (a deed needs no consideration to be valid, being a conveyance, not a contract), but if the loan application sought cash to satisfy the "all cash at closing" provision in Ann's notes, that essential term might be found there. Even if it is, however, the application will be signed by Bob, not Stan — the party to be bound. So if Stan sues Bob, the party to be bound has signed, but if Bob sues Stan, the "party to be bound" will have to be construed liberally, as "the party against whom enforcement is sought." Many jurisdictions will, however, accept such a liberal construction. Thus, it is possible, using the notes and the loan application, that the Statute might be satisfied.

7. Leona will prevail. Even though Leona has fully performed by deeding her interest to Sly, she is not in a position to assert the part performance exception: She has not taken physical possession and she has not substantially improved the knoll. Under the equitable estoppel exception, however, Leona, in reasonable reliance on the oral contract and Sly's continuing assent, had so changed her position that injustice could be avoided only by ordering specific performance of the oral contract for the knoll. Leona's changed her position by deeding her interest to Sly ten years earlier. But even deeding her interest in the property would be insufficient in itself since returning a one-eighth interest in the farm to Leona would undo any harm and Sly's use of the property over the previous ten years is consistent with his being Leona's tenant-in-common. However, Sly's subdividing and conveying away part of the farm prevents Leona's inheritance from being fully restored (leaving Leona with no adequate remedy but specific performance of Sly's agreement to convey the knoll). Further, Leona's joining her siblings on the deed to Sly referred unequivocally to their oral contract. Thus not enforcing the oral contract under these facts would amount to an equitable fraud on Leona.

CHAPTER 22

Executory Period Issues

INTRODUCTION

Not all sales contracts are closed. The contract itself may condition the parties' obligation to close. A party's failure to satisfy a sales contract condition allows the other party to rescind the contract without liability, and in some cases allows the party not meeting the condition to rescind. For example, a clause may allow the buyer to rescind the contract after consulting with an attorney. A common condition, known as the "subject to financing" clause, conditions the buyer's obligation to close on securing a loan commitment under suitable terms, including the amount, repayment schedule, and maximum interest rate. Those terms that are "suitable" are often included in the contract: maximum interest rate, minimum term for the loan, and maximum monthly payment, are often included. Implied in this clause is the buyer's obligation to make a reasonable effort to obtain a commitment. Other clauses may condition the closing on the buyers' selling their current residence, on a third party inspection of the property, on its rezoning, on an appraisal or other report (e.g., a termite inspection report), or on the seller's removing a mortgage or other lien from its title.

MARKETABLE TITLE

(a) Definition of Marketable Title

Title to a property constitutes all the elements or attributes constituting ownership. However, a buyer wishes to know, before closing, that he is obtaining a useful title. To this end, unless the sales contract specifically stipulates a different standard, every land sales contract contains an implied condition that the seller will convey "marketable title" to the buyer.

Marketable or merchantable title, while allowing for the possibility that the buyer's title might be successfully challenged, is a title secure enough that a reasonable person knowing all the facts would accept and pay for it. It is a title free from reasonable doubt as to its validity and reasonably free of the prospect of litigation. Thus a title is unmarketable if there is a reasonable probability the seller does not own the title alleged, the property is subject to an undisclosed encumbrance, or the buyer bears an unreasonable risk he would be subject to litigation related to it in its current condition. A buyer, in other words, is not required to take unreasonable risks or to "buy a lawsuit."

Unless the seller cures all defects before the closing, a purchaser offered an unmarketable title can refuse to close and can rescind the contract. If a buyer intends to rescind a sales contract based on unmarketable title, he must rescind before closing. If closing occurs, courts hold the title required by the sales contract merged with the title taken in the deed; the buyer is thereafter limited to rights flowing from the warranties of title included in the deed. This doctrine of merger does not, however, apply to contract promises concerning the physical condition of the property. These are promises regarded as collateral to the conveyance of the title, and are not merged into the deed.

(b) Examples of Unmarketable Title

Minor encumbrances or unlikely occurrences do not make a title unmarketable. Thus, a mere possibility or suspicion the title is flawed is not enough to make the title unmarketable.

Example: *A*, a single person with no siblings, died intestate 20 years ago. A chance exists some heretofore unknown or long-lost heir may appear claiming an interest in the property. The mere possibility that an unknown or missing heir survived the decedent and, after the probate decree was made final, has a claim to the property does not make a title unmarketable. Likewise, a lien or mortgage long past the statute of limitations on enforcement and involving creditors then dead probably would not make the title unmarketable.

Marketable title is not a title without defects or encumbrances. Most property is transferred subject to encumbrances. It is not the existence of an encumbrance or possible defect that causes a title to be unmarketable; it is the existence of an encumbrance undisclosed to the buyer and thus not made part of his bargain that makes the title unmarketable.

Example 1: A buyer contracts to buy a residential property subject to a restrictive covenant restricting its use to residential purposes. Its title is not unmarketable because of the restriction and the purchaser is legally bound by the sales contract.

Example 2: During the executory period, the buyer discovers a real covenant prohibiting multi-story homes on the property. The title is unmarketable because the sales contract did not disclose the covenant. The purchaser can rescind the sales contract. It does not matter whether the purchaser intends to build a one-story or two-story home, or whether the seller knew of the multi-story covenant. The buyer is not obligated to buy the property unless the seller removes the covenant by the closing.

Example 3: Assume the same facts of Example 2 and a second purchaser contracts to purchase the property. The sales contract makes the transfer of title subject to both the residential-use-only restriction and the one-story-only restriction. The title as to this buyer is marketable because the buyer executed the sales contract aware of both encumbrances.

The buyer in Example 2 did not contract to purchase the property with a restriction that limits houses to one story, so the buyer is not required to complete a contract for something less than he bargained for. The buyer in Example 3, on the other hand, is purchasing exactly what he bargained for and what the contract described. The Example 3 buyer is thus liable on the sales contract.

Typical encumbrances or defects in title are undisclosed co-owners (concurrent or future estates), mortgages or liens, easements,[1] real covenants or equitable servitudes,[2] leases, mineral rights, options, flaws in the deed records, erroneous acreage designations, or ownership based on adverse possession. Violation of a federal or state or local statute, ordinance, or code is a defect in title only if a violation is likely to be prosecuted. Thus the presence of toxic waste on a property does not render the title to it unmarketable. The waste may affect the use of the property, but not its title.

---

1. These are discussed in Chapter 27.
2. These are discussed in Chapter 29.

Example: A buyer contracts to purchase a lot in Blackacre subdivision and discovers during the executory period that because of a flaw in the subdivision process, there is no access to the lot over the streets of the subdivision. The title to the lot is marketable on this account. The title to the lot may be perfectly marketable in the legal sense, but worth nothing in the marketplace. It is legal marketability, not economic marketability, that is at issue.

The title in this Example is marketable for two other reasons: The subdivision process is conducted before a public agency. The rights of the agency to enforce its procedures are not the subject of the marketable title doctrine. The agency's records are not customarily searched in ascertaining whether a title is marketable. Thus violation of a zoning ordinance or a subdivision regulation does not render a title unmarketable. Further, the subdivision process concerns the future use of the property, and the person best suited to know the use is the buyer, not the seller (who is, after all, transferring the right to use it at the closing). Everyone, buyers and sellers, is presumed to know that the use of a property can be affected by zoning and subdivision laws, housing and building codes, and environmental statutes. Absent this public component, as where the buyer discovers that the property is landlocked during the executory period, a few courts have found the title unmarketable, but even here, the traditional rule is that landlocked property is not unmarketable on that account alone.

Example: A buyer contracts to purchase Whiteacre, and inspecting it during the executory period, finds utility poles strung across the property. Does the poles' visibility matter? Yes, but courts split. There are two issues to address: (1) the visibility[3] of the poles puts the buyer on notice that the right of the utility to string the lines might be based on a use right known as an easement, and (2) the fact that the poles go across the property, not strung along one side, might well diminish Whiteacre's value sufficiently to affect the buyer's bargain. The first issue raises the question of whether the duty of a buyer to inspect the property trumps the doctrine of marketability — the second raises the stakes at play in the doctrine: Would the buyer, seeing the poles, rely on the doctrine all the more to release him from the contract.

If in the last Example, the poles ran along Whiteacre's boundary, the situation would be easier to resolve: There would likely be little impact on its value. If in addition the poles provided electricity to Whiteacre, there might even be a benefit in having the easement there. If the utility's lines served

---

3. Visible rights are so apparent upon inspection that the purchaser saw or should have seen evidence of it and is, therefore, to have contemplated purchasing the property subject to the easement. It's not for nothing that a property course begins with a discussion of a possessor's rights, as possession often trumps written rights. Likewise, disclosure of a right adverse to the buyer's title in the sales contract is presumed to have affected the purchase price.

Whiteacre and the utility had a lien for unpaid service charges, the obligation to pay could easily be reduced to money. Monetary obligations secured by the property, such as undisclosed mortgages, liens, or unpaid property taxes, in amounts less than the sales price do not justify rescission of the sales contract because they can be paid off at closing. As to these, a prudent seller, not wanting the pay-off amounts coming out of his proceeds from the sale, will disclose them in the sales contract.

A second title standard, more rigorous than marketable title, is **marketable title of record**: It requires not just marketability, but also that every link in the chain of title a seller presents the buyer at closing be of record — not necessarily recorded, but documented in some fashion, with affidavits or other written evidence admissible in court.

Because a determination of marketability entails ascertaining a reasonable person's response to the likelihood a lawsuit may ensue, sellers sometimes promise to furnish **insurable title,** which is satisfied if a title insurance company will insure the title. The title insurance policy contains a duty to defend the insured should the title prove of questionable marketability, thus anticipating the risk of a lawsuit. This title standard also aids sellers because title insurers are sometimes willing to undertake the risk that litigation will arise over minor or technical defects in title.

(c) Defective Deed Records

Any flaw in the deed records that could lead to litigation makes the title unmarketable. Deeds and other documents (liens, mortgages, etc.) affecting real property are filed ("recorded") in local government offices (in the recorder's office in the courthouse) in the county where the land is situated. A person can trace all filed documents related to a particular piece of land back to the original grant from the state or federal government (that is, he can establish a "chain of title"). These records thus serve an important function in assuring buyers their sellers in fact have title to the property being sold.

Example: A buyer contracting to purchase Greenacre, thinking that the mineral rights underneath its surface are valuable, demands the seller produce an unbroken chain of title tracing title back to the beginning of the time that the property has been in private hands. The demand is reasonable because a title searched back to its root is a title from an unimpeachable source — the government — and is thus marketable.

Deed records can be defective in many ways. The property can be misdescribed in a prior deed, or some names are different from one "link" to the next in the record "chain." A deed may not be properly notarized or otherwise not legally authorized to be recorded, or recorded out of order;

in either case the document will be deemed unrecorded and of no legal effect. A party to a deed may have lacked capacity to transfer the interest in the property (either being a minor, lacking mental capacity, or lacking authorization for a transfer from a corporation by one of its officers, for instance). Any serious flaw or missing link in the deed records makes the title unmarketable.

Searching the records is the customary way of finding evidence the title is marketable or not. Exceptions to the rule that an encumbrance found in the deed records that was not disclosed in the sales contract makes the title unmarketable relate (as we have seen) to rights visible on the ground. In this connection, some courts also find the title to be unmarketable if a structure on the property encroaches on neighboring land or if property on neighboring land encroaches on the property being transferred since, in either case, resolution of the matter could lead to litigation.

(d) Adverse Possession

Adverse possession complicates the determination of marketable title for both the record title owner and the self-styled adverse possessor. Title acquired by adverse possession is marketable in most states, even if the claimant has not filed a quiet title action. At the same time, the mere allegation by a seller that he owns property by adverse possession is insufficient to establish marketable title. Adverse possession must be established by either a preponderance of the evidence or by clear and convincing evidence. Thus controversy as to any element of adverse possession prevents the seller from having marketable title. A seller claiming title by adverse possession bears the burden of proof that he can establish it. Similarly, a record title owner cannot convey marketable title if a third party, especially a present possessor, claims to own an interest in the property by adverse possession unless the claim is frivolous. In this instance, the seller holding a record title might be required to bring a judicial action to defeat the adverse possessor and eject him from the property, if need be, as a trespasser.

CAVEAT EMPTOR AND THE DUTY TO DISCLOSE DEFECTS

The seller's failure to disclose material latent defects is a basis for rescinding a sales contract. Courts imposing a duty to disclose material defects thus abrogate the long recognized doctrine of **caveat emptor — let the buyer beware.** Where courts impose this duty to disclose, buyers can elect either to rescind the sales contract or seek damages from the seller.

(a) Caveat Emptor

In some states, now a minority, caveat emptor reigns. Here, absent some special fiduciary relationship with a buyer, a seller owes no duty to disclose either patent or latent defects to a buyer. The buyer should, all the more carefully, inspect the property before executing the sales contract. A seller who remains silent escapes liability. Even where caveat emptor is the rule, sellers cannot mislead buyers by affirmatively misrepresenting facts or actively concealing facts. Thus a buyer of defective premises in caveat emptor jurisdictions may still bring a claim based on fraudulent misrepresentation.

The elements of fraudulent misrepresentation are (1) a representation of a fact, (2) which is material to the sale, (3) made falsely, with knowledge of its falsity, or with such utter disregard and recklessness as to whether it is true, (4) with the intent of misleading the purchaser into relying on the representation; (5) the purchaser justifiably relies on the representation, and (6) the purchaser suffers some injury proximately caused by his reliance on the misrepresentation (or injury would be suffered if the purchaser goes through with the purchase).

(b) The Duty to Disclose Material Latent Defects

Most states adopt, sometimes judicially and often by statute, a rule requiring sellers to disclose material latent defects to purchasers. Material defects are those that materially affect the property's value, or that could significantly impair the occupant's health and safety, or that the seller knows affects the desirability of the property to the buyer. Latent defects are those defects known to the seller and not discoverable by the buyer upon reasonable inspection.

Example: A buyer contracts to purchase a residence. The sales contract provides that the property is sold "as is." The seller misrepresents the condition of the roof—it is in fact leaky and requires replacement. Does the "as is" provision trump the seller's duty to disclose? No, unless the leaky condition is discoverable. The fraud means that the buyer is not bound by this provision. Only if the seller is silent about the roof and its defective condition is discoverable is the seller not liable: then the provision trumps the duty to disclose. Particularly when the duty of disclosure is mandated by statute, its waiver will not be lightly implied if not expressly permitted by the statute.

Example: Assume the facts in the prior Example. In a jurisdiction recognizing the result in that Example in its case law, a large homebuilder contracts to sell a residence to a buyer. The sales contract provides that any disputes about latent, material defects undisclosed at closing shall be submitted to arbitration and not sued on. Will the arbitration clause trump the duty of disclosure? Maybe. But there is still a chance a court might find the clause unconscionable as applied, an adhesive contract, or a violation of public policy. (Often an arbitration clause is contained in an insurance policy provided the buyer by the seller.)

Courts and states differ on the extent of the required disclosures. A few limit a seller's duty to disclose material latent facts relating to conditions that affect the health or safety of the buyer (meaning that the condition affects the habitability of the property). Some further limit the duty to disclose or transfer habitable premises to professional sellers — builders and developers — of new homes. A few extend this duty to all sellers, as well as to real estate brokers.

In any event, those courts requiring disclosure apply the seller's duty to material latent *physical* defects on the property, including leaky roofs, termites, cockroach infestation, or that the house is built on filled-in or swampy soil. Some courts also require a seller to disclose off-site conditions that may affect the property's value or the occupant's safety or health, such as nearby hazardous waste disposal sites, nearby landfills, noisy neighbors, underground gas pipelines, or proposed developments.

A small minority of courts require sellers to disclose some defects, both associated with the property itself and on nearby properties. In one famous case, sellers were required to disclose a home had a reputation of being haunted by ghosts. Another court required disclosure that a mass murder occurred in the home. However, some state statutes, known as "stigma statutes," specifically absolve sellers from disclosing the home was occupied by a person with HIV or other disease unlikely to be transmitted through occupancy of the home; or that the home was the site of a homicide, suicide, felony, or death by accidental or natural causes.

Even when a seller must disclose latent defects, a seller does not have to disclose non-material patent (or visible) defects. Likewise, a seller must know of the defects before the obligation to disclose arises.

This duty to disclose material latent defects relates only to residential properties. Courts reason commercial purchasers are more sophisticated and can professionally inspect the property. Off-site conditions and non-physical defects, moreover, are not as crucial to commercial owners. Sellers of commercial property may still be liable for affirmative misrepresentations, but caveat emptor remains the rule for commercial properties.

TIME FOR PERFORMANCE

A purchaser cannot rescind a contract as soon as a title defect or physical defect is discovered. The seller has time to rectify or remove the defect. Similarly, the buyer has time to obtain financing, inspect the property, secure government permits, etc. Yet when the sales contract does not specify a time, the parties have a "reasonable time" to perform or to close. A seller may even have time to bring an adverse possession suit without breaching the contract for unreasonably delaying closing. However, when the parties set a date for closing, courts in equity tolerate delays in closing unless the sales contract stipulates that "time is of the essence." Even when time is of the essence, minor delays by one party are permitted if no harm to the other party occurs.

Example: S contracts to sell Whiteacre to B for $100,000 on January 1. The contract calls for a closing by March 31. Because of the large number of loans and real estate purchases being made, and consequent delays by surveyors, appraisers, and title researchers, B's mortgage lender did not approve B's loan until March 15. By the time all documents are drafted, the earliest the parties could close would be April 15. In late March, a second buyer offers S $125,000. B wants to close. S wants to rescind the contract and sell to the second buyer. May S rescind on April 1? Will B be in material breach of the contract by failing to close by March 31? Many unavoidable delays occur in real estate sales. Time ordinarily is not of the essence, absent an express stipulation to that effect. There is no such here: setting a closing date does not make time of the essence. Unless circumstances indicate timing is critical, B has a reasonable time to close. This two weeks' delay, brought on by factors beyond B's control but clearly foreseeable in the contract, is reasonable. A court should refuse to allow S to rescind and give B specific performance.

REMEDIES FOR BREACH OF SALES CONTRACT

If the seller cannot deliver marketable title at closing, the purchaser may elect to rescind the sales contract. Alternatively, the purchaser may choose to go forward with the closing and seek specific performance of the contract. At the same time, if the seller partially breaches the contract — does not disclose a title defect, encumbrance, or acreage, for example — the purchaser can seek an abatement of the purchase price. If a purchaser breaches — generally refuses to close — the seller, like the purchaser, can seek specific performance; but while courts do order specific performance at the seller's request, they often limit the seller to monetary damages.

As to damages, a court could award damages, either (1) nominal, out of pocket or (2) benefit of or loss of bargain damages, the latter being equal to the difference between the fair market value at the time of the breach and the agreed upon contract price. In many cases this is a nominal amount. In some cases, of course, the amount could be substantial. Many jurisdictions provide only nominal damages, while some others (about half) provide loss of bargain damages as well. Nominal damages is limited to closing and settlement costs associated with the sale (e.g., money spent on appraisers, surveyors, lawyers, fix-up costs, utilities, taxes, interest on loans, title examination fees, moving expenses, temporary housing expenses, and increased construction costs). These costs are, after all, incurred, in reliance on closing the sales transaction and awarding them partly puts the non-breaching party back in the financial position he or she would have been had the parties not entered into the sales contract.

Example: V contracts to sell Blackacre to P for $400,000. During the executory period, P discovers an undisclosed easement making the title unmarketable.[4] Blackacre's value has increased to $450,000 since V and P executed the contract. In jurisdictions allowing loss of bargain damages, P can rescind the contract and also collect $50,000 loss of bargain of damages from V. If Blackacre's value had decreased to $375,000 during the executory period, P would not have suffered (and could not collect) any loss of bargain damages.

Example: In the prior Example, when will V sue for damages after P breaches the contract? Only when Blackacre's value decreases between the date of the contract and the date of the breach. That is, only in a falling market is V's suit for damages viable, and worth the time and trouble.

Jurisdictions split on whether a purchaser can get loss of bargain damages when a seller acts in good faith yet fails to deliver marketable title. The majority of courts giving loss of bargain damages allow them even if the seller believed the title marketable when the sales contract was executed. After all, who's to say (except an attorney) whether a title is marketable? Most all jurisdictions, however, give loss of bargain damages when the seller acts in bad faith. Thus, many jurisdictions allow only a buyer's restitution of the down payment and nominal damages. Indeed, it is an assumption that the seller presented the title in good faith that underlies the practice of awarding only nominal damages.

Example: S agrees to sell Whiteacre to B. B breaches the contract. S sues B for damages in a jurisdiction giving only nominal damages but in which S by custom pays the title examination fees associated with a sale. Part of S's complaint asks for these fees. B does not have to pay them because S would incur the same fees in any resale of the property and can reuse the title

---

4. Recall that a marketable title is something the seller must present at closing, thus, although the traditional rule is that damages are measured on the date of the breach, that breach here occurs at closing and so the increase in value to that date carries out the traditional rule.

abstract produced, thus making these fees not just incidental to the sale to B, but to any resale.

In jurisdictions awarding loss of bargain damages, a nonbreaching party may also collect consequential damages for damages foreseeable by the breaching party. Generally, lost profits on anticipated resale of the property or lost rents would fall into this category, as long as they are proven and not merely speculative. Neither will jurisdictions denying loss of bargain damages for good faith defaults award consequential damages on such defaults.

Example: S agrees to sell Blackacre to B. S breaches the sales contract. Between the date of the contract and the breach, the interest rate on the loan B was going to use to make the purchase rises steeply. The difference in mortgage payments reflecting the rate rise is recoverable as consequential damages when B has to finance the purchase of another property.

When damages may be difficult to prove or are speculative, parties (especially sellers) at times insert a liquidated damages clause, either as an option or as the exclusive remedy, into the sales contract. The clause fixes the amount of damages on default (often it will be the amount of the down payment) and often provides that upon the purchaser's default the purchaser forfeits the down payment or earnest money to the seller. As long as the clause is a reasonable estimate of damages, arrived at during good faith negotiations showing actual damages difficult to measure, and does not serve as a penalty, a court will enforce such a clause. If a court finds a clause unreasonable, the seller must then prove actual damages and refund any excess earnest money to the purchaser.

Example: V agrees to sell Greenacre to P. P breaches the sales contract. It contains an optional liquidated damages clause. In some jurisdictions a seller may then elect to retain the down payment and still sue for actual damages. In others retaining the down payment is regarded as an election by V to regard the down payment as full satisfaction of the clause.

EQUITABLE CONVERSION AND RISK OF LOSS

Although the seller holds legal title to and the right to possession of the property until closing, some ownership risks and benefits pass to the buyer immediately upon execution of the sales contract: For example, the buyer suffers or benefits from any changes in the property's fair market value between the date the contract is executed and the closing. This shift of some of the incidents of ownership to the buyer is called **equitable conversion.** The purchaser's interest is deemed an interest in **real property.** Meanwhile, although the seller is still the legal and record owner, the seller no longer is deemed to own an interest in real property. His interest is in the sales contract, which is deemed to be **personal property.** Thus, for example, if a seller or buyer dies intestate during the executory period, the seller's interest passes according to the personal property provision of the intestate succession statute and the buyer's interest passes according to the real property provisions. Similar results follow if the testator's will transfers real property to one beneficiary and personal property to another beneficiary: The seller's interest passes as personalty, the buyer's interest as realty.

Example: V and P execute a brief but enforceable contract for the sale of Blackacre. V has a judgment docketed against him. May the judgment be levied on Blackacre? No, because the doctrine of equitable conversion means that V's interest is personalty. P should not have to research Blackacre's title before making executory period payments of the purchase price. The doctrine gives the contract priority of title over the judgment.

Example: S contracts to sell a rental property to B. Does the doctrine of equitable conversion give B the right to rent upon executing the sales contract? No. Absent a contract provision to the contrary, the doctrine has no bearing on the rents. The rents and profits are B's only at the closing because they derive from the legal title.

Absent a provision in the sales contract, equitable conversion also allocates the **risk of loss** during the executory period if the property is completely or partially destroyed by fire or by natural causes such as by flood, storm, or earthquake, or is affected by government actions such as rezoning, annexation, or condemnation. Here jurisdictions differ. Consistent with the doctrine of equitable conversion — that the buyer is the equitable owner of the property — the traditional and majority rule places the risk of loss during the executory period on the buyer. In contrast, some jurisdictions (a minority) demand the seller deliver the subject of the contract — i.e., the building — and if the seller cannot deliver the building, there is a substantial failure of consideration. In these states, therefore, the seller bears the risk of loss. Yet other states — about a dozen — place the risk of loss on the seller unless the buyer goes into possession, at which point the buyer has the risk of loss. Using its equitable powers, a court may order specific performance, but abate (reduce) the purchase price for the partial loss of value attributable to the damaged or destroyed building. Such an abatement might happen no matter which party, buyer or seller, seeks specific performance.

Example: Does the buyer or the seller have the duty to maintain property subject to the doctrine of equitable conversion? It is the seller who carries the burden of maintenance as well as the duty to pay real property taxes up to the closing. This is true in both majority and minority jurisdictions.

In all states both seller and buyer have insurable interests in the property during the executory period. Both parties might as a matter of prudence, carry insurance during the executory period, but if the party (usually the buyer) bearing the risk of loss carries no insurance, and the other party (usually the seller) carries insurance, some courts adjust the parties' rights accordingly. Some jurisdictions permit a seller both to receive insurance proceeds and collect the full sales price, but the majority require the seller to apply the insurance proceeds against the sales price or hold it in a constructive trust for the buyer's use. When the risk of loss is on the seller and the buyer carries insurance, some jurisdictions allow the buyer both to keep the insurance proceeds and to rescind the sales contract. Other courts impose a constructive trust on the buyer, requiring him to turn the proceeds over to the seller, but allowing an abatement in the purchase price if the purchaser closes the sale, or allowing the buyer to keep the proceeds but allowing no abatement in the purchase price. Still others prohibit the buyer from receiving the proceeds, deeming the seller as legal owner, to receive the proceeds as the third party beneficiary of the insurance policy.

Examples

1. *V* agrees to sell Blackacre to P. The sales contract does not mention the quality of title to be transferred. The sales contract merely says *V* will transfer the property "subject to all covenants, easements, restrictions, and encumbrances of record applicable to this property." While researching the deed records in the county courthouse, P's attorney finds, among other documents, an easement to run a gas pipeline through the northeast corner of the property. Can P refuse to close?

2. S agrees to sell her home to B. B pays S a $2,000 down payment when executing the sales contract, which further provides that the balance of the purchase price is to be paid on delivery of a deed conveying marketable title, free of all encumbrances except those encumbrances enumerated in the contract. One of the enumerated encumbrances was a recorded subdivision plat and its restrictions. The plat contains a restriction prohibiting any building or part thereof from being located within 10 feet of an adjoining property line. S's house is 4 feet from the north boundary line. S obtains written assurances from a title insurer that, for an additional fee that S paid, the insurer would insure the "over the building line" exception. B refuses to close, buying another home instead. S sells her home to another for $5,000 less than B would have paid. S sues B for damages. B countersues to recover the $2,000 down payment. What result?

3. Sellit bought his home in 1955. In 2002 he contracted to sell the home to the Beyers. The sales contract provided Sellit would transfer to the Beyers "good and marketable title, free of liens and encumbrances except for use

and occupancy restrictions of public record generally applicable to properties in the immediate neighborhood or subdivision." A covenant in every deed to every house in the subdivision, including Sellit's, contained the following restriction: "No home shall be erected within 75 feet of the streets and avenues designated in the subdivision plat." The front of Sellit's home was 44 feet from a designated avenue. The four homes closest to Sellit's were 40, 44, 45, and 45 feet, respectively, from the avenue. There never has been any litigation with regard to any of the violations. Two title insurers were willing to insure the property as marketable. A third insurer would guarantee the dwelling could remain as located, but would not guarantee or insure the property's marketability. Beyers refuses to close. Sellit seeks specific performance. Beyers counterclaim for a return of their earnest money. Who prevails?

4. B contracted to buy a 200-acre ranch he intended to use for grazing cattle. Before executing the sales contract, he walked the fence forming the boundary of the farm, at one point standing on some railroad tracks while a ranch hand explained how the current owner used gates to rotate cattle from one field to another. The sales contract provided that B would receive "marketable title free from all restrictions, covenants, easements, and encumbrances except for a utility easement, an easement for an underground gas pipeline, and an easement across the easternmost part of the ranch in favor of a neighbor to reach the county road adjoining the ranch. The sales contract did not mention a railroad easement nor an outstanding $50,000 mortgage. Can B rescind the sales contract, claiming unmarketable title?

5. S plans to sell her home. Which of the following must she disclose to prospective purchasers?
   (a) Basement floods after heavy rains.
   (b) Leaky basement water pipe.
   (c) The home is to be connected to a new sewer system for which a tax assessment is likely.
   (d) Empty, out-of-service underground petroleum storage tanks in backyard.
   (e) The home was the site of a murder 10 years ago.
   (f) The home has a reputation for being haunted by the ghost of the murder victim.
   (g) A landfill is located one-half mile from the home.
   (h) A convicted child molester lives on the block.

6. (a) On March 15, O contracted to sell a cabin on five acres to B. B deposited $1,000 earnest money toward the $100,000 purchase price. Closing was scheduled for May 1. On March 25, the cabin was, through no fault of either party, destroyed by fire. B refuses to close and demands a refund of the earnest money. O seeks specific performance. Who prevails? (b) Under the sales contract, B was allowed immediate possession

of the cabin and five acres. B moved his personal belongings into the cabin on March 20. Does this affect your answer? (c) Assume the sales contract provided that "should the premises be materially damaged by fire prior to closing, this contract shall be voidable at the option of Buyer." Would this clause change the result in (a)? (d) Assume B purchases property insurance on the cabin, $50,000 coverage on the cabin and $50,000 coverage on its contents. B is the insured, with O listed as another person having an interest in the property. Does the existence of the insurance affect your answer? Who receives the insurance proceeds?

7. On May 1, M contracts to sell Blackacre to B for $100,000. On June 1, M dies. M's will directed that all her real property pass to her husband and that all her personal property go to a trust for the benefit of her two children. Who receives the $100,000 at closing? What happens if B is able to rescind the contract?

8. When V and P execute a sales contract for the sale of Blackacre, they agree that purchaser P will assume the risk of Blackacre's loss by fire during the executory period, subject to V's restoration of the property. If P presents you with the contract to review, what advice would you give her?

Explanations

1. No. Even though the sales contract did not mention the quality of title to be transferred, unless otherwise stated, a sales contract contains an implied condition that the seller will convey marketable title. The sales contract did not mention the easement. If the sellers in the sales contract had listed specific covenants, restrictions, easements, and other encumbrances on the property, accidentally omitting the gas line easement, the omission would have made the title unmarketable. In the Example, however, instead of listing covenants, restrictions, easements, and other encumbrances, the sellers transferred the property subject to all restrictions of record. A transfer of this type means the purchaser is willing to accept the property subject to all documents filed in the deed records. The sellers are protected against inadvertent omissions by inserting the general reference to all documents in the deed records. The purchasers, on the other hand, are best served by specific enumerations of the encumbrances.

2. B wins and is entitled to a return of the down payment. S must convey marketable title. Marketable title is not perfect title. It is a title that a reasonable person would accept because the indicated defect would not affect market value or subject the owner to an unreasonable risk of litigation. The title defect here is not the existence of the set-back restriction. B accepted this in the contract. However, the violation of the

setback restriction is a defect that every landowner in the subdivision has standing to enforce. A reasonable buyer understandably might be reluctant to buy the property for fear of future litigation. A reasonable fear of this potential litigation renders S's title unmarketable. The title insurer's willingness to insure the "over the building line" exception does not change this result. Buying insurance would not cure the defect: It may reduce the financial burden of litigation, possibly the cost of reconstructing the home, but it does nothing to remove the specter of litigation. B contracted for marketable title, not the lower insurable title standard. Finally, unless market conditions changed, the purchase price reduction in S's resale may be related to the new purchasers knowing about the violation, another indication the title is unmarketable.

3. Sellit wins and obtains specific performance. Sellit agreed to transfer marketable title. Marketable title is a title that a reasonable purchaser, well informed as to the facts and their legal consequences, would accept. Here, as in Example 2, the defect is the violation of a restriction: the house being 44 feet from the avenue when a covenant mandates any home be 75 feet from it. Not every defect or threat of suit makes a title unmarketable. (Otherwise the doctrine of marketable title would provide an out for a title that a purchaser might prudently accept.) The issue in this Example turns on whether a reasonable purchaser would fear a lawsuit because of the violation. Here the homes have been so situated for more than half a century with no hint of litigation, so the statute of limitations on any lawsuit or its prescriptive analogue in the law of easements would preclude a lawsuit. Moreover, at least the four closest neighbors are estopped from enforcing the covenant since their homes too are in violation of the restriction. Unlike the situation in Example 2 (where a reasonable chance exists a lawsuit could occur since the house may have been the only one in the neighborhood that substantially violated the 10 foot setback), no reasonable purchaser here would anticipate being sued. The title being marketable, the Beyers must honor the sales contract. However, some jurisdictions do not look at the degree of risk of litigation for violations of restrictive covenants or of zoning ordinances: They find the title unmarketable because the *possibility* of a lawsuit exists, so the Beyers should not have to enter into a lawsuit to determine if a court would find a reasonable purchaser would purchase. In those jurisdictions a court might rule in favor of the Beyers.

4. (a) The outstanding $50,000 mortgage does not make the title unmarketable. So long as the sales price exceeds the debt, the mortgage can be removed from the title using the proceeds of the sale. So the seller has until the closing to remove it, using the proceeds to satisfy the $50,000 debt and obtaining a release of the mortgage. (b) After B saw (indeed, stood on) the railroad tracks, most jurisdictions invoke the rule that

visible easements do not make a title unmarketable. If B closes the transaction, these jurisdictions presume that the buyer was willing to take the title subject to the easement and adjusted the sales price to reflect that willingness. Rights that involve possession trump the doctrine of marketable title. On the other hand, some jurisdictions conclude that although B saw the tracks, he is thereafter relying all the more on a general reference to marketability to sweep everything not mentioned in the contract into a *pro tanto* broader definition of unmarketability. When a visible easement is on the edge of the property or benefits the property in some way, such as roads and utility easements might do, they do not make the title unmarketable, but that other visible easements, obstructing the intended use of the property, do. Here, because the railroad easement does not appear to benefit B, the title is unmarketable.

5. In many states, as long as S does not affirmatively deceive the buyer or engage in any active concealment, she would not be required to disclose any of the listed items. Caveat emptor! Because she is selling a used home and is not its builder, she may not have a duty to disclose even in some states imposing a duty to disclose. In states judicially requiring disclosures, she could also avoid a duty to disclose several of the listed conditions because the buyer or his agent by reasonable inspection could spot them. As in Example 4, the risk that a reasonable inspection of the property would reveal the defect makes the visible defect here akin to the railroad easement there: Visible rights as well as limitations on possession trump the record title.

If a state has a statutory disclosure law or form, the statutory provisions control. Under California law, to illustrate, a disclosure form (see West's Ann. Cal. Civ. Code § 1102.6) would require disclosure of the following from the Example: flooding problems, including the basement flooding; plumbing problems, including the leaky pipes; sewer problems, which probably does not reach the prospective future sewer; fuel or chemical storage tanks, which probably reaches the empty, out-of-service tanks; and neighborhood noise problems or other nuisances, which may or may not reach the landfill. By statute, murders and ghosts are not material defects in California. Compare these results to the discussion below when there is no statute on point:

(a) Basement flooding epitomizes defects that can be discovered upon inspection, even when no rain has fallen and the basement is dry. Courts find most basement flooding to be visible and not latent, so there is no duty to disclose.

(b) Leaky pipes in the basement are open and visible if the pipes are visible or if the evidence of previous damage is observable. On that ground, there is no duty to disclose.

(c) There is no duty to disclose future tax assessments if the buyer could have found out about the sewer and the tax assessment by inquiring of government officials, and a seller would not be liable even though the seller had acted deceptively and even if the jurisdiction requires disclosure of material latent defects, as long as the buyer could learn of the situation by inquiring of proper officials. Buyers are responsible for knowing what their duties as landowning citizens are.

(d) As long as the tanks are not being used and pose no health or environmental risks, no disclosure is generally required unless there is some proceeding involving the tanks brought by officials enforcing environmental statutes.

(e) If the state has abolished caveat emptor for material latent defects, the seller may be required to disclose the facts of the murder. Clearly the fact of the murders is not observable by inspection. The remaining issue is whether the fact of the murders is material. Materiality is determined by whether the occurrence of the murder significantly affects the value of the house. The defect involved here is known as a psychological defect. Since some people would not want to live in a house where a murder occurred, and others would not want to have people constantly reminding them they live in the house where the mass murders occurred, a good case could be made that disclosure be made. However, in some jurisdictions, statutes provide that sellers are not required to disclose psychological or stigma conditions. Such a statute would result in no duty to disclose.

(f) If required to disclose under (e), the sellers would be required to disclose here also, particularly when the seller had publicized her haunted house and on this basis is obligated to disclose that reputation to prospective buyers. This obligation might extend to the disclosure of a general reputation in the community, whether or not the seller actively sought the publicity. So a cautious seller would be advised to disclose. In states where caveat emptor survives, no disclosure is required.

(g) Generally, a seller is required to disclose only on-site conditions, not off-site ones. Certainly professional sellers — a developer or builder, or their brokers — might be required to disclose. Such sellers of used houses may have a duty to disclose; other sellers would have no such duty at common law. But if the test is whether the condition is a material latent defect known to seller and important to a reasonable buyer, the status of the seller as a professional or nonprofessional should not matter. The Example also shows why statutory disclosure forms are being enacted in a majority of jurisdictions.

(h) A convicted child molester is not only an off-site matter. He or she is a person, not a condition. Some jurisdictions might require disclosure of noisy neighbors, a noisy nearby bar or dogs, because they might be nuisances. Some jurisdictions have Megan's Laws, statutes designed to inform citizens of sex offenders residing in the community by making offenders register their presence with the government, but buyers as well as sellers can check such registries, so the cases divide on whether there is a duty to disclose in this situation.

6. (a) Under the doctrine of equitable conversion, purchasers are deemed equitable owners of the property as soon as the parties enter into the sales contract, and bear the risk of loss should the property be destroyed or damaged during the executory period. Under the traditional rule, O obtains specific performance. The doctrine developed at a time when land tended to be more important to and a more valuable part of the transaction than the structures on it. Arguably, that situation is often reversed today. Thus the rule in jurisdictions placing the risk of loss on sellers: When the improvements are a substantial part of the bargain, the contract is voidable for a failure of consideration or impossibility of performance. In over 30 jurisdictions, however, equitable conversion prevails: B bears the risk of loss.

(b) It might. What type of possession is the contract calling for? Actual possession by B or constructive possession indicated by moving B's personalty into the cabin. A seller bears the risk of loss if the seller retains "possession" and the risk of loss shifts to B once B takes possession or at closing, whichever occurs first. In these states, most likely B bears the risk of loss. If B's "possession" is insufficient O must bear the risk of loss and B would receive the earnest money back. In most jurisdictions, where the risk of loss passes to the buyers on execution of the sales contract, B as a buyer would bear the risk with or without a right of possession, even if O remained in possession.

(c) The clause could protect B. Equitable conversion is a default doctrine. The parties can override it by drafting a provision in the sales contract. The provision places the risk of loss squarely on the sellers. B can void the contract and have the earnest money returned. The sales contract provides that B has the option of voiding the contract. If B chooses not to exercise this option, an issue arises whether B should receive an abatement in the purchase price, reducing the price by the decrease in value resulting from the destruction of the cabin. Most courts deciding this issue hold that the buyer may receive an abatement.

(d) Land is not insurable. The insurance proceeds on the insurable cabin and its contents are treated in two ways. (1) Once B collects the policy's proceeds and closes the contract, since abatement of the purchase price is an equitable remedy, most jurisdictions either refuse to abate the purchase price or reduce the abatement by the amount of the proceeds paid to B. Otherwise B would receive a windfall ($50,000 insurance and $50,000 price abatement) and the sellers would suffer a $50,000 loss. Insured buyers electing to continue the transaction should pay full price. If B refuses to close, most jurisdictions treat the policy and the sales contract as unrelated agreements, allowing B both to void the sales contract and still collect the $50,000 on the policy. (For insurance purposes, B's having a contract interest in the cabin at the time of the fire gives rise to an "insurable interest.") (2) In some jurisdictions, applicable law considers the two agreements to be related, so when buyers refuse to close, B or B's insurer is required to pay the policy's proceeds to O in order to avoid his suffering a $50,000 loss; it is in this sense that B is said to take the proceeds in a constructive trust payable to the party holding the property. Some jurisdictions apply this theory only if the sales contract requires the buyer to carry insurance.

7. Under the doctrine of equitable conversion, M's contract right to the proceeds passes as personal property. The $100,000 sales proceeds go to the trust for the benefit of M's children. If B rescinds the contract because (say) M's title was unmarketable or B refuses to close based on a clause in the contract, courts treat the property as real property and it would pass to M's husband. On the other hand, if B breaches the contract, M may have the option of either accepting liquidated damages or seeking specific performance, so the property passes to the trust benefitting the children; then the buyer is regarded in equity as a debtor once the contract is executed, and when the buyer breaches, the property is still returned to the trustee for the children to satisfy the debt. All this is premised on the idea that the seller agreed all along to accept money in exchange for the property.

8. Risk of loss rules and the doctrine of equitable conversion are subject to agreements otherwise, but in this agreement, you should ask whether the parties intended to reverse the majority rule, allocating the risk of loss to the buyer, P. If so, they did not do so clearly. While the clause concerning V's restoration of the property imposes a duty on V, it might be a contract duty, rather than an indication that the parties intended to invoke the minority risk. As a contract, P will be put to supervising V's work to ascertain that it is performed in such a manner that the initial expectations of the contract are fulfilled — and suing on the contractual promise when P believes that V is cutting corners in fulfilling his duty. This will produce an arduous and perhaps a longer term relationship than P had expected. However, if the contract was executed in a minority rule jurisdiction, it better fits the purpose of giving V an opportunity (of restoring the property) than the minority rule traditionally provides. Since the minority rule is based on a failure of consideration, this contract would be considered terminated when a fire occurs.

Real Estate Closings

THE CLOSING OR SETTLEMENT PROCESS

A seller or grantor usually transfers title to property to the buyer at a closing or a settlement. Typically at closing, a mortgage lender or other financial institution loans the buyer money to complete the purchase, the buyer pays the seller, and the parties sign a series of documents required by the sales contract, the lender, or applicable law.

The conduct of a residential closing differs by region. In the Eastern, Southeastern, and Midwestern United States, the parties meet face to face and, in the presence of a representative of the lender, exchange the purchase money for the deed. Then the buyer executes a mortgage for the portion of the purchase money funded by the loan. In the Inter-Mountain and Western states, the closing is handled "in escrow" by a closing agent who disburses the money and the deed when all pre-conditions to their disbursal to the seller and buyer are met; here the parties to the contract execute it but never meet thereafter. When they receive whatever documents are required to close, they execute them and send them back to the agent for distribution.

No matter the region, sales of commercial properties are often conducted using an escrow of some type, sometimes with a title company arranging the mechanics of the closing, supervised by the attorneys for the parties.

Whether the transfer is a sale or gift, sellers transfer their interests in property by a deed. The deed must be in writing to satisfy the Statute of Frauds, and must contain (a) the grantor's name, (b) the grantee's name, (c) words that indicate an intent to convey the property or an interest in the property (the "words of grant"), and (d) the interest being transferred (though a fee simple will be assumed by statute in most jurisdictions unless a lesser interest is stipulated). These elements of the deed are typically known as the "premises." It is followed by a description or identification of the property.

The legal description of the property is followed by what is known as the deed's "habendum clause." It typically starts with the phrase "To have and to hold" or "Together with." Here the deed recites any covenants, conditions, easements, equitable servitudes, leases, mineral rights, or other private encumbrances burdening the property. If the grantee is to assume a mortgage or take the property subject to a debt, that too is listed. Often a general reference, such as "subject to all restrictions of record," is adequate to subject the grantee to all restrictions found in the official deed records. The habendum usually contains the seller's warranties of title.

Finally, at the deed's end, comes the grantor's signature. The deed is a conveyance, not a contract, so only the grantor need sign it. However, when it contains promises by the grantee [to (say) not use the property for commercial purposes] it is customary in some regions to have the grantee sign as well.[1]

Most deeds are "recorded" — a matter that is discussed in Chapter 25. State statutes require that all deeds and other documents accepted for recording be acknowledged before a notary public or, in a few states, be witnessed by one or two persons to authenticate the grantor's signature. Even though an unacknowledged and unattested deed transfers title, most purchasers insist on compliance with these further formalities.

Although the format of deeds varies from jurisdiction to jurisdiction, some common forms have evolved. The two most common are the "long form" and "statutory short form" deed. Both contain the four essential parts set out above. The main differences between the two are (1) the statutory short form deed excludes (while the long form incorporates) an habendum clause, and (2) the long form contains express warranties of title, while the short form incorporates into the words of grant some but not all such warranties by reference as mandated by statute.

If the grantor is married, the deed should indicate the grantor owns the property as his or her separate estate (assuming that is the case). If the seller's spouse has an interest under community property laws; is a tenant by the entirety, joint tenant, or tenant in common; or has a marital or homestead interest, the non-granting spouse also must execute the deed in order to release the interest.

Nothing requires the deed to recite the consideration paid for the property. But often to show the buyer is a bona fide purchaser for value, most

---

1. Some jurisdictions do not require grantees to sign even when the deed binds the grantee to honor covenants, conditions, easements, or other encumbrances included in the deed or the grantee in the deed agrees to assume or take the property subject to a mortgage. The rationale is that, by accepting the deed's benefits, the grantee accepts all the obligations in it as well.

drafters include the consideration, or at least a symbolic consideration such as "one dollar and other consideration." Centuries ago in England, grantors embossed their seal onto the deed in lieu of or in addition to their signature. The seal became a requirement for an effective deed. A few states retain this requirement, but the majority of jurisdictions have dispensed with it.

DELIVERY

In general, a deed transfers title only when (1) the grantor intends to convey an interest in property, (2) the grantor manually delivers a deed to the grantee, and (3) the grantee accepts the deed. Each element is necessary to proof of delivery. No deed is considered delivered if the grantor hands the deed to the grantee without intending to.[2] Conversely, without handing the deed over to the grantee, a grantor's recording it may satisfy the second element of a delivery. Thus there are many fact-specific questions involving proof of these three elements. Of the three, an intent to convey an interest is the most difficult to prove, unless a grantor's handing over the deed physically demonstrates an intent to convey title. On the other hand, delivery of a deed to and from an escrow agent provides objective, third-party evidence of the second element.

Courts often resort to rebuttable presumptions to resolve delivery issues. For example, a grantee's acceptance is presumed if owning the property would be beneficial to the grantee; courts will presume a deed in the grantee's possession has been delivered to the grantee; conversely, courts presume the grantor did not deliver the deed if the grantor retains possession of the deed; and courts presume acknowledged and recorded deeds have been delivered. In some jurisdictions, a recorded deed gives rise to an irrebuttable presumption the deed was delivered when one of the parties to a later dispute is a subsequent bona fide purchaser for value. Courts readily find a presumption of delivery or nondelivery rebutted if the facts so indicate. Rebuttable presumptions merely establish who bears the burden of proof and persuasion in the controversy.

Delivery in many situations turns on whether the grantor retains control of the deed and can retrieve it before the grantee takes possession of it. A grantor's giving the deed to the grantor's agent or attorney, for example, is not a delivery until the agent gives the deed to the grantee. Conversely, a grantor's handing the deed to a grantee's agent does constitute its delivery.

---

2. Occasionally someone purloins a deed or tricks the grantor into giving it to him. In these situations there is no delivery unless the grantor intended to convey title when the ostensible grantee took possession of the deed.

SPECIALIZED DELIVERY PROBLEMS

(a) Escrow Transfers

In many commercial transactions and in residential transaction in the Western states, the parties use a third party — an escrow agent or escrowee — to hold the deed and pass the deed to the grantee after the grantee satisfies conditions set out in a valid sales contract. If the escrow is irrevocable and the grantor cannot retrieve or revoke the deed unless the grantee materially breaches the sales contract or fails to satisfy a condition within a reasonable time, the deed will be considered delivered when the grantor deposits the deed in escrow. This is the **doctrine of relation back** and applies even if the grantor dies before the conditions are met: As soon as the grantee meets the conditions, the escrow agent delivers the deed to the grantee and the grantee's title "relates back" to the date of deposit.

(b) Donative and Testamentary Transfers

Problems occur more frequently in informal transfers epitomized by donative or gift transfers related to the grantor's death. A deed does not qualify as the vehicle for testamentary transfers; only documents meeting all statutory formalities under a Statute of Wills serve to transfer property at a grantor's death. A deed to be effective must deliver title during the grantor's lifetime. The deed does not have to guarantee present possession, and may delay the grantee's possession until the grantor's death, but the deed must grant an immediate (if future) interest in the property to the grantee. Thus, though a deed is delivered if it passes either a present or future interest, that interest must pass immediately, not at some future time. If the facts surrounding the handing over of the deed indicate the deed is to take effect at a later date, there is no delivery until that later date. Delivery occurring after the grantor's death in donative transfers does not transfer title. Consider the following examples.

> **Example:**   A grantor executes a deed but does not deliver the deed to the intended grantee. The grantee knows nothing about the deed until the deed is found after the grantor's death. A court in this situation usually will find the deed was not delivered. An executed deed still in the grantor's possession fails the manual delivery element.

> **Example:**   A grantor places a deed someplace under the grantee's control but does not tell the grantee about the deed, knowing the grantee will find the deed later (perhaps after the grantor's death). The grantee finds

the deed after grantor dies. A court might find the requisite intent and delivery under these facts.

Example: A grantor places a deed in a safe deposit box used by both the grantor and the grantee. Grantee finds the deed after grantor dies. Because the grantee has access and control over the safe deposit box, many courts find the grantor's placing the deed in the safe deposit box indicates grantor intended to deliver the deed and gave at least constructive possession to the grantee. Other courts find no delivery since the grantor's access and control over the safe deposit box indicates that he retained a right to revoke the deed simply by retrieving it before grantee takes actual possession.

Example: A grantor hands a deed to an intended grantee with instructions that the grantee is to record the deed if the grantee outlives the grantor. The grantor dies. Since the grantor attempted to pass an interest at some future date after his death rather than to pass a future interest immediately, the grantor had no intent currently to transfer title. So the deed has not been delivered until the grantor died. The grantor cannot use the deed as a will: since it does not meet the statutory prerequisites of a will, the deed cannot operate to effect a testamentary transfer.

Example: A grantor hands the deed to an intended grantee, telling the grantee to record the deed after the grantor's death. The grantor dies. Courts differ on the result. A court rationally could hold, as in the previous Example, that this was a failed testamentary transfer, but many courts uphold the deed as a present delivery of a future interest, holding the oral instruction void as inconsistent with the delivery of a deed. Thus the grantee could record the deed any time after receiving it. An oral condition is nullified by an actual delivery.

Example: A grantor hands the deed to an escrow agent with instructions to deliver the deed to a grantee after the grantor's death. Some courts find the arrangement is a failed testamentary transfer. A few hold the grantor's death terminates the agent's power to deliver the deed, so delivery is impossible. A majority of jurisdictions, however, hold that delivery occurs when the grantor hands the deed to the escrow agent or hold that the delivery relates back to the time the grantor handed the deed to the agent, as long as the grantor cannot revoke the deed and did not condition the agent's delivering the deed on the grantee's surviving the grantor.

Example: A grantor hands a deed to the grantee, the grantor reserving a life estate. The deed here is delivered since the grantee obtains a future interest in the remainder in the property immediately.

Example: A grantor gives a deed to a grantee, the grantor both reserving a life estate and retaining the power to revoke the deed. Some courts hold that the grantee holds no legal future interest: The grantor retains the life estate and current possession and has the power until the grantor's death to revoke the deed. The deed is little more than an expectation that does not ripen into an interest until the grantor dies or releases the power to revoke the deed. Until that time, no delivery occurs. This is especially true when the grantor continues using the property, paying property taxes, and collecting the rents and profits from the property. Other courts find the delivery good as long as the grantor intends to pass the interest immediately to the grantee, regarding the power to revoke as a condition subsequent, giving the grantee an interest until the grantor revokes. Since some interest is currently transferred to the grantee, the deed is delivered. Either result is justifiable. It appears the arrangement is a will substitute. If you believe the Statute of Wills' requirements trump the deed in order to protect decedents, heirs, and devisees from overreaching or fraud, and the grantor has a will, or his heirs are deserving, the deed should not be considered delivered. On the other hand, if the deed is a poor person's version of a trust, a trust being effective even if the grantor reserves a life estate and a power to revoke, the deed carries out the grantor's intent and fits into an overall estate plan, finding that a delivery has occurred is the proper conclusion.

MORTGAGES

(a) Mechanics of Mortgages

Purchasers often borrow money to buy real estate, especially real estate improved with homes or buildings. The most common sources of financing are the seller and financial institutions such as banks and other mortgage lenders. When a person borrows money to buy real property, he or she usually signs two documents. One document is the promissory note, a formal IOU by which the borrower (the debtor) obligates himself or herself to pay the money back to the lender according to certain terms, including the interest to be paid for the use of the money and the timetable for making payments. The other document is the mortgage, which provides collateral for or "secures" the debt: Should the mortgagor (the borrower) default on the loan (or otherwise breach the terms of the mortgage agreement), the mortgagee (the lender) can bring an action (foreclosure) to sell the home based on the lien created by the mortgage and apply the sales proceeds to retire the note. If the seller lends the money and becomes the mortgagee, the mortgage is called a take-back or purchase-money mortgage.

Ordinarily the property pledged as security in the mortgage is the purchased real estate, but that is not essential. Other property may serve as the collateral. To illustrate, a person buying a vacation home may pledge the purchased home to secure the mortgage. Alternatively, for various reasons, the vacation home purchaser may pledge his or her primary residence as the collateral underlying the mortgage. If in this last example the buyer defaults on the note, the mortgagee (lender) under the mortgage has priority rights as to the borrower's primary residence, but not to the vacation home.

Sometimes the purchaser gives promissory notes both to a financial institution and to the seller in order to purchase a home. The financial institution will demand that it receive the "first" mortgage and the seller will take a "second" mortgage. The ranking of mortgages — "first," "second," "third," etc. — establishes which mortgagees (creditors) have the first right (priority) to any sale proceeds should the property be sold in a foreclosure action. Mortgages and liens of a lower priority are known as junior liens or junior mortgages while those of a higher priority are senior liens or senior mortgages. Thus if a person has given three mortgages, the second mortgage is senior to the third mortgage and junior to the first mortgage. A lender should record the mortgage in the local deed records office to protect its status as having first priority to the property.

The party having first priority may use all proceeds from any sale of the home (foreclosure sale) if necessary to satisfy any amounts still owing to the lender. If any sales proceeds remain after satisfying the first mortgage, the money goes to the second mortgage holder, and so on. Any proceeds remaining after satisfying all notes secured by the mortgages belong to the property owner (the mortgagor).

(a) Title Theory and Lien Theory

States fall into two camps concerning the legal ownership of the mortgaged property. A small minority of states subscribe to the title theory of mortgages, meaning the lender (mortgagee) has legal title to the mortgaged property until the debt is repaid. This theory developed at a time when the mortgagee (lender) actually took possession of the property or held its legal title until the underlying note was satisfied. Today, the borrower retains possession of the property. Accordingly, the vast majority of states favor the lien theory, recognizing the mortgage as a security device or an inchoate lien, giving the mortgagee rights to the property when the mortgagor breaches some term of the mortgage. In lien theory states, the mortgagee (lender) has legal title and the mortgagor (borrower) has equitable title in the property. Under neither theory can the mortgagee's creditors force a sale of the collateral to satisfy the mortgagee's debts, and under both theories the mortgagor's creditors can reach the proceeds from the sale of the mortgaged property after the mortgagee's claims have been satisfied. The major difference between the two theories in actual practice is that under the title theory a mortgagee in some states can go into possession of the property as soon as there is a default and remain in possession during the foreclosure proceedings. In a lien theory state, on the other hand, the mortgagor retains possession until foreclosure proceedings are completed.

(b) Deed of Trust

The deed of trust resembles the mortgage. Under the deed of trust the borrower delivers the deed of trust to a third party (the trustee), often the lender's attorney, instead of directly to the lender. If the borrower defaults, the trustee can foreclose on the mortgaged property. The deed of trust allows mortgagees to sell the collateral more quickly and cheaply than under the traditional foreclosure process. Traditional mortgages routinely achieve the same result by incorporating a power of sale right in the mortgage, so there are thus few differences between a deed of trust and a mortgage.

(c) Installment Land Sale Contract (Contract for Deed)

Under the installment land sale contract (or contract for deed), the seller retains legal title and does not deed the property to the buyer until the purchaser pays the full purchase price. In the interim executory period, the buyer takes possession and the parties act pursuant to the sales contract. The payment period under an installment contract (or contract for deed) may be as long as the normal deed and mortgage period — i.e., ten, fifteen, or more years. The buyer has an equitable interest in the property, but unless she records the installment sales contract or a memorandum of contract in the local deed records, she risks losing the property to the seller's creditors or to a bona fide purchaser for value. At one time if a buyer missed a payment, she forfeited her interest in the property and the seller kept the property no matter how wide the disparity between the property's fair market value and the amount of the remaining outstanding indebtedness. Today many courts treat installment land sale contracts like a deed and mortgage transaction, restricting the seller to proceeds of sale equal to the amount of the remaining debt obligation.

(d) Debt Satisfaction and Assumptions

Once a mortgagor (borrower) satisfies (pays) the underlying debt, the mortgagee releases the mortgage. This release should be recorded in the local deed records. Many mortgages and notes contain a due-on-sale clause requiring the entire note balance be paid before the seller can deed the property to a new purchaser. Alternatively, some mortgagees allow subsequent purchasers of the property to continue making payments on the note under the original note terms. The subsequent buyer can assume the note, meaning the purchaser becomes primarily liable on the note: If the underlying property cannot be sold for an amount great enough to retire the secured indebtedness, the mortgagee usually has recourse to the subsequent buyer's other assets for the deficiency. Instead of assuming the note, a subsequent buyer may take the property subject to a note and mortgage. In this situation the mortgagee is limited to taking the proceeds from the sale of the property and cannot go after the subsequent purchaser's other, nonpledged assets. In either situation, the initial mortgagor remains secondarily liable to the mortgagee for any unpaid amounts.

(e) Foreclosure

If the mortgagor (the borrower or debtor) defaults (generally by not making scheduled payments), a mortgagee (lender) has various options based on the mortgage's terms and state law. In earlier times, and in some states today under some circumstances, a mortgagee through an action known as strict foreclosure could petition a court to foreclose a mortgagor from redeeming his property after the foreclosure date: After that date, the mortgagee kept the mortgaged property and the mortgagor was barred (foreclosed) from asserting any rights to it.

The most common method of foreclosure today is judicial foreclosure. It affords the mortgagor (debtor) all the procedural safeguards inherent in a judicial proceeding. The mortgagee files a complaint, the mortgagor answers, and a trial is conducted should the mortgagor allege a foreclosure sale is inappropriate. The court has the title searched and determines what debts are to be paid from the foreclosure sales proceeds. Once the court orders the property sold, pertinent auction information must be posted and advertised as prescribed by statute. The sale usually is by auction (though an auction is not always mandated and in a few states other methods more closely resembling a voluntary sales transaction may be used). Mortgagees are entitled only to the sales proceeds up to the amount owed them. Sales proceeds remaining after all creditors are satisfied belong to the mortgagor. If the sales proceeds are inadequate to satisfy all debts and liens, creditors sue on the note and get a "deficiency judgment" against the debtor's non-pledged assets (if the underlying debt constitutes a "recourse" liability).[3]

---

3. A debtor on a **recourse liability** is personally liable for a debt: A creditor can reach all of the debtor's assets to satisfy the debt. A debtor on a **nonrecourse debt** is liable on the debt; but if the debtor defaults, the creditor can reach only those assets pledged to secure the debt. The creditor cannot reach the debtor's nonpledged assets. To illustrate, suppose a debtor

Mortgagees wanting to avoid the delay and cost of a judicial foreclosure action may try a private foreclosure sale if (a) the state allows it and (b) the parties incorporate a power of sale provision in the mortgage or deed of trust. The mortgagee or the trustee in a deed of trust sells the property in a private sale, often by auction, bypassing the full judicial process. Statutes dictate the process, usually providing for notice and advertising. Some states require a court to approve or confirm the private sale.

Mortgagors can have the private sale voided if the mortgagee or trustee does not adhere to the statutory requirements. As a general rule, the mortgagor cannot protest solely because the sales price was below the property's fair market value unless the buyer at auction or the mortgagee (lender) acted fraudulently or did not comply with the statute or unless the sales price is so inadequate (usually in the 20-30 percent range of fair market value) it "shocks the conscience" of the court. Most courts, then, uphold even very low foreclosure sale prices, recognizing that no involuntary sale will fetch what a traditional purchase and sale will.

The mortgagor enjoys a right or equity of redemption until the property is sold. Thus, a defaulting mortgagor can keep the property by paying off the loan *before* the foreclosure sale. About one-half of the states, by statute, also give the mortgagor a statutory redemption right, which arises *after* the sale. It gives the mortgagor the right to reimburse the high bidder at the sale and undo it. The time in which the mortgagor must exercise his statutory redemption right, depending on the state, ranges from 3 months to 2 years.

Examples

1. S agreed to sell a 1,000-acre ranch to B. They both executed a sales contract for the ranch. S signed not only the contract for a deed but also a warranty deed, intending to leave the deed with his attorney. The two documents were two of the many documents on the attorney's conference table when B picked up the deed, examined it, and put it with his papers. B left with the deed and a year later recorded it. Was the deed delivered?

2. Harry owns Whiteacre. He executes a deed conveying Whiteacre to his sister Sallie. Harry places this deed in his vault for safekeeping. Both Harry

---

borrows $100,000 from Bank A on a recourse note and $100,000 from Bank B on a non-recourse note, pledging $100,000 of common stock to each bank to secure the respective loans, and having $500,000 in cash. When the debtor defaults on both notes, the stock serving as collateral for the two loans falls in value such that the stock securing the note to Bank A is worth $70,000 and the stock securing the note to Bank B is worth $80,000. Since the note to Bank A is a recourse liability, Bank A can sell the $70,000 stock and can force the debtor to use $30,000 of her cash to pay off the rest of the note. But because the note to Bank B is nonrecourse, Bank B can sell the pledged stock for $80,000. That is all Bank B can get from the debtor. Bank B cannot reach any of the debtor's cash to satisfy the remaining $20,000 owed on its note.

and Sallie live on Whiteacre. Harry tells Sallie about the deed and states that she is now Whiteacre's owner. Sallie thanks Harry, agreeing that keeping the deed in the vault is a good idea. Sallie has no access to the vault and has never seen the deed. Harry thereafter destroys the deed to Sallie and executes a new deed conveying Whiteacre to Harry's friend Gloria. Harry manually delivers Gloria's deed to her. Sallie sues Harry and Gloria to quiet her title to Whiteacre. In Sallie's suit, what result and why?

3. Beulah owns her home. For years Elizabeth helped Beulah around the house with repairs and yard work, driving her to the doctor's office and to social, cultural, and church functions. Beulah has two sons and intestate heirs. Elizabeth moved in with Beulah. Five years later Beulah decided she wanted Elizabeth to have her home if Beulah died before Elizabeth. Who owns Beulah's home after Beulah's death in the following situations?

   a. Beulah handwrites a deed giving her home to Elizabeth. She puts the deed with her important papers and tells Elizabeth to read the papers if Beulah dies. Beulah dies. Elizabeth reads the papers and finds the deed.

   b. Beulah drafts and executes a deed. Beulah entrusts the deed to her minister with instructions to give the deed to Elizabeth if Elizabeth survives Beulah. Before Beulah dies, she executes and delivers a deed to one of her sons. When Beulah dies, the minister gives Elizabeth the deed in his possession.

   c. Beulah hands Elizabeth a deed conveying the home to Elizabeth. Beulah orally instructs Elizabeth to hold the deed and to record it only if Elizabeth survives Beulah. Beulah dies.

   d. Beulah drafts a deed granting the home to Elizabeth if she survives Beulah, otherwise the home is to pass to one of Beulah's sons. Beulah reserved a life estate. Beulah hands the deed to Elizabeth. Beulah dies.

   e. Same facts as (d) except Elizabeth, one year after she received the deed, gave the deed back to Beulah (who was still alive). Beulah later dies.

   f. Same facts as (d) except one year after Beulah's death, Elizabeth hands the deed to Beulah's other son (the one without the contingent interest).

   g. Beulah deeded the home to her minister in trust. Beulah was the life beneficiary and retained the right to revoke the trust (and thus to have the home returned to her). Upon Beulah's death the minister (the trustee) was to deed the home to whomever Beulah designated in her will, or, absent such designation, to Elizabeth if she survives Beulah, otherwise to one of her sons. Beulah dies intestate. The minister, Elizabeth, and the sons survive Beulah.

4. Don bought a rental house for $100,000 from Trevor as an investment. Don paid Trevor the sales prices by transferring $5,000 cash from his

savings, borrowing $80,000 from Hometown Bank (HB) and paying that money to Trevor, and giving Trevor an unsecured note for the remaining $15,000. At closing, Trevor deeded the house to Don, and Don signed and delivered a note and mortgage secured by the house to HB. (All these deeds and mortgages are properly recorded.) Five years later when the house's fair market value (FMV) was $150,000, Don borrowed $50,000 from Local Bank (LB) to remodel his personal residence. Don gave LB a note for $50,000 and a mortgage to his rental house (and not to his personal residence). Two years later Don sold the rental house to Zola for $170,000. Zola paid the sales price with $10,000 from her checking account, borrowing $50,000 from Friendly Savings (FS) and paying that money to Don, and agreeing to take the property subject to the notes to HB ($65,000) and LB ($45,000). Don deeded the house to Zola. Zola signed and delivered a note and a mortgage secured by the house to FS. One year later the state suffered an economic recession. Real estate values dropped. Don and Zola each suffered financial setbacks. Assume the following facts:

Balance on Trevor note	$ 5,000
Balance on Hometown Bank note	$ 60,000
Balance on Local Bank note	$ 40,000
Balance on Friendly S&L note	$ 50,000
FMV of Don's home	$200,000
Cash in Don's bank account	$100,000
FMV of Zola's home	$ 90,000
Cash in Zola's bank account	$ 10,000

Please explain what happens when: (a) Don stops making unsecured monthly note payments to Trevor. (b) Zola continues monthly payments to FS but stops making payments to LB and to HB. (c) Zola continues making payments to HB but not to LB or FS.

Explanations

1. No. B's possession of the deed raises a rebuttable presumption that S delivered the deed. The facts, however, easily rebut the presumption: S intended to hand the deed over to his attorney, not to B. No intent to deliver, hence no delivery. B's recording does not alter the result. If B had transferred the property to a bona fide purchaser for value, there might arise an irrebuttable presumption of delivery to such a purchaser. S wins.

2. Sallie loses—judgment for Harry and Gloria. There was no manual delivery and no clear and convincing evidence of intent. Sallie never saw the deed, never touched it, had no access to Harry's vault and

without that access, she cannot even claim to be in constructive possession of the deed. No one changed their position after its execution — so no equities rise to defend Sallie. Her private conversation with Harry was no substitute for the deed's delivery. Sallie's continuing to live on Whiteacre shows her interest, but provides no evidence that the deed had any effect. Harry's access to the vault (and Sallie's lack of access) shows that Harry continues to exercise control and dominion over the property and the deed and raises a presumption of non-delivery. Moreover, without some contract binding Harry to hold the deed for Sallie, Harry cannot be presumed to be Sallie's agent. (Even if Sallie alleged an implied oral contract, it would be presumed revocable before the deed is delivered.) Further, it is no matter that Gloria has not recorded her deed: A deed is valid between the parties to it, even when unrecorded. Recordation only protects against subsequent bona fide purchasers for value. Sallie's failure to record means that she cannot rely on recordation either to substitute for delivery or to create a presumption of delivery. The greatest protection that Sallie could have achieved is to have had her deed recorded.

3. (a) The sons own the home. Beulah attempted a testamentary transfer, using the deed as a will substitute. Elizabeth does not gain access to Beulah's important papers until she survived Beulah. There being no delivery until after Beulah dies, the transfer is void. Beulah's home passes by intestate succession to her sons.

(b) The son's deed trumps Elizabeth's. Beulah delivered the deed to her son during her life, but if the deed to Elizabeth is deemed delivered before the son's deed is delivered, Elizabeth prevails: Beulah cannot revoke a completed gift, and she would have nothing to transfer to the son. So if Beulah's entrusting the deed to her minister constitutes the present delivery of a future interest — i.e., a springing executory interest — the delivery is good and Elizabeth prevails, even though the minister delivered the deed to Elizabeth after the son received his deed. Many courts conclude that the minister is a dual agent, that is, an escrow agent acting for both parties. In this situation, the delivery is good unless Beulah imposed a condition on the transfer other than her death. If Beulah had instructed her minister to deliver the deed to Elizabeth when or after Beulah died, these courts would deem the delivery good. If the minister is Beulah's agent, Beulah had the power to revoke the gift to Elizabeth by asking the minister to return the deed to her. Thus the attempted delivery to Elizabeth was ineffective. The son prevails since his is the only effective delivery.

(c) Beulah has attempted to condition the delivery. The oral condition, being inconsistent with the written deed, is void and unenforceable and does not delay or prevent an effective delivery when the deed is handed over; so the grantee owns the property even if she dies before the grantor. This rule also prevents fraud after a party's death (especially the grantee's death). Elizabeth owns the home.

(d) Beulah has transferred alternative contingent remainders to Elizabeth and the son. Even though the interest to Elizabeth is a contingent interest, Beulah's handing the deed to Elizabeth is still a present delivery of an interest (to Elizabeth and to the son, even though the latter may not have seen the deed), no matter that the interests are contingent, future interests. Delivery is good. Elizabeth survives Beulah, so Elizabeth owns the home after Beulah's death. If Beulah had survived Elizabeth, the son and his heirs would take possession of the home. The deed contained the same condition Beulah put on Elizabeth's interest in (b) above: that Elizabeth survive Beulah before she takes a vested interest in the home. Yet Elizabeth is not Beulah's agent, as the minister was in (b). She is not a third-party escrowee.

(e) Elizabeth owns Beulah's home. Elizabeth's returning the deed does not undo the transfer. To transfer her interest back to Beulah (note Elizabeth could not transfer the son's interest), Elizabeth must satisfy all the requirements for a valid deed, including those in the Statute of Frauds.

(f) Elizabeth owns Beulah's home. When Beulah died, Elizabeth's interest became vested and the alternate contingent remainder was extinguished. Elizabeth handed a deed to Beulah's other son, but unless she gave him some writing (or wrote on the front or back of the original deed) signed by her indicating she was conveying the property to him, the delivery of the original deed transfers nothing to the other son.

(g) Elizabeth owns the home. The trust is a popular vehicle for individuals to avoid the cost, publicity, and delay of probate administration. Courts honor its terms and will hold Beulah delivered the deed to the trustee, even though she retained the right to revoke the trust and all remainder interests, and even though she retained the power to control who would take after her death. She even had the power to sell to a third party during her life simply by revoking the trust and then transferring the property. Nonetheless, the delivery is good. When Beulah died intestate, her home passed to Elizabeth under the terms of the trust.

4. (a) Don is the primary obligor only on the unsecured $5,000 Trevor note. Trevor did not receive a mortgage on the rental house so has no security interest in Zola's house. Trevor is an unsecured creditor, however, and may get a judgment lien against Don's other assets (but not against Zola's assets). Trevor may get his $5,000 from Don's cash in his bank account, depending on how many other unsecured creditors also are looking to it for payment. Don also is secondarily liable on the $60,000 HB note and the $40,000 LB note. As long as

Zola continues scheduled payments, the two banks have no action against Don.

(b) Zola has stopped making payments on the notes secured by the two senior mortgages (HB and LB), and continued paying only on the FS note secured by the junior mortgage. Mortgage agreements normally contain an acceleration clause, which allows mortgagees to seek full payment of the entire outstanding note balance when there is a material default. Zola took title to the house subject to the HB and LB notes. She did not assume any personal liability for the notes, however, so she is not legally obligated to pay the two banks. However, if no one pays off the notes, either of the two banks can bring a judicial foreclosure action in which Zola's house will be sold to satisfy the debts secured by the house. Assuming the house will bring two-thirds of its $90,000 fair market value at auction and ignoring the transaction costs associated with foreclosure, HB, which holds the first mortgage and enjoys the highest priority to the sales proceeds, will receive $60,000 to retire its note.

LB and FS will not receive any foreclosure sale proceeds, will have their liens extinguished, and become unsecured creditors for $40,000 (LB) and $50,000 (FS). LB has no action against Zola because Zola has no personal liability on its note, but Don remains personally liable: As an unsecured creditor, LB will turn to Don. If LB is the only unsecured creditor, it likely will get $40,000 from Don's bank account.

FS still has recourse against Zola personally for the $50,000 because Zola signed the original note. Zola has only $10,000 in her bank account, so FS will not get full payment immediately from Zola. FS does have the option of paying off the notes to HB and to LB (thus "stepping into their shoes"), but because Zola's house's FMV is less than the two notes' balances, that is not a rational solution for FS. Its best hope is that Zola continues making the note payments.

Zola is out a home and still owes FS $50,000. Zola's taking the house subject to the two bank notes was part of the consideration for the house: That is why Zola was able to buy a $170,000 home for $60,000 cash! Zola's taking the house subject to the two bank notes was consideration for the sale of the house. Zola did not obligate herself to pay the banks or Don for the two loans. Zola's only risk is losing the house.

(c) Zola is no better off under this course of action and may even be worse off. LB and FS would accelerate the balance due. HB, however, maintains its senior mortgage status. If the parties notify HB of the lawsuit and HB joins in, HB will insist on and receive $60,000 in sale proceeds. Both LB and FS become unsecured creditors. If HB does not join the foreclosure action, any buyer will take the property subject to HB's mortgage and then must continue paying HB or risk a later foreclosure. At that later foreclosure sale, prospective buyers, aware of HB's rights, would only pay $30,000 ($90,000 − $60,000). So paying HB instead of FS, Zola may still lose the home *and* will still be personally liable to FS: Every dollar diverted from reducing the FS loan balance prior to foreclosure reduces the amount Don ultimately must pay, but does not reduce how much Zola must pay. Paying down the $60,000 HB loan only protects $30,000 in equity in the house, so Zola would need to modify HB's $60,000 loan to make this economically worthwhile, or else rely on the build-up of unsecured equity in the house. By reducing the HB loan rather than the FS loan balance, Zola does not reduce her personal liability one whit, but if Zola pays down the FS loan, on foreclosure she still loses her home, but shrinks her liability to FS.

Post-Closing Title Assurances

MERGER DOCTRINE

The sales contract controls the relationship between the buyer and seller during the executory period, but traditionally, the contract's provisions are no longer enforceable after closing: The contract's provisions for the transfer of title are said to merge into the deed (now the parties might more appropriately be called grantor and grantee) and the buyer's rights were limited to those warranties or covenants contained in the deed or other document transferring the title. Warranties are the grantor's promises either that certain facts are true as of closing, or that the grantor will remedy the problem or pay damages if a third party successfully asserts an undisclosed encumbrance on the title to the property.

Promises in the sales contract that do not pertain to title or are not normally found in a deed are said to be collateral agreements. They are not merged into the deed and are not subject to the doctrine of merger. They may, for example, pertain to the physical condition of the property, enabling a buyer to resort to the sales contract's provisions to remedy a seller's fraud. Alternatively, the sales contract itself may provide expressly that a sales contract provision will survive closing.

TYPES OF DEEDS

Three types of deeds affecting warranties of title are used in this country: the "general" warranty deed, the "special" warranty deed, and the quitclaim deed. Under the **general warranty deed**, the grantor warrants against all defects and encumbrances in title excluding those specifically excepted in the deed itself, no matter whether he or a predecessor in title created the defect or whether the seller even knows of the defect. The grantor in a **special warranty deed** also warrants against defects in title, but the grantor limits his or her warranty to those defects or encumbrances that are attributable to some act of the grantor: The grantor makes no warranties about defects or encumbrances created before he took title. The grantor may refer to any pre-existing defect and encumbrance in the deed, but these representations will not make the grantor liable for them or for other unlisted pre-existing defects or encumbrances.

Example: *A* two decades ago granted Company, Inc., a pipeline easement over Blackacre. *A* conveys Blackacre to B, the deed mentioning the easement. B conveys Blackacre to C without mentioning the easement. C then conveys to D, who conveys to E, all without mentioning the easement. Finally, E conveys Blackacre to F by warranty deed. One year later Company notifies F of its plans to dig up the land to place pipes in the easement. If the warranty deed from E to F were a general warranty deed, E would be liable to F for damages. On the other hand, E would not be liable to F if the deed were a special warranty deed since E did not create or grant the easement.

The **quitclaim** deed contains no warranties. The grantor conveys whatever interest he or she owns, but the grantor does not even warrant he or she has title. In the above example, E would not be liable to F for any defect in title if the transfer was by quitclaim deed. You can recognize a quitclaim deed easily enough because the deed uses the word "quitclaim" or another verb conveying the property that indicates the transfer is without warranties. Quitclaim deeds are especially useful in transfers between family members, short-term ownership situations, and boundary dispute resolutions.

DEED COVENANTS

Deed covenants or warranties are promises or representations that title is as presented at closing and no one will step forward later claiming an undisclosed interest in the property. There are six common deed covenants in "long form" deeds: seisin, right to convey, against encumbrances, warranty, quiet enjoyment, and further assurances. In some states, the grantor must list the covenants in the deed. The grantor is not obligated to make all covenants, and is held only to those covenants specifically included in the deed. States using "short form" deeds provide by statute that deeds containing words of conveyance such as "grant" or "convey" carry some of the six covenants (usually the first three plus the covenant of quiet enjoyment) with them unless the deed expressly excludes them; if the grantor does not expressly limit or exclude these covenants, they are implied terms of the deed.

The first three covenants — seisin, right to convey, and covenant against encumbrances — are called **present covenants**. A present covenant or warranty is breached or violated, if ever, the moment the deed is delivered. A grantor either has seisin and a right to convey the interest, or not, when delivering the deed. Thus present covenants protect against any undisclosed defect or encumbrance that already exists when the deed is delivered, and the grantee can immediately bring suit for breach of these covenants, even though no one has asserted a superior or paramount right to the property. But the grantee's right lasts only until the statute of limitations, running from the delivery date, expires.[1] Consequently, the statute may expire before the grantee discovers the breach — e.g., before a person having a higher priority exercises those rights.

In contrast, the **future covenants** — warranty, quiet enjoyment, and further assurances — are intended to remedy the defect in present covenants just mentioned. They obligate the grantor to perform some act, such as defending against a third party asserting a higher claim to the property, upon some future event. Future covenants cannot be violated until the grantor refuses to act and the grantee has been ousted or evicted by someone having a paramount title or right. Future covenants are mirror opposites of the present covenants in two respects. First, the grantee cannot bring suit against the grantor unless and until the future covenant is actually breached. Second, the statute of limitations does not begin to run until a third party asserts a paramount title or right (in the case of the covenants of warranty and quiet enjoyment) or the grantor refuses to execute a needed document (in the case of the covenant of further assurances).

A grantee may be protected against defects or encumbrances under both present covenants and future covenants. The grantee may assert a breach of the present covenant of the right to convey or of the covenant against encumbrances, for example, if the grantee discovers the encumbrance before the third party asserts a paramount title to the property. Likewise, he may assert either the breach of a present covenant or breach of the future covenant of warranty or quiet enjoyment if the grantee has been evicted as long as the statute of limitations on the present covenant has not expired. If the statute of limitations on the present covenant has expired, the grantee

---

1. A present covenant is sometimes mistakenly called a personal covenant. This is a misnomer in the sense that it is alienable within the statute of limitations applicable to it.

can resort to an action for the breach of a future covenant once the third party asserts his or her paramount title. Sometimes, however, a grantee gets caught without any cause of action. Consider the following Example based on the case of Brown v. Lober, 389 N.E.2d 1188 (Ill. 1979).

Example: Landowners could not sell coal rights to a coal company because, unbeknownst to them, a predecessor-in-interest owned two-thirds of the mineral rights. The landowners sued their grantor for breach of both present and future covenants. The court concluded the landowners could not bring an action on present covenants because the statute of limitations had run. The court also denied the landowners a claim based on breach of a future covenant because the third party had not attempted to mine the coal or to prevent the landowners from mining it, making the landowners' claim for a breach of the future covenant of warranty premature. The mere existence of the superior title and the consequent inability to sell the interest were not breaches of the future covenant.

PRESENT COVENANTS

(a) Seisin

A grantor by the **covenant of seisin** (often stating that the grantor is "well seised" of the interest of estate conveyed) warrants she owns the interest she is conveying. In most states, this means the grantor has legal rights to the estate conveyed. The grantor in this covenant does not warrant that no encumbrances affect the interest conveyed; that is, she can have title giving rise to possession with seisin while the land is still subject to encumbrances. In some jurisdictions, the grantor satisfies this covenant only by delivering both title and possession to the grantee.

Example: A grantor, having no interest in Blackacre, conveys its title to a grantee — and has breached the covenant of seisin.

Example: A grantor, owning Blackacre, conveys its title to a grantee while part of Blackacre is adversely possessed by a third party. The grantor has breached the covenant of seisin because it implies that the grantor is in possession of every part of Blackacre and if anyone else is adversely in possession of any part of it, the covenant is broken.

Example: A grantor, owning Brownacre, conveys its title to a grantee, the deed warranting that the grantor is "well seised and in the event of litigation arising out of this deed, the prevailing party shall be paid attorneys' fees." Part of Brownacre is claimed to be adversely possessed by a third party. The grantee discovers the claim, tenders her suit against the third party to the grantor, who refuses the tender and defense of the grantee's title. The grantee then joins the grantor as a defendant and sues the adverse claimant, who fails to prove adverse possession. Even though the adverse claim failed, the grantee is entitled, as the "prevailing party," to attorneys' fees from the grantor.

Example: A grantor, delivering a deed describing Whiteacre, but in fact deeding a parcel equivalent in size to Whiteacre and encompassing Greenacre and parts of Whiteacre, has breached the covenant of seisin. It is breached by a failure to convey the specific parcel described in a deed, even if the acreage is the same.

(b) Right to Convey

The **covenant of right to convey** parallels the covenant of seisin. The grantor may not have a right to convey when, for example, the purported grantor is not an authorized corporate officer; trust terms limit a trustee's right to convey; a covenant or restraint on alienation is included in the deed; or some other document restricts or forbids the transfer. The covenants of seisin and right to convey are in most jurisdictions regarded as equivalents, but sometimes not.

Example: A grantor, being an adverse possessor of Whiteacre, conveys its title to a grantee half-way through the adverse possession period — and has breached the covenant of a right to convey, but has not breached the covenant of seisin.

(c) Warranty Against Encumbrances

Under the **covenant against encumbrances**, the grantor warrants no encumbrances burden the title except for those mentioned or referred to in the deed. This covenant protects against many interests also covered by the covenant of seisin. Encumbrances include dower and other marital interests, outstanding mortgages, judgment and tax liens, easements, restrictive covenants, and outstanding leases. As can be seen from the foregoing list, they include interferences with both title and use as long as they are the result of voluntarily created interests. Improvements encroaching onto neighboring land are also encumbrances. An encumbrance mentioned in the deed cannot be the basis of a claim for a breach of this covenant. Neither can a government action pursuant to an ordinance or other law.

Many courts allow a buyer during the executory period to rescind a sales contract because of an unenforced violation of a zoning ordinance or environmental law, but those same courts find there is no encumbrance under this covenant. A prospective buyer can rescind the sales contract during the executory period so that the parties return to their original positions; once a closing occurs, however, grantors are no longer liable for all potential violations of government regulations. The grantee must use (and is irrebuttably presumed to have used) the executory period to find all such violations. Thus the definition of an encumbrance under this covenant is narrower than when the term is used in connection with the doctrine of marketable title applicable during the executory period.

Example: A grantee at closing takes a quitclaim deed to Blackacre and later discovers a mortgage on it that is satisfied but not released. This is an encumbrance that renders title unmarketable. May the grantee after the closing sue on an implied covenant of marketable title? No. After the closing, there is no such implied covenant. Agreeing to take a quitclaim does not waive the grantor's obligation to deliver a marketable title at closing, but the grantee's right to object to a known encumbrance ends at the closing. Further, assuming that the satisfaction is proven, there is no breach of the covenant against encumbrances. It is a promise to indemnify, measured by the cost of curing the encumbrance, but there is nothing to indemnify here.

Example: A grantee agrees to buy Whiteacre on which there is a mortgage, unreleased on the records, securing a debt incurred by the grantor. By the time of the closing, the grantee knows of the mortgage but takes title with a special warranty deed anyway. Is the covenant against encumbrances breached? Yes, it is, even if the grantee knows of the encumbrance. The grantee knows the grantor has the power to release the mortgage and has the right to expect that he will do so.

Example: A grantee agrees to buy Greenacre, over which runs a visible easement benefitting the land of a neighbor. The easement is an encumbrance, but this time it is one that the grantor cannot release unilaterally but which interferes with the use of the land so that by closing, the grantee takes subject to the easement. Its visibility makes the grantee's actual knowledge of the easement irrelevant: she is presumed to know of it when closing and to have adjusted the purchase price accordingly, so that there is again nothing to indemnify.

Example: If the easement in the prior Example were not visible, would the grantee have to see the neighbor use it in order to take subject to it? No, because the covenant against encumbrances, being a present easement, is breached if at all at closing—that is, before possession is taken — when an ouster or similar action is not yet possible and when the grantee does not yet know what will interfere with her possession.

The three present covenants discussed so far do not "run with the land" — that is, they do not benefit remote purchasers. Their measure of damages is generally the value of the right, interest, or estate lost by the grantee, with a ceiling represented by the purchase price received by the covenantor and computed as a *pro rata* share of the price.

FUTURE COVENANTS

(a) Warranty

Giving a **covenant of warranty and quiet enjoyment**, the grantor covenants to defend against and compensate the grantee for any lawful claims made against the title that might arise under the covenant of seisin and against encumbrances. A grantee's cause of action under this covenant does not arise until the grantee has been sued, ousted, or evicted by a party asserting a superior interest: There must be either an actual or a constructive eviction first. The mere existence of the paramount interest is not enough. Thus, after the grantor is notified of the eviction and refuses to defend, the grantor must pay attorneys' fees and damages resulting from claims of persons actually owning the property; having any superior interest in the property; or having any interest by way of a lien, life estate, easement, restrictive covenant, equitable servitude, or lease. Similarly, the grantor warrants improvements on the property do not encroach onto neighboring property and, just as with the covenant against encumbrances, government regulations and ordinances cannot form the basis of a covenant of warranty action. Every defect in title or encumbrance breaching a present covenant can become a breach of this covenant, thus allowing the grantee to excuse a breach of the present covenant but saving the possibility of an indemnity once there is an assertion or eviction. "Quiet enjoyment" here connotes an assurance that no one will interfere with the grantee's possession, but contrary to its name, has nothing to do with noise or freedom from noise.

Example: Using a deed with a covenant of warranty and quiet enjoyment, a grantor conveys Blackacre to grantee when a third party is in possession. For purposes of this covenant, the grantee is considered in constructive possession of Blackacre and need not be actually evicted before being able to sue on the basis of this covenant.

Example: Using a deed with a covenant of warranty and quiet enjoyment, a grantor conveys Blackacre to grantee. The grantee takes possession but then leaves Blackacre, yielding to the claim of a third party. Does this count as an eviction? Yes, provided that the grantee proves that leaving was a reasonable action. Once yielding up the property, the grantee has the burden of proof — here of proving that she would have lost a suit litigated with the third party.

Example: Using a deed with a covenant of warranty and quiet enjoyment, a grantor conveys Blackacre to grantee. After the later assertion of an encumbrance, the grantor acquires the interest underlying it and lacking in the conveyance to the grantee. Would the quiet enjoyment aspect of this covenant be satisfied? No, because it does not transfer an after-acquired title or interest. Would the warranty aspect be satisfied? Yes, because in most jurisdictions the after acquired interest would then be transferred to the grantee by the doctrine of estoppel by deed — that is, the grantor is estopped to deny that the acquisition of the interest was for his grantee's benefit. (Some jurisdictions only use this doctrine to protect a bona fide purchaser.) This situation presents a lingering difference between the covenants of warranty and quiet enjoyment.

(b) Further Assurances

The **covenant of further assurances** requires the grantor to execute any document or perform any action needed to cure a defect or encumbrance in the conveyance to the grantee. It also requires a demand by the grantee on the grantor that the latter execute the needed document or perform the needed action. For example, when a technical defect exists in a previously signed document (say a deed was not notarized and acknowledged as it should have been), the grantee may invoke this covenant to have the grantor provide a corrected version. A grantor under this covenant must execute the new deed or other document and cannot demand additional compensation from the grantee for doing so. The grantor may also have delivered a deed to land before the grantor acquired it: A grantee in this situation may insist on the grantor's delivery of a second deed conveying the land from his grantor to him after his grantor purchases the land. This covenant alone among deed covenants can be enforced by specific performance. This covenant is not used in most jurisdictions. Chancellor Kent did not even list it in his discussion of deed covenants in his 1820's *Commentaries on American Law*. It is often called an "English covenant" when it is used.

Example: Using a deed with a covenant of further assurances, a grantor conveys Blackacre to grantee. The grantor's deed is technically defective. Blackacre rises in value to the point where any recovery in damages under the deed's covenants surpasses the price given the grantor. In this event the right to have specific performance of this covenant is most useful.

Example: Using a deed with a covenant of further assurances, a grantor conveys Blackacre to grantee who paid for the fee simple absolute to it. Grantor previously and intentionally did not disclose the grantor's reservation of an interest affecting the grantee's use of Blackacre. Under this circumstance, the grantee need make no demand on the grantee to execute a deed for the reserved interest. No demand need be made on a grantor who acted fraudulently; that would require the grantee to put her trust in the very person who has fraudulently disregarded it. (This exception to the demand requirement applies to any deed covenant.)

DAMAGES

A grantee can receive monetary damages from the grantor for the breach of a deed covenant. The amount of damages depends on which covenant has been breached. A court may allow nominal or actual damages for a violation of the covenant of seisin or covenant of right to convey or may award the property's full value if the grantee transfers the property back to the grantor. The damages for a violation of the covenant against encumbrances will either be the cost of removing the encumbrance or, if that is impractical, the decrease in the property's fair market value. Two caveats apply in calculating damages: First, the maximum the grantee can receive on the breach of a covenant is the original amount the grantee paid his grantor for the property; and second, the maximum the grantee can receive from a remote grantor will be the amount the remote grantor received from a bona fide purchaser.

Example: Grantee pays $10,000 for a lot and later builds a $100,000 home on the lot. On the breach of a deed covenant, the maximum damages a grantor must pay Grantee will be $10,000.

Example: Grantee paid $100,000 for a lot and land, and the value increased to $150,000 before Grantee discovers the breach. The maximum Grantee can receive from a grantor is the $100,000 Grantee paid originally.

Example: Abel sells land to Baker for $100,000. When the land is worth $160,000, Baker learns that Cal owns a one-quarter interest in the property. How much in damages can Baker get from Abel? Since Baker's interest is one-quarter less than she expected, her damages presumably are one-quarter of the property's fair market value. The open question — on which jurisdictions differ — is which number is the fair market value, the price Baker paid for the property or the fair market value when the breach occurred or was discovered? In some jurisdictions Baker's recovery is limited to $25,000, in others to $40,000.

Example: Assume the same facts as in the prior Example, except Cal actually owns a three-fourths interest in the land. What damages can Baker get from Abel? In jurisdictions using the $100,000 original sales price as the relevant fair market value, Baker's damages would be $75,000. In jurisdictions using the $160,000 fair market value on the date the breach occurs or is discovered as the relevant fair market value, Baker suffered $120,000 loss of value, but would be limited to $100,000 damages—the amount Baker paid for the property.

ATTORNEY FEES

In addition to the loss of bargain damages, a grantee, having made a demand for curing a breach of the future covenants of warranty and quiet enjoyment and further assurances and later losing litigation against a third party, can collect attorney fees for the reasonable cost of defending against a third party's lawful claim. The grantor is obligated to reimburse the grantee for these fees that the grantee incurred in defending the claim because the grantor warranted no person had a superior interest in the property, but did not covenant to defend against unfounded claims. The grantee cannot receive attorney fees incurred in a second action to collect the attorney fees incurred in the first action. Nor can the grantee collect attorney fees when successful in the first action.

Example: Suppose in the immediately prior Examples that Baker spent $20,000 in an unsuccessful defense against Cal's claim to a one-quarter interest. Baker's actual loss of value damages were $40,000. In addition, Baker incurred $5,000 attorney fees in a suit against Abel to collect the damages and any attorney fees owed her. Baker should collect from Abel the $40,000 actual loss of bargain damages and the $20,000 attorney fees for the unsuccessful defense. Baker would not receive the $5,000 in attorney fees incurred in the suit against Abel.

Example: Baker incurred $20,000 in attorney fees in a *successful* defense against Cal's claim to the one-quarter interest. In addition, Baker incurred $5,000 attorney fees in a second suit for attorney fees against Abel. Baker would not collect any attorney fees. Baker would not collect the $20,000 since she was successful in her defense. Abel warranted no one had a superior interest in the property, but did not warrant no one would make an unfounded claim. Baker's successful defense is proof Cal did not have a superior interest. So Baker can collect neither the $20,000 for the successful defense nor the $5,000 incurred in the second suit, which he could not collect whether he won or lost the litigation against Cal.

REMOTE GRANTEES

A grantee may transfer the property to other persons, known as remote or subsequent grantees, who will own the property when the breach of a covenant made by a prior or remote grantor occurs or is discovered. To illustrate, assume *A* transfers land to *B*, who later transfers the land to *C*. As to *A*, *B* is the grantee and *C* is a remote grantee. As to *C*, *B* is the grantor and *A* is the remote grantor.

In all states future covenants "run with the land," meaning that a remote grantee can seek relief against any remote grantor in the chain of title who breached his or her deed covenants. As a corollary result, a remote grantor who pays a remote grantee because of a covenant has recourse against any prior warranting grantors (subject to the statute of limitations).

Jurisdictions differ as to the remote grantees' rights to enforce present covenants against remote grantors. Since present covenants are breached immediately on delivery of the deed, the cause of action vests in the first grantee (the non-remote grantee) immediately. At common law, causes of action were not assignable and because of this non-assignability, most jurisdictions held (and still hold) that remote grantees held covenants that were personal to them, did not run with the land, and so they could not bring actions against remote grantors for breaches of the present covenants. That is, a grantee's conveyance did not also assign the cause of action for breach of a present covenant held by its grantee. Only the grantee named in the original deed could enforce a present covenant. Other jurisdictions, by judicial opinion, allow remote grantees to sue remote grantors for breach of present covenants because today causes of action and contract rights are freely assignable, and deed covenants should be no different. A few state statutes embrace the rule that all covenants should run with the land. The statute of limitations for a breach of a present covenant as to remote grantors, however, begins running on the initial transfer out from the defendant grantor, not when the remote grantee receives the deed.

As to maximum amount of damages a remote grantee can receive from a remote grantor when the amount the remote grantee paid differs from the amount received by the remote grantor, the general rule is that the remote grantee is limited to the lesser of (1) the remote grantee's actual damages, (2) the remote grantor's sales price, or (3) the remote grantee's purchase price.

Example: *A* by general warranty deed sold Greenacre to *B* for $50,000. Later *B* by general warranty deed sold Greenacre to *C* for $40,000. The most *C* could collect from *A*, the remote grantor, for breach of a warranty would be $40,000, *C*'s purchase price.

Example: *A* by general warranty deed sold Greenacre to *B* for $50,000. *B* by general warranty deed sold Greenacre to *C* for $60,000.

415

The most C could collect from A, the remote grantor, for a breach of a warranty would be $50,000, A's sales price. C would be better off going against B, from whom C could collect $60,000, and once B paid C $60,000, B could sue A, but only up to $50,000, the amount B paid A, and not the $60,000 B paid C.

IMPLIED WARRANTY OF QUALITY

An implied warranty of quality (a/k/a the warranty of habitability), similar to that existing for leased property, exists in the sale of new and remodeled homes by developers and other commercial vendors. This warranty permits a purchaser to recover from the contractor, developer, or other commercial vendor for defective construction or construction not done in a workman-like quality. It is yet another exception to the doctrine of *caveat emptor*. It extends to latent defects that are discovered within a reasonable period of time. The defect must be due to the builder's poor workmanship, and cannot result in whole or part from subsequent substantial changes to the structure, from misuse of the structure, or from normal deterioration. It extends only to residences and does not apply to commercial buildings.

Thus, most jurisdictions hold that this warranty applies to the sale of new residences (including houses, townhouses, and condominiums), as well as to the sale of commercially renovated or remodeled used homes. So far courts have refused to extend the warranty to the sale of used residences. They imply this warranty is based partly on tort law and partly on contract law. Borrowing from contract law, they allow replacement or repair costs or the decrease in value of the building (known as economic losses) as damages for breach of the implied warranty. If the defect renders the house uninhabitable, some courts allow its buyer to rescind the sale and grant her restitution of the whole purchase price. Borrowing from tort law, a few courts do not allow any recovery of economic losses unless a person has been injured or is likely to be injured. So a latent defect that causes only economic damages does not give the buyer a claim for relief. Most courts question the wisdom of the tort approach, preferring the contract approach allowing economic damages even without physical injury.

Although some jurisdictions find attempts to disclaim void as against public policy, most honor disclaimers that are clear, unambiguous, and conspicuous (e.g., in bold, large, or different colored print), or are otherwise brought to the buyer's attention, particularly when the buyer is informed of the specific defect in advance. General disclaimers, such as a property being transferred "AS IS," do not suffice in most jurisdictions (although effective in some). Courts usually limit the "AS IS" general disclaimer to patent defects, not to the latent defects covered by this warranty.

In jurisdictions where this implied warranty is based on public policy rather than implied contract, any express warranty of quality given by the builder generally supplements but does not negate or override the implied warranty. The implied warranty remains the minimum that the builder offers. In some jurisdictions, however, freedom of contract principles allows an express warranty to trump the implied one if both have the same subject matter, such as the roofing or the heating and air conditioning system.

The statute of limitations for the implied warranty of quality generally runs from the date construction is completed, or from the date the property is sold to the first purchaser, if later. Alternatively, some jurisdictions begin running the statute only when the buyer discovers, or should have discovered, the defect. Many jurisdictions toll the running of the statute from the time the buyer gives the builder notice of the defect.

In most jurisdictions where courts have addressed the issue, this implied warranty is implicitly assigned (within the limits of the statute of limitations) with the house to subsequent buyers. Other courts, borrowing from tort law, have ruled subsequent or remote purchasers are not in privity of contract with the builder and thus the warranty does not run to them, some nonetheless allowing subsequent buyers to proceed in negligence against the builder. Perhaps this implied warranty should run to subsequent buyers: Latent defects often take time to become apparent; subsequent buyers are no more likely than first buyers to discover them before purchasing; and the builder/vendor should expect that homes will be resold and is in a better position to prevent the defect and repair it when discovered.

In any event, the subsequent buyer must prove the vendor/builder caused the defect and show that the suit was brought within the relevant statutory period. The builder can defend by showing he did not cause the defect, that previous owners made substantial changes to the structure, or that the damages were the result of normal wear and tear or other natural causes.

AFTER ACQUIRED TITLE (ESTOPPEL BY DEED)

Sometimes a person conveys property or an interest in property without having legal title, but in anticipation of gaining that title later (this is rare but sometimes happens). Under the doctrine of after acquired title (a/k/a estoppel by deed), the legal title to the property passes to the grantee as soon as the grantor gets it. This doctrine applies only when the grantor warranted she had title. If the grantor quitclaimed the property to the grantee, the grantee acquires no interest if the grantor later acquires the property.

Examples

1. Jen conveyed a building to Turner by general warranty deed. One year later Turner sold the building to Walter by general warranty deed. Walter later learns of a $100,000 note Jen owed Bay Bank. The note was secured by a mortgage on the building now owned by Walter. Bay Bank's mortgage lien is properly recorded in the land records, but neither of the deeds mentioned it. Jen has made all the note payments to date. Bay Bank has no plans to foreclose on the lien. Walter does not want his building to secure the Bay Bank note. What should Walter do?

2. S owns 100 acres of land. He sells three acres to A. Later S sells two acres to B and three acres to C. All three deeds were general warranty deeds. S conveyed easements across his remaining property for egress and ingress to all three grantees' properties. A, B, and C all intended to build homes on their land. Two years later C applies to the County Planning Department for a permit to build his home. The county denies the permit because under its subdivision ordinance, more than one partial sale of land is a "subdivision," and it says that it would continue to refuse to issue any building permit until S, C, and the other partial buyers subdivide S's original property, secure a plat approval, and pave a road as required by the ordinance. When contacted, S refused to do anything about the matter. Do A, B, and C have any rights against S under the deeds' covenants?

3. A by general warranty deed conveyed Blackacre to B for $100,000. One year later B quitclaimed his interest in Blackacre to C for $110,000. Two years later C conveyed Blackacre by special warranty deed to D for $80,000. Six years after the A to B conveyance, Blackacre was worth $90,000 and Trudy Owner, the legal owner, evicted D. Under state law, present covenants do not run to remote purchasers. (a) Explain how all resulting issues among A, B, C, and D should be resolved. (b) How would your answer change if A sold for $100,000, B sold for $80,000, C sold for $110,000, and Blackacre was worth $125,000 when Trudy Owner evicted D? (c) How would your answer change if the actual amounts paid were those set out in the facts but each deed recited consideration received as "$10 and other considerations"?

4. Flawless Construction built a residential townhouse, which it sold to Amos. After living there a few months, Amos noticed excessive humidity and dampness in his basement, accompanied by mold, mildew, and an offensive odor. Some of Amos' personal property stored there was damaged. The moisture originated from the groundwater table underlying the basement. A $2,000 fix would eliminate the problem. Amos wants Flawless Construction to pay to fix the problem. Flawless Construction

contends it bears no liability for this act of nature, especially since Amos can and does still live in the home. What result?

5. Development Inc. contracted with Building Company to build several townhouses. Development Inc. sold one of the new houses to the Sotos. The form sales contract between Development Inc. and the Sotos, among other provisions, contained the following two provisions:

> 17. ONE-YEAR WARRANTY: Development Inc. warrants that it will repair all defects due to faulty materials or workmanship if Development Inc. receives written notice of such defects within one year of the sale to Purchaser.

> 18. ENTIRE AGREEMENT: This contract and the matters referred to herein constitute the entire agreement between the parties. No representations, warranties, undertakings, or promises, whether oral, implied, or otherwise, have been made by Development Inc. or Purchaser to the other unless expressly stated herein, or unless mutually agreed to in writing between Development Inc. and Purchaser.

These provisions were on a standard printed form in like-sized small print. The form contained blanks for the purchaser's name, the house description, the sales price, and the financing terms, if appropriate. A year and a half after buying the home, the Sotos sold the house to Sabrina. A month after moving into the house, Sabrina discovered the exterior walls did not prevent water from coming into the house after a big rain and that the central heating system did not heat one of the bedrooms adequately. There was nothing to indicate previous water damage or heating problems. Sabrina called and wrote Development Inc. demanding Development Inc. repair the house. Development Inc. refused. (a) Sabrina sued Development Inc. Is Development Inc. the proper defendant under the implied warranty of quality? (b) Did Sabrina buy a "new" house for purposes of the implied warranty of quality? Does Sabrina as purchaser from the Sotos have any rights against Development Inc.? (c) How does Provision 17's express warranty affect the analysis? Does an express warranty covering the same subject matter as the implied warranty of quality displace the implied warranty? (d) Was Provision 18 an effective disclaimer of the implied warranty of quality?

6. Adam owns 700 acres. Adam contracts to sell all of them to Len. One month later, and two months *before* closing, Len by general warranty deed conveys 10 of the 700 acres to Marty. Marty records. Two months later, Adam and Len close, Adam delivering a warranty deed to Len for the 700 acres. A year later Len contracts to sell the 700 acres to Nick. When Marty hears Len plans to include the 10 acres Marty had bought earlier in the sale, Marty protests. Who owns the 10 acres?

Explanations

1. Walter wants Jen either to pay off the loan or to substitute other collateral to secure the Bay Bank note. Whether Walter can demand Jen do so under the deed covenants depends on whether the present covenants "run with the land." A mortgage is an encumbrance for purposes of the covenant against encumbrances. A few jurisdictions allow remote grantees like Walter to enforce present covenants: There Walter can enforce the covenant against encumbrances against Jen. In these jurisdictions Jen can either pay off the mortgage or obtain its release from Bay Bank to release the mortgage either by Jen's retiring the debt or substituting with different collateral. If the building is in a jurisdiction in which remote grantees cannot enforce present covenants, Walter has no standing to bring an action for breach of the present covenant against Jen and, in addition, Walter cannot bring an action for breach of the future covenant, which remote grantees can enforce in all jurisdictions, because Bay Bank has not evicted him. Here Walter must enforce the covenant against encumbrances against Turner, who is liable since he gave Walter a general warranty deed not mentioning the mortgage: Then Turner could be either required to pay off the mortgage, leaving him with an action against Jen or required to place funds in trust in case Bay Bank forecloses. Turner might further make Jen a third party defendant to resolve all matters in one proceeding, but that is beyond Walter's control. If Walter cannot locate Turner (say he moved to another state) or Turner is bankrupt, Walter may be left without a remedy unless and until Bay Bank forecloses on the building. At that point he has an action against Jen on the future covenants of warranty and quiet enjoyment.

2. No. S did not violate the present covenant of seisin: S will argue that he owned the fee simple. Neither did S breach the covenant of right to convey: The violation of the subdivision ordinance is not a breach of that covenant. Neither did S, in transferring the land, breach the covenant against encumbrances: The existence of a subdivision or zoning ordinance does not breach that covenant, and the violation of the subdivision ordinance inherent in the land transfers would not change this result in most jurisdictions. In the majority of jurisdictions, therefore, S has not breached any present covenant. (Were this problem to arise during the parties' executory periods, this violation would be grounds for rescinding the sales contracts. During that period, the parties can be placed back into their original positions without much cost, and S could decide how or if to resolve the problem. After closing, however, the grantor's flexibility disappears and in addition, the cost may be too high for the grantor to bear based on the sales price, especially when, as with these facts, both buyer and seller had equal access to the ordinance in question.)

A minority of jurisdictions hold a violation of a land-use regulation like the subdivision ordinance breaches the covenant against encumbrances, especially after the state took action to enforce the provision.

Likewise, future covenants of warranty and quiet enjoyment are not violated since they assure grantees that their enjoyment will not be disrupted by the grantor, by a person acting through the grantor, or by someone having paramount title. The county in denying the permits, is without any claim of title, so future covenants are inapplicable. The covenant of further assurances also does not apply because the facts here do not require S to execute any document or perform some act to perfect the title conveyed. S's deeds granted A, B, and C good title. In any event, deed covenants only (with one exception) give rise to a claim for damages. Damages may be an inadequate remedy here. The exception is the future covenant for further assurances, which may be specifically performed. But specific performance is granted only to obtain a better title — and that's no help to the plaintiffs either.

Equitable rescission of the deeds, when the inability to obtain a building permit and build a home is material to the conveyance that it amounts to a constructive ouster from possession, is perhaps a plausible ground for these plaintiffs' suit. In this regard, plaintiffs might argue that S has denied them seisin of their land, understood as the use of their title so as to be responsive to the government. Distinguishing the traditional use of the covenant of seisin as opposed to the right to convey, then, might provide the plaintiffs with a basis for rescission in the breach of this covenant.

3. (a) D has no claim against C since C, by using a special warranty deed, warranted only against title defects that arose while C owned Blackacre, not any defects already in effect when she acquired her interest. Trudy has owned the land since before the relevant transactions began, so her interest in the land preceded C's purchase. D also has no cause of action on the deed covenants against B since B quitclaimed his interest, meaning he made no warranties whatsoever as to title. Nothing in the facts indicate B (or anyone else) knew of Trudy's interest until the eviction, so no fraud claim arises from these facts.

D can bring an action against A since A conveyed by general warranty deed. D cannot bring a claim based on the present covenants of seisin, the right to convey, or against encumbrances, however, since present covenants do not "run to" subsequent or remote purchasers in this jurisdiction. Fortunately for D, however, future covenants do run; D can seek relief under the covenant of warranty or covenant of quiet enjoyment. D had rights under the covenants of warranty and quiet enjoyment as soon as Trudy evicted him. A owes D $80,000 in damages (the amount D paid) even though A received

$100,000 when he sold Blackacre and Blackacre was worth $90,000 (when Trudy evicted D) because D's damages are limited to the amount he paid.

If D had litigated to defend his interest against Trudy and lost, D could under the covenants of warranty or quiet enjoyment recover reasonable attorney fees and court costs from A. D cannot receive attorney fees incurred in suing A. (NOTE: D would not be able to collect attorney fees for the defense if he had prevailed against Trudy.) In addition, the court may also award D interest on the $80,000, running either from when D bought Blackacre, or when Trudy evicted D. The latter date seems the better rule here since before the eviction D possessed and used Blackacre, especially when Trudy does not seek back rent or profits from D, an innocent trespasser on her property.

C has no claim against B since B quitclaimed Blackacre. C has no claim against A unless and until C becomes liable to either D (and C is not liable to D because she gave a special warranty deed) or to Trudy. Nothing in the facts indicates Trudy sought any damages from C, so C has no action against A.

C lost money on Blackacre, selling Blackacre for $30,000 less than she paid for it, but C cannot demand A reimburse her for this loss. There is a presumption that the loss resulted from a general decrease in Blackacre's market value and not from any title defect. Deed covenants do not warrant against general market changes.

For the same reasons, B has no action against A based on a breach of the future covenants. B may have a claim for breach of a present covenant since he is the only person who could enforce the present covenants against A in this jurisdiction. But B sold Blackacre for a profit before any title defect surfaced and thus he suffered no loss. And even if B sold Blackacre for a loss, since he and his purchaser, C, did not know of any title defect, the decreased value would have again been attributable to general market conditions, and not reimbursable as damages from A.

(b) The answer is the same as in (a), except that D can receive only $100,000 damages in the large majority of states. D cannot recover the full $110,000 he paid for the property or the property's current $125,000 value. His maximum loss of bargain damages is limited to the amount the defendant, A, received for the property. In a minority of states D would be able to collect the $110,000 he paid for the property. In addition to the loss of bargain damages, D may recover reasonable attorney fees incurred in his unsuccessful defense against Trudy, with legal interest.

(c) This Explanation parallels Explanations (a) and (b). D should collect $100,000 in loss of bargain damages with interest and reasonable attorney fees. The parol evidence rule makes oral testimony or other extrinsic evidence inadmissible to construe the plain terms of a contract or deed. This rule causes problems in some jurisdictions for remote grantees. A few jurisdictions adhere strictly to the rule, looking only to the consideration stated in the deed. Some allow the original parties to offer parol evidence to contradict the deed, but will not allow remote grantees that same privilege. However, most jurisdictions allow parol evidence even as to remote grantees, apparently acknowledging a practice of parties' inserting token consideration amounts into deeds. Others feel obliged to honor the rule, yet admit parol evidence as to the actual consideration by treating the amount stated in the deed as a statement admitting receipt of the consideration rather than as a statement of the actual consideration paid, and thus allowing parol evidence to flesh out an unclear fact. This approach is especially likely to be used when the deed recites "$10 and other consideration received" or similar language. Here the $10 stated price was less than the actual consideration. In most jurisdictions, then, the grantor is estopped from limiting his liability to this lower amount.

4. A damp basement is not a title defect, so Amos' case hinges on the implied warranty of quality. Amos must *prima facie* prove (a) Amos bought a "new" home from Flawless; (b) Flawless was the builder/vendor of the townhouse; (c) the townhouse at the time of sale was not delivered in a workmanlike condition; and (d) Amos suffered damages as a result of the defect.

The first two elements are not in dispute. Flawless is a builder/vendor and the townhouse is Amos' home. The townhouse is a new home. The $2,000 cost to fix the defect indicates Amos suffered some damages from the moisture. The damage issue in (d) depends on whether Flawless is responsible for damages caused by moisture from the surrounding groundwater table seeping into the basement. That issue follows from the resolution of the issue in (c), whether the townhouse was delivered in a workmanlike condition. Courts do not demand homeowners prove exactly how the builder failed to build the house in a workmanlike manner: Amos can show either that the home was not built in a workmanlike manner or that the home was not suitable for habitation. Amos proved Flawless did nothing to prevent groundwater from seeping into the basement. He also showed the mold, mildew, and odors made part of his home unusable for its intended purposes. The issue in the workmanlike manner alternative is a question of fact: whether builders in the community anticipate and prevent water seepage into the basement, or whether seepage protection is a nicety some homeowners will pay extra to have. A fact finder might well find a builder should prevent water seepage into basements. Similarly, the alternative question whether the home was suitable for habitation is a fact question: The defect does not have to make the home completely uninhabitable. Instead, the test is whether the home's condition meets the reasonable homeowner's expectations for its intended use. A fact finder here likely would find the leaky basement was ill-suited for use as a bedroom or storage area. Thus the conclusion must be that Flawless did not deliver the home in a workmanlike condition.

Flawless could defend by arguing the leakage was a patent defect. The implied warranty of quality does not cover patent defects. Leaky basements might be deemed patent defects since an inspection would find water stains, molds, mildew, or odors of some sort. In a new house, however, the defect may not have occurred, or not been significant enough to leave such telltale evidence. Nothing here indicates Amos should have discovered the defects prior to closing. Flawless must fix or pay to have the basement fixed.

5. (a) Yes, Development Inc. is a proper defendant. Unlike the situation in most cases, Development Inc. is not the builder/vendor, but it is a commercial vendor. Commercial vendors can be liable under the implied warranty of quality. Building Company, moreover, was Development Inc.'s agent. Development Inc. cannot escape liability by contracting out the work. As a public policy matter, Development Inc. is in a better position to monitor and discover the defects than are consumers.

(b) Sabrina bought a "new" house for purposes of the implied warranty if she is seeking relief from Development Inc. The issue is whether the latent defect existed at the time Development Inc. sold the house to the Sotos. The sale from the Sotos to Sabrina would be deemed the sale of a "used" house if Sabrina tried to sue the Sotos, thus defeating the implied warranty of quality claim against them. The second question is more than a restatement of the first question. Courts disagree as to whether a subsequent buyer can enforce the implied warranty of quality against a commercial vendor if the second buyer is not in privity of contract with the commercial vendor. Most courts support the legal conclusion that Sabrina, as a remote grantee, could enforce the covenant against Development Inc. Only a minority would hold Sabrina, as a remote grantee, did not have standing to sue Development Inc.

(c) Provision 17, "One Year Warranty" is an express warranty covering the repairs of all defects due to faulty materials or workmanship if the purchaser notifies Development Inc. in writing within one year of the sale. If the provision controls, Sabrina has no rights since she did not even buy the house until a year and a half after Development Inc.

sold the house to the Sotos (even if we assume she qualifies as the "Purchaser" under the sales contract). The one year period begins when Development Inc. sold the house to the Sotos. It does not start anew when the Sotos sold to Sabrina. Fortunately for Sabrina, courts likely would interpret the sales contract provision as applying only to *patent* defects, not to the *latent* defects at issue here; they fear a contrary ruling would lead to commercial vendors' effectively negating all warranties by conditioning the express warranty of quality to one year, or an even shorter time. Sabrina has the time set out in the statute of limitations under state law.

The next provision, Provision 18, seemingly disclaims all implied warranties, strengthening Development Inc.'s claim the express warranty of Provision 17 constitutes Sabrina's sole remedy. A court might reject that claim since a reasonable consumer would not associate the two provisions nor appreciate their legal consequences.

(d) No. Development Inc. in Provision 18 attempts to disclaim all implied warranties. Most jurisdictions allow disclaimers or waivers, but they would not approve this one. The disclaimer is part of a boilerplate, preprinted form contract. Its print is small and no different from the rest of the document. To be effective, a disclaimer must be clear and conspicuous, containing some indication the buyer read and understood its legal consequences. Here it did not mention habitability or quality. It is legally insufficient to disclaim the implied warranty of quality.

6. Marty owns the 10 acres. Under the doctrine of after-acquired title or estoppel by deed, title to the ten acres automatically inured to the earlier grantee, Marty, when Len acquired legal title. The legal title acquired by Len is said to "shoot instantly through" Len's hands into Marty's, and Len is estopped, by the fact of his earlier conveyance to Marty, to deny this. Thus Len did not have any interest in the 10 acres when he later contracted to sell to Nick, so those acres were not included in his contract. The recording acts, discussed in the next Chapter, might reverse the result in Nick's favor (if he is a bona fide purchaser). This is so because in some jurisdictions, Marty's deed, recorded before Len purchased the property, will be found to be out of the chain of title; it will be a so-called "wild deed," meaning that it is not properly recorded. Most jurisdictions, however, rule that the recording acts do not repeal the doctrine of estoppel by deed. So it remains an exception to recording act rules, as the next Chapter will make clear.

Recording Systems, Marketable Title Acts, and Title Insurance

INTRODUCTION

The recording system is the principal means by which the title to real property can be determined. It contains a copy of the transfer documents relating to a parcel of land, typically placed in the records by a purchaser[1] or mortgagee seeking to protect the priority of title for a document — be it a deed, mortgage, lease, or other document. Persons using the system have an interest in property that they do not want future claimants to challenge. The statute underlying the system is called a recording act — these acts are everywhere enacted. No state or jurisdiction is without one. Though they are not uniform, the acts vary principally in three ways.

If the recording acts do not protect a person involved in a dispute, common law principles control. The following Examples illustrate these common law principles.

Example: O owns Blackacre in fee simple absolute and conveys it to *A*. O then conveys it to B. At common law, *A*'s title has priority over B's. Why? Because no vendor can convey more than he has, and having previously

---

1. Prior Chapters have routinely used the word "buyer" in regard to purchase and sale transactions, but in this Chapter, because of the traditional use in recording acts of the word "purchaser" — as in "subsequent purchaser" or "bona fide purchaser" — that word is routinely used.

conveyed the fee away to A, O had nothing left to convey to B: The O to B deed was a nullity. First in time, first in right was the common law rule.

> **Example:** O contracts to sell Whiteacre to A. O then conveys Whiteacre to B. At common law, B has priority of title over A. Why? Because B was the first to take legal title from O. Legal titles trump equitable titles, said the common law. A and B were, in effect, in a race to the closing table.

> **Example:** O contracts to sell Greenacre to A. O then contracts to sell it to B. Two equitable interests, like the two legal interests in the first Example, make the first in time, first in right rule applicable again. A prevails over B because O's right to sell by contract, once exercised, makes any second attempt to exercise the right a nullity.

Recording systems often reverse outcomes reached under the common law. If a system protects a person, that person prevails over other claimants having an inferior or competing interest.

> **Example:** O holds title to Brownacre. O conveys it to A, who fails to record her deed. O then conveys it to B, who pays for the deed and promptly records it without having any notice or knowledge of the deed to A. B's deed prevails over the prior, but unrecorded, deed to A. The rule of the recording system is, first to record, first in right — quite different from the common law rule.

A recording system serves two practical functions. First, a recording system assures title or, more accurately, determines a priority of rights to a parcel of land. Generally, a person recording a document in the deed records takes priority over persons later recording an interest in the same property. So many of the cases interpreting recording acts emphasize the concept of proper recording and discerning which persons are protected by the acts. The system's second purpose is informational: A prospective purchaser or lender can search the records to determine whether the prospective seller or borrower has record title, and to locate other recorded interests affecting the property. Gaining knowledge of other record owners, easements, restrictive covenants, cotenants, leases, mortgages, liens, and other recordable encumbrances to title, the prospective purchaser during the executory period may rescind the sales contract if the seller cannot deliver marketable title. These records are accessible to any member of the public: Thus, even before entering into a sales contract, a prospective purchaser can decide if he would be willing to purchase the property subject to the restrictions and encumbrances of record.

The assurance and informational purposes are related. First, a person recording an interest usually can rest assured a subsequent purchaser must honor the previously recorded interest. Second, with actual knowledge or "notice" of the previously recorded documents, a prospective purchaser will be bound by all recorded encumbrances and interests in the property, and cannot later protest he did not think he would be bound by any of the encumbrances. To encourage prospective purchasers to review the deed records, the prospective purchaser is also said to have constructive notice of all properly recorded documents regarding the property. Thus the prudent prospective purchaser checks the deed records and does not rely solely on a seller's representations because even if not doing so, he is nonetheless bound by what he would have discovered had he searched the records.

The concept of the records providing constructive notice gives every purchaser or transferee of an interest in property great incentive to record. Why? Because anyone who fails to record takes the risk that a subsequent bona fide purchaser for value will not have to honor the prior person's interest either because that person did not qualify for protection under the recording act or because, of the two innocent parties, the prior person could have avoided the problem by recording.

Usually one office in each county — titled variously as clerk of the court, or the register, registrar, recorder of deeds, or bureau of conveyances — maintains the deed and other records for all land in that county — or parish, in Louisiana. Each state's recording act specifies the mechanics of the recording process, including the formal requirements needed before the recording office can accept a document for recordation. Once accepted, the recording office dates the document, assigns the document a number, and notes the document in a log. The clerk makes a copy of the document and records pertinent data in appropriate indices: the grantor and grantee index being the most common.

Some recording acts give long lists of documents that may be recorded — e.g., "deeds, mortgages, agreements that convey, transfer, assign, encumber, or affect the title to real property." Other acts permit the recording of "every grant of an estate in real property." Some interests are not recordable. Short-term leases (less than one or two years) are often expressly excluded. In addition, interests that arise from possession (e.g., adverse possession and prescriptive easements) or involve marital property do not arise by written instrument, so there is nothing to record, but interests arising from possession will often trump written, recorded interests.

Before delving into the recording acts, you must be comfortable with the mechanics of a title search conducted by abstractors and the use of a grantor-grantee or tract index to create a chain of title. Governments are quickly placing documents and indices into an electronic format on computers, simplifying the title search. But computers are not changing the rules governing a search: Constructing a chain of title using the traditional indices is still necessary, often because the computerized version of the records is not the official one giving constructive notice of the documents and making it self-proving and admissible in evidence.

A *chain of title* means the series of documents affecting ownership of, rights to, and encumbrances on a parcel of land "linked" together in some manner. Generally, the links are organized by the grantors' and grantees' names. In "searching" title using a grantor-grantee index, the title searcher first checks the grantee indices (moving back in time). This gives him a list of past owners dating back however many years he needs to search. He then searches the grantor index for conveyances made by each past owner in the chain of title, tracing from the earliest grantor to the most recent. This second step tells him whether any owner rendered the title unmarketable in some way by creating an encumbrance on it. The next section of this Chapter discusses the mechanics of the search in more detail.

SEARCHING A CHAIN OF TITLE USING THE GRANTEE INDEX

The grantee index indexes alphabetically by grantees' names. The index includes the name of each grantee for all land in the county for a given period of time — one year, ten years, etc., depending on the volume of transactions. Along with the grantee's name (typically on the left hand column of the page), the grantee index will contain a date and time, the type of document being indexed (deed, lease, easement, mortgage, release, lien, etc.), a brief legal description of the affected property, a reference to an instrument number or the page and book in the deed records where a copy of the document is filed, and the grantor's name (typically on the far right-hand column of the page).

A title searcher or abstractor begins the search by locating the current owner in the grantee index. Since this index lists grantees' names alphabetically, if the current owner is Richard Gray, the searcher would look in the most recent grantee index under "G" or "Gr" for Gray, Richard. Richard Gray may have received several parcels so a check of the brief legal description is important.

A prudent title searcher, looking through the grantor or grantee indices, will be on the lookout for similar names — for example, past owner Johnson Smith may have used the name Johnson A. Smith in a mortgage transaction in the chain of title. In some states, when one name is inconsistent with another, checking the documents involving both may be required. Some other states require that names that sound alike be treated alike: Thus a phonetic search may be required because Johnny Smith should also be searched under the name of John E. Smith.

Once the grantee's name is found, the searcher finds, copies, and reads the complete document (of whatever type — deed, mortgage, lease, etc.) indexed at that entry. The searcher will also locate and read all documents referenced in the indexed document. Next, if the found document was a deed, the searcher notes the name of the grantor and searches the grantee index again, this time using the grantor's name as the grantee. The searcher repeats this process back in time to the **root of title**, which traditionally is the document by which the federal or state government granted the land to a private person, but which may also be a judicial proceeding (say a judgment awarding adverse possession) or some other transfer document treated in the jurisdiction as a root of title.

When the searcher cannot locate the prospective seller in the grantee index, or cannot complete some link back to the root of title, the searcher must inquire as to why the deed records are incomplete. The answer may be found in a judgment or decree of court, a probate decree, a divorce proceeding, a bankruptcy, or some other type of public record. Thus a search (say) of the applicable judgment docket in the clerk's office may be necessary. A prospective purchaser will typically refuse to close a sale until the grantor has completed the chain of title. Why? Because, for the recording system to work, courts often favor maintaining the integrity of the system over seeking equity or justice in any individual case. This attitude puts the onus on the latest person in the chain of title (or their attorneys) to verify that the chain of title is complete and documents are filed properly within it.

SEARCHING A CHAIN OF TITLE USING THE GRANTOR INDEX

The mechanics of searching the **grantor index** are similar to those to search the grantee index, except that the search is now conducted from the root of title forward in time. The title searcher begins with the root of title found using the grantee index and then searches chronologically for grantors up to the present day. A search of the grantor index is intended to disclose documents encumbering the title — easements, mortgages, leases, etc. As with the grantee index, the searcher should find, photocopy, and read each located document. The chain of title resulting from this search leads back to the seller. The title searcher must continue the search up to the day and time of closing to be sure the seller has not granted the property or an interest in the property to someone else.

Example: O agrees to sell Blackacre to Pete. Pete's title searcher finds deeds showing *A* conveying Blackacre to B, and C conveying Blackacre to O, but cannot find a deed from B to C in the records. The searcher may find documents to fill the gap in the judgment docket, probate records, divorce records, or bankruptcy records — but not always. Pete should not purchase

Blackacre if there is an unexplained gap between record owners. He should promptly notify O of all such gaps because the burden is on O to search for, supply, and/or record proper documents to clean up the chain of title before the closing. To make this burden clear, Pete's sales contract should call for O to deliver "a marketable title of record," meaning a record title without any gaps in its chain.

SEARCHING A TRACT INDEX

Some jurisdictions use a **tract index** instead of the grantor-grantee index, and many others supplement their grantor-grantee indexes with a tract index. In a tract index, all documents affecting a parcel of land are indexed on a page for that parcel of land. A searcher in a tract index finds the page for the property in question and copies the page that summarizes all documents affecting the parcel. The searcher then can pull and read all referenced documents.

The majority of jurisdictions retain the grantor-grantee index as their official index. Why? First, most began with the grantor-grantee index system and are reluctant to change. Second, the government employees in a grantor-grantee index system merely index the documents. They do not decide what properties are affected, and thus avoid claims, possible in a tract index system, that their negligence caused a title problem. Third, private abstract companies or title insurance companies, usually maintain a "title plant" in which they reconstruct all public land records, creating the equivalent of a tract index. They update the plant daily for all documents filed that day in the county records. With the equivalent of a tract index available in the private sector, governments perceive no need to change their current recording system. Moreover, private abstractors and title insurance companies lobby zealously against changes.

TYPES OF RECORDING ACTS

Recording acts establish the priority persons have to a parcel of land. Purchasers and creditors must strictly comply with a state's laws regarding recording to be protected by the recording acts. With all the transactions, documents, people, and parcels of land involved, errors and other problems are sure to develop. The first step in resolving many problems is determining the type of recording act adopted in the state. As noted previously, recording acts fall into three categories. They are known as race, notice, and race-notice acts. Categorizing an act before resolving any problems of interpretation or priority of title that arise under it is not always an easy task.

RACE STATUTES

Under a *race* statute, when two persons hold competing claims to real property, the first person to properly record (not the first to close or receive the deed, mortgage, etc.) prevails. For example, N.C. Gen. Stat. § 47-18 provides in part:

> § 47-18 (a) No (i) conveyance of land, or (ii) contract to convey, or (iii) option to convey, or (iv) lease of land for more than three years shall be valid to pass any property interest as against lien creditors or purchasers for a valuable consideration from the donor, bargainor or lessor but from the time of registration thereof in the county where the land lies. . . .

Under a pure race statute, the first person to record wins even if he knows about a previously unrecorded conveyance. The North Carolina statute's key phrase is "but from the time of registration." The statute does not mention the good faith of the parties protected by the statute — the "lien creditors or purchasers." This omission indicates that the statute is not a notice (and so not a race-notice) statute.

The advantage of a race statute is its certainty: The prevailing party is easily determined by seeing who recorded first. A person who delays recording risks having another person's claim to the property take a higher priority than her interest. In effect, a nonrecording owner gives her grantor the power to defeat the conveyance to her; she risks losing her entire interest. That potential power serves as a strong incentive to record a document as soon as it is delivered.

Example: O conveys Redacre to A, who does not record. B learns A has failed to record, and convinces O to convey Redacre to B. B records. Under a race statute, B will prevail because she recorded before A did. (A loses Redacre, but has an action against O on the deed covenants.)

Many states reject the pure race statute because B in the above Example was in a position to avoid the problem since B knew A already had an interest. B's acquiring the property seems unfair at best, and fraud at worst. Most all state legislatures have decided a person with notice of a prior transfer cannot defeat that prior interest. Similarly, a person purchasing without notice of a prior transaction because no notice is available also is at risk in a race jurisdiction.

Example: O conveys Blueacre to A. Before A records, O conveys Blueacre to B, B having no actual knowledge of A's interest. A records before B. Under a race statute, B, the innocent subsequent purchaser, has no interest in the property since A was the first to record.

Many jurisdictions reject the race statute in this situation because *A* was in the better position to avoid the confusion simply by recording quickly and because *B*, being the more innocent of the two, should prevail. The states that reject the race statute adopt one of the two recording acts with a notice component: notice or race-notice.

Today only Delaware, Louisiana, and North Carolina have generally applicable race statutes, and a few states (e.g., Pennsylvania) have race statutes for mortgages and for transactions involving mortgage remedies. The rest of the states divide almost equally between either race-notice or notice statutes.

NOTICE STATUTES

Under a notice statute, a subsequent bona fide purchaser or creditor for value prevails over prior claimants as long as the subsequent purchaser acquires the interest without notice of the prior claim. A subsequent bona fide purchaser without notice prevails immediately upon closing and does not have to be the first to record. In fact, the subsequent purchaser is not required to record at all to prevail against prior unrecorded claimants (although the subsequent purchaser must record to protect his or her interest against yet later subsequent purchasers). Tex. Prop. Code Ann. § 13.001 is a notice statute:

> (a) A conveyance of real property or an interest in real property or a mortgage or deed of trust is void as to a creditor or to a subsequent purchaser for a valuable consideration without notice unless the instrument has been acknowledged, sworn to, or proved and filed for record as required by law. (b) The unrecorded instrument is binding on a party to the instrument, on the party's heirs, and on a subsequent purchaser who does not pay a valuable consideration or who has notice of the instrument.

Subsection (a) says a deed or mortgage is void against subsequent creditors or purchasers for valuable consideration "without notice." The provision is not a race-notice statute: The section does not say anyone must be the first to record. It merely indicates the date the document gives constructive notice to potential purchasers and creditors is the date and time the document is recorded. Subsection (b) of the Texas statute makes an important point, one that courts recognize even if it is not expressly stated: The recording act does not affect the validity of a conveyance between the parties to it. This is important for all types of recording acts because the party not obtaining recording act priority will want to sue his grantor either for fraud or on the basis of deed covenants. The continuing validity of the "instrument" makes that possible.

States with a notice statute reward bona fide purchasers without notice and refuse to condition that protection on the subsequent purchaser's winning the race to record. In a notice state, a purchaser can rely on the deed records as they exist at closing.

Example: O conveys Blackacre to A, then to B, and then to C. Neither B nor C has notice of A's deed. C as the "subsequent purchaser," is protected by the state and C's title has priority over A and B's. If O had not conveyed to C, then B would be the "subsequent purchaser" protected by a notice statute. Thus B has, even in a notice jurisdiction, an incentive to record her deed.

Example: O conveys Blackacre to A, who does not record. O later conveys Blackacre to B, who purchases without notice of A's claim. Then A mortgages Blackacre to C, who does not have any notice of B's interest. If B did not record before C acquired his interest, C prevails since he is a subsequent purchaser for value without notice of B's claim. If B *had* recorded before C purchased, B would prevail since C, the subsequent purchaser, is charged with constructive notice of B's recorded interest.

"Notice" under these statutes can be either actual, constructive, or inquiry notice.

(a) Actual Notice

Actual notice means the subsequent purchaser or her agent had actual notice or knowledge of a prior claim. The subsequent purchaser can gain this knowledge from personal observations, a document in the deed records, or hearing about it either during negotiations or from conversations outside the transaction itself.

(b) Constructive Notice

Constructive notice (a/k/a record notice) refers to notice or knowledge that a purchaser could gain by searching the deed records. The purchaser is deemed to know all matters contained in documents legally recorded in the deed records, even though the purchaser did not search them. In fact, constructive notice or record notice typically is asserted when a purchaser did not search the records (a purchaser who searched the records has actual notice of prior recorded claims).

(c) Inquiry Notice

A prospective purchaser or creditor has inquiry notice when the purchaser hears or observes something that would cause an ordinarily prudent person to inquire further. If a prudent person would have investigated further and that investigation would have revealed some unrecorded interest in the property, the purchaser is deemed to have notice of the unrecorded claim.

The most important source of inquiry notice comes from visiting the property. A purchaser has inquiry notice of all rights belonging to possessors and users of the property. The user may be the owner, a tenant with a long-term lease or with an option to purchase, or the tenant's landlord may own the property (and not be the person trying to sell). If, as in the case of an apartment building, the property contains multiple units, the purchaser must inquire of each lessee.

Structures, railroad tracks, roads, and power lines may also prompt an inquiry. A prospective purchaser also may have inquiry notice based on a common scheme of development, or may be required to check deeds to neighboring property if the properties were conveyed by a common grantor. In summary, the prospective purchaser has a duty to view the property.

A second category of inquiry notice (though it can be considered a type of constructive notice) involves documents mentioned in properly recorded documents. A subsequent purchaser has inquiry notice of all matters specifically identified in properly recorded documents, whether or not the subsequent purchaser read the recorded documents.

RACE-NOTICE STATUTE

Under a race-notice statute, a subsequent bona fide purchaser or creditor who first records prevails against a person claiming a prior, unrecorded interest as long as the subsequent purchaser did not have notice of the preceding interest when she acquired her interest (she can know about the interest when she records the document as long as she did not have notice when she purchased or closed). The race-notice statute is a combination of a race and notice statute. As with the race statute, if the first purchaser in a race-notice state records first, she prevails. The subsequent purchaser in a race-notice jurisdiction, to prevail, must acquire her interest without notice of the preceding interest and must record first. Thus the class of person protected by a race-notice act is narrower than would be protected in a notice act. The race-notice statute therefore resolves the issue of the unscrupulous subsequent purchaser in the race jurisdiction who knew about an unrecorded document and took unfair advantage of the situation. Cal. Civ. Code § 1107 is a representative race-notice act:

> Every grant of an estate in real property is conclusive against the grantor, also against everyone subsequently claiming under him, except a purchaser or incumbrancer who in good faith and for a valuable consideration acquires a title or lien by an instrument that is first duly recorded.

The typical and significant phrases in this statute are "good faith" and "first duly recorded." They establish that the class of persons protected by the act must be without notice and record first.

Example: O conveys Blackacre to A, who does not record. O then conveys to B, who purchases without actual, constructive, or inquiry notice of A's interest. A records. Then B records. In a race-notice jurisdiction, A's title has priority over B's because B to be protected must purchase without notice (which she did) and record first (which she did not). In a notice jurisdiction, in contrast, B, the subsequent bona fide purchaser, would prevail because she purchased without any type of notice of A's interest.

SUBSEQUENT PURCHASERS FOR VALUE

The notice and race-notice recording statutes protect subsequent bona fide purchasers without notice. "Purchasers" include purchasers in the usual sense, as well as mortgagees, lessees, and anyone else who gives value for any interest in the property. Persons who receive an interest as a gift, devise, or inheritance are not purchasers "for value" and thus the recording acts do not protect them or their interests against unrecorded prior transfers. Donees, devisees, and other persons not qualifying as a purchaser for value can prevail over later subsequent purchasers, however, by promptly recording since a subsequent purchaser will have constructive notice of the donee's interest and thus cannot be a protected purchaser without notice. Most statutes provide the subsequent purchaser be a purchaser "for value" or "for a valuable consideration." Even if the statute omits these phrases, almost all courts (except Colorado's) would imply it.

To be a protected subsequent purchaser for value, the purchaser or creditor must furnish some value. It need not be fair market value. Money or other consideration less than the full value of a mortgage will suffice. A promise to pay consideration later is not value. Thus a purchaser who gives the seller a note for a substantial part of the purchase price has not given value yet. If the subsequent purchaser receives *actual* notice of a prior claimant before retiring the note, she loses to the prior claimant, but the prior claimant must reimburse her for all consideration paid prior to her learning of the prior claim.

Often a financial institution or individual that takes a mortgage for a loan, or a home seller who takes back a note and mortgage as part of the purchase price, qualifies as a purchaser for value (the loan or deed to the property being the value). However, this rule does not apply to the creditor who is owed a pre-existing debt and, seeking security for the debt, persuades the debtor to give the creditor a mortgage on land as collateral. The courts demand some new value be given for the mortgage before the mortgagee can qualify as a purchaser for value. The mortgagee (creditor) is not a purchaser for value because the creditor gave no new value for the mortgage and the mortgage was not part of the original loan. Most mortgagees in this situation would thus give the debtor extra time to pay: The time extension then constitutes the requisite "value." "Value" is not limited to more money. Thus, an unsecured creditor with a demand note or a note due and payable who gives the debtor an additional year to pay in return for the mortgage can become a purchaser for value.

PROBLEMS IN GRANTOR-GRANTEE INDICES

The potential for problems in grantor-grantee recording systems is great indeed. One type of problem involves errors in the recorded documents, such as mistaken property descriptions or misspelled names of the parties, or documents that are improperly filed or indexed. Another type of problem involves chain of title problems, such as occurs when a property owner of two adjoining lots transfers one of the lots and incorporates an easement or covenant into the deed of the transferred lot that benefits or burdens the current and future owners of the retained lot.

Example: O, the owner of Lot A and Lot B, transfers Lot B, the deed to Lot B incorporating a provision that both Lot A and Lot B will be restricted to single-family residences (a covenant) and another provision giving the owners of Lot B the right to travel over Lot A to get to a specific road (an easement). Later O sells Lot A to Z without telling Z about the easement or the residence-only covenant. The owner of Lot B wants to enforce the covenant and easement against Z even though Z did not know about the covenant or the easement.

Here Z can dutifully search the grantor-grantee index and not find anything in the chain of title for Lot A that mentions the easement or the covenant. Is Z obligated to check out deeds to Lot B and other surrounding lots? If not, how is the owner of Lot B able to protect her bargain? About half the states conclude Z prevails because he should not be obligated to check on all deeds to surrounding property or on deeds to lots transferred by O, the common grantor, or by other owners of Lot A in the chain of title. In the other half of states, the owner of Lot B prevails (and Z loses) because purchasers and their representatives should know many covenants and easements are included in only one deed from a common grantor. Either way, somebody will be understandably upset.

A familiar problem with grantor-grantee indexes is the so-called "wild deed," a recorded deed or other document that cannot be found easily by a search of the grantor-grantee indexes because a link in the chain of title is not recorded or is recorded out of order.

Example: O deeds Blackacre to A, who does not record. A later deeds to B, a purchaser for value, who records. Still later O deeds Blackacre to X, a purchaser for value with no actual knowledge of the deeds to A and to B. X records. On the one hand, B purchased from A, the legal owner, and recorded, so B is the first of B and X to purchase and to record. On the other hand, though X recorded after B, if he searched the grantee index back from O to the root of title and searched the grantor index forward to the present, X would not find the deed from O to A since it was unrecorded and thus would have no reason to know to look for a deed from A to B. As between B or X, X prevails. Brushing aside the fact that B recorded before X, most courts conclude either that X does not have constructive notice of a deed following a missing link in its chain of title, or that B's deed was not legally recorded. Favoring X is critical to maintaining the conclusiveness and integrity of the recording system. This result gives incentive to a purchaser's demanding a complete chain of title reflected in the records: If B had required A to record the O-to-A deed before B closed, X would have had constructive notice of B's interest and B would prevail.

Documents recorded out of chronological order create more grantor–grantee index problems.

Example: A, anticipating his acquisition of Whiteacre, deeds Whiteacre to B, who promptly records the deed. A subsequently purchases Whiteacre from O and O deeds Whiteacre to A. A records. Later A deeds Whiteacre to X, a purchaser for value without notice of B's deed. X records. Absent the recording acts, B holds legal title. Even though A did not own Whiteacre when he transferred it to B, B takes legal title by the doctrine of estoppel by deed discussed in the last Chapter. B also was the first actually to record. X, however, bought in good faith. Moreover, if X had searched the deed records she would have found the O-to-A deed, but not the A-to-B deed. Courts differ on whether the A-to-B deed is legally recorded or whether X has constructive notice of the A-to-B deed. The majority of cases, including the more recent ones, reject the use of the doctrine of estoppel by deed and hold for X.

The integrity of the recording system requires a purchaser, including B, to ensure all links in the chain of title are properly recorded in order before purchasing: The purchaser (B here) should have re-recorded the A-to-B deed after the O-to-A deed was recorded.

Another problem inherent in the system of deed records is that the deed records do not disclose whether a subsequent purchaser had actual notice or inquiry notice of an unrecorded document or a wild deed, or whether a person in the chain of title bought knowing of an earlier claimant.

Example: O deeds Greenacre to A. Before A can record, O deeds Greenacre to B, who has actual knowledge of the O-to-A deed. B promptly records. Then A records. B later deeds Greenacre to X, a purchaser for value without actual notice of the deed from O to A. X records. B wins between A and B in a race state. B loses between A and B in a notice and a race-notice state because B has actual notice of the O-to-A deed. X, on the other hand, did not have actual notice of the O-to-A deed. When X searched the deed records she would find the deed from O to B and would conclude that B was Greenacre's legal and record owner. So who should prevail between A and X? There is disagreement. In notice and race-notice jurisdictions, some courts favor A because the O-to-B deed is not deemed legally recorded since B had notice of the O-to-A deed. This being so, the O-to-A deed becomes the first legally recorded deed. This result, however, brushes aside the chain of title rules: If A prevails in these jurisdictions, a purchaser to be secure must search all previous owners' names down to the date of closing, a costly and formidable task. X should prevail because she likely would not find the O-to-A deed, it being recorded after the O-to-B deed. X's chain of title appears complete and X prevails to maintain the certainty and integrity of the records and reduce the impact of what are, to X, off-record facts (here B's actual notice of A's deed). This is an instance of B being able to give a priority of title greater than he himself has — an instance of the recording acts creating an exception to the common law conveyancing rule that no grantor can convey more than he has.

A variation of the above facts introduces the **shelter rule**, an important concept in recording acts whereby a grantee can rely on his predecessor in interest taking without notice even if the grantee has notice of an earlier conveyance.

Example: O deeds Brownacre to A, who does not record. O then deeds Brownacre to B, a purchaser for value who has no actual knowledge of the O-to-A deed. B records. Then A records. B later sells and deeds Brownacre to X, a purchaser for value who knows about the O-to-A deed. X records. As between A and X, who owns Brownacre? X prevails over A even though she has actual knowledge of the O-to-A deed and the O-to-A deed was recorded before the B-to-X deed because B, a prior owner in X's chain of title, prevailed over A. As between A and B, B prevails in a notice state because he purchased without notice of the O-to-A deed, and in a race-notice state because he purchased without notice and he recorded first. B therefore owned Brownacre. To protect B in his enjoyment of Brownacre, the shelter rule allows B to transfer Brownacre to whomever he desires, even to those persons knowing of the O-to-A deed. B, therefore, was free to transfer record title to Brownacre to X even though X knew of the O-to-A deed. The recording acts are, in this instance, protecting B's right to alienate Brownacre.

Example: Assuming that facts are the same as in the prior Example, suppose that in addition, A, knowing that he has lost priority to X, buys Brownacre from X and records the X-to-A deed. The shelter rule does not protect A in this situation not because the law won't protect X's right of alienation, but simply because A is attempting to better his priority by changing his chain of title. The shelter rule has limits.

MARKETABLE TITLE ACTS

About 20 states have enacted marketable title acts primarily to facilitate more efficient searches of the records and secondarily to annul some long-outstanding interests in land. Marketable title acts facilitate title searches by stipulating a document conveying title will be the act's root of title even though the common law root of title may have been decades, or even centuries, earlier. Generally, the state marketable title act will specify a period of number of years, ranging from 20 to 50 years, as the marketable title search period. A searcher must trace back in a grantee index to the first document transferring title (the title transaction) that was recorded earlier in time than the earliest date in the marketable title search period. This title transaction becomes the act's root of title.

Example: State has a marketable title act similar to the Model Marketable Title Act: Any person having the legal capacity to own land in this state, who has an unbroken chain of title of record to any interest in land for forty (40) years or more, shall be deemed to have a marketable title to such interest [subject to some exceptions]. The following transactions apply to Whiteacre:

> State gave a patent for Whiteacre to A in 1801.
> A sold to B in 1825.
> B sold to C in 1870.

C granted D an easement in 1900. C died in 1910, devising the property to E. E sold to F in 1940.

F mortgaged Whiteacre in favor of G in 1950.

F sold Whiteacre to H subject to the mortgage to G in 1955.

H sold Whiteacre to I in 1960, the deed not mentioning the 1950 mortgage or the 1900 easement.

I sold to J in 1977. J sold to K in 1998.

L in 2011 wants to purchase Whiteacre from K.

Without a marketable title act, the root of title is the patent from the state to A in 1801. Under the act, however, the searcher need only search to the title transaction recorded at least 40 years earlier. Since the search begins in 2011, the searcher must find a title transaction recorded prior to 1971 — i.e., the deed from H to I recorded in 1960. L can search the grantor index back to 1960 and the grantee index forward to 2011. L has constructive notice of documents recorded or mentioned in documents recorded since 1960, but not of documents recorded before 1960 (unless, as discussed below, one of the act's exceptions applies).

The secondary objective of these acts is to annul interests deriving from documents recorded before the act's root title; they cannot be enforced against a new purchaser unless the documents have been re-recorded after the new root of title or unless the old interest meets one of the exceptions to re-recording. In the Example, since the 1950 mortgage and the 1900 easement were recorded before the statutory root of title, L has no constructive notice of them. If the 1960 "root of title" deed from H to I had mentioned the mortgage or easement, L would have been on inquiry notice of them. Similarly, L would have been on inquiry notice of the easement if he noticed it had he visited the land.

Statutory exceptions to the marketable title act reduce the effectiveness of the act. While the exceptions vary among the states, the exceptions often include interests held by federal, state, and local governments; utility easements; railroad easements; water rights; and mineral interests. A few states except reversions, remainders, rights of entry, and possibilities of reverter. A few states likewise except restrictive covenants. Further, rights acquired by adverse possession or prescription escape the reach of the marketable title acts. Since exceptions recorded long before the statutory root of title remain enforceable, a conscientious searcher will continue searching back into the deed records for them.

TITLE INSURANCE

Title insurance is part insurance, part indemnity contract. Its overriding function, however, is to provide a system for disclosure of the state of a title. Title insurance companies maintain "title plants" where the companies keep real estate records that are the equivalent of a tract index. Each day the company makes copies of all documents filed with the government in accordance with the applicable recording act and incorporates this data into its own records.

(a) Informational Use

When some party to a real estate transaction requests title insurance, the title insurance company searches the title in its plant and issues a preliminary title report or binder setting out the status of the property's record title (not its legal title). Because the title company can issue a preliminary title report, purchasers and creditors can review the record defects and encumbrances and decide during the executory period whether the property is marketable. In practice, the preliminary title report is more useful than the later-issued title insurance policy.

The information furnished in the preliminary title report is limited to information found in the local deed records. The preliminary title report and title insurance policy do not purport to furnish information about or insure against matters created by or that are known by the insured; defects that result in no loss or damage; defects or encumbrances created after the policy date; rights of persons in possession of the property; encroachments, boundary line disputes, and other matters that would be disclosed by an accurate survey; easements not shown by public record; mechanics' liens; and taxes and special assessments not in the public records. Not all policies except all the above, and many companies will (for an extra premium) issue endorsements to a policy providing coverage for many of these matters. However, many policies limit the company's liability solely to damages flowing from the company's not finding documents filed in the deed records (so-called "on record risks") and defects in the title that do not appear on the face of otherwise valid looking documents (so-called "off record risks" — such as the fact that a grantor was incompetent, the document was forged, executed under duress, or was not delivered). The closest thing title insurance comes to being insurance is its coverage of off record risks.

(b) Lender's Policy and Owner's Policy

There are two types of title insurance policies, based on who is insured. Most title insurance policies insure a property's lenders and mortgagees (via a loan policy), not the property's owners (they need a separately issued owner's policy). To facilitate the assignment of mortgages into the secondary market for mortgages, financial institutions condition their mortgage loans on the purchaser/borrower purchasing a loan policy for its benefit that can be assigned to secondary market purchasers and investors. A purchaser also may purchase (or the seller may purchase on behalf of the purchaser) an owner's policy for an additional fee at the same time. Unless the seller is paying for the policy, most purchasers do not choose to purchase an owner's policy.

(c) No Assignment or Running of Benefits

The named beneficiary is the only insured. Owner's title insurance policies are not assignable and do not run with the land. Each new property owner must buy a new policy. Each insured owner is, however, provided "warranty coverage" after selling the insured property: This coverage indemnifies the owner for any liability later incurred under deed covenants that he provides his purchaser.

(d) Insurer's Duty to Disclose Excepted Defects

Title insurance companies argue, often successfully, that their title searches are done for the benefit of the title company to determine whether it will issue a policy. Under this view, the insured's only rights are those provided in a title insurance contract. A bare majority of courts, rejecting the title insurance companies' contract theory, now hold a title insurance company searches the deed records both for its own benefit and for the insured's benefit. The company's failure to disclose defects in these jurisdictions makes a title insurance company liable in tort for negligence in not finding the record defect or for breach of an implied contract to deal fairly and in good faith for not reporting the defect to the insured.

(e) Damages

When a title insurance company pays a claim under its policy, the amount of the claim is measured by the extent the insured property is damaged by the insurer's failure to discover or disclose a title defect. Damages are limited to the amount stipulated in the policy. Subject to the contract maximum, damages are based on the decrease in fair market value resulting from the defect. Most courts use the values as of the date the defect is discovered to calculate the damages. Other courts prefer the purchase date or even the trial date. Notwithstanding their duty to pay damages, title insurance companies usually reserve the right to cure any defect instead of paying for any loss of value.

(f) Other Benefits of Title Insurance

Title insurance policies offer some benefits that make a title insurance policy superior to relying solely on the grantor's warranties of title in the deed covenants. One such benefit is that the insurance company will pay attorney fees to defend the title against third-party claimants, whether or not the adverse claimant has a legitimate claim. Its policy provides for a "duty to defend" that is broader than its duty to pay a claim. Another benefit is that a title insurer provides a deeper pocket than a warrantor and is more readily found and available when a claim must be made. In contrast, a big hurdle in enforcing deed covenants often is finding the warrantor/grantor, and finding him solvent enough to pay a claim.

Title insurance is not, however, a solution for every problem, as the Examples below shows.

Example: In the following situations, O is the owner of Blackacre, whose fee simple absolute title is insured in a standard owner's title policy. Thereafter, the following events occur in the alternative:

1. O is evicted by Blackacre's true owner, who proves that a deed in O's chain of title was not delivered to its grantee. Does O have a claim against the insurer? Yes, because the policy provides more than information about a title, it also insures against off record risks. Non-delivery is such a covered risk. Here O is actually evicted and so can show the insurer an "actual loss" as required by the policy. It is an indemnity agreement, not a guarantee of title, so a loss must be more than theoretical or potential — it must be actual before the insurer will pay a claim.

2. O knew of an easement over Blackacre; it is recorded but does not appear as an exception to coverage in O's policy. Does O have a claim against the insurer? Yes again. Under the policy, the insured has a duty to disclose what she knows about the easement to the insurer (until the closing or the date of the policy), but the insurer also has a duty to discover and disclose what the records would reveal about the title, and it failed in that duty. Only if the easement or other defect were "known to the insured and not in the public records" would a claim based on the known easement be excluded by the terms of the policy. Here it was known, but was recorded, so the exclusion, being narrowly construed, does not apply.

3. The county rezones Blackacre, substantially reducing its fair market value. Does O have a claim against the insurer? No, on two grounds. First, the policy provides title insurance, not fair market value insurance. It insures title, not the use of the property or the property itself. The insurer has no control over public regulation that affects the

445

use of the property (as zoning does). The value of the property could fall to zero, but that would not affect the title insured or the insurer's liability. Second, the rezoning occurred after the policy was issued, and title insurance is retrospective in nature: It indemnifies the insured for defects in title that arose before the policy was issued, not thereafter.

4. O finds that the barn on Blackacre sits partially on a neighbor's land. Does O have a claim against the insurer? No. In its schedule (Schedule A) describing the coverage, the policy will use whatever legal description of the property appears on the insured owner's deed, and if the barn is beyond the boundaries of that description, it is not insured.

5. O is forced to buy a quitclaim deed to the marital rights of a spouse of a grantor in O's chain of title. Does O have a claim against the insurer? Maybe. The existence of a marital interest is an off-record risk; it should have been discovered and disclosed if property in the insured chain of title was purchased by spouses, only one of whom conveyed to the next grantee, or if a grantee who took title and conveyed it later was really married and nothing about the marriage was reflected in the chain. Further, if O bought the pre-existing right without first giving the insurer notice of the claim, O violated the Conditions and Stipulations in the policy: The insurer has the right to participate in the buyout. So the insured O will have to show that the insurer was not prejudiced by anything that O did in the buyout; even then, a few courts might deny the claim as not in compliance with the claims procedure set out in the policy.

Examples

1. Classify each of the following recording acts as either race, notice, or race-notice:
   (a) No sale, contract, counter letter, lien, mortgage, judgment, surface lease, oil, gas, or mineral lease, or other instrument of writing relating to or affecting immovable property shall be binding on or affect third persons or third parties unless and until filed for registry in the office of the ... recorder ... where the land or immovable is situated.
   (b) A conveyance of real property, within the state, on being duly acknowledged by the person executing the same ... may be recorded in the office of the clerk of the county where such real property is situated, and such county clerk shall, upon the request of any party, on tender of the lawful fees therefor, record the same in ... said office. Every such conveyance not so recorded is void as against any person who subsequently purchases or acquires by

exchange or contracts to purchase or acquire by exchange, the same real property or any portion thereof, . . . in good faith and for a valuable consideration, from the same vendor or assignor, his distributees or devisees, and whose conveyance, contract or assignment is first duly recorded.

(c) Every such instrument in writing, . . . recorded in the manner herein prescribed, shall, from time of filing the same with the recorder for record, impart notice to all persons of the contents thereof and all subsequent purchasers and mortgagees shall be deemed, in law and equity, to purchase with notice. No such instrument in writing shall be valid, except between the parties thereto, and such as have actual notice thereof, until the same shall be deposited with the recorder for record.

(d) All deeds, powers of attorney, agreements, or other instruments in writing conveying, encumbering, or affecting the title to real property, certificates, and certified copies of orders, judgments, and decrees of courts of record may be recorded in the office of the county clerk and recorder of the county where such real property is situated. . . . No such unrecorded instrument or document shall be valid against any person with any kind of rights in or to such real property who first records and those holding rights under such person, except between the parties thereto and against those having notice thereof prior to acquisition of such rights. This is a race-notice recording statute. In all cases where by law an instrument may be filed in the office of a county clerk and recorder, the filing thereof in such office shall be equivalent to the recording thereof, and the recording thereof in the office of such county clerk and recorder shall be equivalent to the filing thereof.

(e) Every deed conveying lands shall be recorded in the office of the clerk of the superior court of the county where the land is located. A deed may be recorded at any time; but a prior unrecorded deed loses its priority over a subsequent recorded deed from the same vendor when the purchaser takes such deed without notice of the existence of the prior deed.

(f) A conveyance of an estate in fee simple, fee tail or for life, or a lease for more than seven years from the making thereof, or an assignment of rents or profits from an estate or lease, shall not be valid as against any person, except the grantor or lessor, his heirs and devisees and persons having actual notice of it, unless it . . . , or, with respect to such a lease or an assignment of rents or profits, a notice of lease or a notice of assignment of rents or profits . . . , is recorded in the registry of deeds for the county or district in which the land to which it relates lies.

2. O conveys Blackacre, which he owns in fee simple absolute, to A. A does not record. O conveys Blackacre to B, who does not record. In what type

of recording act jurisdiction does the act resolve the issue of who, A or B, owns Blackacre?

3. M sold her home to A. As part of the purchase price, A gave M a $100,000 note and a mortgage on the home as security for the note. A recorded her deed. M did not record the mortgage. A year later, during the negotiations to sell the home, A told B she still owed $100,000 on the home, but neither the sales contract nor the deed mentioned the note or the mortgage. A sold the home to B for $120,000, with B obtaining most of the purchase price by borrowing $105,000 from Bank. At closing A received the $120,000 and delivered a warranty deed to the home to B; Bank received a note and a mortgage on the home. The closing attorney promptly recorded B's deed and then Bank's mortgage. Then M finally recorded her mortgage. The state in which the home is located has a notice recording act. B and the Bank learn of M's recorded mortgage and bring suit to remove the cloud from B's title. In this suit, what result and why?

4. Velda contracted to sell her home to Albert for $100,000. Albert borrowed $90,000 from Nice Bank. At closing Nice Bank's $90,000 check was given to Velda, a warranty deed was delivered by Velda to Albert, and a mortgage on the home executed by Albert in favor of Nice Bank was delivered to Nice Bank. Nice Bank recorded. Albert recorded his deed one year later. Two years later Albert sold the home to Joe for $125,000, delivering a warranty deed to Joe. To buy the home, Joe borrowed $100,000 from Residential Savings, for which Joe gave Residential Savings a note and a mortgage on the home. Joe promptly recorded his deed. Residential Savings recorded the mortgage the next day. Neither Joe nor Residential Savings knew about Nice Bank's mortgage. Who has what rights to the home?

5. O sold Blackacre to A, a bona fide purchaser. A did not record. A year later A conveyed Blackacre to B, a purchaser for value who lives out of state. B promptly recorded. A year later, O conveyed Blackacre to C, a purchaser for value with no actual knowledge of O's deed to A or A's deed to B. C recorded. A year later B inspected the property and saw C building a house on the land. B brought a lawsuit to evict C. Who prevails?

6. Oscar sold his home at its fair market value to Avery in Year 1. Avery did not record. In Year 5, Oscar sold the home for its fair market value to Mary, who knew about Avery's deed. Mary recorded promptly. Avery finally recorded his deed in Year 7. In Year 8, Mary sold to Nancy, a purchaser for value without actual knowledge of Avery's deed. Nancy recorded. (a) As between Avery and Nancy, who owns the home? (b) What result if Mary did not know about Avery's deed, but Nancy did? (c) What result on the original facts if Avery finally recorded in Year 10, not Year 7?

7. Pop contracted to buy Whiteacre from Owner. Before closing on White-acre, Pop conveyed Whiteacre by general warranty deed to First Purchaser. First Purchaser recorded. Six weeks later, Pop acquired Whiteacre's title from Owner. Pop recorded. Three months later Pop conveyed Whiteacre to Second Purchaser, a purchaser for value who had no actual knowledge of the deed to First Purchaser. Second Purchaser recorded. (a) As between First and Second Purchaser, who owns White-acre? (b) What result if First Purchaser moved onto Whiteacre immediately after receiving his deed from Pop?

8. Mike owned two lots (Lot 1 and Lot 2). Mike sold Lot 1 to Phil by a warranty deed containing the following covenant: "Grantor and Grantee covenant for themselves, their heirs and assigns, that Lot 1 and Lot 2 will be used for single-family residence purposes only." Phil recorded the deed. Five years later Mike sold Lot 2 to Sara by a warranty deed that did not mention the covenant. Sara wanted to build a shop on Lot 2. Phil protested, citing the covenant in his deed. Who prevails?

9. (a) Dad conveyed five acres to Daughter as a gift. Daughter did not record. Daughter immediately moved out of town. Dad, feeling Daughter deserted him, *sold* the five acres to the local School District at its fair market value. The School District did not know about the prior transfer to Daughter. School District recorded. Who prevails as between Daughter and School District? (b) Dad sold five acres to Daughter at its fair market value. Daughter did not record. Daughter immediately moved out of town. Dad, feeling Daughter deserted him, *donated* the five acres to School District. School District recorded the deed. Who prevails as between Daughter and School District? (c) What result in (a) if Daughter recorded before Dad sold the five acres to School District? (d) What result in (b) if School District sold the five acres to Farmer John for its fair market value and Farmer John promptly recorded?

Explanations

1. (a) Race. This is La. Rev. Stat. Ann. § 2721. It is a pure race statute. Notice is never mentioned.
   (b) Race-notice. This is N.Y. Real Prop. Law § 291. The first sentence sets out the requirement for an acknowledgment—essential to make any document recordable in almost all jurisdictions. The second sentence of the excerpt requires, first, that the subsequent purchaser must pay a "valuable consideration" for the interest. If a recording act does not state this expressly, most courts have implied that the person protected by the act must have received the interest "for value" or "for a valuable consideration" as here. Second, although this sentence

never mentions notice, it does mandate that the purchaser must have purchased "in good faith" — the law equates the term "good faith" with "without notice." Finally, the subsequent purchaser's document must be "first duly recorded."

(c) Notice. This is Mo. Ann. Stat. §§ 442.390 & .400. The first sentence expressly states that recorded documents impart constructive notice to subsequent purchasers and mortgagees, who in law and equity will have notice of the recorded document. According to the second sentence, a document is not binding on subsequent purchasers and mortgagees who do not have notice of the document. The last clause "until the same shall be deposited with the recorder for record" mentions "record" but not in the context of mandating a race to record. This last clause refers to a recorded deed giving constructive notice. Earlier language in the last sentence denies protection to subsequent purchasers with actual notice, leaving the last clause to refer to the constructive notice element.

(d) Race-notice. This is Colo. Rev. Stat. Ann. § 38-35-109(a). The second sentence mandates the subsequent purchaser be the first to record to be protected and then excepts from the act's protections those subsequent purchasers who acquired their interest with notice of the prior interest: the classic race-notice statute. To clear up the confusion in its case law, the legislature added the third sentence, startling in its directness: "This is a race-notice recording statute." All recording acts should be so clear! The last sentence, concerning the equivalency of filing and recording, states that the failure of the clerk or recorder to index a document properly, does not affect the priority assigned the recorded document.

(e) Race-notice. This is Ga. Code Ann. § 44-2-1. For a subsequent purchaser to prevail, the purchaser must acquire the deed without notice of the prior unrecorded deed and must be the first to record.

(f) Notice. This is Mass. Gen. Laws Ann. ch. 183, § 4. Under this act, unrecorded deeds are void against all persons except the grantor, his heirs and devisees, and subsequent purchasers having actual notice of the deed, unless the deed is recorded, in which case the recorder of deed prevails against all subsequent purchasers, whether they have actual knowledge or not. Until the deed is recorded, however, any subsequent purchasers without actual knowledge of the deed prevail over the holder of the unrecorded deed. Nothing in the statute requires the subsequent purchasers to be the first to record; hence, no race element.

2. Only a notice recording act resolves the conflict between *A* and B. Neither is protected under a race statute because neither has yet recorded — and the common law rule of first in time, first in right controls and gives *A* priority. Neither is protected under a race-notice statute because if

neither is protected by a race statute, by definition neither is protected by a race-notice statute either. Under a notice statute, however, B could become a subsequent purchaser protected by the statute if he is without notice of A's deed, and so achieves priority over A. Moreover, because it will be A who will have to allege and prove that B had notice, A is unlikely to prevail under such a statute, leaving A to sue O either for fraud or on his deed's covenants of title. Again, though, A will have to allege and prove the fraud existed when O conveyed to A and had not yet conveyed to B, so proving fraud will be difficult as well. All of which makes A's deed covenants A's best remedy. This is why recording acts do not affect the validity of a deed as between the parties to it; were it otherwise, no suit on the covenants would be possible.

3. Judgment for Bank. B recorded before M, so B did not have constructive notice of M's mortgage. B was only told that A owed money "on" the home. This is not actual notice of M's mortgage, but since the act is a notice statute, the remaining issue is whether A's telling B of her note to M constitutes inquiry notice of M's mortgage: Would this information induce a reasonably prudent person to inquire about a mortgage to secure the $100,000 debt? This may be a factual issue in some jurisdictions, but the answer is probably that it would give inquiry notice, putting the burden of inquiry on B. If so, B would have notice of the mortgage when B acquired title and so not be protected by the notice recording act. So long as B owns the home, it would continue to secure the $100,000 note and mortgage. (If M the mortgagee prevails, B still has an action against A based on the A to B deed covenant against encumbrances.) If instead B has no inquiry notice, M still has a right to collect the note from A, but cannot foreclose on B's home if A defaults on the note. M becomes an unsecured creditor, sharing rights with A's other unsecured creditors. However, none of this matters to Bank. It prevails over M in either situation: It took the mortgage without actual or inquiry notice of M's mortgage since no one, according to the facts, told the bank about M. Also, since the Bank received its mortgage before M recorded, Bank could not possibly have had constructive notice of M's mortgage. So while M may have a higher priority than B, M has a lower priority than Bank. In a foreclosure action, M does not have any rights to the sales proceeds until Bank's note is satisfied. In practical terms, however, since B's priority with M is subject to the litigation risk involving inquiry notice, B and the Bank share a common goal of having A satisfy the debt to M.

4. The issue turns on whether the Nice Bank mortgage is in the chain of title or whether subsequent purchasers and creditors must search the deed records for documents filed before the prior fee owner (Albert) recorded his interest. A title searcher must examine documents filed from the date

the record title owner acquired his interest and not just from the date the deed was recorded. Both Joe and Residential Savings should have searched from the date Albert acquired the title to the home. That search would have uncovered the Nice Bank mortgage. So Joe and Residential Savings had constructive notice of the Nice Bank mortgage; it has priority over Joe's deed and Residential Savings' mortgage. (Joe will continue living in his home until Albert defaults on the note to Nice Bank and Nice Bank forecloses; meanwhile Joe has an action against Albert for either breach of the covenant against encumbrances or the covenant of warranty and quiet enjoyment.) Nice Bank also prevails in a race jurisdiction since Nice Bank recorded before Joe and Residential Savings recorded, and also in a race-notice jurisdiction since Joe nor Residential Savings can satisfy either element of such a statute: They did not record first and when they did record, they did so with notice.

5. C prevails under all types of recording acts. In a notice jurisdiction, B's deed, though recorded, is a "wild deed," meaning it is not legally recorded. B's deed will be deemed recorded only when all links needed for the chain of title to be traced to B's deed are recorded. The deed from O to A is not recorded, so all conveyances out from A, including B's recorded deed, also must be deemed unrecorded. Since B's deed is deemed unrecorded, B's deed cannot give constructive notice to subsequent purchasers like C. In a race jurisdiction, because B's deed is still unrecorded, C also prevails just by being the first to record. Even if C, in searching the deed records, actually happened upon or found B's deed from A, C would not have to take notice of it; that is, it is still not in the chain of title that C would search while looking for conveyances out of O in the grantor index. The facts say C did not have actual knowledge and C (again) would not have found B's deed using grantor-grantee indices. In a jurisdiction using a tract index, C may have found the deed had he actually searched, but the use of such an index is no reason not to construct a chain of title and use it. (Thus are chain of title rules useful to cleanse titles of adverse interests, even in jurisdictions using a tract index.) Moreover, in fairness, B was in the best position to prevent the problem by requiring A record A's deed before B would agree to close. The integrity and workability of the grantor-grantee indices depends on each person in every real estate transaction demanding a complete chain of title.

6. (a) Nancy prevails in a race jurisdiction because Mary was the first to record. Because Mary has priority, her successors continue forming the links in the chain. The principle that subsequent purchasers can profit from a predecessor's being protected by the recording statute is known as the shelter rule. In effect, once a person, like Mary, has perfected her priority under the recording acts against a prior

claimant, like Avery, all persons (like Nancy) claiming through the perfected interest (Mary's interest) also prevail against the prior claimant (Avery).

In notice and race-notice jurisdictions, Mary's actual notice of Avery's deed raises the issue of whether her notice affects Nancy's title priority. The better rule (with a majority of older cases to the contrary) is that Nancy's title is "freed of the equities" preventing Mary from winning. Searching the records, Nancy would find nothing amiss: Nancy would find the deed from Oscar to Mary and would not have discovered the deed from Oscar to Avery unless Nancy extended her search of Oscar's transactions all the way to Nancy's closing. Unless Mary tells her she has notice, Nancy is not bound to question her, there being no basis for inquiry notice and for assuming that she is not a bona fide purchaser. Unlike the situation under the shelter principle, Nancy prevails on her own merits. She has followed the rules and recorded. In a race-notice state, Nancy wins because Mary recorded first and, as before in a notice jurisdiction, takes free of the equities affecting Mary's title. For all purchasers subsequent to Mary, Avery's deed is outside the chain of title. In addition, Avery's late recording was the reason the problem occurred. Thus, as between Avery and Nancy, Nancy is the more innocent; so she prevails to guarantee the integrity of the recording system by playing down the role of off-record facts (here Mary's actual notice of Avery's deed).

(b) Nancy prevails in all types of jurisdictions because, under the shelter rule, Nancy prevails if Mary prevails. Mary prevails in a race state because she recorded before Avery. Mary prevails in a notice jurisdiction as soon as she receives her deed because she acquired her interest without notice of Avery's deed (which was still unrecorded when Oscar sold to Mary). Mary prevails in a race-notice jurisdiction because she prevailed in the two other types of jurisdictions.

(c) Nancy wins. Under race statutes, both Nancy and Mary recorded before Avery. Under a notice statute, Nancy prevails because she acquired the property without notice of Avery's deed. The fact that Mary knew of Avery's adverse claim does not prevent Nancy from prevailing in her own right. Under race-notice statutes, Nancy wins because she recorded before Avery and had no notice of Avery's deed.

7. (a) A majority of jurisdictions would hold for Second Purchaser as the subsequent purchaser. On the one hand, First Purchaser, the first purchaser, properly recorded, and is deemed the legal owner under the doctrine of estoppel by deed. On the other hand, First Purchaser's deed is not in the chain of title and Second Purchaser likely would not find the deed in a search. Most courts find in Second

Purchaser's favor to ensure the integrity of the recording system (and to lessen the significance of the doctrine of estoppel by deed). As between First Purchaser and Second Purchaser, First Purchaser was in the better position to avoid the problem by re-recording his deed after Pop acquired Whiteacre from Owner. In race and race-notice jurisdictions, Second Purchaser was first to record within the chain of title. Further, Second Purchaser prevails in a notice jurisdiction because she purchased without actual notice and with no constructive notice of First Purchaser's deed since First Purchaser's deed was filed outside the chain of title. A few jurisdictions would find in favor of First Purchaser by reading the recording acts literally as protecting persons who record, not just those who record in the chain of title. It is better, however, to take account of chain of title rules when interpreting the recording statutes since they don't work well without those rules.

(b) Second Purchaser would now have inquiry notice of whatever interest First Purchaser possessed. That being so, Second Purchaser loses in both race-notice and notice jurisdictions, but prevails in a race jurisdiction since she was the first to record.

8. Jurisdictions are evenly divided on this question. Owning both lots at one time, Mike is a common grantor. When searching the grantor index, a searcher would find Mike's name associated with his conveying Lot 1 to Phil. The property description in that index may mention the covenant as affecting Lot 2, but most typically the index's brief description will describe Lot 1 but not Lot 2. Assuming this so, the issue becomes, does the subsequent purchaser of Lot 2 have the duty to search deed records for all transfers from a common grantor of neighboring properties? Is the fact of a common grantor, coupled with the knowledge that many restrictive covenants and easements are contained in only one deed out from the common owner, enough to put all subsequent purchasers on inquiry notice of all restrictions in deeds of neighboring lands? Extending the required search does not require searching all deeds in the record, and searching the common grantor's name from the time the common grantor originally acquired the property to the closing of the subject property narrows the search. If a jurisdiction places the burden on the subsequent purchaser to read deeds of neighboring lands from a common grantor, Sara would have constructive notice of the deed restrictions, and thus be bound by the covenant in notice and race-notice jurisdictions. Since Phil was the first to record, Sara also would be bound under a race statute. About half the jurisdictions in the country would rule in favor of Phil and hold Sara bound. The other half find the deed to Lot 1 outside the chain of title of Lot 2: There it is more efficient to require the person receiving the benefit in the first deed (Phil here) to be

sure the deed was properly indexed as affecting both Lot 1 and Lot 2 than to require subsequent purchasers to search old deeds from the common grantor. In these states Sara as the purchaser of Lot 2 would not be bound by the covenant contained in the deeds to Lot 1. The use of a tract index does not avoid this problem: The problem of indexing Lot 1's deed to Lot 2 remains. Upcoming Chapter 30 explains that for the residential restriction to "run with the land" so as to bind the subsequent purchaser (Sara here), the subsequent purchaser must have notice of the restriction on her lot, either by it being recorded in the deed records (constructive notice) or by a common development scheme (inquiry notice).

9. (a) Local School District prevails. Daughter did not record, so School District prevails in a race jurisdiction because it recorded first. School District has no actual or constructive or inquiry notice of the deed from Dad to Daughter, so School District also prevails in notice and race-notice jurisdictions.

(b) Daughter prevails. School District as a donee is not a "purchaser for value." Thus it cannot seek protection under the recording statute. Resort to common law principles favors Daughter since she acquired her title first.

(c) Daughter prevails. Daughter would have been the first to record and School District would have had constructive notice of her interest. Her receiving the property as a gift is immaterial. Daughter as donee (protected) differs from the School District as donee in (b) above (not protected) because Daughter was the first to receive the property and sought protection against subsequent grantees: A prior grantee (even a donee) who records in the chain of title prevails against subsequent grantees. It is subsequent grantees who seek protection that must be purchasers or creditors for value. Daughter having received and recorded her interest prevails against School District.

(d) Farmer John prevails. Since he is a subsequent purchaser for value without actual notice of Daughter's unrecorded deed and he was the first to record, he will prevail against Daughter under all types of recording statutes. Farmer John's rights are not tainted by School District's failure to qualify as a purchaser for value. He would have benefitted from the shelter rule if School District was protected under the recording act, but he still can prevail even if the recording act does not protect School District. Farmer John qualifies for protection based on his own merits and prevails.

Private Land
Use Controls

PART V

26

Private Nuisance

INTRODUCTION

A **private nuisance** is an act or condition on the defendant's land that **substantially and unreasonably interferes** with the plaintiff's use and enjoyment of plaintiff's land. The **interference** is usually an **intangible invasion** such as smells, light, sounds, vibrations, dust, and pollution of air and water rather than a **physical invasion**, which is subject to strict liability in an action in **trespass**. For instance, a person who walks his dogs on his neighbor's land trespasses and will be liable for at least nominal damages. If that same person allows his many dogs to bark all night, the barking dogs may be a nuisance if a court determines the barking substantially and unreasonably interferes with his neighbors' use and enjoyment of their property. Although both trespass and nuisance are actions to protect possession, trespass is more easily proven than nuisance: Only the invasion need be shown in a trespass action, not the substantiality and unreasonableness of the invasion.

Early private nuisance cases looked solely at the interference with plaintiff's use and enjoyment of his land, much the way courts evaluate trespass actions today. An injunction, rather than damages was the usual remedy for a nuisance. The injunction, however, became subject to a **balancing of the utilities**. As industrialization and urbanization proceeded, each landowner had to tolerate some inconveniences and annoyances for the benefit of technological advances, and only if the harm to the plaintiff outweighed the social utility of the defendant's activity would an injunction issue. Otherwise the defendant could continue his activity and the plaintiff was not entitled to damages. More recently, courts recognized the new balancing rule favored a finding of no nuisance when plaintiff landowners were harmed by major economic entities. Courts then began allowing damages (measured by the diminution in market value) if the plaintiff seemed entitled to some relief but an injunction seemed inappropriate. Recent judicial decisions can be found using each approach, though there is today a trend toward refusing an injunction but allowing damages.

In many cases, the plaintiff's and the defendant's uses both are socially beneficial, but the two uses are incompatible. The one labeled a private nuisance is the one the court finds less suited to the locale. Only in close cases will the use in place first prevail over a later use: The second party came to the nuisance.

INTENTIONAL AND UNINTENTIONAL INTERFERENCES

Interferences with a plaintiff's use and enjoyment of the plaintiff's land may be either an **intentional** or an **unintentional interference**, the latter usually resulting from negligent, reckless, or abnormally dangerous activities. These activities are either disfavored as falling below expected standards of conduct (negligence and recklessness), or they may be **nuisances per se** or nuisances as a matter of law, involving malicious actions, spite fences and structures, nuisances forbidden by law (houses of prostitution, crack houses, setting off fireworks), pollution, or abnormally dangerous activities, on which is imposed such a high standard of care that a strict liability standard applies to them as long as the interference is substantial.

> **Example:** O uses Blackacre for breeding foxes. N owns adjoining property and fires off guns intending to interfere with the foxes' breeding. The malicious gunfire is a nuisance *per se*.

> **Example:** N generates cooking smells, principally onions, on her property intended to annoy her neighbor O. O then generates the smell of french fries that wafts over N's property. O sues N in nuisance to abate N's activity. Since O retaliated, she will not win: He who seeks equity must do equity.

With regard to intentional interference, "intentional" does not necessarily mean that the defendant's use and enjoyment of land was meant to interfere with the plaintiff's; instead, it distinguishes the acts or conditions from negligent acts or conditions. Proof of intent is not an element of nuisance. An "intentional invasion" occurs when the defendant in fact knows or should know his activities or property condition will affect the use or enjoyment of neighboring property, but feels society should tolerate or encourage his activity or condition despite the inconveniences to his neighbors.

Example: A person mowing his lawn knows or should know the noise from the lawnmower and some dust will pass over the property line to neighboring property, and that the exhaust from the lawnmower pollutes the air flowing over that property. Despite this knowledge, the person probably considers the invasions normal, acceptable consequences of mowing the lawn (even though his innocent neighbor may have to turn up the sound on the television he's watching). He means his neighbor no harm. His interference and invasions are, nonetheless, characterized as "intentional." They probably are not unreasonable (or even substantial) interferences with his neighbors' use and enjoyment of their lands, but they are intentional.

Example: N mows his lawn at daybreak close to O's bedroom window, leaving the mower running there with the choke pulled all the way out. As O gets out of bed and shuts the window, N gestures obscenely at her. This is proof of malice and a nuisance as a matter of law.

SUBSTANTIAL INTERFERENCE

Only a **substantial interference** with the use or enjoyment of property will amount to a private nuisance. As members of the community, individuals must tolerate certain annoyances, such as children at play during daylight hours or the noise of passing automobiles. "Substantial" does not necessarily mean egregious. It means that persons of normal sensitivities would consider the interference to be substantial. This substantiality element deters complaints by petty or overly sensitive plaintiffs. Once a defendant's activity was found to have substantially interfered with his neighbor's use and enjoyment of the neighbor's land, a court would enjoin the activity. Although early cases often made this a primary inquiry, today courts consider the next factor, unreasonable interference, more important.

Example: O is annoyed by his neighbor's flying radio-controlled model airplanes over O's property. This activity may be annoying, but does not meet the substantiality element required for a private nuisance claim.

Example: The roots and branches of a neighbor's trees encroach on O's Blackacre above and below the surface of its land. The encroachments may be annoying, but are not substantial enough to meet this element of a private nuisance claim.

UNREASONABLE INTERFERENCE

While courts and commentators agree on the necessity of finding a substantial and unreasonable interference with the use and enjoyment of neighboring lands, they disagree on how exactly to determine unreasonable interference and what remedies are available once a private nuisance is found. The following, drawn from the Restatement (Second) of Torts, seems to be the current but not universal trend: Defendant's acts or the condition on defendant's property will be a private nuisance if: (a) the **gravity of the harm** to plaintiff's use and enjoyment outweighs the **social utility** of defendant's conduct or the condition on defendant's property; (b) the harm to plaintiff is sufficiently grave and greater than the plaintiff should be required to bear without compensation; (c) the harm to plaintiff is sufficiently grave and the financial burden on the defendant compensating for the harm, and for similar harm to others, would not make the defendant's continuing his activities impractical; (d) the harm to plaintiff is sufficiently grave and the defendant could avoid the interference in whole or in part without undue hardship; or (e) the harm to plaintiff is sufficiently grave, plaintiff's use is well-suited to the character of the locality, and the defendant's conduct or property condition is unsuited to the locality. See Restatement (Second) of Torts §§ 825-831.

Not all courts have adopted the Restatement's view. Some limit the definition to situation (a) and deny relief in the other four situations. A few states look solely at the severity of the interference with the plaintiff's use and enjoyment of his property without considering at all the social utility of the defendant's activities.

In evaluating the **gravity of the harm to plaintiff**, a court considers the extent and the character of the harm, the social value attached to the plaintiff's use or enjoyment, the suitability of the use in the character of the locality, and the burden on the plaintiff forced to avoid the harm. In regard to the character of the locality, courts look to whether the plaintiff **came to the nuisance** as one of the factors considered (though it is only one factor and not determinative). In evaluating the **social utility of the defendant's conduct**, courts consider the social value the law attaches to the defendant's conduct, and the suitability of the defendant's activities or property condition to the character of the general locality. Zoning ordinances may help ascertain the suitability of the location for the defendant's and the plaintiff's uses, but zoning status is only one factor and not determinative.

Example: O and her neighbors live nearby a Brick Kiln. Kiln emits a fine red powder that coats their homes and lawns. If the Kiln is liable in nuisance, what consequences flow from an injunction given to O *et al* to force abatement of the nuisance? An injunction in this situation would give the Kiln a strong incentive to buy the emissions right needed to continue its operations. If the injunction did not issue, O and neighbors would have to buy a right to clean(er) air from the Kiln. But should the rights involved be awarded to those who put the highest value on them? Or should they be given to those who would buy either of them anyway (the law thus saving the parties the trouble of bargaining)? With its multi-factor approach, nuisance law seems to put its emphasis on answering the last question first, and then, if the parties wish to bargain further, they can do so—but with the knowledge that one party has the right to an injunction, or not. This is not a level playing field—but was it that to start?

INJUNCTIONS AND DAMAGES

As to remedies for a private nuisance, some courts hold that once a private nuisance is found by **balancing the utilities**, the plaintiff is entitled to an **injunction**. Probably most courts today would engage in a second, more critical **balancing of the equities** during the remedy phase to determine the appropriate relief. An injunction seems appropriate if the harm to the plaintiff outweighs the social utility of defendant's conduct, where the defendant can avoid the harm without undue hardship, or where the plaintiff's conduct is suited to the locale and the defendant's activity is not. While some courts will grant injunctive relief only, the vast majority will grant damages, sometimes in addition to injunctive relief, and sometimes in lieu of it. "In lieu" damages may seem appropriate where the defendant provides significant social utility and cannot prevent the nuisance. In many jurisdictions, a defendant can escape an injunction only if the social utility of the defendant's primary activity benefits the public at large rather than merely benefitting the defendant personally (this is known as the **rule of necessity**).

Nuisance remedies can also involve both injunctions and damages. A court might give the plaintiff an injunction continuing until the defendant pays the plaintiff's damage claim, or might give the plaintiff damages, but hold that if the nuisance worsens, an injunction will issue. A court's options needn't be just an injunction/no injunction choice.

LIGHT AND AIR

No American jurisdiction accepts the English **doctrine of ancient lights**. English landowners could by the passage of time, obtain rights to the free flow of light and air over their property. In the United States, no such rights in the enjoyment of light and air are available, no matter how long continued.

463

However, a structure placed solely to deprive an owner of light and air may be actionable as a **spite fence**. Such a fence need only interfere with light and air to qualify as a private nuisance in most all jurisdictions. Otherwise, a landowner may build anywhere on his property so long as the location is consistent with public land use regulations, regardless of the impact of the building on the light, air, or view previously enjoyed by neighbors: Only a structure built solely out of malice can convert a lawful act into a nuisance.

Example: Tenants and property owners in nearby high-rise buildings bring suit in nuisance to enjoin the construction of a skyscraper that would interfere with their radio and TV reception. For this purpose, the surrounding airspace is like a public highway and there is no right to exclude the defendant's encroachment on it. Judgment for the owner of the skyscraper.

LATERAL SUPPORT AND SUBJACENT SUPPORT

Related to private nuisance because it relates to rights and obligations between owners of neighboring property, is the landowner's right to **lateral and subjacent support**, and the concomitant obligation not to do any act that causes neighboring lands to subside or move. The right to have one's land supported to the side and from below is often referred to as a natural right, meaning that it will be strictly enforced.[1] A landowner in hilly terrain cannot remove so much dirt on his land that the uphill land shifts, subsides, or gives way. A landowner can remove soil from his property but not so much or so near his property line that it changes his neighbor's land. Likewise, the owner of underground minerals may not mine them in such a manner as to cause the surface of over-lying lands to subside.

The rights and obligations relating to lateral support vary depending on whether the supported land is in its natural state or if structures or other improvements have been built on the supported land. The owner excavating or changing his land so as to cause a shift of the soil of the supported land is strictly liable for damage caused by removing the lateral support if the supported land is in its natural condition, and is liable for damages to improvements on the supported land if his excavation would have caused the supported land in its natural condition to shift or move.

If the supported land has been improved such that the land needs support greater than if the supported land was in its natural state, the supporting land owner's standard of care changes from a strict or absolute

---

1. That is, a rule of strict liability is used (though damages are not presumed to follow every violation of the right).

liability to one based on negligence. The standard of care to which an excavator is held anticipates the excavator considering the effect the excavation has on neighboring property. If the excavating landowner can or should foresee that an excavation will cause the soil to shift or subside, his removing the soil will be negligent. If, however, the excavation benefits the supporting land, the landowner must use accepted engineering methods of excavation, must give notice to the supported land owners, and must allow the supported land owners sufficient time to take steps to prevent harm to their land and improvements. It is a defense to a negligence claim that the owner of the supporting land gave sufficient notice and time to the owner of the supported land, and the owner of the supported land did not shore up his land.

In contrast to lateral support rights and obligations, which relate to the removal or changing of soil on the supporting property, the rights and obligations related to **subjacent support** involve actions that may cause the land surface to subside. Two variations of subjacent support cases can be found. In the first, the owner of a mineral interest can be liable to the surface owner if the mineral owner in extracting the mineral removes the subsurface support resulting in the subsidence of the surface land. The second variation occurs when pumping water from one parcel of land leads to the subsidence of neighboring land.

Water flows underground (a/k/a groundwater) are similar to those above ground. It is either in an underground reservoir or watercourse, or is **percolating water**, seeping through the soil or sub-strata and flowing toward areas of low pressure. If enough groundwater flows from one area to another, the underground strata will collapse and the surface subside. Under the traditional or English Rule, a landowner owns all the percolating groundwater he can capture or pump from the ground. Under this rule of capture, the landowner can remove any amount of water for any purpose without regard to the effect on neighboring land.

Most American jurisdictions reject the English Rule and substitute one of several approaches. One approach, called the American Rule, limits the landowner to removing only so much water as can be used to reasonably benefit the landowner's above ground property. Another approach views the percolating water as jointly owned by all the surface owners. A landowner can take out only his correlative share, having due regard for the needs of the other owners. Under a third approach, landowners can withdraw water as long as the removal does not affect other landowners' beneficial use of the water. Under these approaches, as long as the landowner does not exceed the amount of water he legally can remove from his sub-strata and does not act maliciously or waste the water, he is not liable for the subsidence of neighboring land. A fourth approach is to apply a negligence standard that addresses the subsidence issue directly, holding that a landowner is negligent, and hence liable, if he withdraws water in a manner that negligently damages or destroys land of others. In some western states a landowner whose removal of water from under his land causes his neighbor's land to subside is strictly liable for any damages to his neighbor's property.

Examples

1. Five plaintiffs and the defendant, Sam, live in a semirural area with homes in close proximity. The closest of any plaintiffs' home to Sam's is 50 yards. Plaintiffs already lived in the area when Sam moved in. Two years ago Sam built a dog kennel for his 16 Australian Shepherd show dogs. The dogs stayed penned outdoors during the daytime. Sam moved them indoors each evening, and the dogs remained inside the kennel all night. The dogs barked all night and much of the day. Plaintiffs could not sleep, perform yard work, or enjoy their porches or yards because of the dogs' constant barking. The plaintiffs became sleep-deprived, easily annoyed, irritable, and physically run-down. Sam says the dogs never woke him. The five plaintiffs brought a private nuisance action. What result?

2. Sid and Rob are neighbors, sharing a back property line. A six-foot-high solid adobe wall separates the two lots. Sid built a one-basket basketball court in his backyard 60 feet from the back property line. Rob's house is ten feet from the back property line. His spouse was pregnant and became nervous when she heard Sid or Sid's son, Jonathan, playing basketball. In addition, their weekend basketball games, lasting between 5 and 30 minutes, interrupted Rob's naps. Since the court was not lighted, the games were only played during the daylight. Rob complained to Sid about the noise. Sid poured additional concrete into the hollow pole supporting the backboard and added several inches of foam rubber and plywood behind the backboard to deaden its sound. The noise still annoyed Rob. Twice, to abate the noise, Rob sprayed the basketball court with water while Sid and Jonathan were playing. Rob also hired an acoustic engineer, who concluded the noise was below the municipal code maximum noise level, but that the noise could exceed the maximum noise level if more people played. Rob's spouse could hear the noise in her bedroom if the window was open. Closing the window substantially reduced the noise. Rob, extremely distressed and frustrated because Sid continued playing basketball, brought a private nuisance action to halt Sid's basketball games. What result?

3. The Carpenters and five of their neighbors brought a private nuisance action against Sunnyland Feedlot, a feedlot that services approximately 9,000 head of cattle daily. Plaintiffs allege the manure, pollution of river and groundwater, odor, pest infestation, increased concentration of

birds, dust, and noise caused by the feedlot constitute a private nuisance. The state's economy depends largely on agriculture. What result?

4. Airport leased property in the northwest quadrant of the airport to Sna-fuel, an operator of a fuel storage facility servicing the airport. Snafuel built three 300,000-gallon above-ground fuel storage tanks on the leased premises. Studies indicated the tanks present a severe and unnecessary risk of a potential disaster. Federal regulations stipulated the tanks should have been placed underground. Office Park is located on the northwest border of Airport, about 100 feet from the three fuel storage tanks. Office Park tenants fear that, in the case of an explosion, they and their property will be burned to a crisp. They also worry their insurance premiums will become unaffordable. Office Park also contends its proximity to the fuel storage tanks has decreased the property's market value. Office Park, for itself and its tenants, brings an action alleging a private nuisance. What result?

5. Landowner conveyed all the coal, minerals, oil, gases, iron ore, and stone to Coal Company. Two years later Landowner conveyed the property to New Owner, excepting the rights transferred to Company. Company wrote New Owner that Company planned to strip mine the coal (strip mining destroys the land surface). New Owner brought an action to prevent Coal Company from strip mining the coal. What result?

6. Quarry Company has operated a stone quarry for 40 years on a 100-acre parcel of land adjoining Farmer's land. The quarry covers the entire 100 acres and is about 80 feet deep. Water seeps into the quarry. To mine the quarry, Company must continually pump water from the quarry. Company has drained so much water from its pits that the water table beneath Farmer's land has dropped and the water support for the clay under Farmer's land has been destroyed, resulting in a series of sink holes up to 10 feet deep and 30 feet wide on Farmer's land. Farmer brought an action against Quarry Company for damages to his land. What result?

Explanations

1. Plaintiffs will win. A private nuisance is a condition on defendant's land that substantially and unreasonably interferes with the plaintiff's use and enjoyment of the plaintiff's property. Generally, there must be some invasion. Here that invasion was noise — 16 dogs' barking. The interference was substantial: a normal person of the community would regard the noise as seriously annoying or intolerable. Sam's hobby is raising the show dogs. The harms to the plaintiffs are serious disruption of sleep and social activities, and some physical and mental stress and anxiety. The balancing result is that the condition, the dogs'

barking, constitutes an unreasonable interference with the use and enjoyment of the neighboring property. A 16-dog kennel is ill suited to the locality. An injunction will issue limiting Sam to a reasonable number of dogs—say two.

2. Sid prevails. The most that can be said for Rob is that noise invaded his property. Some doubt exists whether the noise substantially interfered with Rob's use of his property. Mr. and Mrs. Rob's statements that they lost sleep and suffered emotional distress sound like the noise was substantial to them, but it is doubtful persons of normal sensibilities would have been disturbed by Sid's basketball playing. Reasonable people realize that complete emotional tranquility is seldom attainable: There are few if any places where a person may possess his property free of all interference, and transitory emotional distress is the natural result of many interferences, so an interference must be substantial to be found a private nuisance. A reasonable person probably would not find the noise to be substantial. Even if the "substantiality" factor is conceded, however, here Sid's conduct does not appear unreasonable. Basketball is good exercise and furthers family cohesion as long as Sid plays alone or with his son. Sid made changes to soften the sound of the backboard, but the noise was not greater than expected for reasonable use and was below the municipal code noise level maximums. Play occurred during the daylight hours when such noise normally occurs. Rob, moreover, could eliminate much of the noise simply by closing his windows. On balance, Sid's basketball playing was not an unreasonable interference with Rob's use and enjoyment of his property.

3. The issue here is what to do when the social utility of defendant's conduct outweighs the harm to the individual plaintiffs. Here the feedlot certainly interferes substantially with the plaintiffs' use and enjoyment of their property. The harder question is whether the interference is an unreasonable one. Under the Restatement, a court would balance the social utility of the feedlot against the harm to the plaintiffs. If the court determines that the social utility of the feedlot, as an essential activity in the local economy, outweighs the harm it causes, this determination might end the case, and the feedlot as a matter of law would not be a private nuisance, no injunction would issue, and no damages would be awarded. Here the feedlot would likely be determined to be a critical component of the jurisdiction's economy, requiring some of its citizens to suffer some inconveniences so that all the people in the long run are better off. However, the Restatement envisions a situation where an injunction may not be appropriate, but where damages would be in order if the harm to plaintiffs' use and enjoyment was severe and greater than the plaintiffs should bear without compensation, or if the harm was serious and the defendant's paying damages would not make the

defendant's activities infeasible. If either of these two situations fits the facts, Sunnyland Feedlot should pay the plaintiffs' damages. Otherwise the feedlot could "externalize" the cost onto its unfortunate neighbors.

A few jurisdictions would find for the plaintiffs by looking exclusively to the interference with the plaintiffs' use and enjoyment of their land: Their courts would order Sunnyland Feedlot to cease the activities constituting the private nuisance — the feedlot in the Example — due to the interference with plaintiffs' use and enjoyment of their properties. The injunction issues, end of matter. Any other response would give the defendant a private right of eminent domain or an easement over neighboring property. The injunction returns the parties to a non-nuisance status. The parties are then free to contract to resolve the issue amongst themselves: If they cannot agree, the feedlot must close. In most jurisdictions today, however, a court would balance the equities to determine if an injunction or damages or both is the most equitable remedy. The facts in the Example do not develop the nature of the surrounding locale: Residences may be moving toward the feedlot; so that at some later point in time the feedlot will become a private nuisance and thus be forced to relocate.

4. The result depends on whether the jurisdiction recognizes an action for private nuisance when interference or invasion of the plaintiffs' property has not yet occurred. Some jurisdictions hold that a private nuisance action cannot be maintained for an interference with the use and enjoyment of land caused solely by the fear of a future injury. This rule is used when, as here, an alternative option is to enforce federal regulations. Other jurisdictions do not require an invasion as an essential element of a private nuisance: All that is required is a condition on the defendant's land that unreasonably interferes with the plaintiff's use and enjoyment of its land. So stored explosives or above-ground fuel storage tanks could be the grounds for a private nuisance action. Conditions that constitute a similar private nuisance have been houses of prostitution, crack houses, and funeral homes. Even these jurisdictions, however, may not find the interference here to be "substantial" if the parties merely fear for their lives and property. It is only when that fear is reflected in the decline in the property's fair market value that many of these jurisdictions conclude the interference would be considered substantial to the normal person in the community. Assuming the tanks are a private nuisance, a court would issue an injunction only against the use of the above-ground fuel tanks. The airport itself could continue and underground tanks would be allowed as more suited to the locale.

5. New Owner as the surface owner has a right of continued subjacent support, and Coal Company as the owner of a mineral estate and miner of the minerals has an obligation not to remove or destroy that

support. New Owner prevails since Coal Company by strip mining would destroy the surface and its subjacent support. The parties can contract to allow Coal Company to strip mine but it is not an inherent right of ownership of the coal or other minerals.

6. The result depends on the jurisdiction. Jurisdictions focusing on a landowner's right to withdraw water, such as those states employing the English Rule (not many states) or the American Rule, allowing a landowner to remove as much water as it needs to reasonably benefit the use of the land, would hold Quarry Company is not liable for the damages to Farmer's land. Other jurisdictions hold a landowner strictly liable for causing harm to neighboring land by removing the subjacent support and would find Quarry Company liable for damages to Farmer's land. Those states adopting a nuisance standard likely would find Quarry Company liable to Farmer.

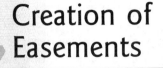

Creation of Easements

CHAPTER 27

INTRODUCTION

An *easement* is a nonpossessory interest one person has in the property that another person possesses. It is a right to use another's land for a specific purpose. The Restatement of Property § 450 (1944) offers the following definition:

> An easement is an interest in land in the possession of another which (a) entitles the owner of such interest to a limited use or enjoyment of the land in which the interest exists; (b) entitles him to protection as against third persons from interference in such use or enjoyment; (c) is not subject to the will of the possessor of the land; (d) is not a normal incident of the possession of any land possessed by the owner of the interest; and (e) is capable of creation by conveyance.

Example: O owns Blackacre. She records a deed with herself naming herself the grantee of an easement for a road over Blackacre (from an adjacent property that she also owns). Is the easement valid? No, one cannot create an easement in one's own property.

The most frequently encountered easements give the holder a right to travel over another's land, or a right to place utility lines, sewer lines, pipelines, or railroad tracks across another's property, but easements may be used for many other purposes. The easement holder and the landowner both may use the same area of land, but the landowner's use may not unreasonably interfere with the easement holder's use of the easement for its intended purposes.

In a deed granting a strip of land for a "right-of-way," it is unclear whether the interest granted is an easement, a fee simple absolute, or a fee simple determinable. This issue often becomes a matter of dispute when its user (say a railroad) abandons it and plans to sell the strip (or many adjoining strips) to a third party, or a valuable mineral is found under the strip. In drafting easement deeds, the prudent attorney should clearly identify easements as such.

Example: O deeds a "strip for right of way" over Whiteacre to E and E1, both adjacent neighbors of O. Is the easement valid? Possibly. No particular words of art are necessary to create an easement: indeed, the word "easement" needn't be used. Any words showing an intention to create an easement will suffice. Here the last three words express an intent to limit the first. Further, the common law says that "easements lie in grant," meaning that a deed must be used.[1] Moreover, that the easement is intended to benefit more than one party (here E and E1) is no bar to its validity. Easements often benefit more than one piece of property. Finally, a phrase like "strip," without further explanation, will usually not expand an easement into fee simple absolute ownership of the strip. Instead, it suggests that the easement itself is to be held in fee.

TERMINOLOGY

An easement may be an **easement in gross** (or personal easement) or an **easement appurtenant.** An **easement in gross** benefits a person, while an **easement appurtenant** benefits the owner or possessor of a particular parcel of land. The easement appurtenant is implicitly conveyed with the property it benefits, whether or not the conveyance expressly mentions the matter; it has the potential to continue indefinitely. An easement in gross, on the other hand, unless assignable, ends at its holder's death.

Example: O deeds to his next-door neighbor, E, the right to park in his parking lot. E has an easement. E sells her home to P and moves to a house five miles away. The easement is an **easement in gross** if, under the terms of the

---

1. Why must easements be written? Because they are nonpossessory interests and cannot be conveyed (thought common law judges) orally and have the conveyance be clear at the outset. They'd be a litigation-breeder otherwise. Being interest in land, today easement deeds (a/k/a express easements) must satisfy the Statute of Frauds and, to provide their holders with protection against bona fide purchasers, must also be recorded.

deed from O to E, E can continue parking in O's lot after she sells her home to P. On the other hand, the easement is an ***easement appurtenant*** (benefitting P as the current owner of the home) if the deed provided that any new owner of the house succeeded to the right to park in O's parking lot. The easement will not be interpreted to benefit both E and P.

In deciding whether an easement is an easement in gross or appurtenant, courts have a constructional preference for the easement appurtenant, which means an easement in gross must be clear from the express grant or from surrounding circumstances. Why this preference? First, it serves to prevent obsolete in gross easements from having only a dog-in-the-manger, nuisance value and, second, to make sure that the dominant estate's owner is around to bargain over changes needed in the use of the servient estate.

Property burdened by the easement is called the ***servient estate*** or ***servient tenement.*** The land benefitted by the easement is the ***dominant estate*** or ***tenement.***[2] Though the law speaks of benefitted and burdened property, it is the owners of the properties whose uses are actually benefitted or burdened. In the previous Example, O's land was the servient estate, and the E-P property was the dominant estate. The term "servient estate" describes the burdened property for both easements appurtenant and easements in gross. The term "dominant estate" is used only when discussing easements appurtenant. An easement in gross has no dominant estate. Why? Because an easement in gross benefits a specific person and not the owner of a particular property.

Example: O deeds an easement over Blackacre to E, the owner of adjacent Whiteacre. E rents Whiteacre to T. Does T have the right to enforce the use given in the deed? Yes, because it is the holder of the benefit of the easement that has standing to enforce its terms.

Example: Suppose E, the owner of Blackacre, the dominant estate, buys adjacent land and attempts to use his otherwise valid easement for the benefit of his newly acquired land. Can he? No. Once the dominant estate has been identified in the easement deed, it has been identified for all time. This type of deed, like any other deed, is interpreted at the time of its execution and delivery. So the dominant estate cannot be enlarged thereafter. This is why it is necessary and prudent for the deed to identify the dominant estate with precision — and the servient estate too, for that matter.

---

2. Thus an easement appurtenant is one that is useful to, enhances the enjoyment of, or is a useful adjunct to the dominant estate. It is (again) not necessary that the easement deed contain the word "appurtenant" (though that would be prudent on its drafter's part) so long as the intent of the grantor is clear.

A final bit of terminology for easements distinguishes affirmative or positive easements from negative easements. **Affirmative easements** give the holder the right to go onto the servient estate for a specific purpose. E, in the prior Examples, has an affirmative easement to use or park on O's property.

Example: E has a right of way through a building on O's adjacent land. O demolishes the building and builds a more up-to-date one in the same location. Does E's affirmative easement survive the demolition of the building on the servient estate? If the easement is appurtenant to the land, not the structure, E's easement survives. Otherwise the servient estate has been destroyed, and with it the easement. Thus when such an easement is created, defining the servient estate is all the more important. Because O's right to redevelop his land is a crucial right, absent a clear indication of a contrary intent, the servient estate is destroyed.

A **negative easement** gives the holder the right to prevent the possessor of the servient estate from doing some act on the servient estate. English courts recognized only four negative easements: (1) rights pertaining to light (duty not to block light or the easement holder's windows), (2) airflow (duty not to interfere with airflow), (3) water channels (duty not to interfere with water flow in artificial streams on the dominant estate), and (4) lateral support (duty not to remove support from a house on the dominant estate). All of them were easements appurtenant.[3] American courts have refused to recognize easements for light and air not expressly bargained for or deeded, have accepted the one for water channels if the dominant estate had a water-wheel on it, and called the right to lateral support (as discussed in the previous Chapter) a natural right rather than an easement. They have also recognized view easements (duty not to block view), solar easements (to protect access to solar energy), and conservation easements (usually given to a government or charity to protect or maintain open, historic, or scenic areas). They are reluctant to recognize still other negative easements because they impinge on the fee ownership of the servient estate and should be expressly bargained for in the most precise terms if they are to result in the efficient use of both estates.

Because negative easements are not an observable use of the servient estate, their nature and scope must be precisely defined in the deed creating them. Thus, a landowner needing air flow for a windmill or to cool her house cannot object to a neighbor's new wall or building just because it blocks the flow. Only if the neighbor or one of the neighbor's predecessors deeded the landowner or one of the landowner's predecessors a negative easement will the landowner have an enforceable right.

---

3. Great Britain had no recording acts when these four were recognized, so an easement in gross would have created problems of disclosure that the common law sought to avoid.

Example: O promises not to permit trees on his property to grow more than 30 feet tall in order to preserve the view that E has over O's land. Is this easement an affirmative or negative one? It is negative if O will do the tree trimming involved, but if E is permitted to enter O's land to trim the trees, it is affirmative. Is this easement otherwise valid? Not in all states. Not because of its subject matter, but because words of promise, contractual language, and not words of conveyance, are used. In some jurisdictions, because easements "lie in grant," words of conveyance must be used.

Example: In the previous Example, the promise is made on a document formatted like a deed, and O and E are referred to as grantor and grantee respectively, but the verbs in the granting clause are still those of promise. Is the easement valid in all jurisdictions? Probably. This certainly would be the case if the words of promise were used in the *habendum* of the deed, but words of conveyance were used in the granting clause. Why? Because the latter controls the former if there is a conflict between them. So beware of possible conflicts between rules stating easements "lie in grant" and "no words of art are necessary to create an easement."

OTHER NONPOSSESSORY INTERESTS

Besides easements, there are two other nonpossessory interests a person may have in another's land. One is a **profit a prendre** or "profit." It is the right to enter another's land, without liability for trespass, and remove minerals, timber, or other natural resources constituting a natural part of the land. It might give a right to hunt, fish, or remove topsoil from the land. A person with a profits interest has an easement to venture onto the property as necessary to enjoy the profits interest. Thus easements are sometimes described as a use right without a profit.

When a landowner permits another person to use his property, but the permission is revocable or terminable at the landowner's will, the user has a **license.** A person invited to swim in his neighbor's pool has a license. Tickets to see a movie, concert, or sporting event often are characterized as licenses, as are many short-term parking arrangements. A license needs no writing or consideration, can be implied, usually from conduct or custom, and so long as the user stays within its terms, the license gives its user immunity from a suit in trespass. Indeed, some definitions of a license consider this immunity the essence of a license, along with its revocability.

Some jurisdictions do not consider a license to be an interest in land. Others call a license a revocable, nonpossessory interest in land. Described either way, it remains revocable at will. However, licenses can become irrevocable through the doctrine of estoppel, and so become indistinguishable from easements.

An express easement that fails for some technical reason (e.g., it does not satisfy the Statute of Frauds) becomes a license.

Example: L gives O $1,000 for a license giving L the right to cut timber on Blackacre. Does the money turn O's right into an easement? No. O's permission is still just that, permission. What if L assigns his right to timber Blackacre to A? The traditional rule was that the assignment automatically revokes the license. Today in a majority of states the assignment would just be a nullity. However, if the license were for commercial purposes, it would be assignable in some jurisdictions.

Example: O leases Greenacre to T for the sole purpose of T's timbering the property. Why would T prefer this arrangement to a profit? A lease is a possessory interest in land. A license is nonpossessory. Moreover, a lease is an exclusive right to use the land for the term of the lease. A license is not an exclusive right unless expressly made so. Thus, using a lease, T is assured that he will have no other lumbermen competing with him and that he has the full term of the lease to complete the job.

EXPRESSLY GRANTED OR RESERVED EASEMENTS

Most express easements result from an **express grant** or **express reservation** in a deed. Express grants usually are created by deed: The grantor often sells only part of her property and grants the purchaser an easement over the seller's retained land. Then the grantee owns the dominant estate and the grantor retains the servient estate.

Conversely, if the grantor was to have an easement over the grantee's land, the deed likely would incorporate a clause **reserving** an easement or **excepting** an easement. At one time, in some jurisdictions, which word chosen ("reserve" or "except") was key to whether the deed created an easement in favor of the grantor at all. A reservation created an easement; an exception did not. The theory was that a **reservation** was a grant of the property to a purchaser and a regrant of the easement back to the original grantor. An **exception**, in contrast, was merely a statement the property might be "subject to an easement." The proof the outstanding easement existed could only then be found in another, independent, pre-existing deed. Because most people, including lawyers and judges, are unaware of this distinction, and after a while used the terms concurrently and interchangeably, today the two terms are synonymous.

Example: *A* sells Blackacre to B, reserving in the deed an easement for parking automobiles on Blackacre for *A*'s neighbor N. Is the easement valid? No. Not in most jurisdictions. An easement or interest in land may not be reserved in favor of a third person (that is, a person neither the grantor nor grantee to the deed). This rule is known as the "stranger to the deed" rule.[4]

While enforcing an easement reserved to a third party seems sensible, a large majority of jurisdictions still follow this rule. While sometimes acknowledging that the rule forbidding a reservation to a stranger is counterintuitive[5] and a "vestige of feudalism," the majority of courts retain the old rule because, as explained by one court, "Where it can reasonably be assumed that settled rules are necessary and necessarily relied upon, stability and adherence to precedent are generally more important than a better or even a 'correct' rule of law." Estate of Thomson v. Wade, 509 N.E.2d 309 (N.Y. 1987). There are several further rationales for this rule. (1) Having three parties to a deed may give title searchers and the recorder of deed fits when the public records are maintained using grantor and grantee indices. (2) The stranger has no interest in the land from which the easement is carved, so who knows if he wants it, can use it, or that it results in the efficient use of the property involved? (3) Reserving an easement contravenes the rule that easements "lie in grant." (4) The dominant estate may prove difficult to define. A few states, such as California and Montana, will enforce a reservation to a stranger to the deed if the deed clearly identifies the third party, the deed specifically locates the easement on the servient estate, the grantors testify that they intended to create the easement, and the price paid was less than if the easement had not been reserved.

However, in Willard v. First Church of Christ, Scientist, 498 P.2d 987 (Cal. 1972), a landowner sold property on the condition a church located across the street would have an easement to park on the transferred property. The court interpreted the deed transferring the property as reserving a parking easement to the church. One of the issues in the case was whether a grantor can reserve an interest (here an easement) to a "stranger to the deed" (here the church). The grantor's intent clearly was that she wanted the church to have the easement. A primary rule of construction is to ascertain and carry out the grantor's intent. The grantor's intent controlled: The church got its parking easement. This case is typical of about ten jurisdictions rejecting the stranger to the deed rule: The minority "welcome stranger" rule uses one document instead of two, it's cheaper, and it carries out the grantor's intent.

---

4. Note that the rule is applicable to easements and *interests* in land. It might also be used when the reservation in a deed is in favor of a third person's life estate.

5. Counterintuitive? Yes. Aren't remainders, executory interests, and other types of future interests all typically created in favor of third persons?

EASEMENTS BY ESTOPPEL AND IRREVOCABLE LICENSES

Express easements may prove ineffective because a document does not qualify as a writing under the Statute of Frauds or because the parties may never have reduced it to writing in the first place. When the owner of the servient estate otherwise authorizes the owner of the dominant estate to use the burdened property for a specific purpose, a license has in effect been created, the putative grantee receiving a license. As previously discussed, a license is revocable at will, but to be more specific, the license is revocable at will *at law*. However, a court of equity will in some situations enforce the license as either an ***easement by estoppel*** or an ***irrevocable license***. No matter the name, three elements must be present: (1) the owner of the servient estate consents to the dominant estate holder's use of the servient estate; (2) the servient estate owner knows or should know the dominant estate owner will materially change his position, believing the permissive use will not be revoked; and (3) the dominant estate holder, reasonably believing the permission will continue, substantially changes his position by investing in improvements on either the servient or the dominant estate.

The dominant owner's reliance must be justifiable. Most jurisdictions refuse to find an easement by estoppel if its claimant should have verified the fact represented before relying on it.

With these elements met, courts conclude that under the facts, the servient estate holder cannot deny the existence of the easement. Broadly applied, an easement by estoppel will result when a person uses another's land and a court finds that person will be inconvenienced if stopped. Saying that they disfavor easements by estoppel, courts choose different ways to rein in their use: (1) Some courts require the servient estate owner's representation specifically be that an easement exists. One jurisdiction requires that the initial entry be expressly permitted. In these jurisdictions, mere permission to use property will not ripen into an easement, even if the claimant materially changes his position on the expectation his right to use the property would continue. (Others extend the easement by estoppel theory to all representations of fact. In some of these, even silence may be the basis for an easement by estoppel.) (2) Another group of jurisdictions permit estoppel only when the speaker intended that the claimant act in reliance on the statement. (3) Still other jurisdictions require that the servient estate's owner benefit in some way from the dominant owner's reliance investments. (4) Still others permit estoppel only if the representation occurred in a purchase and sale of property.

Example: S sells Blackacre to B, saying nothing about T's right to use Blackacre to hunt and fish. B is otherwise a bona fide purchaser of Blackacre.

Does B take its title subject to T's right? Yes, if the right is an easement by estoppel, no if it is an irrevocable license.

The character of the transaction and the relationship between the parties are critical factors in determining whether an easement by estoppel exists. Purchasers from a developer, who buy after seeing a plat or a brochure purporting to show streets in the subdivision, often gain an easement by estoppel to use the depicted roads. When evaluating actions between neighbors, courts more willingly enforce informal agreements as easements by estoppel if the claimant made a long continued use of the claimed easement and spent money to improve, repair, or maintain the claimed easement. Overall, courts in most jurisdictions evaluate the facts and find an easement by estoppel where they feel the claimant acted in good faith on the servient estate owner's words or actions, and the servient estate owner's words or actions are such that he rather than the claimant should bear the consequences of any confusion.

A few jurisdictions, adhering to the rule that an express easement must be in writing to satisfy the Statute of Frauds, refuse to recognize the *easement* by estoppel. They recharacterize whatever writing they have as the grant of an *irrevocable license* — which, as a practical matter, is the same as an easement by estoppel, though recognized in a way that preserves the integrity of the Statute of Frauds.

Example: O owns Blackacre. R has a right of first refusal to purchase Blackacre when O offers it for sale. O grants L an irrevocable license to use Blackacre for hunting and fishing. R insists on exercising his right of first refusal. May he do so, purchasing free of L's rights? The answer is no if the irrevocable license is an easement by estoppel, but yes if it is a license. The former is an interest in land, the latter is not.

Some jurisdictions prefer a third theory, based on the part performance exception to the Statute of Frauds. It excuses the dominant estate owner from complying with the Statute, but it still permits the court to craft the easement as if there had been a writing.

No matter which theory is used, the easement or irrevocable license becomes irrevocable, although how long it becomes irrevocable is subject to dispute. Some courts hold that once the easement or irrevocable license is conceded, it continues as long as would any express easement — i.e., potentially forever. Other courts allow it a more limited life, allowing it to continue "for its natural life" or "to the extent necessary" for the dominant estate holder to amortize his expenditures. This last approach leaves open issues as to how future repairs and improvements affect the duration of the easement, and how to measure when a dominant tenement owner has amortized his expenditures. Amortization might be measured, for instance, by either the fair market value of the investment or its replacement cost, and cover either the period that it takes the original improvement to become unuseable or the period that the parties might reasonably expect.

A final, fundamental issue is whether courts should permit easements by estoppel at all. How can reliance on a revocable interest be reasonable? Once the parties intend a license, no unilateral change by either party should make it anything else. Moreover, recognition tempts licensees to enlarge their interests and creates an unwritten exception to the Statute of Frauds. Thus a few jurisdictions acknowledge neither the easement by estoppel nor the irrevocable license. The large majority, however, recognize its essential function: One party has so substantially changed his position in reasonable reliance on his neighbor's consent that it is unconscionable not to enforce the agreement. Recognition gives flexibility to the law, prevents the dominant owner from obtaining a windfall from the servient owner's investments, insures that the Statute of Frauds does not itself give rise to a fraud, and is consistent with general estoppel theory.

IMPLIED EASEMENTS

Implied or non-express easements are not favored, are strictly construed, but may be created under two sets of circumstances not involving a writing or bargain struck between the dominant and servient estate owners. These circumstances are well embedded in the law of easements. One involves a land transaction carving one parcel out of a larger property, and the second involves a particular transaction of the same type, but which leaves part of the larger property landlocked. Both are exceptions to the general rule that easements "lie in grant" and require a writing.

EASEMENTS IMPLIED FROM PRIOR USE

Easements implied from prior use — a/k/a quasi-easements[6] — arise when a use was in place at a time a single parcel of land was severed or divided into two adjoining parcels, leaving one parcel benefitting the other in some way, even though the seller and purchaser did not discuss or even think of it when

---

6. Why *quasi*-easement? Because no one can create an easement in his or her own property, it is improper to call them easements as such. So courts referred to the use on the unified parcel as a quasi-easement and to various parts of the pre-divided property as the quasi-dominant estate and the quasi-servient estate. This visualizes the situation existing before the common owner sold part of the land.

they bought and sold the land. This type of implied easement remedies this all-too-human oversight and permits courts to reach results reasonable parties would have reached had they discussed the matter, emphasizing the parties' likely intent at the time of severance (not at time of trial). The following Example's scenario is typical.

Example: O owned two adjoining lots. He sold one to Meg. A driveway and a sewer line ran from Meg's house to the street. After the sale, part of the driveway and part of the sewer line ran over (and under) O's lot. The deed conveying the lot to Meg did not mention the driveway or sewer line. Does Meg have a right to continue using the driveway or sewer line? Since the deed did not expressly give Meg an easement over O's land, Meg can continue the prior driveway and sewer uses only if all the elements of an easement implied from prior use are present.

All of the following elements must be present for an easement implied from prior use:

(1) The unity of ownership is severed;
(2) The use was in place before the severance;
(3) The use was visible or apparent at the time of severance; and
(4) The easement is necessary for the enjoyment of the dominant estate.

This type of implied easement is premised on one person owning the whole parcel of land when the pre-existing use was in place, hence the first, common ownership or **unity of ownership** element. The second element requires the use pre-date the severance, hence the **pre-existing or prior use** element: The common owner must have engaged in the use just before the severance occurred, no matter how long pre-existing. Some courts explain this second element further by stating that the pre-existing use be continuous and permanent, not temporary or casual, so that a reasonable person would expect the use to continue no matter who owned the property. The third element requires the pre-existing use be **visible** or **apparent** at the time of severance. Driveways, roads, and other quasi-easements on the surface easily satisfy this requirement. Potentially more difficult are underground sewers, water or utility lines. As to the last, visible or apparent means uses or conditions discoverable by a reasonable inspection. Thus a purchaser seeing an indoor toilet might reasonably assume that it is connected to a sewer line.

The fourth element — **necessity** — is the most complex. Jurisdictions may impose a different standard of necessity depending on whether the easement arose in an **implied grant** or an **implied reservation**. The degree of necessity will be less for an implied grant. Why? Because the grantee of the dominant estate can be excused for not knowing the location of a use on the adjoining parcel. The common owner who tries to reserve an implied easement, on the other hand, is not so easily excused since she had greater knowledge, plus she executed the deed transferring the property without reserving any easement.[7] So some jurisdictions set a **reasonable necessity** standard for an **implied grant**, but require **strict necessity** for an **implied reservation**. Most jurisdictions use reasonable necessity, no matter whether the easement arises by implied grant or reservation.

A common definition of reasonable necessity is "reasonably necessary for the fair enjoyment" of the dominant estate. Strict necessity, on the other hand, mandates a finding that the dominant estate owner cannot fairly enjoy the property without the easement. It must be absolutely necessary to that enjoyment. Most jurisdictions today subject both the grantor and the grantee to a standard of reasonable necessity. Influenced by the Restatement, Property, § 476 (1944), some jurisdictions also evaluate the totality of the facts to determine whether the parties would have intended the easement if they had thought of it at the time of severance: This means adding to the discussion thus far factors involving the consideration for the severance deed, the weighing of the benefits and burdens involved, and the extent to which the parties knew of the prior use.

> **Example:**   O owns Blackacre and Whiteacre, the latter benefitting from a drainage ditch originating on Whiteacre and proceeding across Blackacre. O sells Whiteacre to B, saying "make your own arrangements for draining Whiteacre. I don't want Blackacre burdened any longer by the ditch." B agrees, but later, investigating the matter, decides that the ditch is necessary for draining her land. Does B still have an easement implied from prior use? Arguing that she does, she might note that all of the elements are objective in nature. None are overtly intent-based. In response, O might point out that the whole basis for these elements is that they represent the inferred intent of the parties at the time of the severance, and assume that the parties did not negotiate, bargain, or otherwise indicate their intent to continue the prior use, or not. Implying a license might give the parties time to work this matter out.

EASEMENTS IMPLIED BY NECESSITY

The second category of implied easement is the **easement implied by necessity,** also known as a way of necessity. It is an easement implied for egress and ingress, establishing a right-of-way for landlocked property. Land-locking a property destroys so much of its use that the law, as a matter of either public policy or

---

7. This suggests an element of estoppel in a court's thinking about this matter.

implied contract, presumes that the parties to the landlocking transaction could not have intended *not* to include a right-of-way onto the land.

The elements for any easement implied by necessity are as follows:

(1) A common owner severed the property;
(2) The necessity for egress and ingress existed at the time of the severance; and
(3) Ingress and egress are strictly necessary for the landlocked parcel.

As with the easement implied from prior use, the easement implied by necessity requires there has been a common owner who must have conveyed part of the property to another person and in severing the property caused one of the parcels to become landlocked. The severance must cause the dominant estate to be landlocked.

Example: O carves a land-locked parcel out of a trackless wilderness parcel and conveys the parcel to E. How is E's way of necessity different from an easement implied from prior use? A way of necessity need not be in existence at the time it is created.

No easement will be implied by necessity unless the easement is **strictly necessary** for egress and ingress.

Example: The deed from O to E land-locking E's property provides for access to E's land that is narrow, steep, and very inconvenient for E to use. E later protests that she needs better access and asserts a way of necessity. In this situation there is no strict necessity for implying an easement. E must have no access in fact for a way of necessity to be implied.

Example: Suppose that the access in the deed in the prior Example is blocked several years after O delivered the deed to E. Would that matter? No, because strict necessity, like the other elements necessary to establish this easement, must exist when E's parcel is severed. E's remedy lies in trespass.

Example: Suppose that the O-to-E deed gave E a license to use the inconvenient right of way. A license (being revocable) is not access for the purpose of determining whether the easement is necessary.

The party seeking the easement (which can be either the grantor or the grantee) must show the easement is strictly necessary. Strictly necessary can mean absolutely necessary, but many courts interpret strict necessity to mean strictly necessary for the enjoyment of the property or invoke a standard of reasonable necessity. Courts in some jurisdictions, for example, may imply an easement by necessity even if a property has access over publically-owned navigable water. Easements by necessity will not be implied for mere convenience. Property that has access, but only by foot, by a roundabout route, or over a wide, deep ravine spanned at considerable expense, present cases about which outcome prediction is difficult.

This implied easement lasts only so long as the necessity (of whatever degree) lasts. Once a new road is built or a new way is available, the easement ends.

Example: A deed from O to E land-locks E's land, but at the time E has an alternate route off her property that is blocked years later after E has sold her property and its title has come into E1's hands. May E1 assert a way of necessity? Yes: any subsequent owner of E's land may do so and, when doing so, is not subject to a defense of laches or a statute of limitations. So long as the necessity (of whatever degree) would have been present at the delivery of the O-to-E deed, the way of necessity may lie dormant in a chain of title until needed.

A problem peculiar to easements by necessity is physically locating the easement on the servient estate. Generally, the servient estate owner has the first opportunity to locate the easement, having due regard for the dominant estate holder's situation. If the servient estate owner's location is unreasonable or the servient estate owner delays its location, the dominant estate holder has the right to locate the easement at some reasonable location, having due regard for the servient owner's use of the land. As with other easements, once an easement by necessity has been located, it can be moved only with the consent of both parties.

About 20 states have a statutory easement implied by necessity.

PRESCRIPTIVE EASEMENTS

A person can gain an **easement by prescription** by long-continued adverse use. The elements for an easement by prescription parallel in most respects those of adverse possession, substituting "use" for "possession": The use of the servient estate must be actual, open and notorious, hostile and adverse, continuous and uninterrupted, and (in a minority of jurisdictions) exclusive — each element being present for the statutory prescriptive period.

In addition to these six elements, at least one state requires color of title as an element of easement by prescription. Since this is definitely the minority view, color of title will be discussed under hostile use rather than on its own.

(1) *Actual use* demands a physical presence on the servient estate. No *negative* easements may be gained by prescription, only *affirmative* ones.

Thus a claimant cannot compel his neighbor to take down a fence, wall, or building because the claimant has an implied negative easement to light and air.

(2) *Open and notorious use* means the use must be so open and visible that the landowner will or should notice it. The landowner's actual knowledge suffices even if the use is not noticeable by anyone else. Absent actual notice, something observable on the claimed estate (such as a roadway, utility lines, or paths) gives constructive notice to the landowner. Likewise, the presence of a residence, a manhole cover, or valves and pipes, may provide notice of an underground utility, water, or pipeline. In contrast, a concealed or nighttime use does not satisfy this element.

Example: O asserts that his neighbor's development of property threatens O's 100 year old tree whose roots and limbs extend over their common boundary. Does O have a prescriptive easement for the roots and limbs? No. Roots are not an open and notorious use, and the limbs do not put the neighbor on notice of a claim for surface use.[8]

(3) *Hostile and adverse use*, sometimes known as a use by **claim of right**, means the claimant uses another's property without regard to the owner's rights and without permission. No personal hostility is required. A person who receives permission from the servient owner to be on the property cannot gain an easement by prescription, no matter how long the claimant uses the property. A person who enters pursuant to a defective deed enters by claim of right, for example, and not by permission. His use is hostile and adverse. On the other hand, the existence of a gate or similar obstruction is evidence of a permissive use on servient land: They notify strangers that their use of the servient estate is by permission.

Acquiescence or tolerance of the use by the servient owner is not permission. The claimant's use remains hostile. For hostility to be destroyed once it begins, the claimant must renounce his claim of right or concede he uses the land by permission. Oral or written consent given after the use began may or may not constitute permission, depending on how the claimant reacts. A claimant who concedes he is a wrongdoer or trespasser and agrees, preferably in writing, that he will continue the use only as a licensee is no longer hostile. He cannot change his mind later. The claimant who either denies he needed permission or remains noncommittal in the face of the landowner's attempt to consent remains hostile.

---

8. Likewise, a claim for an easement implied from prior use would also fail.

Possession that began as permissive use can become adverse use if the claimant acts beyond the scope of the permitted use or otherwise has made a definite, identifiable assertion of greater rights than he originally received. The expanded claim must be so open and notorious, however, that it gives actual notice to the landowner. Gradual expansion will not qualify.

Courts often create rebuttable presumptions to determine whether a claimant's entry was permissive. Some jurisdictions presume that an open and notorious use is also hostile, and some presume that a continuous use is also hostile, unless the landowner can prove the entry was with permission. Other jurisdictions, noting that prescriptive easements are disfavored at law, refuse to make such presumptions and place a heavy burden of proof (to produce clear and convincing evidence) on the claimant as to all elements. This issue often arises in cases concerning a common driveway.

Example: Two neighbors jointly build a driveway along their mutual property line, part of the driveway on one lot and part on the other. The neighbors do not discuss whether any easement exists, much less put it in writing. Years later (after the statutory period has run), one neighbor will attempt to stop the joint use of the driveway. Courts that presume hostility will likely find that a prescriptive easement arose. Those courts that presume a permissive use will hold the use to be an easement by estoppel or a revocable license.

Many courts consider use by immediate family members (parents, children, brothers, and sisters) to be permissive unless evidence to the contrary is furnished. Similarly, evidence of a neighborly relationship is presumed permissive in some jurisdictions.

Courts in some jurisdictions will presume the use of unenclosed and unimproved property to be permissive unless the claimant affirmatively can prove hostility. The corollary in these jurisdictions is the use of enclosed, improved, or cultivated property will be presumed to be hostile, absent evidence to the contrary.

When a claimant has color of title — a defective deed or other writing, for example — that is evidence of hostility. It also shows when the prescriptive period started to run, and may also show the location and scope of the easement. (Color of title is not the same as claim of right or claim of title. See Chapter 8, supra.) Color of title is not an element for a prescriptive easement in any jurisdiction save one. This approach authorizes prescriptive easements only if the claimant asserts a right under color of title.

Some states also impose shorter statute of limitations periods for easements with color of title. This is consistent with similarly shorter periods afforded adverse possession actions with color of title. Recognizing an innate difference in character of use between prescriptive use and adverse possession, however, most states that have addressed the issue do not shorten the statutory period in a prescriptive easement case for someone holding under color of title, but this remains an open issue in many states.

(4) Continuous and uninterrupted use does not mean the claimant uses the easement all the time. It means only that the claimant's use has not been abandoned and is consistent with that of a reasonable easement holder's use. A prescriptive easement may, for example, be periodic or seasonal—the use of a logging road, a beach in the summer, or a fire escape down an abutting building. This element also requires that the servient owner not effectively interrupt the claimant's use. The interruption must be permanent, not just temporary or attempted. A successful ejectment or trespass action by the landowner destroys the continuity. A fence that interrupts the claimant's use of a road also will defeat the continuous use element. However, a servient owner's erecting a fence to block a roadway is not an interruption if the claimant removes the fence or installs a gate in the fence within a reasonable time. Finally, a claimant's changing the location of a claimed right of way may be interpreted as the abandonment of the road in the first location and the start of a new easement at the new location. If the claimant discontinues her own use of the road, the statute of limitations must begin running anew on the new location.

(5) Exclusive use is not a necessary element for a prescriptive easement claim in most jurisdictions. If it were, the concurrent use of the easement by the dominant and servient estate owner would prevent a prescriptive easement from arising in most situations. Most jurisdictions therefore omit the exclusivity element or else define exclusivity as requiring only use by the claimant.

A sizeable minority of jurisdictions impose an exclusive use element, but limit it in two ways. First, some require that the claimant's use be independent, distinguishable and unique from the use made by the general public. This interpretation makes it harder for a person to claim an easement in gross by prescription. Second, other jurisdictions require that the servient owner not use the property in a way that would prevent the claimant from enjoying the easement. A claimant's failure to meet this second requirement also defeats the continuous and uninterrupted use element. A few jurisdictions find no exclusive use if the claimant uses the claimed easement for the same purpose as the servient owner. A few even conclude a similar use of the land by the claimant and the landowner, especially as to a road, constitutes permissive and nonexclusive use, thus defeating the prescriptive easement claim.

(6) The **prescriptive period** is the time a claimant must use the property before a court will award an easement by prescription. Generally the time is the same as a jurisdiction's statute of limitations period for adverse possession.

Examples

1. Common Owner owned two adjoining parcels (Parcel A and Parcel B). Parcel A abutted Major Road. Parcel B bordered a river and a public timber road that meandered ten miles to a county road. Common Owner never used the timber road, preferring to cross Parcel A to Major Road. Four decades ago, Common Owner sold Parcel B to Chad. The deed to Chad did not grant Chad an easement over Parcel A. Five years later, Common Owner sold Parcel A to Dan, the deed to Dan "excepting and reserving to Chad, his heirs and assigns, a right-of-way located at [a description locating the roadway over Parcel A]" from Parcel B to Major Road. In the ensuing years, members of the public generally and the various owners of Parcel B used the right of way to get to and from Major Road. After several interim conveyances, Ed bought Parcel A. Last year Hilton bought Parcel B and built River Inn, a 50-room motel, on Parcel B. Ed sought to bar Hilton from using the right-of-way over his land to reach Major Road. All of these deeds were properly recorded. (a) What type of easement is Hilton claiming? If there is an easement, would Ed's land (Parcel A) be the dominant or servient estate? (b) Explain why your answer would change if Common Owner first conveyed Parcel B to Chad, then later deeded an easement to Chad, and still later deeded Parcel A to Dan? (c) Does Hilton have an easement by estoppel (or an irrevocable license)? An easement implied from prior use or by necessity? (d) Does Hilton have an easement by prescription? (e) What should Hilton do if a court rules he has no easement of any type over Parcel A?

2. Paul owned two adjoining lots thirty-five years ago. He built a house and a detached garage on each lot. Paul built one driveway between the two houses leading to the two garages. Paul lived in a house and rented out the second home. A decade later, Paul sold the rent house to Tim. The property line between the two lots was placed so that the driveway was located exclusively on Paul's land until it reached the back of the houses, where it widened giving access to both garages. The deed did not mention the driveway, but Paul orally assured Tim he could continue using the driveway to get to his garage. This year, Tim sold his home to Mary by a deed transferring the lot "with all easements, rights and appurtenances." A week after moving into her new home, Mary went out of town for the weekend. She left her car in the driveway, thereby preventing Paul from driving his car out the driveway. As a consequence, Paul missed church services that Sunday morning. When Mary came home that Monday, Paul told her she could not use his driveway anymore. Mary brings suit for the right to continue using the driveway.

(a) Is Mary claiming an easement appurtenant or an easement in gross? If the easement is appurtenant, does Mary own the dominant or servient estate? (b) Is Mary seeking an affirmative or negative easement? Does Mary have an express easement? (c) Does Mary have an easement by estoppel? (d) Does Mary have an easement implied from prior use? (e) Does Mary have an easement implied by necessity? (f) Does Mary have an easement by prescription (assume a 10-year prescriptive period)? (g) Assume no garage and no driveway existed when Paul sold to Tim twenty-five years ago. Twenty-four years ago, Paul and Tim agreed to build a driveway, and shared the cost for a contractor to build the driveway in the same location stipulated in the main facts. Paul and Tim contracted with separate builders to build their detached garages at the back of their respective lots. Would these facts change your answer to any of the questions?

Explanations

1. (a) An express, affirmative, appurtenant easement. Why appurtenant? Because it benefits owners of specific land, Parcel B. Four reasons support this: First, the deed reserving the easement reserves it to Chad, his heirs, and assigns, which is traditional language indicating an easement will run with the land. Second, the surrounding facts indicate the main reason for the easement is to gain access to Parcel B from Major Road for all purposes and not for a use peculiar to Chad. Third, an easement appurtenant is presumed unless there is some indication an easement in gross was intended. Nothing indicates such an intent here. Fourth, there is a servient estate (not possible with an easement in gross). Why affirmative? Because Hilton asserts his rights as the current owner of Parcel B. Hilton's right-of-way would go over and use Ed's property—so the easement is affirmative. Ed's land is burdened. The owner of the burdened property owns the servient estate. The owner of the benefitted property has the dominant estate. Finally, Hilton claims an express easement, but does not have one in a majority of jurisdictions. Courts in those jurisdictions hold that Hilton did not have an express easement because the deed from Common Owner to Chad did not *grant* Chad, Hilton's predecessor in interest, an easement. It only reserved an easement in favor of Parcel B for a right-of-way over Parcel A in his deed conveying Parcel A to Dan. Chad was a stranger to the deed. The controversy then turns on whether the jurisdiction would allow Common Owner to reserve an easement to a stranger to the deed. Courts using the majority rule conclude that the Common Owner could not reserve an easement in land that he no longer owned, and

that even though this sometimes frustrated the Common Owner's intent, the frustration could easily be avoided by the Common Owner's conveying the easement directly to the third party. In a minority of jurisdictions, courts adopt the welcome stranger rule and give effect to Common Owner's intent, particularly when the purchase price paid the Common Owner reflects the imposition of an easement.

(b) Hilton would then have an express easement in all states and no longer relies on the reservation in the easement to Dan. Instead, his easement comes from a deed specifically granting Chad, Hilton's predecessor in interest, an easement appurtenant. Chad recorded the deed and the deed to Ed excepts the easement. The answer would be the same if Common Owner had deeded the easement to Chad one nanosecond before delivering Parcel A to Dan. Using two documents instead of one makes all the difference in outcome.

(c) Assuming the jurisdiction recognizes an easement by estoppel or an irrevocable license, on the facts given, Hilton would have neither. Nothing in the facts indicates Hilton's use would not be revocable, something he must have known when building the motel, and the current use of a license does not imply its indefinite continuance. If Hilton used the right-of-way as a license, it would be a revocable one, despite its long-standing use. On the other hand, Hilton should prevail on claim for an easement implied from prior use. The easement will be an implied grant. Common Owner owned both parcels. He crossed Parcel A to reach Parcel B. The quasi-easement was apparent, probably by some trail or road so long as the Common Owner used it. This claim may turn on the necessity element. If the state demands strict necessity, Hilton probably loses since Hilton can use a winding timber road that was in place when the property was severed; in addition, courts in a few jurisdictions might require Hilton to use the river. Because this is an implied grant and not an implied reservation, however, most states require reasonable rather than strict necessity. Since the roadway over Parcel A seems reasonably necessary for the fair enjoyment of Parcel B, Chad likely received an implied easement from prior use, which passed with the property to Hilton. Further, Hilton does not have an easement implied by necessity. Two elements for implying the easement by necessity for right-of-way took place: Common Owner was the common owner and the severance of the property caused the necessity, but the necessity for this easement was at most a reasonable and not strict necessity since the owner of Parcel B, Chad, could have left and entered Parcel B by way of the timber road, time consuming as that may have been.

(d) Hilton may have an easement by prescription. Parcel B landowners have been traversing Parcel A for four decades, when Common Owner initially sold the property to Chad. (Common Owner himself traversed Parcel A, but Common Owner's time cannot be tacked to determine the time of actual use.) All Parcel B owners' use from Chad to Hilton can be tacked to satisfy the statute of limitations period and other elements. Use continued over four decades satisfies even the longest statutory period. In a few states, Hilton could benefit from a shorter statutory period if the reservation to Chad in the deed to Dan constituted color of title. Many of the elements are noncontroversial: Actual use, open and notorious use, and continuous and uninter-rupted use are all met, the facts not indicating otherwise. Adverse and hostile use, as well as (where applicable) exclusive use are more difficult. Most states do not require exclusive use, so the exclusive use element would be no problem in those states. The exclusive use element in the states that do demand exclusive use may be a problem because the facts say the general public used the right-of-way. Chad and all successors, as far as we can tell, used the right-of-way as the owner of the adjoining tract rather than as a member of the general public. Hilton should persuade a court he and his predecessor satisfy the exclusive use element. The hostile use element should be satis-fied, also. Common Owner's attempted reservation of an easement to Chad indicates he recognized a claim by Chad to an easement over his land at least as of the day the reservation was included in the deed to Dan. (Alternatively, a court easily could conclude Chad claimed a right from the date he bought the property.) No evidence even suggests Chad or anyone else in the chain of title renounced the claim to the right-of-way.

In summary, Hilton should have an easement over Parcel A, either as an easement implied from prior use or by prescription. In some states Hilton would have an express easement, though in a majority of states he does not qualify since his predecessor was a stranger to the deed reserving the easement.

(e) Assuming Hilton exhausts all of these options and all his appeals, Hilton could negotiate with Ed to purchase either an easement over Parcel A, Parcel A itself, or an easement over other adjoining lands for access to Major Road. Some western states by statute authorize private condemnation actions under certain circumstances. Hilton may have such a right under the statute. If he exercises this right, he will have to pay Ed the fair market value of the roadway, but at least Ed could not refuse to complete the transaction. Hilton might convince the local government a road along his property line would serve a public need, and have the local government purchase the land and build a road. This may take longer than Hilton wants to wait, however. If all else fails, Hilton apparently could rebuild the bridge, then grade and use the meandering ten-mile timber road.

2. (a) Easement appurtenant. An argument could be made that, if Tim had an easement at all, it was an easement in gross. Paul told Tim that Tim could use the driveway to reach his garage. Paul may have meant Tim and not anyone else could use the driveway. This then would sound more like a revocable license. On the other hand, Paul may have meant Tim could use the driveway as long as Tim used the house, and whoever possessed it after Tim would have the right to use the driveway. That would be an easement appurtenant. This second scenario rings truer. Courts have a construction preference for easements appurtenant. So a court would likely find any easement here to be appurtenant. More importantly for Mary, she will have a right to use an easement appurtenant, whereas an easement in gross may be used by Tim but not by Mary. If the easement is appurtenant, Mary is claiming the dominant estate. Mary's property is the one benefitted by any easement. The benefitted property is the dominant estate. Paul's property, burdened by the easement, would be the servient estate.

(b) Because Mary wants to drive over Paul's land, she seeks an affirmative easement, but she does not have an express easement. An express easement must be in writing to satisfy the Statute of Frauds. Paul did not deed Tim the easement. He merely told Tim that Tim could use the driveway to reach his garage. The deed from Tim to Mary could not create an easement over Paul's land.

(c) Mary probably does not have an easement by estoppel. Paul made no statement to Mary before she bought the house or otherwise gave her any indication she might be able to drive over his property. She therefore cannot gain an easement by estoppel based on anything Paul said to her. On the other hand, Mary succeeds to any easement that Tim had in the property. If Tim had an easement by estoppel, Mary also owns the easement. Tim's claim is based on Paul's oral statement that Tim could use Paul's driveway. It appears Paul made the statement after Tim decided to buy the home. If so, then Tim could not have changed his position based on the statement and thus he does not qualify for the easement by estoppel.

If, however, Mary can show Tim purchased the house only because of Paul's assurances that Tim could use the driveway, she should get her easement by estoppel. Paul made a representation to persuade Tim to commit to the house purchase. He should have known that Tim would rely on the representation in buying the home, and that it was an important factor in Tim's decision to buy the home. Finally, Tim bought the home as a consequence of relying on the representation. While some courts might find an easement by estoppel here, the surrounding circumstances seem to indicate Tim was going to buy the house, and Paul's assurances were just a neighborly act. From the facts, it appears that if Tim was relying on the assertion, and the assertion was as critical as Mary needs a court to believe, Tim should have fleshed out the matter more at the time, asking his attorney how best to document his rights. Not doing so, Tim should be denied the easement rather than having Paul lose his right to exclude others from his property. The facts are even less supportive of Tim and Mary because they do not indicate that Tim expended any money on the easement.

(d) Mary probably does not have an easement implied from prior use even though the elements may seem satisfied. Paul was the common owner. The use was in place at the time the commonly owned parcel was divided in two, it was visible at the time of severance, and it seems reasonably necessary for the enjoyment of the dominant estate. However, the fact that Paul told Tim that Tim could drive over Paul's driveway to reach his garage is evidence that Tim used the driveway pursuant to Paul's permission. The conversation indicates the parties did not overlook the issue. The opposite seems true. The two presumably believed the right to use the driveway was not part of the transfer to Tim. If so, the presumed intent underlying the easement implied from prior use theory disappears. Tim did not receive an easement implied from prior use, only a revocable license. Since Tim did not get an easement from prior use, neither will Mary.

(e) Mary does not have an easement implied by necessity. Her property borders a street so she does not need a way of egress and ingress.

(f) Mary does not have an easement by prescription. She has been on the property less than a month. The only way she could prevail is by tracking Tim's use. Tim did use the driveway long enough to satisfy most state's statutory period. His use was open, continuous, and exclusive, but not hostile or under a claim of right: The facts indicate Tim used the driveway with Paul's permission. A person who begins using property pursuant to a landowner's permission cannot gain an easement by prescription, no matter how long the use. This type of easement may hinge on Tim's state of mind: Did he begin using the easement because he thought he had a right, an easement in legal parlance, to continued use as the new owner of his house, or was he grateful for the kindly gesture of his saintly grantor/neighbor? A court's conclusion as to Tim's state of mind affects dramatically the outcome.

(g) Mary's chances increase tremendously under these facts. First, the facts increase the likelihood that a court will find an easement by prescription. Tim spent money to build the driveway and built his garage, indicating that Tim believed that he could use the driveway for a long time. Tim's use, therefore, was hostile and under claim of right based on his reasonable belief that the agreement was that he would have a long continuing use. Tim's claim is hostile even if the word "easement" was never spoken between Paul and Tim. Once Tim used the driveway for ten years, he had an easement by prescription. Since Tim's easement is appurtenant, he could transfer it to Mary. Second, Tim also may have had an easement by estoppel. Paul and Tim discussed jointly building a driveway for their common use. Paul must have known (in fact Paul encouraged Tim) that Tim would expend money to pay for the driveway and to build a garage based on Tim's right to continue using the driveway. Tim in fact spent the money. Tim's actions indicate that he reasonably believed that Paul would not attempt to revoke Tim's right to use the driveway. Thus, it seems Mary has an easement by estoppel. However, the new facts lessen the chance Mary will prevail in an easement implied from prior use action since the use was not in place when the property was severed. The change in facts will not affect any discussion of an easement by necessity.

Assignability, Scope, and Termination of Easements

ASSIGNABILITY OF EASEMENTS

Most easements are assignable. Some are not. **Assignable** means the easement can be sold, gifted, devised, inherited, or otherwise conveyed. Rules concerning assignability of easements depend on several factors, the major factor being whether the easement is an easement in gross or appurtenant.

Easements appurtenant run with the land: Whoever possesses the dominant estate (by purchase, gift, devise, or inheritance) has the right to use the easement over the servient estate. A person conveying the dominant estate loses her easement rights to the person to whom it is conveyed. Likewise, the servient estate remains burdened with the easement no matter who owns the servient estate. Moreover, an easement appurtenant is implicitly assigned with the dominant estate, whether or not the deed mentions it

An **easement in gross** benefits a person whether or not he owns a particular parcel of land. It lacks a dominant estate. The law relating to the assignability of easements in gross is evolving. Rules are developing separately for **commercial easements in gross** and for *noncommercial*, or personal, easements in gross. *Commercial* easements in gross further a money-making activity (as opposed to noncommercial or personal easements in gross, granted for the owner's personal enjoyment or pleasure). Railroad, utility, and pipeline easements are commercial easements in gross. A commercial easement in gross also might be the right to use a lake to run a fishing, boating, or swimming operation, or the right to remove timber or minerals from the land (the latter being **profits a prendre** or profit — and profits are everywhere assignable).

Unless expressly made nonassignable or the circumstances surrounding the creation of the commercial easement in gross indicate otherwise, commercial easements in gross are assignable. For instance, a telephone company with easements in gross throughout the region for its telephone poles and lines can assign its easements in gross to a successor telephone company. The same goes for easements for railroad companies assigning railroad easements for tracks or water companies assigning easements for water lines. The circumstances giving rise to the right to assign here are obvious: If the easements were nonassignable, the purchasing telephone company (or railroad or water company) would not be able to use any of the poles or lines (or tracks or pipes) on any servient estate. Without those wires (or tracks or pipes) the company could not operate.

Example: E holds a commercial easement in gross over Blackacre. E dies, leaving H as her sole heir. O (the owner of the servient estate) refuses to let H use the easement. If an easement is assignable, it is also likely to be inheritable too — but don't count on it.

Noncommercial easements in gross (or personal easements) are a different matter. Many jurisdictions prohibit their assignment even if they allow assignability of commercial easements in gross. A few jurisdictions permit holders to assign noncommercial easements in gross. The majority rule is that a noncommercial easement in gross is not assignable unless circumstances or the document creating the easement expressly stipulates the easement in gross is assignable.

Example: E holds a noncommercial easement in gross, non-assignable in the jurisdiction, but assigns it anyway. The assignee either holds a license, or nothing (the assignment being a nullity), or (worse yet) the attempt at an assignment destroys E's easement.

DIVISIBILITY AND APPORTIONMENT

An issue distinct from assignability concerns the **divisibility** or **apportionment** of easements. In the assignability discussion, the holder of the easement transferred all her interest in an easement to one other person. When divided or apportioned, the easement holder attempts to share the easement with others or to assign, divide, or apportion the easement to multiple grantees. The issue is whether an easement holder can divide or apportion an easement among several grantees — i.e., whether a person owning an easement can transfer an otherwise assignable easement to more than one person.

(a) Easements Appurtenant

The holder of an *easement appurtenant*, by subdividing and selling parcels of the dominant estate, transfers the easement with each parcel. Each resulting parcel becomes a dominant estate and the owner enjoys the easement over the servient estate so long as the several dominant estate owners do not overburden the servient estate.

Example: E owns Blackacre, and as its owner has an easement for egress and ingress over Greenacre. E subdivides Blackacre, selling subdivided lots to 20 different people, and retaining a lot for herself. Who has a right to cross Greenacre? It could be E as long as she owns any part of Blackacre, or the new owner of the lot where the right of way enters Blackacre from Greenacre, or all 21 owners, or no one if in subdividing Blackacre (the dominant estate) E might have destroyed the easement. The answer is that all 21 property owners have an easement over Greenacre. Easements appurtenant are divisible and apportionable.

(b) Easements in Gross

Easements in gross that are not assignable obviously are not divisible or apportionable, either. Since most noncommercial easements in gross are nonassignable, the following discussion applies to *commercial easements in gross*.

In jurisdictions where commercial easements in gross are assignable, courts often distinguish between exclusive easements in gross and nonexclusive easements in gross. *Exclusive* easements in gross are those where the easement holder has the sole right to use an easement. A person owning an exclusive easement in gross has the sole power to authorize others to use it. Even the servient estate owner cannot allow others to use the easement. If a person (or a company) has an exclusive easement in gross, that person may permit many others to use the easement as long as the total burden on the servient estate does not amount to a surcharge or misuse of the easement.

Most jurisdictions do not presume that an exclusive easement is intended, absent clear language to the contrary. Persons granted nonexclusive easements in gross, on the other hand, cannot subdivide or apportion any rights to the easement. A *nonexclusive* easement in gross is one in which the easement holder has the right to use the easement, but the servient estate owner (or other exclusive easement holder) can authorize others to use the easement and the holder of the nonexclusive easement in gross cannot prevent the servient estate owner (or some other person having the exclusive easement) from granting the right to use an easement to other persons. The servient estate owner (or other exclusive easement holder) in effect retains the power to decide how many persons can use the easement.

When two or more persons inherit or otherwise share the exclusive right to an easement, at least one court has concluded the multiple owners must act with one voice (known as the **one-stock rule**). See Miller v. Lutheran Conference & Camp Association, 200 A. 646 (Pa. 1938). Each of the multiple owners under a one-stock rule has a veto on any action taken with regard to the easement or profit. This resolution is thought to encourage reasonable exploitation without overutilizing the easement or profit. As developed more fully infra, should the exclusive holder, a "one-stock" group, or the many nonexclusive users of an easement or profit overburden the easement, the servient estate owner has a right to enjoin the uses that overburden or exceed the scope of the easement.

SCOPE OF EASEMENTS

The *scope* of the easement delineates the extent of use an easement holder may make of the servient estate. The scope refers to the location, intensity, and manner of the use. An easement holder's use cannot exceed its scope. The general rule is that the holder may make such use of the easement reasonably necessary for the enjoyment of the dominant estate and not unreasonably burdensome to the servient estate.

(a) Location

The location of an easement must be identified and described at its inception. Once the location is established, the easement owner must remain within the located easement. The easement owner's use of the servient estate outside the boundaries of the easement, even for the same purposes authorized in the easement, is a trespass.

Example: E holds a roadway easement over Blackacre and wishes to install drainage ditches on either side. E may not do so if the ditches are outside the easement's original location.

If an easement is expressly located, the terms of its grant or reservation control. If the location is unspecified, usage can generally establish its location. Thus an express grant or reservation should describe the precise location of the easement. In a few jurisdictions, an express grant or reservation that does not locate the easement is invalid. In most jurisdictions, however, the easement is valid even though its location is unspecified.

The location of easements implied from prior use and by prescription are fixed by the use made at severance or the start of the prescriptive period.

Easements implied by necessity (as well as express easements not specified in the grant or reservation) must be physically located after the easement is recognized. The general rule is that if the location cannot be ascertained from its deed or other document, the servient estate owner can within a reasonable time locate the easement, but if the servient estate does not locate the easement or if the proposed location is unreasonable, the dominant estate holder (or holder of an easement in gross) can locate the easement, having due regard for the convenience of the servient estate owner. And so on, back and forth, until the estate holders reach agreement.

In most jurisdictions, an easement once located, is forever located, absent an agreement otherwise by both estate holders. Several states and the Restatement (Third) of Property (Servitudes) permit the servient estate owner to move the easement at the servient owner's own expense as long as moving the easement does not inconvenience the dominant estate owner's or easement holder's use of the easement. An easement holder's unilateral change in location of the easement constitutes a **misuse** of the easement. The misuse may be from one part of the servient estate to another, or from the surface to an underground location (or vice versa). Thus an easement for a ditch may not be deepened or widened after its initial location.

Example: A utility company owns an easement to place poles and wires over property. The easement to place poles over property does not give the utility company the right to move the wires underground.

(b) Intensity of Use

When the intensity of the use is specified in the grant or reservation, those terms control. However, even express grants or reservations do not address every potential problem (and usually address no potentiality beyond stating the easement's basic purpose). The general rule, that an easement holder can use the easement as long as the use is reasonably necessary for the dominant estate and does not overburden the servient estate, has both flexibility and uncertainty. Its stress is often upon the original parties' unexpressed but presumed intent in determining what qualifies as an authorized use of an easement. In ascertaining the original parties' intent, courts presume the parties intended the scope of the easement would evolve to accommodate reasonably foreseeable changes in the surrounding area and in society.

Example: O in 1900 granted E an easement appurtenant over O's land so E could reach a public road. In 1900, both properties were rural, and travel was by foot, horse, and buggy. One hundred years later O's heirs and E's successors and assigns own the respective properties. Are E's successors limited to using foot, horse, and buggy to travel over a dirt path easement? No. Cars, trucks, and even motorcycles are natural developments and the scope of the easement will be adjusted to accommodate progress.

Example: As in the prior Example, E's successors-in-interest, reacting to urbanization of the neighborhood, subdivide E's original property into 100 homesites. They sell the individual lots to individuals who build residences. Each new homeowner uses the easement to travel to the public road. The owners of each and every lot within the original benefitted property have the right to use the easement appurtenant over O's property. Subdivision of the dominant estate does not in itself result in an easement's misuse. It is a reasonably foreseeable use of the easement, one not overburdening the servient estate.

Example: E's successors build a retaining wall along and widen the easement to prevent its surface from eroding. There is no misuse of the easement on this account, but O's heirs would have a cross easement, over the wall for access to the easement's right of way.

Example: E's successors wish to widen what was once an eight-foot-wide easement to a twenty-foot-wide easement. They can lay shell, asphalt, or concrete to make a modern road out of the initial easement, but what about the widening? Some states would permit it as an incidental improvement, consistent with the original parties' presumed intent and taking into account neighborhood conditions. Other states recall their rules on location and refuse to permit the widening.

The easement holder's use is not unbounded. She is limited to using the easement only for the authorized purpose of the easement. A logging road easement could not be used for residential purposes. But a residential roadway easement, though it is originally for seasonal access, might eventually be used all year. A dominant estate owner having a right of egress and ingress through an alleyway over a neighboring lot, for example, cannot use the alleyway to park vehicles, even though those same vehicles may be driven through the alley.

Example: Suppose that in the prior O-E Examples E's successors, instead of subdividing the property, build a shopping mall, with hundreds of cars daily streaming across the servient estate. A court would find either (a) that the intended use was for access to residential not commercial property or (b) that the intensity of use with the resulting noise, pollution, and traffic was beyond O and E's presumed intent, even if the neighborhood, including the servient estate, was commercial.

Example: E's successors trim the trees along the easement for twenty years. By doing so, they have expanded their use. An easement express at its creation may be expanded by prescription.

(c) No Benefit Allowed to Nondominant Property

An easement appurtenant may benefit only the dominant estate. It cannot benefit adjoining property, even if the owner of the dominant estate also owns the adjoining property, and even if the adjoining property is used in a manner integrated with activity with the dominant estate. Any extension of the benefit to another property is a misuse of the easement.

Example: Wilson owns land he wants to develop into a residential subdivision. He would like access to Main Street. Wilson discovers an adjoining lot owner that has an easement appurtenant over Jack's land for access to Main Street. Wilson buys the lot. Can Wilson use the easement over Jack's land to get to Main Street? Wilson can use the easement to benefit his newly acquired lot, but not to benefit his adjoining land: Wilson, his workers, and his prospective purchasers cannot get from the back property to Main Street by going over the newly acquired lot.

Example: Ed owns a restaurant with the easement for egress and ingress over Otto's property. Ed's restaurant is successful and he plans to enlarge it. If the enlarged restaurant remains on the dominant estate, Ed and his customers can continue using the easement over Otto's land. If, however, Ed buys a 50-foot-wide strip behind his lot to accommodate the larger building and to provide extra parking spaces, Ed and his customers will not be able to use the easement over Otto's property to reach the part of the building and parking area on the adjoining 50 feet. Ed must take steps to prevent the misuse. If Ed cannot effectively do so, he and his customers may not be able to continue using the easement at all!

(d) Improvements, Maintenance, and Repair

An easement holder (the dominant estate holder) has the right to improve the easement as long as the improvements promote the use of the easement, are within its scope, and do not unreasonably burden the servient estate owner's use or enjoyment of her property. Prior Examples involved an asphalt right-of-way and a retaining wall. Similarly, a company or individual having the right-of-way for utility lines or pipelines has a right as necessary to install the pipes, poles, and wires essential to the enjoyment of the easement. In contrast, a utility company that has the surface rights to install utility poles and lines cannot remove the poles and place the wires underground. Placing the wires underground exceeds the scope of the easement and hence is a misuse of it. The utility company in this case must secure a grant of the underground easement.

Conversely, the easement holder has the (default) duty to maintain and repair the easement and any improvements placed on it, as well as liability for negligent repairs, for slip and fall events on the easement, and for injury to the servient estate done in the course of fulfilling this duty. This duty follows the privilege of use and in exercising the duty, the easement holder has a right to enter the servient property to maintain the easement. In some jurisdictions, this duty is imposed regardless of the extent of the servient owner's use of the easement, but in most jurisdictions, since the duty follows the privilege of use, multiple users share the costs of repair in proportion to their use. The terms of any maintenance and repair agreement do not affect the scope of the easement.

Example: A utility company that installs poles and overhead wires has a right to enter the property to repair and maintain the poles and wires, to remove or replace the poles or wires, to clear out undergrowth, and to cut back trees endangering the wires. Likewise, a pipeline company with a pipeline easement or a person having an underground sewer or water line easement has a right to go onto the servient estate and dig up the ground as necessary to maintain its pipes and lines.

TERMINATION OF EASEMENTS

An easement, whether express or implied, potentially lasts forever. Nonetheless, easements can be extinguished or terminated.

1. **By the Terms of the Grant.** The deed or will granting or reserving the easement may set an expiration date, a term of years, or a condition. The grant may allow an easement of egress and ingress as long as the grantee continues mining operations or until a highway opens; or a landowner may grant an oil company a pipeline easement for 50 years. The easement expires automatically according to the express terms of the grant or reservation.

2. **Purpose for Easement Ends.** An easement terminates when the purpose for the easement ends. For instance, an easement to enter an apartment complex to install and service cable lines ends if the apartment building is destroyed. Although the doctrine has been applied to all types of easements, it is most often applied to terminate easements implied by necessity. The easement implied by necessity

ends as soon as another way to enter the property appears and the strict necessity for the easement for egress and ingress ends.

3. **Merger.** An easement is a right to use another person's property. Once a person gains concurrent ownership of both the dominant estate and the servient estate, the estates merge and the easement disappears. If the common owner later severs the property, the old easement does not reappear automatically, absent an agreement otherwise.

4. **Forfeiture for Misuse.** A court may declare an easement forfeited for misuse. This is an extraordinary remedy, only imposed in the most egregious cases of misuse. The more common action is an injunction halting the misuse. Where the easement cannot be used without benefitting property adjoining the dominant estate, a court will enjoin all use of the easement until the easement holder can stop the misuse.

5. **Release.** An easement is an interest in property of another. As such, the easement holder by deed can transfer part or all of the easement to the servient estate owner. This transfer is called a release and must be in writing to satisfy the Statute of Frauds.

6. **Abandonment.** An easement holder may abandon an easement. Abandonment has two elements: intent to abandon and subsequent nonuse. Intent to abandon is often hard to prove. It must be evidenced by some identifiable and unambiguous act inconsistent with continued ownership of the easement. Nonuse, no matter how long continued, is neither an identifiable event or an unambiguous fact, nor an act inconsistent with the ownership of the easement. Nonuse for a long enough time, however, does give credence that some oral pronouncement or action taken long ago constituted the requisite unambiguous act denoting the intent to abandon. This is a thin reed, and not often a fruitful one. The best evidence of intent to abandon is a deed or other written document, which makes abandonment close to release.

7. **Estoppel.** Just as an easement by estoppel may be created, in some jurisdictions the servient estate owner can extinguish an easement by estoppel. The same standards apply at termination as at creation: The easement holder consents to the servient estate owner's use of the easement location in a manner inconsistent with the easement's use; the easement holder knows or should know that the servient estate owner, believing the consent will not be revoked, will materially change her position; and the servient estate holder, reasonably believing the consent will not be revoked, substantially changes her position, usually by constructing improvements over the easement.

8. **Prescription.** Just as a person can gain an easement by prescription, a servient estate owner can terminate an easement by prescription.

Easements of all sorts, whether express, implied, or prescriptive, can be extinguished by prescription. Terminating an easement by prescription is not as easy as it sounds: The servient estate owner must use the easement in a manner adverse to the easement holder's right. This is not easy to do. Recall the servient estate owner has the right to use the easement as long as her use does not unreasonably interfere with the easement holder's use. Thus, to terminate an easement by prescription, the servient estate owner must prove her use of the property was inconsistent with continuation of the easement. Improving the right-of-way before a pipeline company "installs" its pipes is not adverse enough. Neither is farming over an easement during a period the easement holder is not using it. A fence blocking a road usually is not adverse enough, especially if there is an unlocked gate over the road. If a fence blocks the easement holder's anticipated use, however, it may be adverse. A stone wall over the roadway might be adverse use if the easement holder attempts to use the road after the wall has been constructed: Until then, the servient estate owner's wall is consistent with the easement holder's nonuse of the easement.

9. **Recording Acts.** The easement as an interest in property is subject to a state's recording acts. A subsequent bona fide purchaser who takes without actual, constructive, or inquiry notice of the easement is not bound by the easement. Likewise, a creditor that records a mortgage before an express easement is recorded is protected by the recording acts and, if necessary, may sell the property in a foreclosure action. The purchaser at the foreclosure sale is not bound by the easement. If, on the other hand, the easement was recorded before the mortgage (or the easement holder is otherwise protected under the recording act, such as the mortgagee having actual or inquiry notice of the easement), the easement holder has priority and the purchaser at the foreclosure sale takes the property subject to the easement. In states having marketable title acts, an easement recorded prior to the "root of title" faces extinguishment unless one of many possible exceptions in the act applies.

10. **Eminent Domain.** Federal, state, and municipal governments through a process known as eminent domain or condemnation can force landowners to sell property to the government as long as the government pays for the property. The government in an eminent domain action takes the whole property, including any easement. This has two consequences for the easement holder. First, the easement is extinguished. Second, because the government took the easement, a property interest, the government must compensate the easement holder.

Examples

1. Landowner's 200 acres include a 50-acre lake. Landowner deeds Marty the right to fish and boat on the lake. (a) Marty wants to hold a ski show on the lake. Can he? (b) Marty wants to bring his friend, Catfish, along to go fishing with him. Landowner does not like Catfish and wants to prohibit him from using the lake. Can he? (c) Marty planned to take two working buddies fishing. Marty awoke, feeling ill. He gave his buddies a map to the lake and a note giving them permission to fish without him. Landowner does not want anyone using the lake unless Marty accompanies them. Can Landowner refuse to let the two buddies use the lake? (d) Marty died, devising his fishing rights to his fishing pal, Catfish. Does Catfish have an easement to fish on the lake? (e) Assume Landowner sold Marty ten acres of adjoining land, and the deed conveyed the easement to fish and boat on the lake on Landowner's property. Marty died, devising the ten acres to Catfish. May Catfish fish and boat on Landowner's lake?

2. Debbie granted Seashore Pipeline an express easement across her property for the construction, maintenance, and operation of pipelines. Debbie gave Seashore the exclusive right to install additional pipelines as long as Debbie and the company negotiated an additional compensation arrangement for each extra pipeline that was laid within the easement. Seashore constructed a 12-inch pipeline through the easement. Two years later Seashore constructed a 20-inch pipeline within the easement. Seashore compensated Debbie when it added the second pipeline. Twenty years later Seashore sold and assigned the 12-inch pipeline and the easement to Triton Company. Seashore reserved an undivided one-half interest in the easement. Seashore Pipeline did not assign any interest in the 20-inch pipeline. (a) Debbie brought a trespass action against Triton and sought to terminate Seashore's easement. What result? Why? (b) Instead of giving Seashore an exclusive easement, Debbie deeded separate easements to Seashore for each pipeline, one for the 12-inch pipeline and one for the 20-inch pipeline. Seashore later sold the 12-inch pipeline and the easement for the 12-inch pipeline to Triton, which attempted to dig up the pipeline and replace it with a 20-inch pipeline. Debbie protests. What result? Why?

3. Optics Cable Network plans to offer television, telephone, and Internet cable services. It is critical to the company's success that it be able to lay cable either underground or over poles to businesses, schools, and residences. Optics contracted with Flat Hills Electric Company to attach cable lines to existing poles on easements the electric company assembled years ago. Optics entered into a similar contract with Statewide Telephone Company. Landowners have challenged these arrangements, arguing that Flat Hills and Statewide cannot authorize Optics to string or lay its

cable in the easements, and that Optics therefore was trespassing. (a) The original easement grant to Flat Hills was worded as an easement "for the purpose of constructing and maintaining an electric transmission or distribution line or system." Can Optics use the Flat Hills easement without compensating the servient landowners? (b) The original easement grant to Statewide was worded as "the right to construct and operate equipment for the distribution of electricity and messages upon or across the" property. Can Optics use Statewide's easement without compensating the servient landowners?

4. Ben bought two five-acre parcels. Parcel I is east of and adjacent to Route 53. Parcel II is a landlocked tract just east of Parcel I. Shortly afterward Ben deeded Parcel I to Cal, reserving an easement for himself, his heirs, and assigns, to use a right-of-way running from Route 53 across the southern boundary of Parcel I to Parcel II. Ben stored equipment and sewer pipes on Parcel II. Cal owned and operated a construction company on Parcel I. The construction company's office building was located 20 feet from the easement. Five years later, Ben sold Parcel II to Asphalt Road Graders, the deed including the easement over Parcel I. Over the next ten years Asphalt trucks made an average of 200 daily round-trips from Parcel II to Route 53. Asphalt bought Parcel III (not landlocked) ten years after it bought Parcel II. Parcel III is directly east of Parcel II. Asphalt built a new asphalt plant on Parcel III. Trucks going to the asphalt plant entered and exited from Route 53 over Parcel I and Parcel II. Asphalt's business increased after the new plant opened, and so the average number of trucks using the easement on Parcel I doubled. As traffic increased, the trucks began driving faster and raised dust. Dust entered Cal's showroom through the ventilation and air-conditioning system. Dust also fell on employees' and customers' cars. Although Asphalt paved the road when it bought Parcel II, it had not repaired the road since then and the heavy truck use caused the pavement to deteriorate, adding to the dust problem. The parties agree the road had deteriorated so much it had to be rebuilt completely.

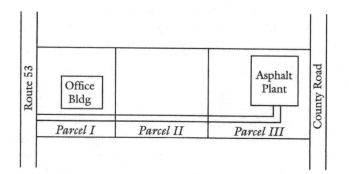

This year Cal installed four eight-inch high-speed barriers on the easement in an effort to slow the trucks. Asphalt built up the road on either side of the four speed barriers with asphalt in an effort to minimize the damage caused to its trucks when the trucks went over the speed barriers. Cal removed the asphalt gradings, leaving the barriers with eight-inch-high horizontal edges. When Asphalt attempted to replace the asphalt inclines, Cal parked his truck on one of the barriers, locked the gate on the easement for one hour, and told the Asphalt workers to remove the asphalt. The parties end up in court. (a) Cal claims Asphalt's almost constant running of trucks over the easement is a misuse. How would a court rule? (b) Cal claims trucks cannot use the easement to get to the asphalt plant on Parcel III. How would a court rule? (c) Cal claims the facts justify terminating Asphalt's easement over Parcel I. How would a court rule? (d) Asphalt wants the speed barriers removed. Cal wants the speed barriers to stay. How would a court rule? (e) If the easement continues, who should pay to rebuild the road? Once the road is paved, who should pay for the repairs and maintenance of the road?

5. Farmer sold Erin a landlocked lot. He deeded Erin a ten-foot-wide easement for ingress and egress over Lot 24 to reach Cove Road. Farmer continued selling lots. A year later he deeded Lot 24 to Wilbur subject to Erin's easement. Wilbur has always wanted to get rid of the easement. (a) Erin purchased Lot 35, which adjoins her original lot and fronts on High Street. Does her easement over Wilbur's property end? (b) The county constructed a road fronting on Erin's original property. Does her easement over Wilbur's property end? (c) Assume both (a) and (b) occur and Erin fences in her yard, without a gate in the fence at the point where her easement begins. Does the easement over Wilbur's property end? (d) Assume all the above, plus Erin plants a hedge along the fence. Is her easement still in existence? (e) Assume all the above, plus Wilbur built a storage shed on the easement and ten years pass (the statute of limitations period is ten years). Is Erin's easement still in existence? (f) Assume all the above occurred. Wilbur sells his property to Erin, who moves into Wilbur's home. Six months later Erin sells her old home to Wilbur's son, who wanted to move back to the old neighborhood. Is the easement still in existence? (g) What result in (f) if Erin sold her home to the son one day before she closed on Lot 24? (h) Would any of the answers above change if Farmer's deed to Erin had granted her a right-of-way over Lot 24 as long as Erin's property remained landlocked?

Explanations

1. (a) Marty has an easement in gross. The easement is a noncommercial easement for Marty's personal pleasure and enjoyment rather than a commercial easement in gross. The scope of a personal easement for fishing and boating normally would not include such an intense use by the easement holder as holding a ski show. Marty cannot hold a ski show on the lake. The ski show may have other problems. Since the easement is personal and not commercial, Marty's use of the easement for commercial purposes probably exceeds the scope of the easement. In addition, the ski show would use much of the land surrounding the lake for both participants and spectators. The easement to use the lake for fishing and boating carries it with it the right to travel over the land and use it as reasonably necessary to enjoy the fishing and boating rights, but it does not carry with it the right to use the grounds for other reasons, such as accommodating large crowds.

   (b) Marty has a noncommercial easement in gross. The easement in gross, even a personal or noncommercial easement in gross, includes reasonable ancillary use by the easement holder beneficial to the use of the easement. Unless the grant specifically limited access to Marty to use the lake alone, an easement to fish and boat includes the right to bring a reasonable number of others (for social, safety, or other practical reasons). Catfish can accompany Marty.

   (c) Noncommercial, nonexclusive easements in gross are not apportionable. Marty, for example, could not give his buddies the right to fish on the lake anytime they wanted. The Example is narrower than that, however, with Marty allowing his buddies to go just this one time without him. They could argue Marty has not assigned them any rights, and that they came as Marty's guests even though Marty himself could not come. A court probably would hold the easement is personal to Marty, and buddies can fish on the lake only when they accompany Marty. Landowner can refuse to let Marty's two buddies fish on the lake.

   (d) Noncommercial easements in gross generally are nonassignable unless the circumstances or the grant indicates the easement is assignable. Nothing in the facts even hints at Marty's easement being assignable. Marty cannot assign the easement in gross during his lifetime or by will at his death. Marty's easement terminates on his death. Unfortunately for Catfish, he loses this one hook, line, and sinker.

   (e) Marty had an easement appurtenant. The easement appurtenant is assignable and passes with the dominant estate. When Marty devised the ten acres to Catfish, Catfish acquired the easement to fish and boat on Landowner's lake.

2. (a) Seashore Pipeline has an exclusive commercial easement in gross. Seashore has the right to assign its easement to Triton Company. Seashore assigned one of the pipelines to Triton, but only made a partial assignment of its easement; stated otherwise, Seashore attempted to subdivide or apportion its easement. The issue becomes whether Seashore can subdivide or apportion its easement rights as long as it compensates Debbie for each additional pipeline. Yes it can. Seashore has an exclusive easement. Unless the deed or contract specifies the easement is nonassignable or nonapportionable, most jurisdictions will conclude Seashore can assign, subdivide, or apportion its rights in a commercial easement in gross so long as the total use does not overburden the servient estate. A court would be more sympathetic to Seashore here because the pipeline itself limits the amount of usage that can be made of the easement and Debbie would be additionally compensated for each additional pipeline. The partial assignment to Triton is valid. No new pipeline was added so Debbie is not entitled to extra compensation. Triton's use did not cause a surcharge or overburdening of the easement since total volume of use is circumscribed by the size of the pipeline in place.

   (b) Debbie granted Seashore two nonexclusive easements in gross to place pipelines through her property. Seashore cannot subdivide or apportion a nonexclusive easement, but it can assign it. Seashore owns two easements and can assign each independently of the other. The assignment of the easement and the 12-inch pipeline was valid. Triton Company owns the easement. A second issue is whether Triton can expand the size of the pipeline in the easement from a 12-inch to a 20-inch pipeline. The grant for the easement stipulated a 12-inch pipeline. That stipulation established the scope of the easement. Triton's attempt to enlarge the pipeline is a misuse of the easement. Debbie can enjoin Triton from putting in the 20-inch pipeline. If Triton wants a 20-inch pipeline through Debbie's property, it must negotiate with Debbie for the right to an easement for that purpose. Debbie prevails.

3. (a) Some courts would hold that the easement was for electrical transmission only: Cable use exceeds its scope. Optics might argue that cable is just a technological development that did not exist when the easement was granted and the phrase should include cable today as either a natural extension of the original easement or should favor the extension of cable services as a public benefit. Some courts accept such arguments, others do not, finding that an easement is an encumbrance on the servient owners' title and not so expansive.

   (b) Courts usually extend easement for transmitting "messages" and "communications" to include cable. With that issue resolved, courts address whether the easement holder, Statewide, can apportion its easement. The courts typically find the easement is an assignable commercial easement in gross; and the easement is exclusive, giving the easement holder the power to apportion the easement as long as the easement is not overburdened. Because the cables attach to existing poles, the additional cable does not overburden the easement. Judgment for Optics.

4. (a) Asphalt prevails. Asphalt had an easement appurtenant for the benefit of Parcel II. As owner of the dominant estate, Asphalt can make such use of the easement as is reasonably necessary for the full enjoyment of the dominant estate as long as the use does not unreasonably burden the servient estate. In evaluating reasonableness of both the use and the burden, the original parties' intent is presumed to accommodate normal development of the property in the general vicinity. Not much has changed since the easement was granted. Nothing in the facts indicate the parcels are not suited for industrial uses. Cal operated a construction company on Parcel I. Ben stored pipes on Parcel II. Asphalt operated its asphalt business for 10–20 years before the case came to trial: Even if the truck use exceeded the scope of the original reservation, Asphalt may have gained the expanded scope by prescription. The number of trucks traversing the easement seems to be a normal development of industrial use over the five-acre tract. The trucks traveling over Parcel I are not an unreasonable use or burden. The dust might be another matter. A person must use an easement in a manner not to unreasonably burden the easement or the servient estate. Asphalt's stirring up dust may be an unreasonable interference with the servient estate owner's use and enjoyment of his land, especially since the dust can be controlled by repairing the road, which the parties apparently agreed should be done.

(b) Cal is correct. While an easement holder can use the easement for the general benefit of the dominant estate, the holder's use of the easement for the benefit of any nondominant land, even if the same person owns both properties and even if, as is the case here, the two properties are used as an integrated unit, is a misuse of the easement. Trucks going to the asphalt plant located on Parcel III cannot go over Parcel I. Asphalt, therefore, must find another way for its trucks to get to the asphalt plant. The facts say Parcel III is not landlocked, so finding a new entrance and exit may not be a problem (though it may be inconvenient and may increase the distance that the trucks must travel to get from the asphalt plant to work sites). If all trucks go to the asphalt plant, which is possible, then all or virtually all truck traffic over Parcel I must end; then Cal may achieve a complete ban on trucks.

(c) Asphalt will retain its easement. A court will terminate an easement for misuse of the easement, but termination for misuse is not favored. A complete impossibility of use, or evidence the dominant estate holder will intentionally continue misusing the easement, or some such circumstance is required before a court will terminate an easement for misuse. Nothing in the facts indicates any reason to terminate the easement.

(d) The speed barriers must go. A servient estate owner cannot interfere with the dominant estate owner's use of the easement. The court may direct Asphalt, the dominant estate owner, to control the trucks' speed by putting up speed barriers or enforcing a speed policy for its employees and contractors, but self-help by Cal, the servient estate owner, is inappropriate.

(e) Since Asphalt's trucks cause the dust and Asphalt is the main user of the easement, Asphalt should pay to rebuild the road. Similarly, the persons using the easement have a duty to maintain the easement and any improvements they make to it. Asphalt should maintain the road. The costs of rebuilding and maintaining the road will be allocated between Cal and Asphalt based on each one's percentage of the total use.

5. (a) No. The easement continues. While the strict necessity ends, the easement still serves a purpose of accessing Cove Road. The only time an easement ends when the strict necessity ends is when the easement was implied by strict necessity for egress and ingress. Erin's easement was an express easement, not one implied by necessity. The mere existence of an alternate route over Erin's other property will not terminate the easement over Lot 24.

(b) No. The easement continues. Even though Erin has a road in front of her house that she probably will use most of the time, the easement across Wilbur's land remains valid. It still serves a purpose of getting to Cove Road, and will as long as there is a Cove Road.

(c) No. The easement continues. Erin seemingly stopped using the easement. The fence certainly makes it inconvenient for her to use the easement and indicates she does not intend to use the easement, but for the easement to terminate a court must conclude Erin abandoned it. Erin's putting up the fence does not unambiguously signal that intent. Mere nonuse is not an abandonment. If need be, Erin may remove the fence and drive over or otherwise reasonably use the easement.

(d) The easement continues. A hedge adds an extra dimension of nonuse and difficulty to Erin's reopening the way, but in and of themselves planting the hedge and building the fence do not amount to an abandonment of the easement. See (c), supra.

(e) The easement continues. The shed would block Erin's use of the easement if she tried to drive on the easement. Erin has not tried to use the easement. Wilbur has the right to use his property any way he wishes as long as he does not interfere with Erin's using her easement. Until Erin tries to use the easement, Wilbur's putting a shed there is not hostile enough to start the running of the ten-year prescription period.

(f) No. The easement is terminated. When Erin bought Lot 24, she became the owner of both the dominant and the servient estate. A person cannot have an easement over her own property, so the easement merged into the fee simple. Once terminated, it disappeared. It does not spring up again when Erin sells her original home to Wilbur's son.

(g) The easement would continue. Erin never owned both lots simultaneously, so the easement did not merge into the fee simple. It is an easement appurtenant and runs with the land. Wilbur's son owns the dominant estate and would have an easement over Lot 24.

(h) Erin's easement would have ended by its own terms as soon as she bought the adjoining Lot 35 with frontage on High Street (or as soon as Erin cleared a way to the avenue). At the latest, the easement would have terminated as soon as the county built the road in front of Erin's home.

Real Covenants and Equitable Servitudes: Running with the Land

---

INTRODUCTION

Landowners may contract among themselves as to the use or nonuse of their properties, and courts will enforce the contracts as between their original parties. At one time, however, neither contract rights nor obligations could be assigned to third parties. Courts would enforce contracts only if there was **privity of contract** between the parties (i.e., both parties were principals to the agreement). A person could assume the obligations by executing an assumption agreement or a new contract, but he could not become liable solely by purchasing the affected property.

Today courts (1) give subsequent purchasers of property standing to enforce the agreement against other landowners who were parties to it, and (2) obligate subsequent purchasers to honor the obligations affecting their property, even though they had no interest in the land affected by the agreement at the time it was executed and were not a party to it. In this sense, the law refers to such purchasers as "remote" purchasers. Building on the concept of **privity of estate**, discussed last in the context of landlord-tenant law, **courts of law** established elements for **real covenants** — a/k/a **covenants that run with the land** — that made some contracts or promises affecting property bind and benefit subsequent owners of the affected properties.[1] And **courts of equity** expanded the number of subsequent purchasers who would be bound

---

1. Covenants that "run" with the land are routinely referred to as real covenants, meaning that a successor in title may be substituted for his or her predecessor regarding the right to enforce

and burdened using what came to be known as **equitable servitudes**. There is some overlap, and some critical differences, between real covenants and equitable servitudes.

TERMINOLOGY

Real covenants and **equitable servitudes** are agreements, promises, or deed provisions that relate to real property and that bind or benefit subsequent owners of the respective properties solely because they own the property. Real covenants and equitable servitudes, because they benefit and obligate subsequent landowners, are said to **run with the land** (more precisely, real covenants burden estates in land, not the land itself, and equitable servitudes bind subsequent owners but are not referred to as running with the land). The objective of the law of real covenants and equitable servitudes is to distinguish those covenants that bind and benefit subsequent grantees from covenants benefitting or obligating only the original promisees or promisors.

The property whose owner **benefits** from a covenant or servitude in any controversy is called the **benefitted** estate. The property whose owner is bound by a covenant to act or not act is called the **burdened** estate. A covenant often will both benefit and burden a piece of property. Whether the property is labeled the benefitted or burdened property in any controversy depends on whether the property owner is trying to enforce a covenant against another landowner, or other persons are trying to enforce the covenant against the property owner.

Example: Every deed conveying lots in a subdivision contains a covenant providing that only "a two-story home can be built on the property." Chris owns a lot in the subdivision. If Chris wants to prevent a neighbor from building a single-story house, Chris owns the benefitted estate and the neighbor owns the burdened property. If it were Chris planning to build a single-story house, Chris' lot would be the burdened estate, and the neighboring lots are the benefitted estates.

Covenants can be **affirmative** or **negative** (negative covenants are commonly called **restrictive covenants**). Affirmative covenants and negative

---

and the obligations of a covenant. Such substitutions are present in many other settings in the law of real property, as with the concepts of voidable and derived title in personal property, the doctrine of tacking in adverse possession law, the Statute *Quia Emptores* in the transfer of freehold estates, the doctrine of equitable conversion in land transactions, and the idea of a bona fide purchaser under the Recording Acts. In each instance, the purchaser of an interest takes title subject to whatever liens, encumbrances, and obligations applied to the vendor.

covenants indicate the type of **burden** binding the landowner. *Affirmative covenants* require the owner of the burdened estate to perform some act or to pay money. Affirmative covenants include the duty to maintain a wall or a dam. *Negative covenants* restrict or prohibit the uses that can be made of the burdened property. They include, among many other possibilities, covenants restricting property to single-family residences, covenants prohibiting farm animals on the property, and covenants prohibiting the sale of alcohol there. Sometimes it is difficult to tell the difference between an affirmative and a restrictive covenant.

Example: Two adjoining landowners are bargaining over the obligation to maintain a boundary fence separating their properties. One wishes the other "to maintain the fence." The other counters that she will "not permit the fence to fall into disrepair." The first is an affirmative covenant, the latter a negative one.

Today both affirmative covenants and negative covenants may be enforced both as either real covenants or equitable servitudes if their respective elements are proved.

IDENTIFYING REAL COVENANTS AND EQUITABLE SERVITUDES

Real covenants and equitable servitudes are interests in land. Like all interests in land, the creation of the real covenant or equitable servitude must satisfy the Statute of Frauds — i.e., the covenant must be expressly created in a writing, usually a deed. The Part Performance doctrine and the equitable estoppel exceptions to the Statute (see Chapter 21, supra) apply here as well. Likewise, real covenants and equitable servitudes to be binding on subsequent bona fide purchasers must comply with the state's recording statute. See Chapter 25, supra. Notwithstanding the Statute of Frauds, courts will imply equitable servitudes in certain situations.

The following elements are necessary for a real covenant or an equitable servitude to bind and benefit subsequent owners:

Real Covenant	Equitable Servitude
1. Intent to Bind Successors	1. Intent to Bind Successors
2. Touch and Concern	2. Touch and Concern
3. Privity of Estate	3. Notice
a) Horizontal Privity	
b) Vertical Privity	

Two elements — **intent to bind successors** and **touch and concern** — are the same for real covenants and equitable servitudes. The two diverge as to their third elements. The **notice** requirement for **equitable servitudes** is easier to satisfy since all it requires is that the successor owner of the **burdened property** have actual, constructive, or inquiry notice of the covenant. Both aspects of the **privity of estate** requirement for real covenants, as discussed later in this chapter, have narrow technical meanings. Generally, a covenant that meets the real covenant's privity of estate requirement also satisfies the equitable servitudes' notice requirement (especially in conjunction with the recording statutes). However, the reverse is not true: Few covenants meeting the notice requirement for an equitable servitude also will satisfy the privity of estate element necessary in most states for a real covenant to run with the land.

Classification as a real covenant or an equitable servitude matters when considering the remedies for their breach. In many jurisdictions monetary damages and injunctive relief are available for breaches of real covenants, but only injunctive relief is available for breaches of equitable servitudes. Since most plaintiffs only care to enjoin prohibited uses and activities and are not interested in monetary damages, the more easily proven equitable servitude action serves their purposes.

Even if an element for a real covenant or an equitable servitude is not satisfied, the covenant remains enforceable and binding on the original parties to the agreement. The purpose of its "running with the land" is to determine whether subsequent purchasers can enforce or be obligated to honor the covenant, not whether the covenant constitutes a valid contract between the original parties.

INTENT TO BIND AND BENEFIT SUCCESSORS

For a covenant to run with the land, the original parties must **intend** that the covenant benefit and/or burden subsequent purchasers rather than that it merely be a personal agreement between the original parties. The intent that the covenant will run with the land must be ascertainable from the deed setting out the covenant. Intent is the easiest of the three elements to prove for real covenants to run with the land.

Several words serve as rebuttable presumptions of the parties' intent to burden and benefit successors. First, the parties may stipulate that a promisor agrees for himself, his heirs and assigns to be bound by the covenant. The courts interpret "heirs and assigns" as proving the requisite intent (absent evidence to the contrary). A common and straightforward statement such as "This covenant shall run with the land" also shows intent. So does a statement that "[t]he covenant is appurtenant to the land" conveyed or retained.

So a covenant is often included in a deed (often in its *habendum*), and the intent for the burden to run is made clear by one of the statements listed in the above paragraph. Sometimes the deed also states who can enforce the benefit (i.e., whether it is personal to the promisee or whether it runs to the owner of promisee's nearby land or to subsequent owners of the nearby land). In many cases the deed stipulates only that the burden runs with the land. An issue then remaining is whether the benefit runs with some other property or whether it is enforceable only by the original promisee. Often this issue is resolved with an inference that the benefit will run with the land if the promisee owns neighboring property. Conversely, the benefit is considered personal to the promisee (even if the burden runs with the land) if the promisee retains no land near the burdened estate. If the promisee is subdividing land, a presumption arises that the benefit is to run with all properties in the subdivision still owned by the promisee.

As the above discussion indicates, the running of the *benefit* must be analyzed separately from the running of the *burden*. One may run while the other does not. A separate analysis is required for all other elements as well.

TOUCH AND CONCERN

Real covenants and equitable servitudes must **touch and concern** the burdened property before a court will enforce the covenant against subsequent purchasers. There are many views of the role touch and concern plays in evaluating covenants. Touch and concern at one time meant physically touch and concern property. Many covenants do physically touch and concern land, such as limiting the property to single-family residences, prohibiting improvements from being built closer than five feet from the property line, or requiring all structures to have brick exteriors. Other agreements, such as a covenant to pay a homeowner's association fee or a covenant not to compete against the seller's nearby business may not physically touch the property, yet still will "touch and concern" the property. Thus restrictions on the use of land clearly satisfy this element, but affirmative covenants are less likely to.

The "touch and concern" element is premised on the presumed intent of the original parties to the covenant. It asks whether a reasonable person upon reflection and hindsight (knowing what has transpired since the original promise) would have intended the covenant to run with the land. Thus it focuses on the reasonableness of having the covenant bind successors. That reasonableness is often indicated when the subject of the covenant under review is so connected to the use of the land that the original parties must have expected it to run.

(a) Burdens That Touch and Concern Land (or Don't)

As discussed previously, the frequently encountered covenant restricting the land to residential uses touches and concerns the burdened estate. Likewise, a covenant that the grantee not operate a business that competes with the grantor's nearby business for five years touches and concerns the burdened estate.[2]

However, a covenant for the payment of money does not touch and concern the burdened property. Similarly, a covenant that a named management company will manage the property for a percentage of rentals does not touch and concern the land. Covenants providing that the seller will build a house on the lot when the buyer decides what kind of house to build does not touch and concern land; thus subsequent purchasers will not be forced to use the seller as their builder. Likewise, a contract that the seller would deliver water for a fixed price does not touch and concern the land (the burdened property's owner can as easily dig a well). Finally, a covenant promising to support (or not oppose) a rezoning application does not touch and concern the land (the right to appear in an administrative proceeding is too important).

A major exception to the general rule that payment of money does not touch and concern land is a contractual requirement that the burdened property owner pay money to a homeowners association, which will be upheld as touching and concerning the land because the money will be spent to maintain the property or a common area. Since a covenant requiring the landowner to pave parking areas, maintain shrubs, etc., would touch and concern the property, the required homeowner's fee used to pave driveways, maintain shrubs, etc., also touches and concerns the land. Even if, in the case of a homeowners association, the money is used to maintain common areas, such as roads, parks, pools, and parking areas, and not the burdened property itself, courts conclude that members have undivided interests in the common areas or that the common areas make the burdened property more enjoyable. Moreover, observe many courts, the homeowners are paying the money to themselves in the guise of the homeowners association. Whatever the courts' legal rationale, homeowner's fees to a homeowners association controlled by the homeowners touch and concern the land.

---

2. A non-compete covenant may also be invalid on a policy ground, as an **unreasonable restraint on competition**. If invalidated on this ground, the agreement is unenforceable against the original promisor. Generally, noncompete agreements must not last for more than a reasonable period of time, must be limited to a reasonable geographic area, and must be narrowly tailored to suit its purposes. To illustrate, if Pizza Man sells a lot on the same block as his popular pizza parlor, he might include a covenant the transferred lot shall not be used to operate a pizza parlor for five years. A court would find this covenant touches and concerns the transferred burdened land as well as the retained benefitted land.

A covenant to maintain insurance for improvements on the land is taken, by most courts, to touch and concern it. True, when a claim on the insurance is payable, the proceeds are money, not the improvement, but any required application of the proceeds to rebuilding the improvement is a sufficient connection to the land for most courts considering the matter. They find that a reasonable implication of the covenant's requiring insurance is that the proceeds will be used on the land to rebuild, keeping the improvements in a condition similar to the way they were when the original promise was made.

At one time most jurisdictions did not allow affirmative covenants to run at all, because they feared covenants would encumber title so much that no purchaser would buy the land. Although all recognize affirmative covenants today, their courts remain more wary of affirmative covenants than they do of restrictive covenants. (As previously discussed however, several rationales justify courts' finding that money obligations touch and concern the burdened property.) First, courts may not wish to depart from their precedents. Second, they dislike covenants that are open-ended, in the sense that they impose costly, uncertain, and unforeseen financial burdens. (Recall the covenant requiring the buyer to employ the seller to build a house.) Here a court may look for a time limit on affirmative covenants requiring subsequent owners to pay money (although homeowner associations may escape the intense scrutiny imposed on other payees). Third, the original landowners entering into the covenant and subsequent purchasers may not have the sophistication or take the time to appreciate the long-term consequences of a promise. A covenant that runs with the land, unlike the typical contract, does not give a subsequent landowner an opportunity to rectify her predecessor's mistakes, since real covenants may continue indefinitely. Finally, many affirmative covenants calling for burdened property owners to purchase goods or services from the promisee are little more than ingenious marketing tools for the promisee's business and as such might be considered unreasonable restraints of trade.

(b) Benefits that Touch and Concern Land (or Don't)

The preceding paragraphs discussed whether the covenant or servitude touched and concerned the burdened property. Whether the covenant touched and concerned the *benefitted property* is a separate issue and must be analyzed separately. The covenant must touch and concern the benefitted property for the benefit to run with the land, no matter whether the burden is personal to the promisor or is a real covenant or equitable servitude running with burdened property.

Example: O owns two adjoining lots. O transfers one of the two lots to P. The deed restricts the transferred land to single-family residences and provides that the restriction shall run with the land. O then transfers his retained lot to T. P attempts to build a grocery store. The issue is who can enforce the single-family residence covenant: T, the subsequent and current owner of the adjoining lot; or O, who no longer owns any property in the area. The answer depends on whether the covenant touches and concerns T's land. If the benefit touches and concerns T's land, T can enforce the covenant. If, on the other hand, the benefit does not touch and concern T's land, O (but not T) can enforce the covenant. In this Example all jurisdictions hold the covenant touches and concerns the benefitted property. T (but not O) can enforce the covenant.

Whether T, the subsequent purchaser in this Example can enforce the covenant against P depends on the meaning of "touch and concern." A requirement that the covenant actually produce a physical presence on the land will lead to a conclusion that the covenant does not touch and concern the benefitted property. Courts using the "touch and concern" element determine whether a reasonable person upon reflection and hindsight would have intended the benefit to run, leads to the conclusion that the legitimate purpose of the restriction on P's property is to improve the use and enjoyment of the second lot, whether O or some person owned the lot. Guaranteeing nearby property will continue its residential character furthers a property owner's enjoyment of the benefitted property. Once O sold the second lot, his interest in maintaining the residential nature ended. The person with an interest in maintaining the residential character would be the current owner of the second lot (here T). The benefit touches and concerns the second lot. This is not to say that all residential restrictions are appurtenant to some land: If, for instance, O initially owned and sold only the first lot and his nearest property was five miles from it, the nexus for the benefit disappears. The benefit in this situation would be personal to O.

In the other situations discussed above in "Burdens that Touch and Concern (or Don't)," the noncompete covenant could touch and concern benefitted land. The homeowners association fee would touch the benefitted land since the money must be spent for the upkeep of the property. A court probably would find that the management contract covenant is a personal benefit. The benefit of a construction contract in nearly all cases likewise will be personal. The benefit of the water supply contract may touch and concern specific property if the contract stipulated the water was to come solely from identified land. In some jurisdictions, a covenant does not touch and concern purported burdened property unless the covenant also touches and concerns some benefitted property (i.e., the court will hold the covenant does not run even if it does touch and concern the burdened property). In these jurisdictions, once the benefit of the covenant is found to be personal, the burden will not be binding on subsequent purchasers: That is, if the benefit is in gross, the burden does not run.

However, most jurisdictions favor a rule that a burden that touches and concerns land can run even if the benefit is personal. They seem to follow one of three approaches: (1) The burden may run even if the benefit is personal or touches and concerns benefitted property. (2) The burden will not run unless the covenant touches and concerns both burdened and benefitted land. (3) The burden will not run as a real covenant unless the covenant touches and concerns both burdened and benefitted land, but an equitable servitude will be enforced even if the benefit is personal as long as the burden touches and concerns the burdened land. The third approach is likely to be used when either of the original parties is either a defendant or plaintiff in a lawsuit to enforce the covenant.

> ***Example:*** *A* and *B* own adjoining properties in a summer cottage community around a lake. The lake water becomes unfit for *B* to drink. *A* agrees to supply water from her well for the summer to *B* for a fee for use in *B*'s cottage. *A* and *B* sell their properties. Assuming only the touch and concern element for a running covenant is in doubt, does this agreement touch and concern their land? Can *B*'s purchaser compel *A*'s purchaser to supply the water? That the water is drawn from the well on *A*'s purchaser's land is to a degree a restriction on its use otherwise. But the water, once drawn from the well, is no longer part of the land: it is personal to *B*'s purchaser. It might as well be treated as personal property. Moreover, the seasonal nature of the agreement and confining use of the water to *B*'s purchaser's cottage, indicates that the benefits and burdens of ownership of each property are not substantially affected. This agreement does not touch and concern the land.

(c) The "Legal Relations" Test

The legal relations test provides that a covenant touches and concerns the land when it affects the legal relations — the benefits and the burdens — of the promisor and promisee as owners of their respective properties. This restated test is an effort to judge the effect of the covenant, not common law technicalities. This test originated in a 1938 New York opinion validating homeowners association fees. It has proven influential but has not relaxed traditional touch and concern analysis sufficiently to claim that it has achieved its objective. This failure may be because it says too much. If the covenant's benefits and burdens are evaluated together, then any burden is a benefit to the promisee's property, and thus every covenant touches and concerns the land, and then all judicial discretion to invalidate a covenant is gone. And judicial discretion may be what the touch and concern element of a real covenant is about.

Example: Developer inserts, in every deed in a residential subdivision lot, a covenant providing that on any subsequent resale of the lot, Developer shall receive 1 percent of the appreciated sales price. This covenant does not touch and concern the land: the first homeowner, when accepting the deed, cannot know its effect on land values, nor how long and when in the future it will apply. It may enable Developer to sell lots more cheaply, but who knows? Homeowners may make decisions to buy too hastily, without evaluating the effect of the fee. A covenant that benefits promisees so much and promisors so little, and that burdens promisees so much and promisors so little, does not touch and concern the land.

REAL COVENANTS AND PRIVITY OF ESTATE

The conditions for real covenants and equitable servitude share the first two elements, intent and touch and concern. They diverge on the third element. In many jurisdictions, the benefitted party must prove there was **privity of estate** before a **real covenant** will bind the subsequent owners of the burdened property. Two separate privities must exist before a court in these jurisdictions will find privity of estate: horizontal privity and vertical privity. Vertical and horizontal privity are evaluated under different rules.

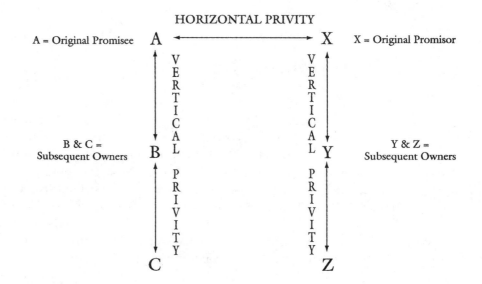

(a) Terminology

(1) Original Promisee

The **original promisee** is an original party to the agreement creating the covenant. The original *promisee* can enforce the covenant (assuming another person is bound), either because the benefit is personal to the promisee or because it is appurtenant to the promisee's property. A person can be both a promisee and a promisor under a covenant; that is, a covenant, such as a residential-use-only covenant, may both benefit a person (so the person is the promisee) and burden the same person (so the person is the promisor).

(2) Original Promisor

The **original promisor** is an original party to the agreement creating the covenant. The original *promisor* is always *bound* by the covenant (assuming another person is benefitted), either because the burden is personal to the promisor or because the burden is appurtenant to the original promisor's land.

(3) Subsequent Owners

Subsequent owners (also known as purchasers, remote purchasers, owners, assigns, or successors in interest) are those persons who were not original parties to the contract, but who now own property that may be benefitted or burdened by a covenant entered into by a previous owner (the original promisee or original promisor) if the covenant runs with the land. Since a subsequent owner cannot be bound or benefitted under traditional **privity of contract** theory, the subsequent owner will benefit or be bound only if the benefit or burden runs with the land (i.e., is appurtenant to the land). Of course a subsequent purchaser can enter into a new contract and be bound by it, but the issue in real covenants and equitable servitudes is whether the remote subsequent purchaser can enforce or be bound by a predecessor's deed covenant even if the subsequent purchaser does not enter into the new contract.

(4) Horizontal Privity

Horizontal privity refers to the necessary relationship between the original parties to the agreement for the covenant to run with the land (i.e., to bind and/or burden subsequent owners of the property). It is measured at the time of the original agreement that created the covenant. Horizontal privity is not necessary for its enforcement between the original parties: No "privity of estate" is needed since the original parties are bound and benefitted by "privity of contract." Jurisdictions have three different standards for horizontal privity of estate. See (b) Horizontal Privity, infra. All three are not hard to understand, although all exclude more covenants that you might expect. The adjective "horizontal" here signifies the relationship between the original promisee and the original promisor. *A* and *X* in the diagram are in horizontal privity.

(5) Vertical Privity

Vertical privity refers to that relationship between an original promisee or promisor to the contract and those subsequent purchasers tracing their interests in the benefitted or burdened property back to either of them. It requires that a transferee take substantially the same estate as the transferor. Typically vertical privity is found on sales, gifts, devises, and inheritances of real estate, but not in leases.

(b) Horizontal Privity

In the majority of jurisdictions retaining the horizontal privity element, **horizontal privity** is either *instantaneous* privity or *mutual* privity. Instantaneous privity exists when the original promisor and promisee transferred a property interest of some type: That is, they must be in a grantor-grantee relationship in a deed transferring the fee simple, or a landlord and tenant in a lease. Here it is the interest transferred in the deed, or the transfer of possession in the lease, that meets the requirement of this type of privity. It exists only in the nanosecond of delivery. However, all but a few jurisdictions go further and require mutual privity as well: That is, most all jurisdictions require that both parties have an ongoing, simultaneous interest in some piece of property. Mutual privity is also known as *tenurial* privity. It arises when one original party transfers an interest in land (other than the covenant itself) to the other original party. Generally it can be created only in conjunction with grants of less-than-fee, present, freehold estates; leases; or easements. The transfer of the property and the creation of the covenant must occur simultaneously.

Example: Abbott and Costello are neighbors and execute a document limiting their respective properties to single-family residential use. There is no horizontal privity because the document, even if it is a deed, does not transfer a fee, a life estate, an easement, or a leasehold. Abbott and Costello may have intended the covenant to run, and the covenant does touch and concern both properties, but Abbott and Costello already owned their respective properties when they made the agreement. Thus, there could be no mutual, horizontal privity of estate. Consequently, the covenant will not run to successors in interest.[3]

Example: Abbott, owning two adjoining lots, transfers one lot to Costello, incorporating a covenant limiting both lots to single-family residential use only. Both Abbott and Costello are promisors and promisees of the covenant: Each has interest in the other's property — that is, the right to enforce the covenant. Here both instantaneous and mutual horizontal privity exist because the covenant was included in a transfer of a fee interest. This privity is sometimes referred to as successive interest privity.

Example: Abbott, owning two adjoining lots, transfers one to Costello, the deed containing no covenants. Six months later Abbott and Costello each give the other a deed restricting their respective lots to single-family residential use. There is no horizontal privity, because the restrictions were not created in conjunction with the initial transfer of a lot to Costello.

A few states require horizontal privity for the *burden* to run, but not for the *benefit* to run. In these states, the original promisor would be burdened no matter whether the original promisee or a subsequent owner enforced the covenant, but horizontal privity would be necessary to enforce the covenant against subsequent purchasers of the burdened property.

A number of states loosen horizontal privity in another way: They require only that the burdened party have actual, constructive, or inquiry notice of the covenant. As to constructive notice, these jurisdictions rely on a combination of the Statute of Frauds and the recording statutes, relying on the ubiquity of their use in creating covenants. This approach has the advantage of merging real covenant and equitable servitude law into a single law of servitudes running with the land. But if notice of some type is present to satisfy the privity requirement, then it could as easily be said, as later discussion will show, that horizontal privity is not required for the creation of an equitable servitude.[4]

---

3. There are those commentators who maintain that property law is a subspecies of contract law: For them, instantaneous privity would suffice, but if it did, any set of neighbors, each owning their land in fee, could create covenants among themselves that would bind future neighbors, and the agreements of the moment would last indefinitely, with unpredictable results for the value of each benefitted and burdened property.

4. One jurisdiction, Massachusetts, has a narrower rule. Horizontal privity of estate will be found by a Massachusetts court only when the covenant is created in the grant of an easement or a lease. So, in Massachusetts, none of the residential-only covenants in the three Abbott and Costello Examples would run to successors since none of the three scenarios involved easements or leases.

(c) Vertical Privity

Vertical privity denotes the relationship between an original party to the covenant and her successors in interest. All vertical privity requires is that the subsequent, remote property owner succeed to an original party's entire estate or ownership interest in the property, either directly from an original party or through persons on the same chain of title, tracing their interests back to an original party to the covenant.

> **Example:** In the Abbott and Costello Examples above, Costello sells his fee to Gracie. Costello and Gracie are in vertical privity.

Many jurisdictions distinguish between what constitutes vertical privity for a *burden* to run and what constitutes vertical privity for a *benefit* to run. For a *burden* to run to a successor or remote party, the party must have succeeded to the original promisor's **entire estate** or **ownership interest**. This type of privity exists when the successor has succeeded to substantially the entire estate of his predecessor. The "entire estate" requirement means tenants are not in vertical privity with their landlords. On the other hand, all that is required for a *benefit* to run is that a remote or subsequent purchaser have a **possessory interest** in the property. This relaxed requirement for benefits to run rests on the premise that possession is the ability to control use, and land use restrictions are most often the subject of covenants. Under this analysis, tenants are in vertical privity if they wish to enforce or benefit from the real covenant. They do not take the original party's entire estate, but do have physical use and possession of the land, and so can enforce the benefit of a covenant.

In some jurisdictions, adverse possession defeats the running of both benefits and burdens because the adverse possessor does not succeed to any party's interest. The adverse possessor is regarded as starting a new chain of title and hence is not in vertical privity with an original party to the covenant. Another rule, just as sensible, might state that the adverse possessor dispossessed the true owner, but not the rights and obligations consistent with the adverse possessor's use of the property: That is, the title of the true owner is by operation of law transferred to the adverse user, but it is transferred just as it was in the hands of the true owner.

EQUITABLE SERVITUDES AND NOTICE

The third element for an **equitable servitude** (in place of a real covenant's privity element) necessary to bind a subsequent purchaser is for the purchaser to have **notice** of the covenant when he or she buys the burdened property. The rationale underlying equitable servitudes is that a subsequent, remote landowner should be bound by a covenant, maybe not for damages, but at least for injunctive relief, if the original parties intended the burden to run, the covenant "touches and concerns" the land, and the person to be bound knows about the covenant when he or she buys. As with recording statutes, notice as an element of equitable servitudes can be either actual notice, constructive notice gathered from the land records, or inquiry notice gathered from viewing the premises and surrounding properties. We return to inquiry notice in the next chapter in the discussion of subdivisions and common schemes.

The notice requirement applies only to the burdens not to the benefits. Benefitted owners do not have to take with notice of the servitude: As long as the intent and "touch and concern" elements are present, a benefitted subsequent owner can enforce an equitable servitude whether or not he had notice of the covenant when he purchased.

Fairness and sense of unjust enrichment underlie this notice element for an equitable servitude. Why permit a subsequent remote purchaser to buy with notice of the covenant and then proceed to ignore it? Moreover, when the purchaser paid value for burdened land, it would be a windfall to her to ignore the burden. Thus all jurisdictions and commentators favor dispensing with the privity of estate as a necessary requirement for a real covenant to run. Abolishing the privity requirement means relying instead on the omnipresent Statute of Frauds and recording statutes to give notice to subsequent purchasers or to protect subsequent purchasers from covenants in deeds not properly recorded. A person held bound by a real covenant must here have taken the deed with actual, constructive, or inquiry notice of a previously recorded document incorporating the real covenant.

THE RESTATEMENT (THIRD) OF PROPERTY: SERVITUDES

The Restatement (Third) of Property: Servitudes, published by the American Law Institute, advocates replacing most of what is presented in this chapter with a unified approach to servitudes on land. It is unclear what effect this Restatement will have on pre-existing law.

This Restatement attempts to simplify the law of covenants and servitudes by discarding historic labels such as restrictive covenants, affirmative covenants, real covenants, equitable servitudes, and negative easements. A single term — servitudes — encompasses them all. It also eliminates the horizontal privity element, the vertical privity requirement, the in gross and appurtenant designations, and the touch and concern requirement. While technically abolishing the touch and concern element, the Restatement uses a functionally equivalent concept whereby a court can declare a covenant invalid as illegal, unconstitutional, or against public policy. Thus courts would honor any covenant creating a servitude as long as the covenant is in a writing satisfying the Statute of Frauds, the beneficiaries are those intended to be benefitted by the contracting parties, and the servitude is not illegal, unconstitutional, or against public policy. All servitudes are presumed to be assignable and divisible unless a contrary intent is discernible. Covenants are interpreted based on the parties' intent rather than strictly and narrowly. A person enforcing a servitude may seek both monetary damages and equitable relief.

Further, this Restatement gives more unilateral latitude to a servient estate owner to relocate an easement, at his own expense, as long as he does not hinder or prevent the use of the easement. The Restatement also encourages affirmative covenants such as historic preservation and conservation servitudes. It also approves of creating rights in strangers to the deed. Similarly, special rules apply to life tenants, lessees, and adverse possessors, who may be subject to servitudes and be able to enforce them.

Examples

1. David owned two lots on a heavily traveled industrial road. David sold one lot to Austin by a deed containing a covenant prohibiting the sale of beer, wine, and intoxicating liquor on the lot. Later David sold the second lot to Tyler, the deed also containing a covenant prohibiting the sale of beer, wine, and intoxicating liquor. Both deeds provided the alcohol ban would be binding on the purchasers (Austin and Tyler respectively), their heirs, and assigns. David inserted the covenant into the deeds because he staunchly opposes alcohol consumption. All deeds were properly recorded. Austin sold his lot to Oren, who wanted to open a convenience store and sell beer and wine in the store. (a) Is the benefit personal to David or appurtenant to Tyler's lot? (b) If David chooses not to enforce the covenant, does Tyler have standing to enforce the covenant? (c) If Tyler chooses not to enforce the covenant, does David have standing to enforce the covenant? (d) Does the burden of the covenant bind Oren? (e) Would your answer to (d) change under the following facts: David included the covenant in the deed to Austin because David operated a bar and grill on the second lot and did not want Austin or anyone else selling beer and alcohol in competition with David's bar. David later sold the bar and grill to Tyler by a deed that did not contain the covenant. (f) Assume, instead of inserting a covenant prohibiting the sale of beer, wine, and other alcoholic beverages, the deed conveyed the lot to "Austin, his heirs, and assigns, as long as no beer, wine, or other alcoholic beverages are sold on the premises," and David deeded the second lot to Tyler with the same restriction. Austin sells to Oren,

who wants to operate a convenience store that sells beer and wine. What result?

2. Judy and Carrie own adjoining lots. They enter into an agreement that their lots would be restricted to single-family residential use only and that no mobile homes would be located on either lot. The agreement provided, "The covenants will run with the land." The agreement was properly recorded in the local land records. Judy subsequently sold her lot to Tai, the deed restricting the lot to single-family residential use only and prohibiting mobile homes on the lot. Carrie sold her lot to Curtis, the deed containing the same two restrictions. Curtis bulldozed all the trees on the lot and moved six mobile homes onto his lot. When Curtis cut the trees and situated the mobile homes, the value of Tai's lot dropped $10,000. Tai sues Curtis seeking $10,000 in damages and an injunction requiring Curtis to remove the six mobile homes. What result?

3. Terry owned two adjoining lots. Terry's house was situated on Lot 1, except his house encroached one foot onto Lot 2. Terry contracted to sell Lot 1 to Gerard. Gerard was concerned about the one-foot encroachment. To allay Gerard's apprehension, at closing Terry executed a "Declaration of Restriction" providing that no improvements be made on Lot 2 within three yards of the house on Lot 1. Terry was named grantor in the declaration, but the declaration named no grantee. Also at the closing, Terry executed and delivered a deed conveying Lot 1 to Gerard, the deed being made subject to and including all rights accruing from all recorded conditions, restrictions, covenants, and easements affecting the property conveyed. Both documents were recorded in the local land records that same day. Two years later Terry sold Lot 2 to Kim, the deed being made subject to "easements, covenants, and conditions of record." Kim contracted with House Builders to construct a house on her lot. When Gerard saw the house was going to be built within one yard of his home, he brought a lawsuit to enjoin the construction as a violation of the three-yard setback in the Declaration of Restriction. Was the Declaration of Restriction a real covenant running with the land?

4. Guy owned 400 acres. He sold 150 of the acres to Chad. The sales contract, but not the deed, stated, "Guy covenants he will offer Chad a right of first refusal for all or part of the remaining 250 acres owned by Guy when Guy receives an offer to buy the land." Chad filed a memorandum of the right of first refusal in the local deed records. Guy received an offer from Holt Investments for the remaining 250 acres. Guy notified Chad of the offer. Chad declined to exercise the right of first refusal. Five years later Holt Investments sold 100 acres (out of the 250 acres) to Timber Paper Co. Six months later Chad filed a suit alleging Holt Investments' sale to Timber Paper Co. was made in violation of his right of first refusal. Who prevails?

Explanations

1. (a) The deed does not say that the benefit runs with the land, but that is not unusual and has not prevented courts from implying that the benefit runs. A court might resort to the rebuttable presumption that the benefit is appurtenant if the promisee owns nearby land that could be benefitted. David owns the adjoining lot. On these facts, the presumption will be rebutted. When David later sold the adjoining lot, the deed included the same covenant, and David owned no more land at that time. It appears David did not insert the covenant into either deed to benefit his retained land, but for reasons personal to him (i.e., his staunchly prohibitionist convictions). The land, moreover, is on a "heavily traveled industrial road," which seems to indicate that David did not intend to benefit Tyler's lot by burdening Austin's lot. Under this interpretation, the benefit is personal to David.

   (b) If the benefit of the covenant is personal to David, Tyler would not have standing to enforce it. On the other hand, if the analysis in (a) is incorrect, and the benefit is appurtenant to Tyler's land, Tyler would have standing to enforce the covenant. The intent to run would be implied since David owned property when he burdened Austin's lot. Horizontal privity existed because David inserted the covenant into the deed transferring the lot to Austin. Vertical privity existed since Tyler acquired David's entire interest in the lot. Touch and concern may be a slight problem, but a court probably would hold the benefit touched and concerned Tyler's lot since the restriction affects the enjoyment of the benefitted land and is a commonly encountered restriction.

   (c) Again the answer depends on the answer in Explanation (a) above. Only one person, David or Tyler, has standing to enforce the covenant. If the benefit is personal to David, he can enforce the covenant against Oren in most jurisdictions. In some states, however, the burden will not touch and concern the burdened property (or at least the burden will not run with the land) unless the benefit also touches and concerns benefitted property. In those states, since David asserts the benefit is personal to him and not appurtenant to Tyler's land, the burden will not run to Oren at all. Thus, even though David has standing, there is no covenant to enforce. If the conclusion in (a) is incorrect, and the benefit is appurtenant to Tyler's land, David would not have standing to enforce the burden.

   (d) This Explanation also depends on Explanation (a) and the law of the jurisdiction. For the burden to run, the original parties must have intended the burden to run. The intent to run element is met: The deed provided the covenant would bind Austin, his heirs, and assigns. Also required for the burden to run are horizontal and vertical privity. In all states except Massachusetts, the horizontal privity of estate element is satisfied since the covenant was created in a deed transferring the property from David to Austin. Since Austin transferred his interest to Oren, vertical privity of estate exists, too. Normally a covenant prohibiting the sale of alcohol would touch and concern the burdened land, and so a majority of courts would find. Thus, in a majority of states the burden runs with the land and is binding on Oren. The notice requirement for the equitable servitude also is met since Oren at a minimum had constructive notice of the restriction in a recorded deed in his chain of title. In a few states, however, if the benefit was personal to David rather than appurtenant to Tyler's property, a court might refuse to enforce the burden against subsequent purchasers. See Explanation (c) supra. If the benefit was appurtenant to Tyler's property, the burden would run with Oren's land in all states.

(e) The new facts simplify the analysis. All the elements for the burden to run are met as in Explanation (d). Moreover, the new facts support an argument that the covenant was for the benefit of the retained lot, protecting David's bar and grill operations. Thus, a court would find the benefit was appurtenant to the lot now owned by Tyler. Since the burden and benefit touched and concerned adjoining properties, the burden ran with Oren's land and would be binding on Oren.

(f) The Example explores the difference between a covenant studied in this chapter, and a condition subsequent studied in Chapters 9 and 10, supra. David in Example (f) did not give Austin a fee simple absolute subject to a covenant. Instead, he granted Austin a fee simple determinable. David retained a possibility of reverter. The condition subsequent is the sale of beer, wine, or other alcoholic beverages on the premises. If alcohol is sold on the premises, Austin (or his heirs or assigns: Oren here) loses all interest in the land, and the property automatically reverts to David or his heirs. Tyler as the owner of the adjoining lot has no rights to Oren's land. In contrast, the sale of alcohol on the premises under the original facts would breach a covenant. Oren still would own the land. David (if the benefit was personal to him) or Tyler (if the benefit was appurtenant to his land) could enjoin the sales or seek monetary damages. So the consequences flowing from a violation of a condition are much more draconian than the consequences resulting from the breach of a covenant. Most restrictions on use today are expressed as covenants. Purchasers understandably are not willing to purchase property subject to conditions subsequent.

2. For Tai to collect damages, she must prove that a real covenant ran with the land so as to burden Curtis. Tai cannot do this. For a real covenant to run in this case, the original parties must intend the covenant to run, the

covenant must touch and concern Curtis' property for the burden to run, the covenant must touch and concern Tai's land for the benefit to run, and there must be horizontal and vertical privity. The intent to run is easily satisfied because the agreement stipulated, "The covenants will run with the land." Touch and concern also is met. The burden definitely touches and concerns Curtis' land since the land can be used only for single-family residences and no mobile homes can be located on the lot. The benefit touches and concerns Tai's land since the restriction on Curtis' land makes Tai's use of her property more enjoyable. A court, moreover, would conclude that the covenant is the kind that reasonable landowners would impress upon their property and intend to bind remote purchasers. Vertical privity of estate is met in both cases as Tai succeeded to Judy's estate and Curtis succeeded to Carrie's estate.

However, the horizontal privity element fails in most jurisdictions. In most states, horizontal privity will be found only when the covenant is included in a deed transferring the property, in a lease, or in a grant of easement. In this case, the lots were separately owned when Judy and Carrie agreed to restrict their two lots. Thus, courts in most states will find there was no horizontal privity of estate. A few jurisdictions require horizontal privity only for the burden to run. Even in these jurisdictions, however, since Curtis was a remote purchaser, there must be horizontal privity for Curtis to be burdened, and as just noted, there was no horizontal privity in this case.

Tai could only enforce the covenant as a real covenant if she lives in one of the few states that has abolished the horizontal privity of estate requirement altogether. Tai would prevail in these states since Curtis had notice of the restrictive covenant (it was in his deed) and all other elements for a real covenant to run could be proved.

All is not lost for Tai. While Tai's claim for damages is doomed in most jurisdictions because she cannot prove the horizontal privity necessary to enforce a real covenant, she will prevail in her quest for injunctive relief. To get injunctive relief, Tai needs only to prove the elements for an equitable servitude. As discussed above, the intent to run and the touch and concern elements, common to real covenants and equitable servitudes, are met. Horizontal privity of estate is not necessary for an equitable servitude to bind remote purchasers. Since the first two elements can be proved, the equitable servitude will be enforced against Curtis if he had notice of the restriction. The notice could be actual, constructive, or inquiry notice. Whether or not Curtis had actual or inquiry notice, he definitely had constructive notice. The restriction was in his deed and in the original agreement, which was recorded. Curtis must remove the mobile homes. But Curtis does not have to plant new trees, since no covenant addressed trees on the properties: Mere loss in value does not entitle a landowner to damages or injunctive relief unless the defendant was under a legal or contractual duty not to cause the injury.

3. The Declaration of Restriction is a real covenant binding Kim. To enforce a real covenant, Gerard must prove the following: The original parties intended the covenant would run with the land, the covenant touched and concerned the burdened land, both horizontal and vertical privity exist, and the covenant is in a writing satisfying the Statute of Frauds. Horizontal privity is at issue here. Kim would argue that the covenant was not included in the deed and so Terry attempted to burden his own land, which cannot constitute horizontal privity. But horizontal privity is established when a restriction is created in connection with the conveyance of an estate in land. There is no requirement the restriction be incorporated into the deed itself. The Declaration of Restriction was executed in connection with the overall conveyance of Lot 1 to Gerard. That was enough. Gerard prevails.

4. Timber Paper Co. prevails. The vertical privity is met. So is the notice element. Holt Investments had constructive notice of the right of first refusal during the activity surrounding its own purchase of the 250 acres. Not so clear are the intent to run and the touch and concern elements, common to both real covenants and equitable servitudes. The right-of-first-refusal covenant does not affect the nature, quality, use, enjoyment, or value of the property. As such, the agreement in the sales contract was collateral to the land and did not touch and concern it. This being so, it was a personal covenant binding on the original promisor, Guy, but not on subsequent purchasers. Second, even when exercised, the right is the equivalent of an option to purchase, does not work an equitable conversion, and so does not give the parties to it and their successors any mutual or successive interest in property. So there is no horizontal privity. Third, it is not the type of restriction that should be allowed to continue indefinitely. It is too open-ended and to allow it to stand would violate the common law Rule Against Perpetuities. Fourth, the Restatement (Third) of Property (Servitudes) gives courts the option to declare that the covenant does not run or to limit its running to a reasonable time. Its duration might then be limited at least to the period of time permitted in gross — 21 years — by the Rule or to some shorter period. Fifth, this right of first refusal was personal to Chad and not appurtenant to the 150 acres. In some jurisdictions, a burden will not run with the land unless the benefit also touches and concerns land. In these states, the burden of the covenant would not run with land. There is no such thing as a covenant in gross. Finally, nothing in the documents indicates the right of first refusal was to bind any person other than Guy, the original promisor. The court, therefore, would find that the original parties had not intended the covenant to run with the land in the first place.

30

Real Covenants and Equitable Servitudes: Common Schemes and Termination

The previous Chapter discussed the elements essential for benefits and burdens of a covenant to run with the land to subsequent property owners. This Chapter discusses common covenant schemes used in subdivisions and the termination of covenants.

THE COMMON SCHEME AND SUBDIVISIONS

A large proportion of all United States homeowners live in urban condominium complexes or suburban subdivisions whose parcels or lots are subject to a common scheme of covenants, restrictions, and conditions (CCRs), all set out in one large document or declaration and administered by a homeowners' association (HOA). Such environments are sometimes referred to as common interest communities.[1] They typically result from a land developer or common owner subdividing a large parcel of suburban land in accordance with local subdivision ordinances and selling lots to individuals or builders. The common owner sometimes builds roads, sewers, and drainage systems and works with utility companies to insure each lot has access to essential services. The developer may build homes on each lot before selling, or may sell unimproved lots to individuals or builders. He

---

1. This term refers not just to CCRs administered by HOAs, but also to community members acting collectively. The same is true of the discussion in this Chapter. It is applicable not just to HOAs, but also to the owners of any subdivision with a common set of servitudes.

may incorporate covenants into deeds to promote residential use, maintain value, preserve aesthetics, promote safety, and for other purposes the sub-divider believes will increase the value of the lots.

Invariably, problems arise. Some deeds, for instance, may not incorporate all or any of the covenants, the covenants might vary from one deed to another, or the developer may try to sell some retained land for a purpose inconsistent with the use (typically residential) being made of the sold properties. The law of equitable servitudes has adapted to these problems. As a result, courts have developed rules for a **common scheme** or *general plan of development* to impose burdens and grant standing to enforce the servitudes. The common scheme, then, is a device used only when the remedy sought is an equitable one — e.g., an injunction.

THE COMMON SCHEME AND STANDING TO ENFORCE A SERVITUDE

Let's first review the rules affecting subdivisions based on traditional real covenant and equitable servitude analyses.

Example: Developer owns Blackacre and deeds one of its lots subject to a restrictive covenant to Bailey. Bailey's property is the burdened estate. If Bailey breaches the covenant, Developer can enjoin the violation. Whether any subsequent purchaser of Developer's retained land can enjoin Bailey's breach depends on whether the benefit of the covenant is personal to Developer or is appurtenant to the subsequent purchaser's land. If the covenant is appurtenant and not personal to Developer, Developer's remaining land in the larger parcel is the benefitted property. Each lot sold later by Developer remains benefitted, and all new owners have standing to enforce the covenant against Bailey.

Example: A year after selling the lot to Bailey, Developer sells another lot in Blackacre to Cricket, the deed subject to the same restrictive covenants included in Bailey's deed. Cricket breaches a covenant in her deed. Bailey seeks to enjoin Cricket's breach of the covenant. Using traditional analysis, Bailey cannot enforce the covenant against Cricket (or any other subsequent purchaser), even if Cricket's deed included the covenant, for two reasons. First, the covenant in Bailey's deed burdened Bailey's land. It did not burden Developer's remaining property, including Cricket's lot. Second, most jurisdictions have strict laws prohibiting a grantor (like Developer) from granting the benefit of covenants to strangers to the deed. Bailey would be a stranger to the deed transferring the lot to Cricket. So even if Developer inserted the same covenant in Cricket's deed, traditionally neither Bailey nor any subsequent owner of Bailey's property could enforce the covenant against Cricket (no intent to run and no privity of estate).

Example: The covenant in all the deeds out from Developer restricted each lot to single-family residential use. Fargo purchased the last lot and wants to build a gas station on it. Developer either waives the restriction in a writing or orally assures Fargo he can build the station. Bailey, Cricket, and the other landowners want to enjoin Fargo's building the gas station. Traditionally they have no standing to prevent the gas station from being built. First, the benefit is personal to Developer since he owned no other property to which the benefit might become appurtenant; and Developer has indicated he will not enforce the covenant. Second, all previous purchasers are now strangers to the deed to Fargo. So Bailey, Cricket, and the other landowners cannot stop Fargo from building the gas station.

The **common scheme** concept is primarily used to overcome most of the legal obstacles in the prior Examples in order to give all subdivision owners *standing* to enforce the *benefit* but not the burden of the covenant. Second, in perhaps a majority of jurisdictions, it can also (though not in as many jurisdictions) be used to imply, not just a mutuality of benefits, but also a mutuality of burdens. Third, in a few jurisdictions, it can be used to permit any lot owner in a subdivision to sue any other lot owner. The important point is that a common scheme does not itself create a restriction or burden; instead, it tells a plaintiff alleging the benefit of a covenant whether she has standing to sue a burdened lot owner.

Once a court finds a common scheme, it will conclude that the common owner, Developer in the Examples, intended to impose the identical covenant in all parcels from the time the common scheme began. Thus the lots within the scheme, and sometimes the entire subdivision, became *burdened* and/or *benefitted* as soon as the common owner sold the first lot as part of the *common scheme*. The entire tract is both benefitted and burdened, and each landowner, from Developer to Bailey to Fargo, enjoys the benefit and has standing to enforce the common servitude against all other landowners in the subdivision, no matter who bought in what order. Even to confer standing, however, these burdens and benefits must be implied. How this is done is the subject of the next section. For now, applying this common plan concept to the Examples, the finding of a common scheme results in holding the *benefit appurtenant* to all lots in the subdivision rather than *personal* to the Developer. In addition, all purchasers, including Bailey and Cricket, and Fargo, have a right to enforce the servitude against the owner of any property subject to the common scheme. Again, their order of purchase does not matter.

THE COMMON SCHEME AND NOTICE FOR RECORDING ACTS AND EQUITABLE SERVITUDES

Most courts will impose the burden on all land in the common scheme once they find a common scheme exists. The imposed burden is not automatic, however, since many courts fear that implying the burden weakens the integrity of the *recording systems* and the elements required for **equitable servitudes**. Moreover, the recording statutes require a bona fide purchaser for value have **notice** of the burden before a court will subject the subsequent purchaser to the burden. Likewise, as the discussion in the last Chapter shows, the critical element in *equitable servitudes* is *notice*.

Example: Building on the prior Examples, Developer deeded property to Bailey, Cricket, and others incorporating the same covenant into most of the deeds. For reasons unknown, Developer's deed to Jones omitted the covenant. Jones later conveyed his lot to Rich, the deed omitting the covenant. Rich wants to do some act that would breach the covenant if the covenant burdened him and his lot. Can Developer, Bailey, Cricket, or any other landowner enforce the covenant against Rich?

While Developer and maybe others have standing to enforce any covenant, the threshold issue is not whether anyone has standing to sue, but whether Rich is subject to the covenant at all. When the title searchers searched the deed records they would not have found the restriction in the Developer-to-Jones-to-Rich chain. Because nothing in Jones' deed mentioned the *covenant*, Rich would prevail under traditional analysis in pure notice or race-notice states as a bona fide purchaser for value without notice. Hence he would be protected under the recording statutes unless a common scheme somehow gives constructive notice.

Similarly, in the last Example, Rich, the subsequent bona fide purchaser for value, did not have the notice necessary for the covenant to be enforced as an *equitable servitude*. Rich probably had no actual notice of the covenant because he had no contact with Developer and may not have seen or heard of any plat or covenant. Since the covenant was not in any deeds in Rich's chain of title, he did not have constructive notice in the usual manner of a recorded deed. Some jurisdictions require title searchers to search deeds out from a common owner. Most do not. See Chapter 25, supra. However, a jurisdiction requiring searchers to read deeds out from a common owner might find that Rich had inquiry notice.

However, when (as in the last Example) some of the deeds in the subdivision do not contain the covenant in dispute, or the covenants in some lots are not identical to other covenants with the same subject matter, the implied burden and benefit are known as **implied reciprocal negative easements** or **covenants**. ("Easement" is a misnomer.) The primary rationale for creating this type of implied interest in land is that by creating a substantially uniform set of covenants that permit similar uses and impose similar restrictions on every lot owner, all of them are benefitted and burdened in equal measure. Additional rationales are that (1) each owner, upon buying the lot, may have been put on *constructive* notice through the recording statutes that covenants were uniformly or substantially applicable — thus, taking delivery of the deed was presumed acceptance of the scheme; and (2) if the subdivision had assumed its land use character by the time the owners bought, they were on *inquiry* notice of the covenants that required that the subdivision look the way it did — houses uniformly set back from the street, all being built in the same architectural style, and so on. An implied reciprocal negative (or restrictive) covenant "runs with the land."

When a lot owner who seeks the benefit of a covenant purchased his or her lot before a burdened lot owner, another theory aids the early purchaser in gaining standing. This theory is not as commonly used as the implied reciprocal negative easement or covenant, but it makes the burden of a covenant run backwards. It relies on a finding that the lot owner was the **third party beneficiary** of the covenant between Developer and the prior lot owner.

The discussion in the prior paragraph shows that later lot purchasers (that is, later than the burdened lot owner) have an easier time gaining standing. Why? Because as previously discussed, it is easier to find that the benefit of a covenant was transferred to later purchasers. Why else would Developer impose a covenant on early purchasers if not to transfer its benefits to those to whom he later sold lots? A recognition of this implied transfer is often known as the **retained land theory**. Often this is also a recognition that the title transferred to a lot comes with all the "appurtenances attached thereto" (a usual term in any deed).

Most jurisdictions have adopted subdivision ordinances. These ordinances require that a subdivider file documents including a map or plat. The plat looks like a combination of an engineer's and a surveyor's view of the subdivision. It contains the metes and bounds of each lot. It assigns each lot a number that may thereafter be used to transfer the title to the lot. On it usually appears a reference to the deed book and page at which a declaration of the covenants (CCRs) has been recorded. Sometimes the plat itself shows the dimensions of any express easements affecting the subdivision, and it may even incorporate phrases with the gist of the major provisions of covenants in the declaration. Most courts hold this recorded subdivision plat constitutes the notice necessary to satisfy the notice requirement for an equitable servitude and to deny the subsequent purchaser any protection under the recording statutes. The notice is either constructive notice if the recorded subdivision plat details the covenants, or inquiry notice that uniform covenants may apply to all lots, including the purchaser's lot.

Even without using the rationales provided by the recording of subdivision plats, jurisdictions find the notice needed to overcome recording acts and equitable servitude obstacles by concluding uniform neighborhood characteristics gave the subsequent purchaser inquiry notice of the covenant. Obligating purchasers to inquire about observable conditions to gain knowledge of restrictions serves to imply residential-use-only covenants, setback requirements, height limitations, brick exterior requirements, and prohibitions against mobile homes and farm animals. Other covenants may not be such that a reasonable person would have inquired about them. Examples of these might be covenants requiring that a house have a minimum square footage or maximum number of bedrooms or occupants per square foot. If a reasonable person would not have inquired, the purchaser did not have inquiry notice of the covenant or servitude. Further, if the subsequent purchaser bought early enough, before neighboring lots were developed, the subsequent purchaser may not have had inquiry notice of the omitted covenant at all.

THE COMMON SCHEME AND THE STATUTE OF FRAUDS

Servitudes are interests in land and, as such, must be created in a writing to satisfy the Statute of Frauds. The normal exceptions to the Statute of Frauds for part performance and estoppel apply. In addition, a few jurisdictions straightforwardly hold a covenant established pursuant to a common scheme constitutes an exception to the Statute of Frauds. More courts, however, hold that once it can be shown that the common owner indicated the land was to be restricted, either orally or by showing the prospective purchaser a plat, the purchaser has notice of the common scheme and will be estopped to deny the covenant or servitude's existence. In these jurisdictions, marketing pamphlets, and advertisements, as well as deed provisions, can provide evidence of a writing.

Other jurisdictions, such as California, demand some writing to satisfy the Statute of Frauds. A developer's recording a subdivision plat constitutes an acceptable writing, however, even if nothing is inserted into the purchaser's deed. In all these situations, the covenant burdens the purchaser just as though it were included in the original deed.

Still other states, such as Massachusetts, refuse to resort to the common scheme theory to impose restrictions at all. In these states, the purchaser with no covenant in his deed is not bound by the covenant.

WHAT CONSTITUTES A COMMON SCHEME

(a) Common Covenants

Determining what the common scheme is, which lots are included in the scheme, and when the common scheme began, however, is fact sensitive. The common scheme may be used to find the existence of an implied reciprocal negative easement or covenant. That finding, however, may not be made as often as one might expect. A variation in the terms or incidence of the covenants may indicate a common owner did not intend a common scheme. How many lots or what percentage of lots must be burdened is a facts-and-circumstances inquiry.

Example: In Sanborn v. McLean, 206 N.W. 496 (Mich. 1925), 53 of 91 lots transferred by a common owner were restricted to residential use only and all lots on the street, including the 38 lots not expressly restricted to single-family residential use, were single-family residences. That was enough for the court to find a common scheme using an implied reciprocal negative covenant for all lots visible from that burdened lot along the same street in the subdivision. Most courts addressing this matter have required that over half of all lots be expressly burdened before finding a common scheme. Depending on the specific facts of the controversy, some courts may demand a higher (or lower) percentage of burdened lots to infer an intent to establish a common scheme.

(b) When a Common Scheme Begins

A second issue concerns the exact point in time when the common scheme begins. A common owner may own a tract and sell lots from it before the common plan is developed. Since these lots were sold before the common scheme of development began, they are not part of the common scheme. Consequently, covenants not included in their deeds will not be implied, nor will the owner of those lots have standing to enforce any later burdened properties that are part of the scheme. Even when an implied reciprocal covenant is found, the implied covenant is not retroactive.

(c) Geographic Boundaries of Common Schemes

A third issue concerns the geographic boundaries of the area encompassing a common scheme. A developer may own multiple tracts and treat each tract separately. Similarly, the common owner may own just one tract, but intend to develop only part of the tract under the common scheme. A common scheme on part of the tract will not burden the land not made a part of the common scheme. Finally, a common owner may intend to develop an entire tract, but put different covenants on different parts of the tract: e.g., some single-family residences, some apartments, some retail shops, and some commercial ventures. No hard and fast rule applies as to deciding what commonly owned land belongs to a common scheme. A court will evaluate all the facts and circumstances.

Example: In Snow v. Van Dam, 197 N.E. 224 (Mass. 1935), a developer owned a tract of land. The northernmost part of the property, constituting approximately 10% of the property, was separated from the rest of the tract by a major road. In addition, the land north of the road was swampy. The developer subdivided and sold lots south of the road, but not north of the road. After selling all lots south of the road, decades later the developer sold the land north of the road by a deed containing the same restrictions as contained in the deeds to the southern lots. The new owner of the northern land wanted to operate a commercial business in violation of the covenant. Owners of the lots south of the road sought to enjoin the business. The case turned on whether the northern lots were in the same scheme as the southern lots. The court concluded both northern and southern lots were part of the same common scheme, explaining that the northern part was at the gateway of and provided access to the whole subdivision, so that the use made of that lot tends strongly to fix the character of the entire subdivision. Moreover, the northern land was shown on all the plans and plats from the beginning. The failure to subdivide it sooner was apparently due to a belief that it was unmarketable, not out of any intent to reserve it for other than residential purposes, so that from the beginning the scheme contemplated that no part of the northern land should be used for commercial purposes. When the lot of the defendant was later restricted, the restriction was in pursuit of the original scheme and gave rights to earlier as well as to later purchasers. See *Snow*, 197 N.E. at 228. Finally, since they had covenants expressly conferring the benefit, the owners of the southern lot had standing to sue the northern lot owner because of the third party beneficiary theory for establishing the common scheme.

THE RESTATEMENT (THIRD) OF PROPERTY (SERVITUDES)

The American Law Institute published the Restatement (Third) of Property (Servitudes) in 2000. This Restatement seeks to formulate a law of servitudes unhindered by the many common law rules. The Restatement, for instance, eliminates the horizontal and vertical privity elements, as well as the touch and concern element. See the last Chapter, supra. Importantly, for owners of land in subdivisions, the Restatement favors creating rights in strangers to the deed, which would eliminate many of the problems discussed in this Chapter. Instead, the Restatement would allow any person who has a legitimate interest in enforcing a servitude to have standing. The Restatement relies on a common scheme or general plan to create benefits and burdens, similar to the common law.

TERMINATION OF COVENANTS AND SERVITUDES

Real covenants and equitable servitudes can be terminated. There are 12 commonly mentioned ways this happens. They apply to easements as well.

1. **By the Terms of the Covenant.** Many covenants by their terms continue for a specific number of years or until the occurrence of some event. The deed or CCRs creating the covenant stipulates the event that causes the covenant to automatically terminate. By its terms, a covenant may be renewed periodically, either by its term or the vote of all benefitted and burdened owners.

2. **Merger.** Because a real covenant or an equitable servitude envisions rights and obligations between landowners, once a common owner acquires both the benefitted and the burdened property (and no one else owns benefitted or burdened property), the covenant or servitude terminates through merger. If that common ownership ends, the covenant is not revived, even if the common owner later sells part of it. Merger applies whether the common owner previously owned the benefitted property, the burdened property, or is a third party purchaser of both.

    Example: Common owner dies, and his heir O becomes the fee simple absolute owner of Blackacre. Blackacre is subject to a covenant for the benefit of Whiteacre, in which O holds a life estate under the provisions of Common Owner's will. Is the covenant subject to merger? Yes. The common owner must have either a beneficial or freehold ownership of both properties. A life estate is a freehold.

3. **Release.** Covenants and servitudes are interests in property. As such, owners of the *benefitted* property can grant a written release to the owner of the burdened property. Like other transfers of real property interests, the release must satisfy the Statute of Frauds and

should be recorded in the land records. If more than one lot is benefitted, all benefitted lot owners must join the release to terminate the covenant (though those landowners signing a release may be estopped from enforcing the covenant later).

4. **Rescission.** It is a mutual release. As with releases, landowners can execute a document rescinding the covenant so that the covenant no longer binds any property. If the document is not effective as a release, it is regarded as promissory and contractual in nature. It is effective only if all persons with standing to enforce the covenant join in executing the document. The most common use of the rescission is by a developer when all purchasers to that date ask or agree that a covenant is not appropriate for the subdivision and should be rescinded.

> *Example:* Abe and Ben execute a release of a covenant benefitting and burdening their respective properties. It does not satisfy the Statute of Frauds. What is the release's status? It is an agreement that either might breach and be subject to damages: Its failure to satisfy the Statute is no reason not to enforce it as a contract. If it does satisfy the Statute, there may remain a question in some jurisdictions about whether it is recordable.

5. **Unclean Hands.** Courts will not allow a benefitted owner to violate a covenant and at the same time to enjoin another landowner from violating it: The plaintiff cannot enforce a covenant if he has unclean hands. A plaintiff's minor infraction, however, does not foreclose an action against a neighbor's egregious violation.

6. **Acquiescence.** Acquiescence is intentional tolerance of a covenant's violation. It results when a benefitted property owner passively endures multiple violations of a covenant. The owner, even though not violating the covenant herself, by her acquiescence to or tolerance of violations, may be estopped from enforcing it against yet another violator. Acquiescence envisions such a pattern of violations that enforcing the covenant in this one instance would serve no purpose. It can be a defense to enforcement at the level of both an individual covenant and a common scheme. Acquiescing in too many violations of a covenant approaches abandonment (discussed next). Acquiescence in the violation of one covenant will not prevent a landowner from enforcing other covenants.

7. **Abandonment.** Abandonment requires both an intent to abandon and an act of abandonment. Individual covenants as well as a common scheme may be abandoned. The latter abandonment occurs when such a high number of landowners in a common scheme violates the common covenant that it becomes

unenforceable by any of the benefitted landowners. Generally, for a court to find an abandonment, the violations have caused such a substantial change in the neighborhood that the original purpose of the covenants has been subverted. Minor changes in the use of the benefitted or burdened land are not an abandonment.

> **Example:** C owns Whiteacre and adjoining Blackacre. C conveys Blackacre to O, and in order to benefit C's residence on Whiteacre, inserts a covenant in the deed prohibiting O from using Blackacre for any commercial use. C conveys Whiteacre to T, who tears down the residence and builds a shopping center. Once the statute of limitations runs out, C has abandoned the covenant and it is terminated.

8. **Laches.** Laches occurs when a benefitted owner waits so long to bring suit to enjoin a covenant's violation that the burdened owner is unduly harmed by the delay itself. The delay must be unreasonably long under the circumstances. Laches does not actually terminate a covenant. It merely prohibits the covenant's enforcement for a specific breach. The benefitted owner is free to enforce it upon subsequent breaches. Laches is seldom a successful defense to an enforcement suit. This is because a defendant's argument is that plaintiff waited too long to bring suit, even though the plaintiff brought suit within the statute of limitations period. Thus a defense of laches is seldom more than a variation of estoppel.

9. **Estoppel.** A benefitted owner may not act in a way indicating that she does not intend to enforce a covenant, and then enforce it. So an action reasonably calculated to induce reasonable reliance by the burdened owner, resulting in substantial injury to the latter, constitutes an estoppel on the right to enforce a covenant.

10. **Changed Conditions.** Equity will not enforce a covenant if the conditions in a covenanted subdivision have so changed that its benefit is no longer substantial enough to justify the burden. The covenant then no longer serves its intended purpose. In this situation, no injunction for violating the covenant will issue. This defense is thus a remedial one, balancing the equities. The majority of jurisdictions consider only changes occurring within the subdivision. Changes in the conditions on land outside of or external to the covenanted neighborhood are irrelevant. Why? Because the benefitted owners cannot control external changes and further, they contracted for the right of enforcement. Even when they make some "border" lots poorly suited for permitted uses, no injunction will issue. The border lots remain a buffer, preventing gradual encroachment of outside development into the subdivision.

If the injunction is denied, the benefitted owners may receive damages.

> ***Example:*** Benefitted owner *A* sues to enjoin B's violation of a covenant. B defends the suit with evidence of the substantial harm that would occur if the covenant were to be enforced and of changing conditions within the covenanted subdivision in which both *A* and B reside. *A* then presents substantial evidence that the covenant is still of value to her. B's defense will fail. Evidence of the covenant's continuing benefit to *A* need not rise to a preponderance of all the evidence. In most jurisdictions, substantial evidence will suffice. B's evidence of substantial harm is irrelevant, as the remaining benefit is the focus of this defense. Thus speaking of the doctrine as "balancing the equities" can be misleading in this context.[2]

> ***Example:*** Benefitted owner *A* sues to enjoin B's violation of a covenant as in the prior Example. B responds, alleging that a changed conditions defense is applicable and that *A* is relying on changes that had already occurred at the time *A* purchased her lot in the covenanted subdivision. If *A* had an opportunity to inspect the violating owner's lots, determine the applicability of the covenant, and purchased anyway, *A* has acquiesced in the violations. Will this defense succeed? Probably not. The key lies with *A*'s seller. Didn't he have the right to convey his right to enforce the covenant with the lot? Yes, he did.

11. **Recording Acts.** Real covenants and equitable servitudes are recordable. A subsequent bona fide purchaser who takes without actual, constructive, or inquiry notice is not bound by them.

12. **Eminent Domain.** Federal, state, and local governments through eminent domain or condemnation can force landowners to sell their property to the government as long as the government pays for the property. When the government buys burdened property, the covenant burdening the land is extinguished. However, jurisdictions

---

2. Some jurisdictions do, however, balance the equities. They use the doctrine of "relative hardship" to do so. They consider this latter doctrine a subset of changed conditions. Jurisdictions using it balance the benefits of maintaining the covenant against the harm to the burdened property if it is enforced. If the harm to the burdened property is disproportionately great compared to the benefit to the neighboring properties, a court of equity may decide not to enforce the covenant. Generally, courts use this doctrine when the violation of the covenant has been an innocent and unintentional one. More specifically, they are more likely to apply this doctrine to release a border lot from a covenant. But jurisdictions not considering external changes in evaluating changed conditions will not use the doctrine this way.

disagree about whether the government must compensate owners of benefitted property for the loss of their right to enforce the covenant against the government in its use of the formerly burdened lot. A majority of jurisdictions, viewing the benefit as a property right, will find a "taking" of the benefit, thus requiring the government to provide compensation. A significant minority, in contrast, conclude the benefit is too attenuated, the covenant was never intended to apply to condemnors, the covenant was a contract right, not a property right, or that the compensation is against public policy.

Examples

1. John owned land on a hillside overlooking a bay. He subdivided it into 12 lots, six lots (Lots 1-6) on the uphill side of Bay View Road, and six lots (Lots 7-12) on the downhill side of Bay View Road. John recorded a subdivision plat clearly setting forth a 15-foot setback but containing no height restrictions to any lot. Because the lots are on a hill, Lots 1-6 are on a higher elevation than Lots 7-12. John sold Lot 4 by a recorded deed to Fran. The deed contained the following covenant: "At no time shall any building or structure be erected or placed or allowed to remain on Lot 4 within 15 feet of the property line bordering on Bay View Road. This covenant shall run with the land." Deeds to all twelve lots carried some version of this 15-foot setback restriction. The deed did not mention any height or view restrictions. On September 1, 2004, Fran conveyed Lot 4 to Dale (the plaintiff).

   A year after conveying Fran's lot to her, John conveyed Lot 11 to Lucy. Lot 11 was the first of the lower-slope lots to be sold. The deed contained the following covenants: "(a) At no time shall any building or structure be erected or placed or allowed to remain on Lot 11 of more than one (1) story in height, nor shall any building be located within fifteen feet of the property boundary line on Bay View Road. (b) The foregoing covenant shall run with the land hereby conveyed and shall be equally binding on all subsequent owners." Within the year, John sold Lots 7-10 and Lot 12 by deeds containing the same restrictions contained in the deed for Lot 11. Lucy conveyed Lot 11 to Connie, the deed stating the conveyance was subject to the covenants in Lucy's deed. Connie deeded Lot 11 to Val "subject to all grants, easements, covenants, restrictions, liens, and encumbrances of record." Last year Val began building a two-story home on Lot 11. Dale was dismayed the house would interfere with his view of the bay. The owner of Lot 10 mentioned to Dale her deed contained a one-story restriction, and so Val's house might be "too high." Researching the land records, Dale discovered the one-story restriction on Lot 11. Dale brought an action seeking to enjoin

Val from constructing the two-story house. (a) Who prevails if there is no common scheme? (b) Who prevails if there is a common scheme? (c) Is there a common scheme? (d) If there is a common scheme, when did the scheme begin? (e) Lot 11 was the last lot to be improved. Two-story homes have been built on Lots 1, 5, and 7. Single-story homes have been built on the remaining lots. Assuming the one-story restriction applied to Lot 11, does the existence of the three two-story homes result in the termination of the one-story height restrictions?

2. Vicky owned 100 acres of land. Fifteen years ago, she began selling portions of the 100-acre parcel. Although no formal subdivision plat was ever filed, about half of the parcels contained a covenant requiring grantees not to use their property for commercial development. Some of these deeds contained a covenant that specifically ran with the land conveyed, some did not state the covenant ran with the land. About half of the deeds contained no restriction whatsoever. Sherry purchased a lot from Vicky ten years ago, the deed containing a covenant prohibiting commercial use of the lot. Two years later, Sherry purchased an adjoining parcel from Vicky, the deed containing a restrictive covenant prohibiting Sherry and any future grantees from using the parcel for commercial purposes. On the same day, Vicky conveyed a lot to Wallace, the deed containing no restrictions on commercial use. Ed then purchased the parcel from Wallace, the deed containing no restrictive covenants. Ed opened a restaurant on his land. Sherry brings an action to enjoin Ed from operating the restaurant. What result?

3. Suburban Builders has owned 50 acres of land for ten years, expecting someday to subdivide the land into lots for residential use. The 50 acres are subject to covenants limiting the property to single-family residential use only. The city recently annexed the 50 acres, and zoned the land "R-3, Retail." Property zoned "R-3, Retail" can be used for retail shops, small offices, restaurants, gas stations, banks, apartments, duplexes, and single-family residences. Suburban Builders, Inc., submitted a subdivision plat, which the city approved, that calls for retail shops along the two sides of the subdivision bordering on major roads adjoining the land, with a transition area dedicated to apartments, and the remaining 70 percent of the land to be used solely for single-family residences, a park, and an elementary school. Dan, who has standing to enforce the original covenant, sues to enjoin Suburban Builders' development scheme. Suburban Builders claims the city's annexing the property, zoning the land "R-3, Retail," and approving the subdivision plat resulted in the residential use only covenant being terminated. What result?

4. Henry owned a 15-acre strip of land. Between March and December 1975, Henry sold five three-acre parcels (Tracts A, B, C, D, and E),

each deed containing the following restriction: "Grantees, their heirs, or assigns, agree not to erect on the property any building intended for any purpose except as a single-family private residence." The purchasers of Tract A and Tract B built homes, currently valued between $500,000 and $600,000. Tract C remains unimproved. Tracts A, B, and C are heavily wooded, and egress and ingress to them is by way of a private road. The State Highway Commission in 1987, through an eminent domain action, purchased Tract D pursuant to its plan to build Clarkson Road, a four-lane highway. Clarkson Road now runs across Tract D and intersects Highway 40 less than one-eighth of a mile north of Tract D.

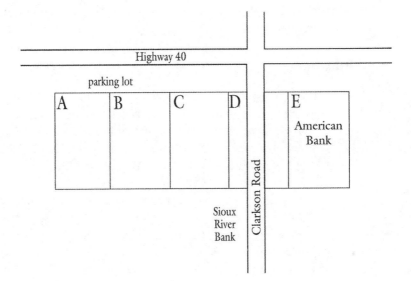

The year Clarkson Road opened, the owners of Tract E sold Tract E to American Bank. The deed expressly released Tract E from the single-family residence-only covenant. The owners of Tract A, Tract B, and Tract C likewise executed releases from the covenant to American Bank. When Henry sold them, the five tracts were part of a rural, agricultural community. No commercial or retail businesses operated in the surrounding area. Only a small number of homes dotted the area. The opening of Clarkson Road began a period of rapid commercial development. Today a mall, several large office buildings, and a condominium development are all within a half-mile of the five tracts. American Bank operates a bank on Tract E. The increase in volume of traffic and commercial activity caused a substantial increase in the noise levels on Tracts A, B, and C. The county, moreover, has plans to widen Highway 40. A parking lot for an office building abuts Tracts A and B.

Tess bought Tract C in 2000. Sioux River Bank plans to build an office building on Clarkson Road on land abutting Tract C and approached Tess about leasing or purchasing her land to construct a paved parking lot on Tract C, to be used by tenants and customers of the new bank (no part of the bank building would be built on Tract C). The transaction is contingent on River Bank's being able to construct a parking lot on Tract C. Tess brings this action. Tess makes three arguments. Please evaluate the following three theories. (a) Tess argues the other tract owners have waived or abandoned their right to enforce the covenant. (b) Tess argues the covenant is unenforceable due to changed conditions within and without the 15 acres. (c) Tess argues a surface parking lot would not violate the restrictive covenant even if the covenant is enforceable.

Explanations

1. (a) Assuming Dale is the only plaintiff, Val will prevail if there is no common scheme. John sold Lot 4 to Dale's predecessor in interest, Fran. There was no one-story height restriction on Lot 4 or on John's retained land. John no longer owned any interest in Lot 4 when he later deeded Lot 11 to Lucy. When John burdened Lot 11, he benefitted the lots he still owned on that date, but not the lots he had already sold. In most jurisdictions, he could not benefit the owner of Lot 4 since the owner of Lot 4 was a stranger to the deed. No owner of Lot 4, like Dale, therefore, has standing to enforce the one-story height restriction.

   (b) Dale prevails if there was a common scheme with the one-story height restriction in effect when John sold Lot 4 to Fran in 1974. For the covenant to run, the intent, touch and concern, horizontal privity, and vertical privity elements must be met. The intent for the burden to run was found in the deed itself. More uncertain is who was to be benefitted by the covenant. The topography strongly suggests the height restriction was to protect the upslope homeowners' (including the owner of Lot 4) view of the bay. The burden and benefit of the covenant easily touched and concerned the separate properties since only one-story homes could be built on Lot 11, and the view from Lot 4 is preserved by the covenant. With a common scheme, all lots are benefitted and burdened by the covenant from the start of the scheme. The benefit of the restriction is appurtenant to all lots within the scheme transferred from John to the new owners, including John's transfer of Lot 4 to Fran. Horizontal privity existed on the transfer from John to Fran. Vertical privity can be linked from Fran to Dale and from John to Val. Since the elements of a real covenant are satisfied, Dale could enforce the covenant as either a real covenant or an equitable servitude with an injunction. As to the servitude, because Val had constructive and maybe actual notice of the one story only restriction, and the other elements for an equitable servitude are met, Dale can enjoin the building of the two-story home on Lot 11 if the restriction was part of the common scheme.

(c) This is a close question. The subdivision plat is evidence of a scheme of development as is John's selling the lots within a relatively short time period. Included in the common scheme is the 15-foot setback requirement. The tougher issue is whether the one-story height covenant was part of a common scheme. Since all the lower slope lots were subject to the one-story height restriction, and there seems to be no reason to have inserted a similar covenant in the deeds to upper slope lots, it appears John intended a common scheme of restricting the lower slope lots to one-story homes. In the case on which this Example is loosely based, only three of the lower slope lots were restricted (rather than all six lower slope lots as in the Example). A court might conclude that no restriction was needed or appropriate to the upper slope lots since they did not block any other subdivision lots' view. The test is whether "lots of like character or similarly situated property" were burdened. Since half of the lower slope lots were burdened, the appellate court found a common scheme. However, a court might disagree, concluding three restricted lots were an insufficient number to support a common scheme. Further, the piecemeal restrictions in the conveyances plus John's not including the height restriction on the subdivision plat indicates no common height scheme. However, more favorable to finding a common scheme is the fact that all lower-slope lots were similarly restricted and John had no reason to place height restrictions on the upper lots. Either a conclusion of common scheme or no common scheme is reasonable.

(d) The issue is critical. Only if a common scheme was in effect before John sold both Lots 4 and 11 will Dale be able to enforce the height restriction against Val. Clearly, the common scheme with the fifteen-foot setback was established before John sold his first lot. Not so obvious is whether the height restriction was part of the original scheme or whether John began a second scheme of development that imposed the height restriction to the lots in that second scheme. If the height restriction was part of the second scheme and not part of the initial scheme, that second scheme began after John sold Lot 4 to Fran (Dale's predecessor in interest), so Dale would not have standing to enjoin Val's building a two-story home. However, if a court might reasonably conclude the height restriction was part of the initial scheme, notwithstanding its not being included on the subdivision plat, John intended to preserve the upslope lots' view of the bay all along and his waiting to sell the first downslope lot before incorporating the height restriction into a deed was consistent with that intent.

(e) No. The one-story height covenant has not been terminated. It has not been acquiesced in or abandoned. Of the three lots with two-story houses, only the deed to Lot 7 actually was burdened with the one-story-only restriction. Acquiescence does not apply because the house on Lot 7 did not block the view from Lot 4. The covenant had not lost its purpose. Abandonment fails because the Lot 7 violation had not worked such a substantial change in the subdivision that the purpose of the covenant has been subverted. Dale can enjoin the building of the two-story house.

2. Ed can operate the restaurant. The deed to Ed did not prohibit commercial activities on his lot. The only way Ed's lot could be burdened is if Vicky's land had been restricted; and if the benefit of the prohibition against commercial use ran to Sherry. Sherry can prove both matters only if Vicky's land was restricted pursuant to a common scheme. The problem is that Vicky's course of conduct does not establish an intent to establish a common scheme. Some deeds contained the non-commercial use restriction, but many did not. Even those that limited commercial uses imposed varying restrictions, some restricting only the original purchasers and some purporting to run with the land. Given the absence of uniform covenants, there seems to be insufficient evidence to support a finding that a common scheme existed. Without a common scheme, Sherry has no case. Judgment for Ed.

3. Dan can enjoin Suburban Builders' development. Deed covenants and zoning ordinances both regulate land use. Private parties use covenants. Governments regulate through zoning laws. The landowner is subject to both. The landowner must honor the more restrictive of the two. Here the deed covenants permit only single-family residential use. Restaurants and retail shops are not allowed. Zoning laws do not overrule or terminate the covenants.

4. (a) Tess's best argument that the other owners waived or abandoned the covenant is based on the facts that they (1) expressly released Tract E from the covenant so American Bank could build its bank and (2) did not object to the State Highway Commission's acquiring Tract D for the purpose of constructing Clarkson Road. Her arguments are not good enough. A court will find a waiver or an abandonment only when the violations are so pervasive as to indicate an intent to abandon the covenant. The facts here do not indicate the requisite intent. The landowners cannot prevent a state's condemning

property to be used for public purposes. The State Highway Commission's purchasing the property in an eminent domain action extinguished the covenant on Tract D. The other landowners could do nothing about that and so cannot be said to have consented to it. The state's taking Tract D for road purposes will not terminate the covenant as to the remaining lots. Further, the release of Tract E from the covenant will not constitute an abandonment of the covenant as it affects Tracts A, B, and C. Once the state builds four-lane wide Clarkson Road, separating Tract E from the rest of the affected lots, as a practical matter whether a business or residence sat on Tract E, became irrelevant to the beneficial uses made of Tracts A, B, and C. The four-lane highway had so separated Tract E, that the owners of the four lots could reasonably conclude it no longer shared an identity of interest with the remaining three lots. The release of Tract E under these circumstances was not an abandonment of the covenant as to the remaining three tracts.

(b) For a covenant to be terminated by reason of changed conditions, the changes must be so radical as to defeat the essential purposes of the covenant. If the covenant retained some substantial value to the landowners, a court will enforce the covenant even though some landowner, Tess here, suffered a hardship from the covenant's continued vitality. Here the changed conditions occurred on Tracts D and E, but those two tracts could be effectively severed from the remaining three tracts, which remained primarily wooded and residential. The substantial changes on the surrounding lands transformed the area from rural and peaceful to a commercial use area. Yet the changes to the surrounding area were external changes, and external changes usually will not justify terminating a covenant. The affected three tracts retain their essential character. The covenant, in fact, may be more important now than ever to preserve the essential character of the land from further commercial intrusions. The covenant remains enforceable.

(c) Tess is correct. Courts strictly interpret restrictive covenants. A court will not rewrite a covenant to say something the covenant does not itself say. The covenant prohibited the erection of "any building intended for any purpose except a one-family private residence." A paved surface parking lot is not a "building." Even without pausing to interpret the words of the covenant, however, some jurisdictions preclude the use of a parking lot that serves a non-residential use on the theory the parking lot must further a permitted dominant use before the parking lot is allowed. Here the parking lot would further a nonpermitted use and thus not be permitted in those jurisdictions.

Public Land
Use Controls

PART VI

Constitutional and Statutory Constraints on Zoning

INTRODUCTION

Municipal governments—cities, counties, towns, villages, and townships—have no inherent powers. They derive all their powers from state government. As authorized and enabled by state statutes, they are the primary regulators of land use, through zoning ordinances, housing, and building codes. They often administer more specialized ordinances as well, for purposes such as historical and landmark preservation and aesthetic regulation.

Early ordinances controlled **nuisances**, such as stables, slaughterhouses, and pool halls, and promoted fire safety. By the 1920s, municipalities were enacting **comprehensive** zoning laws, regulating land use throughout the city. Comprehensive zoning laws regulate all uses within a zone, not just those that may be nuisances. Zoning ordinances impose restrictions on buildings other than use restrictions. The most common such other restrictions relate to **height, bulk, area**, and **exterior design** of structures.

AN INTRODUCTION TO CONSTITUTIONAL LAW

The state constitutions grant powers to the state legislatures. Primary among these is the power to regulate activities that affect the "public health, safety, morals, or general welfare." Collectively, this regulatory power is known as the **police power.** Only coincidentally does it have anything to do with the power of the police. This power is both plenary (meaning that it is inherent in the function of a legislature) and reserved (meaning that it is retained by the legislature if not delegated to municipal governments — just as the states under the Tenth Amendment to the federal Constitution have reserved all powers not delegated to the federal government).

Municipal governments, having only the power delegated to them by a state constitution or by legislation, received their authority to enact a zoning ordinance through a state's zoning **enabling act**. Unless either expressly delegated in a state statute or reasonably necessary for achieving an expressly delegated activity (often this is evidenced by the express purposes of the act), the municipality is without power to legislate. This rule is called **Dillon's Rule**. Some municipalities exercise the power to zone as if they were state legislatures; these are known as **home rule** jurisdictions.

The federal and state governments' power to regulate (and so to delegate) is limited by the federal constitution. Some of its provisions, invoked to review and invalidate zoning ordinances, are the Substantive Due Process Clause, the procedural Due Process Clause, the Takings Clause, the Equal Protection Clause, or the First Amendment. All state constitutions have provisions analogous to the Due Process, Equal Protection, and Takings clauses. The federal Takings Clause, which requires governments to give "just compensation" to landowners when the government "takes" property, has been the center of recent judicial developments. See Chapter 34, infra.

THE STANDARD STATE ZONING ENABLING ACT

The U.S. Department of Commerce in 1922 drafted a **Standard State Zoning Enabling Act** (Standard Act). It was adopted or was the model for enabling acts in over 35 of the states. Its key phrases are still in use today. It is the city or county council, the township or village board, or other legislative body that enacts a zoning ordinance. The ordinance divides the municipality into use districts — e.g., residential, commercial, or industrial district — and locates each district on a zoning map. It also adopts procedures for enacting, enforcing, and amending it. Further, it recognizes that the administration of the ordinance will require that it be amended. Thus the Standard Act offers a system of appeals to an administrative body, known typically as the **board of zoning adjustment** or **board of zoning appeals** (BZA). For example, if a landowner wants to build a deck, but the zoning administrator finds that a deck is a prohibited "structure" as defined in the ordinance, the owner may appeal that decision to the BZA. The language authorizing the BZA to hear such an appeal is often taken from the Standard Act. A right to appeal also arises if the landowner challenges an administrator's refusal to grant a building permit.

The Standard Act also grants the BZA the power to hear and grant a landowner a variance. A **variance** excuses a landowner from some provision of the zoning ordinance if compliance with the ordinance would cause the landowner **unnecessary hardship or practical difficulties**. These hardships and difficulties are often not further enumerated in the ordinance. Further, a BZA also has the power to grant a **special exceptions or conditional use**. It is a land use expressly allowed in a use district only if certain conditions spelled out in the ordinance are met. For example, a special exception may be granted for a library, private school, hospital, church, gas station, apartment, funeral parlor or private club to locate in a district zoned for single-family residences.

Because the BZA is an administrative body, a landowner may appeal any of its decisions to a court. Upon judicial review, the court will require that the BZA have substantial evidence to support its decision. Substantial evidence is what a reasonable person would accept and act on, more than a scintilla but less than a preponderance of all evidence that might be produced. The burden of proof at a BZA hearing or upon judicial review is on the applicant or the appellant.

ENACTING A ZONING ORDINANCE

When a municipality acts within the police power and its state's enabling act, it may enact a zoning ordinance just as it would any other ordinance: that is, subject to the notice, hearing, and procedural requirements required by state law. In some jurisdictions (comprising about a dozen states), a zoning ordinance must be preceded by a comprehensive planning process, resulting in a separate document known as the General or Comprehensive Plan. Thus the Plan is a precondition to zoning in these jurisdictions. This precondition is derived from the statement in many zoning enabling acts that zoning must be "in accord with the comprehensive plan," a phrase taken from the Standard Zoning Enabling Act. In most jurisdictions, there is no such precondition: A zoning ordinance is judged in accord with the comprehensive plan when its provisions are reasonable in themselves and consistent inter se. Nonetheless, even though it is not mandatory, many municipalities develop a comprehensive plan and use it as a guideline for their zoning ordinances. The plan generally has several components, including a land use component, establishing the goals that the ordinance should strive to achieve, such as preserving the character of the district, maintaining property values, determining the suitability of each district for various purposes, and promoting the health, safety, morals, and general welfare of the municipality. In some jurisdictions, the plan is developed by the municipality's planning commission and then adopted as an ordinance by the municipal legislature — e.g., the city council, the town commissioners or supervisors, or the village trustees.

CUMULATIVE AND NONCUMULATIVE ZONING

In Village of Euclid v. Ambler Realty Co., 272 U.S. 365 (1926), the Supreme Court, by a vote of 6 to 3, upheld the Village of Euclid's zoning ordinance against a challenge the zoning law violated the **Due Process Clause** and the **Equal Protection Clause** of the U.S. Constitution.

Euclid reviewed a simple but typical zoning ordinance, which consisted of two documents — a zoning map and the text of the ordinance. The Euclid ordinance mapped the whole village into districts, meaning that it was a **comprehensive** ordinance. This zoning map showed the boundaries of each district. Then in the text of the ordinance, each district was restricted based on 3 factors. First, each district was limited to certain **uses**: U-1 was limited to single-family residences; U-2 added duplexes, so single-family residences and duplexes were permitted in U-2; U-3 added apartments, hotels, schools, churches, libraries, museums, and government buildings; U-4 permitted, in addition to the above uses, such uses as retail stores, banks, restaurants, law offices, theaters, stores, and gas stations; U-5 allowed all of the above plus billboards, warehouses, and light manufacturing; and U-6 allowed heavy industrial plants, junkyards, and gasoline storage facilities, while U-7 listed uses prohibited in the village altogether.

A similar classification scheme restricted building **heights**; and another classification scheme required minimum lot sizes (**area** restrictions). In addition to these 3 major classification schemes — use, height, and area — the ordinance contained other restrictions dealing with lot width, setbacks, etc. Because of this case, zoning by districts is called **Euclidean zoning**.

The zoning used in Euclid is known as **cumulative zoning**. Under cumulative zoning ordinances, the different zones or districts are ranked in a hierarchy. Uses allowed in a less dense zone are allowed in all denser zones, but no use may be located in a less dense zone than the zone in which it is first assigned. So higher uses may be located in all lower zones. Thus, in the Village of Euclid, a landowner can build a single-family residence in all other use districts U-2 through U-6. Likewise a retail store can be built in U-3 as well as in U-4 through U-6, but is prohibited from U-1 and U-2. The cumulative zoning applies to height and area restrictions as well: Buildings in the least restrictive area can be any height allowed in the municipality whereas a ten-story structure, as an example, cannot be located in an area district restricted to two-and-one-half stories.

Example: A municipality enacts a tree-preservation ordinance, the purpose of which is to preserve the tree canopy of the jurisdiction. It requires that every landowner whose land has a tree with a trunk whose diameter is over two feet obtain a permit before cutting it down. Your client wants to expand his house, taking out several large trees in the process. Is this ordinance authorized by the *Euclid* opinion? Maybe not: The tree is not a land use whose existence might become a nuisance or conflict with other uses, thus needing to be separated from them. It does not involve the police power triad of health, safety, or moral concerns. Joining the *Euclid* majority were three justices, including Justice Oliver Wendell Holmes, who probably would not have voted to uphold this ordinance: At the time of the *Euclid* case, the police power clearly encompassed that triad of powers, but not the fourth, the general welfare power, that is routinely added today. Currently the ordinance would be valid, but before the 1930s, it might not have been. It is not *Euclidean* zoning.

In the alternative, some jurisdictions adopt **noncumulative** or **exclusive** use zoning, especially for commercial and industrial districts. Exclusive zoning recognizes that a single-family residence or an apartment may be just as incompatible when surrounded by industrial or commercial uses as a manufacturing plant would be in a residential district. The exclusive zoning ordinance permits only expressly authorized activities in each district.

THE CONSTITUTIONAL LAW IN *EUCLID*

Euclid v. Ambler Realty Company confronts constitutional issues arising under the Due Process Clause. In *Euclid*, the landowner claimed the Village of Euclid's enactment of the zoning ordinance ran afoul of the Due Process Clause of the Fifth Amendment, which guarantees that no person shall "be deprived of life, liberty, or property, without due process of law...," U.S. Const., Amend. V, and of the Fourteenth Amendment, which reads in part, "nor shall any State deprive any person of life, liberty, or property, without due process of law...." U.S. Const., Amend XIV, § 1. The harm Ambler Realty alleged that it suffered was a substantial loss of its land's value and loss of the right to use its land for otherwise legal purposes.

Euclid involved **substantive due process**.[1] A court will review a law (either a state statute or ordinance) challenged as unconstitutional as a violation of substantive due process in three steps. First, it asks whether the law advanced the public health, safety, morals, or general welfare — that is, whether a state or municipality in enacting a law or ordinance is promoting a **legitimate state interest**. Second, once the state shows it is attempting to further a

---

1. A second aspect of the Due Process Clause is **procedural due process**, which requires a government to give notice and an opportunity to be heard on any administrative matter affecting an individual before the government can deny or revoke the person's rights or privileges. Procedural due rights form a cornerstone of American law and play a major role in implementing zoning ordinances.

legitimate state interest, the law will be upheld if the **means** chosen to achieve the legitimate state interest is **rationally related** to that interest. A court will declare the statute unconstitutional only if the provision is **arbitrary and capricious**, having no relation to the promotion of the claimed legitimate state interest. Third, even if the ordinance advances a legitimate state interest and is rationally related to it, the person challenging the ordinance is still given an opportunity to prove that it is not sufficiently narrow in its reach and thus is overbroad and *ultra vires* its purpose. In sum, a court will uphold a law if the state shows (1) a legitimate state interest, (2) achieved by means rationally related to the promotion of that interest, and (3) **narrowly tailored** to promote that interest.

When the ordinance infringes upon a **fundamental constitutional right**, e.g., infringes political speech, the burden on the state increases: The state then must convince a court the state's interest outweighs that right. That is, the state must prove that the ordinance advances a compelling state interest. If the state cannot show the state's interest outweighs the individual's fundamental right, a court will invalidate the statute or ordinance as unconstitutional. And even when the state's interest outweighs the infringement upon an individual's fundamental right, the statute must be narrowly tailored to achieve the state's interest while infringing as little as possible upon the right.

Example: City Council wants to reduce the costs of removing litter from the city streets. Pursuant to the above analysis, the first question is, does the city have a legitimate interest in reducing the cost of cleaning litter from the streets? The answer is yes, a city has a legitimate interest in preventing litter and saving taxpayers' money.

Example: Now assume City Council passes an ordinance making it illegal to distribute leaflets on city streets and sidewalks. The council was reacting to evidence that substantial litter results when persons receiving the pamphlets drop or toss them on the sidewalks or streets. The next question is: Is the ordinance rationally related to reducing the cost of removing the litter? Again, the answer must be "yes, it is."

Example: Police ticket a person for distributing leaflets. The person challenges the ordinance as unconstitutional. What result? The antilitter ordinance infringes upon the individual's right to free speech and freedom of the press. The distribution of leaflets is protected by the First Amendment. Because the antilitter ordinance infringes on a constitutionally protected right of free speech and freedom of the press, and the city can offer only a legitimate interest and not a compelling interest to justify the ordinance, under the approach developed above, a court will hold the antilitter statute is unconstitutional.

Example: Same facts as in the prior two Examples. Can City Council enact any antilitter ordinance? Yes. The Council might enact an ordinance making the throwing of leaflets on the pavement illegal or it could place trash baskets on the sidewalks, but it may not prohibit the distribution of leaflets in the first instance.

In *Euclid*, Ambler Realty argued the Euclid zoning ordinance's depriving Ambler Realty and other property owners of their right to use their property as they desired and decreasing their property's value greatly amounted to an impermissible interference or "deprivation" of the individual's constitutional right of property ownership. In response, the Supreme Court in *Euclid* enumerated several **legitimate state interests** furthered by zoning ordinances: Zoning promotes safety and security, reduces street accidents, decreases noise, preserves an environment in which to raise children, and aids in fire prevention. The Court then likened zoning ordinances to nuisance control statutes (which were constitutional) and declared the ordinance was **rationally related** to the furtherance of legitimate state goals. The Court next concluded the ordinance did not implicate any fundamental constitutional right. Thus only a rational relationship between the ends to be achieved (the legitimate state interest) and the means chosen to achieve those ends (the zoning law is the means) is all that is required to uphold the law under a substantive due process inquiry.

UNCONSTITUTIONAL *ON ITS FACE* AND *AS APPLIED*

Constitutional challenges to a statute or ordinance can be framed in two ways. The Supreme Court in Euclid v. Ambler Realty considered only whether the statue was constitutional **on its face**. A court evaluates a statute for its "facial validity" based on the statute's operation in most cases. In *Euclid*, once the Court found the zoning ordinance was a rational means to achieve a legitimate state interest, and no other specific constitutional right was implicated, the Court found the ordinance on its face did not violate the U.S. Constitution.

Because Ambler Realty had no plan to develop its property, it challenged the zoning ordinance on its face and not as applied to any specific development of its land, so the Supreme Court did not need to address whether the zoning ordinance **as applied** to Ambler Realty's land was unconstitutional:

> It is true that when, if ever, the provisions set forth in the ordinance in tedious and minute detail, come to be concretely applied to particular premises, including those of the appellee, or to particular conditions, or to be considered in connection with specific complaints, some of them, or even many of them, may be found to be clearly arbitrary and unreasonable.

Euclid, 272 U.S. at 395.

Two years after *Euclid*, the Supreme Court in Nectow v. City of Cambridge, 277 U.S. 183 (1928), concluded the zoning ordinance **as applied** to plaintiff's property was unconstitutional. The plaintiff in *Nectow* owned a large tract of land. Land on the opposite side of an adjoining street was used for residential purposes. Land on plaintiff's side of the street was used for (or intended to be used for) industrial purposes. The city included in a residential zone a 100-foot-wide strip of land (65 feet wide after an expected road expansion) that was a small part of plaintiff's larger tract. The rest of plaintiff's tract was zoned industrial.

The Supreme Court recited two facts found at trial. The first was that no practical use could be made of the 100-foot strip of land in question for residential purposes because, among other reasons, plaintiff could not earn an adequate return on any development of the property. The second finding was that placing the plaintiff's 100-foot strip of land in a residential district would not promote the health, safety, convenience, and general welfare of the inhabitants of that part of the city, taking into account the natural development of the land, the character of the district, and the resulting benefit that would accrue to the whole city.

After reciting these two findings, the Court relied on *Euclid* for a substantive due process argument that the zoning ordinance in *Nectow* failed as a means to promote a legitimate state interest. The Court held that a zoning regulation "cannot be imposed if it does not bear a **substantial relation** to the public health, safety, morals, or general welfare." Since zoning the 100-foot strip of land would not promote any legitimate state interest, and the invasion was serious and highly injurious, the zoning ordinance was unconstitutional **as applied** to the 100-foot strip.

NONCONFORMING USES

Uncertain about the constitutionality of demanding a landowner stop any existing use of land or to tear down any structure not in conformity with a municipality's zoning ordinance or amendment, municipalities routinely enact ordinances allowing existing nonconforming uses to continue. **Nonconforming uses** are legal and in place when an ordinance takes effect and that, except for already being in the district, would not be permitted in that district under a newly enacted zoning ordinance.

Example: A grocery store is located in a single-family residential use district the municipality zones exclusively residential. The store is a nonconforming use. Absent the legal rules applicable to nonconforming uses, it would be forced to relocate outside the residential-only district.

The nonconforming use must exist at the time the ordinance takes effect. Mere ownership of the parcel or having a plan to use it for a non-conforming use is insufficient. Many jurisdictions by ordinance or judicial decree in equity will grant a person an equitable or vested right to build an already permitted nonconforming use under certain circumstances: The claimant must have acted in good faith, meaning the claimant had no good reason to believe the ordinance would be enacted or amended to prohibit the intended use. In addition, the claimant, before the ordinance was enacted, must have made or committed to make substantial expenditures toward building or operating the nonconforming use. Most courts must also find that the claimant in good faith had received a building permit for any nonconforming use.

Most jurisdictions allow the expansion of existing nonconforming uses if the expansion is no more than required by the growth of the business on the land. Such courts are following the "natural expansion" doctrine. However, most prohibit a landowner's expanding the use by increasing the number of buildings or starting new businesses, or substantially changing the hours of operation. Likewise, an owner can replace old equipment or substitute more efficient equipment.

Example: A land owner owns a quarry that is a nonconforming use under its municipality's zoning ordinance. The owner may expand the quarry even though as it grows it comes close to nearby existing houses.

Example: A land owner owns a tavern that is a nonconforming use under its municipality's zoning ordinance. He may not present live entertainment in it.

A change of ownership does not end the nonconforming use status: It "runs with the land," not the landowner. Once a landowner abandons a nonconforming use, however, the right to use property for a nonconforming use ends and neither the owner nor any subsequent owner can resume the nonconforming use. Instead of a facts-and-circumstances test as to whether the owner has abandoned a use, most ordinances stipulate a period of nonuse — ranging from 60 days to a year — as presumptive of abandonment.

An owner of a nonconforming structure can engage in normal maintenance and repairs. A few states allow replacement of a nonconforming structure as long as the new one does not increase nonconforming uses. Other jurisdictions, eager to eliminate nonconforming uses, do not allow landowners to replace or substantially alter nonconforming buildings, even if destroyed by fire. Ordinances sometimes replace a facts-and-circumstances test as to what is a "substantial" alteration by restricting the cost to one-fourth or one-half the value of the current structure's fair market value (not cost) or limit alterations to those needed to meet updated health or building codes.

AMORTIZATION

Legislatures and courts hoped nonconforming uses would "wither away." That is not often the case. Indeed, some become more valuable just because they are nonconforming. So many states and municipalities enact amortization provisions; these allow nonconforming uses to continue only for a specified maximum period of time, after which the nonconforming use will no longer be permitted in the district. The period of use allowed usually is based on the time necessary for the owner to recoup the cost of improvements made to the property. Depending on the type of improvements and the jurisdiction, this amortization period is typically several years.

A minority of courts hold the amortization provision to be unconstitutional on its face, under the U.S. Constitution or, more likely by a state court, under its state constitution. These courts liken the amortization provision to a "taking" of the property under the Takings Clause of the U.S. Constitution or its analogue in the relevant state constitution, so the municipality must either pay just compensation to the landowner or not enforce the provision. In such states, a court presumably would approve the amortization provision if the provision incorporated an obligation for the state to compensate the landowner for the loss of the nonconforming use. The majority of state courts, however, uphold reasonable amortization provisions as legitimate regulatory tools that do not implicate the Takings Clause, analogizing these provisions to provisions that prohibit the expansion of nonconforming uses or that prohibit the renewal of abandoned uses. The reasonableness of an amortization provision is based on the time needed for the landowner to recoup the investment in the use or structure.

In recent decades, many municipalities, recognizing that nonconforming uses are not going to wither away, have focused the application of amortization ordinances on troublesome uses like adult bookstores or billboards. Here courts are sensitive to protecting constitutional rights where a city amends a zoning ordinance to rid the city of undesirable yet legal activities by establishing a blatantly short (say 90 day) amortization period. Some courts declare amortization provisions unenforceable because they are not authorized by the state's zoning enabling act: The Standard Act, for example, authorizes states to "regulate" land uses, but not prohibit them.

Examples

1. A municipality enacts an ordinance that prohibits the overnight parking of any truck, trailer, or commercial or recreational vehicle on the street in any single-family residential use district of Town. O is fined for parking his truck overnight outside of his house in such a district and challenges the ordinance. Is this ordinance valid?

2. O applies for a variance for a backyard deck he wishes to construct. The municipality's Board of Zoning Appeals denies his application. O appeals its decision, asking for judicial review by a court, where O raises constitutional due process issues concerning the denial. In defense, the municipality responds that O did not raise these issues before the Board and so cannot raise them in court. Will the municipality's defense succeed? Will O's appeal be heard as a prima facie or "as applied" case?

3. A municipality's amortization ordinance provides that a nonconforming use can be rendered illegal by abandonment or destruction by fire if not rebuilt within a year. Abandonment is not further defined in the ordinance. Oliver owns a nonconforming shed that is totally destroyed by a fire; he does not apply for a building permit until 11 months after the fire, and rebuilding will take a year. The municipality's Board of Zoning Appeals refuses to approve the permit, so Oliver sues for mandamus ordering them to approve his application, alleging that their refusal denies him substantive due process. Does it?

4. A concrete plant has been operating a ready-mix concrete plant in a municipality for 20 years. Last year the municipality amended its zoning ordinance to no longer permit concrete plants to operate within its limits. The municipal council rezoned the property on which the plant operated to R-4, Multifamily Residential, to provide space for high-density, low-income housing. Under the ordinance, the city council could set reasonable amortization periods for nonconforming uses on a property-by-property basis, considering the height of structures used; the nature of the use; the surrounding land uses; the character of the neighborhood; the cost of the property and of any improvements; any benefit to the public if the use continued or ended; the burden on the property owner who is required to terminate the nonconforming use; and the length of time the use has existed. After a public hearing, the council decided the concrete plant be given a two-year amortization, at the conclusion of which the plant was to cease to operate within the district. A major factor in the council's decision was the company's having used the concrete plant for nearly 20 years, finding that 20 years was long enough for the plant's owner to recoup its investment. The plant's owner challenges the exclusion of concrete plants from all locations in the municipality. Does

the council have a legitimate state interest in excluding concrete plants from the city? Is the zoning ordinance rationally related to the promotion of any claimed legitimate state interest?

Explanations

1. The ordinance is invalid on substantive due process grounds. (1) If challenged in court, the ordinance might first be justified as a means of restricting a residential district to residential uses, but the ban is not restricted to commercial vehicles, so, second, a truck for the personal use of a resident of the district would be prohibited too; thus there is no police power nexus between the terms of the ordinance and its purpose; third and moreover, it is not narrowly tailored: A Ford F-150 is no larger than a Ford Crown Victoria. (2) The ordinance might also be justified as an aesthetic regulation, but that a truck "looks commercial" is insufficient and the ordinance does not distinguish between a resident's new clean truck and an ugly, rusted, dilapidated junker — thus no nexus exists here either. The municipality might have banned overnight parking by large 18-wheel rigs, but a clean, new F-150 is no larger than an old, dirty Crown Vic, so again the ordinance is not narrowly tailored. (4) Further, a fundamental right of association claim might be made if O's friends were not able to visit him, or if he was not able to visit them in the district.

2. The Board of Zoning Appeals is an administrative agency and if it heard constitutional issues, it would be acting ultra vires, beyond the scope of its enabling act or ordinance authority, so the defense will fail. Moreover, a variance requires a showing that the ordinance applied to a particular parcel like O's, as opposed to many parcels, and resulted in an inability to use the parcel. So the appeal should be regarded as an "as applied" one.

3. Not likely. Abandonment at common law requires an act of abandonment, taken with an intent to abandon. But if the ordinance defines abandonment by the mere passage of time, the elimination of nonconforming uses thereby is nonetheless rationally related to the purpose of the ordinance to bring all parcels into conformance with the ordinance. Writ denied: The face of the ordinance gives the officials the authority to interpret the ordinance as repealing the common law definition of an abandonment.

4. The council's decision is entitled to a presumption of validity and constitutionality and the council can offer several legitimate state interests. Any goal that promotes the health, safety, morals, or general welfare qualifies, so housing low-income persons will qualify. One legitimate goal was to remove the source of dust and other air pollution associated with concrete plants. Similarly, trucks to and from the plant may cause

dangerous traffic conditions. Further, providing housing for all segments of citizens residing in the municipality promotes its general welfare and qualifies as well. Moreover, zoning is the means to achieve the state's legitimate ends. Rezoning to prohibit the operation of the concrete plant within the city is rationally related to health (cleaner air), safety (safer traffic conditions), and the general welfare (housing low-income persons). So the amortization provision also is a means rationally related to the promotion of the legitimate state interests.

32

CHAPTER

Variances, Special Exceptions, and Zoning Amendments

Flexibility is added to zoning ordinances through variances and special exceptions, both administered by the Board of Zoning Appeals or Adjustment, and zoning amendments enacted by the municipal legislature.

VARIANCES

Zoning ordinances permit the board of adjustment to grant variances. A *variance*, if granted, allows a landowner to build on land or use the land in a manner otherwise not permitted by the zoning ordinance. The variance is an administrative order waiving application of the zoning ordinance in order to keep the ordinance from denying a landowner all reasonable use of his property. It also serves as a safety valve that prevents the city or county from being held liable under the Takings Clause of the Constitution, or the zoning ordinance from being declared unconstitutional under the substantive Due Process Clause of the Constitution.

Variances are categorized as either use variances or area variances. **Use variances** permit a use otherwise prohibited in the district. A few states prohibit use variances altogether. **Area variances** permit deviations from area, bulk, setback, street frontage, floor space, and height and other nonuse requirements of the zoning ordinance. Boards of Adjustment or Zoning Appeals (and courts) are more receptive to area variances since they usually do not change a district's essential character.

Zoning ordinances authorize both types of variances by a provision similar to §7 of the Standard State Zoning Enabling Act discussed in the last Chapter, which authorizes the Board to permit such variances from the terms of the ordinance as will not be contrary to the public interest, where, owing to special conditions, a literal enforcement of the provisions of the ordinance will result in unnecessary hardship or practical difficulties, and so that the spirit of the ordinance shall be observed and substantial justice done.

A Board will grant a variance only if there is substantial evidence[1] that the following elements are met:

1. The variance is not substantially incompatible with the comprehensive zoning plan;
2. The landowner is affect in a unique way by some provision in the ordinance;
3. The landowner applying for a use variance suffers an unnecessary or undue hardship in the use of the land or, in the case of an area variance, a practical difficulty if the variance is denied; and
4. The grant of the variance will not be detrimental to the public welfare.

The first requirement — that the variance would not be substantially **incompatible with the comprehensive zoning plan** — guarantees that the variance will not be inconsistent with the zoning ordinance's overall plan. Moreover, too great a departure from the zoning scheme looks like an **amendment** to the zoning plan itself. Boards of Adjustment have only the powers given to them by the ordinance; they do not have the legislative authority to amend the zoning ordinance; that is a power reserved to the municipal legislature.

The second prerequisite is that the landowner would suffer a **unique** difficulty or hardship in the use of the land in question if the variance is not granted. The hardship usually arises from some unique physical condition of the land. Uniqueness involves some particular condition that justifies treating it differently from other land in the district. It does not mean that the lot is the only lot in the district suffering from the hardship, but the hardship cannot be one generally characteristic of land in the district. If many land parcels suffer from the same disabling condition, the matter is one for the municipal legislature to address by rezoning the parcel or parcels.

---

1. "Substantial evidence" is a critical mass of evidence, what a reasonable mind would accept as adequate, more than a scintilla but less than a preponderance of all the evidence available and providing a reasonable basis for a decision though that decision may still be fairly debatable. It is enough to deny a motion for a directed verdict upon judicial review. This evidentiary standard applies to all Board decisions.

Example: O applies for a variance because her land parcel is affected by a sulfurous odor emitted by a nearby paper mill. This application will be denied because the odor is not unique to her parcel.

Example: O applies for a variance because her parcel is affected by the fumes and noise from heavy traffic traveling a road abutting her land. This application will be denied if many parcels along the road in her zoning district are affected in the same manner.

Example: O is zoned in a residential-use district and applies for a variance because the closeness of an abutting commercial-use district makes her property much less valuable as a residence. Her application will be denied because mapping use districts is a legislative matter and the Board is not authorized to change the boundaries of a district. If the lessening of the property's value is such that O cannot reasonably make use of it as a residence, the application may be denied because each of the 4 elements for a variance must be satisfied in its own right: one cannot be balanced against the others.

Third, the hardship suffered must be an undue or unnecessary hardship. **Undue or unnecessary hardship** is a condition of the lot such that the owner could not make effective use or make a reasonable profit from owning the lot put to a reasonable use unless a variance is granted. Most states apply this standard in evaluating petitions for use variances. A more lenient standard, the **practical difficulty** standard, is used to evaluate petitions for an area variance. In any event, the hardship suffered must go to the use of the land: A mere decrease in value of the property will not justify a variance. A landowner is not entitled to the most profitable use of the land.

Example: A local zoning ordinance requires a minimum of 60 feet along an abutting road or street before a parcel can be improved: At least 60 feet must abut the street. An owner could build on a parcel having a frontage of more than 60 feet, but could not build if the frontage was 59 feet or less. The original subdivider sold a lot with a 40-foot frontage to a landowner before the city enacted the zoning ordinance. Since the lot has a 40-foot frontage and not the 60-foot frontage necessary to improve a lot under the ordinance, the landowner suffers a hardship, which would be considered unnecessary but for the ordinance.

Not all hardships qualify. A hardship, for example, will not be considered unnecessary if it was **self-created**, meaning self-imposed. In other words, the hardship cannot be the result of some action by a landowner (or predecessor in interest) knowing of the zoning ordinance. In some jurisdictions, it is the landowner applying for the variance who bears the burden of proof on this point — in which case it becomes another element necessary for granting a variance; in others, it is a "defense" to an order granting the variance, meaning that the self-created nature of the hardship or difficulty will be raised by neighbors opposing the application. Still other jurisdictions require that the applicant make an effort to eliminate the hardship or difficulty before applying for the variance. If no such effort is made, the applicant runs the risk of the Board's finding that the need for the variance is self-created. (Often the effort involved is an attempt to buy enough neighboring land to bring the lot into compliance with the ordinance.)

Example: The zoning ordinance requires a 60-foot frontage and O has a parcel with a 100-foot frontage. O sells part of her lot to P. P's lot has a 60-foot frontage while the portion that O retains has a 40-foot frontage. O sells the retained portion to B. Having a lot with a 40-foot frontage creates a hardship since B cannot improve the lot under the zoning ordinance. O and B suffer a unique hardship because of the 60-foot frontage requirement, but will not be considered to suffer an unnecessary hardship: O's hardship is self-created and B should have checked the ordinance before purchasing: He might have a remedy against O, but by purchasing, B is responsible for checking the ordinance and after the transfer is deemed to have checked it. A "subject to zoning" condition should have been in B's sales contract.

Similarly, an owner cannot intentionally construct a structure in violation of the ordinance or build before securing a building permit and subsequently seek a variance claiming that destruction of the structure would be an unnecessary hardship. Such a hardship is self-created. Even if the building permit was issued illegally, no owner may rely on an illegal permit.

The fourth element for securing a variance is to show that the grant of a variance would not be **detrimental to the public welfare**, meaning that granting the variance would not harm the use and enjoyment of neighboring properties, would not detract from the character of the neighborhood, and otherwise would not be contrary to the public health or safety of the area. A decrease in the value of adjacent property, as well as aesthetic, safety, environmental, or traffic concerns, may be considered harm preventing the issuance of a variance.

A variance need not be narrowly tailored. That is a due process requirement for legislative, not administrative, actions. But variances should be, collectively and individually, selectively granted and deviate from the ordinance only so much as is necessary to make the affected property usable or reasonably profitable. In this sense, the variance is meant to provide a buffer against the ordinance's application working a taking of an owner's property.

Most ordinances give the Board, when granting a variance, the authority to impose conditions, usually taking the form of a real covenant. The conditions must be reasonably related to the promotion of the objectives of the ordinance. Conditions might include building and maintaining fences or planting hedges to preserve the district's aesthetics, or grading the land to improve its drainage.

SPECIAL EXCEPTIONS

The Board also has authority to grant or deny a **special exception** (a/k/a special use, special use permit, or conditional use). It is a use expressly provided for in the text of an ordinance, but not located on the zoning map that accompanies the text. They are land uses permitted not as of right, but instead permitted only conditionally: that is, permitted only after the Board considers and applies the conditions expressly set out in the ordinance's text. In contrast to the variance, which permits deviation from provisions of the ordinance, it lists as special exceptions those uses that *may* be located in the district. Typically uses listed as special exception generate heavier than usual traffic, involve a high volume of users, or are likely to have detrimental effects on surrounding parcels. Banks, social clubs, churches, nursing homes, convenience stores, child care facilities, and funeral homes are often the subject of special exceptions, each listed with distinct conditions tailored to that use.

The Board may approve only those uses specially mentioned in the ordinance. It must apply all the conditions and may not vary or add to them. It has no authority to deny the special exception if all the conditions are met; in that sense, a special exception is a permitted use, just not one permitted as of right. These express conditions can be quite specific, involving such things as fences, set-back lines, minimum number of occupants, and the maximum percentage of the lot covered by the specially permitted use. The specific standards are sometimes followed in the ordinance by a general standard, e.g., that the use has "no adverse impact on surrounding lots," providing the Board with discretion to grant or deny the application after considering the degree of impacts on surrounding parcels that cannot be mitigated, as well as the benefit of permitting the use relative to the impacts it would create — say, in extra traffic or pollution.

Thus, to qualify for a special exception, a landowner needs to show that (a) the ordinance lists the use as a special exception; (b) the use will meet all conditions set out in the ordinance; and (c) the special exception will not detract from the area's health, safety, and public welfare beyond that inherent in the normal conduct of the activity itself. Since the special use is a permitted use and its location is entitled to a presumption of validity, the applicant does not have to prove that the special exception benefits the neighborhood: the municipality's legislature has already decided that it might and in that sense it carries a presumption of validity. Because the substantial evidence standard is again used in hearing and deciding the application, the applicant's evidence and experts do not have to be more creditable than that of the opposition: They only have to present substantial evidence.

JUDICIAL REVIEW OF VARIANCES AND SPECIAL EXCEPTIONS

The Board is an appointed administrative body. The zoning ordinance (or the state enabling act) sets out the standards and conditions needed for all variances and special exceptions, and the Board's function is to determine whether the conditions and standards have been met. Once the board concludes the law's requirement or conditions have been met, the board must grant the variance or special exception application before it. If they are not met, the Board must deny the application. Anything else would be ultra vires or beyond the scope of its authority.

Parties disappointed by the board of adjustment's decision may appeal to a court. A court will review, either as an administrative appeal or *de novo*, the record developed at the Board level to ensure that its decision was based on finding of fact and the law and the conditions in the zoning ordinance. For this to occur, several preliminary matters must have occurred.

First, the zoning ordinance (or the state enabling act) must enumerate the standards and conditions controlling the board's discretion. Generally this is no problem with variances, since ordinances often mimic the standards in the enabling act and the courts hold that the unnecessary hardship and practical difficulty language in the enabling act or other language in the ordinance provide adequate guidance. Some courts, however, have had trouble with the standards for a special exception. If an ordinance's conditions or standards are too general or the Board mimics them in its findings, it is impossible for courts to know the grounds for the Board's decision. In addition, one or more of the standards may give the Board insufficient guidance and too much discretion. If put in this position, a court may hold that those provisions are an unconstitutional delegation of legislative power. They are then struck from the ordinance, since the court will be forced to evaluate the Board's decision and findings without the excluded provision. Moribund at the federal level of our government, this delegation doctrine lives on at the state and municipal level.

Example: The mop up or general condition for granting a special exception for a nursery school in a residential-use district is that the grant "be for the benefit of the community." Too broad: It is the municipal legislative body that must decide on whether the community benefits, and thus the last condition on special exceptions is likely to be of the "no adverse impact" type.

Second, the Board must provide an applicant with procedural due process: The applicant and persons (including neighboring landowners and the general public) interested in the decision must be given an opportunity to be heard and an opportunity to present and rebut evidence. The Board must keep a written record of its findings of fact and an explanation of its decision in every case. A court will not review a Board's decision unless the court has before it a written record including findings of fact and the reasons for the Board's decision. Otherwise, a court will remand the matter to the Board to prepare a record. A decision based on a factor not included in the written record is *per se* arbitrary and capricious, requiring a reversal of the Board's decision.

If a court is satisfied it has a complete written record, the court begins with the presumption the Board's decision is correct, and will reverse the verdict only if (a) the ordinance is unconstitutional; (b) the Board's finding of facts are clearly erroneous; (c) the court finds the Board did not adhere to the procedures and guidelines contained in the ordinance or its own operating procedures; or (d) the board's decision was arbitrary, capricious, or discriminatory or was not supported by substantial evidence.

AMENDING THE ZONING ORDINANCE

Municipalities (city councils or county commissioners) must, when enacting zoning ordinances and amendments, follow procedures in effect for every type of ordinance — notice, hearing, and multiple readings in different sessions for enacting and amending zoning ordinances. In doing so, they are acting in a legislative capacity, so no formal written record of findings is necessary. They must, however, make ordinances available to the general public after enactment. Any zoning amendment is entitled to the same presumption of validity and correctness that was given to the original ordinance: it need only be supported by substantial evidence.

The Standard Zoning Enabling Act and most enabling acts today require that the zoning ordinances be "in accordance with" a master plan or comprehensive plan of development. In a dozen or so states, statutes make the existence of a plan a mandatory precondition to a zoning ordinance. Absent a state statute to the contrary, when no master or comprehensive plan exists, most courts overlook this failure: they accept the zoning ordinance itself and all the decisions made under it as a "plan." In any event, many courts require zoning ordinances and amendments add up to a consistent land-use policy — that is, that the ordinance and amendments to it be consistent *inter se*.

Thus courts will void a zoning ordinance provision or amendments thereto only (a) if the ordinance, provision, or amendment is not enacted pursuant to the state's enabling act or the local zoning authority's comprehensive plan of development; (b) if the ordinance, provision, or amendment is arbitrary, capricious, or discriminatory; or (c) if the ordinance, provision, or amendment violates some provision of the federal or a state constitution or statute.

In most states, there is no one test for the validity of a zoning amendment: furtherance of the public or general welfare is the best that many states do. Among the factors that a court might balance and consider upon judicial review of any amendment are the size of the requested rezoning, the compatibility of the rezoned property with its neighboring land uses, the benefits and detriments resulting from approval of the rezoning application, and the compatibility of the rezoning with the comprehensive plan. These criteria are flexible.

In a few states, an ordinance can be amended only if either (1) there is a mistake in the original ordinance or (2) there are changed conditions in the actual land uses in the neighborhood of the applicant's parcel since the enactment of the original ordinance that justify the amendment.

THE PROBLEM OF SPOT ZONING

One exception to the general rule that a rezoning amendment is given a presumption of validity is the doctrine of *spot zoning*. Spot zoning occurs when the municipal legislature rezones a parcel or parcels into a more intensive or less restrictive use and the property is rezoned for the benefit of its owner and not for the public. Because nearby similarly situated property is not similarly rezoned, such a rezoning is "not in accord with the comprehensive plan" and also in violation of the provision the Standard Zoning Enabling Act and many enabling acts today, that use districts "be uniform for each kind or class of building throughout each district." Violating this uniformity provision requires analysis like that given under the equal protection clause, requiring that classifications made in an amendment be reasonable. The spot zoning doctrine is a judicial gloss on these enabling statutes. Thus when a court feels the amendment favors one landowner over neighboring property owners, the court will invalidate the amendment as spot zoning.

Most jurisdictions, finding spot zoning, invalidate the rezoning as illegal. In other jurisdictions, spot zoning merely identifies a situation in which the municipality loses the presumption of validity; here the doctrine is a burden-shifting device, and once a landowner (usually a neighbor of the applicant) meets an initial burden of proof showing that the application will result in spot zoning, the burden shifts to the municipality to justify its approval of the application. Courts in these jurisdictions then review the same factors that are used for any rezoning to decide whether the spot zoning is illegal.

No single factor determines whether a zoning amendment constitutes spot zoning, but four factors are commonly used in spot-zoning cases. One is whether the land to be rezoned is owned by one person or involves rezoning a relatively small parcel. A small parcel owned by one person is a likely signal that the amendment is spot zoning. A second factor is whether the amendment is "in accord with the comprehensive plan." (This phrase is taken from the Standard Zoning Enabling Act and is found today in many such acts.) Courts are prone to defer to the Board if the amendment accords with the plan. A third factor is whether the land use when rezoned will be compatible with surrounding uses. Compatibility is a particularly useful factor when no comprehensive plan exists. The greater the incompatibility, the more likely it is that spot zoning will be found. A fourth and final factor is whether the rezoning confers some general benefit on the community or merely confers a benefit on the applicant for the rezoning. If the latter, then the rezoning is likely spot zoning. No one factor is determinative.

Example: Landowners own a corner lot in a residential neighborhood one mile from the business district. All lots for five blocks in any direction are used for single-family residences. Landowners petition the town council to rezone the corner lot from single-family residential use only to commercial use so landowners can open an ice cream parlor. Since the single corner lot is in the middle of a residential district and surrounded completely by homes, the court will invalidate the rezoning as illegal spot zoning. The neighbors' need for ice cream is irrelevant, the benefit to the owner is what counts.

Example: Landowner owns undeveloped property originally zoned residential use only. The property is bounded by a railroad, commercial property, a state highway, and a U.S. highway. Assuming rezoning the property to commercial would not materially benefit the community or harm the community, the fact that the property is surrounded by busy roads and commercial activity favors the landowner in her rezoning effort. This is not spot zoning. To prevail, protesting landowners must identify some harm significant enough for a court to override the municipality's presumption of validity.

INITIATIVE AND REFERENDUM

Initiative and referendum refer to legislative actions taken by a vote of a municipality's citizenry. As applied to zoning, an **initiative** describes the process through which citizens petition to have a proposed zoning amendment placed on a ballot, and voters adopt or reject the zoning amendment. A **referendum** occurs after the local zoning authority enacts or amends an ordinance. No successful applicant for a rezoning is home free in jurisdictions where a municipality's legislative actions are subject to referendum. Either the municipality or a citizens group, by a petition containing a required number of signatures, may have the zoning amendment placed on the ballot; and the voters decide whether to ratify or repeal it. The U.S. Supreme Court upheld zoning by initiative and referendum. It held that a referendum requirement is not *per se* a violation of due process: what the voters can delegate to a municipality's legislative body, they can also withhold or reserve. *City of East Lake v. Forest City Enterprises, Inc.*, 426 U.S. 668 (1976). In contrast, several state constitutions have been interpreted to prohibit zoning by initiative and referendum.

Likewise, several state constitutions have been interpreted to limit referenda requirements to legislative actions, but in *City of Cuyahoga Falls, Ohio v. Buckeye Community Hope Fdn.*, 538 U.S. 188. 199 (2003), the Supreme Court said:

> As a matter of federal constitutional law, we have rejected the distinction . . . between legislative and administrative referendums. In Eastlake . . . , we made clear that because all power stems from the people, "[a] referendum cannot . . . be characterized as a delegation of power," unlawful unless accompanied by "discernible standards." The people retain the power to govern through referendum 'with respect to any matter, legislative or administrative, within the realm of local affairs.' *** The subjection of the site-plan ordinance to the City's referendum process, regardless of whether that ordinance reflected an administrative or legislative decision, did not constitute *per se* arbitrary government conduct in violation of due process.

Zoning by referendum, though constitutional as a process for amending a zoning ordinance, remains subject to other constitutional challenges as would any zoning action.

Example: Before seeking a rezoning, a landowner decides to seek an amendment to the municipality's comprehensive plan from its planning commission. The commission grants the owner the amendment she sought, but neighbors knowing about and opposing her plan to seek a zoning amendment from the municipality's legislature petition for a referendum on the plan amendment. The planning commission is clearly an administrative body, and the plan's amendment is only a guide for the legislature (unless this is a mandatory planning state) and does not preclude the owner's seeking the rezoning, but nonetheless under *City of Cuyahoga Falls*, the referendum petition (if available by statute or provided by the state constitution) may put the plan amendment to a vote. This is too much of a good thing and suggests why many states do not subject administrative decisions to referenda requirements.

CONTRACT AND CONDITIONAL ZONING

Sometimes a municipality sees merit in a landowner's application to have her property rezoned, but either wishes to limit potential uses of the property or to place some affirmative obligation on the landowner to protect owners of surrounding property, thus demanding she comply with **conditions** when her application is approved. For example, she may be required to build a fence or plant hedges, to accept increased setbacks, to reduce the building-footage-to-lot-size ratio, or to limit the property to certain uses such as a grocery store. Typically these conditions are provisions of the rezoning amendment's text and documented in real covenants filed in the land records. Most (but not all) courts approve such conditions as an exercise of the police power.

While most jurisdictions approve the use of conditions, a few states reject all conditions to a rezoning, and yet other states reject contract zoning but permit conditional zoning. Under **contract zoning**, the local zoning authority agrees to rezone property if the landowner agrees to certain conditions. Courts distinguishing between contract zoning and conditional zoning invalidate **contract zoning** because the municipality's legislature has by contract bargained away its power, which it cannot do. Under **conditional zoning**, on the other hand, the local zoning authority does not consider a rezoning application until the landowner has recorded specific affirmative or negative covenants on the use of the property or, alternatively, the zoning authority incorporates the restrictions into the zoning amendment. The zoning authority is not legally bound to rezone even if the landowner records the stipulated covenants. Courts invalidate contract zoning as an unauthorized delegation of the municipality's legislative authority to those who can enforce the covenants, but approve conditional zoning.

Conditional zoning (and contract zoning where valid) also may face attack on the basis of being illegal spot zoning. Then the zoning amendment must (again) conform to the comprehensive plan of development, be compatible with the uses being made of surrounding property, and benefit the neighbors as well as the applicant.

FLOATING ZONES, CLUSTER ZONES, AND PUDS

Land-use planners have developed zoning techniques in addition to Euclidean zoning. A **floating zone** is a zoning district authorized in a zoning ordinance (where standards for its use are expressly set out) but not located on the zoning map, so that it does not yet encompass any land. In this sense, it is like a large special exception: express in the text of an ordinance, but unmapped. The municipal legislature uses its power to map the zone after the text of the ordinance is enacted as the need arises and when the proper location becomes apparent. The floating zone is particularly useful for things like garden apartments and commercial office parks. It is more responsive to market forces than Euclidean zoning, allows both for legislative reflection about the location of a use on the zoning map and for thoughtful site planning, is not inconsistent with the vast majority of zoning enabling acts, and enjoys the presumption of validity accorded legislative actions. On one or all of these grounds, most courts considering the validity of floating zones approve them. Since mapping a floating zone is also fraught with opportunities for abuse or favoritism, it is typically open to a change of subject as spot zoning (and may be invalidated on that ground).

Cluster zoning allows a developer to overdevelop some land within a larger parcel, increasing the density beyond that allowed in the district, while underdeveloping or dedicating other land in the parcel to parks or leaving it in its natural undeveloped state such that the density for the parcel as a whole stays within the zoning ordinance standards.

The **planned unit development (PUD)** is an extension of cluster zoning that also allows a range of varying uses within a large tract of land. The developer can coordinate single-family and multi-family uses with commercial uses to meet the needs of the residences. Zoning ordinance provisions authorizing PUDs may incorporate density flexibility similar to those allowed under cluster zoning, but the PUD's main attraction is the multiplicity of *uses* allowed on the tract. This technique is used mostly for large parcels of land, converting them into very large subdivisions or even new towns.

Examples

1. O purchases a house designated as an eighteenth-century historic building and located in a modern single-family residential-use district under the applicable zoning ordinance. O seeks to convert the house into two dwelling units so that the property can pay for the maintenance of its historic features, and seeks a variance to do so. Will the variance be granted?

2. The Board of Zoning Appeals grants O the variance for which she applied "for her life." O seeks to sell the subject land parcel and the purchaser asks you whether the limitation on the duration of the variance is valid. Is it?

3. O applies to the Board of Zoning Appeals for a variance and proves that she cannot earn a reasonable return on the subject parcel if the application is denied. Has O suffered a taking of her property?

4. "Landfills" are designated as special exceptions in a zoning ordinance that prescribes set-back, minimum acreage, and landscape screening along the municipality's roads, as well as authorizing the Board of Zoning Appeals to prevent its "adverse impacts" on surrounding parcels. The Board grants a waste disposal company a special exception permit for a landfill, limiting the company to accepting only trash from its residential customers and preventing it from accepting used construction materials. Is the limitation valid?

5. At the hearing on O's application for a special exception, O presents, among other things, data comparing the adverse effects of her proposed use with the effects of other permitted-as-of-right uses. Neighbors opposing the application present data showing that the effects of O's proposed use are greater than the effects of other, previously granted, special exceptions for the same use. The Board of Zoning Appeals in its denial of the application regards O's data as irrelevant. Is the Board correct?

6. At the hearing on O's application for a special exception, O presents, among other things, data showing that the effects of O's proposed use are no greater than the effects of other, previously granted, special exceptions for the same use. The neighbors opposing the application present data showing that the effects of O's proposed use are above and beyond the effects inherently associated with such a special exception no matter where it is located. The Board of Zoning Appeals in its denial of the application disregards O's data. May the Board do this?

7. O owns a parcel in a residential use district. O's parcel abuts a commercial district. O seeks to have her parcel rezoned from a residential to a retail commercial use. At the hearing on his application, O presents data on the need for his proposed use due to the increased population in the municipality and points out the need for her proposed use recognized in the municipality's comprehensive plan. Neighbors opposing the proposal point out that there have been no rezonings in O's district for any type of commercial use, and that before O's data on population needs is considered, she must show a shift in land uses away from residential uses, among the land uses present in the district. Are the neighbors correct?

8. In a small municipality, O owns a residential parcel that she seeks to have rezoned to a commercial use. At the hearing on her application, she presents data showing that her proposed use is compatible with surrounding uses, but including in her comparisons land uses from an abutting municipality. The municipal council, sitting as a hearing

examiner on her application, refused to consider the extraterritorial uses in reaching a decision. Is the council correct?

9. O owns a parcel in the downtown area of a municipality attempting to replan its downtown. At the hearing on O's application for a rezoning, she presents data showing that her rezoning proposal better fits this replanning effort than do the land uses presently surrounding her parcel. Is O entitled to have her application granted?

10. At the late night hearing on O's application for a rezoning, the municipal council's members are inattentive, some appearing to be asleep or discussing other legislation amongst themselves, all the while O's opposing neighbors are shouting and catcalling to council members to deny O's application, which the council in time does. O's petitions for a rehearing. Is she entitled to have her application reheard?

11. The municipality's Planning Commission grants O's application for a multi-use planned unit development in an otherwise large lot, single-family residential zone. Under the laws of the state, the citizens of the municipality are entitled to file a petition to put the grant to a referendum of all the municipality's citizens. Does the municipal board of elections have to accept and consider the petition?

12. O owns a parcel abutting a municipal street scheduled for widening under the municipality's capital budget. O and the municipality agree in writing that in exchange for conveying that portion of the parcel necessary for the widening, O will be permitted to develop the remainder of the parcel at a density no less than permissible under the Euclidean zoning ordinance in effect just before the conveyance. The municipal council enacts the substance of the agreement as an amendment to its zoning ordinance. Several years later, the zoning ordinance has been amended — and O's parcel downzoned — so that the same land area that accommodated four lots now only can accommodate two. O seeks to enforce her agreement with the municipality. Can she?

13. O owns a parcel located in a Euclidean R-3 residential-use district in which a planned unit development (PUD) is permitted as an overlay zone. O applies to the municipal planning commission for a PUD permit, proposing development of his parcel as a density permissible under the applicable PUD ordinance but greater than that permitted in the R-3 district. The neighbors object to O's overdevelopment of his parcel and appeal the commission's issuance of O's permit. On appeal, what result and why?

Explanations

1. To the extent that the house predates the zoning ordinance, its non-conformance with the set-back, area, and dimensional requirements of the ordinance are likely grandfathered as nonconforming uses, so an application for an area variance is probably not necessary, although there is often a permit required to establish a base line for the allowable nonconformance. An application for a use variance is still necessary — however, the issue will be whether the uniqueness element of a variance application is satisfied. This surely is a "unnecessary hardship" not shared by surrounding parcels. The variance will be granted. Because the variance is to pay for the maintenance of the historic features of the house, the "no reasonable return" element for a use variance is established as well. Likewise, the applicable comprehensive plan has been drafted with existing structures in mind, so that variance is conformable to the plan. Finally, as to the hardship being self-created, the obvious answer is that O didn't build the house.

2. No. A limitation on a variance for the life of the applicant is invalid. A variance "runs with the land" and may not be made personal to the owner. It must be based on the objective facts unique to the land's condition. Just as an owner's personal hardships provide insufficient grounds for issuing a variance, the application should be checked again to determine whether the grounds for granting the variance affected the land use, not just the owner: Variances affect the use, not the user. Reliance on an illegal permit based on the variance's issuance subjects the purchaser to the risk it might be revoked. No one may rely on an illegal permit unless it provides a basis for estopping the municipality from revoking it — and estoppel is a doctrine that few jurisdictions would use in this situation. By the same token, a condition on a variance that the subject parcel not be rented and would be invalid as well. The Board has exceeded its delegated authority.

3. No. The pre-existing use of the property is not diminished by the denial. Moreover, no finding of an administrative body like the Board of Zoning Appeals is a substitute for a judicial finding that a taking under the Fifth Amendment occurred. The Board is not competent to make such a finding. It is a lay body, there is no uniform procedure for it within any state, and in any event its decisions are not final, but are instead subject to judicial review. We do not delegate decisions on constitutional matters to it. A claim alleging a taking and review of the Board's variance decisions are distinct causes of action. Likewise, an application for a variance is not a precondition to making a takings claim later. It could thus be brought after the statute of limitations for an administrative appeal has run. When brought, it is an "as

applied" takings claim, as opposed to a facial challenge to the zoning ordinance: a variance requires a detailed look at particular and unique parcels as opposed to a general inability to use many parcels in order the make a reasonable return on them. That detail is grist for an "as applied" claim.

4. No. Unless the ordinance in its definition of a landfill limited the type of waste the permit holder could accept, the Board may not do so. It must impose only the conditions listed in the ordinance. Otherwise a "land-fill" is regarded as a permitted use and the company is entitled to a liberal reading of the definition. The Board might decide that run-off from certain types of waste will pollute the groundwater of the neighborhood, and that is an "adverse impact" over which the Board has authority that might be implied from the conditions set out in the ordinance, but a blanket prohibition on types of acceptable waste is beyond its authority.

5. The Board has a point: Why compare uses permitted with a special exception with uses permitted without it? Both are already permitted uses and entitled to a presumption of validity. The neighbors have devised a more relevant set of comparisons, one that better accords with the presumption of validity. Assuming that the neighbors' evidence is substantial, this application will be denied. The Board is not charged with rebutting all the data presented to it. It merely needs to assemble substantial evidence that the application should be denied to survive a rational basis, not-arbitrary-and-capricious judicial review of its decision.

6. Yes. The neighbors have figured out a comparison that is once again more substantial than the one O presents. A special exception is a permitted use anywhere in the use districts designated in the ordinance, so the comparison of O's proposed uses with previously granted special exceptions is not as telling a reason for denial as an argument that no matter where located, O's proposed use has effects that are not inherent in that use. The municipality's legislatures must have assumed that a specially permitted use will have some inherent adverse effects on its neighbors, thus only those uses that have effects beyond those the legislature foresaw should be denied entry to any designated use district. This evidentiary standard for special exceptions best accords with the presumption of validity accorded a special exception.

7. No. An applicant for a rezoning has the burden of proof, but in most states, it does not include making a change in the actual land uses a precondition to the presentation of further data. O must in general show that the rezoning will have little impact on the existing use district, be compatible with surrounding uses, be consistent with the comprehensive

plan, and will benefit the community more than detract from its general welfare. Each one of these factors is balanced against all the others, no one being a threshold test for the application. What the neighbors have proposed is certainly protective of the existing population's expectations as to what their surroundings will be when they purchased their parcels, but only few jurisdictions accept their argument.

8. Nothing in most if not all of the enabling acts for zoning ordinances precludes consideration of extraterritorial land uses, and such consideration is appropriate in a small municipality. So the council should not refuse O's data, but is entitled to weigh it lightly in the balance when balancing it with other factors.

9. No, not entitled, but O's data shows compatibility with the replanning effort and the council would be within its rights if they gave it extra weight on that account. Her neighboring commercial owners, however, when considering her application's compatibility with surrounding uses, would be right to insist that her comparisons be between her proposed use and the existing, actual land uses surrounding her.

10. Yes, she is. O has been denied the most basic due process.

11. Yes, it does. The board of elections must accept petitions to ratify or annul all legislative actions, and rezoning to a planned unit development use is such an action. The fact that the Planning Commission is an appointed administrative body, normally considering administrative matters, is not relevant — it is the type of action taken that controls the board's decision on the petition.

12. She can enforce the agreement: It is no more than would be accomplished by cluster zoning, reasonable as conditional zoning, and well within the police power. If properly executed by the official with the power of eminent domain and reviewed by the municipal council, it is not contract zoning: If the agreement was considered on its merits as a zoning matter, it is not an impermissible delegation of the council's zoning authority. It is instead seen as the municipality's reserving to itself the authority to enact cluster zoning. Neither is it spot zoning since the municipality avoided paying compensation for the widening and so received a benefit: spot zoning must benefit the landowner at the expense of the public. Not the case here. (In a few jurisdictions, the doctrine of governmental estoppel would allow enforcement as well.)

13. Judgment for the neighbors. Absent express, overriding provisions of the PUD ordinance, the PUD may not have a lot density greater than the underlying Euclidean zoning. The Euclidean provision of its zoning

code trumps its non-Euclidean provisions, which are not repealed by the conflicting provisions in the PUD ordinance. PUD's are intended as supplementary, but not overriding, law. A PUD ordinance is in this respect a glorified cluster zone, meant to prevent land use spill-overs or externalities affecting neighboring land while providing flexibility to zoning administrators in varying Euclidean requirements.

CHAPTER 33

Zoning Extended and Challenged

Zoning ordinances sometimes are challenged on constitutional grounds other than those based on the Due Process and Takings Clauses. This chapter discusses some frequently encountered disputes.

HOUSEHOLD COMPOSITION AND SINGLE FAMILY RESIDENCES

The highest zone or district in cumulative, Euclidean zoning ordinances is the "single family" residential-use-only district. Defining a "single family residence" is thus an important, oft-litigated issue. The definition excludes apartments, boarding houses, multifamily residential uses, and "non-residential" uses, including retail and other commercial activities. But a boarding house, group home, or student housing may have the outward appearance of a single family house, but not be inhabited by a family. Many ordinances, however, define single-family residences in terms of the number of people and the legal relationships of those persons as constituting a "single family," often also limiting the term to persons related by blood or marriage, or to a maximum of three to four persons unrelated by blood or marriage. The issue is the extent to which the state may regulate the composition of households as "single families."

(a) Village of Belle Terre v. Boraas

In Village of Belle Terre v. Boraas, 416 U.S. 1 (1974), the Supreme Court approved as constitutional an ordinance that defined "family" as follows:

> [O]ne or more persons related by blood, adoption, or marriage, living and cooking together as a single housekeeping unit, exclusive of household servants. A number of persons but not exceeding two (2) living and cooking together as a single housekeeping unit though not related by blood, adoption, or marriage shall be deemed to constitute a family.

The landowner in *Belle Terre* rented a home to six unrelated college students. The village ordered the landlord to comply with a single-family residential ordinance. Instead, the landlord and three of the tenants challenged the ordinance. The Supreme Court found a legitimate state interest in controlling noise, traffic, and parking, and in promoting quiet seclusion, clean air, family values, and youth values. The means chosen, the definition of "family," was rationally related to the promotion of the legitimate state interests. The Court found no infringement on a fundamental constitutional right (students not being a specially protected or "suspect class"), nor was the categorization based on blood and legal relationships a violation of the Equal Protection Clause of the Constitution (unrelated persons not being specially protected either).

(b) Moore v. City of East Cleveland

In Moore v. City of East Cleveland, 431 U.S. 494 (1977), the city's ordinance defined family in "single-family" to include a head of the household and spouse and all their unmarried children who did not themselves have any children living with them. The ordinance then provided that one dependent married child and his spouse and their children or an unmarried child and his or her children also could live in the home. The elderly Mrs. Moore had two sons, one of whom went away to find work, leaving his son (Mrs. Moore's grandson) to live with Mrs. Moore. Her household then consisted of one son, his dependants, and the grandson. This violated the ordinance. The city issued an "illegal occupant" notice to Mrs. Moore, and when she did not send the grandson away, the city brought criminal charges against Mrs. Moore. She was convicted, fined $25, and sentenced to five days in jail. The Supreme Court held "the Constitution protects the sanctity of the family." The family includes persons related by blood and marriage and extends at least to uncles and grandchildren.

So *Belle Terre* permits municipalities to limit the number of unrelated persons that may live in a house as a single family, while *Moore* prohibits them from limiting the number of related persons that can constitute a "family." *Belle Terre* gives municipalities latitude under the U.S. Constitution to restrict the composition of "family" as long as it does not limit the number of persons related by blood, marriage, or adoption from being a "family." Some state constitutions and state statutory laws offer more protections in this area. Some state courts have interpreted their own constitutions to prohibit ordinances approved in *Belle Terre*.

(c) Fair Housing Act and Group Homes

Congress enacted the Fair Housing Act, 42 U.S.C. §§3602 et seq., to prohibit discrimination in the sale or renting of property on the basis of race, color, religion, sex, handicap, familial status, or national origin. Handicap means, with respect to a person, (1) a physical or mental impairment which substantially limits one or more of such person's major life activities; (2) a record of having such impairment; or (3) being regarded as having such impairment; but the term does not include current, illegal use of or addiction to a controlled substance. "Discrimination" includes not only active discrimination, but also "a refusal to make reasonable accommodations in rules, policies, practices, or services, when such accommodations may be necessary to afford such persons equal opportunity to use and enjoy a dwelling." 42 U.S.C. §3604(f)(3)(B).

Although the Fair Housing Act applies to all states and municipalities, the Act itself specifically exempts "any reasonable local, State, or Federal restrictions regarding the maximum number of occupants permitted to occupy a dwelling." 42 U.S.C. §3607(b)(1). The Supreme Court has interpreted the Fair Housing Act to prohibit cities from passing zoning ordinances that discriminate against group homes[1] housing protected individuals. In City of Edmonds v. Oxford House, Inc., 514 U.S. 725 (1995), the city defined "family" as "an individual or two or more persons related by genetics, adoption, or marriage, or group of five or fewer persons who are not related by genetics, adoption, or marriage." Oxford House opened a group home for adults recovering from alcoholism and drug addiction. The number of residents ranged from 10 to 12 persons at any given time, greater than the 5 unrelated occupants permitted under the city's ordinance. The city issued a criminal citation to Oxford House. Oxford House in response argued that the city must accommodate the group

---

1. "Group homes" refer to houses where a relatively small number of people with some common attribute live together instead of living in a larger institution. It helps the residents maintain or adjust to a normal life in the community. Group homes generally house foster children, juvenile offenders, recovering drug addicts, alcoholics, disabled persons, and criminals ready for release (halfway homes).

home under the Fair Housing Act. The city countered, citing §3607(b)(1)'s exemption. The Supreme Court held the Fair Housing Act exemption did not protect the city, concluding that the city could not restrict the number of unrelated handicapped persons in a household, who were protected under the Fair Housing Act, while imposing no similar restriction on families. According to the Court, the exemption encompasses ordinances that cap the number of persons who may occupy a dwelling, whether or not related. The city could still limit all homes of a certain size to a maximum number of bedrooms, number of people, or square footage (which it did elsewhere in the ordinance). It also could enforce the five-unrelated-persons ordinance against persons not part of a protected class. Fraternity and sorority houses, for example, are not protected, and the six students in *Belle Terre* would not be protected either.

AESTHETIC REGULATION

Municipalities often enact **aesthetic** ordinances, regulating the architectural appearance of signs and billboards, structures, historic districts, and landmarks.

(a) Signs and Billboards

Municipalities ban or restrict the use and placement of signs and billboards. Ordinances regulating them have been challenged on **substantive due process** and on First Amendment, **free speech** grounds. Early cases generally invalidated all ordinances regulating aesthetics and signs on substantive due process grounds because the state had only the authority to regulate matters that impaired the public "health, safety, and morals." Only if a specific sign or billboard became a nuisance could a government take action against the sign owner. After Village of Euclid v. Ambler Realty Co., 272 U.S. 365 (1926), upheld zoning ordinances on broader health, safety, morals, and **general welfare** grounds, municipalities justified sign regulation as promoting the general welfare. In early cases, aesthetic concerns, standing alone, was held to be an insufficient basis for an exercise of the police power and for such regulation, but along with other concerns, such as preserving the value of surrounding parcels, solving traffic problems, and promoting tourism, many ordinances were later upheld, and finally aesthetics alone came to be a sufficient basis for regulation in more than 30 states. About 10 states consider aesthetics permissible as a supplemental factor to bolster other factors such as economic or traffic goals.

Permitting local zoning authorities to regulate signs and billboards shifted the constitutional argument from substantive due process to the speech grounds. All such ordinances must be the **means** to promote a **legitimate state interest**. A court will uphold an ordinance if the regulation **rationally relates** to the accomplishment of the stated legitimate purpose unless the law or ordinance infringes upon a constitutionally protected right. If the ordinance infringes on the constitutionally protected right of free speech, the state must show that (1) the interest it is trying to achieve is a **compelling state interest** and that (2) the ordinance is **narrowly tailored** to **substantially advance** the state's compelling state interest, while (3) infringing as little as possible on the free speech rights.

Five factors are important: (1) Whether the ordinance regulates **commercial speech** or **noncommercial speech**. Noncommercial (political) speech receives great protection, whereas commercial speech is afforded only "intermediate" protection. (2) Whether the signs and billboards all are on-site (on-premises) or off-site (off-premises). On-site signs identify, promote or refer to some business or activity conducted on the premises where the sign is located. Signs located on another's land or along the street or highway promoting a business located elsewhere is an off-site sign. On-site signs (even commercial on-site signs) receive more protection than off-site signs. (3) Whether the regulation is content-based or content-neutral. Content-based ordinances affect the sign's message. Courts are more likely to invalidate content-based ordinances than content-neutral ordinances. Content-neutral ordinances regulate a sign's location, size, height, or other aspect having nothing to do with its message. (4) Whether the sign is located on a residential lot: Most protected are noncommercial signs on a residential lot. (5) Whether the state is attempting merely to regulate the time, place, or manner of sign placement, or whether the state is attempting to ban a category of signs or billboards. An ordinance that aims at the content of a sign's message will be struck down as unconstitutional. In contrast, an ordinance that regulates land use (time, place, and manner regulation) will be upheld as constitutional if the regulation is unrelated to the suppression of the speech involved.

Laws regulating commercial use of signs and billboards, including absolute bans on certain types of signs, will be upheld if the government offers a legitimate state interest; and the law substantially advances the legitimate state interest. The required means/end relation demands more than the typical rational relationship. The distinction between the "rational relationship" and the "substantially advances" standards puts a greater onus on the government to show that it has not overregulated the placement or physical appearance of commercial signs. Likewise, courts scrutinize more closely those ordinances aimed at commercial speech that are content-based in order to guard against the "rationalization of an impermissible purpose." For example, courts have struck down ordinances, ostensibly enacted for aesthetic or safety reasons, that really overregulate and so in effect ban adult bookstores or ordinances overregulating "for sale" signs in order to stop "white flight."

Judicial scrutiny increases dramatically when the ordinance infringes upon noncommercial speech. Noncommercial speech includes political speech, which is afforded absolute protection. The first question concerning ordinances that infringe on noncommercial speech is whether the statute or ordinance at issue is content-based or a content-neutral. Courts invalidate content-based regulations that are not narrowly tailored to promote a compelling state interest: here aesthetic, traffic safety, and economic concerns do not qualify as compelling state interests. Courts declare nearly all content-based regulations of noncommercial speech to be unconstitutional.

Example: A municipality, citing traffic safety and aesthetic reasons, enacts an ordinance prohibiting all outdoor commercial and noncommercial signs. Its ordinance exempts all on-site commercial signs that relate to the activities conducted on the property from the prohibition. It is permissible to ban all off-site commercial signs, but impermissible to ban on-site or off-site noncommercial signs. Metromedia, Inc. v. City of San Diego, 453 U.S. 490, 514 (1981).

Example: A municipality enacts an ordinance banning almost all signs on residential property, including a small anti-war sign in the front window of O's house. Showing a "special respect for individual liberty in the home," recognizing a "venerable means of communication that is both unique and important," and stressing the uniqueness and affordability of noncommercial signs on residential property, a court on judicial review would hold that the municipality could not ban residential signs. No adequate substitute exists for noncommercial residential signs. Ladue v. Gilleo, 512 U.S. 43 (1994). Thus, an ordinance must be a content-neutral regulation that promotes substantial aesthetic, traffic, safety, or economic state interests unrelated to the sign's message and is narrowly tailored so as to minimally affect the individual's free speech, when other reasonable methods of communicating the same information are available.

(b) Architectural Controls

Architectural design ordinances require that a proposed structure conform to minimum architectural design standards before a municipality will issue the owner a building permit. That is, the structure's external appearance and function must not be so at variance with other structures in a use district as to cause a substantial depreciation in values of neighboring properties, in turn diminishing the real property tax base of the municipality. Architectural design ordinances may either mandate a variety of architectural plans to prevent a monotonous sameness of homes or promote uniformity of appearance and function.

Challengers to these ordinances argue that (1) the state enabling act does not authorize aesthetic regulation (this argument is usually rejected, either because acts today provide express authorization or authorization can be "reasonably implied" from the express provisions of an act); (2) the ordinance does not set out sufficient standards to guide the planning commission or administrators and thus is an unconstitutional delegation of legislative authority (this argument is sometimes successful when the standard involves untutored discretion, but is usually met by restricting board members to design professionals); (3) the standards in the ordinance are void for vagueness. (this argument will be successful when (say) the standard is "to use natural materials" in a structure; otherwise it rarely prevails); (4) the external architectural design of a home or structure should be protected under the First Amendment free speech, broadly construed as freedom of expression. (In the hands of just any owner, this argument will likely fail, but in the hands of the Society to Preserve Frank Lloyd Wright Homes, it might succeed. If accepted, this argument produces legal analysis comparable to that relating to the regulation of signs. The likely result would severely restrict architectural board's considerations: They likely would be limited to a review of architectural designs for safety, fire hazard, or under other standards unrelated to how the structure compares with those surrounding it if any of these arguments succeed.) The effort to maintain aesthetic uniformity and harmony in a use neighborhood or use district would then be left where it is found most often, in deed covenants between private landowners.

(c) Historic Districts

A specialized form of architectural design ordinance concerns historic districts. Historic district ordinances often predate more general architectural design ordinances. Municipalities enact historic district ordinances to preserve the exterior appearance of historical or architecturally significant buildings, monuments, and districts in a colonial, Spanish, or French style. The ordinances typically prohibit demolition of structures in the district, restrict owners' renovation of structures, and ban the introduction of new architectural styles. Preservation of historic districts for aesthetics, historic, cultural, and tourism reasons is a legitimate state interest.

Historic district ordinances are constitutional. Each parcel owner in the district is regarded as receiving a benefit (in the form of similar restrictions on her neighbors) roughly equal to the burden of the regulations—a fair swap of benefits and burdens satisfying the substantive due process clause. The administrative board reviewing and approving (or disapproving) all plans for demolition, renovation, and construction in the district is guided by the appearance of all the other structures in the district, and is thus seldom found to be too vague or to be an unconstitutional delegation of legislative power on that account: the standards are found on the ground.

Denial of permits for structures in these districts may result in a takings claim when the structure cannot yield a reasonable return in rent or other income. Usually these claims fail because the owner always has the pre-existing use to fall back on, so that assuming that there is a taking, it is not of all economically viable uses of the structure.

Example: O owns a historic district structure that has deteriorated but the body overseeing the district, the municipal Board of Zoning Appeals, has found that it is economically feasible to restore it to the standards prevailing in the district. Only when the deteriorated condition of the structure precludes any reasonable use should its demolition be permitted. An economical restoration plan must lift the value of the existing building plus the cost of restoration to at least a level attained by other structures in the district. Its restored value must be higher than its replacement cost to satisfy the due process clause.

(d) Landmarks

The preservation of landmark structures, associated with historical events shaping a municipality or with persons influential in shaping that history, embodying distinctive styles of construction or design or possessing highly artistic qualities as a whole, is of great concern to municipalities. Sustaining their form, structural integrity, and material is the work of "historic" preservation. Distinguished from zoning, it seeks to preserve both the exterior and the interior of a structure. The aesthetic considerations involved provide a substantial state interest energizing landmark ordinances. Under these ordinances, modification of a designated landmark requires an owner to obtain a "certificate of appropriateness" before proceeding. Substantial contrasts with the pre-existing exterior, or incongruity of detail, are deemed inappropriate. In this regard, congruity standards are regarded as contextual, surviving even when a melange of styles exist in the same district. The leading case on historic preservation is Penn Central Transportation Co. v. City of New York, 438 U.S. 104 (1978). It upheld the preservation of Grand Central Terminal as an historic landmark against challenges based on the Due Process, Takings, and Equal Protection Clauses. It also marked the withdrawal of federal courts from aesthetics regulation cases.

Example: O wishes to demolish a landmark to replace it with a structure yielding a higher rent. He may not do so: no owner is entitled to a more profitable use if the regulation is otherwise valid.

Example: O objects to regulation of the size and type of window panes used in his landmark structure. She may not object on that account alone because it is the details of the structure than make up its whole. Whether in a historic district or on a landmark, it is the ensemble of details that counts.

When regulating historic landmarks used for religious purposes, care must be taken that the ordinance is content-neutral, or it may be challenged as an infringement of the free exercise clause of the First Amendment, although analogous state constitutional provisions may invalidate landmark designation more readily.

Example: A church objects to a landmark designation of its worship space. Its objection is given more careful judicial review when the nave or sanctuary of a church or synagogue is involved than when the objection concerns a church hall, mission, or office. The free exercise clause requires a compelling state interest, a narrowly tailored regulation, etc. In addition, the common focus on the exterior of a structure has led some courts to find no authority for the regulation of interior spaces, even when an ordinance does not expressly prohibit such regulation.

TWO FEDERALLY FAVORED LAND USES

(a) Religious Uses

In the Religious Land Use and Institutionalized Persons Act, 42 U.S.C. §2000cc, municipalities are prohibited from applying a zoning ordinance in such a way that a "substantial burden" is placed on the "use, building, or conversion of real property for the purpose of religious exercise," unless the municipality (1) demonstrates "a compelling interest" in doing so and (2) uses "the lease restrictive means of furthering that compelling governmental interest." This statute shifts the burden of proof to the municipality to justify its restriction and creates a heightened standard for judicial review of its decision. The municipality when denying a religious applicant for a zoning decision will have to make an individualized assessment of the application. Moreover, a landowner does not need to have its own religion affected by the restriction: an owner losing a contract to donate or sell property for religious purposes has standing to bring a claim under this statute. Even a facially neutral ordinance *may* offend the statute.

Example: A municipality permits houses of religion in its residential use districts only by special exception. Requiring a permit is not a substantial burden. Neither is a scarcity of large parcels available for religious uses or the cost of obtaining a permit (such burdens fall on religious and non-religious users alike). Further, this ordinance is facially neutral: This means that the applicant for the special exception has an initial burden to show that a substantial burden is placed on religious exercise. Once this showing is made, the municipality must meet the demands of the statute. So this restriction is not an impermissible one, absent evidence that religious exercise is the restriction's target or that the costs of obtaining the permit are prohibitive. In any event, administrative remedies must be exhausted before bringing a RLUIPA claim: Only after that can it be determined whether the restrictions placed on the religious property are the least restrictive.

A municipality's protecting its real property tax base from tax-exempt land uses such as houses of religion is not a compelling interest, but imposing a floor area ratio (limiting a structure's square footage to a proportion of its surrounding land area) to reduce the impact on surrounding properties or public infrastructure, or a concern for neighborhood parking and traffic safety, can be.

(b) Wireless Communication Facilities

The Telecommunications Act of 1996 (TCA) has several substantive and procedural requirements that apply to municipal zoning for cell towers. (The land use term for them is sometimes "Frankenpines.") It preempts statutes and local ordinances that violate the Act. However, municipalities have the first opportunity to decide how to regulate towers as long as they do not regulate towers because of the environmental effects of radio frequency emissions complying with FCC regulations. The Act provides a cause of action in federal court for "any person adversely affected by an final action" inconsistent with its provisions. Most courts have held that the Act does not shift the burden of proof from the applicant to the municipality, although courts have held to the contrary. The Act's intent is to refocus municipalities on the rule that the location of the towers must be "in accord with their comprehensive plan" and to force them to plan for these uses, giving procedural due process to applicants seeking to place a tower in the municipality.[2] It may also force cell phone companies to choose sites for towers carefully.

---

2. The Act requires that municipal decisions be made within a reasonable time and that any denial be "in writing and supported by substantial evidence contained in a written record." This is sometimes taken to require formal findings of fact — but sometimes not: The courts are split as to whether this provision requires formal findings and a written explanation of the decision. Stamping "denied" on the application satisfied one court. A municipality may not deny permission for a tower to restrict market entry. Denials have been upheld when existing facilities were adequate, or when the proposed tower would create aesthetic, risk, or compatibility problems.

The Act prohibits the "prohibition" of towers by a municipality. That prohibition need not be express on the face of the ordinance, and in some courts it may be inferred from a series of denials, or even one denial. But courts are divided: One view is that there is prohibition when a local government does not allow service providers to fill gaps in wireless telephone coverage. Another view is that the Act is not violated by an individual decision, but only by a blanket prohibition and a general ban or policy. Some courts, in other words, use a "prohibitive effect" test when examining an ordinance, but others require that the prohibition be explicit, as in the instance where no provision is made for location of a tower or when the municipality demonstrates a general hostility to towers: No towers located in the municipality and no service in a neighborhood might show this. The applicant must often make a showing (1) of a gap in coverage and (2) that the gap will be filled (by the applicant) in the least intrusive manner. Often these elements are balanced, but sometimes both must be shown, There is no prohibition in the Act of the municipality's assessing the adequacy of service. Courts have divided on the issue of whether a temporary moratoria on locating cell towers violates the Act.

While a municipality may not ban towers, it may prohibit them *as of right* and subject them to special exception procedures. The intent of the Act is to respect municipal land use ordinances, but to give a hard look to tower denials. Thus, if the tower is too tall and the parcel too small, there may be danger of its falling onto adjacent property, and that safety factor is sufficient substantial evidence for a denial at the proposed location. When the tower is lit with flashing lights 24 hours, has red lights at the top and middle, is so tall that it could be seen in the whole municipality, and is located at the gateway to the municipality, there is likewise substantial evidence sufficient for a denial. However, the citizenry's generalized concerns about aesthetics are insufficient to constitute substantial evidence justifying a denial.

Example: Neighbors opposing a cell phone tower operator's application for a special exception state at the applicant's hearing that (1) "This tower is a monstrosity and an eyesore. . . ." (2) "This tower destroys our reputation as a beautiful community for tourists. . . ." (3) "This tower blocks the view of Mt. Smoky. . . ." Which are more objectionable? Number 1 is definitely objectionable under the Act. Number 2 invites the opposition to muster further evidence: Evidence that the tower will be located nearby a prominent feature of the community, in a historic district, or where it is out of character with the surrounding properties (as in, being taller than the surroundings). Number 3 is therefore the least objectionable.

Aesthetic objections coupled with evidence of an adverse impact on property values may constitute substantial evidence justifying a denial. But then appraisal evidence will be necessary for the municipality to justify a denial.

Example. A real estate broker testifies that . . . "[f]or sure the presence of the tower will decrease the ability of a homeowner in the area to sell their house in a shorter period of time and at the asking price." Is that a basis for substantial evidence? This is not an opinion that property values would be impacted adversely: It is only to say that achieving the asking price will take longer — that's not an impact that amounts to substantial evidence.

Example. In an area variance proceeding involving a tower's height, there is testimony of a church leader that the rental from the cell phone company would keep the church's budget in the black for the coming year. This might constitute substantial evidence of a practical difficulty and for containing the "tower" in a church steeple.

Courts have often been willing to grant the mandatory relief, saying that a (1) writ of mandamus frequently employs a mandatory injunction and that the Act authorizes a federal court to act "on an expedited basis." Likewise, a court might issue an injunction against any collateral attack on the placement of the tower, providing virtual immunity for an applicant against further litigation aimed at thwarting the placement of the tower.

ADULT ENTERTAINMENT

Adult entertainment facilities include movie houses; adult bookstores; adult video stores; strip, nude, and topless clubs; massage parlors; and escort services. The Supreme Court has held that the First Amendment protects adult entertainment as free speech or freedom of expression. Hence an outright ban on adult entertainment establishments because city leaders oppose it in all of its forms is unconstitutional. The constitutional analysis to be applied in the regulation of adult entertainment establishments parallels the analysis set out above on the regulation of signs and billboards.

An ordinance that aims at the content (pornography) will be struck down as unconstitutional. Obscenity is illegal and the state or municipality has the right to prohibit or broadly regulate it in connection with adult establishments. An ordinance that regulates land use (time, place, and manner regulation) will be upheld as constitutional if the regulation is unrelated to the suppression of the speech involved. Specifically, (1) the state must be trying to promote a substantial state interest (higher than a legitimate state interest) unrelated to the suppression of the speech; (2) the means chosen (the ordinance) must advance the interest; (3) the ordinance must be narrowly tailored to achieving that interest, infringing as little as possible freedom of speech or expression.

Substantial state interests include protecting the quality of residential settings and minimizing the problems associated with traffic, parking, prostitution, crime, juvenile delinquency, vagrancy, depreciation of property values, and deterioration of retail areas. Substantial state interests also includes the promotion of health, safety, *morals* (e.g., public decency ordinances, including bans on prostitution), and the general welfare. Courts uphold long-standing decency laws of general application as long as the laws are not aimed at adult establishments alone.[3] Thus, in Barnes v. Glen Theatre, Inc., 501 U.S. 560 (1991), three justices called the ordinance prohibiting nude dancing one of general application promoting the public decency. Justice Scalia agreed, saying that nude dancing is not speech or expression protected by the First Amendment. Justice Souter also agreed, saying that nudity is a condition not the expression: it is the dance that is the protected expression, not the condition of being nude. In contrast, in Schad v. Mount Ephraim, 452 U.S. 61 (1981), an ordinance prohibiting all live entertainment but which was enforced only against adult entertainment establishments, was held unconstitutional.

The second element — that the ordinance advance a substantial state interest unrelated to suppression of free speech — prevents officials from rationalizing a law actually aimed at the content of adult entertainment rather than at its secondary consequences. It permits courts to determine the officials' predominant purpose in enacting the ordinance despite their stated purpose.

Courts approve many ordinances regulating adult entertainment. The Supreme Court, for example, has approved ordinances that disperse adult entertainment businesses to minimize the harm to any one part of town. The opposite strategy, requiring all adult entertainment businesses to concentrate into one (or one of several) locations (often referred to as "combat zones") also have been approved.

The Supreme Court's tendency to underenforce constitutional restrictions on adult entertainment derives from its treatment of such entertainment as a lower class of commercial speech deserving some scarce protection. In the City of Renton v. Playtime Theatre, Inc., 475 U.S. 41 (1986). The ordinance in *Renton* prohibited the location of adult movie theaters within 1000 feet of all residential areas (including apartments), churches, and parks, and prohibited locating an adult theater within one mile of any school, ostensibly to offset the negative secondary effects of adult movie theaters. The Court approved the ordinance as a reasonable time, place, and manner regulation. That the ordinance effectively restricted the theater to about 5 percent of the land area of the city and

---

3. The Twenty-First Amendment gives states the right to regulate the sale of alcoholic beverages. The states enjoy latitude in regulating the sale of alcoholic beverages. Many states use this power to prohibit the sale of alcoholic beverages in adult establishments, or to regulate the entertainment offered in the establishment as a condition of receiving a license to serve alcohol.

that the 5 percent were not viable locations for the theaters was irrelevant: the Court said the 5 percent (or 520 acres) allowed reasonable alternative avenues of communication.

EXCLUSIONARY ZONING

Euclidian zoning is an exercise in separating land uses into districts. A municipality may exclude many activities and structures from its various districts. In *Village of Euclid v. Ambler Realty Company*, for example, the Supreme Court favored the separation of apartment dwellers from families living in houses. Many ordinances also exclude mobile homes from single-family residential districts. Because the socioeconomic status of the persons differ among persons likely to live in houses, apartments, and mobile homes, zoning on these bases segregates classes of people. How far may a community go to exclude people rather than structures and uses from the city or zones within the community?

An ordinance based on a **suspect class** (race, color, religion, or national origin) will be struck down as unconstitutional on equal protection or substantive due process ground, or as illegal on a statutory basis. Subtle racial discrimination provisions and ordinances may be invalidated as unconstitutional if the aggrieved person proves the city acted with a **discriminatory intent** or **purpose**. Village of Arlington Heights v. Metropolitan Housing Development Corp., 429 U.S. 252 (1977). A plaintiff class may submit statements of political leaders or associations with past discrimination practices as evidence of the leaders' discriminatory intent or purpose. A mere **discriminatory impact** or **effect**, however, does not warrant constitutional relief.

Without proof of intentional discrimination, plaintiffs may still bring suit under the federal Fair Housing Act (FHA) or comparable state laws. Courts hold aggrieved plaintiffs may prevail under the FHA by showing **discriminatory impact** or **effect** rather than the harder to prove **discriminatory intent**. Likewise, some state courts interpret their state constitution or state statutes such that discriminatory impact or effect, especially if the ordinance continues past discriminatory practices, will be enough to violate the state's constitution or statute.

Municipalities struggle to offer services while keeping taxes low. Most try to offer the highest quality of life and governmental services at the lowest cost to citizens. The ideal mix is a high property tax base from clean industry coupled with a low need for public services. Education is a major expense for municipalities. A major portion of their budgets is allocated to schools, so they often can maintain low real property taxes by keeping the number of school-age children low. To achieve an optimal mix of high-income citizens needing a minimum of municipal services, an ordinance may specify larger-than-needed minimum lot sizes and minimum floor area for all new homes. These zoning standards increase the cost of land and structures, making moving to the community viable only for people with moderate or high incomes. Prohibiting mobile homes and apartments also serves to exclude poorer families, who probably do not pay enough taxes to fund the costs of educating their children. Do such provisions serve legitimate state interests? Some courts say no.

Socioeconomic class (or being poor) is not a suspect class, so the federal Constitution's Equal Protection Clause does not prohibit zoning ordinances that disfavor the poor. Neither does the FHA protect the poor from exclusionary zoning practices. In several states in the Northeast, courts have found their state constitutions' general welfare clause or state zoning enabling acts impose a duty to provide a realistic opportunity for all citizens to live in every municipality. Southern Burlington County NAACP v. Township of Mount Laurel, 336 A.2d 713 (N.J. 1975) is the most famous of these cases. It started with a review of a Mt. Laurel's zoning ordinance. Mount Laurel was a small bedroom community whose community leaders were worried about urban sprawl from nearby Camden. The Township's zoning ordinance aimed at keeping government expenditures low and the value of land high. It imposed minimum lot sizes, minimum lot widths, and minimum floor area for houses so that as a practical matter only middle- and upper-income families could afford homes in the Township (and low- and moderate-income families could not afford to live there).[1] Developers were required to dedicate 15-25 percent of all developed land to public uses, such as schools, parks, public buildings, etc., as required by the planning board. Apartments and other multi-family units were allowed in a few areas. With an eye to keeping the number of school-age children to a minimum (to save on education expenses), the Township limited apartments to one and two bedrooms; no school-age children could live in a one-bedroom apartment; and no more than two school-age children could live in a two-bedroom apartment. The net effect of these provisions was to force developers to raise the price of land sold, thereby limiting purchasers to upper- and middle-income persons who had no more than a certain number of school-age children.

The New Jersey Supreme Court concluded New Jersey's zoning enabling act and its state constitution both required zoning ordinances to promote the general welfare. The "welfare" contemplated was of all citizens and areas of the region, not just those within the township's boundaries.

---

1. The minimum sizes were not outrageously large, and in the South and West, they might seem reasonable or even downright small. The minimum floor area, for example, was 1,100 square feet for a house. The minimum lot size in the most restricted area was one half acre (smaller lots were allowed in other zones).

Mount Laurel's exclusionary ordinance affected other municipalities in the region. Once enough facts were introduced to show an ordinance's presumptive invalidity by not serving the general welfare, the burden shifted to the Township to justify its zoning. Mere fiscal reasons would not serve to justify the exclusionary practice. Mount Laurel offered ecological and environmental justifications, which the court brushed aside under the facts of the case (but which the court said could be a legitimate consideration in some cases). As a remedy, Mount Laurel was required to take appropriate action to fulfill "its fair share of the regional need for low and moderate income housing."

Zoning remedies in these exclusionary cases might include: First, plaintiff home builders are often given a "builder's remedy" — that is, the right to build as they proposed. Such a remedy is preferable to invalidating the zoning and remitting the builder once more to a balky legislative process, and it is aimed at giving plaintiffs an incentive to challenge exclusionary ordinance provisions. Second, the defendant municipality may be rezoned such that the beneficiaries of the suit — typically, these are (besides the plaintiff) the would-be purchasers of "affordable housing" excluded by ordinance provisions that raise the cost of housing beyond what they can afford — can afford to purchase housing there. Affordable housing is not least-cost housing or low-income housing; it is generally a stripped-down version of what the builder would otherwise construct. Third, remedies often impose mandatory duties on municipalities to rezone land for affordable housing — adding, say, a townhouse-use district to a single-family residential community. In order to impose such duties, however, a court first has to figure out how many dwelling units of various types fulfill the defendant municipality's obligation to provide its "fair share." Its share may be figured on the basis of a whole metropolitan region, or on the basis of the land available in urbanizing areas of the region, or on the basis of the land available within commuting distance of the jobs that persons able to afford such housing might hold. These are complex remedial issues, and though they may be triggered by a court case or the denial of a rezoning involving affordable housing, the task of resolving them often winds up as an administrative matter handled by a state planning office or department.

Examples

1. Maui quarreled with his neighbor for several years concerning the neighbor's dog (which was always on the verge of attacking Maui) and the neighbor's wood-burning stove (which, as operated, polluted the air). Maui finally brought a nuisance action to force the neighbor to get rid of the dog and the wood-burning stove. The court dismissed both complaints. Maui posted signs in his front yard to protest the court's decision

and to condemn his neighbor's failure to control his dog and his neighbor's wood-burning stove. The signs read: "Warning: Town Justice Allows Neighbor's Biting Dog to Run Loose!"; "Tie Up Your Biting Dog"; "Poison Your Own Air, Not Ours!"; "Stop Smoke Pollution"; and "Neighbors and Town Want to Do Away with Our Freedom of Speech and Our Right to Protest!" The municipality's building inspector ordered Maui to remove the signs for violating the local zoning ordinance. The zoning ordinance permitted several types of signs without a permit, including all on-site advertising, address signs, identification signs for hotels and non-dwelling buildings, and for sale and rental signs. A section of the ordinance also allowed signs and billboards "in the interest of public information and convenience, [if] the Building Inspector upon approval of the Zoning Board of Appeals, issues a temporary permit for a period to be designated by the Board. Such temporary signs shall be completely removed by the property owner at the termination of the permit." Maui applied for seven permits for each of the signs. At a hearing before the Board, several neighbors opposed the application because they believed Maui's signs were dangerous and could cause accidents. The Board granted Maui a temporary permit allowing him to post all five signs for two weeks. The two-week period was not acceptable to Maui and he filed suit seeking a restraining order to prevent the municipality from enforcing the ordinance against him. Is the sign ordinance constitutional as applied to Maui?

Bedford's municipal zoning ordinance limits occupancy of homes and apartments. There must be a minimum of 200 square feet of habitable space for the first occupant and 150 additional square feet for each additional occupant. Thus, for four occupants, a house or apartment must have 650 square feet. (Nationally recongized housing associations have proposed standards requiring some 400 square feet, or more variable standards requiring some 500 square feet, depending on the number of persons sleeping in one bedroom.) Bedford enacted its ordinance in part due to residents' concern that too many people living in one apartment, unsupervised children, children playing in unsafe environments (e.g., balconies, parking lots, hallways, elevators), noise, and overcrowding were dangerous and unhealthy conditions. Bedford has a good school system and many people moved there because of the schools and there is some indication some people favored the ordinance to stop this influx of people, but that was not the main reason given for enacting the ordinance. A landowner wishing to development multi-family housing challenges Bedford's ordinance as violating the Fair Housing Act prohibition against discriminating against tenants and purchasers based on familial status. Bedford defends, citing the Fair Housing Act §3607 exemption. Does §3607 serve as a defense for Bedford?

Explanations

1. The ordinance is unconstitutional. The Supreme Court has said noncommercial residential signs are entitled to the highest protection afforded by the Constitution. While a city can regulate the size of residential signs and otherwise can regulate signs if the regulation is content-neutral, the ordinance in the case distinguishes signs based on content. The ordinance allows on-site advertising, for sale signs, etc., without a permit, whereas other signs, such as Maui's political speech signs, are subject to regulation. The ordinance, therefore, is content-based and not content-neutral. A court will evaluate the content-based ordinance under a strict scrutiny standard. Since the regulation is content-based, the ordinance is presumptively invalid. To prevail, the municipality must show the ordinance serves a compelling state interest (and not just a substantial state interest) and the ordinance is narrowly tailored to achieve the compelling state interest. The facts do not give the reason for the ordinance, but aesthetics and maybe traffic and safety concerns are viable, substantial, but not compelling state interests here. Moreover, the ordinance is not narrowly tailored to achieve aesthetics, traffic, or safety concerns. In addition, it allows some commercial signs to be permanent whereas noncommercial signs "in the public interest" are only allowed temporarily and then only if the Board of Zoning Appeals in its discretion allows the signs. The Board's unbridled discretion also may constitute an unconstitutional delegation of legislative authority to an administrative body.

   The ordinance is valid. The Fair Housing Act prohibits discrimination based on "familial status," meaning no person, including the municipality, may discriminate in the sale, rental, or regulation of dwellings based on the occupancy of dependent children under the age of 18. The landowner will argue, however, that these occupancy requirements force parents with children to pay for larger units than if they had no children or than they would have had the ordinance not been in effect. Larger units are more expensive, and the difference in price could force some parents, especially lower income parents, to seek housing elsewhere. However, Section 3607 exempts "any reasonable local . . . restriction regarding the maximum number of occupants permitted to occupy a building"; §3607's exemption thus requires (a) a reasonable (b) ordinance (c) regarding the maximum number of occupants permitted to occupy a building. As to element (a), §3607 demands the restriction be "reasonable." The stated purposes of protecting health and safety by preventing overcrowding are legitimate state interests and the means chosen are rationally related to achieving those ends. That the restrictions apply to all persons, related or not, lends further credence to the occupancy limits being geared to achieve legitimate ends and not to discriminate against any group based on familial status. Bedford enacted an ordinance and it regulates the number of people allowed to occupy a building — so elements (b) and (c) are met. In *City of Edmonds*, the Supreme Court noted Congress meant the exemption to apply to ordinances that limit the number of persons who may occupy a dwelling based on the number of persons per square footage or per number of bedrooms. There is no national standard that a municipality must adopt. The Bedford ordinance limits the number of persons entitled to live in a dwelling based on the dwelling's square footage. Thus facially the ordinance falls within the exemption.

However, the owner might also argue that Bedford adopted its square footage requirement such that the ordinance had a discriminatory impact or effect: here he might show that after its enactment came a reversal of population trends so that, instead of growing, Bedford's population decreased. All that the plaintiffs must show under the Fair Housing Act is discriminatory effect or impact. If the ordinance is facially neutral, however, the owner would also proof that the ordinance caused the decrease in families living in Bedford.

Finally, there are no constitutional issues here because families are not protected classes under the Constitution (though some are under the Fair Housing Act): Nothing in the Constitution or the Fair Housing Act grants an unlimited number of family members to live together in one dwelling.

Takings

Federal, state, and municipal governments can buy private property, either in fee simple or less than fee interests, such as easements, and either whole lots or strips of land. Unlike private purchasers who must find a willing seller, governments have the power to force unwilling persons to sell property to them. This power is called **eminent domain.** It is a power so well established that the framers of the federal and state Constitutions assumed it to be an inherent right of government, so the Fifth Amendment's **Takings Clause** simply states, "nor shall private property be taken for public use, without just compensation." This clause is applicable to the states through the Fourteenth Amendment. It mandates that **reasonable compensation** be paid for the property taken. The process by which the property is taken and compensation paid is called **condemnation**.

This chapter introduces takings issues associated with both **conventional condemnation** — i.e., when the state admits it is taking private property and uses its right of eminent domain, embodied in its state code, to effect the condemnation — as well as **inverse condemnation** — arising when a state occupies or invades private property without initiating condemnation, including **regulatory takings** — takings occurring when a government's regulation of private property "goes too far." Finally, the chapter reviews **exactions**, a regulatory action occurring when a government imposes a condition or exaction on a landowner in return for issuing a building permit.

CONVENTIONAL CONDEMNATION

Often the condemnor government and the property owner agree on a price such that the transaction resembles a private sale and purchase. If the parties disagree over the compensation due the owner, the government brings the condemnation to a court for trial.

(a) Public Use

The Takings Clause restricts condemnation to takings "for public use." This restriction prohibits a government from taking property for any *private use*. In Berman v. Parker, 348 U.S. 26, 33 (1954), however, the Supreme Court expanded on the phrase and ruled that a government's taking and transferring private property to private third parties as part of an urban development project of a blighted area of Washington, D.C., was a constitutional means to effect a public use, even though Mr. Berman's property was not itself blighted. The government, it said, had a legitimate interest in making the community healthy, spacious, aesthetically pleasing, clean, sanitary, and well-balanced; all these interests can be achieved using the police power. Taking and transferring the property to private parties was a rational means to advance those legitimate state interests. So long as the government bene-fitted from the taking, the "public use" clause was satisfied.

In Hawaii Housing Authority v. Midkiff, 467 U.S. 229 (1984), the Supreme Court further interpreted public use as equivalent to the achieve-ment of a public purpose, regarding condemnation as the means to accom-plish a legitimate governmental purpose. Once the state identifies a legitimate state interest or purpose, the state has the power to take private property if taking the property is rationally related to the furtherance of the legitimate purpose, so long as the interests identified are within the police power. This inquiry again proceeds as does a substantive due process anal-ysis of a statute or ordinance, but here courts do not substitute their judg-ment for a legislative determination unless the stated purpose is "palpably without reasonable foundation" or the taking is not rationally related to the promotion of any legitimate purpose. In Midkiff, the Supreme Court con-cluded that the State of Hawaii could condemn land then lease it to private parties and immediately transfer it in fee simple to the same parties to use as private residences. Even though the land would ultimately be used by private persons for private uses, the state had a legitimate state interest in bolstering its economy by diversifying land holdings and having their occupants own them, so condemnations of the leasehold lands was a legitimate means to accomplish that goal. Thus the public use clause was deemed coterminous with the police power.

Fifty years after *Berman*, the Supreme Court held that legitimate public uses or purposes include promoting economic development and increasing tax revenue. *Berman* implied as much, but did not say it. In Kelo v. City of New London, 545 U.S. 469 (2005), the city agency was held able to take nonblighted property and transfer it to private developers to achieve the legitimate public purpose, again deferring to state and municipal officials' discerning public needs. In *Kelo*, the city condemned 115 privately-owned properties and transferred them to a private nonprofit entity that planned to build a new multi-use development, including a conference center, a marina, a pedestrian riverwalk, new residences, walking trails, office spaces, restaurants, and retail shops. The legitimate state interest was to revitalize its waterfront area, to attract tourists and businesses, to create jobs, and to increase tax revenues.

Reacting to *Kelo*, some state legislatures enacted statutes prohibiting condemnations for economic development. Most state courts have followed *Kelo* in interpreting their state constitutions. A few states, however, interpret their state constitution public use requirement as requiring use by the public or by the government. Others allow a transfer to private citizens only when something significant about the property, beside the fact that it will be in private hands, justifies the taking (as with a health or safety concern); thus condemnations of "blighted" property, or of property whose use will be supervised by some regulatory body (as with a water line maintained by a public utility), or of a nature requiring public action (as with the provision of roads or sewers), are justifiable even though their overall purpose is economic development.

Example: Mayor Blunder convinces the city council that the mayor should live in a city-owned mansion to host dignitaries on behalf of the city. He proposes that the city acquire a suitable home to be used by himself and all succeeding mayors to be used in part for entertaining or meeting persons doing business with the city. The council agrees and the city begins condemnation proceedings to acquire the most stately mansion within five miles of city hall. The mansion's owner challenges the city's right to take his house. The city can force the current owner to sell the mansion since it will serve a legitimate purpose of providing a home for the current and future mayors to use for city needs.

Example: Ten years later, Mayor Blunder decides not to run for reelection. He tells the city council he would like to retire to a particular house on the seventh hole of a private golf course. The council agrees to use its eminent domain power to acquire the house and sell it to Mayor Blunder. The homeowner challenges the city's right to take his home. The homeowner prevails since the city cannot use its eminent domain powers to take property for private use. Here the city tried to acquire the house strictly to benefit the mayor in private life.

(b) Just Compensation

The Fifth Amendment provides that no taking is effective "without just compensation." Thus, even if the state has the power to take private property for public use or purpose, the state must pay the current owner just compensation. The just compensation that must be paid is the property's fair market value. If only a portion of the property is taken, the state must compensate the owner for the fair market value of that portion.

INVERSE CONDEMNATION

In contrast to the conventional condemnation process where the governmental body identifies property and begins proceedings to acquire it, paying just compensation before putting the property to public use, *inverse condemnation* occurs when a landowner claims the government has physically occupied or taken some property right from the landowner without compensation and without initiating the condemnation process, or has regulated the property is such a way that the government has constructively taken the property. Whereas in a conventional condemnation proceeding the government initiates the action, in an inverse condemnation action the landowner brings the action against the government, claiming the government has taken the landowner's property and must compensate her.

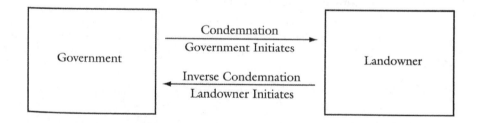

A landowner must have standing to bring an inverse condemnation against a government entity. Most often, the landowner when the regulation is passed is the person with standing to bring the inverse condemnation action. However, in Palazzolo v. Rhode Island, 533 U.S. 606, 630 (2001), the Supreme Court decided that a purchaser or successive title holder, even one who purchases with notice of a regulation enacted earlier, is not barred from challenging a regulation as a taking. The State argued that because the purchaser bought with knowledge of the regulation, the regulation was "a principle of state law" binding on the purchaser. The Court rejected that argument. If accepted, the government could validate any regulation just with the passage of time and title and so make constitutional a regulation otherwise unconstitutional, meanwhile leaving a landowner with unacceptable options: hold the property for years until litigation resolves the issue or sell the property (for less) to a purchaser who would not have standing to challenge the regulation. So the Court refused to permit an unconstitutional regulatory taking to become "transformed into a background principle of the State's law by mere virtue of the passage of title."

CATEGORICAL OR PER SE REGULATORY TAKINGS

(a) Physical Invasions

The inverse condemnation occurs when the government physically invades or occupies private property, or by statute or regulation authorizes a third party to do so. **Physical invasion** and **occupation** cases are **categorical** or **per se takings**. The government has no defense for such an invasion: Once a landowner shows that his property has been physically invaded or occupied by a government body or by a private party acting under its authority, the landowner has a successful categorical takings claim.

Example: State buys a strip of land from the record title owner to construct a new road, unaware that A was its owner by adverse possession. A returns home from vacation to find that his backyard had been dug out and dirt removed. Because the state physically invaded A's property, it is liable to A for taking his backyard. Its categorical physical invasion is similar to a trespass by a private party who had invaded A's land. Even through A may not oust the state, he may sue it in an "inverse condemnation" action, forcing it to use its eminent domain code to determine the compensation he is due.

Example: O raises chickens on her land. An airport runway ends 2,200 feet from O's house and her chicken shack. Government planes approaching the airport fly low feet over the house, just above the highest tree in her yard. The planes blow leaves off trees and create loud noises, cause the chickens to die of fright, and deprive her family members of sleep and make them nervous, worrying that planes might crash into the house. Because of the planes, O no longer can raise chickens and her land has depreciated in value. The government has "taken" an easement by physical invasion. While airspace above the immediate reaches of the land is part of the public domain, an intrusion so close to the ground interferes with and affects O's normal use of her land. Even though the planes never touch the house, ground, or trees, the continuous and recurring invasion affects the use and value of the land.

The invasion is in the same category as telephone wires that overhang property where no wires or poles actually touch the land. O has an inverse condemnation claim against the government for the physical invasion. See United States v. Causby, 328 U.S. 256 (1946).

Example: A state statute provides that a landlord must permit a cable television company to install its cable facilities on and in rental units. Pursuant to this statute, a cable company installs a cable less than one-half inch in diameter across the rooftop of a landlord's apartment building, installs cable boxes on the rooftop, and strings cable to tenants subscribing to the cable service. The landlord has a takings claim for this permanent physical invasion. A permanent physical invasion by or under the authority of the state is a *per se* taking. That it is the company's invasion, not the state's, is irrelevant to the claim. That the cable service attracts tenants and benefits the landlord is likewise irrelevant. Once the invasion is physical or categorical, the benefits and the burdens of the statute are not balanced against one another. This lack of balancing is what distinguishes a categorical from a regulatory taking. See Loretto v. Teleprompter Manhattan CATV Corp., 458 U.S. 419 (1982).[1]

In these three Examples, the good faith or the public benefit derived from the governmental action makes no difference. There is no balancing of private injuries against the public benefits involved; there are no degrees of invasion. A taking occurs, or not. A related consequence of this all-or-nothing analysis is that no matter how small the damage to the property invaded, just compensation must be paid. A further consequence is that just compensation is payable, no matter that the landowner whose property is invaded is also benefitted.

There is long established precedent for compensating physical invasions in this way. If property is a metaphorical bundle of sticks, a physical invasion doesn't just remove one stick from the bundle; instead it shortens each of them. With a physical invasion, the government has taken away the right to possess, denied the right of use, and decreased the right to sell — hence the justification for the *per se* categorical rule for physical takings. Finally, the rule presents few problems of proof and can easily be black lettered and understood — further justifying its unique status in the law of takings. When the government enters an owner's premises, the government must pay for the privilege.

---

1. The statute's constitutionality is unaffected by the success of the claim. It has educational and community benefits that advance a legitimate state interest and allowing cable companies to string their cable is rationally related to the accomplishment of this interest. The statute is constitutional and a state willing to compensate affected landlords can continue to enforce it or in the alternative, may choose to repeal or amend it to require companies to pay just compensation on its behalf.

Example: State law prohibits mobile home park owners from requiring removal of such a home when the home owner moves out, provides that leases of the space for the home may not be terminated for any reason other than nonpayment of rent, and provides that such a lease is freely assignable. A municipality in the State has enacted a rent control ordinance, rolling back the rent for park space to the rent charged two years ago: all further rent increases must be approved by the municipal council. In this situation, a leasehold transfer brings a premium price. Park owners bring suit, contending that their inability to repossess leases between transfers is a physical invasion of their property. Is it? No, The regulation of this type of lease is extensive, but not so extensive as to amount to a physical taking: giving the mobile home owner the advantage of transferring a lease may transfer a benefit from owners to tenants, but that does not convert the regulation into a physical invasion. Unless the park owner is compelled to submit to the physical occupation of his land or unless he is compelled not to continue the present use of his land perpetually, there is no physical invasion. See Yee v. City of Encondido, 503 U.S. 519 (1992). As we shall see, however, the benefit transferred may be relevant to the proof of a noncategorical taking.

(b) Total Takings

A *per se* or categorical taking also occurs when a government regulation prohibits all economically beneficial or productive use of private land, the prohibition amounting to a "total taking" of the use value of the land. See *Lucas* v. *South Carolina Coastal Council*, 505 U.S. 1003 (1992). In *Lucas*, for example, a state law forbade the construction of all new permanent buildings on some beachfront lots. Two lots costing nearly $1 million were rendered valueless by a Council regulation enacted under the law and prohibiting all construction seaward of an erosion line mapped on the lots' landward side. The Supreme Court concluded that such a complete loss of value amounted to a taking requiring compensation.

This "total taking" rule is subject to two exceptions. First, all laws and regulations that duplicate results reached under common law as to the regulation of nuisances do not amount to a taking.

Example: Kathleen owns land, some of which is lakefront land, but a large part of which is the bed of the lake. Kathleen decides to fill in the bed, causing other lakefront lots to flood. A land use regulation that denies Kathleen's application for a landfill permit will not amount to a taking.

Example: Third Eye Nuclear Power Plant is located on an earthquake fault. The state can order the plant be shut down and the state will not have to compensate Third Eye even if shutting down the plant eliminates the land's only economically productive use because the state did "not proscribe a productive use that was previously permissible under relevant property and nuisance principles." See *Lucas, id.* at 1029. Building the plant on the fault was a nuisance to begin with.

A second exception arises when a regulation or restriction, even one that eliminates all economically viable use, "inheres in the title itself, in the restrictions that background principles of the State's law of property and nuisance already place upon land ownership." *Id.* Adverse possession, prescription, implied easements, riparian rights, natural rights of lateral and subjacent support, customary rights, state and federal navigational servitudes over a watercourse, Native American hunting and gathering rights, as well as wildlife and public trust rights fall into this exception. These background principles of law adhere in everyone's title to land, trumping the rights of possession that every citizen has.

Example: The case law of a state has long held that a regulation that preserves the natural use of a wetland is not a taking. This case law restriction on title is a "background principle" of the law in that jurisdiction, so that even in the face of a "total taking," no compensation need be paid. The "background principle" is an "implied limitation" on title.

Example: As a British colony, a state enacted a statute giving the public access rights to all "Great Ponds" — lakes over 10 acres in size. This statute, received into the law of the state at the creation of the United States, is a "background principle" of that state's law.

Example: Pierson v. Post, 3 Cai. R.175 (N.Y. 1805), establishing the common law rule of capture for wild animals, sprang from the "background principle" that a wild animal before its capture was the "property" of the state. From that principle sprang the rule that a statute could regulate the capture of wild animals. See Geer v. Connecticut, 161 U.S. 519 (1896). From that case in turn sprang statutes protecting endangered species. At each step of the law's progress, the background principle of the common law provides a defense for a governmental defending against a "total taking" claim.

Prior to *Lucas*, statutes, ordinances and regulations that restrict or abate nuisances did not result in takings, public nuisance control being a traditional function of government exercising the police power. Hence early ordinances prohibited stables in certain parts of town or barred brick manufacturing plants from residential areas; See Hadacheck v. Sebastian, 239 U.S. 394 (1915). The *Lucas* opinion makes this regulatory power of government a defense that the government may raise when a regulation effects a "total taking," but beforehand, the person claiming a total taking has an opportunity to show that all economically viable use is prohibited.

Thus *Lucas* has been most used to devise governmental defenses to takings claims. Few "total taking" claims succeed.

Example: O owns several seams of coal underlying Blackacre and other properties, whose surface is owned by S. Because the environmental damage that underground mining will cause S's surface, O's mineral estate is designated unsuitable for mining by government regulators, completely prohibiting O from mining under S's surface. So O brings a "total taking" claim to court, but if the regulation is akin to the protection that the common law provided against loss of subjacent support for the surface, O's claim will fail, even though coal mining is completely prohibited. However, O's claim may still be evaluated as a regulatory taking, as discussed in the next section.

REGULATORY TAKINGS — THE *PENN CENTRAL* AD HOC FACTORS

Inverse condemnation actions not involving categorical types of takings just discussed, involve a residual type of takings known as **regulatory takings**. This type of takings claim stem from two sentences from Pennsylvania Coal Co. v. Mahon, 260 U.S. 393 (1922), that sum up the conflict: "Government hardly could go on if to some extent values incident to property could not be diminished without paying for every such change in the general law" and "The general rule at least is, that while property may be regulated to a certain extent, if the regulation goes too far it will be recognized as a taking." The fact-based inquiry provoked by these sentences is, in regulatory takings cases, whether the particular regulation at issue has gone "too far." These inverse condemnation claims may thus be tried either before a judge or jury.

The most used test for a regulatory taking is based on three factors enunciated in Penn Central Transportation Co. v. New York City, 438 U.S. 104 (1978). The first *Penn Central* factor examines the "character of the government's action." The second examines the effect the regulation has on the remaining use and the value of the regulated property, examining "the economic impact of the regulation" on the burdened or affected landowner. The third factor examines, more particularly, "the extent to which the regulation has interfered with distinct investment-backed expectations" of the owner. The key inquiry is the burden the government imposes upon the affected private property owner as compared to the burden on all owners. See Lingle v. Chevron U.S.A., Inc., 544 U.S. 528, 542 (2005).

(a) Character of the Government Action

The "character of the government action" refers to either (1) physical invasions and occupations by the government, (2) the misuse of the regulatory authority of the government, (3) uncertainty in the application of regulations so that an owner is unable to plan for the use or development of property, or (4) the importance of the governmental action (as where the regulation prevents a significant threat to the environment).

As to the first characterization, a plaintiff will bring a categorical takings claim for a physical invasion, as discussed previously in this Chapter.

As to the second characterization, if a government body misuses the regulatory process to benefit the government's later use or acquisition of the land, a landowner can assert a takings claim. For example, if the government, (a) intending to condemn land, denies its owner public services in the hope of decreasing its fair market value in advance of paying just compensation, or (b) plans to condemn an owner's land for a park, but finds its plans too expensive and then restricts the owner's land to "parkland uses" in its zoning ordinance, a taking occurs.

As to the third characterization, if the government proposes a park, but abandons its plans in an on-again, off-again manner that goes on for a decade, a temporary taking occurs during the time that the owner cannot use or sell the land because of the uncertainty of governmental action.

Example: In City of Monterrey v. Del Monte Dunes at Monterrey, Ltd., 526 U.S. 687 (1999), the city denied the landowner permits and repeatedly demanded additional concessions because of the city's long-time interest in acquiring the property for public use rather than for its stated purposes of protecting the environment, providing public access to a public beach, or protecting the habitat of the endangered Blue Butterfly. In the case, the landowner over a five-year period submitted nineteen plans, most of them drafted to meet the city's demands, while the city rejected every application and added new demands. The Supreme Court accepted the landowner's theory that the city's acting in bad faith and failing to follow its own zoning ordinances and policies could amount to a temporary taking. See *Del Monte Dunes*, 526 U.S. at 722.

As to the fourth characterization, consider municipal ordinances enacted to prevent health and safety problems. They are more easily justified than those that merely confer a benefit on the municipality, particularly one that burdens a few landowners and benefits many surrounding owners: The Takings Clause is here a check on governmental action that forces private citizens to bear what should be borne by the public as a whole. This is often referred to as the Takings Clause's "fairness rationale." The phrase thus invites an analysis balancing various factors.

Example: A state enacts a statute designed to prevent underground coal mining beneath buildings, regardless of the severance of a mineral estate from the right to possess and occupy the surface. The statute is enacted to prevent the subsidence of buildings. Its character justifies a finding that the statute is constitutional. See Keystone Bituminous Coal Ass'n v. DeBenedictis, 480 U.S. 470 (1987) (distinguishing *Mahon*, op. cit., as involving a statute benefitting the owner of a single building).

(b) The Economic Impact of the Regulation

The second *Penn Central* factor — **the economic impact of the regulation** — examines the economic loss to the landowner. Here "use" and "value" are used interchangeably: That is, the loss of "use" is the loss of "value." Courts look at whether an owner is left only with an "unreasonable number of uses" once a regulation is imposed. Conversely, no regulatory taking occurs if the landowner can make economic use of the property with the regulation in place.

The diminution in value must be great — indeed, it must be a near complete loss of value. For example, the zoning ordinance in Village of Euclid v. Ambler Realty Co., 272 U.S. 365 (1926), see Chapter 31, infra, decreased Ambler Realty's property value 75 percent (i.e., its property after the zoning was worth only 25 percent of its prezoning value), yet no compensable takings occurred. See also Hadacheck v. Sebastian, 239 U.S. 394 (1915) (92.5 percent diminution in value did not result in a taking). The impact of the regulation must be "functionally equivalent to a classic taking" (*Lingle*, op. cit.), leaving the owner with a value in the affected property only slightly above its *de minimis* value. Absent such an extreme situation, this factor argues against the success of a regulatory takings claim.

Why is this second factor so unfriendly to takings claims? In part because it is an invitation to courts to measure the damage done the owner at the same time as it considers whether there is a taking in the first place. Normally, damages are measured only after the court decides that there is a successful claim, so why should it inquire into the merits of the claim and the remedy for it all at once?

(c) Investment-Backed Expectations

This third *Penn Central* factor attempts to balance the second — if the second was unfriendly to owners, the third is a method for introducing the owner's point of view into the balance. This factor says that a regulation may be deemed a taking if the regulation interferes with the landowner's *distinct investment-backed expectations*. Courts interpreted subjectively "distinct" to mean objectively "reasonable" and gave "expectations" three meanings, depending on whether (1) the claimant was aware of the problem that produced the regulations, (2) the claimant could reasonably have foreseen the enactment of the regulation, and (3) the claimant knew that his use was highly regulated to begin with. Thus an owner aware that his use will pollute a nearby waterway, aware that filling in a wetland will require state and federal permits, and aware that his use makes him a player in a highly regulated industry like surface mining, is unlikely to have his investment-backed expectation given much weight. But a claimant improving property in justifiable reliance on regulations in effect at the time the improvements were made, without any notice of new regulations in the offing and not participating in a highly regulated industry, will have the opportunity to recoup the fair market value of the improvements. However, when a claimant can, after the regulation is imposed, still use the property as he used it beforehand, there is no taking: He has, by his own admission, not been denied the reasonable use of his property.

Example: An investor in real property reasonably expects to make a reasonable return, but abandons his plans to do so. Does abandoning his plans mean forfeiting a regulatory takings claim when the regulation is otherwise unreasonably burdensome? No, there is embedded in the idea of an "investment" a vested right in that investment, entitling him to consideration of this third factor.

Example: An investor seeks to build a marina and seeks a permit for doing so, but is told by regulators not to bother and that the marina is not under their jurisdiction. He proceeds with construction and the regulators change their mind. Are his investment-backed expectations violated? Yes, they are: the investor reasonably relied on the government position (he expected its decision on jurisdiction to be final) and its change of mind may give rise to a successful regulatory takings claim. See Kaiser Aetna v. United States, 444 U.S. 164, 176 (1979).

Example: Should a landowner lose his reasonable investment-backed expectations and a taking claim depending on whether the regulation was enacted before or after the landowner's purchase of affected property? No, otherwise the Takings clause would be rendered toothless by the passage of time and title. See Palazzalo v. Rhode Island, 533 U.S. 606, 626-630 (2001).

Example: A chemical company wishing to market a pesticide discloses a trade secret to a regulatory agency for such products. Is the public disclosure of the secret by the regulator a taking? There is no reasonable expectation of secrecy in a public process when disclosure is necessary for regulatory approval. See Ruckelshaus v. Monsanto Co., 467 U.S. 986 (1984).

CONCEPTUAL SEVERANCE

The economic impact and interference with investment-backed expectations analysis assumes courts know what the "property" is that is claimed to have been taken. This issue involves determining the denominator in a fraction representing the property taken divided into the whole parcel owned by the claimant. This fraction is computed in order to calculate whether the property has been occupied physically, its owner denied all economically viable uses, or regulated too far.

(a) The Surface as Denominator

Property can be conceptually severed based on how much of the surface is affected. This usually happens in eminent domain actions when a state wants to acquire a strip of land at the edge of a larger parcel to build or widen a road. Because the state will permanently occupy the land, the state will purchase the strip, leaving the landowner with the remaining land. The state acquires the strip's surface, subsurface, and air rights. Alternatively, the state may pass a law or ordinance restricting the use of part of the parcel. The taking analyses differ dramatically depending on whether a physical occupation or mere regulation is anticipated, as the following Examples illustrate.

Example: City intends to widen a street abutting Blackacre. City plans to use a 20-foot strip across the front of O's lot for the widening. City must compensate O for the strip because City intends to permanently occupy it. Its duty to compensate O does not depend on O's retaining 90 percent of the original lot, even if O's retained land becomes more valuable because of the wider street.

Example: City passes an ordinance prohibiting requiring that all improvements on O's land be more than 20 feet from the abutting street. O will receive no compensation when this ordinance is enacted, even though O cannot use the 20-foot strip of his land. As a practical matter, the 20-foot strip's value is close to zero. A court will evaluate the regulation's impact on O's entire lot, not just on the 20-foot strip. The surface area of O's land will not be considered severed in evaluating the regulation. Instead, the economic impact analysis will be applied to a lot as a whole. This is often known as the "whole parcel" rule. In Palazzolo v. Rhode Island, 533 U.S. 606 (2001), a landowner argued that his property should be severed into the small portion which he could develop under state wetland regulations, and a much larger portion, which he could not develop because of those regulations. The Supreme Court acknowledged the severability issue and said its cases indicate the whole parcel rule controls, but that it has "at times expressed discomfort with the logic of this rule." 533 U.S. at 631. The next term, in Tahoe-Sierra Preservation Council, Inc. v. Tahoe Regional Planning Agency, 535 U.S. 302 (2002), the Court emphatically stated that, in regulatory takings cases, the whole parcel controls.

(b) Airspace, Surface, and Mineral Rights as Separate Interests

Property can be conceptually severed into airspace, surface area, and subsurface or mineral interests. Once severed, the surface, mineral, and air rights can be considered separate properties for takings purposes. Courts in a regulatory taking analysis will sever a person's interests in these interests only in unique cases. As a rule of thumb, surface rights are critical. The regulation that prohibits all use of surface rights, fully allowing mineral extraction, likely will constitute a taking. In contrast, a restriction on mineral production that permits full surface use likely will not amount to a taking unless either (a) the property owner has made substantial improvements to extract the minerals and can claim he was deprived of his investment-backed expectations, (b) the surface is unusable and the regulation makes the mineral estate valueless, or (c) the property owner holds only the mineral interest and the regulation makes the mineral interest valueless. Severance is only an issue in regulatory takings analysis. A physical invasion into any of the three is a per se taking.

Example: A government aircraft landing approach to an airport carries planes to within 80 feet of a private house. This is a physical invasion of airspace affecting a landowner's use of her surface area and thus constitutes a taking. See United States v. Causby, 328 U.S. 256 (1946).

Example: City passed a landmark preservation ordinance prohibiting substantial changes to the exterior of historical buildings. Pursuant to the ordinance the owner of a railway terminal could not construct an office tower in the airspace above the terminal. The law does not effect a taking because the terminal owner can continue operating the terminal and receive a reasonable return on its investment in the terminal. The airspace above the terminal is not a separate property interest. The whole property (airspace, surface use, and subsurface use) is the whole parcel. See Penn Central Transportation Co. v. City of New York, 438 U.S. 104 (1978).

Example: In State A, persons owning mineral rights in land often do not own the surface rights. State A enacts a subsidence statute requiring coal mining companies to keep up to 50 percent of the coal in place to prevent land subsidence, protect the environment, insure the state's economic future, and safeguard its citizens' well-being. The statute will not effect a taking since the coal that must remain in place cannot be conceptually severed from all the coal in the ground. See Keystone Bituminous Coal Association v. DeBenedictis, 480 U.S. 470 (1987) (a 5-4 decision). If, however, the law as applied to any particular company reduces the value of extractable coal to zero, a taking will be found unless the company also owns the surface rights.

Example 4: In State B, persons owning mineral rights often do not own the surface rights. State B's law traditionally recognizes a separate property interest called the support estate, permitting coal mining companies to mine without liability for subsidence. State B enacts a statute prohibiting mineral owners from removing coal within 150 feet of any improved property belonging to another, whether or not the mineral owner owns the support estate. This statute effects a taking. It made the coal in the support estate valueless and in effect took the support estate from the coal company and gave it to the surface owner. Even assuming the law served a public purpose, this transfer from one private citizen to another is a taking. See Pennsylvania Coal Co. v. Mahon, 260 U.S. 393 (1922).

The majority opinion in *Keystone Bituminous Coal Association* distinguished the statutes in Examples 3 and 4. It said the government action in Example 3 was to "arrest what [the state] perceived to be a significant threat to the common welfare" (a legitimate state interest) whereas in Example 4 the law "merely involve[d] the balancing of private economic interests of coal companies against private interests of the surface owner" (thus subject to a takings claim). The Court noted the coal companies in Example 3 continued profitable operations while the coal companies in Example 4 could not begin to extract the coal as they expected to and thus there was "undue interference with their investment-backed expectations." This last observation requires a conceptual severance of the mineral and support estates in Example 4, while refusing to sever them in Example 3.

(c) Temporal Severance

(1) Permanent Takings

Property can be conceptually severed on a timeline. If a state takes land for a highway, for example, and the property is owned by a life tenant and a remainderman in fee simple, the purchase price would be allocated between the owners of the two interests. Likewise, a regulation that permanently reduced the property's value to zero would be compensable, each interest holder receiving a proportionate share of the award.

(2) Temporary Takings

Either a permanent physical invasion, a total taking, or a regulatory taking is compensable. So is a temporary regulatory taking; that is, the government is liable in damages for the time during which an unconstitutional regulation is in effect. See First English Evangelical Lutheran Church of Glendale v. County of Los Angeles, 482 U.S. 304 (1987). The measure of damages for a temporary taking is the fair rental or option value. The temporary taking may result from either a temporary physical occupancy or a complete denial of use (a total taking). The latter was the situation in First English. A temporary taking may also result from a bad faith abuse of the regulation or licensing process. See City of Monterey v. Del Monte Dunes at Monterey, Ltd., 526 U.S. 687 (1999) (where the city repeatedly denied the landowner development permits without showing that the landowner failed to meet all requirements for the permits).

Necessary administrative delays and not-unreasonably-long emergency moratoria are not temporary takings. Tahoe-Sierra Preservation Council, Inc. v. Tahoe Regional Planning Agency, 535 U.S. 302 (2002), held that a temporary, 32-month moratorium on development while the Agency formulated a comprehensive plan for affected property was not a taking. Just as property rights might be conceptually severed, they can also be temporally severed, but the "whole parcel" for this case was the petitioners' right to develop their property both before, during, and after the moratorium. Just impacting that right during the moratorium is not a regulatory taking, even if the development right is completely taken for that limited period of time. The Court held that a moratorium's validity is to be evaluated using a Penn Central regulatory takings analysis, not under a Lucas total takings, categorical analysis. The moratorium's length and effects are to be balanced within Penn Central's analytical framework. By recognizing the distinction between temporary and permanent regulatory takings in Tahoe-Sierra, the Supreme Court limited the reach of both First English and Lucas, bringing claims that would be brought under either case under the aegis of Penn Central.

JUDICIAL TAKINGS

"The Takings Clause . . . is not addressed to the action of a specific branch of government. It is concerned simply with the act, and not with the governmental actor ('nor shall private property be taken' (emphasis added)). There is no textual justification for saying that the existence of the scope of a State's power to expropriate . . . varies according to the branch of government effecting the expropriation." See Stop The Beach Renourishment, Inc. v. Florida Department of Environmental Protection, 130 Sup. Ct. 2592,

2601 (2010) (Scalia, J., writing for a plurality of four Justices). In this case the state had restored a beach with dredged sand, denying littoral owners direct access to the ocean. The owners claimed that the denial of direct access was a taking, but eight Justices thought not. The owners were denied future accretions of beach front by the dredge and fill. The state, however, was only protecting a public asset — here the publicly owned submerged land filled in. Justice Scalia's quoted words are logical and controversial and may be broadly applicable, but it remains to be seen if they have traction in the law of takings.

REMEDIES

What remains of First English is its discussion of regulatory takings remedies. The traditional remedy in inverse condemnation cases was invalidation of the statute, ordinance, or regulation: The law was said to be repealed nunc pro tunc, as if it had never been enacted. After First English, courts may award money damages once they find a taking. Once a taking is found, the government has the option of compensating the landowner or repealing the statute, ordinance, or regulation. If the government chooses repeal, it pays compensation only for the time period that the unconstitutional law was in effect. This is payment for its temporary taking. So the Takings Clause requires no statutory sanction for the damage remedy, measured either as (1) difference money (comparing the fair market value of the property before the taking with its value just after the effective period), (2) the fair rental value for the effective period, (3) a property's option price during that period, or as (4) the value of any opportunity to use the property lost during the period, always subtracting its value during the time consumed by normal administrative and judicial procedures. Even assuming that Tahoe-Sierra has not severely limited First English, bringing a temporary takings claim is seldom worth the time, trouble, and costs the cause of action will consume.

EXACTIONS

Exactions are conditions imposed by a government that a landowner or developer must meet before the government will issue the landowner or developer a subdivision or building permit. The exaction may be a dedication of land to public purposes, a restriction on development, or a required improvement. A city, for example, may require a developer when subdividing a parcel to dedicate land for a school, road, or park; or a developer may be required to incorporate flood control measures, connect the property's streets to public streets, or furnish sufficient parking when applying for a building permit. An exaction must further a legitimate state interest, and cannot be a pretext to avoid the Takings Clause compensation requirement.

To satisfy substantive due process, ordinances must serve a legitimate state interest. Exactions can be the means to achieve that interest. The **essential nexus** or relationship between the end to be achieved (the legitimate state interest) and the means chosen to achieve that end (the exaction) must be close enough so that the exaction substantially advances the legitimate state interest. Nollan v. California Coastal Commission, 483 U.S. 825 (1987) (involving a beach house renovation and enlargement).

Two Supreme Court cases developed the line between legitimate government exactions and an exaction that constitutes a taking. In Nollan v. California Coastal Commission, 483 U.S. 825, 837 (1987), the Nollans bought and sought to demolish a beach home and replace it with a larger, more modern home. Their property was located on the Pacific coast on a strip of land between two public beaches. The Coastal Commission conditioned the grant of a building permit on the Nollans' granting the state an easement for the public to walk on the Nollans' property to go from one park to the other. The Court concluded the exactions "utterly fail[ed] to further the end advanced." The Commission's stipulated state interest in *Nollan* was guaranteeing persons driving along the coastal highway were able to see (have "visual access" to) the beach. The Court accepted visual access goal as a legitimate state interest. The Commission, however, chose to guarantee the public's visual access by conditioning the building permit on the Nollans' granting the state an easement for the public to walk along the beach along the Nollans' property. The Court found a logical flaw here: It said there must be an "essential nexus" (relationship) between the legitimate state interest and the means (the exaction demanded), but could not find this "essential nexus" here, between the easement along the beach and visual access from the highway. Instead, the Court saw the exactions as a preconceived attempt to gain easements for the public from all beachfront owners without having to compensate the owners. The Court found a taking had occurred.

To date, the U.S. Supreme Court has not found a taking for an exaction beyond physical dedications or physical intrusions as conditions of development to public use. In City of Monterey v. Del Monte Dunes at Monterey, Ltd., 526 U.S. 687 (1999), the Court said that the law of exactions was not readily applicable to and was not designed for situations involving nondedicatory fees and "money exactions."

The overall concern with exactions is that government might cite a legitimate fault with the landowner's proposed use of his property to exact a dedication of land to the public that does more than is necessary to mitigate the harm caused by the landowner's development. Such overreaching was the Supreme Court's concern in Dolan v. City of Tigard, 512

U.S. 374, 391 (1994). There the Supreme Court adopted a rough proportionality test that demands the municipal agency (there a planning commission) make "some sort of individualized determination that the required dedication is related both in nature and extent to the impact of the proposed development." Thus, after *Dolan*, exactions are analyzed in a two-step process: (1) Courts determine whether an **essential nexus** exists between the legitimate state interest and the condition exacted (as required in *Nollan*). (2) If the essential nexus exists, courts then determine whether there is **rough proportionality** between the condition exacted and the projected impact of the landowner's proposed development (*Dolan*).

To illustrate, Dolan's development and expansion of a hardware store located along a creek contributed (said the city) to potential flooding in a nearby creek and increased traffic on local streets. The city conditioned Dolan's building permit on Dolan's dedicating land in a flood plain along the creek to the city so the city could improve its storm drainage system along the creek. In addition, the city conditioned the grant of a permit on Dolan's dedicating 15 more feet of its land outside the flood plain to the city so the city could build a pedestrian/bicycle path to help reduce auto traffic on nearby streets. Both the drainage system and the bicycle path had already been included in a master plan developed well before Mrs. Dolan applied for her building permit.

The Supreme Court first concluded there was an essential nexus between the dedication of the flood plain land and flood control; and the Court also found the essential nexus existed between the dedication of the additional 15 feet of land for the pedestrian/bicycle path and the reduction of traffic congestion problems. However, as to the second step in its analysis, the Court went on to conclude the demanded exactions failed the rough proportionality test.

As to the flood plain dedication, the Court, citing the importance of a landowner's right to exclude others from his property, felt that there was no reason for the city to demand a public access greenway as opposed to a private greenway to serve its legitimate interest in flood control. The landowner's right to exclude others and monitor her property was not being regulated, said the Court; it was eviscerated! In addition, the Court believed the city could achieve its aims by forbidding Mrs. Dolan from building on the flood plain.

As to the pedestrian/bicycle path, the Court noted that dedications for streets, sidewalks, and other public ways generally are reasonable exactions to avoid excessive congestion resulting from the development, but on the record before the Court, the city had not met its burden of demonstrating that increased traffic use to be generated by the landowner's development was roughly proportional to the city's requirement that an easement be dedicated for a public pedestrian/bicycle path. After all, how many customers bike to a hardware store to shop?

Several years later, in City of Monterey v. Del Monte Dunes at Monterey, Ltd., 526 U.S. 687, 702-703 (1999), the Supreme Court revisited its exactions jurisprudence, and stated:

> Although in a general sense concerns for proportionality animate the *Takings Clause* (citation omitted), we have not extended the rough-proportionality test of *Dolan* beyond the special context of exactions — land-use decisions conditioning approval of development on the dedication of property to public use (Citing both *Nollan* and *Dolan*). The rule applied in *Dolan* considers whether dedications demanded as conditions of development are proportional to the development's anticipated impacts. It was not designed to address, and is not readily applicable to, the much different questions arising where, as here, the landowner's challenge is based not on excessive exactions but on denial of development. We believe, accordingly, that the rough-proportionality test of *Dolan* is inapposite to a case such as this one.

As previously discussed, this discussion can be read as limiting the reach of exactions claims.

Example: A municipality asks a land developer, as a condition for obtaining a subdivision plat, to pay a fee it says it will use to purchase parkland made necessary by the presence of subdivision residents in the municipality. The developer shows that the amount of the fee will purchase an amount of raw land larger than the subdivision itself. She asks you what she should do and whether you would bring a lawsuit alleging an unconstitutional exaction. Will you? *Del Monte* states that "we have not extended" the law of exactions beyond the realm of dedications or exactions of *land*. Is this more than a statement of historical fact? That is an open question and lower federal and state courts are split on the issue. Some say that there is no such thing as a money exaction because it is only when *land* is "taken" that there is a need for greater judicial scrutiny. Others say, land or money, there's no difference: both affect developer's bottom line. So the suit is a chancy one.

Example: A municipal council asks a land developer, before it rezones her land, to record a negative covenant restricting the developer of part of the land for which the developer seeks the rezoning. The developer refuses to record the covenant. The council refuses to rezone. The jurisdiction permits conditional zoning. The developer asks you to bring a lawsuit alleging a unconstitutional exaction. Will you? Again, a chancy thing. *Del Monte* states that exactions law applies to "decisions conditioning approval. . . ." *Nollan* and *Dolan* both are the decisions of administrative bodies, not legislative ones. Most lower courts, therefore, have limited the reach of exactions law to administrative decisions and refused to extend that law to legislative matters.

Example: A land developer's subdivision plat is conditionally approved and she asks you to bring an exactions claim. Will you? A denial after repeated attempts to placate the municipal planning commission was what was involved in *Del Monte*. A close reading of that case's discussion of exactions might lead you to say that exactions law applies only to denials, but not to conditional approvals.

Examples

Physical Invasions

1. (a) Government drug enforcement officers decide to use remote unproductive land owned by a private citizen to store, fuel, and repair airplanes used to search out drug smuggling activities along the border. Over a two-year period, an average of four planes land on the makeshift airstrip. Trucks are used to supply fuel, food, and supplies. May the landowner bring a successful takings claim? (b) An airplane engaged in government drug enforcement operations along the border develops engine trouble, forcing it to land on private land. Government employees using government vehicles drove onto the private property to repair the airplane. Once repaired, it resumes its flight and the government vehicles left the land. May the landowner bring a successful takings claim?

2. A state statute provides that farmers may burn the stubble in their fields without liability for ensuing trespass and nuisances. The smoke from a burn causes a neighboring farmer to die of an asthma attack. Does the dead farmer's family have a successful takings claim for a physical invasion?

3. Government by statute provides that abandoned railway easements shall be used as trails for walking and bicycling. R & R Railroad files documents with the regulators to abandon its easements over a long rail line. Government began converting the easements into hiking and bike trails. The owners of the land over which the easements ran bring suit alleging a taking. What result?

4. Government restricts landowners abutting Deepwater Creek from using wells or pumping water directly out of the creek in order to protect an endangered species of fish found there. Owners bring a physical invasion takings claim against the government. Will it succeed?

5. State Highway Department purchased a strip of land abutting one side of Grubb's farm. The deed from Grubb to the State Highway Department reserved an easement for access to the highway to be built on the strip. Grubb used the easement at the location specified in the deed for a dirt road to access the highway for the next 39 years. The Department then

condemned another strip to widen the highway further. Grubb applied for a permit to construct a concrete access road to the highway where the current dirt road was located. The state denied the permit application, citing public safety concerns. In addition, the state denied Grubb access to the highway over the dirt road, digging a ditch on the most recently condemned strip to prevent Grubb from entering the highway from his land, asserting that Grubb could access the highway by traveling over other county roads that ran by his land. Grubb sues the state, alleging inverse condemnation from being denied the permit. What result?

Total Takings

6. O owns a land parcel suitable for a landfill, but is denied municipal permits for it based on neighbors' opposition. The parcel is wooded, and the trees could be harvested for pulp to make paper. O claims that he has been denied all economically beneficial uses of the parcel and brings a total takings claim. The municipality defends arguing that the value of the harvested trees means that O's parcel has not been taken. Will the defense succeed?

7. O owns a ranch on which he raises captive elk under a license from the state. He has invested hundreds of thousands of dollars a year in keeping the elk healthy and strong, developing special feeding stations, hiring a veterinarian, and developing monitoring systems for his elk herds, all so that he can provide hunters with opportunities to shoot the elk for fees totaling more than a million dollars a year. The state in which the ranch is located then prohibits fee-shooting of the elk and other game animals and prohibits the transfer of O's game farm license. O brings a total takings claim against the state. Will it succeed?

Regulatory Takings

8. O owns a lot in a single-family use district. O is denied a zoning variance to build a single family home on an under-sized lot. O thereafter brings a regulatory takings claim and moves for summary judgment. On his motion, what result and why?

9. A drug wholesale company's pharmaceuticals, left at a pharmacy engaged in filling prescriptions for controlled substances illegally, were seized by the government under the police power. The company brings a regulatory takings claim. Will its claim succeed?

10. A municipality down-zones O's and many other parcels of land from a multi-family to single-family use district. Several years later, O is denied a rezoning from a single-family to multi-family use. O brings a regu-latory takings claim. Will O's claim succeed?

11. O owns 150 acres of land. She operated a private golf course on 110 of the acres for decades. The other 40 acres surrounded were unimproved. The golf course was located in a district zoned "Residential," in which golf courses were permitted. O hired a firm to plan a residential development on the 40 acres surrounding the golf course and submitted her plans to develop the 40 acres to the town board. The town board requested certain revisions, which O incorporated into her plans. While O was making her plans to develop the 40 acres, the town hired a private planning firm to help formulate a comprehensive plan taking into account the town's growth patterns. The firm made three observations that affected O's golf course and remaining 40 acres. First, urbanization had resulted in overdevelopment of the town, reducing the open space in the town's watershed below acceptable levels. Second, additional residential development could lead to increased flooding. Finally, because of current overdevelopment, the town needed to preserve recreational opportunities for its residents. Based on these findings, the town rezoned O's golf course, including the 40 acres surrounding the golf course, from "Residential" to "Solely Recreational Use" (as it did three other golf courses in the town). The town refused to issue building permits to O because the 40 acres were zoned Solely Recreational Use. O brings an action against the town alleging an unconstitutional taking of her property without just compensation. What result?

12. Assume the same facts as in Example 7 (under the heading of total takings), but in addition assume that O brings a regulatory (not a total) takings claim. What result and why?

Conceptual Severance

13. O owns land in a state in which the right to capture the groundwater underneath one's land is included in surface ownership rights. O leases this right of capture to a water bottling company. The state enacted an ordinance prohibiting the pumping of groundwater for uses not on the overlying land. O claims a categorical taking of all economically viable uses of her groundwater rights. Will O's claim succeed?

14. P purchases a parcel of land intending to develop a subdivision on it. P's lender says that financing it requires a loan too small to meet its lending minimums, so P purchases a second abutting parcel containing steep slopes, and then a third parcel contiguous only along a small part of its eastern boundary, and then a fourth contiguous parcel containing several acres of wetlands. P decides to develop them all as a single development. When he learns that he cannot build on the steep slopes and cannot fill in the wetlands, his lender figures that although the

development now meets its lending criteria, the steep slope and wetlands regulations will render much of P's acreage unavailable for the project. As much as 75 percent of the second parcel is steep slopes and 50 percent of parcel number four is a wetland. P claims a taking has occurred on these two parcels. Will his claim succeed?

15. O purchases the fee simple absolute to Brownacre and thereafter conducts a sand and gravel excavation on land surrounded by residences. The municipality in which Brownacre is located permits sand and gravel excavation only by special exception on all of its residential-use districts. All the surrounding parcels (along with Brownacre) are zoned in such a district. O applies for a special exception and his application is denied. O brings a regulatory takings claim. Will his claim succeed?

16. Owen owns two parcels of land bisected by a use-district boundary on the zoning map of a municipality. One parcel is zoned commercial, the other residential. The commercial parcel is down-zoned so that it may only be used for professional offices. Owen brings a takings claim, alleging that the commercial parcel has been taken. Will his claim succeed?

Temporary Takings

17. Dan receives a low-interest mortgage loan for the development of multi-family, low-income housing from a municipal fund for such developments. The mortgage contains a covenant providing that the sole use of the mortgaged property is to be low-income housing. Dan's loan was to be repaid over the next 20 years. The development's neighborhood changes. The supply of low-income housing in the municipality dwindles. The municipality then by ordinance freezes the use of Dan's property in its current use and prohibits the prepayment of Dan's and other similar loans in order to preserve the remaining supply of such housing. Five years after taking the loan, Dan wants to prepay the loan in order to let other private investors join Dan in operating the housing. The prepayment prohibition prevents the private investors from joining Dan and subsequently the market for such investments dries up. Dan brings a temporary taking claim, claiming that prepayment prohibition ordinance's effect over the time the investors wanted to join Dan was a taking. Will Dan's claim succeed?

Exactions

18. During the course of a negotiation with a municipal planning commission over a developer's obtaining a subdivision approval, the commission staff makes a demand for a land dedication that clearly is not roughly proportional to the impact of the subdivision on the municipality. Will you advise the developer to protest the exaction?

19. Refined Oil owns a gas station at the intersection of two heavily traveled, congested streets. Because of the surrounding municipalities' growth, many intersections, including Refined Oil's, are experiencing above-capacity traffic during rush hour. The municipality wants to widen both streets by adding extra lanes of through traffic and dual left-turn and right-turn lanes at this intersection. Meanwhile, Refined Oil wants to modernize its service station. Gas stations are permitted as a special exception in the use district in which Refined Oil's station is located: This means that Refined Oil's needs a special use permit from the municipality's Board of Zoning Appeals. The Board issues the permit under guidelines set out in the zoning ordinance if and on the condition that Refined Oil dedicate a 40-foot by 40-foot triangular piece of land at the intersection of the two abutting streets, comprising about 20 percent of the station's total land area. Studies indicate the modernized station would increase traffic at the intersection about 0.4 percent. The Board's policy was to require dedications along congested streets as a condition of land use permits without regard to whether the exactions related to the intended use of the property. The municipal Capital Improvement Budget has contained an item for this street widening for the last five years. Refined Oil brings a takings claim against the municipality. What result?

Explanations

Physical Invasions

1. (a) The government will be liable to the landowner in an inverse condemnation suit for a physical invasion of private property. The taking was temporary. Damages are allowed for temporary takings. The amount of the damages should approximate a fair rental amount of the land plus the cost of repairing the land since the government acted as a trespasser. (b) No taking. Just as common law recognizes an exception to trespass actions in emergencies, a government's temporary invasion of private property because of an emergency should not amount to the intentional action characterized as a taking. Nonetheless, the government should still be liable for any damages its invasion actually caused on the private property.

2. Yes, in an inverse condemnation action, if the smoke is classified as a tangible invasion of the neighboring farm. The immunity provisions of the right-to-burn statute provide immunity from some types of private actions, but not from claims of a constitutional nature. The Takings Clause is self-executing and unaffected by statutes of this type.

3. R & R abandoned the easements, so they revert to the fee simple owners of the underlying land. Since the government is denying the fee owners

the abandoned land and plans to allow members of the public to use it, there is a physical taking. The government may have a legitimate public purpose rationally advanced by its program, but it still must decide whether to pay compensation and continue the program, or amend or repeal it.

4. Yes. The restriction is a denial of one of the rights in their bundle of sticks comprising the owners' property: That is, the right to possess the groundwater underneath their land and assert their riparian right to use the water of an abutting water course. That the government's purpose is a legitimate one and is rationally related to the restriction is irrelevant to the claim. If the government had condemned the subsurface for storage of water or natural gas, the effect on the owners would be the same. Compensation may be hard to measure, but that is no reason why a court should not find that a taking occurred.

5. The state is liable to Grubb. The Department may argue that a landowner has a common law right of access to a public road, but that this right can be denied if the owner has other access to the highway, even if it is not as direct. The Department may also argue that the state could deny Grubb all access to the highway for safety reasons. Neither argument is relevant. Grubb was not relying on his common law right to access, but on an express reservation of an easement in the deed granting land to the state decades earlier. An easement is a property right. The state sought to redo its earlier bargain with Grubb and took the easement without compensating him. The result is a taking. Even though the Department has the right and power to deny Grubb access to the highway, whether it has the power to deny Grubb access to the highway is a different issue from whether the state must compensate Grubb. Here it must compensate Grubb for taking his easement.

Total Takings

6. The municipality's claim will fail: The test for a total takings is the denial of "all economically beneficial uses." It is the lack of an economically beneficial use, not the impact of the regulation on property values, that is relevant to a total taking claim. While the complete elimination of value is sufficient for such a claim, the lack of value is not necessary to establish it. Categorical takings analysis is appropriate even when the parcel retains a nominal value. Thus a property can be sold when it lacks economically beneficial uses.

7. No. It is the value of the elk to O that is affected, and while it is conceptually possible that a total taking of personal property is actionable, the elk have a beneficial use in an alternative market: They might be sold to out-of-state breeders and elk ranchers, or harvested on O's ranch for their

meat and antlers. While these alternatives may not earn O a million dollars, they are sufficient to show the O has not been denied *all* economically beneficial use of either the herd or the ranch. Taking a property's *most* beneficial use does not constitute a taking. Moreover, the right of a landowner to hunt game on his land is a common law right and may therefore be a background principle of state law, but that is not what the state prohibited here: It prohibited hunting for a fee, the rationale for which might encompass the very concerns that made O hire a vet and develop special feeds.

Regulatory Takings

8. Motion denied. A regulatory takings claim requires an ad hoc factual inquiry using the three factors explained in the *Penn Central* opinion. A court will seldom enter summary judgment on a regulatory takings claim without considering them on the merits. Never say never, but it will be the rare case in which such a motion succeeds.

9. No. There is no reason why the takings clause need be limited to real as opposed to personal property, but even so, if the government acted under the police power and was within the scope of its authority, then its seizure, retention, or damage of the drugs were seized in pursuance of police activity. This being so, they were not seized for a "public use." Thus the takings clause is inapplicable.

10. No. O has not been deprived of all economically viable use of his land, even if O is not able to sell or rent the land at substantially less than its appraised fair market or fair rental value. A failure to show a total taking is not evidence of a regulatory taking, but a generous appellate court might allow amendment of the complaint to allege a total takings, categorical claim.

11. O might prevail under a *Penn Central* regulatory takings analysis that considers (1) the character of the government action and (2) the economic effect of the regulation on the owner, particularly the owner's (3) reasonable investment-backed expectations. The character of the government's action does not aid O: There is no physical invasion. Moreover, zoning through comprehensive planning is not a taking. The effect on O's use of her property does not aid her either: O's reasonable investment-backed expectations center on the improvements made to operate the golf course. The zoning ordinance anticipates the golf course's ongoing operations. O suffers no loss of investment-backed expectations on the course itself. Her real loss is on the 40 acres not directly related to the golf course. She has expended money in anticipation of building homes but has not built any yet. That is not enough for her to have investment-backed expectations in the 40 acres.

The town's refusal to grant a building permit may reduce the value of the 40 acres, but the land still has value. Mere diminution in value is not a taking. Even if the 40 acres are valueless (which is unlikely), O could prevail only if the court conceptually severs the 40 acres from the 110-acre golf course, but this a court will not do. If the 150 acres are evaluated as one whole parcel, a court would conclude O can make a reasonable return on the full 150 acres by operating the golf course. The rezoning does not amount to a regulatory taking.

12. O will not prevail on his *Penn Central* takings claim. (1) The character of the governmental action analysis is not an inquiry into the purposes of the prohibition of fee-hunting (it might well have been to protect the state's fund from hunting licenses for wild game on unenclosed land); instead, it is an inquiry into the abusive or intrusive nature of the prohibition. If enacted to prohibit the "hunting" of captive animals not free to roam, it is not abusive of the state's authority to regulate the taking of wild game. (2) The economic impact or effect on the owner is minimal if O can still sell his specialized equipment and elk out of state: There are many valuable sticks in O's bundle of sticks left in his hands. Likewise, under the claim's (3) investment-backed expectations analysis, the fact that O's operations required a state license to start with means it is unlikely that he has a reasonable investment-backed expectation in the continuation of the operations of a fee-for-shooting game ranch. Couldn't the state quarantine diseased poultry, forbidding their shipment off a farm and ordering their destruction? The state did less than that here. Captive elk may likewise pose significant health hazards for wild elk that are the state's property until captured. Thus none of the three Penn Central factor argue in favor of O's claim.

Conceptual Severance

13. O's claim to a total taking of her groundwater rights will not succeed. The court hearing her claim will use the whole parcel rule, evaluating her loss of this right of capture against all of her common law rights of ownership and conclude that a reasonable number of uses remain in her hands. As a matter of fact, in this case and regardless of any severance, reasonable uses of this particular right remain: She can use the groundwater on her land for any number of agricultural or domestic uses.

14. P's claim is unlikely to succeed. He acquired all four parcels aiming to build a single development. A common development plan shows that the whole parcel rule will apply to all four, considered as one piece of property for takings purposes. He did, however, acquire them at different times: When the dates of acquisition are different, this tends to show that each parcel should be treated separately. Also

relevant might be whether the steep slopes enhance the value of the remaining parcels: If they do, then this tends to show that they should be treated as one whole parcel. That three of the four parcels are contiguous also tends to show that they should be treated as one parcel. Thus the court will weigh the common development plan, the dates of acquisition, the interrelated land values, and the degree of contiguity — all are factors used by courts deciding whether or not conceptual severance will be permitted before it considers the merits of P's takings claim. No one of these factors is likely to be controlling, but here the common plan of development and the contiguity of the parcels likely give rise to a presumption that the whole-parcel rule applies.

15. O's claim will fail. When property is under a single ownership, the entire land area encompassing the two parcels will be treated as one whole parcel. The different zoning classifications of each are irrelevant. Likewise, no conceptual severance is likely when the parcels have different street addresses or are different property tax lots.

16. O's claim will likely fail. Taking title to the fee, instead of to the sand and gravel separately, creates a presumption that the whole parcel rule controls.

Temporary Takings

17. Eliminating the right to prepay a loan is not itself a taking. The court will resist formulating such *per se* rules. The investors were not excluded from investing in Dan's development by undertaking some of Dan's loan obligations. The fact that they might have wanted to avoid the effect of the mortgage's sole use covenant does not show that they were excluded from investing in Dan's development, with the prospect that the prohibition on prepayment would someday be lifted. But a temporary taking claim is a subset of regulatory takings law. Here the main issue centers on the reasonable investment-backed expectations that Dan had when undertaking the development. His primary expectation might be said to be to run the development for 20 years. At the same time, the facts show that "but for" the prohibitory ordinance, Dan would have reaped a profit in selling part of his development to investors. Any expectations that Dan had must, under *Penn Central*, be evaluated in the context of the severity of impact caused by the ordinance. In that broader context, a court might embrace a "but for" instead of a "primary expectation" analysis when evaluating Dan's claim. If there is an express prepayment right in the mortgage, the character of the governmental action may more readily be shown to be abusive (the municipality having broken its agreement with Dan),

but Dan will still have to establish that he would not have developed the low-income housing without the prepayment right. So the answer is that it depends.

Exactions

18. It might be best not to protest at this point, when negotiations are ongoing. It is not clear that exactions law applies to anything but final administrative decisions. Extending exactions law as you are asked to do here might tempt the developer to argue that the demanded then withdrawn exaction was the real reason for a later denial. Courts might well be hesitant to address such issues of motivation. And if courts were willing to address such issues, would that hamper a municipality's ability to negotiate? It might wind up demanding less than is necessary. Finally, exactions law shouldn't swallow up the field of regulatory takings, and it might if exactions law reached as far as your client asks it to.

19. The dedication requirement is an exaction or condition for a special-use permit. An exaction may constitute a taking if the exaction bears little or no relationship to the harm caused by the proposed development. Exactions review entails two steps. First, there must be an essential nexus between the exaction and a legitimate state interest. The dedication of land to help reduce traffic problems is logically related to ameliorating increased traffic resulting from a larger service station. Hence, the first element favors the municipality. However, the municipality loses on the critical second analytical step: Once the essential nexus is found, a court must decide if there is a rough proportionality between the condition exacted and the development's projected impact on the area. In this case, the municipal Board had a policy of conditioning grants of special permits along congested streets on dedication of land for street widening. The increase in traffic by less than 0.4 percent does not justify dedication of 20 percent of the gas station's land when, as would occur here, the municipality and the public would physically invade property formerly owned by Refined Oil, even though only a small percentage of the travelers were there because of Refined Oil's service station. Finally, the Board demanded the exaction as part of a general program of requiring dedications when *Dolan* demands that the Board made an individualized determination as to whether the impact of the modernization on traffic is tailored or roughly proportional to the required dedication.

Index

Index

Index

Index